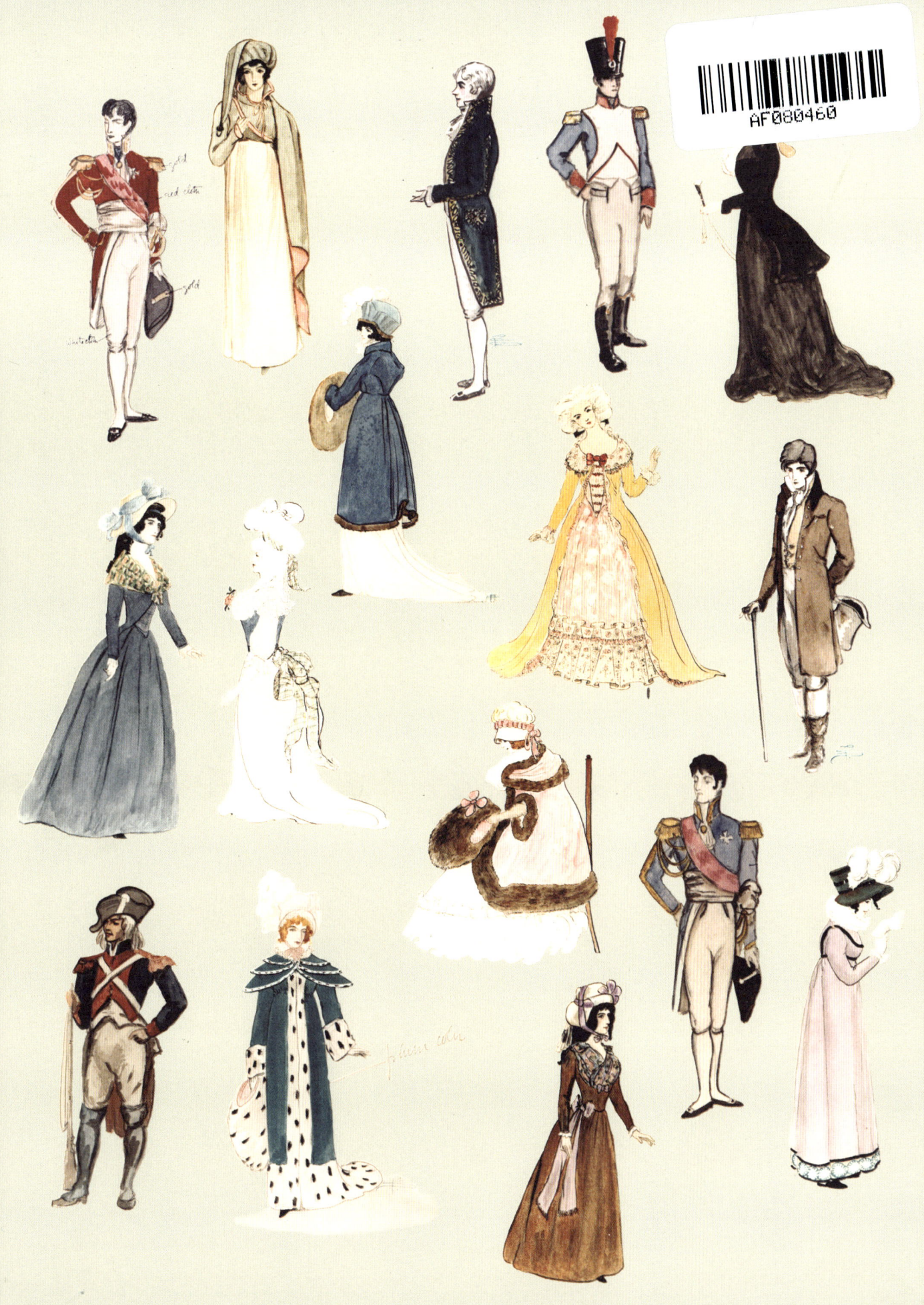

Pamela Colman Smith

Copyright © 2018 U.S. GAMES SYSTEMS, INC.

All rights reserved. The illustrations, cover design, and contents are protected by copyright. No part of this book may be reproduced in any form without permission in writing from the publisher, except by a reviewer who wishes to quote brief passages in connection with a review written for inclusion in a magazine, newspaper or online.

Unless otherwise indicated, the illustrations in this book are from the Library of Stuart R. Kaplan. Further reproduction prohibited without written authorization from the publisher.

10 9 8 7 6 5 4 3 2

Library of Congress Control Number: 2018902159

Hardcover Edition: ISBN-13: 978-1-57281-912-2
Clothbound Limited Edition ISBN-13: 978-1-57281-944-3

U.S. GAMES SYSTEMS, INC.
179 Ludlow Street
Stamford, CT 06902 USA
www.usgamesinc.com

Cover design by Paula Palmer
Book design by Clive Jacobson
Edited by Lynn Araujo, Jennifer A. Kaplan and Paula Palmer
Photography by Andrew D. Sullivan
Bibliography by William G. Miller
Index by Peter Rooney
Printed by Global PSD
Made in China

Cover portrait of Pamela Colman Smith by Alphaeus P. Cole
Costume designs on endpapers courtesy © National Trust, UK

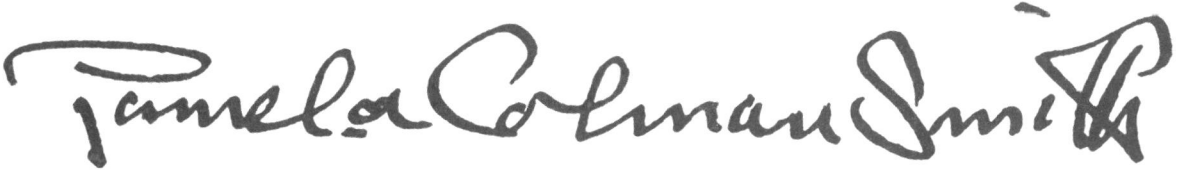

Pamela Colman Smith

The Untold Story

by Stuart R. Kaplan

with

Mary K. Greer

Elizabeth Foley O'Connor

Melinda Boyd Parsons

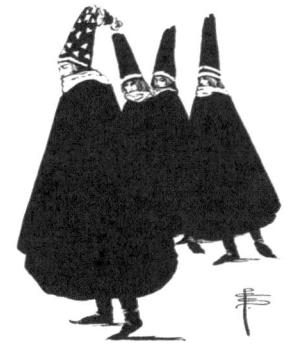

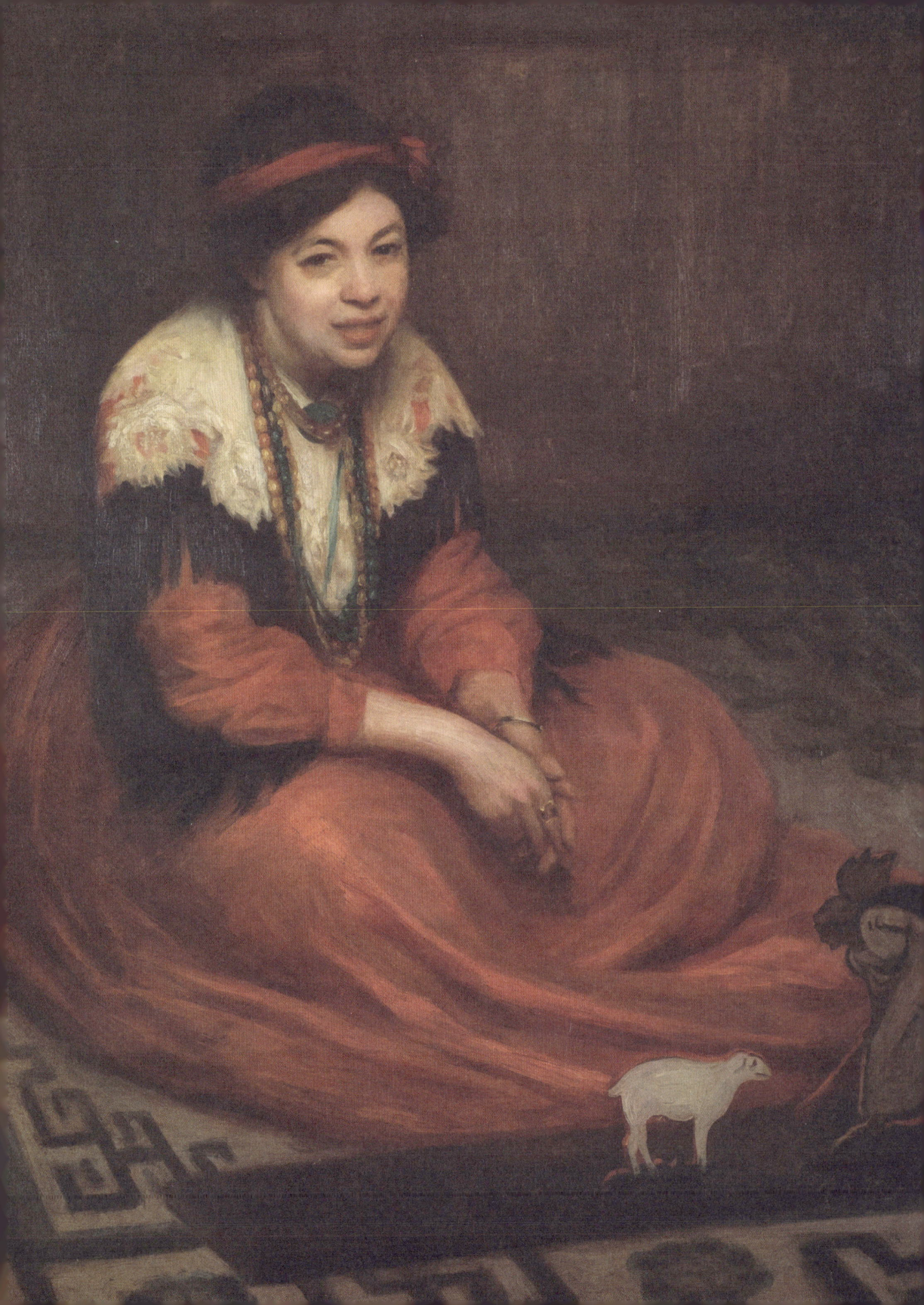

Table of Contents

ABOUT THE AUTHORS 8

PAMELA'S LIFE *by Elizabeth Foley O'Connor* 11

    Family and Childhood 15

    Life in Jamaica 17

    Miniature Theatre 19

    Art Student and Reception 21

    Emergence as a Professional Artist 25

    Return to England 40

    Problems with Publishers 44

    A Broad Sheet and The Green Sheaf 46

    The Green Sheaf Press 56

    Music Pictures 60

    Jamaican Folktale Performances 70

    Rider-Waite Tarot Deck 74

    Involvement in the Suffrage Movement 76

    Illustrations and Other Projects 79

    World War I 84

    Move to Cornwall 86

    Final Years 89

FOLKTALES, ART & POETRY *by Stuart R. Kaplan*

    Prior to 1902 100

    1902 to 1904 166

    1905 to 1906 198

    1907 to 1909 216

    1910 to 1951 288

continued on Page 7

Opposite: Portrait of Pamela Colman Smith by Alphaeus P. Cole, 1906

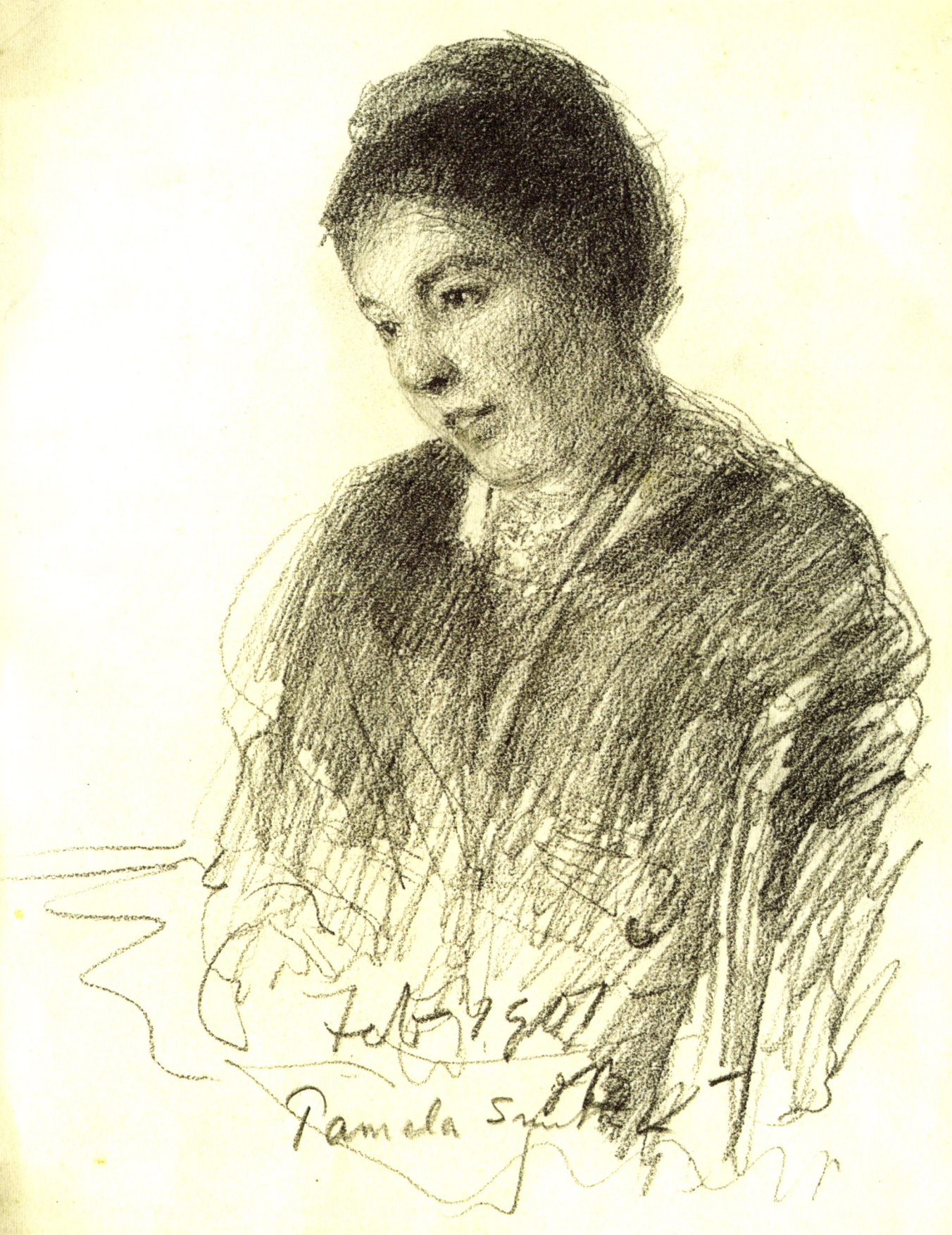

INFLUENCES & EXPRESSION IN THE RIDER-WAITE TAROT DECK *by Melinda Boyd Parsons* ..350

    Introduction 350

    Pamela Colman Smith and Arthur Edward Waite 352

    The Secret Tradition 353

    Chislehurst 355

    Spiritualism and Arts and Crafts Movement 357

    The Pratt Institute 359

    Theatrical Influences 359

    Tarot Drawings 361

    Friendships 365

PAMELA'S LEGACY *by Mary K. Greer* 371

    Innovative Tarot Deck 371

    Cards in Film, Media and Poetry 376

    The Rider-Waite Deck as Experienced by Tarot Readers 377

    A Therapeutic Tarot 378

    The Mid 20th Century Tarot Renaissance 379

    Waite and the Secret Tradition 380

    Pamela's Non-tarot Legacy 381

    Jamaican Folktales: The Annancy Stories 382

    A Legacy of Crossed Boundaries 382

    The Artist 383

    Our Lady of The Lizard 384

    Pamela's "Other Worldy" Senses 385

    Critical Commentaries on the Works of Pamela Colman Smith 386

    Conclusion 386

ADDENDUM 388

PORTRAIT OF PAMELA COLMAN SMITH 410

BIBLIOGRAPHY *by William G. Miller* 412

INDEX 425

Opposite: Pencil drawing of Pamela Colman Smith by John Butler Yeats, February 1901

About the Authors

THIS PAMELA COLMAN SMITH BOOK BRINGS TOGETHER FOR THE FIRST TIME A VAST AMOUNT OF information about a turn of the 19th century artist/author who up to now was primarily known to the public only for her Rider-Waite Tarot deck. The authors chosen to contribute to this book were carefully selected based on their expertise and scholarly research. The release of the book in 2018 is especially timely as it is the 140th anniversary of the birth of the artist, and the 50th anniversary of U.S. Games Systems, Inc., publishers of the Rider-Waite Tarot deck.

Mary K. Greer

Mary K. Greer's introduction to tarot occurred in the 1960s when she would watch the TV soap opera "Dark Shadows" that featured tarot readings as part of its plot. When Mary was in college, her best friend received Eden Gray's *Tarot Revealed* as a Christmas gift. Mary was intrigued from the moment she saw the book as the images "spoke" to her. She located a metaphysical bookstore in Tampa, Florida and went on her first spiritual quest to find a deck. Mary discovered not only the Rider-Waite deck in the store, but the whole world of the occult and metaphysical.

Mary was drawn to the idea that that you could reveal something about a person based on the story-telling images revealed in the tarot. It fit right in with her English major college studies in symbolism and Jungian archetypal studies. It also complimented the kind of exercises she was doing in theater improv classes. Making associations between images and a person's life came naturally to Mary, and she decided that she would teach tarot and make it her life's work. Mary has a total of ten books published, an internet tarot blog and webinars, and she travels the world teaching tarot. She has a collection of nearly 2000 decks, and almost as many books on tarot and its history.

Stuart R. Kaplan

Stuart R. Kaplan saw his first tarot deck at the Nuremburg Toy Fair in Germany in 1968. At the AGMuller booth, Stuart came across a Swiss 1JJ tarot deck printed with medieval images that was used for playing Tarock, a popular card game in Europe. Stuart returned to the states with the deck and established U.S. Games Systems. Henry Levy, the buyer at Brentano's ordered 100 decks which promptly sold out. Customers, however, weren't purchasing the deck to play Tarock; instead, they were using the cards for fortune telling. Henry asked Stuart to write a book about the cards, which fit into Stuart's propensity for historical research. Within several years, Stuart's sales of the deck and his subsequent book, *Tarot Cards for Fun and Fortune-Telling* exceeded 700,000 copies.

Stuart's first introduction to the Rider-Waite tarot came in 1971 through Donald Weiser, owner of Weiser's bookstore. Donald was publishing "The Pictorial Key to the Tarot" with the Rider-Waite images, and Donald suggested to Stuart that he obtain the rights to the deck, which he did. U.S. Games Systems currently publishes over 120 different tarot decks sold throughout the world. Stuart's collection of rare books covering the history of tarot and playing cards remains in his personal library along with an extensive collection of original Pamela Colman Smith material.

Elizabeth Foley O'Connor

Elizabeth Foley O'Connor's encounter with tarot began in 1998 when her college roommate offered to read her cards, but Elizabeth refused. While intrigued by the cards, she did not know the name of the deck, the artist who designed the deck, or the significance of the cards. Seven years later, Elizabeth encountered the Rider-Waite deck again when writing a paper on T.S. Elliot's 1922 poem "The Waste Land" for a graduate school class. She was intrigued by the figure of "Madame Sosostris, famous clairvoyant," and her "wicked pack of cards." Further research by Elizabeth uncovered some rudimentary information about Pamela Colman Smith, a forgotten woman artist and writer.

Elizabeth was interested in a host of women who had been active in the fin de siècle period and the early years of the 20th century. In 2011 Elizabeth completed a dissertation for her PhD in English at Fordham University, which explored depictions of women in Irish and Caribbean texts during the early 20th century and Pamela's name again appeared. Elizabeth quickly became interested in learning more about Pamela. She has spent the last six years researching Pamela's life and work. She is currently at work on a literary biography entitled *Pamela Colman Smith: An Artistic Life* to be jointly published by Clemson University Press and Liverpool University Press, England. Currently, Elizabeth is an Assistant Professor of English at Washington College, Maryland.

Melinda Boyd Parsons

Melinda Boyd Parsons was a graduate student at the University of Delaware in the 1970s, majoring in art history, when she attended a seminar on "Artists of the Stieglitz Circle." When the class instructor flashed a slide on the screen of a blue-violet sphinx with a piercing gaze (Pamela's painting "Blue Cat"), Melinda knew that the artist was the one she wanted to study. Melinda eventually authored a paper about the artist, and later wrote an MA thesis and catalog in 1975 for two exhibitions of Pamela's works, one at The Art Museum, Princeton University and the other at the Delaware Art Museum. She later earned a PhD in 1984. Melinda remained unaware that Pamela had drawn a tarot deck until an art history friend told her about the deck.

Melinda went to the Newark Department Store where she purchased the Rider-Waite tarot deck in a yellow box published by U.S. Games Systems. The same friend suggested that Melinda go for a tarot reading. Melinda found a tarot reader named Rusty Carnarious who did a reading. Rusty's last words—in reference to Pamela—were "It's time to pull together what has been scattered." Melinda is a collector of Pamela Colman Smith books and decks, and a retired professor of art history at the University of Memphis.

Each author of this book has traveled extensively to Bude, Cornwall, England, and to The Lizard and London, retracing Pamela's life and, alas, searching in vain for Pamela Colman Smith's gravesite, which remains unknown to this day.

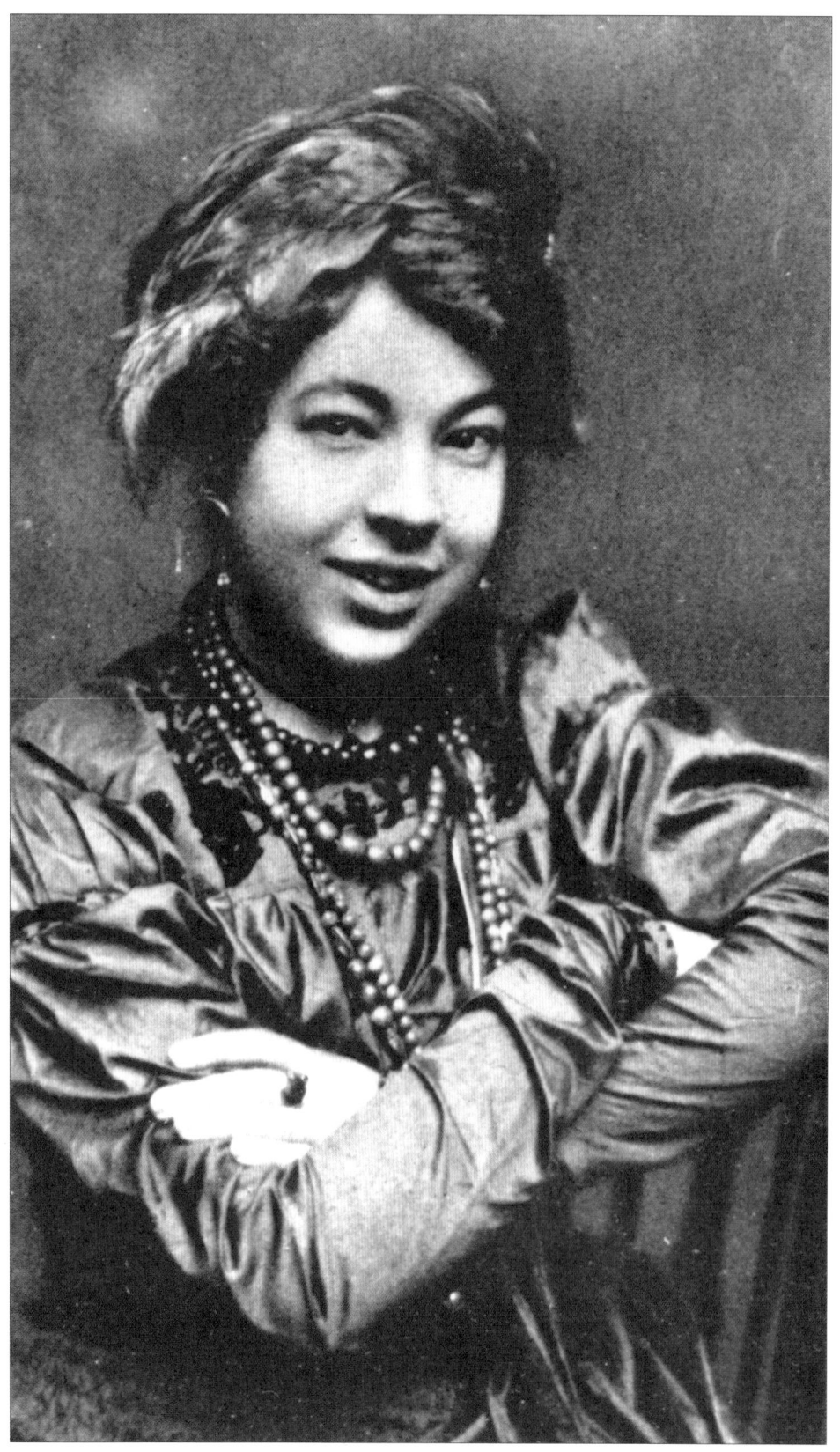

PAMELA'S LIFE

Corinne Pamela Colman Smith was an artist, poet, folklorist, editor, publisher, and costume and stage designer who was active from the mid-1890s through the 1920s. Born in London to American parents, Pamela traveled widely, spent a significant part of her youth in Jamaica, was educated as an illustrator at the highly-regarded Pratt Institute in Brooklyn, and died in her beloved Cornwall, England. Her paintings were exhibited in many galleries in the U.S., Continental Europe, and England—where she lived the majority of her life—including several international art exhibitions. She also has the distinction of being the first non-photographic artist to have her work shown at Alfred Stieglitz's "Little Galleries of the Photo-Secession" in New York.

Pamela illustrated more than 20 books and many magazine articles, wrote two collections of Jamaican folktales, co-edited *A Broad Sheet* with Jack Yeats from 1902-1903, edited *The Green Sheaf* from 1903-1904 by herself, and, after its demise, ran the Green Sheaf press, which focused particularly on women writers, including her own work. Her venture into publishing appears to have emerged as both a calculated business move and a reaction to the frustrations she encountered when dealing with the virtually all-male publishing establishment. She occasionally referred to publishers in letters as "pigs" and vented her frustrations over failing to place work and not receiving royalties to which she considered herself entitled.[1] Active in the theatrical world, Pamela staged her own "miniature" theatre performances, traveled with the Lyceum Theatre Company, contributed set and costume designs to several plays, and performed Jamaican folktales and other poems for public recitals in both England and the U.S.

Pamela was an irrepressible spirit. This is reflected in both her nickname "Pixie" and her deviation from the standards and expectations for women of her time. She pursued a career and did not marry or have children; instead, she surrounded herself with like-minded female friends and companions. As a teller of West Indian Anansi stories at public performances in both London and New York, Pamela blended her interest in Irish and Jamaican folktales into a personal mythology that celebrated freedom, fearlessness and independence of spirit. These characteristics are evident in much of her work and are especially apparent in her two published collections of Jamaican folktales *Annancy Stories* (1899) and *Chim-Chim* (1905). The latter was published by her own Green Sheaf press and includes several traditional tales that emphasize the agency of the female characters.

Throughout her life, Pamela struggled with those who did not understand her and who had a hard time positioning her within existing gender, class and racial categories. John

Opposite:
From *The Craftsman*, October 1912

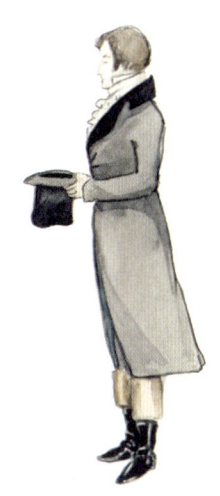

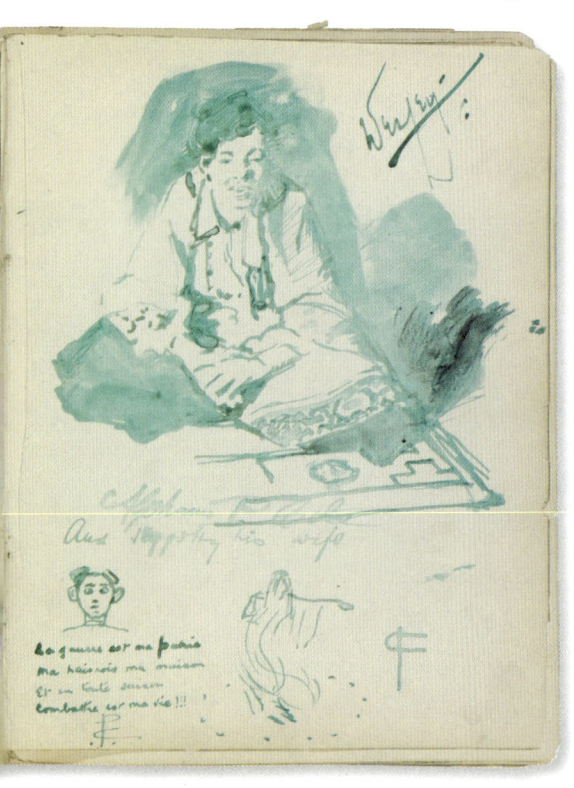

Sketch of Pamela Colman Smith by Alphaeus P. Cole. From Pamela Colman Smith's Visitors book, 1901-1905

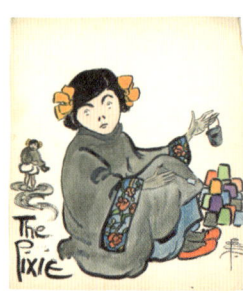

Playful caricature of Pamela Colman Smith drawn by herself. Courtesy © National Trust, UK.

Yeats had this assessment in the summer of 1899 after meeting her to arrange a possible literary venture with his son W.B. Yeats:

"Pamela Smith and father are the funniest-looking people, the most primitive Americans possible, but I like them much… Her work whether a drawing or the telling of a piece of folklore is very direct and original and therefore sincere—its originality being its naïveté. I should feel safe in getting her to illustrate anything. . . . She looks exactly like a Japanese. Nannie says this Japanese appearance comes from constantly drinking iced water. You at first think her rather elderly, you are surprised to find out that she is very young, quite a girl . . . I don't think there is anything great or profound in her, or very emotional or practical."[2]

At the time of her visit to Yeats, the "rather elderly" Pamela was just twenty-one. John Yeats's assessment reflects both his paternalism and his biases against "primitive" Americans, especially those whom he assumed to be a class below him and whose racial origins he had trouble ascertaining. However, his comments are characteristic of the uncertainty and confusion contemporaries had in placing her into conventional categories like age and ethnicity. Perhaps in response to his—and others'—assertion that she had Asian origins, Pamela created a sketch of herself in a kimono that was published in *The Critic* magazine in 1900. In the accompanying article, Pamela explains that the Japanese influence on her work is "'not so much as people suppose.'" The article adds that the caricature was created "[w]ith a merry recognition of the association;"[3] moreover, it is characteristic of Pamela's irreverent humor.

Published accounts of Pamela's art and life also exhibited a tendency to exoticize her background and depict her, and often by extension her art, as simple and naïve. A full-page 1904 *Brooklyn Daily Eagle* article is representative: "There could be no greater contrast to the ordinary dainty young Heights girl, of pretty manners, or normal tendencies, conventional ways and the usual ambitions. Yet were an Iphetonga to be danced to-day, Pamela Coleman Smith [sic], this odd-artist mystic girl, would be trebly qualified for its inmost place."[4] Pamela is described as different from most young women of her time due to her focus on an independent life and an artistic career rather than marriage and children.

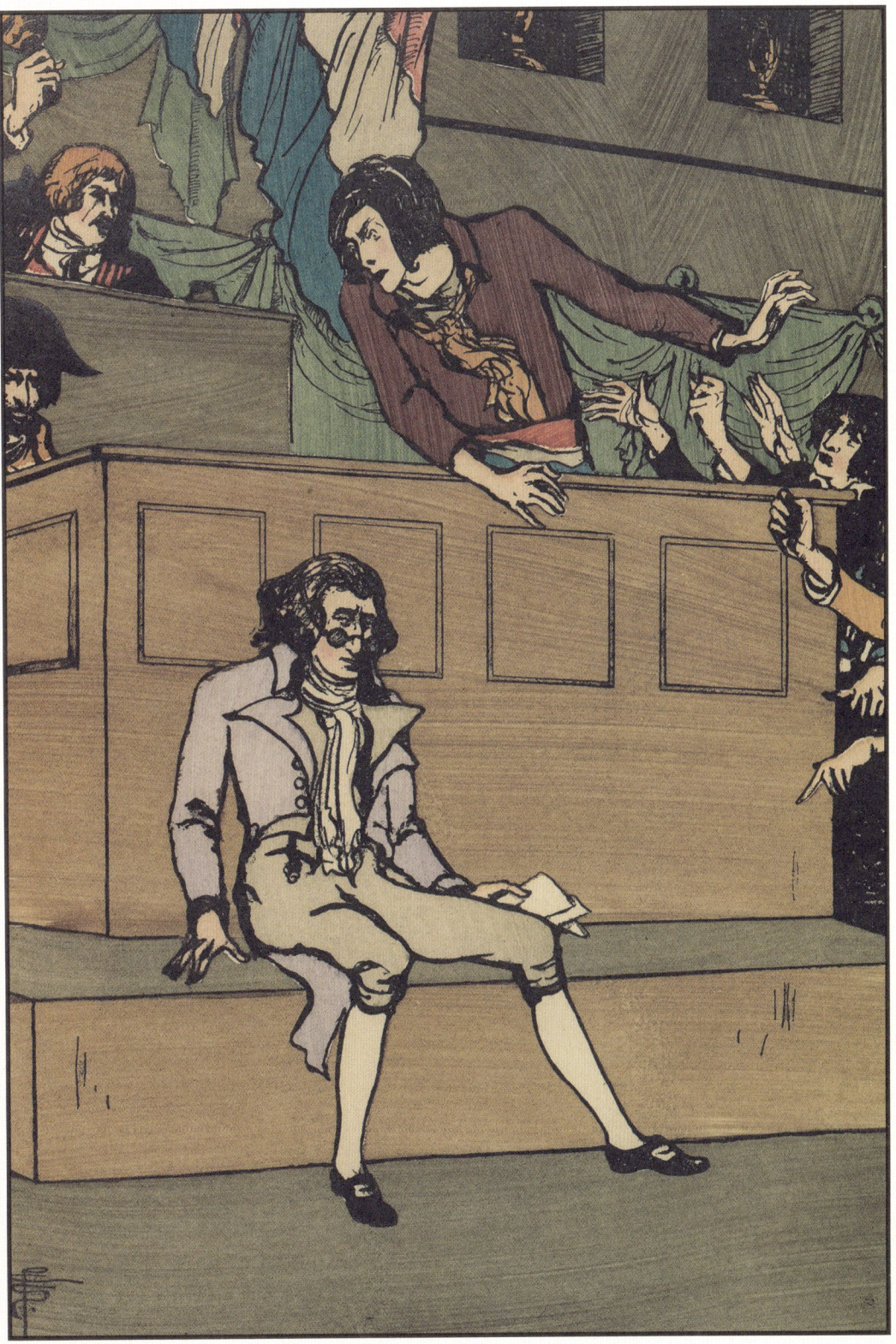

Sir Henry Irving as Robespierre. From *The Brooklyn Daily Eagle*, 1904

The unnamed writer appears to insinuate that she may have Native American blood as "Iphetonga" is both the Native American word for Brooklyn Heights and refers to the indigenous tribe who inhabited Brooklyn before the arrival of the Europeans.[5] However, "Iphetonga" also refers to a series of exclusive balls held in Brooklyn Heights in the 1880s and 90s that were eventually ended because of disagreements over which families had high enough social standing to attend. Both Pamela's maternal and paternal relatives inhabited the highest echelons of Brooklyn society, which would have guaranteed her an undisputed place at these soirées.[6]

The clearest written reference to Pamela's possible mixed race comes in Henry Wood Nevinson's 1923 memoir, *Changes and Chances*, which recalls his time in London in the early 20th century. Nevinson terms Pamela an "exciting little person" and notes that he "supposed" she was "touched with negro blood."[7] A year later, Pamela's fellow Pratt student, Earnest Elmo Calkins, in his memoir, *'Louder Please!' The Autobiography of a Deaf Man*, likens Pamela during her folktale performances to "a strange African deity."[8] He references Nevinson's book and states that while he had "never heard" that Pamela was of mixed race, it would "account for her peculiar dramatic power."[9]

Other contemporary articles passed beyond questioning Pamela's racial origins and described her as more animal or even ethereal than human. A 1912 *Delineator* profile states that she resembled "a brown squirrel, and a Chinese baby, and a radiant morning...."[10] As the article acknowledges, Pamela defied convention and easy categorization and, most importantly, blazed an important path for female artists: "Before she was twenty she was an inspiration to American women painters who were working toward something different. Many of our women have since done notable decorative work, but she was the pioneer who gave them courage."[11] Similarly, Arthur Ransome's generally complimentary description of her in his 1907 *Bohemia in London* veers into this territory when he terms her a "strange little creature" and states that upon welcoming him into her London salon she describes herself as a "goddaughter of a witch and sister to a fairy."[12] While it is impossible to know whether Pamela actually uttered these words or if they are Ransome's interpretation of what she would have said, it does seem in keeping with her known tongue-in-cheek type of response. What is clear is that people who met Pamela were uncertain about her exact racial makeup. Questions about her physical appearance seem to have affected the way Pamela and her work were received, possibly explaining her lack of sustained success in her artistic and publishing pursuits.

Family and Childhood

PAMELA'S ABILITY TO ADAPT TO A VARIETY OF PEOPLE, PLACES AND SITUATIONS IS SOMETHING that seems to have been ingrained in her through her peripatetic childhood. When she was 24-years-old, she wrote to an acquaintance, "I have been on a good many long voyages—twenty-five beginning when I was 3 months old..."[13] While it is unclear where Pamela went on her infant voyage, it is possible that she traveled to Brooklyn Heights, New York where her parents, Charles Edward Smith and Corinne Colman Smith, grew up and had many relatives. The pair married on September 28, 1870 in New York but the details of their courtship are unknown. Charles Edward was 24 and Corinne, 34. It is also unclear why the couple settled in England or how long they had been living there before their daughter's birth on February 16th, 1878 at 27 Belgravia Road in the Pimlico section of London, a few blocks from Victoria Station.

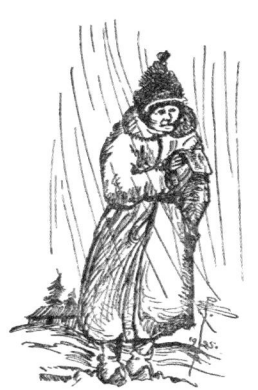

Both Pamela's parents came from prominent Brooklyn Heights' families. Her maternal grandfather, Samuel Colman, was a well-known bookseller, publisher and etcher, in both Boston and New York City, who is credited with publishing the first illustrated volume of American verse.[14] His New York store became a haven for writers and artists, especially those associated with the Swedenborgian religion. The Colman family were members of the Swedenborgian New Church and Samuel published several works by Swedenborg and his Manhattan store served as a depository for New Church material.[15]

Pamela's maternal grandmother, Pamelia Chandler Colman was a prolific author of children's books, many of them collections of translations of French and German fairy tales. The unusual spelling was a family tradition; as a child Pamela was also known as Melia in honor of her grandmother.[16] Writing as Mrs. Colman, Pamelia Chandler Colman collaborated on several of these, notably the long-running *LuLu Tales* series, with her eldest daughter, Pamela Atkins Colman (later Howard). Pamelia's oldest son, Samuel Colman, was a noted landscape artist of the Hudson River School. A world traveler, he was an avid collector of Chinese and Japanese prints, a love that Pamela shared and whose influence can be seen in her art. Pamela's mother, Corinne Chandler Colman, was not as illustrious as her siblings but newspaper accounts state that as a young woman she was "very beautiful" and a "great drawing room actress of Brooklyn" whose performances in a private theatre hosted by her sister, Pamela Atkins Colman Howard, were well acclaimed throughout the borough.[17] It is unknown how Charles and Corinne first became acquainted, but it is fascinating to consider that it was at one of these private theatre performances.

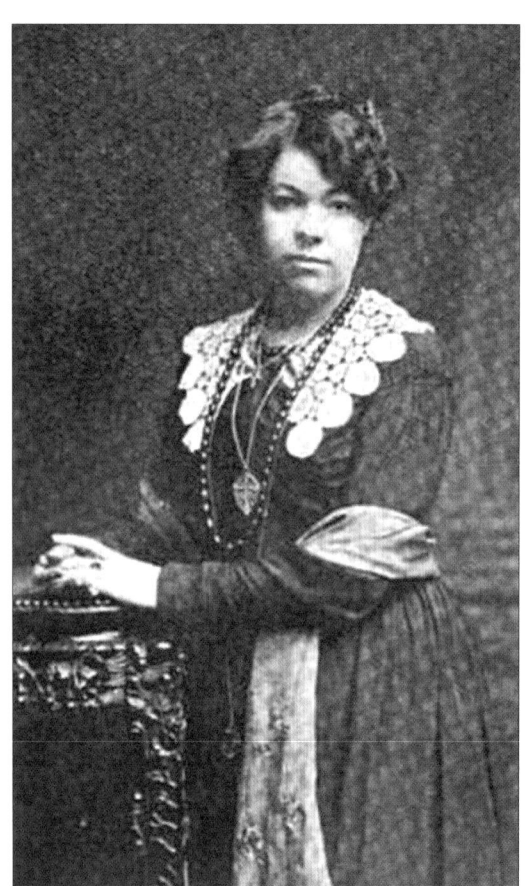

Pamela Colman Smith in a shawl. Photo by Russell & Sons, circa 1904-1905

While Pamela's maternal relatives included well-known artists and writers, her paternal family was distinguished for their contributions to government and business. Her father's mother, Lydia Lewis Hooker, was a direct descendant of Thomas Hooker (b. July 5, 1586 – d. July 7, 1647), a Puritan clergyman, who was a founder of the Connecticut Colony. He was a staunch advocate of removing the requirement of church membership from a citizen's eligibility to vote, which was his chief disagreement with the Puritan leadership of the Massachusetts Bay Colony that he left.[18] Pamela's paternal grandfather, Cyrus Porter Smith (b. April 5, 1800 – d. February 13, 1877), was an important figure in the development of Brooklyn from a small village in the early 19th century to a bustling borough at the time of his death in 1877. He was the fourth appointed mayor of Brooklyn in 1839 and a year later was the first to be popularly elected to that position. Cyrus held the office until 1842 and later served as a state senator from New York.[19] A prosperous businessman, he helped found the first gas company in Brooklyn, was director of Brooklyn's Union Ferry Company, president of the Brooklyn City Railroad Company and one of the founding directors of Brooklyn City Hospital.[20] While an older son, Bryan, followed him into business in Brooklyn, his youngest son, Charles Edward, "artist rather than businessman, hardly met with the material success of his brother."[21] According to the *Brooklyn Daily Eagle*, Charles Edward, Pamela's father, spent much time in London and at one point worked for the celebrated London design firm of Nichols, Colshaw & Co.[22] Another older brother, Theodore Eanes, known as Teddy, became a merchant but never married. He remained close to Charles Edward and Pamela throughout his life and left her a bequest in his will.

Pamela and her parents lived in the London suburb of Chislehurst until 1881 and then moved to Manchester where Charles Edward worked as a "manufacturer of upholstery."[23] When she was ten, the family moved to Jamaica after her father took a job as an auditor with the West India Improvement Company, an American concern that took over completion of the railroad on the island from the colonial government. During this period, Pamela often returned to New York "under the entire charge of a Jamaica negro nurse" where "she made long visits at more than one [Brooklyn] Heights house."[24]

Life in Jamaica

ALTHOUGH PAMELA'S LIFE-LONG INTEREST IN THE CULTURE OF JAMAICA INDICATES A formative role, scant information about her early years in Jamaica has survived. We do know that she traveled from her home in St. Andrew's Parish, Jamaica—a suburb of Kingston, the capital of the Crown colony—to New York in October 1893 and enrolled at the Pratt Institute in Brooklyn later that month. Pamela's registration card notes she was 15 and that the purpose of her studies was art teaching or illustration.[25] She attended Arthur Wesley Dow's first composition class at Pratt in the fall of 1895 and his applied design course in the spring of 1897; through these courses Dow's views on composition and design were to become central to Pamela's early work.[26] The June 1896 issue of the *Pratt Institute Monthly* relates that two of her posters were included in the *Century* magazine poster exhibition.[27] One is described as "pretty and fanciful" and depicts fairies dancing around a toadstool. The other, termed "most originally worked out," shows the reflection of a child picking tiger lilies beside a pool.[28] Neither of these, nor any of the other entries by Pratt classmates, won the competition.

By the summer of 1896 Pamela had returned to Jamaica to help nurse her sick mother. After her mother's death on July 10, 1896, she ran the household for her father. It is also during this period that Pamela's voice first emerges in a series of letters to her cousin, Mary Bidlack Reed. Pamela recounts making breakfast for the household, counting the washing, paying wages for the workers on the estate, and allocating money for groceries. At one point, she laments that "I get <u>terrible</u> [sic] mixed up on farthings and am often short."[29] However, her life in Jamaica did not consist entirely of domestic duties. Pamela frequently drove around the island in her "little buggy—with her little horse- Grog" who was occasionally spooked. As she notes in a letter to Mary, "the only thing that Grog seems afraid of is oxen fastened together and then he stands on his hind legs!"[30] The daughters of the U.S. Consul in Jamaica, Quincy Oliver Eckford, often joined her on these outings.[31] The family frequently entertained, and Sir Henry Blake, who served as Governor of Jamaica from 1889-1898, came to visit, as did his elderly parents and Lord George Fitzgerald who served as Blake's private secretary. A Kingston *Daily Gleaner* article notes Pamela and her father were "both well known in Jamaica during their sojourn, and she was quite a figure in the society of St. Andrew, especially in artistic circles."[32]

Pamela's art is a frequent subject in her missives to her cousin. Early in the series, she expresses frustration at not having been more productive since her return to

Jamaica: "I have done very little work since I've been home only a few comps—All the time I am doing anything the old telephone keeps ringing and I get so mad! And I just begin to have a good time and the mosquitoes begin to bite like mustard!"[33] Pamela did draw a few posters for local businesses; she reproduces one for a millinery shop in a letter to her cousin.[34] After the death of her mother, Pamela increasingly discusses drawings she has undertaken, such as those of Merlin, Vivian and Guinevere, based on suggestions of Pre-Raphaelite-influenced Pratt friends, and she urges Reed to offer potential topics.[35] During her time on the island, Pamela also became a member of the St. Andrew Sketching Club.[36]

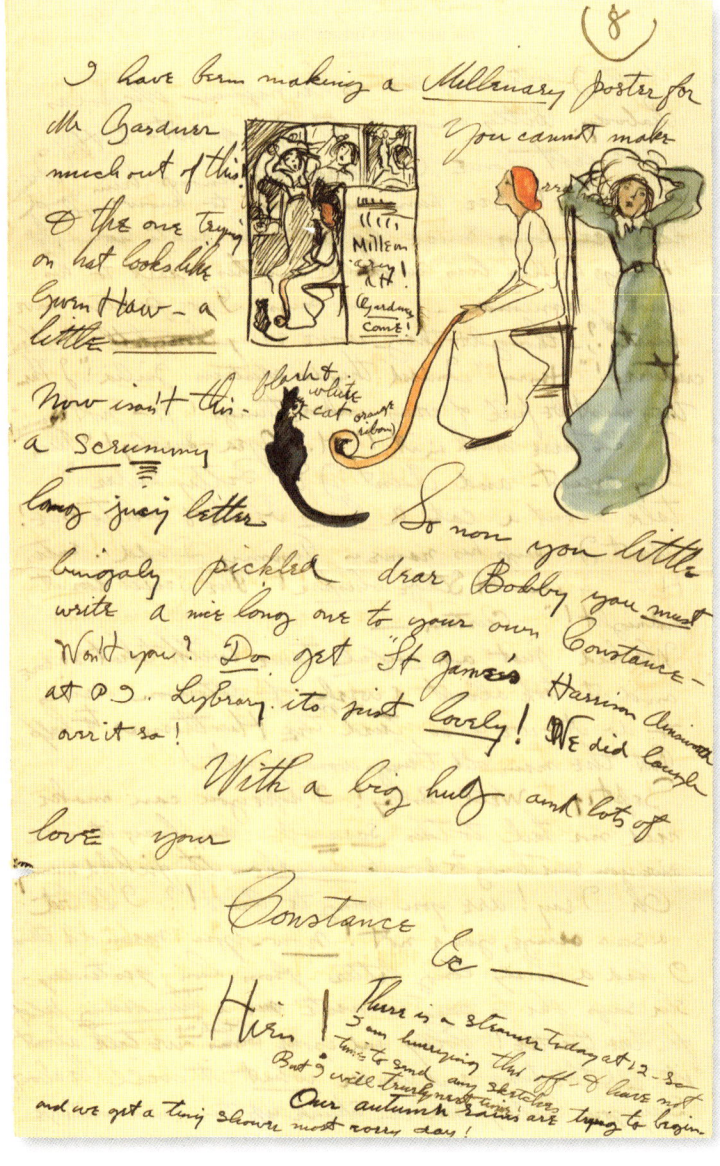

Millinery poster from a letter to Mary B. Reed. Signed by Pamela with pen name Constance, September 17, 1896. Pamela Colman Smith Collection, Special Collections Department, Bryn Mawr College Library

Miniature Theatre

PAMELA'S LETTERS TO REED ARE PEPPERED WITH ACCOUNTS OF BOOKS SHE HAD READ AND her thoughts on the New York theatre scene, which she followed by reading the *New York Herald* and magazines that arrived in Jamaica a few weeks after their publication. However, the most popular topic in her letters is her miniature theatre and the plays she wrote and produced for it. The tiny dramas took place on a stage that measured approximately 18 inches square and the theatre was equipped with elaborately painted sets and figures that were moved by means of grooves and strings.[37] A 1899 *Washington Times* article termed it "one of the completest miniature theatres ever seen."[38] Pamela manipulated the figures herself, which she named and often reused in multiple plays; by 1899 she had created more than 300 of them.[39] As Gardner Teall in *Brush and Pencil* explains, "The knights and ladies of the buskin are first drawn on stiff paper and colored, then cut out and made to lead upright lives with a bit of glue and proper manipulation."[40] Teall adds that "I have never seen a more gorgeous presentation on any stage." Pamela created the sets and figures herself, but often had help from her father, servants, and friends who contributed the musical accompaniment and special effects, as well as read the play's narration.

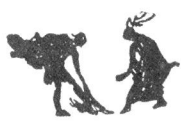
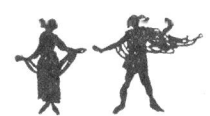
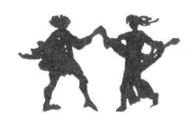

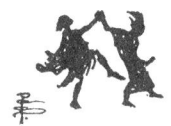

The most popular of Pamela's miniature theatre plays, and the one that she went on to perform in public for paying audiences, was *Henry Morgan*, which was loosely based on the life of the Welsh privateer and later Lieutenant Governor of Jamaica.[41] She performed it several times at home in Jamaica during the fall of 1896—often to a wide assortment of guests—but the play had its first public performance on December 10, 1896 at the Half-way Tree Infant Kindergarten in Kingston, Jamaica.[42] As letters to her cousin reveal, Pamela was "awful busy" making groups of people for the procession before Morgan is knighted, including 39 additional pirates, nine guardsman, multiple children, and "three Indians with feathered headdresses."[43] More than 200 children and their parents were in attendance, and the performance was accompanied by a guitar, flute, and piccolo that, according to Pamela, "make cold shivers run down your back—!"[44] An article in the Kingston *Daily Gleaner* praised her artistic talents and stated that "the beauty and clearness of the performance of the little play called forth unqualified expressions of appreciation and delight from all present."[45] More than a week after the performance, Pamela recounts to her cousin that she is still meeting people who say her play was a "great success."[46]

A year later Pamela performed *Henry Morgan* in Brooklyn for her fellow students and teachers as part of the Pratt Art Students' Fund Association's annual Christmas social. Although one performance was initially planned, the demand for tickets was so great

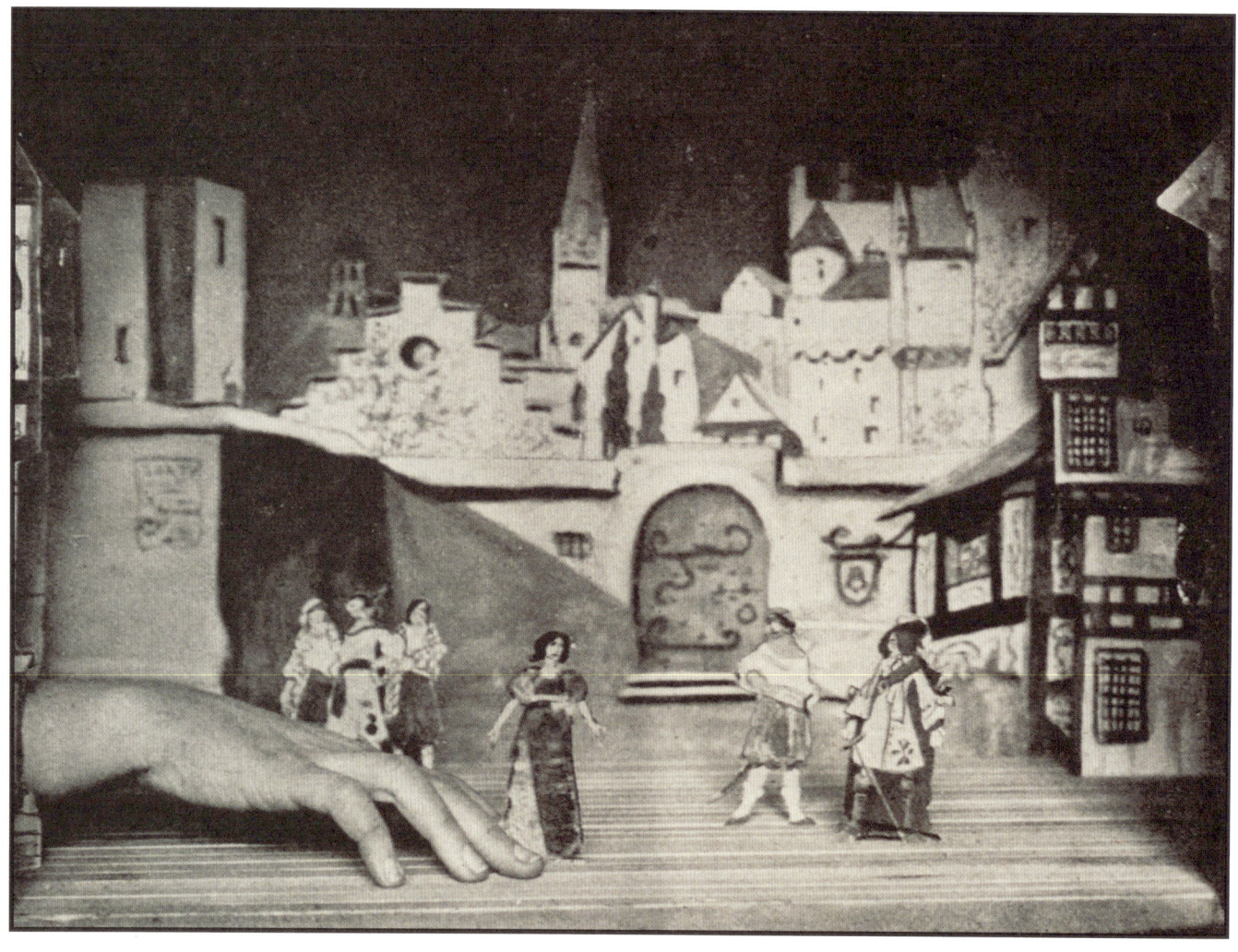

Miniature theatre created by Pamela Colman Smith for the play *Henry Morgan*. From *Brush and Pencil*, June 1900. Image provided by The Metropolitan Museum of Art, New York, Thomas J. Watson Library

that three performances were given.[47] The *Pratt Institute Monthly* states the play netted $95 and terms *Henry Morgan's* 15 scenes and 13 acts "a most original and charming entertainment."[48] The unnamed writer stresses that it is difficult to fully express the artistic beauty and effectiveness of the scenes and states that "[w]hether one sees the interior of the heroine's chamber, or the blue waters and sunny hillsides of the tropical island, each is a delicately-balanced harmony, constructed on the most refreshingly-original lines, yet so simply and unerringly true that one feels is a new faculty for seeing life, though it be that of two centuries ago."[49] This difficulty to put into words the full effect of Pamela's work and simultaneous focus on the originality and "truth" of her compositions was to become typical of assessments of her work.

Art Student and Reception

At Pratt, Pamela studied composition, drawing and painting and was widely regarded as a child prodigy. She was the first student to have feature articles written about her in the *Pratt Institute Monthly*. She earned what may have been her first commission when a fellow Pratt student, Earnest Elmo Calkins, paid her $10 for a poster of a Crow and Pitcher to illustrate Aesop's fable of the same name, for which he had devised "some advertising use."[50] Pamela remained matriculated at the Brooklyn art school until June 1897 but did not receive a degree. A 1902 article in *The Reader* states that she studied at Pratt for only two years; "[a]s no noticeable change showed itself in the character of her work under this tutelage, and as she became more determined to work out her own problems in her own way, she ended her connection with the school."[51] While Pamela's resolve to do things her own way seems to be a hallmark of her personality, she does seem to have been influenced by at least one of her Pratt professors, the artist Arthur Wesley Dow. Dow, who was also influential in Georgia O'Keeffe's training, taught his students that rather than imitating nature, paintings could be composed by using color, tone, shape and line.[52] Through Dow, Pamela became acquainted with both symbolism and the emerging concept of synesthesia. She also studied 19th century Japanese *Ukiyo-e* prints, with their flat shapes, bright colors, and subjects in action-filled poses that she was already familiar with and had collected with her father.[53] Pamela assimilated all these elements into her work in an original and highly creative manner. I.C. Haskell, writing in the *Pratt Institute Monthly* in 1897, compliments both her "feeling for color arrangement" and her "comprehension of form in line and design" but reserves her strongest praise for Pamela's originality: "No doubt she has been influenced and helped by study of the art world; but she seems to have the power of assimilating these influences and using them as a stimulus in her own growth, not wearing them like a borrowed garment."[54] Thus, what set Pamela apart was the originality and uniqueness of her paintings, which the January 1898 edition of *The Studio* magazine describes as "extremely interesting, though it is difficult to classify them."[55]

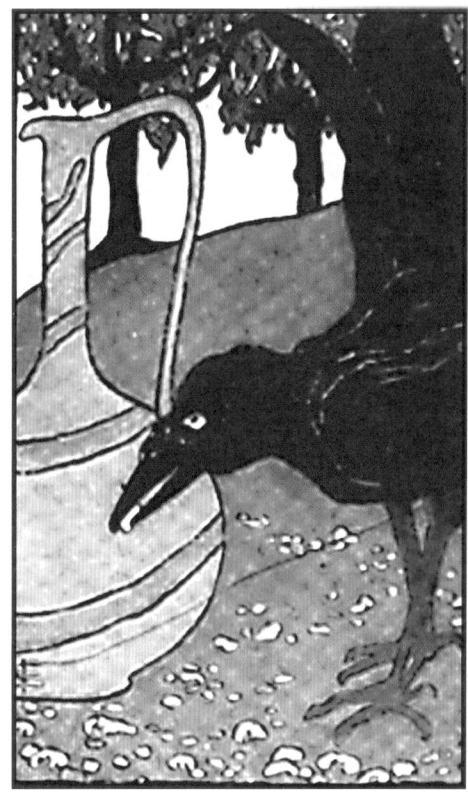

"The Crow and the Pitcher," cover design. From *American Printer and Lithographer*, December 1900

Audiences and critics were receptive, at least initially, and in 1897, Pamela, who was only 19, had her first feature exhibition at William Macbeth's Gallery in New York, where

"Tropical Fruits," a composition. From *Pratt Institute Monthly*, December 1897. Courtesy of Pratt Institute Archives

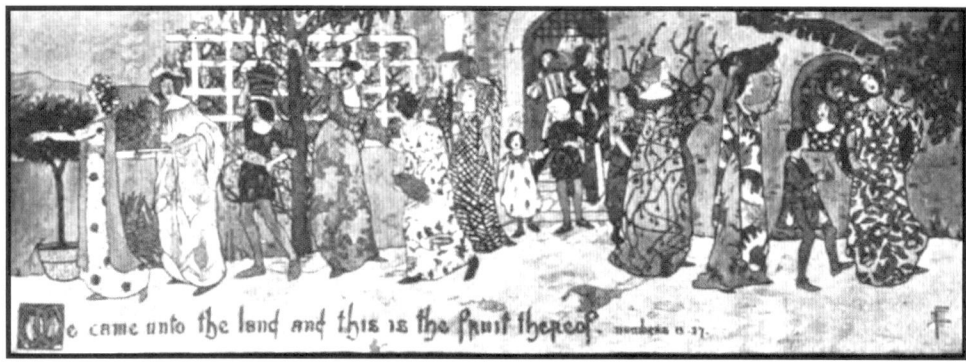

"The Wind" from *Pratt Institute Monthly*, December 1897. Courtesy of Pratt Institute Archives

Far right: "Recess" from a drawing by Pamela Colman Smith. [Also called "Our Pets" in *Pratt Institute Monthly*, December 18, 1897]. Art & Architecture Collection, Miriam and Ira D. Wallach Division of Art, Prints and Photographs. The New York Public Library, Astor, Lenox and Tilden Foundations

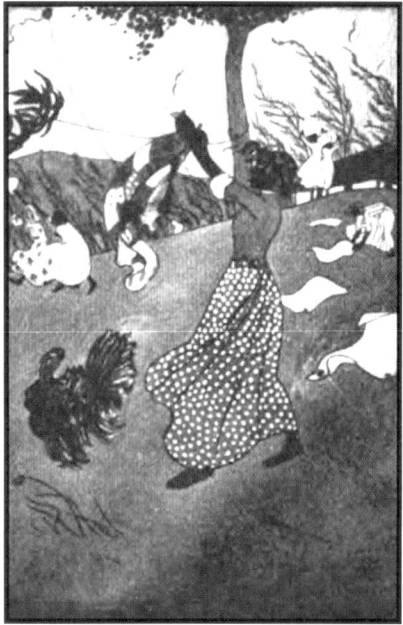
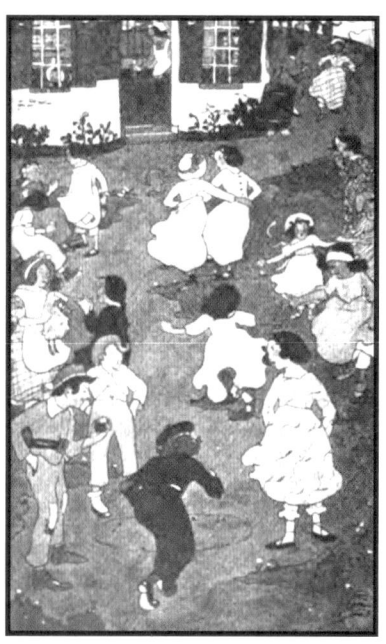

Miniature stage setting by Pamela Colman Smith. From *Pratt Institute Monthly*, December 1897. Courtesy of Pratt Institute Archives

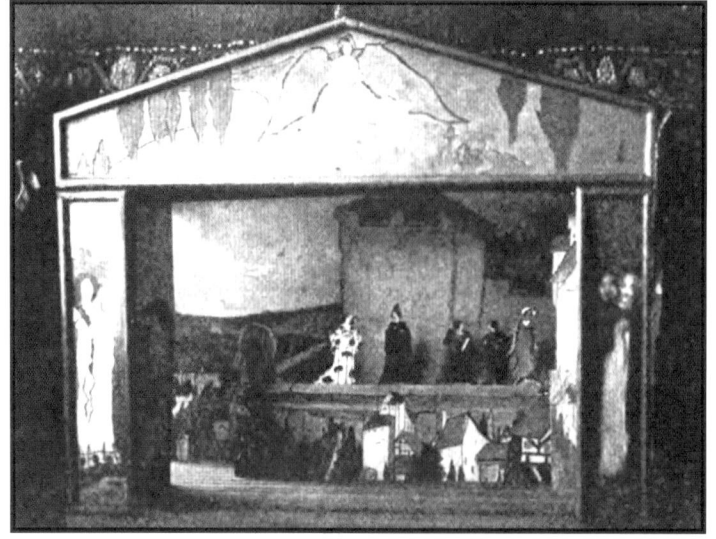

she sold four of her watercolors.[56] By the end of 1897, Smith's Christmas cards, illustrations, and prints were being sold regularly through the gallery. Several critics heaped praise on her work, such as Gardner Teall in the June 1900 issue of *Brush and Pencil*. He writes:

> Even in this day of unusual movements in art… it is not an ordinary thing to find one so absolutely untrammeled by Traditions of the Schools, so unhampered by the whisperings of convention in art, so undeterred by any dictates of precedent from venturing farther afield, and one so masterfully conquering color and tactfully forcing an allegiance of it to purpose which has come whole-souled, as has Pamela Colman Smith, whose work stands unique in America, and certainly as unique everywhere.[57]

Thus, Teall, like Haskell before him, views Pamela's work as unique and uninfluenced by the major artistic developments of the time. Other critics, however, disparaged her drawing, terming it "naively crude," "unformed," or too reminiscent of the Victorian illustrator Walter Crane.[58] Teall himself says that the "draughtsmanship" of her work "would be rather open to controversy" and that her "lines are not of the same defined sort that characterized the drawings of Aubrey Beardsley," an artist with whom she was often unfavorably compared.[59] Similarly, James McNeill Whistler states that "She does not know how to draw or paint, and she does not need to do either."[60] Whistler, who was at the forefront of the fin de siècle Anglo-American art scene, voices the unspoken view that seems to characterize much of the contemporary criticism of Pamela's art: that it is not her technique—or lack thereof—that matters; the value of her work is purely imaginative. Although never explicitly stated, this is heavily implied as a feminine characteristic, which may have contributed to her work being dismissed and overlooked both in America and England.

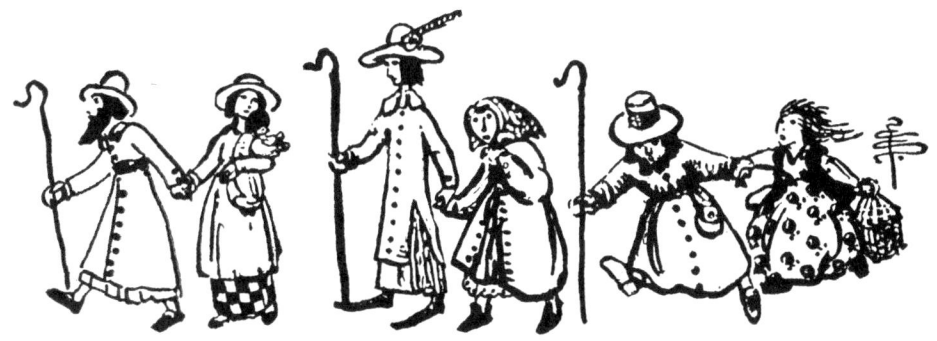

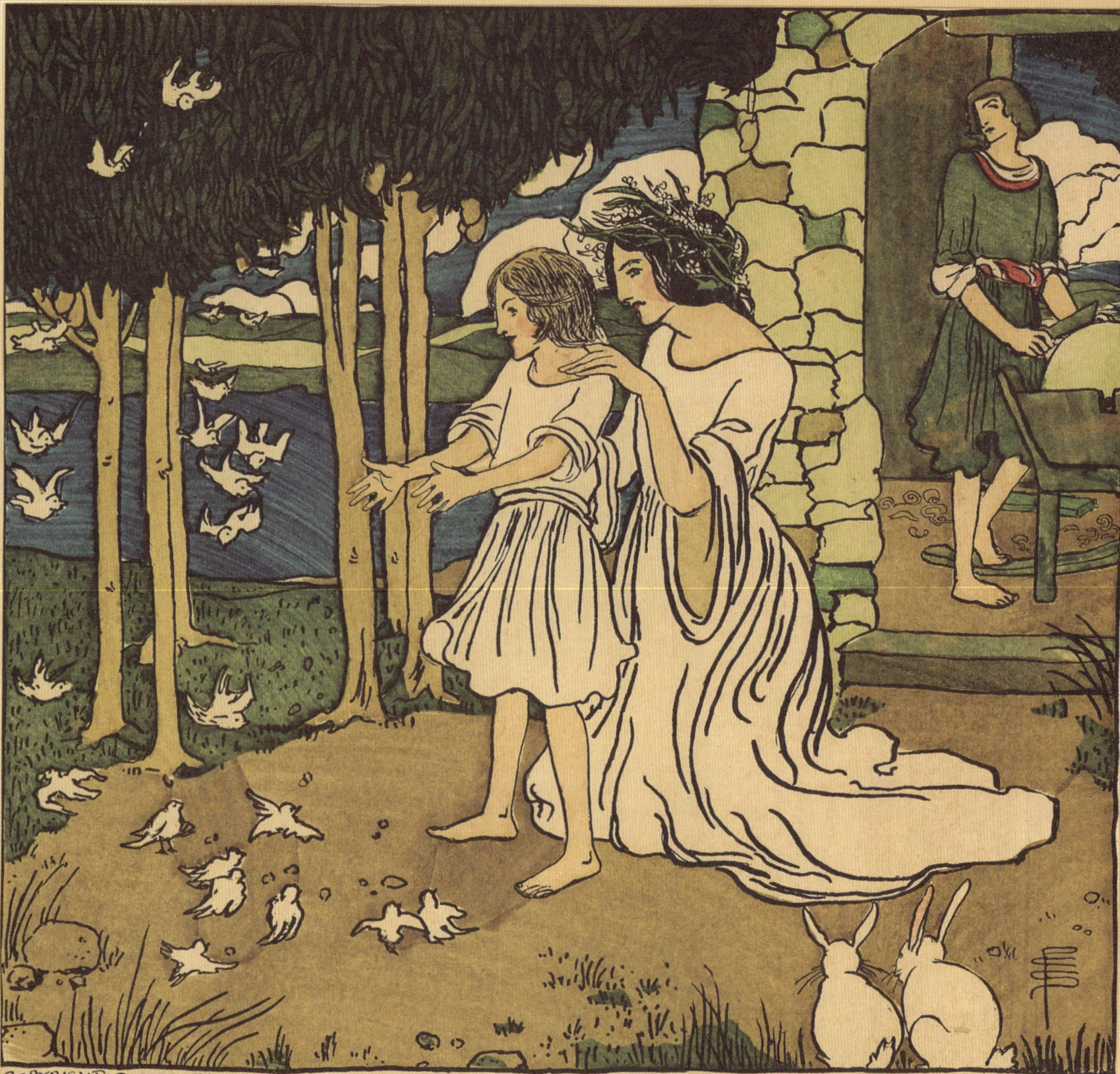

COPYRIGHTED. 1898. BY W. MACBETH.

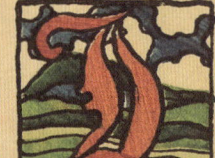n gentle thought, and gentle deed,
His early days went by;
And the light His youthful steps did lead
Came down from heaven on high.

Emergence as a Professional Artist

During the late winter of 1898 Pamela and her father returned to Jamaica. Letters reveal that she had collaborated on what appears to be an unfinished play with the headmaster of the Kingston Grammar School and had begun work on a Shakespearean alphabet for children.[61] She had already completed drawings of Banquo from *Macbeth*, Caliban from *The Tempest*, and Hotspur from *Henry IV Part 1* and had planned illustrations of Katherine from *The Taming of the Shrew*, Viola from *Twelfth Night or What You Will*, and Mistress Quickly who appears in *Henry IV Parts 1 and 2, The Merry Wives of Windsor,* and *Henry V*.[62] Pamela was in talks with publishers to issue a deluxe edition of this work but the project apparently never came to fruition. By late spring, she and her father had returned to New York and settled in the Stuyvesant Apartments at 142 East 18th Street in Manhattan. The building was constructed in 1870 and is held to be the first multi-level apartment building for the middle class in New York City with artists' lofts on the top floor.[63] It was from this central location that Pamela's goal of becoming a professional artist began to take shape. With the help of her father, she attempted to leverage a network of friends and familial acquaintances in order to market her art to both publishers and influential personages, such as the famous actress Maude Adams who achieved her greatest fame in J.M. Barrie plays, especially her role as Peter Pan. This put into motion several projects that would come to fruition in the next two years. More immediate results included an illustration in the Christmas number of *Collier's Weekly*; a color advertisement on the cover of the Christmas *Book Buyer*; and several of her Christmas cards sold by William Macbeth in New York, Boston, Chicago, and San Francisco.[64] R.H. Russell published Pamela's *Shakespeare's Heroines* calendar for 1899, of which only the poster promoting it survives. The publisher also issued a series of her color prints in time for the Christmas holidays that were on sale at Macbeth's Manhattan gallery and other New York stores.[65]

The Russell portfolios included "Recess," which had previously been exhibited at the Pratt Institute and depicted children at play, "Twelfth Night Merry Makers," a "Christmas Carol," which shows the Holy Family and contains sheet music for the poet Edwin Waugh's adaptation of the song, an illustration from Shakespeare's *Macbeth*, and a triptych based upon W.B. Yeats's 1894 play *The Land of Heart's Desire*.[66] The *Macbeth* drawing depicts an ornately clad Lady Macbeth declaiming lines, printed below her, from Act 1, scene 4: "The service and the loyalty I owe,/ In doing it pays itself."[67] In Shakespeare's tragedy these famous lines are spoken by her husband. This subtle change suggests that Pamela believed that a woman's actions—and not those of men—were key to understanding the play and

Opposite:
"Christmas Carol"
by Edwin Waugh.
Published by R.H.
Russell, 1898

Lady Macbeth from *Macbeth*, Act I. From the Russell portfolio, courtesy of Folger Shakespeare Library

the demise of Macbeth and his kingdom. It foreshadows Pamela's frequent portrayal of women in more independent and active roles throughout her career.

Pamela's interest in Irish myth and fairies is most evident in her triptych for Yeats's *The Land of Heart's Desire.* This interest seems to have taken root during her teenage years in Jamaica in the early 1890s where she read W.B. Yeats' *Wanderings of Oisin and Other Poems* (1889), *Celtic Twilight* (1890), and *Irish Fairy and Folktales* (1892). Pamela's piece is notable for the extreme movement of her riotously dancing female subjects. In the center image, one of the two lone males in the composition is a black-frocked priest who is physically restrained by two women, ostensibly over his horror over the indecorous merrymaking. The second male, Shawn Bruin, is trying to restrain his wife, Maire, from romping with the barefoot and red-headed fairy child who leads the white-gowned pixies who dance in the side panels.[68] Shawn implores his now energized wife, who was previously withdrawn and listless, to remain with him in the real world instead of giving in to the false escape of laughter and dancing of the fairies. However, she succumbs to the spirits' charms and dies in her husband's arms. The play marked the first time Yeats drew on Irish folklore as living mythology, an idea which influenced Pamela greatly and resonated with her own growing interest in both Jamaica's rich pirate and seafaring history and its folklore. The history and lore of these two traditions, which are generally separate, were both extremely important to Pamela and are fused in her work.

The following year—1899—was a particularly productive one for Pamela. She published the *Annancy Stories*, *The Golden Vanity and The Green Bed*, *Widdicombe Fair*, *Fair Vanity*, and illustrations for the play *Trelawney of the 'Wells'*. She also provided illustrations for both Seamus MacManus's *In Chimney Corners*, a collection of Irish folktales, and a commemorative brochure featuring the actors Sir Henry Irving and Ellen Terry of the Lyceum Theatre Company. Arguably, the most important work Pamela published during this prolific year was her book of Jamaican folktales, *Annancy Stories*, which she wrote as well as illustrated.[69] Her interest in the tales had begun several years earlier during her sojourn in Jamaica. Pamela's transcriptions of two short Jamaican folktales—"Annancy An' De Nyam Hills" and "De Story of De Man An' De Six Poach Eggs"—were included in the October-December 1896 issue of Franz Boas's *Journal of American Folklore*. The stories are credited as the first transcriptions that use Jamaican pidgin, rather than standard English. Pamela revised and significantly expanded these stories as well as added twenty others for her own book-length collection—her first—which was published by R.H. Russell. She also added

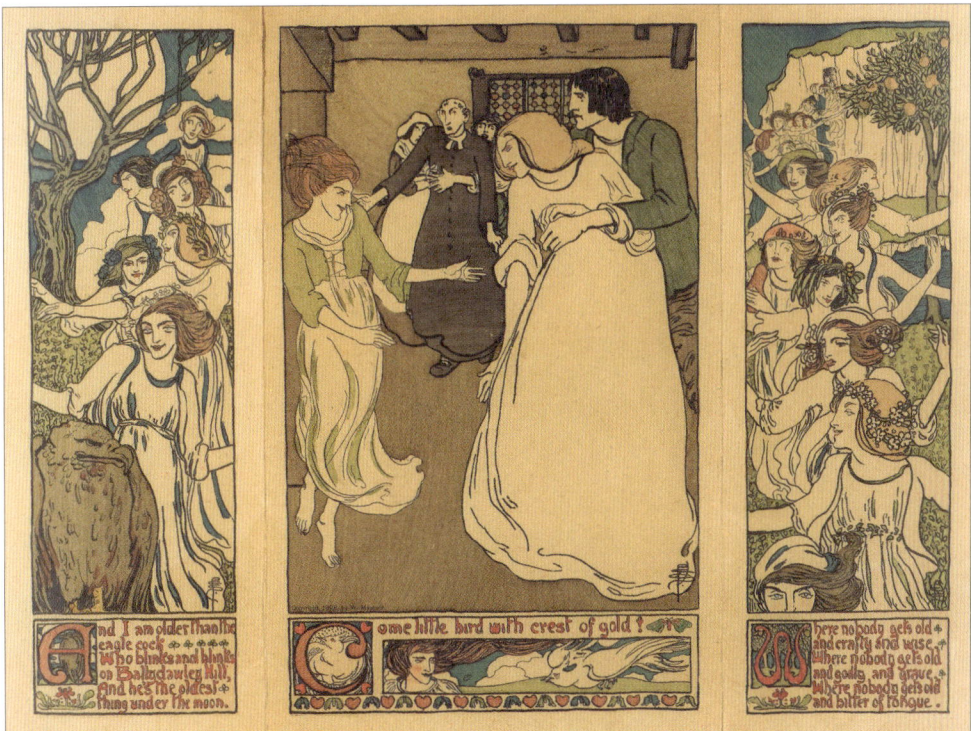

"The Land of Heart's Desire," a triptych. Possibly intended for inclusion in Illustrated Verses of W.B. Yeats (unpublished). Published by R.H. Russell, 1898

liberal illustrations and her depictions are the first known published drawings of Anansi, a traditional African folktale character who is also one of the most important characters in Caribbean folklore. This trickster figure can assume the form of both a man and a spider. Pamela calls this figure Annancy and highlights his wily tricks, a pronounced sense of humor, and a deliberate refusal to follow established rules. Unlike other contemporaneous accounts, Pamela's Annancy is not as aggressive and is often bested by other animals. This can be seen in the first story of the collection, "Annancy and Chim-Chim," where Annancy attempts to trick Chim-Chim bird who was beating him at cards but is thwarted at every turn. Thomas Nelson Page, a prominent writer of the time who wrote the introduction

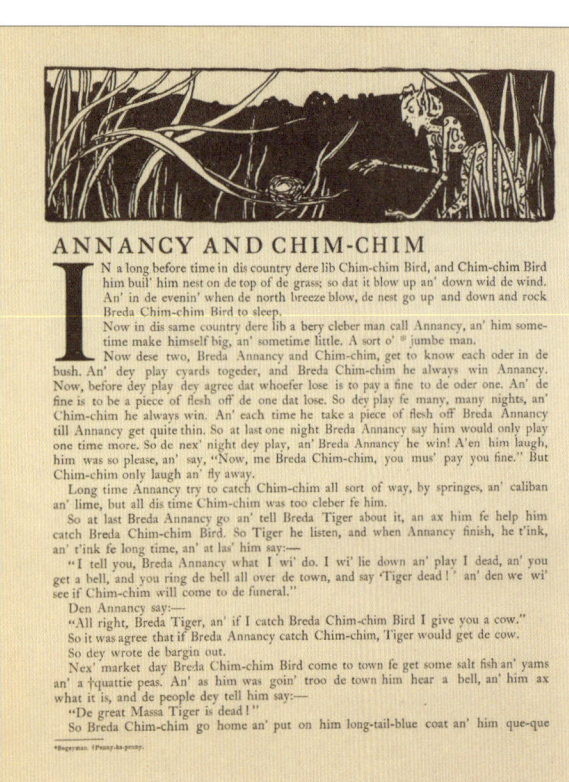
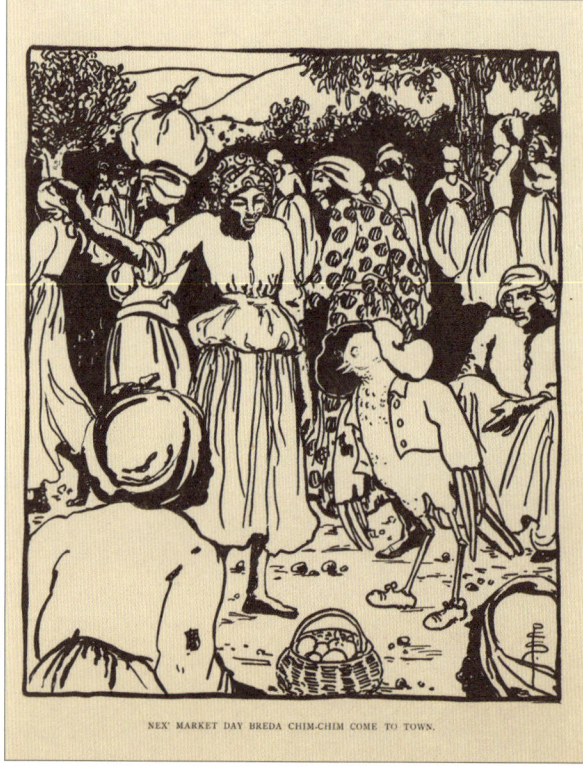

"Annancy and Chim-Chim," from *Annancy Stories*. Published by R.H. Russell, 1899

for the collection, stated that Pamela's *Annancy Stories* "are perhaps the most original contribution to negro folk-lore literature since the day when "Uncle Remus" gave us his imperishable record of "Brer Rabbit."[70]

The setting of Pamela's tales is distinctly Jamaican, with several references to the practice of *obeah*. The term refers to a series of magical and religious practices that were popular in the Afro-Caribbean, notably Jamaica, but were outlawed during British imperial rule. While obeah is most commonly associated with a male practitioner, several of Pamela's *Annancy Stories*, such as "Why Toad Walk 'Pon Four Leg," "Haylefayly An' Pretty

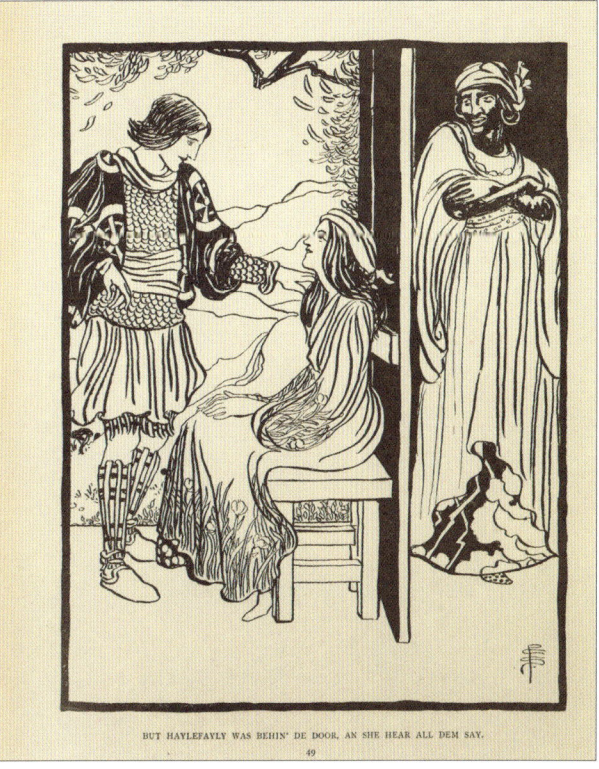

Obeah Woman from "Haylefayly An' Pretty Peallope." From *Annancy Stories* with original caption "But Haylefayly was behin' de door, an she hear all dem say." Published by R.H. Russell, 1899

Peallope," "Bull-Garshananee," "Annancy An' De Nyam Hills," and "The Three Sisters," all feature an "Obeah woman." This is in keeping with the collection's focus on strong female characters. Other stories include more familiar figures in West Indian folktales like Annancy, Chim-Chim, Gingy Fly, Guinea Fowl, Paarat, Tiger, and Toad. However, Pamela clearly also draws upon folklore traditions from around the world such as *Aesop's Fables* and *Arabian Nights* as well as European fairytales by Hans Christian Andersen, the Brothers Grimm, and Charles Perrault. Excerpts from Pamela's *Annancy Stories* were included in the December 1898 editions of the *New York Herald* and the *Pittsburgh Daily Post*.[71] An effusive article about Pamela and the collection, which was syndicated in several newspapers across the country, noted that "With the most astonishing invention, imagination, and humor she has pictured a series of strange, alluring little people who cannot fail to win the childish heart, and at the same time delight appreciative grown folks."[72]

Pamela's illustrations for her *Annancy Stories* bear several similarities to the female dancing figures in her triptych of Yeats's *The Land of Heart's Desire* and her drawings for Seamus MacManus's *In Chimney Corners: Merry Tales of Irish Folklore*, 1899.[73] For example, her final illustration of three sisters seemingly bewitched by Anansi's fiddling in "How Annancy Win De Five Dubbloon" is very similar to the riotous dancers in her illustration

Opposite: "The Giant" from *In Chimney Corners: Merry Tales of Irish Folk Lore* by Seumus MacManus. Published by Doubleday & McClure Co., 1899

for Yeats's play; both groups of figures are touched by magic and Pamela may have viewed them similarly.[74]

There is also a notable resemblance between the white male and female figures for her illustrations for "Annancy An' Tiger Ridin'," "Haylefayly An' Pretty Peallope," "De Golden Water, De Singin' Tree An' De Talkin' Bird," and "The Three Sisters," from *Annancy Stories* and the male and female figures in illustrations for "Billy Beg and the Bull," "The Queen of the Golden Mine," and "The Black Bull of the Castle of Blood" from *In Chimney Corners*.[75] All three works were completed in the 1898-1899 period and show similar stylistic inventions. Most surprising are the similarities between Pamela's drawing of Annancy and the Irish giant whom she includes in illustrations for the cover and beginning pages of the book. Interestingly, the giant only appears in the final story of the collection, "The Giant of the Band Beggar's Hall," and is not physically described other than the repeated refrain that he is "the greatest giant over all of them."[76] Despite having a fondness for human flesh and engaging in trickery while playing cards, the giant is ultimately bested by Jack, the king of Ireland's son. Pamela's drawings of both Annancy and the giant include large ears, upturned eyes, sloping brows, and flyaway hair to indicate that, despite their culturally specific differences, she saw both of these characters as trickster figures.[77] It is particularly interesting that the central figure for the frontispiece of *In Chimney Corners* is the giant rather than Jack, who is the protagonist of several of the tales and the closest to a unifying figure for the

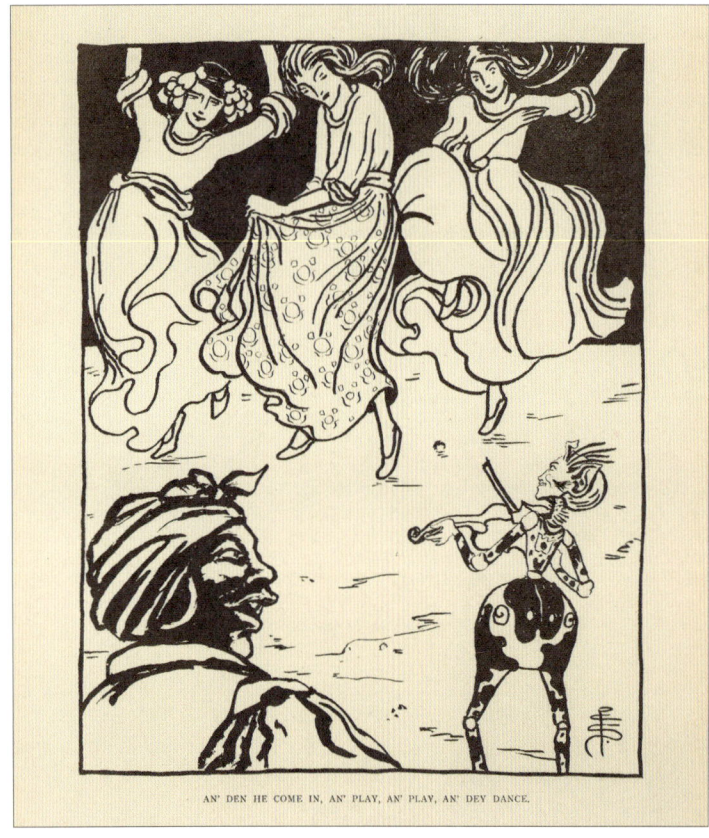

Dancers from "How Annancy Win De Five Dubbloons." From *Annancy Stories*. Published by R.H. Russell, 1899

collection. A much smaller male figure, who may be Jack, appears in the center bottom of the frontispiece but rather than aggressively confronting the giant, he is staring at him with upturned eyes, seemingly in amazed admiration.

There is no known extant correspondence between Pamela and Seamus MacManus, and we do not know how Pamela came to illustrate the collection. In the late 1890s,

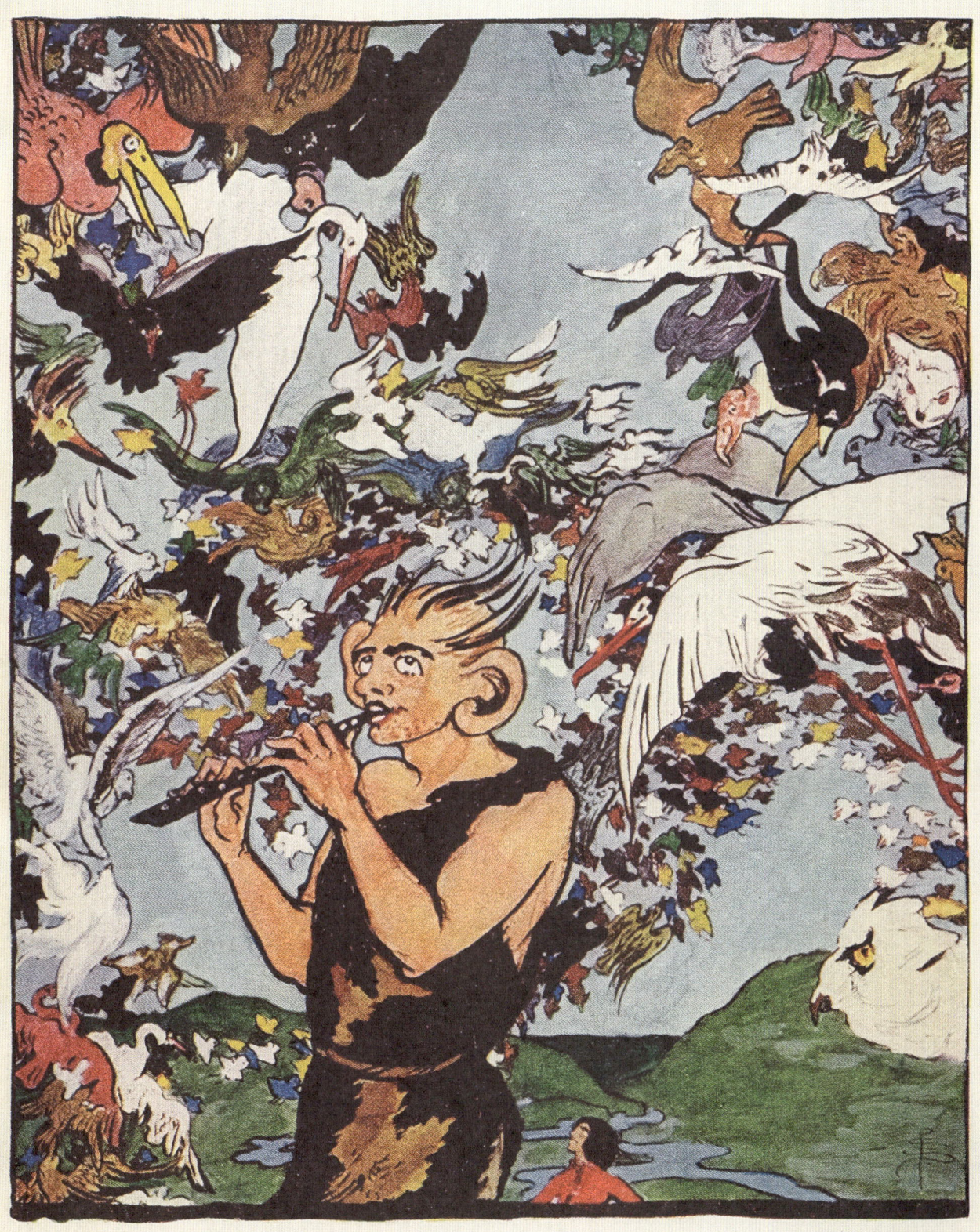

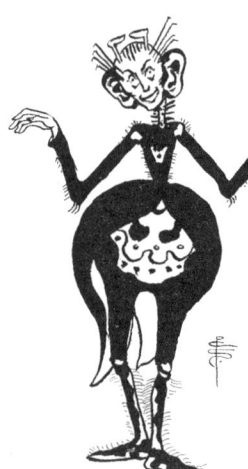

"Annancy" from *Annancy Stories*. Published by R.H. Russell, 1899

MacManus, who was married to the Irish Literary Revival poet Ethna Carbery, was at the beginning of his literary career but he would go on to gain a wide following for his retellings of Irish folklore in America in the first part of the 20th century. Although he had lived in New York in the 1890s, where he published his first two collections, in the spring of 1899 he had returned to his native Donegal and resumed work as a schoolteacher as he prepared *In Chimney Corners* for publication. Pamela notes in an August 1899 letter to Alfred Bigelow Paine that she and her father had traveled to Mountcharles, a village in County Donegal, Ireland, to meet him and were not impressed: "he is a bloomin school master and <u>awful</u> stupid."[78] She does not elaborate, but it is fascinating to consider that some of her negative opinion of him might be due to disagreements over their varying approaches to the folklore collection.

Much more so than the *Annancy Stories*, or any of Pamela's other publications up to this point, *In Chimney Corners* had a truly international presence. The collection was widely reviewed in Irish, English and American newspapers. There were multiple advertisements for it in the *Dublin Daily Mail*, the *Dublin Daily Express*, and the London *Morning Post*. The reviews for *In Chimney Corners* were more mixed. While the *St. Louis Post-Dispatch* noted that "MacManus has caught the elusive spirit of folk lore" and the *Pall Mall Gazette* declared that an "excellent racy teller he makes," the *Brooklyn Life* reviewer stated the stories "lack imagination" and were "full of repetitions, not only of incident but of phrase, which become wearisome in the reading."[79] The critical responses for Pamela's illustrations were even less positive. The *Pall Mall Gazette* states that [o]ne doubts that the grotesques of Miss Pamela Colman Smith will add to the book's attractiveness."[80] The *Brooklyn Life* reviewer noted that Pamela's illustrations "arrest the attention immediately" but quickly adds that "If by some blunder of the binder they had been included in a copy of the 'Arabian Nights,' they would have seemed more appropriate than they do here."[81] However, the *Dublin Daily Express* devoted an entire short article to Pamela's work, praising her "fantastic imagination" and predicting that her illustrations "will make the book." The unnamed reviewer concluded

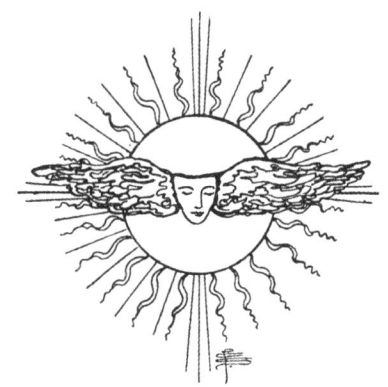

by suggesting that "We hope that some day she will venture into the higher sphere of mythical legend."[82] In fact, Pamela proposed several ideas for collaborations with W.B. Yeats's poetry and his retellings of Irish myth, but none of these found their way to print. However, in May of 1899 Pamela met W.B.'s friend and collaborator Florence Farr Emery in New York and was asked to create additional stage designs for a proposed New York run of W.B.'s *The Countess Cathleen*.[83]

Like her *Annancy Stories* and illustrations for *In Chimney Corners*, Pamela's twelve full-color illustrations for the two Old English ballads, *The Golden Vanity* and *The Green Bed* reflect her growing interest in folktales and folk culture of all sorts. With their focus on her interest in sailors and nautical themes, they also are products of her interest in Jamaica's rich seafaring and pirate history.[84] A distinctive feature of Pamela's works during this period is a union of foreground and background to create an almost two-dimensional effect due to complicated compositions of swirling lines and areas of pattern and texture. The *Critic* noted that Pamela's *The Golden Vanity and The Green Bed* "shows a quality of Hogarthean humor, which from her former work, she would hardly be suspected of possessing."[85]

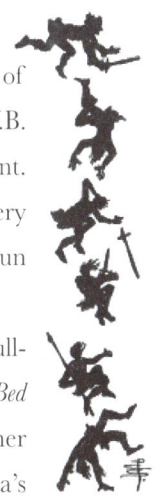

Book cover from *The Golden Vanity and The Green Bed*. Published by Doubleday & McClure Co., 1899

Widdicombe Fair and *The Golden Vanity and The Green Bed* were both issued as limited editions, with only 500 numbered copies published in cloth portfolios. The combination of high production quality and limited edition status resulted in a relatively high price. These ventures appear to have introduced Pamela to the value of creating deluxe editions in small runs that would fetch higher prices, something she would explore further in her little magazine, *The Green Sheaf* and her Green Sheaf press. However, neither *The Golden Vanity and The Green Bed* nor *Widdicombe Fair* sold their 500 copies. Pamela struggled for years to extract the

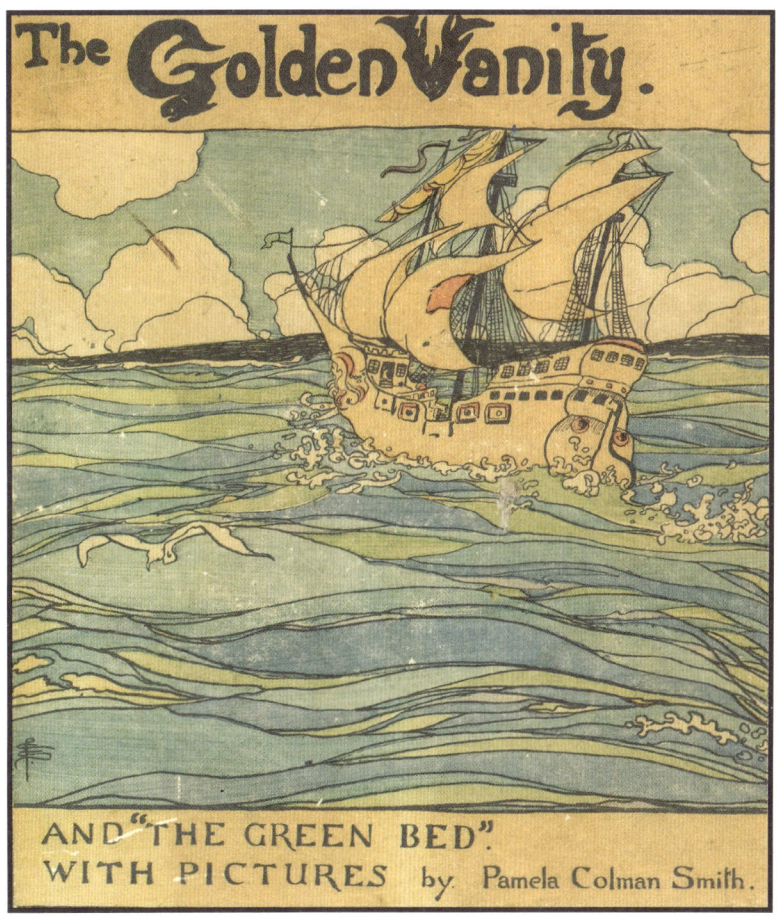

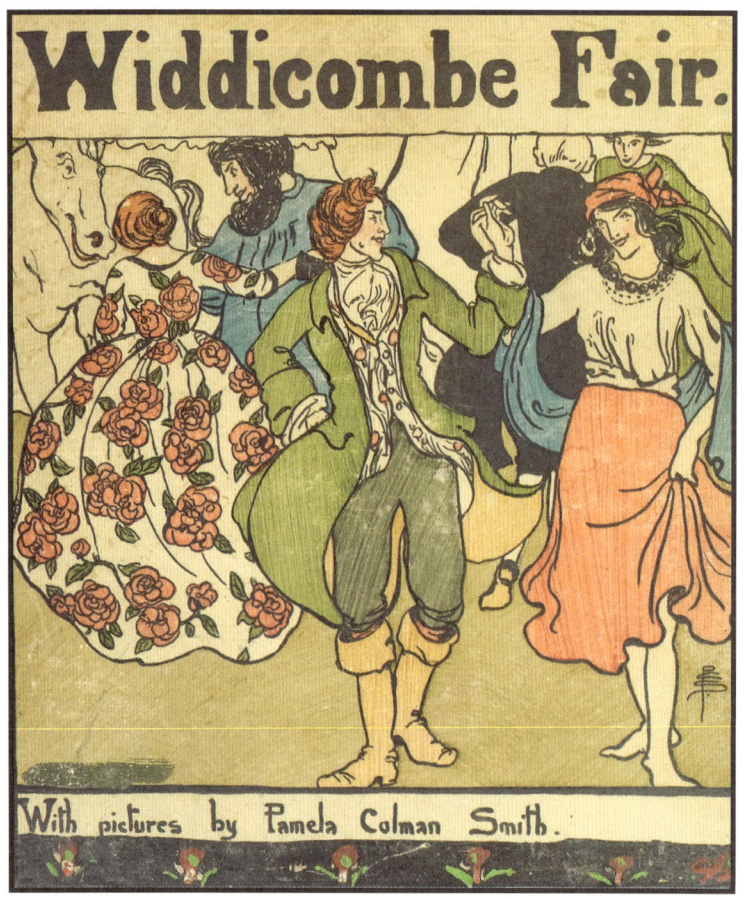

Book cover from *Widdicombe Fair*. Published by Doubleday & McClure Co., 1899

royalties she was due from both R.H. Russell and Doubleday & McClure, the works' respective publishers.

The variety of Pamela's subjects is most clearly evident in her 1899 illustrations for the Old English ballad, *Widdicombe Fair*, which depicts a diverse group of men and women from all walks of life.[86] Her illustrations show women blushing under the gaze of a nearby male, or boldly staring at potential suitors, and still others teasing men as they dance, riotously enjoying themselves, or disdainfully observing the throng. There are several pirates in attendance and at least one dark-skinned performer. The figures in Pamela's drawings display a characteristic energy of movement. Significantly, a large number of these figures are female and their active and almost taunting gaze is unusually bold for the period. Her subjects typically defy Victorian feminine stereotypes and are far from languishing decadent damsels. The *International Studio* magazine commended Pamela's "coloured stencil-pictures," stating that they "are quite astonishing in their ingenuousness and in their force of delineation."[87] For these early works, Pamela created a printmaking technique that fused mechanical reproduction with hand stenciling.[88] This technique, and the works themselves, were influenced by her studies with Arthur Dow at the Pratt Institute.

Pamela loosely based her illustrations for *The Golden Vanity and The Green Bed* as well as *Widdicombe Fair* on Old English ballads that the Rev. Sabine Baring Gould had transcribed from West Country English oral tradition.[89] Pamela and her father had met with Baring Gould, a prolific hymnist, novelist and folklorist, at his Devonshire home during their summer 1899 trip to England and Ireland.[90] Pamela's illustrations were part of a fin de siècle movement of increased interest in traditional West Country English ballads and folklore that spanned the Atlantic Ocean. A company of English singers debuted these songs replete with period costumes and scenery in Boston in the fall of 1899.[91] Interestingly,

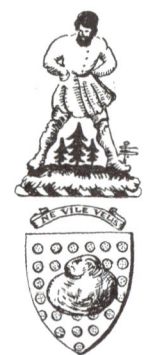

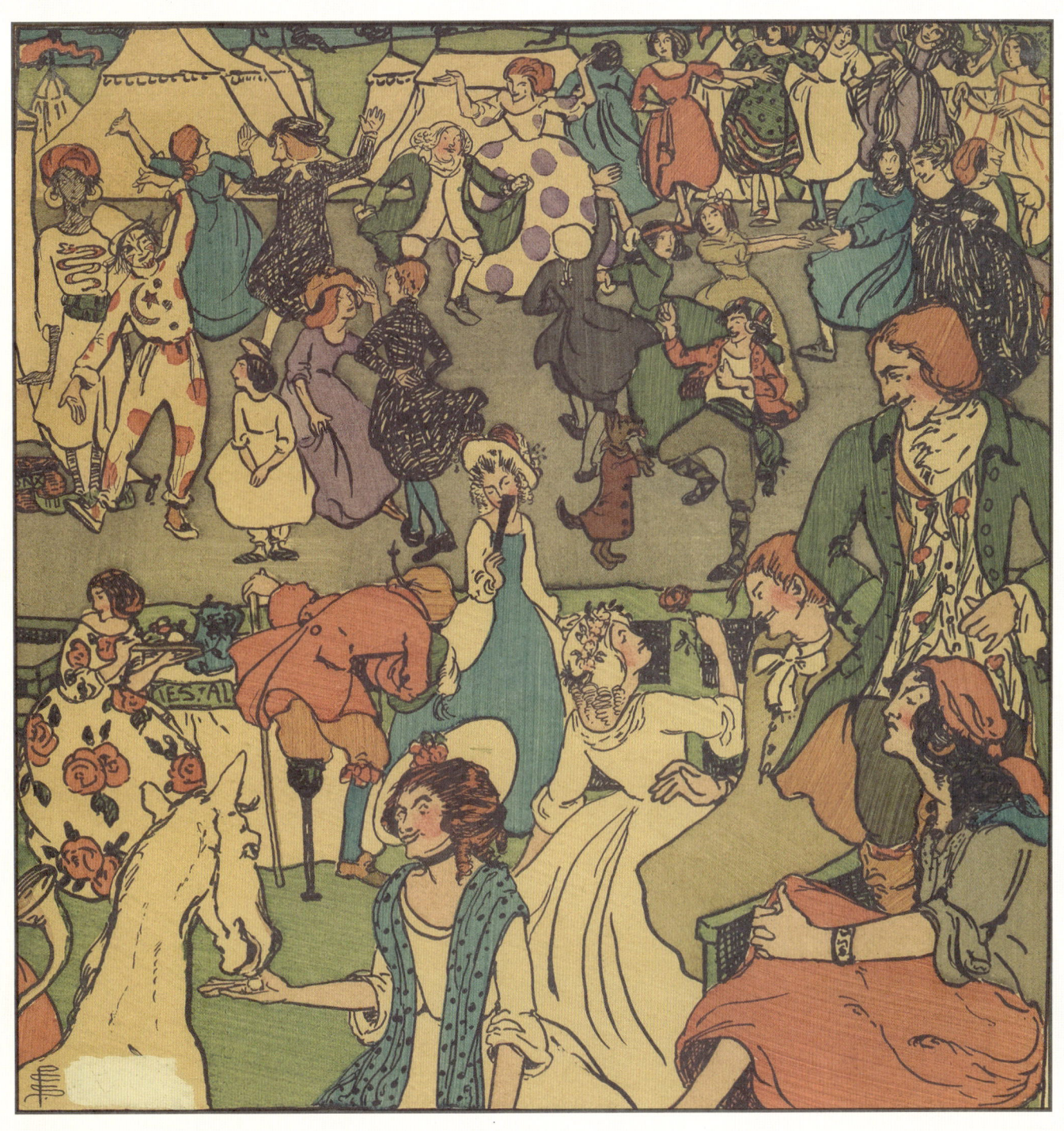

Group of dancers
from *Widdicombe Fair*.
Published by Doubleday
& McClure Co., 1899

the *Philadelphia Inquirer* and the *Washington Times* both noted that it was at Baring Gould's residence that Pamela was first formally introduced to Sir Henry Irving, the famous English actor and owner of the Lyceum Theatre Company. Sir Henry, along with Ellen Terry and Bram Stoker, were to become a central part of Pamela's subsequent personal and artistic life.[92]

Pamela's remaining two 1899 publications were tied to her interest in the theatre world. In February, R.H. Russell released a souvenir collection of several characters from Arthur Wing Pinero's 1898 comic play about the 1860s London theatre scene *Trelawney of the 'Wells'*.[93] Pamela's meeting with Sir Henry Irving in England resulted in her providing him with four large color illustrations and several black and white drawings and sketches for an 18-page souvenir brochure that was published in November by Doubleday & McClure to coincide with the Lyceum Theatre Company's American tour in the fall of 1899. These included Sir Henry in *Robespierre*, Sir Henry and Ellen Terry in *Nance Oldfield*, Ellen in *The Amber Heart*, and Sir Henry and Ellen in *Merchant of Venice*.[94] As a syndicated newspaper article on the souvenir brochure relates, Pamela was allowed "unusual opportunities to study [Irving's] characters, and those of Miss Terry, from 'behind the scenes.' The result is a collection of drawings altogether remarkable."[95] The text of the souvenir booklet was written by Bram Stoker, Irving's longtime manager who is best known for his 1897 novel, *Dracula*. The experience also allowed Pamela to develop a friendship with Sir Henry, Ellen, and Bram as well as other members of their families.

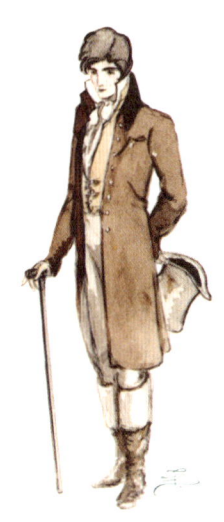

In January 1900 Pamela's involvement with the theatre continued as she worked on "two sets of costumes" for Charles Frohman, a well-known New York producer.[96] She also contributed to another souvenir theatre booklet, this one for her cousin, William Gillette, who achieved prominence in several stage versions of Arthur Conan Doyle's *Sherlock Holmes*.[97] Gillette, who was Pamela's paternal cousin, was the first to portray the fictional detective and endowed him with several attributes that, although absent from the novels, are now commonly associated with him: deerstalker hat, pipe, smoking jacket, patterned socks, striped slippers, multiple rings, and a messy Victorian study. The result, as Heather Campbell Coyle notes, is "a rather louche and bohemian Holmes—more Robert Downey Jr. than Basil Rathbone—who is immediately familiar over one-hundred years later."[98] This image of Gillette as Holmes was to become cemented in the public consciousness through illustrations in *Colliers* and *The Strand* but Pamela's cover depiction, published in 1901, is believed to be the first.[99] Several examples of Pamela's watercolors were collected by Gillette and are today prominently displayed in Connecticut's Gillette castle, which is now a state park.[100]

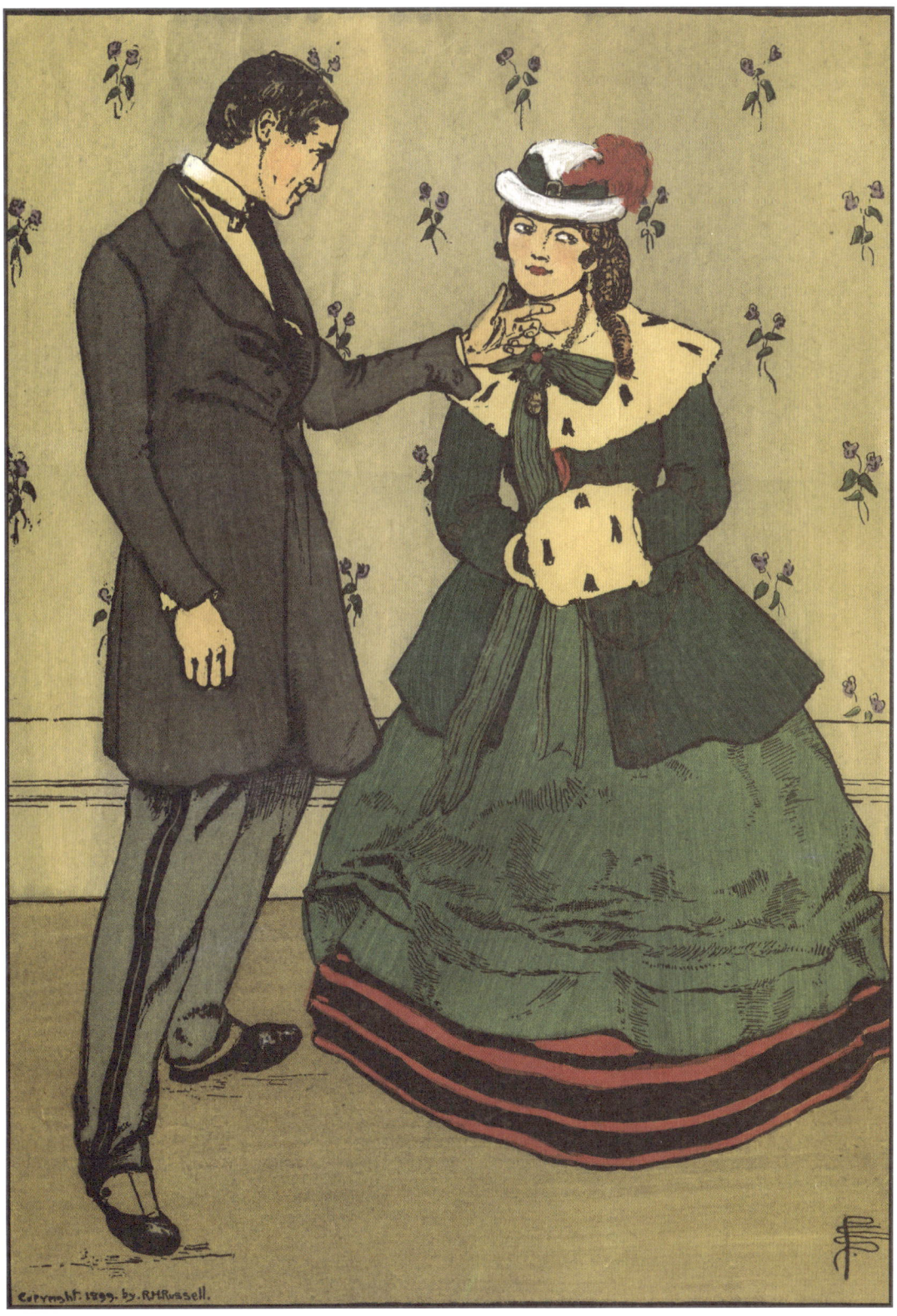

Tom and Imogene from *Trelawney of the Wells, Act III*. Published by R.H. Russell, 1899

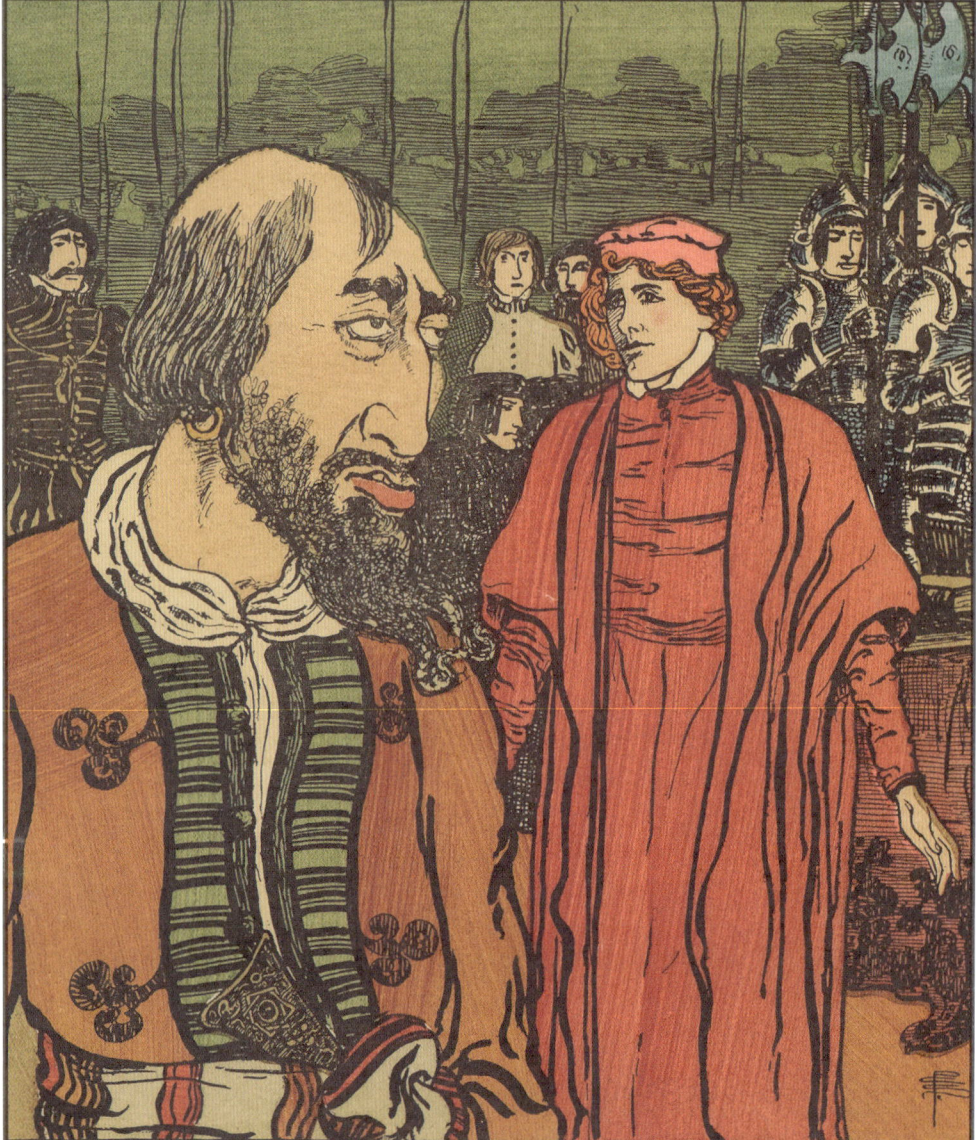

Sir Henry Irving as Shylock and Miss Ellen Terry as Portia in *Merchant of Venice*, Act IV, from *Lyceum Souvenir* by Bram Stoker. Published by Doubleday & McClure Co., 1899

Pamela's art was also included in two exhibitions in the spring of 1900. In January, her watercolor "London Bridge," was on display at Macbeth's 5th Avenue Manhattan gallery. Pictorial in style, the painting displays different types of Londoners, such as the Lord Chancellor, Salvation Army men, society swells, and beggars, all making their way across the busy crossing.[101] In June, some of her drawings were included in an exhibition and sale at Pratt Institute for the benefit of the Art Students' Fund Association.[102]

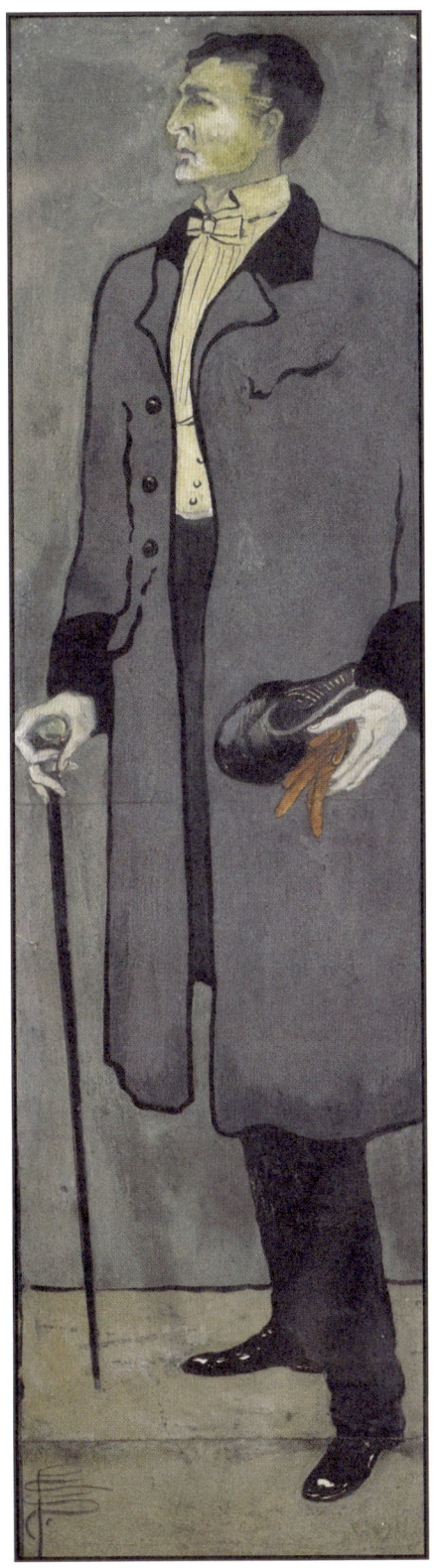
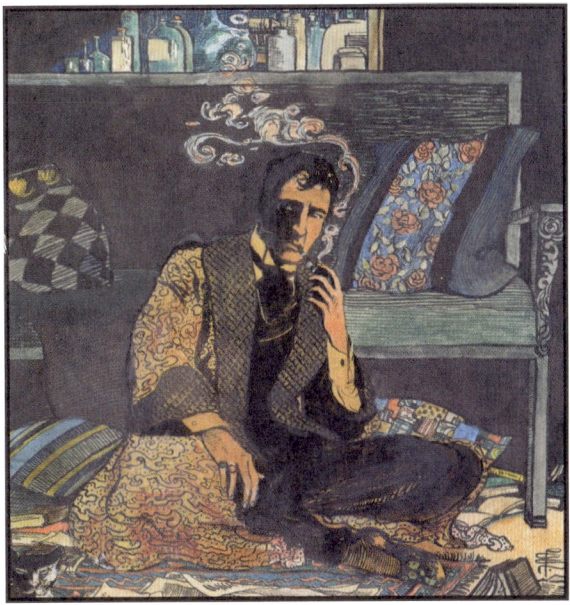
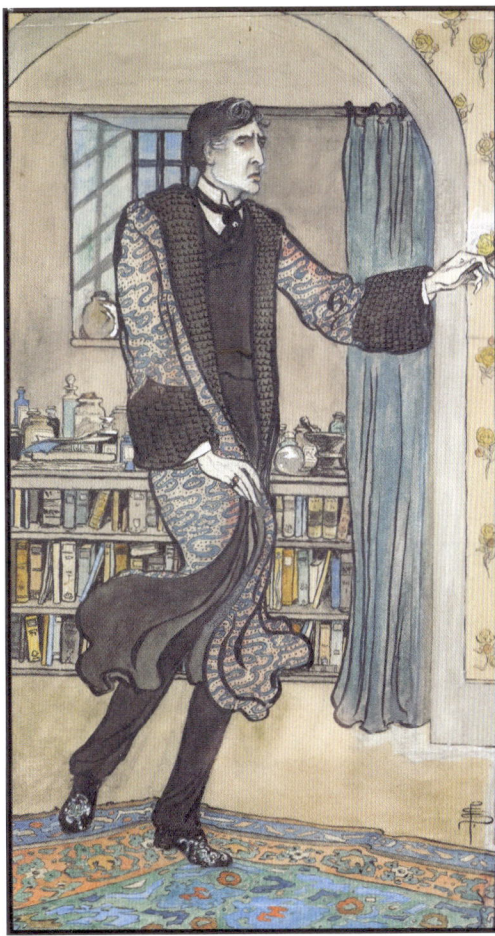

Sherlock Holmes from *William Gillette as Sherlock Holmes*, produced at the Garrick Theatre, New York. Published by R.H. Russell, 1900

Return to England

The Bramy Joker from "Ellen Peg's Book of Merry Joys," an unpublished folio that Pamela collaborated with Edy Craig, circa 1900-1901. Courtesy © National Trust, UK

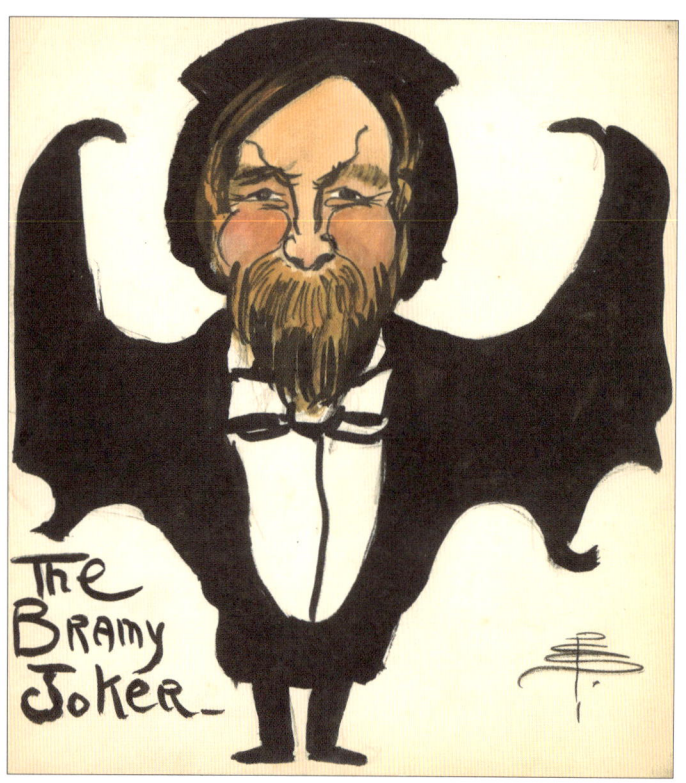

On December 1, 1899, Pamela's father, Charles Edward, died in New York unexpectedly.[103] The *Brooklyn Daily Eagle* notes that his passing was a "severe bereavement" for his daughter and that "the companionship between the two was very close and affectionate."[104] He was 53. Pamela's short letter to her cousin Mary Reed on his passing does not dwell on her father's demise but instead expresses her happiness at her cousin's projected visit and refuses a Christmas invitation as she would be "rushed with orders" for lampshades, little boxes, and other decorative items.[105] Much of Pamela's letter details her growing friendship with Ellen Terry, whom she refers to as ET and terms "a dear," and a trip that she is planning with her to Philadelphia.[106] Interestingly, Pamela signs the letter "Pixie Pamela"—the nickname that she will use for more than a decade—and notes "That's my name ET gave me."[107] In a January 15, 1900 letter to her son, Edward Gordon Craig, Ellen Terry is impressed by Pamela's work ethic and states that "[s]he is extraordinarily industrious & is ever-lastingly making & selling as fast as she makes."[108] Ellen goes on to detail the prices Pamela gets for her handiwork and concludes that she is "a funny little creature."[109] The friendship between the two deepened over the winter, with Pamela appearing in performances of *Robespierre*, *Merchant of Venice*, and *The Bells* as part of the crowd. This culminates with Pamela telling her cousin that "I am going home with Miss Terry?!!!!! Isant [sic] it lovely!!!!???!!!"[110] Home, of course, was England where Pamela had spent her childhood and where she would remain, interspersed with extended trips to the U.S., for the rest of her life.

Pamela set sail from New York on May 19, 1900 on the S.S. Menomenee with Sir Henry Irving, Bram Stoker and Ellen Terry.[111] Upon Pamela's arrival in England, she quickly became friends with Ellen's two grown children, Edith Craig, known as Edy, and Edward Gordon Craig, known as Gordon. She also became friendly with many of their friends and acquaintances, most notably Christopher "Chris" St. John, formally Christabel Marshall, who was to become Edy's longtime partner. Shortly after arriving in England, Pamela collaborated with Edy on the unpublished portfolio, "Ellen Peg's Book of Merry Joys," which describes the authors as "the 2 little devils Pixie & Puck."[112] During Pamela's transatlantic voyage, she began work on another portfolio that included scenes from a shipboard concert by Ellen and Sir Henry as well as a caricature of the "Bramy Joker" as a bat. In the fall of 1900, Pamela embarked on a tour of England with the Lyceum Theatre Company for which she played in crowd scenes.[113] During the nine-week tour, she visited Brighton, Edinburgh, Glasgow, Manchester, and Liverpool, "a very American place—and of <u>course</u> I didn't like it."[114] In Manchester, Pamela "went all over the house I lived in till I was 10."[115]

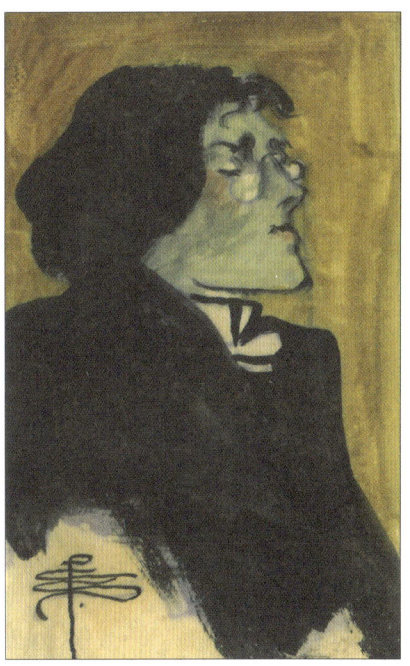

Portrait of Laurence Irving by Pamela Colman Smith painted inside the front endpaper of her personal copy of Godefroi and Yolande, a Medieval Play in One Act, published in 1908

One of Pamela's first projects after her return to England was a series of illustrations for *Kensington Magazine*, a short-lived publication that was edited by Beatrice Erskine and R.J. Richardson. These included a wash drawing of Peg Woffington, the eponymous protagonist of Charles Reade's 1853 novel about an Irish actress; Ellen Terry in the "Strolling Players" and a two-page cartoon entitled "Our Adventures" that detailed the experiences during their American tour; a depiction of Sarah Bernhardt in Edmond Rostand's *L'Aiglon*, and a Japanese-inspired illustration, "The Faithful Wife Dancing Before the Robbers."[116] Edy and Chris also contributed to the publication.

During this period, Pamela often contributed to projects that Ellen Terry's children Edy or Gordon Craig were working on. In May 1901, Edy designed 39 dresses for the English actor Sir Johnston Forbes-Robertson's new play, *The Sacraments of Judas*. Pamela did sketches of the designs and earned eight shillings, which she termed "bus fare if nothing more!"[117] An illustration by Pamela that had been previously exhibited, "The Wind," appeared in Gordon Craig's little magazine, *The Page*.[118] She also designed bookplates for friends and acquaintances. One of these, for the actor Frank Tyars, was included in Wilbur Macey Stone's 1902 collection *Women designers of book-plates*.[119] In January 1902, a poster she had designed advertising a dramatic performance on board the S.S. Menominee—the ship on which she, Ellen Terry and Sir Henry Irving crossed the Atlantic—was included in the Grantham Industrial Exhibition.[120]

By the winter of 1901, Pamela had settled at 14 Milbourne Grove, The Boltons, in South Kensington. After a short time, Pamela rented the flat next door for her studio. These rooms soon became the focus of a weekly gathering of artists, writers, actors, and other Chelsea bohemians. In his 1911 memoir of his life in England in the early years of the 20th century, Arthur Ransome recalls his first visit to Pamela's salon and refers to her as "Gypsy." Ransome describes her as "a little round woman" who "looked as if she had been the same age all her life, and would be so to the end." He notes that she "was dressed in an orange-coloured coat that hung loose over a green skirt, with black tassels sewn all over the orange silk, like the frills on a red Indian's trousers."[121] Her greeting was "a little shriek," a sound Ransome describes as "oddest, most uncanny little shriek, half laugh, half exclamation."

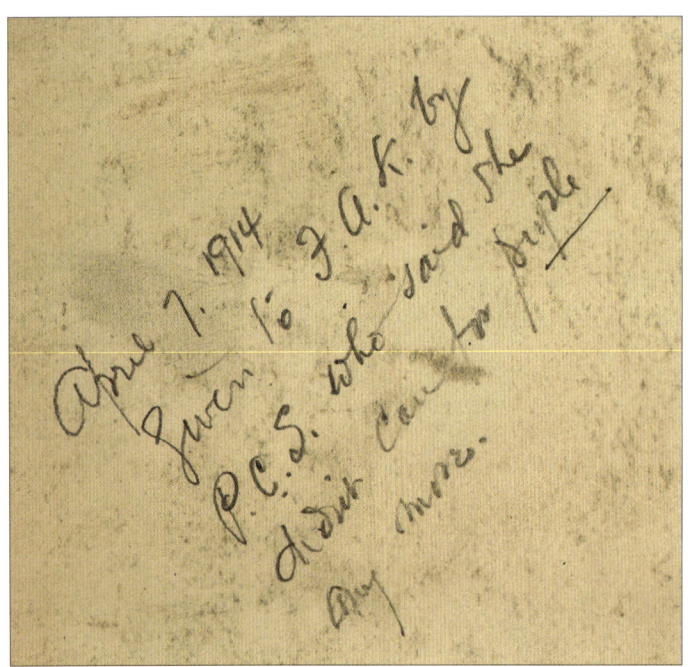

Handwritten inscription by Pamela Colman Smith dated April 7, 1914 from the inside back cover of her Visitors book, 1901-1905

The room was filled with a group of artists and writers and on every surface there were books, art supplies, china toys, and piles of portfolio; perched "ridiculously" on top of one pile was a woolly monkey. The group drank opal hush, claret mixed with lemonade, "so that a beautiful amethystine foam rose shimmering to the brim." Pamela told those assembled that it was the favored drink of the Irish poets. After refreshments, she, and others, sang songs, played piano, and recited poems. The evening ended with Pamela telling some of the Annancy tales she had previously published and she would use to entertain groups of paying customers with at recitals in the U.S. and England. Ransome recalls that she "flopped down on the floor, behind a couple of lighted candles" and "told story after story, illustrating them with the help of wooden toys she had made herself."[122] Although Pamela's studios would frequently change location, this weekly gathering continued well into the next decade, with friends memorializing the salon with drawings and poems in her guest book. On April 7, 1914 the Visitors book last entry notes "Given to F.A.K. by P.C.S. who said she didn't care for *people* anymore." The F.A.K is Frederick Allen King who was a literary and dramatic editor of *The Literary Digest* and likely Pamela's New York agent until the 1930s.

In addition, to hosting a weekly salon at her Chelsea studio, Pamela also began to take part in the wider London social scene. At a studio tea in a mews, she finally met W.B. Yeats in March 1901. She described her encounter this way:

> W.B.Y. was there and he is a rummy critter! Seemed most stupid and had on a tea party air and posed about and looked bored—And when all the ladies with ermine collars had gone, who all told him how very much they liked his bloomin poetry, which probably they had never read or heard of… then WB began to talk! Folklore—songs, plays, Irish, language, and lots more—reciting a sort of folksong which was splendid.[123]

What is striking about her hard-headed account—even more than her preference for W.B.'s folklore over his poems—is that it is hardly that of a naïve child. Shortly after this initial meeting, he saw her stage designs for *The Countess Cathleen* and watched parts of a performance of the play in her miniature theatre with which he was "much pleased."[124]

Pamela quickly became part of the constellation of artists, writers, and musicians associated with W.B. Yeats and his family. She joined first the Irish Literary Society and then the Masquers.[125] The latter group also counted among its key members Florence Farr, Edy Craig, and the artist Walter Crane, who was an important early influence for Pamela.[126] Pamela's friendship with George Russell (A.E.), led to her contributing the cover design for the *Celtic Christmas*, the holiday number of the *Irish Homestead*, from 1903-1906.

One of the most important connections for her artistic career and long-term reputation occurred in the fall of 1901 when Pamela joined the Isis-Urania Temple of the Order of the Golden Dawn; W.B. Yeats and Florence Farr Emery were also members. Pamela's motto was *Quod Tibi Id Allis* or "To Yourself as to Others." Through this group she also met Arthur Edward Waite who would commission her now famous tarot deck in 1909.

During this period, a close mentorship developed between Pamela and W.B. Yeats, and she consulted him in all of her major editorial endeavours. Pamela frequently discussed plans for a projected illustrated edition of Blake—someone they both admired—and suggested she design a book of Gaelic mythology for children but nothing came of either plan.[127] She did the stage makeup for W.B.'s *Cathleen ni Houlihan* and three years later her way of blackening Kathleen's face had become "a holy tradition."[128] In 1904 Pamela collaborated on stage designs and costumes with her close friend Edy Craig for W.B.'s *Where There is Nothing* in a production that premiered at the Royal Court Theatre in London in November 1904.[129] Yeats termed parts of these designs "impressive" and wrote to Lady Gregory shortly after the play's opening that "Pixie Smith…alone seems to understand what I want."[130]

Problems with Publishers

DURING THIS FIN DE SIÈCLE PERIOD, PAMELA CONCEIVED OF SEVERAL BOOK LENGTH PROJECTS, including an illustrated collection of 60 fairy poems tentatively titled *Pixie's Poetry Book*, and an illustrated edition of Anna Laetitia Barbauld's 1778 *Lessons for Children*, that never made it into print.[131] She attempted to place this last project with multiple publishers to no avail. Pamela's ventures into the world of publishing yielded a range of emotions, frustration chief among them. She vented her annoyance in a series of letters to Alfred Bigelow Paine, whom she affectionately referred to as "Dear Tutter." Paine was the children's page editor of the *New York Sunday Herald* in 1898, and from 1898-1909 was an editor at *St. Nicholas Magazine*; in 1901 he became a reader and solicitor of material for the Henry Altemus Publishing Company and is most famous for his multi-volume biography of Mark Twain. While none of Paine's letters to Pamela are preserved, the comfort and intimacy between the two evident from her replies are remarkable. A March 1901 letter to Paine saw her anger and annoyance bubble to the surface of the usually upbeat and pragmatic tone of most of her letters. She writes, "Pigs! The publishers are all pigs!?!"[132] At times her inability to place her work led her to humorously negotiate as she does in an August 1899 letter to Paine: "We are…dead broke so will give St. Nick some old bargains cheap! Ha!"[133] In other letters, she celebrates small victories: "I got $89.80 royalty on Irving Souvenier!! Ha! Much forced!! Perhaps I shall someday get as much as $50.75 out of RHR."[134] RHR refers to Robert H. Russell, representative of the William H. Russell publishing firm that put out some of her early work. Pamela's frustration over her difficulty placing her edition of Barbauld's *Lessons for Children*, which she endearingly refers to as Little Charles, with a publisher is indicative. As she writes to Paine on May 28, 1901, "That bloomin pig!... [Grant] Richards! Kept Little Charles 6 weeks and then returned him! Then sent him to Heineman and Lane and Duckworth in turn. & he came back from each! An older & a wiser Charles!- but still he is in a neat little red portfolio & no publisher is likely to take him! jam!!!!!!!!!!!!"[135] Later that same summer she expressed her exhaustion over the whole process, especially her distance from many of the New York publishers: "Has RR [Russell] been over here [England] this year? Or Doubleday? I can't find out anything! Dam publishers any way! –I am tired of 'em."[136] Thus, it is not difficult to see why Pamela would be interested in gaining more control over the publication process, first by becoming editor of two literary magazines and then, eventually, owning and operating her own small press. One of Paine's short stories, "The Boat of Dreams," was included in the ninth issue of *The Green Sheaf*.

Far right: Facsimile of letter by Pamela Colman Smith dated May 28, 1901 to Alfred Bigelow Paine, aka Tutter. Courtesy of The Huntington Library

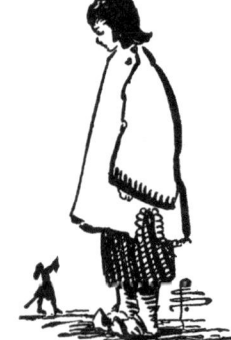

14. Melbourne Grove –
The Boltons S.W.
London
May 28. 1901.

Dear Tutter –
 Howdee ! — Your letter of April 8.
came weeks ago ! —
 Been very busy! Dress rehearsals & new plays,
helping Edy – and getting my office &
theatre in order – we call it "The Henrietta
Theatre"! — Yeats came & saw part of
"The Countess Cathleen" and seemed much
pleased with the theatre! So is also
Robert Taber & Forbes Robertson – they
want to see a play soon too – old "Harry
Morgan" is being called to rehearsal —
Edy seems to think he is great fun! —
"Here we are in old London again!" in sooth
"'tis a merry town!"
You'd better make your always thought of
trip & "it shall be a roaring spree!" &
I like your description of the Studio tea!
Thank goodness I have not been to any
more! Sent you a Kensington some weeks
ago – hope it reached you —
First blooming "Richards" kept "Little
Charles" 6 weeks & then returned him!
Others sent him to – Heinemann & Lane &
Duckworth in turn

& he came back from each! an older & a
wiser Charles! – but still he is in a neat
little red portfolio & no publisher is likely
to take him! – Jam!!!!!!
 "Coriolanus" is rather nice – not very! – and only
ran 6 weeks! — And yesterday they began
"Robespierre" again! – and in a week or so. "Madame
Sans Gene" — and "Charles I" & "Louis XI"
H.I. did not seem to speak as plainly as usual
& when saying wretch – says rats!! — E.T.
as skipping as Volumnia — She is very
well! better than she has been for months!
— I saw Heinemann after the first
night – a supper on the stage – and asked him
why he did not take "Charles". He began
to stammer a lot about the War!
(Blow!) Norman Hapgood — is in town & is
rosier than ever! — See him at first nights
& things — Tacoma Laurance's latest – seems
to be Alice Neilson — She's a darn little
thing! — I saw Pelleas & Melisande a
week or so ago – Harry awfully good in it
& Mrs Pat Campbell looks godly —
Forbes Robertson has a new play the Laurance
of Judas" – and Edy did 39 dresses for
it & helped – & did sketches for it for
8 shillings! So you see bus fare – if nothing
more!

a ripping good play! – The last act
stunning! Brittany in 1791! & ladies dresses
like this — Gertrude Elliot! each eye bigger than
her mouth! very nice
& quite good for the part

"Santos I have met!"
Hope old mc'Cann is OK
it is be ?

I don't know if I shall be over in Oct. or
not — it seems a long way I can't say! —
Thanks for papers you sent. I should like
magazines! Chris dipped into them freely for
"Far & Near" which she writes for The Lady
every week – we all liked 'em & wish you'd
send more! – please! You did not Eleanor
& had you did – the idea of calling anything or
anybody! Brooklyn!
Next time you see G.W.E. (his) tell
him a merry (forced) howdee from me!
Ask Hackett if he remembers sitting next
only to Dattley & I in the stalls at "The Only
199 Way"? – & if he ever got the set of
Trelawny prints I sent to him care of the
Greenroom club — ?

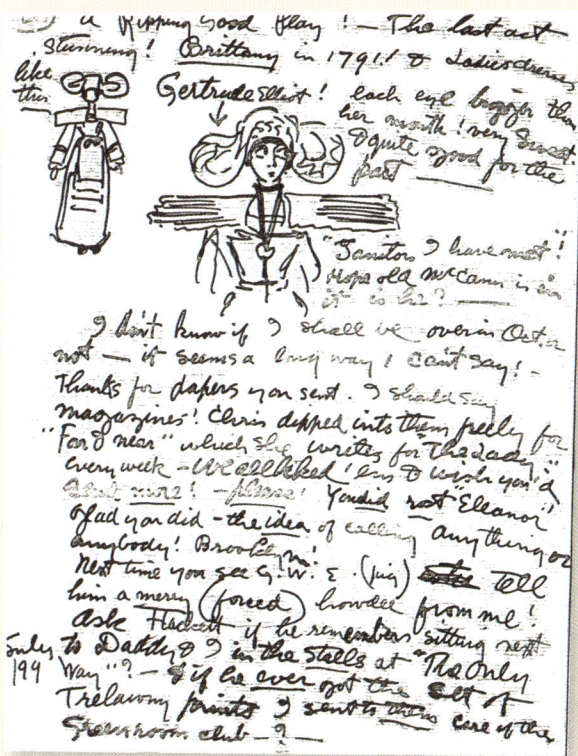

4) They say "Lady Huntworth" was good I didn't
see it &
 I told Teddy Craig some weeks ago – to write
you and send some drawings – he is so very
cracky! You'd better write him & ask him to
write again – think you might get an idea
for a sort of mad person for a book!
from his letters —
 Lots of new plays here – mostly bad. some
good – mighty few! —
 I have been to Chislehurst – over Sunday –
a nice place – lovely woods – clouds of bluebells
& I stayed with the Wards – Marcus Ward's brother
& they lived there when we did – in 1790 & 80 &
81. — & I was about 2 or 3! —
 Love to all gang when you see 'em!
no more news now — so will stop.
  Write some more amusing letters
please!
  Pinkie
  Pamela

A Broad Sheet and The Green Sheaf

PAMELA'S OWN LITTLE MAGAZINE, *THE GREEN SHEAF*, GREW OUT OF HER EXPERIENCES AS co-editor with Jack Yeats of *A Broad Sheet* during 1902-1903. This partnership appears to have served as her first-hand introduction to the world of little magazines. Her role in this publication began after she struck up a friendship with Jack and his wife, Mary "Cottie" Yeats, cultivated by their shared love of miniature theatre. In June 1901 Pamela visited the Yeats's cottage in Devonshire, watched Jack's performance of his miniature circus, and then dressed up and regaled them with performances of Jamaican folktales replete with handmade cardboard cut-outs of the key characters.[137] In an August 1901 letter to Tutter, Pamela fondly recalls her trip and how nice Jack and Cottie were, noting approvingly that Jack "draws such bully things!"[138]

A Broad Sheet, as its name implies, was a one-page publication that was published and sold by Elkin Mathews. Originally a format for public notices it was favored in the 17th and 18th centuries by balladers, poets, and political activists. A subscription was 12 shillings a year and $3 in the United States. It primarily featured large, hand-colored drawings by Jack Yeats and Pamela accompanied by poetry and prose from many prominent figures of the Irish Literary Revival. Notable highlights from Pamela's tenure at *A Broad Sheet* include her illustration of the "Blood Bond" passage of George Moore and W.B. Yeats's play *Diarmuid and Grania*, her illustration of George Russell's (A.E) "The Gates of Dreamland" and her drawing, "A Cobweb Cloak of Time" accompanied by a short poem she had written. It is noteworthy that prominently displayed in seven of the eleven issues that Pamela co-edited with Jack Yeats, are large drawings prepared by her at the top of the page, which might have contributed to some of the conflict between her and Jack Yeats. A December 15, 1902 letter from Jack to John Quinn hints at personal discord between them:

> Between you and me and the wall, as they say, Miss Pamela Smith (though I think her a fine illustrator with a fine eye for colour and just the artist for illuminating verse) is a little bit lazy, and she being a woman I can't take a very high hand with things, so there is often a lot of fuss about the numbers, and I don't like to be responsible for anything that I have not got absolute control of.[139]

Jack Yeats continued to edit this iteration of *A Broad Sheet* without interruption until December 1903 and did contribute a drawing to the tenth edition of *The Green Sheaf*.

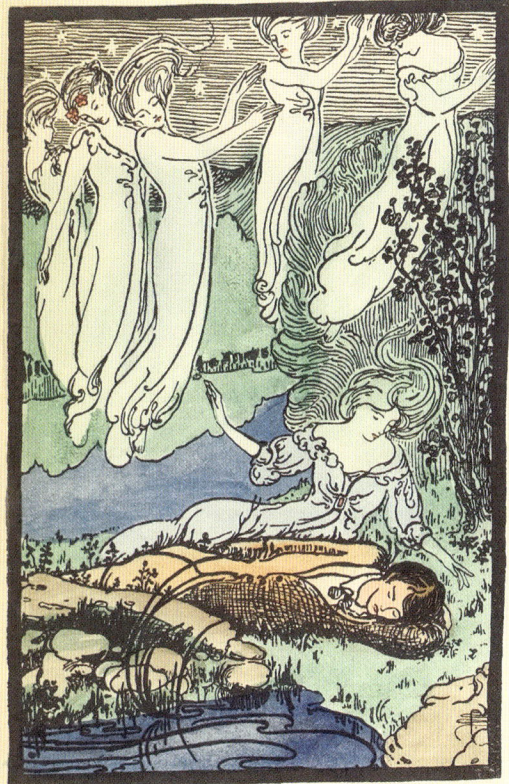

A BROAD SHEET
JUNE, 1902
PICTURES BY MISS PAMELA COLMAN SMITH AND JACK B. YEATS.

THE GATES OF DREAMLAND.

It's a lonely road through bogland to the lake at Carrowmore,
And a sleeper there lies dreaming, where the water laps the shore.
Though the moth wings of the twilight in their purples are unfurled,
Yet his sleep is filled with music by the masters of the world.

There's a hand is white as silver that is fondling with his hair,
There are glimmering feet of sunshine that are dancing by him there,
And half open lips of faery that were dyed to richest red
In their revels where the Hazel Tree its holy clusters shed.

"Come away," the red lips whisper, "all the world is weary now,
'Tis the twilight of the ages, and it's time to quit the plough.
Oh, the very sunlight's weary ere it lightens up the dew,
And its gold is changed to grey light before it falls to you."

"Though your colleen's heart is tender, a tenderer heart is near;
What's the starlight in her glances when the stars are shining clear?
Who would kiss the fading shadow, when the flower face glows above?
'Tis the Beauty of all Beauty that is calling for your love."

Oh, the mountain gates of dreamland have opened once again,
And the sound of song and dancing falls upon the ears of men;
And the Land of Youth lies gleaming, lit with rainbow light and mirth,
And the old enchantment lingers in the honey heart of earth.

A. E.

In January 1903 Pamela struck out on her own and launched her own little magazine, *The Green Sheaf*. During the planning stages of this magazine she consulted W.B. Yeats repeatedly; ultimately, however, she did not incorporate many of his suggestions. She replaced his choice of *Hour-Glass*—the title of one of his plays—with *The Green Sheaf* and dedicated the little magazine not to "the Art of Happy Desire," as he suggested, but more simply to "pleasure."[140] Where W.B. Yeats wanted the subject matter to be confined to dreams of an ideal state, "beautiful or charming or in some other way desirable," Pamela chose to have her title page proclaim "pictures, verses, ballads, of love and war; tales of pirates and the sea . . . ballads of the old world."[141] An enigmatic title, *The Green Sheaf*, and its accompanying image of a sheaf of green-colored pages tied with a red ribbon, brings to mind U.S. currency, of which Pamela often lamented her shortage, but also the green

"The Gates of Dreamland" by George Russell, aka A.E. From *A Broad Sheet*, June 1902 sheaves of grain that in the Bible the Israelites offer to God in order that He may bless the spring harvest.[142] While grain is the most commonly discussed sheaf, as the *Oxford English Dictionary* notes, it can also refer to "a cluster or bundle of things tied up together."[143] In this respect the title is quite apt, as the magazine contained a range of art, poetry, fiction, translations, and non-fiction prose of a wide variety of styles. In addition, green, a color traditionally associated with health and fertility, also had a long association with homosexuality. In ancient Latin the adjective *galbinatus* meant both a shade of green and effeminate.[144] This association became prominent in the 1890s through the work of Oscar Wilde, who habitually wore a green carnation to identify his orientation.[145] While Pamela's familiarity with this practice is unclear, she did like the color and wrote almost all of her business and personal correspondence in green ink during this period.

Notably, *The Green Sheaf* did not include any of Pamela's retellings of Jamaican folktales. One possible explanation for this omission is that Pamela felt strongly that her retellings of Anansi stories needed to be written in a language that reflected, but did not completely mimic, the patois of the Jamaicans from whom she first heard the tales. While this is now standard practice, it was not the case when Pamela first began publishing her versions of these tales in the mid-1890s. *The Green Sheaf*, as its editorial statement affirms, was very catholic in its content and printed a wide variety of fairy and folktales from several different countries. However, all of its content was written in standard English and it may be the fear of losing subscribers that caused Pamela to refrain from publishing any of her retellings in the pages of her magazine. Despite having persistent problems with money throughout her adult life, Pamela's letters reveal that she was attuned to financial concerns and quite savvy in at least some of her financial decisions.

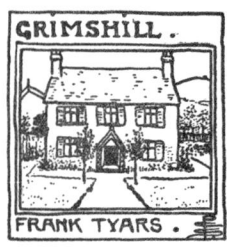

Bookplate by Pamela Colman Smith

While *A Broad Sheet*, the magazine on which she collaborated with Jack Yeats, was closer in spirit to the fine art small press publications of the 1880s and 90s, such as the *Hobby Horse*, *The Green Sheaf* can clearly be seen as a forerunner of the little magazines of the 1910s-1920s. Instead of *A Broad Sheet's* single page, *The Green Sheaf* was generally 12 pages with a few issues as large as 16 and some as small as eight pages. It was priced at 13 shillings for a yearly subscription—one more than *A Broad Sheet*—but offered 13 issues for that price instead of the 11 of *A Broad Sheet*. Pamela's publication also provided readers with the option to purchase individual issues for 13 pence each. Both magazines were published on a letterpress printer on thick, hand-made paper, and colored by hand. *A Broad Sheet* was published and sold by Elkin Mathews and printed by Farncombe & Son, Printers, Croydon. Mathews, in concert with John Lane, published the infamous *Yellow Book* in 1894 and after their split became the first publisher of such authors as W.B. Yeats, James

Joyce, Ezra Pound and Robert Bridges. In contrast, *The Green Sheaf* was edited, published, and sold by Pamela herself. There is no reference as to who printed the magazine; the one exception to this appears to be the supplement to the ninth number that contained John Todhunter's "A Dream," which is credited as being printed by the Farncombe firm. This supplement seems to be a bit of an anomaly as the back advertising page notes that "After Thirteen numbers of the First Volume have been completed *The Green Sheaf* will be published Quarterly."[146] This did not happen nor was the notice repeated in the tenth or eleventh numbers.

Early issues of *The Green Sheaf* saw poetry, fiction, and drama by many of those who graced the pages of *A Broad Sheet* such as W.B. Yeats, A.E. [George Russell], and F. York Powell. It also continued and extended the earlier journal's practice of publishing work from now-deceased artists and writers. To that end, *The Green Sheaf* printed several works by William Blake, short stories by Anna Laetitia Barbauld, and poems by John Keats as well as a short translation of a work by Friedrich Nietzsche and a painting by Dante Gabriel Rossetti. And just like the earlier publication, each issue featured multiple drawings and poems by Pamela. Numbers of *The Green Sheaf* also included work by such figures of the Irish Literary Revival as Lady Augusta Gregory and J.M. Synge. Names more commonly associated with the theatre, such as Edward Gordon Craig, Martin Shaw, Christopher St. John, and E. Harcourt Williams graced the pages of the magazine. While Pamela's close friend Edy Craig did not contribute any signed entries for the magazine, almost every issue of *The Green Sheaf* contains an advertisement for "Edith Craig & Co." which provided costumes for private and public theatricals. Other contributors included Victor Bridges, Lady Alix Egerton, Cecil French, W.T. Horton, Laurence Irving, John Masefield, Yone Noguchi, Ernest Radford, Reginald Rigby and John Todhunter. *The Green Sheaf* also published the work of a host of seemingly unknown women writers—many of whom may have been pseudonyms—as well as anonymous contributions that increased as the numbers progressed.

Although some issues of *The Green Sheaf*, have a unifying theme, such as the second that focuses on dreams and the supernatural, most numbers of the magazine were more loosely conceived. Pamela's editorial direction seems to have been to present the widest range of content possible. For example, the third issue begins with "The Harvest Home Masque" by Edward Gordon Craig and Martin Shaw, which is partly an explanation of this dramatic representation of the peasant celebration of the end of harvest and part advertisement for a modern version the authors could present in a home or theatre setting.[147] This is followed by Alix Egerton's poem "The Lament of the Dead Knight," which explores the supernatural

Opposite: "Eventide" poem by Ernest Radford. From *The Green Sheaf* No. 3, 1903

love between the dead speaker and his bereaved lady love; a Cecil French drawing of grieving lovers separated by coils of snaky brambles that seems more in keeping with the nineteenth century than the twentieth is at the bottom of the page.[148] Ernest Radford's poem "Eventide" follows and is joined by one of Pamela's more mystical illustrations—an androgynous figure wrapped in a shawl who is being pulled along by cavorting redheaded pixies while pairs of lovers embrace on clouds scattered throughout the darkening sky.[149] Sheet Music for the folk song "Spanish Ladies," which was arranged by Martin Shaw, is accompanied by a rectangular illustration done by Pamela.[150] Her drawing brings to mind her work on *The Golden Vanity and The Green Bed;* while one of her Spanish ladies has downcast eyes and a raised fan in response to the blandishments of a seaman ready to set sail for England; the other stares disinterestedly into the distance.

While the majority of the content of *The Green Sheaf* pertains to legend, fantasy, or the distant past, a few issues of the magazine contain poetry and drawings that deal with contemporary life and, notably, they are created by Pamela herself. For example, the fourth issue contains her stark illustration of a woman walking by herself in a field that is barren except for two leafless trees standing watch. It is complemented by the poem, "Alone" in which the speaker laments that she feels alienated regardless of the setting: "In cities large—in country lane,/ Around the world—tis all the same;/ Across the sea from shore to shore,/ Alone—alone, for evermore."[151]

Although it is tempting to read into this work Pamela's own isolation and alienation, the poem can definitely be seen as foreshadowing the bleaker, more introspective turn in poetry of the modernist period. Pamela returns to the hazard of city life in the penultimate issue, number 12, through the large illustration and accompanying poem, "The Town." Featuring the profile of a woman caught in a rare moment of repose while she contemplates the talking men and dancing lovers that surround her, the vividly-colored drawing conveys the glamour and bustle of city life as well as the dissatisfaction many of its inhabitants experience.

The brief poem, unlike almost all of the other poems in the magazine, features enjambment—the running of a line into the next—which was to become a central feature of modernist poetry: "O deary me how idle is/ This great and weary town./ For people talk and never do/ As they go up and down."[152] In this work, even "the great" town is "weary;" interestingly, this lassitude is not due to the hustle and bustle of the thousands of people who flood its streets every day, but by the emptiness of their talk and their complacent failure to do anything they say they will.

The Green Sheaf

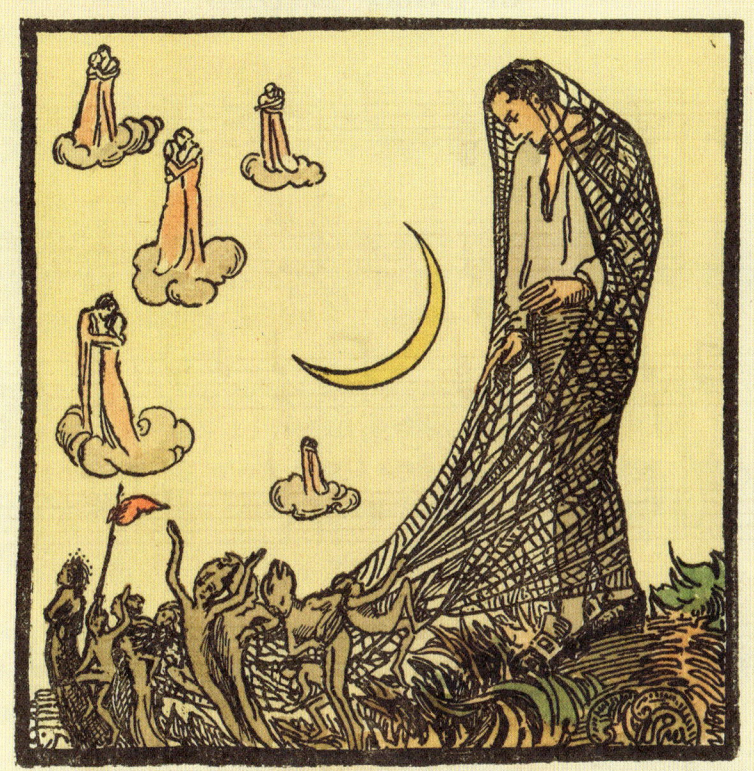

EVENTIDE.

The lonely path that I would tread
At night-fall by the pixies led,
It leadeth to the no-man's land
Where plighted, linkèd lovers stand :—
Lips sealing lips, in silence they
Give ear to what the heavens say :—
The evening star to setting sun—
" The day has half its course to run."

Ernest Radford.

The Green Sheaf

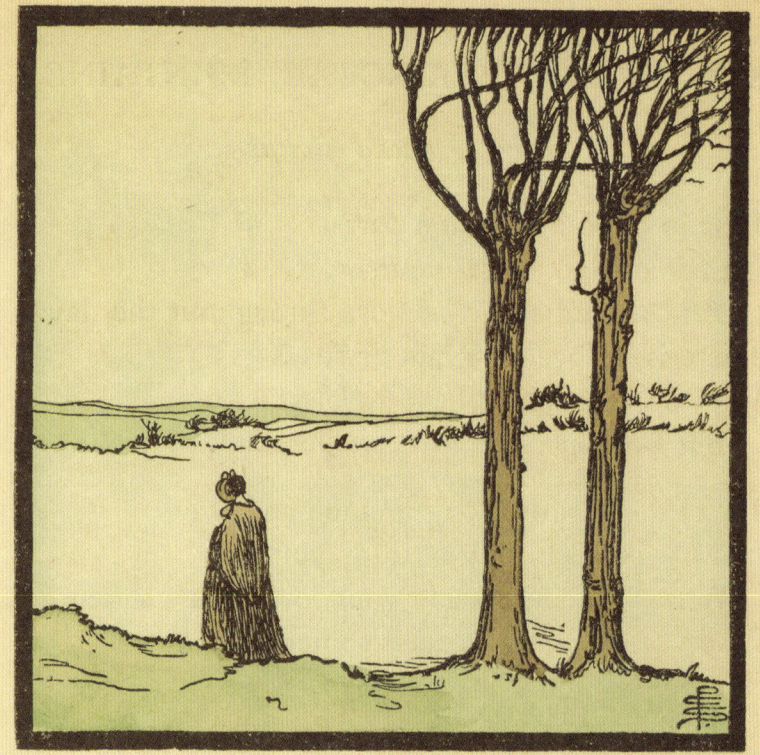

ALONE.

Alone and in the midst of men,
Alone 'mid hills and valleys fair;
Alone upon a ship at sea;
Alone—alone, and everywhere.

O many folk I see and know,
So kind they are I scarce can tell,
But now alone on land and sea,
In spite of all I'm left to dwell.

In cities large—in country lane,
Around the world—'tis all the same;
Across the sea from shore to shore,
Alone—alone, for evermore.

P. C. S.

The Green Sheaf

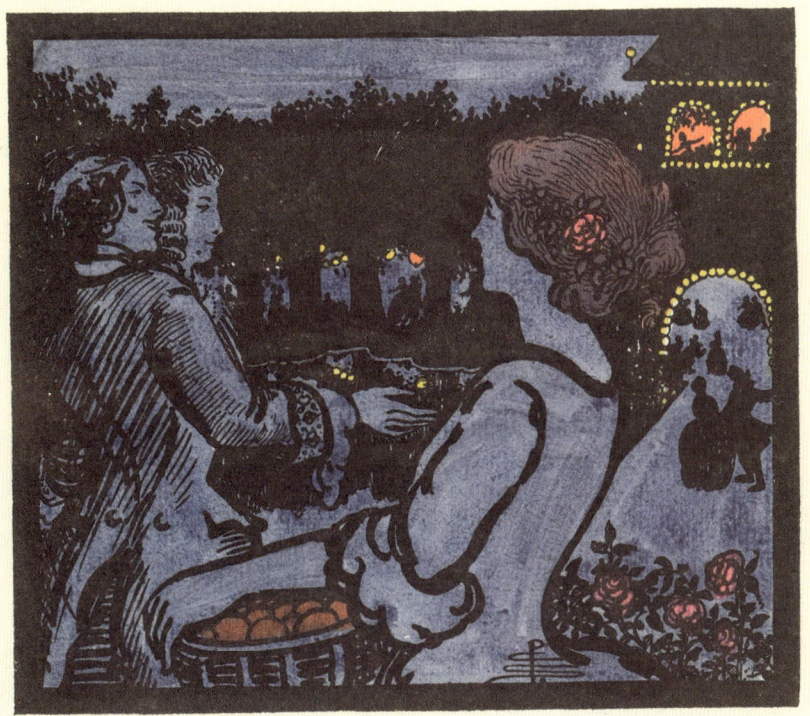

THE TOWN.

O DEARY me how idle is
This great and weary town.
For people talk and never do
As they go up and down.

P. C. S.

Far left: "Alone" written and illustrated by Pamela Colman Smith. From *The Green Sheaf* No. 4, 1903

Left: "The Town" written and illustrated by Pamela Colman Smith. From *The Green Sheaf* No. 11, 1904

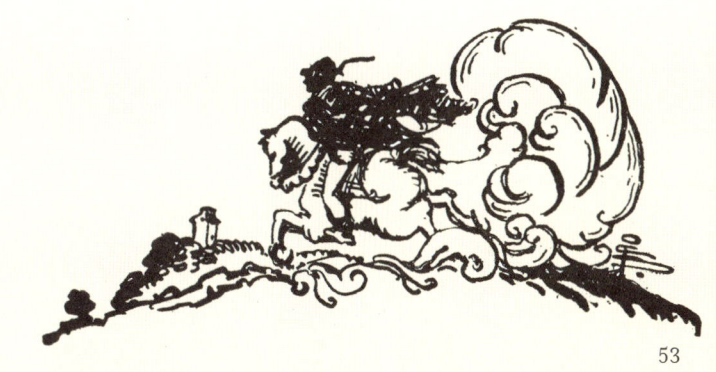

Early 20th century reviews of *The Green Sheaf* appear to have been infrequent. A small mention of the magazine did appear in the February 6, 1904 issue of *The Academy and Literature*. The unnamed writer notes that "The Green Sheaf is a refreshing publication, as its name implies....the literary contents are quaint and sometimes beautiful, but the chiefest charm lies in the hand-coloured prints, which are highly-decorative, simple in treatment and of a pleasant old-world flavor."[153] The note erroneously comments that the little magazine was published by Elkin Matthews who is listed on the title page as only selling it. However, a month later another unnamed writer (or possibly the same person who has undergone a change in view) in the same publication corrects the error but strikes a very different tone: "I have been flipping through the dandified leaves of the ninth number of that strange little periodical 'The Green Sheaf' published and edited and sold by the strange personality whom we call Pamela Colman Smith."[154] The author goes on to state that "some of the designs, by far the best, are from her own whimsical hands," but it is impossible to ignore the repeated use of "strange" to describe both Pamela and her publication. Moreover, this bemusement, which often manifests in condescension and infantilization, is in keeping with other Anglo-American views of her and infiltrates assessments of her magazine. While the first account stressed the beauty and "old world charm" of *The Green Sheaf's* contents, the second terms it "dandified" and that even the best drawings are merely "whimsical." Although it is impossible to know—bearing undiscovered letters—what could have accounted for this change, it is also possible to infer that Pamela's unconventionality and free-spiritedness might have ruffled more than a few feathers.

Pamela's own views of the magazine also changed dramatically over the course of its publication. In April 1903 she wrote to gallery owner William Macbeth, thanking him for subscribing to *The Green Sheaf* and agreeing that "it <u>does</u> look well!" and adding that "It is exciting getting it out every month—planning it all out…"[155] She also points out that she has recently opened a school for hand coloring, a venture that "I have had in mind for long."[156] The school is frequently advertised in the back pages of *The Green Sheaf* and seems one of several money making ventures that Pamela conceived of during this period. It is also possible—although not addressed in this letter nor any others we have found—that pupils of the school may have helped her color *The Green Sheaf's* illustrations as part of their training, thus lightening the burden of having to color each copy by hand and providing them valuable experience. However, it is unclear how many students, if any, signed up for this school. In November 1903, Pamela had an exhibition of her drawings at The Gallery in Bayswater, London, which depicted "dreams out of the ivory gate, and visions before midnight." Terming Pamela's art "utterly lawless," the *Morning Post* reviewer

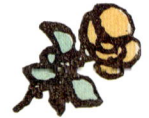

notes "In the setting out of such imaginings the canons of art are massively futile. The measure of a vision is not to be told by perspective; nor the dimensions of a pixie by the anatomical laws of flesh and blood."[157] By February 1904, Pamela's initial optimism and excitement regarding *The Green Sheaf* had cooled considerably. As she writes to Paine, "The Green Sheaf will probably go on semi annually because there are many other things to do more important. … I am telling Annancy stories very often now and hope in time to make some money by it—Green Sheaf does not pay yet—It is most discouraging to go on working at it."[158]

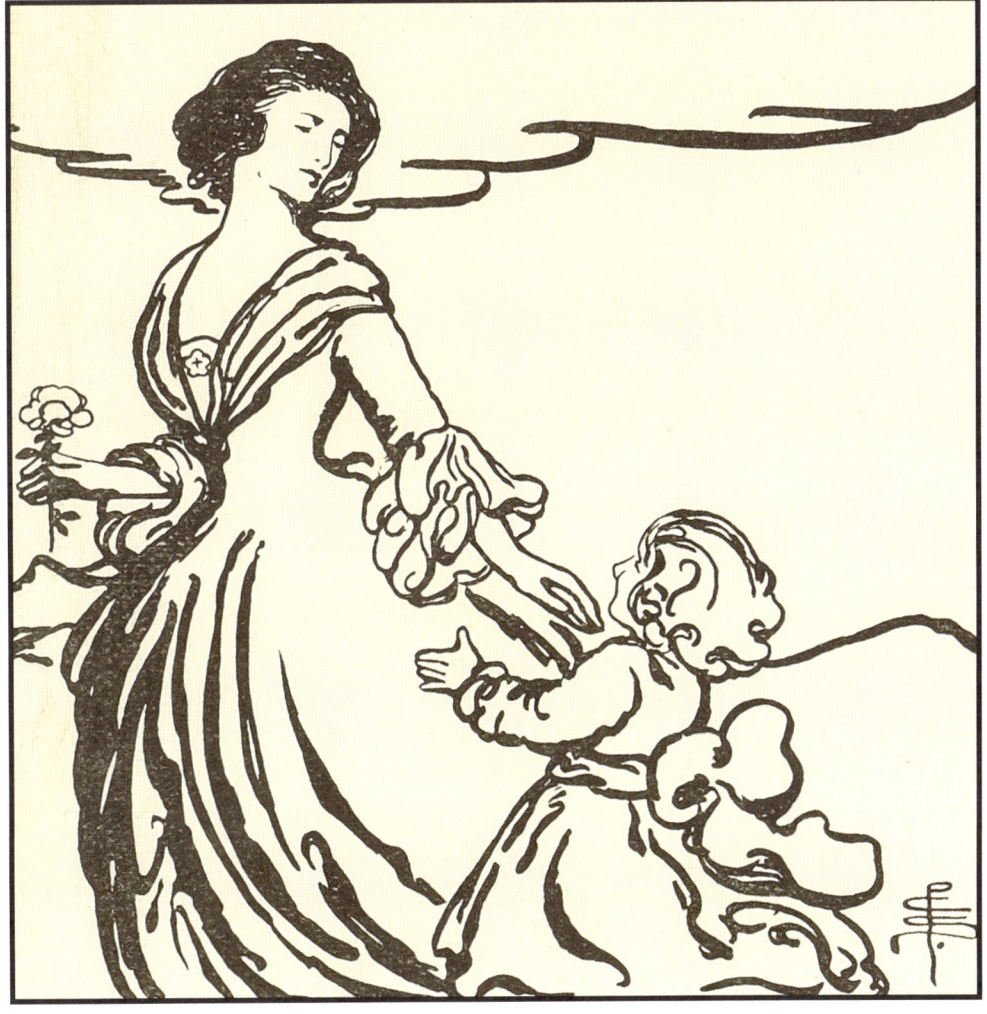

From an announcement inviting subscribers to visit her new print and book store in Knightsbridge, London.
From *The Green Sheaf* No. 13, 1904

The Green Sheaf Press

Opposite: Book covers from *Four Plays* by Laurence Alma Tadema, 1905; *Chim-Chim: Folk Stories from Jamaica* by Pamela Colman Smith, 1905; *In the Valley of Stars There is a Tower of Silence* by Smara Khamara, 1906; and *A Sheaf of Songs* by Alfred C. Calmour, 1904. All published by the Green Sheaf press

DISCOURAGED AND FRUSTRATED BY *THE GREEN SHEAF*'S INABILITY TO LIVE UP TO HER ECONOMIC dreams and, undoubtedly, by the amount of work it took to single-handedly edit, publish, and sell even a small circulation literary magazine, Pamela wrote W.B. Yeats in February of 1904 with a new plan. She wanted his advice on a scheme to set up a small press with her close friend, Mrs. Fortescue: "We want very much to set up a hand press to print small editions of books (by subscription) hand-coloured."[159] She raises two potential projects as a possibility—William Blake's *Songs of Innocence* and *Songs of Experience* and a book devoted to the work of the Victorian painter, printmaker, and engraver, Edward Calvert. She astutely knows that other publishing companies are working on editions of each; Methuen for the *Songs of Innocence* and *Songs of Experience* edition using a three-color printing process and joined by an introduction by Laurence Binyon and a long-announced edition of Edward Calvert engravings by the Unicorn Press. Pamela requested W.B. Yeats's help, in the form of an introduction for the Blake and "what text there is" for the Calvert and, almost undoubtedly, the prestige—and accompanying sales—his name would bring to either project. She knows that secrecy is important and implores W.B. to "<u>Please</u> keep this to <u>yourself.</u>"[160]

The last number of *The Green Sheaf* ends with a short advertisement that informs readers:

> Miss Pamela Colman Smith begs to inform the *Green Sheaf* subscribers, and other friends and customers, that she, in conjunction with MRS FORTESCUE has opened a shop for the sale of Hand-Coloured Prints and other Engravings, Drawings, and Pictures, Books, &c, at the foregoing address. Orders taken and promptly executed for Christmas and Invitation Cards, Menus, Ball Programmes, Book Labels, and every kind of Decorative Printing and Hand-colouring.[161]

While readers may have been surprised at this somewhat unexpected new direction, this was far from the only personal advertisement that appeared in the pages of the magazine. Early numbers contained more traditional ads for other books published by Elkin Mathews. However, beginning with the fourth issue, other advertisements highlighted a service to make custom costumes by Edy Craig, and a personal jewelry gallery by John Baillie that also offered classes in metalworking and various forms of painting. In the sixth issue, Pamela begins hawking her own services as "Gelukiezanger;" the name the female Tiger declares is her own in "Paarat, Tiger, An' Annancy" from the *Annancy Stories*.[162]

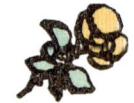

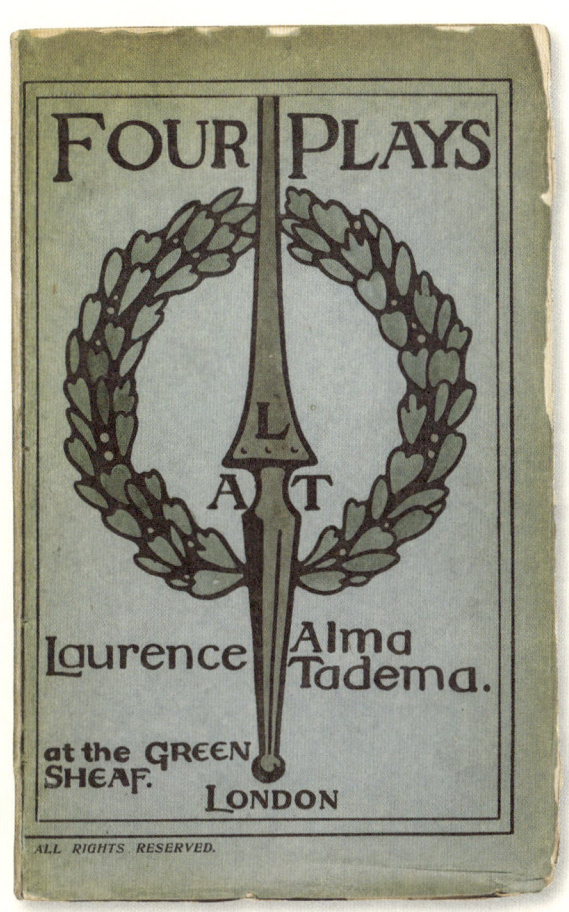
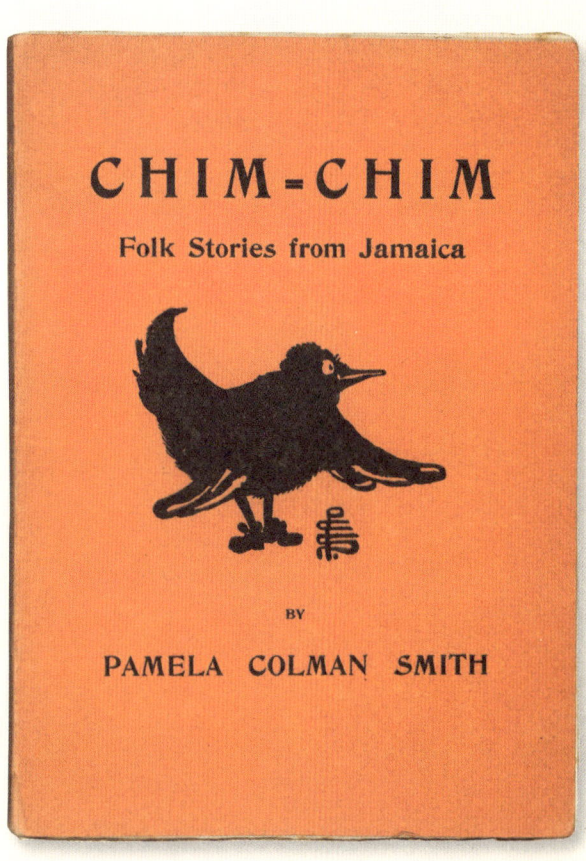
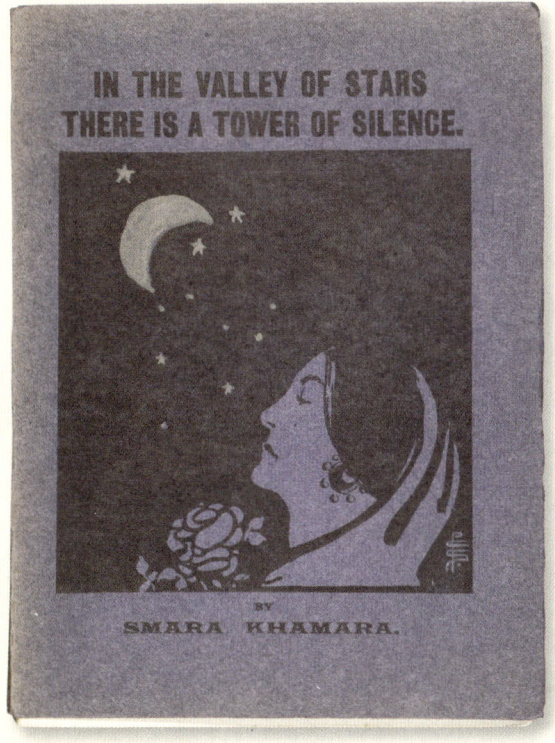
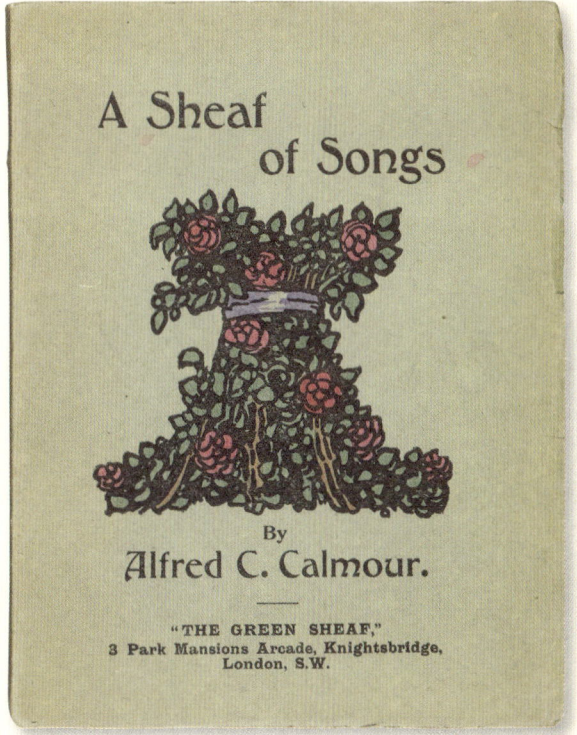

Pamela was to continue to refer to herself by this name throughout her public and private performances of West Indian folktales.

While it is unclear how long the Green Sheaf shop operated or if it was ever financially successful, Pamela did operate her Green Sheaf press until at least 1906.[163] The press published a range of novels, fairy tales, folktales and poems by predominately women writers. Although her planned editions of William Blake's *Songs of Innocence* and *Songs of Experience* and Edward Calvert's engravings never materialized, Pamela published several books, most of them by contributors to *The Green Sheaf*. They include: *Shadow Rabbit: A Story of Adventure* by Dolly Radford and Gertrude M. Bradley; *A Sheaf of Songs* by Alfred C. Calmour; *Saints Among the Animals* by Margaret Ward Cole and Alphaeus P. Cole; *The Book of Hours* by Lady Alix Egerton; *The Book of Good Advice* by Reginald Rigby; *Henry Irving* by Christopher St. John (Christabel Marshall); and *In the Valley of Stars There Is a Tower of Silence: A Persian Tragedy* by Smara Khamara. The latter work contains a full-color frontispiece by Smith. The press also published two works by Laurence Alma Tadema; *Tales from My Garden,* which are also illustrated by Pamela and *Four Plays.* Furthermore, the press issued Pamela's *Chim-Chim* in 1905, which was the most experimental of all of her prose work. In addition to writing and illustrating works published by her press, Pamela also illustrated Edith Theobald's "Letters from the Beasts to Dina," which was included in John Baillie's *The Dream Garden: A Children's Annual* in 1905.

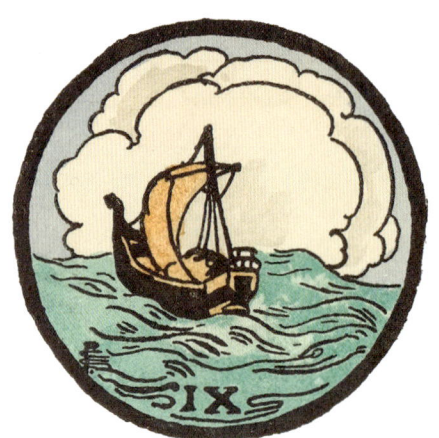

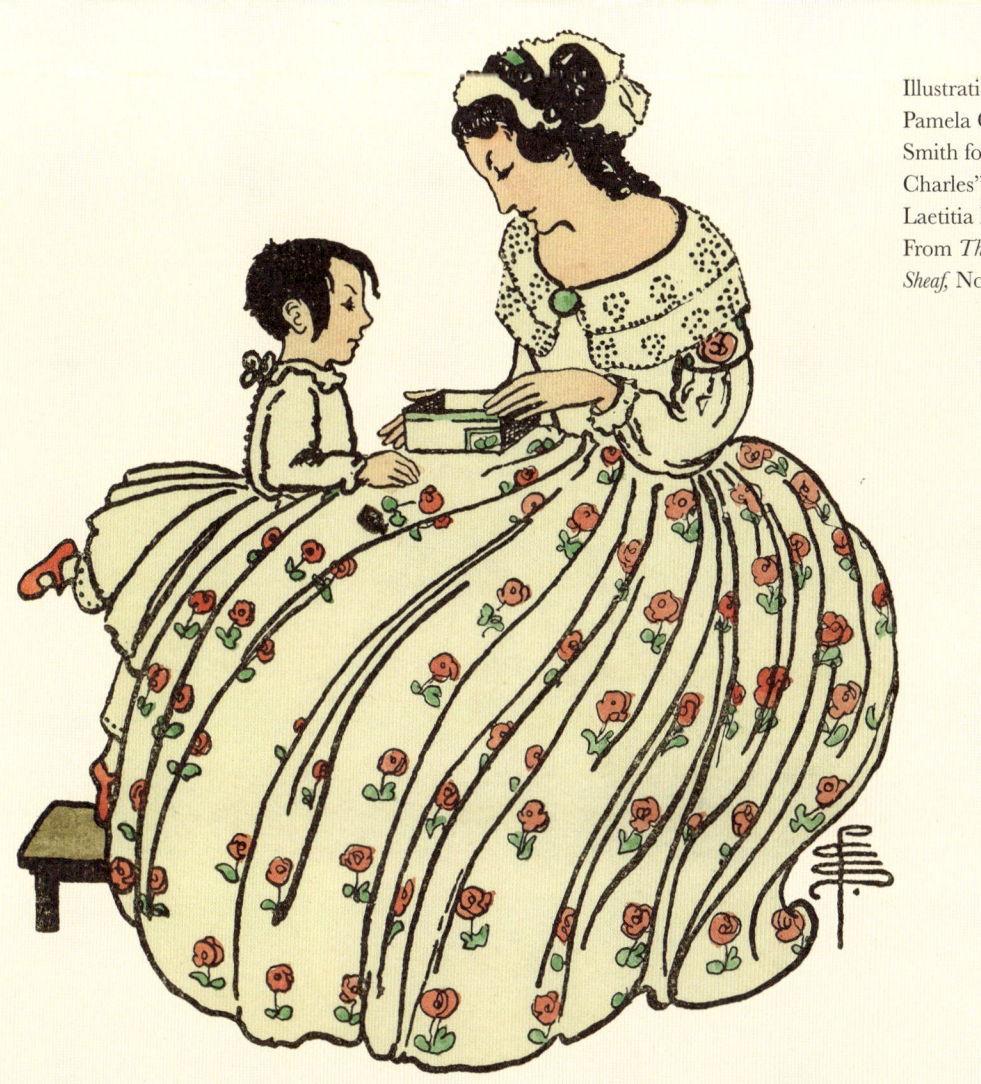

Illustration by Pamela Colman Smith for "Little Charles" by Anna Laetitia Barbauld. From *The Green Sheaf*, No. 1, 1903

Music Pictures

AFTER THE DEMISE OF THE GREEN SHEAF PRESS, PAMELA APPEARS TO HAVE FOCUSED MORE attention on pursuing a fine art career. For several years her "music pictures" catapulted her to avant-garde artistic prominence. Pamela had her first vision at Ellen Terry's house on Christmas day 1900 while listening to Gordon Craig play Bach. Years later Pamela described the experience this way in a 1927 article by the Hon. Mrs. Forbes-Sempill in *The Illustrated London News*:

> 'a shutter clicked back and left a hole in the air about an inch square, and through it I saw a bank and broken ground, the smooth trunks of trees with dark leaves; across from left to right came dancing and frolicking little elfin people with the wind blowing through their hair and billowing their dresses. The picture was very vivid and clear, and a beautiful colour, with bluish mist behind the tree trunks. I drew an outline in pencil of what I saw on the edge of a newspaper, and as I finished—in perhaps a minute—the shutter clicked back again.'[164]

After this first experience, Pamela did not compose any drawings to music for about two years. However, the images returned when she attended a series of concerts by the composer Arnold Dolmetsch, a friend of W.B. Yeats. Arnold, like Pamela, was associated with the Masquers, a group who chanted W.B.'s poetry. Shortly thereafter, Pamela began making larger drawings at Queen's Hall concerts in London, producing as many as 20-30 drawings in one sitting. During a prolific week in February 1908, she noted that in the past week she had done 94 drawings "almost all of them useable ones."[165] After the fact, she would then return to certain sketches, enlarging and finishing them as well as adding color.[166]

Pamela's ability to visualize music she heard is one of the most important keys to her artistic ability. It is evidence that she had synesthesia. People with synesthesia most commonly perceive letters or numbers as colors, but synesthetic associations can occur with any number of crossed senses or cognitive pathways. However, Pamela appears to have had a very atypical form of synesthesia where music conveys a complex visual image. A French critic, G. Jean-Aubry, who was Joseph Conrad's friend and translator, observed Pamela creating her "music pictures" and described the process this way:

> She comprehends music visually, whether a symphonic piece or a piano composition. For her the musical impression is immediately transformed into a graphic image. I have seen her curled up in a corner at a concert

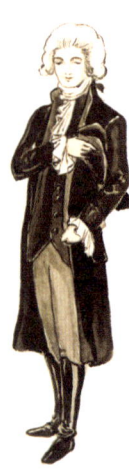

Original 1913 watercolor, painted to Bach's Aria in G. This painting was included in an article "Music Made Visible" by Mrs. Forbes-Sempill in the February 12, 1921 issue of *The Illustrated London News*.

with her sketch book on her knees, a sepia brush in her hand, listening to the work, following the rhythm, and smiling, working without haste, as if she had the time to put down her impressions in a few seconds, the time of twenty measures, the scarred page, caressed, scratched, shows varied sketches, some like one of the charming series of Schumann's Carnaval, others in the style of Song of the Land by Severac, the Valley of Clocks by Ravel, the images or prints of Debussy or those reminiscent of Dvorak's Symphony from the New World or Beethoven symphonies, and works by Bach, Scarlatti, Purcell or Byrd.[167]

The musician Claude Debussy was a friend of Pamela's and said that her drawings to his compositions were his "dreams made visible."[168]

Pamela's "music pictures" took several forms.[169] While the most common was the "living and moving picture" which immediately appeared to her upon hearing a musical piece, at other times the picture appeared and grew in color and form upon the page as Pamela drew.[170] Speed was of the upmost importance for this "lightning artist," as the images would disappear as soon as the last notes of the music faded. According to Mrs. Forbes-Sempill, the action of drawing these images was entirely subconscious and that "if she ever alters her drawing in the least detail from what she sees, the picture instantly

"Music Pictures," original handwritten manuscript by Pamela Colman Smith. Courtesy of The Beinecke Rare Book & Manuscript Library Yale University. Portions of this manuscript reproduced in "Pictures in Music." From *The Strand Magazine*, June 1908 breaks up and disappears."¹⁷¹ If the music did not appeal to her, she either drew nothing at all or left only a half-finished sketch. Furthermore, Pamela stressed that these drawings were not illustrations. In a 1908 *Strand* article she explained: "They are not pictures of the music theme—pictures of the flying notes—not conscious illustrations of the name given to a piece of music, but just what I see when I hear music—thoughts loosened and set free by the spell of sound."¹⁷²

Some of the early "music pictures" portray relatively mundane surroundings in bright watercolor, such as the 1905 "Catch Me" based on Schumann's Opus 10, No. 4, which depicts a mother and child playing on a windy day.

Others are more mystical but still retain the vibrant color, such as the 1907 "Sea Creatures," which in purple, blue, and silver depict a veiled, human woman riding the crest of a wave, followed by several female water spirits.

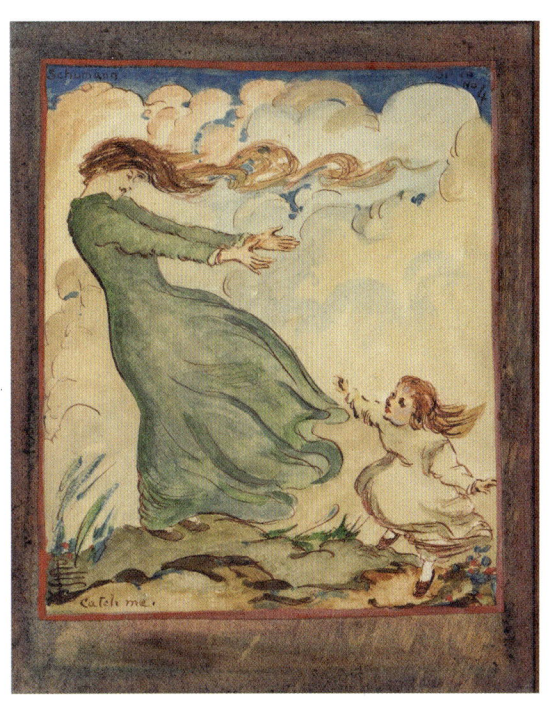

"Catch Me" original watercolor painting by Pamela Colman Smith, circa 1905, painted to Schumann's Opus 10, No. 4

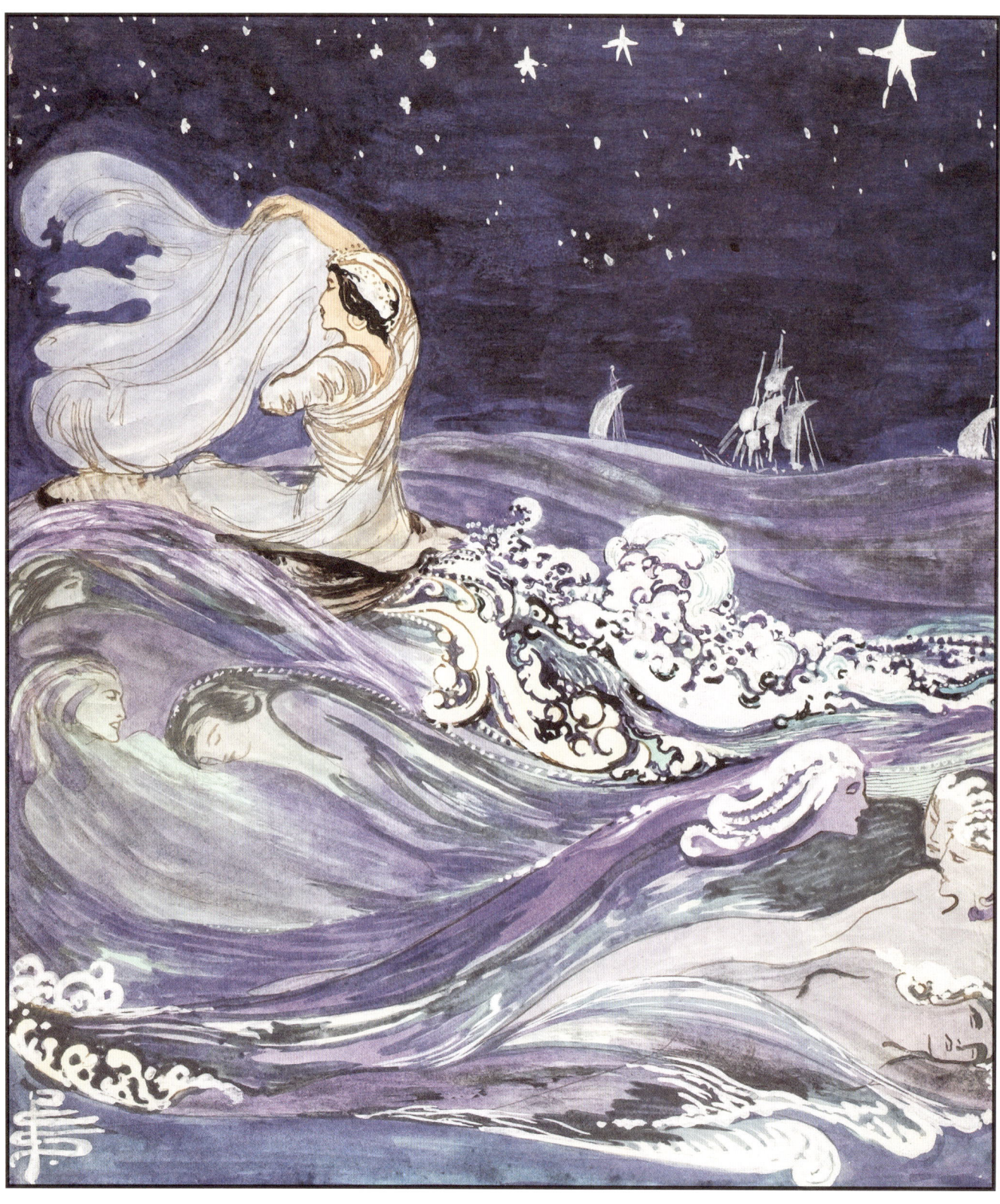

In a 1908 article in *Strand Magazine*, Pamela likened her visions to "unlocking the door into a beautiful country" peopled with a range of fascinating characters from land and sea:

> There stretched far away, are plains and mountains and the billowy sea, and as the music forms a net of sound the people who dwell there enter the scene; tall, slow-moving stately queens, with jeweled crowns and garments gay or sad, who walk on mountain-tops or stand beside the shore, watching the water-people. These water-folk are passionless, and sway or fall with little heed of time; they toss the spray and, bending down, dive headlong through the deep.[173]

Like dream images, these music-fueled visions transcended the logic of space, time, and the normal limitations humans usually experience. However, one striking commonality is the prevalence of women, often depicted in active, powerful roles. Some of these images were associated with specific pieces of music. For example, Pamela's drawing for Beethoven's *Sonata Pathetique* featured "slow-moving stately queens," while her image for Beethoven's Symphony No. 5 in C minor depicts the Queen of Tides, "who carries in her hand the pearl-like moon."[174]

Increasingly, Pamela drew her "music pictures" in black, India ink, and sepia tones rather than brilliant washes of color. They also became more personally symbolic as she began to associate different composers with specific images. Bach's *Chromatic Fantasy* was linked with brown-clad maidens ringing bells, while Chopin's Ballade No. 1, Opus 23 in G Minor called to mind gardens at night "where mystery and dread lurk under every bush, but joy and passion throb within the air, and the cold moon bewitches all the scene."[175] The catalog to Pamela's 1907 exhibition lists this painting as "The Fugitive," which more closely calls to mind what the piece represents for her. Writing in *The Craftsman* in 1912, M. Irwin Macdonald noted that just as the subjects of the paintings varied with the different composer, Pamela's method of handling the compositions also changed. "Even the quality of line in the original sketches, which is broad, powerful and sweeping when it represents Beethoven's titanic emotions, becomes dainty and precise under the influence of Mozart, sensual and freakish in the portrayal of certain moods of Richard Strauss, and vague, delicate and at times austere when it endeavors to define and fix the well-nigh formless musical fancies of Debussy."[176] Only the music of Wagner consistently failed to elicit any images but, instead, made her enraged. Pamela explained in *The Illustrated London News* that when she listened to Wagner: "my scalp tingles and my hair pricks; I feel so full of rage that I want to crack the heads of people together like nuts. When it is played in a room, thick curtains of brown spiders' webs appear; sticky and evil smelling."[177]

Opposite left: "Sea Creatures," original watercolor on paper by Pamela Colman Smith, circa 1904-1905. Courtesy of The Beinecke Rare Book & Manuscript Library, Yale University

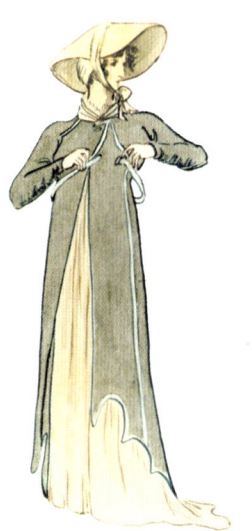

In January 1907, the New York photographer Alfred Stieglitz exhibited 72 of Pamela's watercolors at his 291 Gallery in Manhattan. Pamela's paintings replaced a show of Rodin's drawings that Stieglitz had planned as his first fine art exhibition.[178] The show drew more journalists than art patrons until James Huneker praised Pamela's art in *The New York Sun*:

> You read the titles and dream of Blake, of Fantin-Latour, of the Japanese, of De Groux, of James Ensor, of Beardsley, of Edvard Munch, of Maeterlinck and of Chopin. But your eyes tell you that Miss Smith is in every design, many of them mere memoranda of a spiritual exaltation, of the soul under the influence of music, or haunted by some sinister imagining.[179]

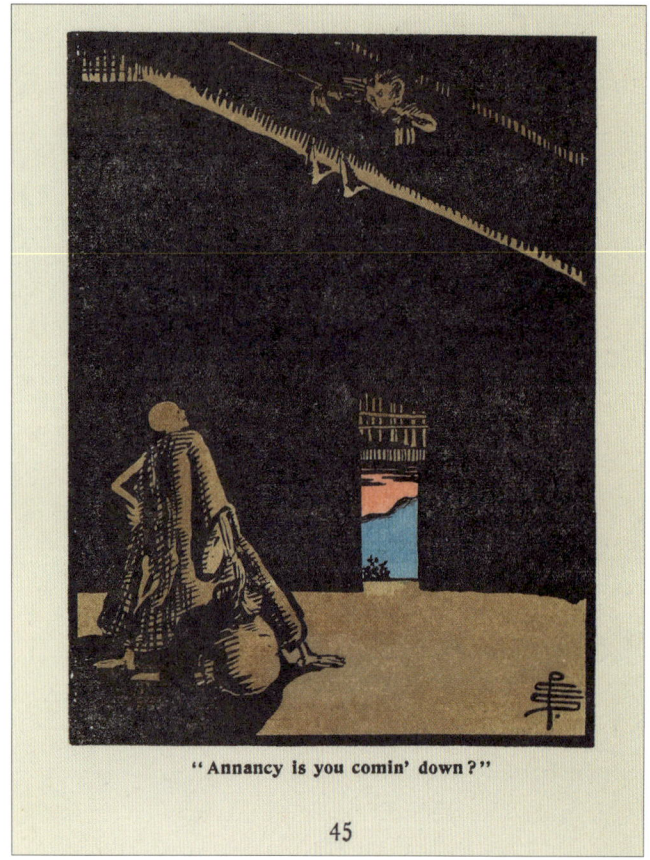

"Death in the House" from *Chim-Chim: Folk Stories from Jamaica*. From Green Sheaf press, 1905

Huneker singled out Pamela's "Death in the House" as "absolutely nerve shuddering." The work was not typically gruesome but, like the work of Munch, subtly conveyed a sense of horror through suggestion. The image was first included in "Annancy and Death," a story that was part of Pamela's 1905 *Chim-Chim and Other Stories* published by the Green Sheaf press.

The comparisons to famous European artists, notably William Blake and Aubrey Beardsley, generated much buzz and resulted in the extension of the exhibition, which was originally set to last for a week, for an additional ten days.[180] As Alfred Stieglitz remembered, "The exhibition created a sensation… [bringing] the Whitneys and Havemeyers, Vanderbilts and all classes of people into these tiny rooms of ours. The place was literally mobbed."[181] The majority of the pictures from the collection sold and "nearly all of the most significant magazines" purchased her drawings for publication.[182] One of the very few non-musical pictures in the collection depicted Maude Adams as Peter Pan in J.M. Barrie's 1905 play. Alfred Stieglitz issued a portfolio of platinotypes, or platinum prints, of some of Pamela's drawings, including the *Peter Pan* illustration.[183] The 291 Gallery show was quickly followed by one at the Pennsylvania Academy in Philadelphia in March.[184] Once she returned to England, she had exhibitions in London in November and Edinburgh in December; the latter was a joint show with James Patterson, the Scottish landscape painter.[185]

The rush of success that resulted from the January 291 Gallery show emboldened Pamela to write a brief manifesto in support of American artistic freedom. Entitled "A Protest Against Fear," it was published in the March 1907 issue of *The Craftsman* and began this way:

> It seems to me that fear has got hold of all this land. Each one has a great fear of himself, a fear to believe, to think, to do, to be, to act.
>
> Who dares to do anything without fear of what some other will think or say? How can a country have a living, growing art when it is so bound down by fear, the most dreadful of all evils?[186]

The statement boldly addresses all people whose creativity is stymied by fear—and one can easily infer—artistic and social convention. These were customs that Pamela herself disregarded and, ultimately, her nonconformity negatively affected both her artistic and personal life. Terming this type of fear as "the most dreadful of all evils," Pamela views it as one of the limitations that has prevented "[t]his marvelous, great country, big in all its feeling and full of energy" from "producing almost no freedom of thought or work." She concludes by exhorting art students to look within:

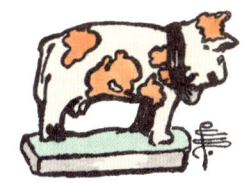

> You, younger students, who are entering this garden of toil, where flowers are grown by love and patience, why do you not try to be true to your better selves, why do you not try to see the finer, bigger things that are all about you, and to kill in your garden those mawkish weeds of sugar-sweet sentimentality and shallow feeling. Try to feel truly one thought, one scene, and make others feel it as keenly as you do—thus is art born.

Pamela appeals to each art student to resist conformity, which may well yield financial remuneration and professional success, and, instead, look inside to create art that comes out of truth and helps share experiences and ideas.

In a February 21, 1908 letter to Alfred Stieglitz, Pamela sounds an even more dire note, stating that "All art—pictures and illustrations—with the exception of a very few things! is a hollow sham! The more students put off the better! I feel a very revolutionist that would make the hair of any self-respecting art instructor <u>rise</u>."[187] Pamela also continued to submit both art and prose to newspapers, magazines, and journals during this period with mixed results. As she wrote to Alfred Stieglitz in March 1908, "The publishers are as dull here as elsewhere! Except for the usual <u>harmless</u> dull insipid stuff by feeble females! I know plenty of 'em who are living <u>well</u> by the <u>inanities</u>! We disgruntled devils don't please anybody!—"[188] While her humor is still visible, the anger regarding the actions of publishers that she expressed to Paine and others is now less obvious. In its place is an almost cheerful resignation. Having lived in London for the better part of eight years, she now knows how the system works and that it is indeed possible for a woman writer to survive—even live well—by their "inanities." However, Pamela is not "feeble" and willing to guide her artistic and literary output to conform to popular taste. She is a "disgruntled devil" who will remain true to herself and her art.

Pamela's initial success at 291 led to two more exhibitions at Alfred Stieglitz's gallery: a group show with Willis Geiger and D.S. McLaughlin in 1908 and another solo show in March 1909.[189] She was one of only six women given a featured exhibition by Stieglitz between 1905-1917; Georgia O'Keeffe was the only other woman to have a solo show during this period.[190] Pamela's last show at the Little Galleries of the Photo-Secession took place in March 1909 and received far less media attention than her first appearance. A brief mention in *The New York Times* noted that "Miss Smith's style has always a touch of the bizarre united to elements of greater dignity."[191] Writing in the July 1909 issue of *Camera Work*, Benjamin De Casseres praised Pamela's one-woman show, stating that "[n]o more curious and fascinating exhibition has ever been held in New York." He continued:

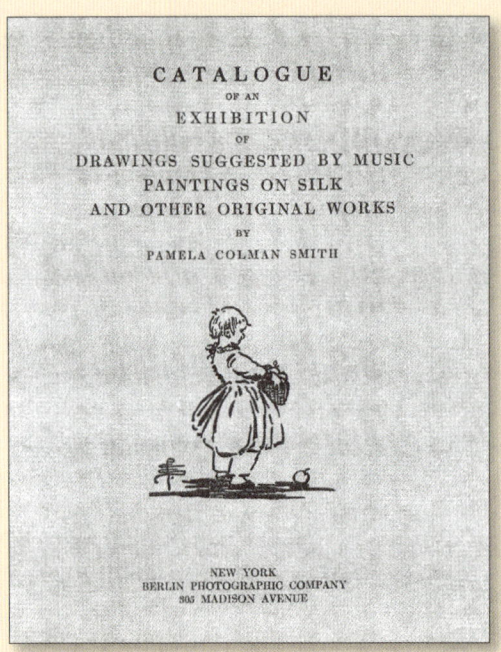

"Catalogue of an Exhibition of Drawings Suggested by Music: Paintings on Silk and Other Original Works" by Pamela Colman Smith. Published by Berlin Photographic Company, 1912

> She is a blender of visions, a mystic, a symbolist, one who transfigures the world she lives in by the overwhelming simplicity of her imagination. To me, these wonderful little drawings are not merely art; they are poems, ideas, life-values and cosmic values that have long gestated within the subconscious world of their creator—a wizard's world of intoxicating evocations—here and now accouched on their vibrating, colored beds, to mystify and awe the mind of some few beholders; to project their souls from off this little Springboard of Time into the stupendous unbegotten thing we name the Infinite.[192]

Pamela's art, suffused with a mysticism and symbolism that tapped into the great uncharted unconscious, appeared as "modern" to an art world struggling to cast off the strictures of 19th century impressionism and still unaware of the coming abstract phase. Over the next few years, Pamela's "music pictures" were exhibited in London, Cambridge, Stratford-Upon-Avon, Belfast, Edinburgh, Paris, and Ghent. In 1912, she had another solo show in New York at the Berlin Photographic Company.

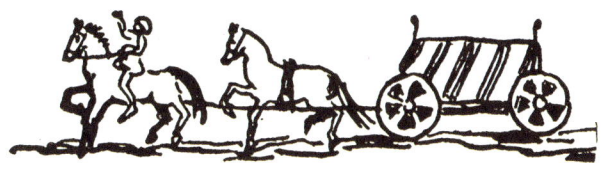

24. Page of Cups		⎫
25. Page of Pentacles		⎬ Designs for a Set
26. Ace of Swords		⎬ of Tarot Cards
27. Nine of Swords		⎬
28. Five of Cups		⎬
29. Four of Wands		⎭
30. Birth of the Sun.		
31. "Little Charles"	Mrs. Bardauld	
32. "In the Fields"	Mrs. Bardauld	
33. Weeping Trees and Falling Stars.		
34. Vas Spirituale		⎫
35. Rosa mystica		⎬ Designs for
36. Turris Davidica		⎬ The Litany of Loretto
37. Turris eburnea		⎬
38. Stella matutina		⎭

DRAWINGS SUGGESTED BY MUSIC

39. Piano Sonata, Op. 57, Second Movement	Beethoven
40. Piano Sonata, Op. 57, First Movement	Beethoven
41. Piano Sonata, Op. 57, First Movement	Beethoven
42. Piano Sonata, Op. 57, First Movement	Beethoven
43. Piano Sonata, Pathétique	Beethoven
44. String Quartet in D Major	Mozart
45. Concerto No. 4 in D Major	Mozart
46. Concerto No. 4 in D Major	Mozart
47. Concerto in A Major	Mozart
48. Concerto in A Major	Mozart
49. Intermezzo No. 5	Schumann
50. "Warum"	Schumann
51. Symphony No. 1	Schumann
52. Symphony No. 2, Op. 61	Schumann
53. Symphony No. 2, Op. 61	Schumann
54. Symphony No. 2, Op. 61	Schumann
55. Papillon	Schumann
56. Quartet, Op. 15	Glazounow
57. Variations, Op. 33	Tschaikowsky
58. Violin Concerto in D, Op. 35	Tschaikowsky
59. Violin Concerto in D, Op. 35	Tschaikowsky
60. Till Eulenspiegel's Merry Pranks, Op. 28	Richard Strauss
61. Don Quixot	Richard Strauss
62. Fantasia in G Minor, Op. 24	Josef Suk
63. Russian Airs	Glinka
64. Sonata for Violin, Last Movement	Cæsar Franck
65. Prelude Corale and Fugue	Cæsar Franck
66. Quintette	Cæsar Franck
67. Quintette	Cæsar Franck
68. Prelude	Cæsar Franck
69. "Il pleure dans mon coeur"	Claude Debussy
70. "En Sourdine"	Claude Debussy
71. Chant de la Terre	Severac

HAND-COLORED PRINTS

72. Alone.
73. Charles and Auntie.
74. The Recitation.
75. Romantic Landscape.
76. Four Place Cards.
77. Christmas Card.

Jamaican Folktale Performances

ALTHOUGH PAMELA HAD FIRST LISTENED TO THE TALES OF ANANSI AND HIS FRIENDS AS A child in Jamaica and had first published her book-length collection—*Annancy Stories*—as a fledgling artist in New York, it was only after she returned to England in the spring of 1900 that she began to tell these stories. At first, the performances were largely confined to her weekly salons. However, within a few years Pamela began to perform them in public and by 1904 was advertising her services at parties and other gatherings in the pages of her *Green Sheaf* and had hopes that this venture would be more financially remunerative than her

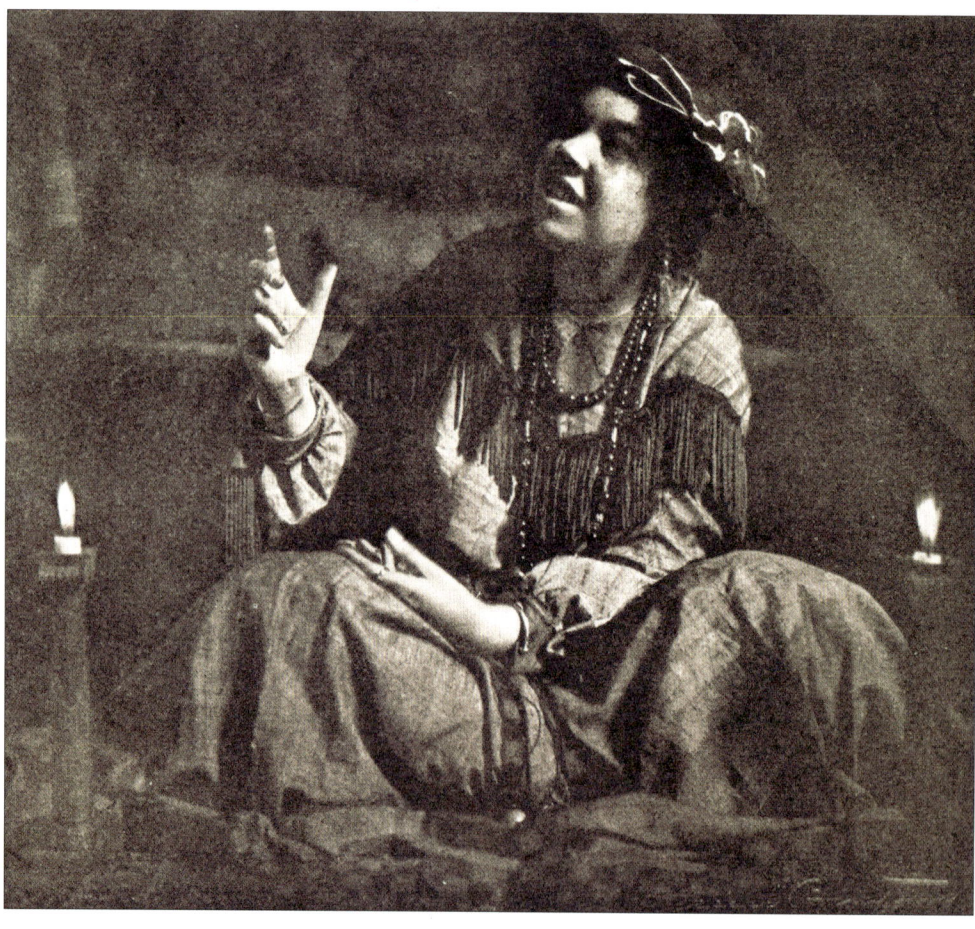

Pamela Colman Smith as she recites a folktale. Photograph by Alice Boughton. From *Brooklyn Life* magazine, January 1907

little magazine.[193] One of her first public appearances telling these tales was at a Christmas 1903 Hans Andersen Bazaar in London held to support the Girls' Realm Guild of Service. Pamela, "who already has won a reputation for the telling of quaint West Indian stories of the 'Brer Rabbit' order," delighted the children in attendance.[194]

In October 1904, the American *Lady's Home Magazine* devoted an article to Pamela's London performances noting that "clad in a loose, flame colored robe, she sits in Eastern fashion on the floor" and transfixes her listeners with tales of the adventures of Anansi, the spider-man, Chim Chim Bird, Brodda Gingy Fly, and the Dibby Dibby Tree.[195]

Instead of the more traditional "Once upon a time," all of her stories began with "In a long-before time—before Queen Victoria came to reign over we," which both transports listeners back to a simpler time before the hegemony of British imperialism and highlights Jamaica's colonial status and, thus, the "otherness" of these simple stories.[196]

As the 20th century progressed, story-telling in England became a very popular entertainment. As *The Sketch* magazine notes, Pamela was the "most noteworthy of Society story-tellers" as she most effectively conveyed the charm of the old stories to modern audiences. She is helped in this endeavor "by her voice, which is exquisitely modulated, and while penetrating, remains low and tuneful."[197] In January 1904 she was included in a Café Chantant honoring Princess Christian's infant nursery at the White Hart Hotel in Windsor.[198] Often Pamela's performances were included as part of benefit programs. She told her Jamaican stories to a large League of Mercy meeting—a British foundation established in 1899 by Royal Charter to aid the sick and suffering in charity hospitals—held at her friend the photographer Kate Pragnell's studio in Brompton in April 1908.[199] In December she was the featured entertainment at the Hartwell and Stone school Christmas program in Buckinghamshire.[200] Even Pamela's exhibition at the John Baillie Gallery in Baker Street was enhanced by a "charmingly unconventional little entertainment" in which she both told her Annancy stories and sang Old English folk songs such as "Little Sir William" and "All Round My Hat."[201]

Pamela also gave several performances in conjunction with other female story-tellers. In July 1906, she participated in a recital with Marion Gordon Kerby and Lillian Woodward at the Aeolian Hall in London. Pamela is cited as excelling in the telling of "negro tales; she is, perhaps the champion narrator of dusky folk-lore. She does not only impersonate, she portrays."[202] In the summer of 1912 she teamed up with the actress Jean Sterling Mackinlay, who was married to the actor Harcourt Williams, for a series of recitals in London, Bath, and Eastbourne, among other locales.[203] The concert in Eastbourne was repeated the following winter.[204]

A 1912 brochure advertises Pamela's services as a storyteller for children's and adults' parties that she operated out of her Battersea Park Studio. The four-page flyer includes testimonials from several of her famous friends. J.M. Barrie declared that "I know of no more delightful entertainment for children than yours, so quaint, so simple; and it is the prettiest of pictures, the children sitting agape around you." Ellen Terry simply revealed that "Since hearing your stories I have told no other!"

When Pamela returned to the U.S. in 1907 and 1909 for her two solo shows at Alfred Stieglitz's Little Galleries of the Photo-Secession in Manhattan, she also made several public appearances in which she told Jamaican folktales. In late January 1907, she performed at a reception hosted by the Entertainment Club at the Waldorf Astoria in honor of the Italian Ambassador, Baron Mayor des Planches.[205] In February, Pamela returned to Brooklyn Heights and regaled alumnae at the Packer Institute, then a secondary school for girls,

"Folk Stories from Jamaica, West Indies" told by Pamela Colman Smith with photo of artist by Kate Pragnell, 1912

with her Annancy stories "given in most artistic manner and with a fascinating accent."[206] She was accompanied by the Boys' High School orchestra. A stuffed alligator that she had brought with her from Jamaica joined her on stage.[207] In March, Pamela helped celebrate the 25th anniversary of the Photoerone Reading Club by entertaining those assembled with her folk stories, singing Old English ballads, and chanting several of W.B. Yeats' poems.[208]

However, the highlight of Pamela's U.S. visit was her New Year's Eve performance for Mark Twain. As the *New York World* notes, "an exotic young woman with melting dark eyes and a sweet, crooning voice made the veteran humorist laugh like a child, and all his distinguished company of guests forgot time, space and the everyday world of commonplace reality."[209] She entertained those assembled with the Annancy story "De

Man An' De Six Poach Eggs," among other stories and songs. While more details of the event are not discussed, Pamela explained that while some stories can be painted, sung, or written, the spoken word transcends the limitations of the other medium.

> "All stories can be told, and told so that every human being can understand them. When I tell the Jamaica stories to very young children I illustrate them with dolls, which I make myself—saw them out of wood with a fret-saw, then paint them and stick on feathers and beads, Jamaica mammy style. These are to the little kiddies what book illustrations are to grown-ups. But the real, universal world-old way is to tell the stories orally, and put the illustrations in as you go along, by sign language, facial expression, intonation, gesture, and all that sort of thing."[210]

Pamela's focus on the similarities between different modes of artistic output is key here as it highlights that she viewed these very different modes of expression as part of the same continuum. The accoutrements—be it dolls, images, animals, or words—only serve to enhance the experience. Moreover, it's the human element of the oral performance that she views as most important in order to connect with audiences and transmit ideas and emotions.

Photo of Pamela Colman Smith with her small theatre figures, circa 1912

Although Pamela's 1909 New York visit was not nearly as filled with public appearances as her 1907 sojourn, she did return to the Pratt Art Club to deliver a lecture on the importance of imagination in art. Entitled, "Magic Spectacles," her talk illustrated examples of French, Italian, Chinese and Japanese art, highlighting that in each case the imagination dominated. She went on to affirm her belief in fairies and goblins, which she said is captured in her work.[211] A return trip in April 1910 resulted in Pamela participating in an ambitious program hosted by the Educational Theater that featured a new fairy place, a pantomime, and Mother Goose rhymes as well as costumed performers and a children's orchestra.[212]

Rider-Waite Tarot Deck

WHILE CROWDS FLOCKED TO PAMELA'S TELLING OF ANNANCY STORIES IN THE U.S. AND England and journalists devoted pages of their magazines to discussions of her "music pictures," perhaps her greatest claim to lasting fame, ironically enough, came from what she termed "A big job for very little cash!"[213] In November of 1909, Pamela finished a set of 78 card designs that had been commissioned by Arthur Edward Waite. The deck was published in December 1909 by William Rider and Son, London, and was sold both as a stand-alone deck of cards and together with a book of instructions written by Waite entitled, *The Key to the Tarot: Being Fragments of a Secret Tradition Under the Veil of Divination.* The backs of the

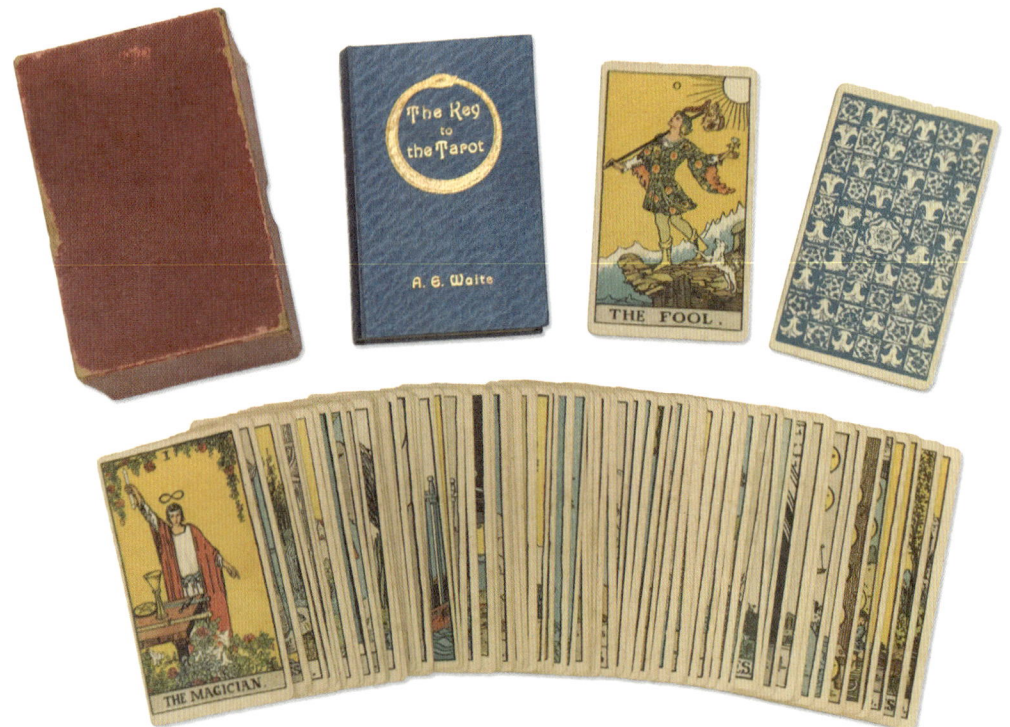

Original Rider-Waite tarot deck and book with box, 1909

original cards featured a repeating blue and white roses and lilies pattern, and the deck was packaged in a two-piece cardboard box. The Rider deck, as it was initially known, was reissued in 1910 on superior paper stock with a brown "crackle mud" pattern back, and the cards have been reprinted many times ever since. It is now the most popular tarot deck in England and America.

Pamela initially met Waite after she joined the Isis-Urania Temple of the Golden Dawn in 1901. Although it is unclear how invested she was in the organization, she never advanced beyond the first degree Zelator level. Pamela followed Waite when he seceded from the Isis-Urania Temple in 1903, which at the time was headed by W.B. Yeats, and created his Independent and Rectified Order of the Golden Dawn.[214] Waite wanted to create a more spiritual Rosicrucian-Christian order, and it is possible that this focus influenced Pamela's decision to convert to Roman Catholicism at the Farm Street Church in the Mayfair section of London in July 1911. In contrast, W.B. Yeats favored a Hermetic orientation that put a greater emphasis on magic and the occult; he resigned from the Isis-Urania Temple in 1905. After this split, Pamela's friendship with W.B. and several members of his family gradually waned.

Arthur Edward Waite first conceived the idea for the tarot deck after discovering a group of old occult manuscripts relating to tarot cards and felt that the deck could be made more meaningful by adding pictorial images to the forty pip cards. As he notes in his 1938 autobiography, *Shadows of Life and Thought*, he soon thought of Pamela:

> Now, in those days there was a most imaginative and abnormally psychic artist, named Pamela Colman Smith, who had drifted into the Golden Dawn and loved the Ceremonies—as transformed by myself—without pretending or indeed attempting to understand their subsurface consequence. It seemed to some of us in the circle that there was a draughtswoman among us who, under proper guidance, could produce a Tarot with an appeal in the world of art and a suggestion of significance behind the Symbols which would put on them another construction than had ever been dreamed by those who, through many generations, had produced and used them for mere divinatory purposes. My province was to see that the designs—especially those of the important Trumps Major—kept that in the hiddenness which belonged to certain Greater Mysteries, in the Paths of which I was travelling. I am not of course intimating that the Golden Dawn had at that time any deep understanding by inheritance of Tarot Cards; but, if I may so say, it was getting to know under my auspices that their Symbols—or some at least among them—were gates which opened on realms of vision beyond occult dreams. I saw to it therefore that Pamela Colman Smith should not be picking up casually any floating images from my own or another mind. She had to be spoon-fed carefully over the Priestess Card, over that which is called the Fool and over the Hanged Man.[215]

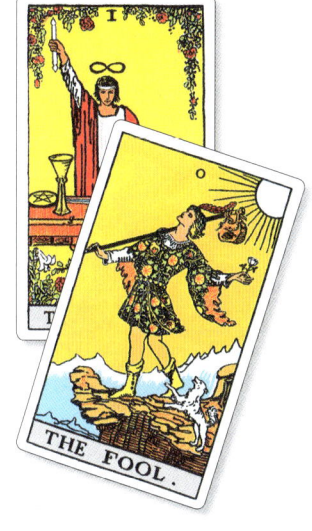

While Waite viewed Pamela as "a most imaginative and abnormally psychic artist" whose work had found success in the art world, he dismisses her as not being sufficiently aware of or interested in the deeper meaning of the mysteries of the deck and in need of "guidance." However, there has been much debate among scholars of the tarot regarding how much Waite "spoon fed" material to Pamela and how much control she had over the designs. What is clear is that he put most of his emphasis on the Major Arcana and that Pamela had much more freedom over the Minor Arcana. In fact, one of the most unique features of the deck is imagery of the pip cards of the Minor Arcana. Only one other deck, The Sola-Busca, created in Italy in 1491, had previously illustrated these cards and several designs were incorporated by Pamela. The British Museum exhibited the deck in 1907 and it is possible that Pamela saw it on display and was inspired to illustrate her own Minor Arcana.[216] In 1910 she contributed a cover design to a reissue of the 1892 *Tarot of the Bohemians* by Papus (Gerárd Encausse).

Involvement in the Suffrage Movement

IN ADDITION TO HER DESIGNS FOR THE TAROT DECK, PAMELA'S OTHER MAJOR PROJECT AFTER her return to England in 1909 was becoming active in the Suffrage Atelier, a group of political artists formed by Laurence and Clemence Housman—siblings of the poet A.E. Housman—to prepare for the June 1909 Women's Social and Political Union (WSPU) demonstration.[217] The Atelier produced plays as well as artwork for the movement and Pamela's friend, Edy Craig, was a key link in bringing the Suffrage Atelier, and the closely aligned Artist Suffrage League, together with the Actresses' Franchise League.[218] The organization became a major political entity and encouraged professional and non-professional artists to submit work—and paid them a small percentage of the profits—which was unusual for suffrage organizations at the time.[219]

Most of the posters and postcards that the Suffrage Atelier produced were unsigned in order to emphasize the communal nature of women's struggle for enfranchisement. However, Pamela did contribute at least one clearly identifiable poster and postcard, which is signed P.S., and created in an avant-garde style popularized by the Beggerstaff Brothers (William Nicholson and James Pryde).[220] The poster, which is entitled "A Bird in the Hand is worth Two Mocking-Birds in the Bush," depicts a woman in profile firmly holding a bird while two sneering birds with human faces—handily identified by tags around their necks as the Liberal Prime Minister Herbert Henry Asquith and the Chancellor of the Exchequer David Lloyd George—perch in what appears to be an ivy tree. Text on the bottom attributed to "A. and L.G." states: "If you drop the Conciliation Bill we may do something for you in the dim and speculative future."

The poster was created in response to the 1st Conciliation Bill of 1910, which would have given women the right to vote. Supporters of the bill had collected over 250,000 signatures and Asquith had agreed to give the bill a discussion in Parliament. However, the general election intervened and the discussion did not take place. The poster alludes to an offer Asquith and Lloyd George had made about attaching women's suffrage as an

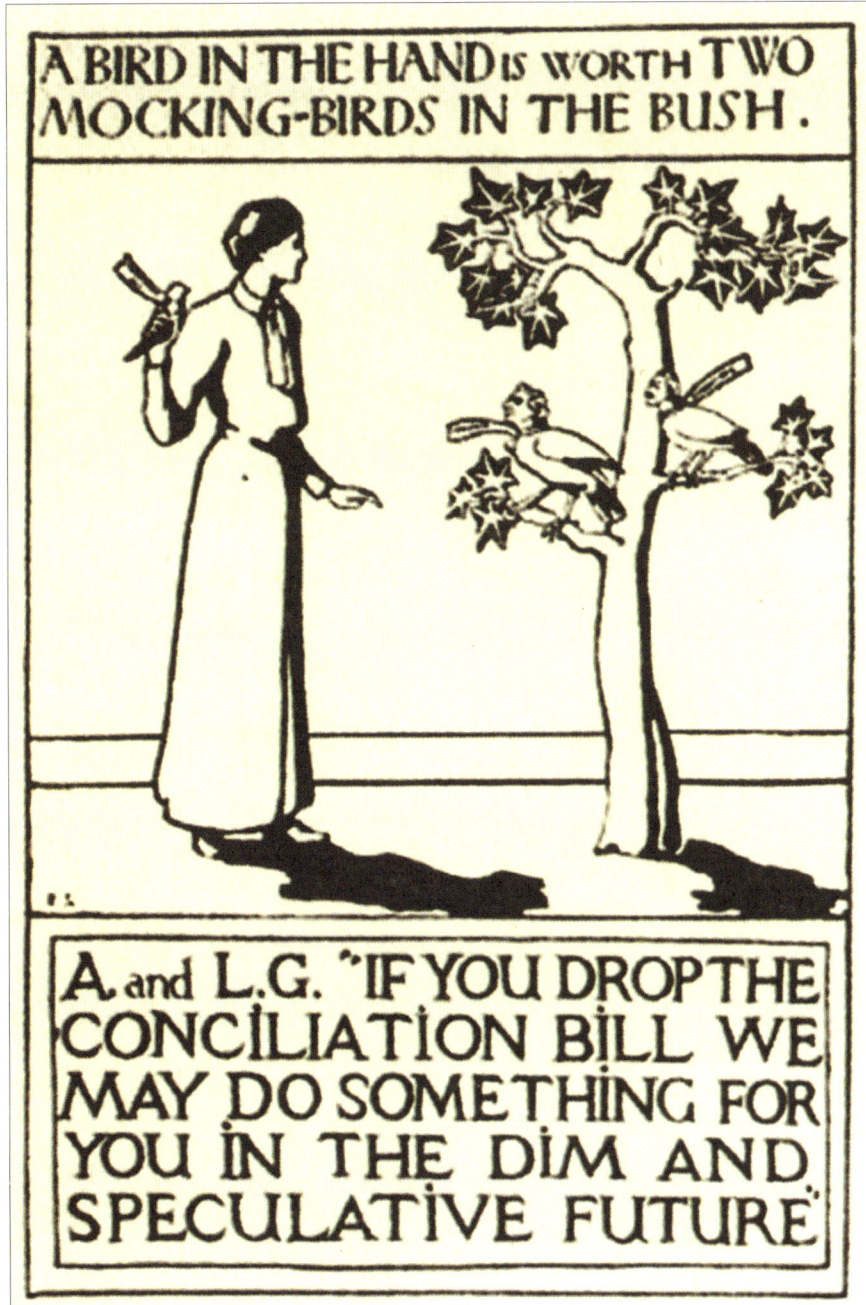

"A Bird in the Hand" poster and postcard designed by Pamela Colman Smith for the Suffrage Atelier. The Conciliation Bill would have given women limited rights.

amendment to the Reform Bill "in the dim and speculative future." With her characteristic pragmatic sense of humor, Pamela's poster urges women not to give into the false promises of the "mocking-birds" but instead push forward with the Conciliation Bill. Unfortunately, her advice was not followed.

In addition to the poster, Pamela appears to have contributed many more unsigned posters and handbills in support of both suffrage and women's rights more broadly defined. There are no extant records for the Suffrage Atelier to verify the authorship of the majority of the group's output during this period. Pamela is known to have contributed stencil designs, along with Ada P. Ridley and Alice B. Woodward, for Laurence Housman's 1911 *Anti-Suffrage Alphabet*.[221]

Opposite: Illustration of Lady Arabella from the *Lair of the White Worm* by Bram Stoker. Published by William Rider and Son, Limited, 1911

Pamela's friends Edy Craig and Chris St. John were also very involved with dramatic performances in support of the suffrage movement. This took the form of processions and tableaux as well as full-length dramatic productions. Chris co-wrote with Cicely Hamilton at least two suffrage plays during the 1908-09 period: *How the Vote Was Won* and *The Pot and the Kettle*.[222] Edy, Chris, and Cicely collaborated on the 1910 *A Pageant of Great Women*, which was put on many times at multiple locations with local participants.[223] It is unclear what Pamela's participation was, if any, in these projects. An advertisement for her "afternoon of folklore" with Marion Gordon Kerby did appear in the program for Chris's July 1906 play, *The Decision: A Dramatic Incident*.[224] Building on the success of *A Pageant of Great Women*, Edy and Chris formed the Pioneer Players in 1911.[225] From 1915-1918, Pamela was on the organization's executive council and also designed costumes for several productions. She designed the cover for a December 1915 production of *Theatre of the Soul* produced and directed by Edy.[226]

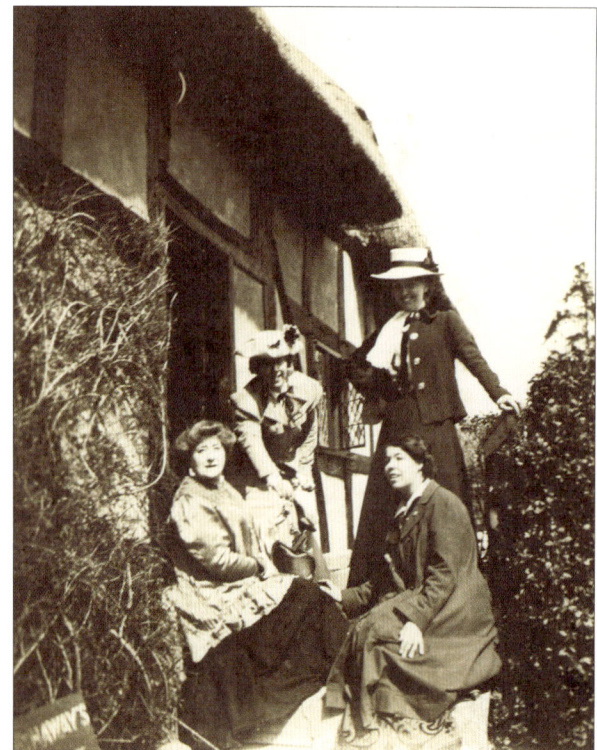

Photograph of Pamela Colman Smith, seated right, and Ellen Terry, seated left, with Edy Craig and Chris St. John. Courtesy of the Royal Shakespeare Company

Illustrations and Other Projects

DURING THE EARLY 1910S, PAMELA BECAME INVOLVED IN SEVERAL BOOK-LENGTH PROJECTS. SHE contributed six color illustrations to Bram Stoker's 1911 *Lair of the White Worm*. Although not nearly as successful as Bram's earlier *Dracula*, this final novel shared an interest in the supernatural and Pamela's drawings were touted as highlighting "the attractiveness as well as the weird character of the book."[227] The central character of the novel, Lady Arabella, has the ability to transform into a serpent who wreaks havoc on all she encounters. Pamela's illustration of a silver-clad Lady Arabella dancing in "a fantastic way" with outstretched arms brings to mind a costume sketch Pamela did with Edy Craig for Russell Vaun's *Nicandra*.[228] Like Bram's novel, Vaun's 1901 play rewrites the Egyptian myth of the serpent-eyed goddess Hathor "who embodies female power manifested by desire and anger." However, while the Egyptian original highlights "the beneficent value of female power," both Stoker and Vaun highlight the snake woman's danger which, ultimately, leads her to her destruction by the male protagonist.[229]

In 1912, Pamela's lavishly illustrated short story "Susan and the Mermaid" appeared in the December edition of *The Delineator* magazine, complete with a two-page spread of paper dolls. The fairy tale describes a young girl's journey to a magical undersea world unlocked by her Grandmother's magic pearl. Populated by mermaids, pompous dolphins, sociable seahorses and excitable pugfish, the Coral City of Oceana also contains "great

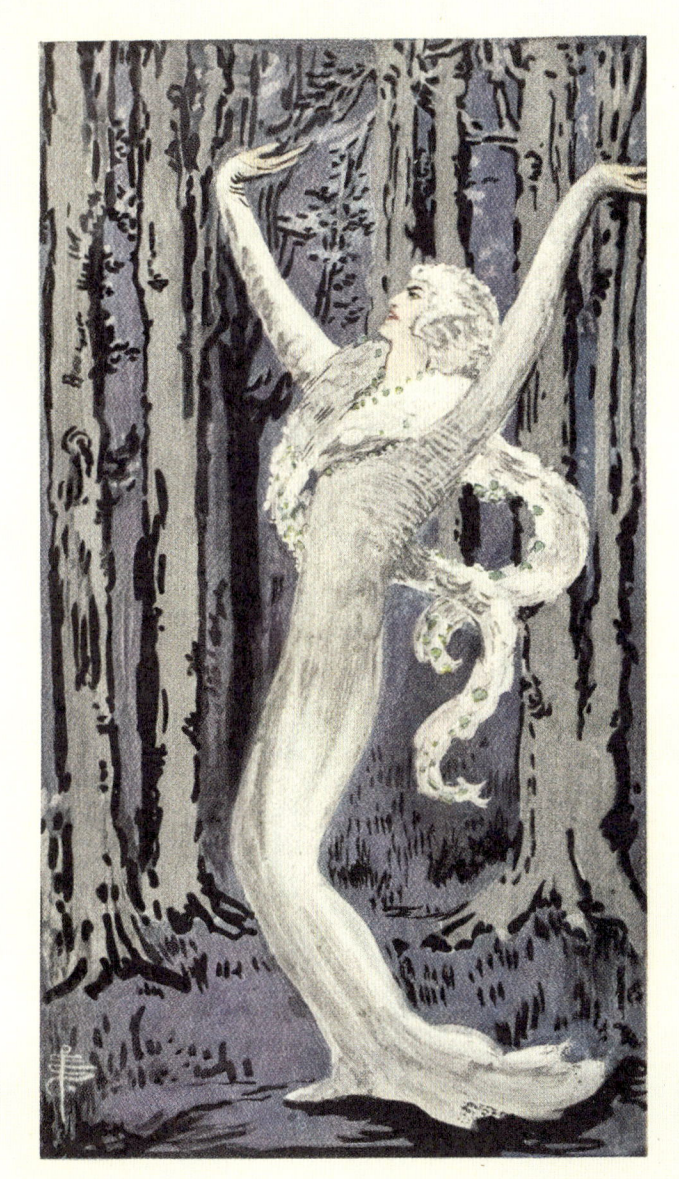

"Lady Arabella was dancing in a fantastic sort of way."

galleries of pictures, and the national theater, and a large concert-hall with notes painted outside that played themselves when you looked at them."[230] The mermaid abruptly leaves, and Susan is almost engulfed by the water. She is narrowly saved by her grandmother who at first hesitates before saying the magic words that return Susan to her human form.

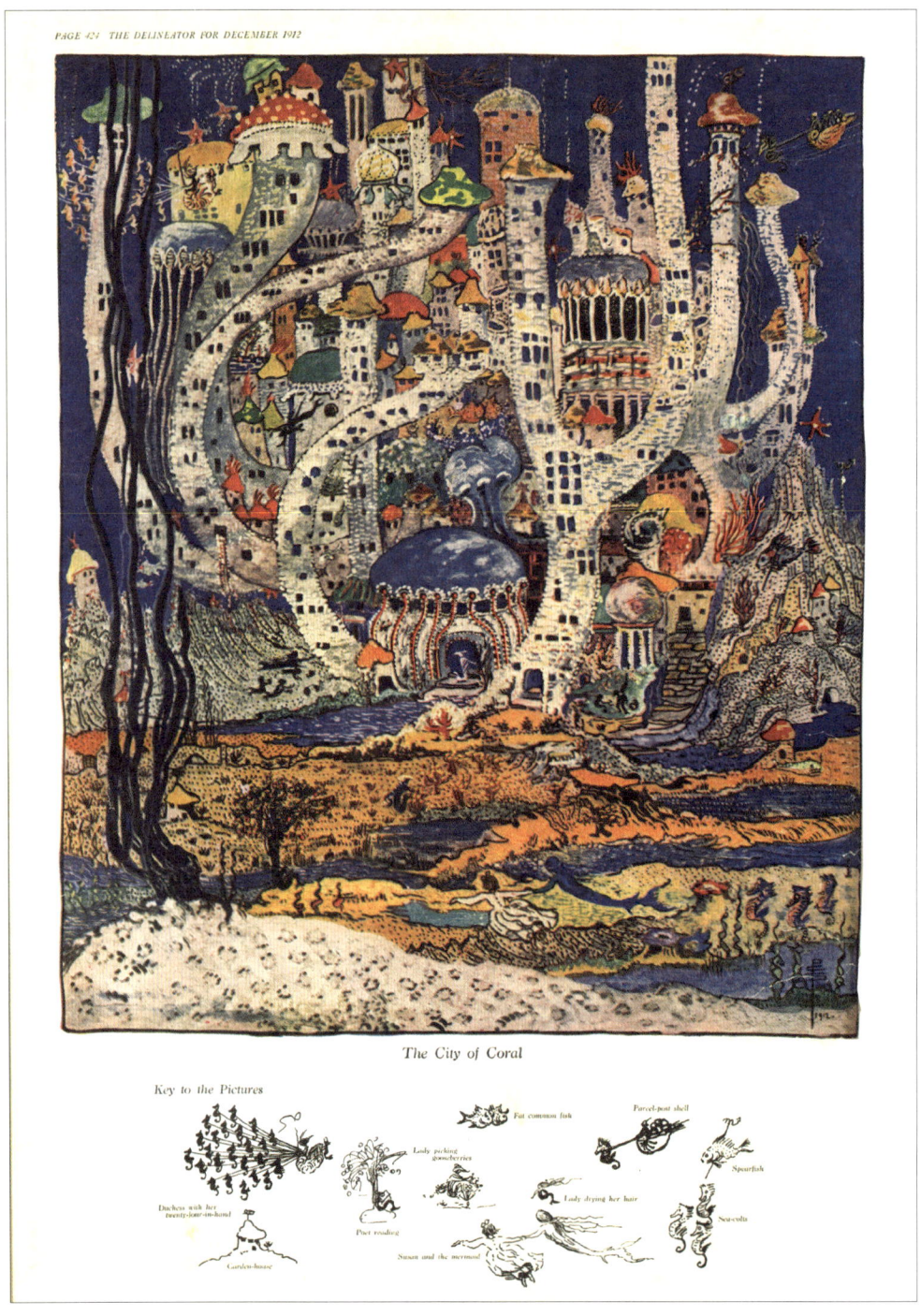

The City of Coral

The following year, Pamela fuses her interest in both the magic of the fairytale and the limitations of female agency through her illustrated edition of *Blue Beard*. Recommending the book for children, *The Brooklyn Daily Eagle* declares it is "a dainty little edition with spirited full-page illustrations," an assessment that completely overlooks the work's dark tone.[231] From the stark cover design that features a man's disembodied head, complete with vacant blue eyes and blue-tinged beard, the edition highlights the dangers of unchecked patriarchal power and the irrational expectations imposed on women to obey their husbands over their own safety and welfare. Young and impoverished, the unnamed female protagonist learns to look past her husband's ugly facial hair and spurred on by his wealth and the lavish lifestyle "begins to think the master of the house a very civil gentleman."[232] They quickly marry, and the husband soon needs to go away on business. Before leaving, he informs his wife she can invite all her friends and gives her free range of the house and all his wealth with the exception of a "little closet" on the ground floor. As he exhorts her, "Open them all; go into all and every one of them, except that little closet, which I forbid you, and forbid it in such a manner that, if you happen to open it, there's nothing but what you may expect from my just anger and resentment."[233] The woman quickly gives in to her curiosity, disobeys her spouse, and enters the secret closet only to be confronted by quantities of clotted blood and the dead bodies of Blue Beard's previous wives. Interestingly, Pamela's illustration for this grisly scene superimposes elements from Bram Stoker's *The Lair of the White Worm*. All of the wives have long, tube-like bodies and outstretched arms that are reminiscent of Lady Arabella. Several of the women appear to have exchanged their humanity for patterned scales and serpent-like facial features.

The magical key quickly becomes stained with blood that will not wash off, and, upon the husband's return, its red hue immediately alerts him to her disobedience. Sentenced to die, she manages to trick her husband into allowing her a little more extra time with her sister, Anne, only to be rescued by their brothers who unceremoniously run her spouse through with their swords. The widow inherits her husband's wealth: "She made use of one part of it to marry her sister Anne to a young gentleman who had loved her a long while; another part to buy captains' commissions for her brothers; and the rest to marry herself to a very worthy gentleman, who made her forget the ill time she had passed with Blue Beard."[234] Pamela's very material elaborations to the traditional *Blue Beard* fairytale clearly highlight that despite the old adage, wealth can be leveraged to achieve happiness and the wife's disobedience does not result in any permanent punishment.

Turning from narrative toward the fluidity and power of dance, Pamela's other book-length work in 1913 was twenty-seven black and white drawings to illustrate *The Russian*

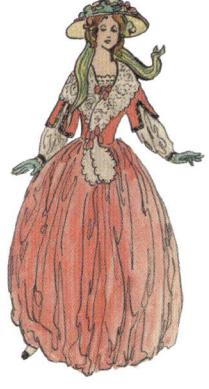

Ballet. Ellen Terry was listed as the author, but she was in ill health and her memory failing, the volume was ghost written by Chris St. John. In England, it was published by Sidgwick and Jackson and in America by the Bobbs-Merrill Company. The book details the rise of the Ballet Russe, which was founded in 1909 by Sergei Pavlovich Diaghilev, the Russian ballet impresario and art critic. St. John's text focuses on the attention in the Russian system to developing both the "virile agility of their steps" and the dramatic intensity of male dancers in a profession that often privileged prima ballerinas and their seductive

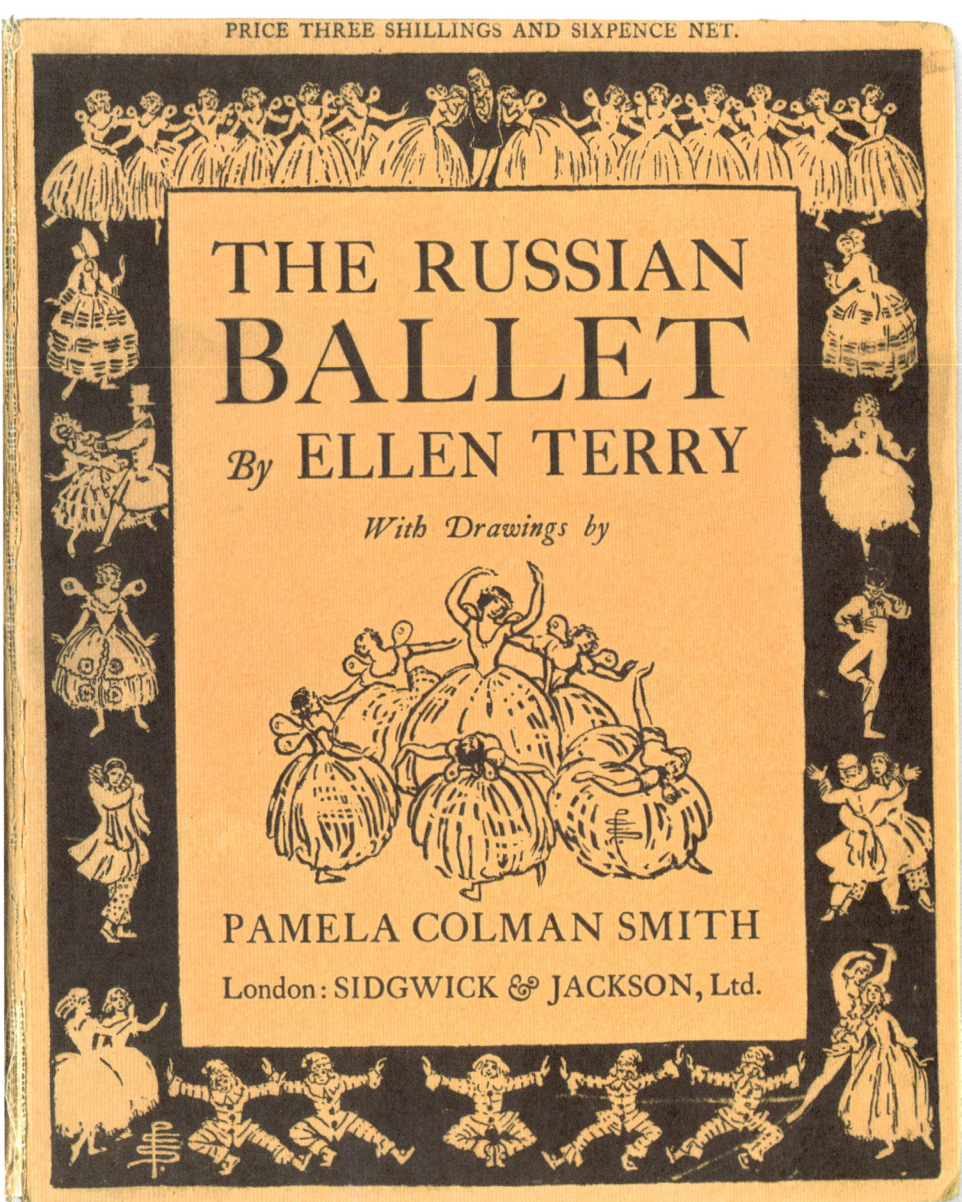

Cover of *The Russian Ballet* by Ellen Terry with drawings by Pamela Colman Smith, 1913

en pointe maneuvers.²³⁵ In her illustrations Pamela captures the lithe grace and emotional intensity of the company's principal male dancer, Vaslav Nijinsky, in several performances, including *Scheherazade*, *Spectre de la Rose*, and *Le Carnaval*. Other illustrative highlights include Anna Pavlova in *Les Sylphides* and *Spectre de la Rose* as well as a quartet of sinister men in long cloaks and tall hats who introduce the Stranger in *Tamar*. Writing in *The Guardian*, Horace Taylor praises Pamela's "decorative drawings, all with a strong sense of black and white," and concludes that in spite of "some clumsiness of form and carelessness of proportion," her illustrations "often succeed quite wonderfully."²³⁶ The *Globe* review is less qualified, stating that "The pen and ink sketches of Miss Smith are a sheer delight. There is not one of them that does not reproduce for us the very spirit of the dancer."²³⁷

Pamela's other projects during this period include designing costumes for a 1914 Easter-season "musical frolic" in London entitled "Brer Rabbit and Mr. Fox" based on the "immortal stories" told by Joel Chandler Harris's Uncle Remus.²³⁸ Also in April, she gave away the guest book she had kept since 1901. An inscription notes that Pamela was releasing the book as "she didn't care for people any more." This change signals a shift in her social demeanor and possibly foreshadows the change in focus many experienced during World War I. Later that year, Pamela contributed more than 100 black and white drawings to Eunice Fuller's *The Book of Friendly Giants*. Upending persistent stereotypes regarding the wickedness of ogres, Fuller collects folktales from Hungarian, Norse, Celtic, German and Chinese sources to provide a new assessment of this material.²³⁹ The title page is dedicated "To All Believers" and depicts three beneficent towering figures smiling down on miniscule humans cavorting in a peaceful valley.

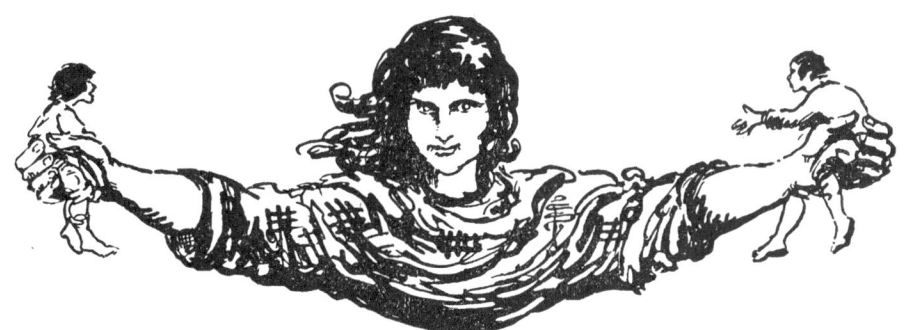

Sometimes he would hold them at arm's length

World War I

After Great Britain declared war on Germany on August 4, 1914, Pamela, like many in England, turned her attention to charitable activities. She hosted bazaars in her studio and donated the proceeds to the Red Cross and other groups. Pamela's final public art endeavors were created during this period as she contributed several wartime posters. One of the most famous features an array of smiling male serviceman encircling a glowering white bulldog. In support of the Bulldog Soldiers & Sailors Club, the poster urges citizens to donate the dogs on June 16th, 1915 in order to "make our Brave Boys comfortable." She also contributed posters for both the War Refugee Relief Fund and the Polish Victim's Relief Fund; her close friend, Laurence Alma Tadema, was the latter organization's Honorary Secretary.

Following Pamela's conversion to the Roman Catholic faith in 1911, the religious dimension of her work became more apparent. Pamela's poster for the Polish Victim's Relief Fund implores the Blessed Virgin Mary, through her title of Most Holy Virgin of Czestochowa, for aide and assistance during this difficult period. It was similar to a series of now lost paintings dating from 1912 based on the Roman Catholic Litany of Loreto. A popular prayer of supplication, the Litany was first used at the famous Marian shrine in Loreto, Italy and is one of only six litanies approved for public recitation by the Vatican. Set to music by Palestrina, Charpentier, and Mozart, the Litany calls on the Virgin Mary using her titles as Spiritual Vessel, Mystical Rose, Tower of Ivory, Queen of Peace, and Morning Star.[240] In 1917, Pamela illustrated a set of 30 cards that mapped the Stations of the Cross. The cards, entitled "The Way of the Cross," were accompanied by verses by the French writer Paul Claudel and translated into English by Rowland Thurnam.

During this period, Pamela also continued to tell Annancy stories, at least occasionally. She appeared in a matinee performance at the Savoy Hotel in February 1917 in support of the Women Wartime Workers.[241] In June 1916 she headed the picture makers at the annual Chelsea Fair.[242] And later that month Pamela took part in the art tent at a Temple of Mystery bazaar that provided "high class astrology plus demonology."[243]

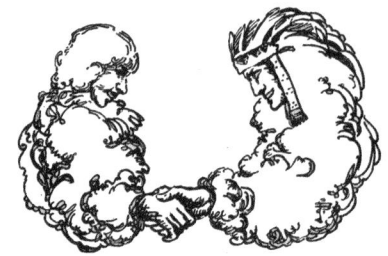

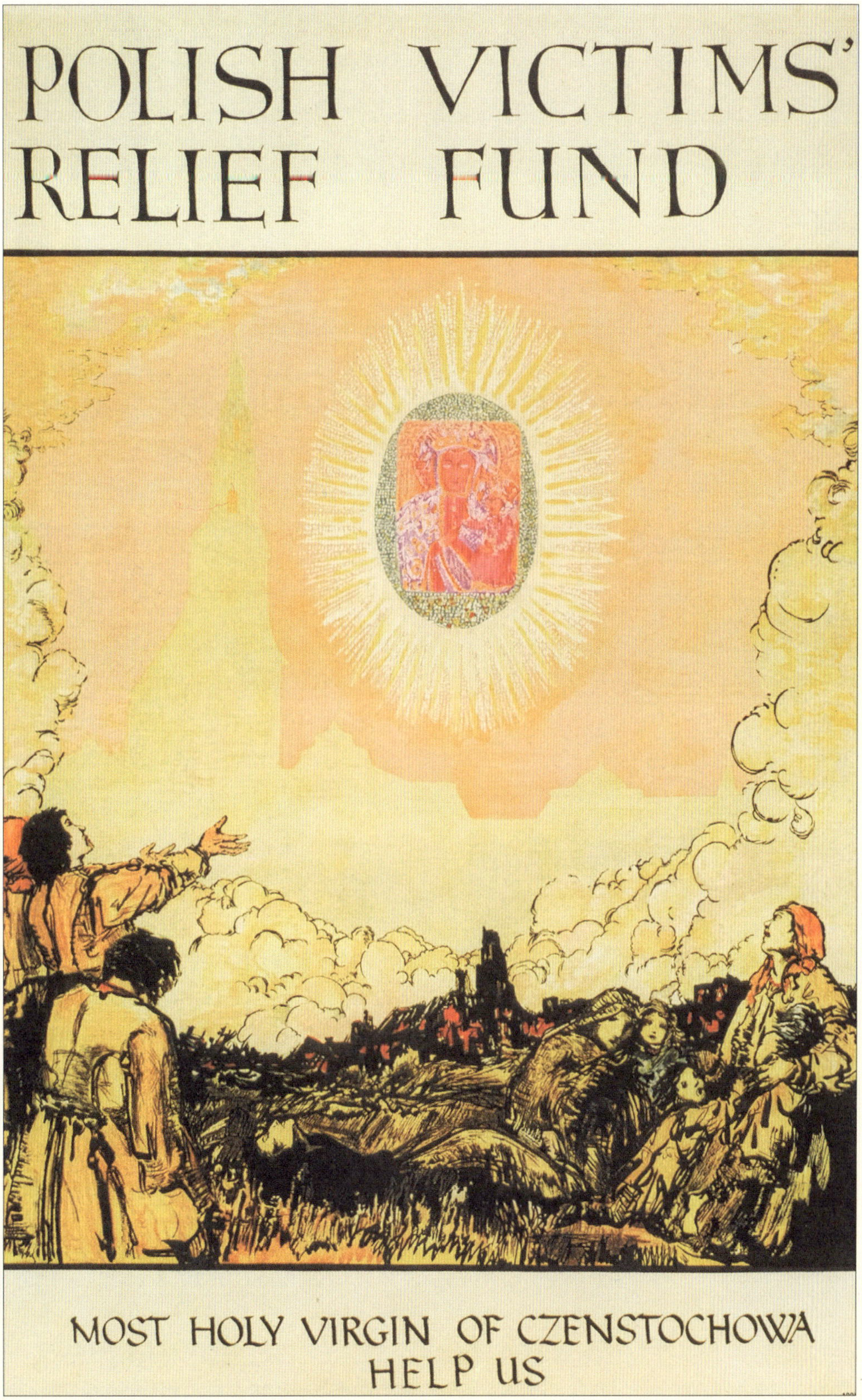

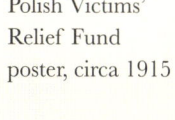

Polish Victims'
Relief Fund
poster, circa 1915

Move to Cornwall

AFTER THE END OF WWI, PAMELA RECEIVED A BEQUEST FROM HER UNCLE TEDDY SMITH IN New York. In March 1919 she used the funds to sign a long-term lease on Parc Garland, a large house with two additional buildings and two acres of land, at the Lizard on the tip of Cornwall in southwestern England. In 1899, a Roman Catholic chapel had been established on the property and there had been plans to open a rectory and day school, which apparently never materialized.[244] Once Pamela took residence, she resurrected the chapel, which she called Our Lady of the Lizard, and supported herself, in part, by operating a summer resort home for Roman Catholic priests on the grounds. She was eventually joined in this pursuit by Nora Lake, her longtime friend who lived with her for many years.

Parc Garland house and chapel, The Lizard, Cornwall, England, circa 1920s

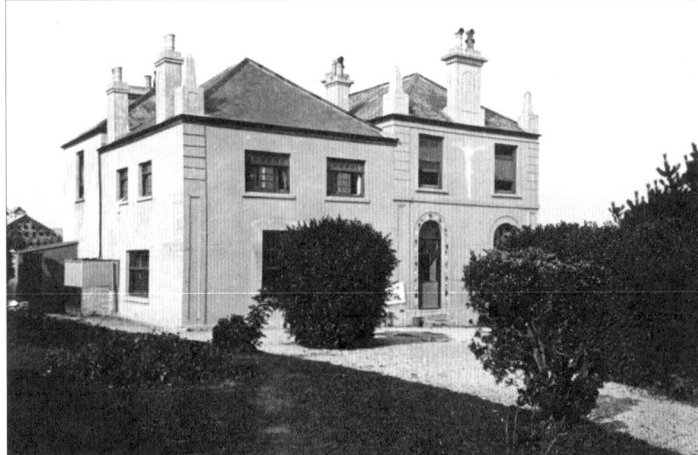

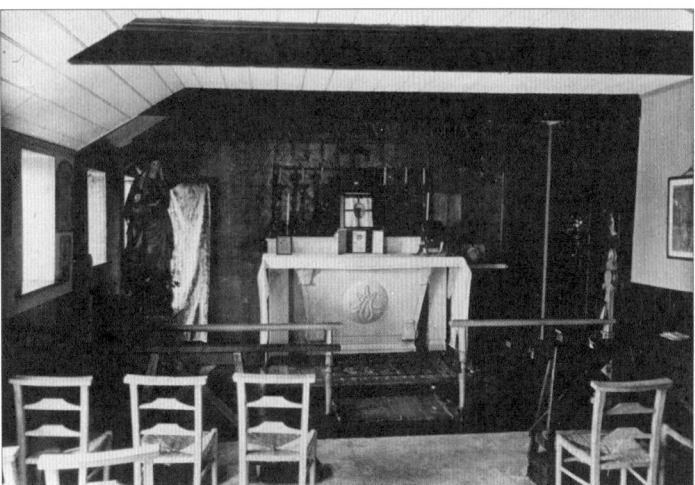

In February 1923, the Bishop of Plymouth, writing in *The Tablet*, England's Catholic newspaper, noted that "for some years, through the personal devotion and very difficult struggle of two ladies, this chapel (recently renewed) has been kept open."[245] The Bishop explains that there were only around 30 scattered Catholics in this "out-of-the-world-spot," summer holiday folk, "the Coastguard, oddments of military and naval forces, and the Marconi employees of Poldhu" all utilize it.[246] However, he announced the establishment of an Our Lady of the Lizard Fund by which to purchase a cottage for a permanent priest and to establish Foundation Masses so the Eucharist can be regularly celebrated.[247]

Little is known about Pamela's daily life at the Lizard. She was within walking distance of the rugged Atlantic Coast with a nearby secluded beach and around the corner from the local Landewednack Primary School. In the December 1919 issue of *Drama Magazine*, Pamela recounts her experience putting on a Nativity play in a village hall with local schoolchildren. She adapted the play from a synopsis published in a magazine. As she notes, "There were no stage directions. They had to be made, and the play written and made actable and speakable."[248] She added that while the children learned their parts relatively quickly, she called regular rehearsals because she "tried to make it as like the real thing as one could, and the children felt that it was like a 'real, live' play, though, I think, not one of them had ever been in a theatre."[249] Pamela goes on to detail the play, scene by scene, discussing everything from scenery and stage props to the placement of the child actors and even includes patterns for the various costumes. She concludes her narrative by discussing the costs.

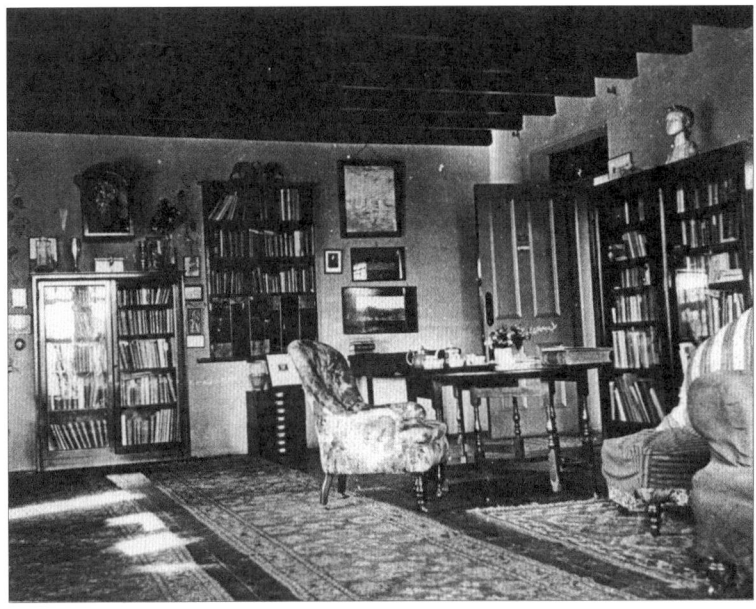

View of Pamela Colman Smith's sitting room at Parc Garland displaying personal possessions and hundreds of books, circa 1920s

"The materials for the dresses for this production came to about five pounds. In other days it would have cost somewhat less. But the skilled labour of the production—re-writing the play, rehearsals, cutting out the dresses, making some and showing others how to make them, making and collecting the properties and 'hand properties', posters, &c.— was all unpaid labour and would work out to a good sum if paid even at an hourly wage."[250]

She concludes with the rather tongue-in-cheek assessment that "When one plans out a production of any kind, one is apt to leave out the question of paying for these things."[251] While it is unclear if Pamela ever attempted to produce another such play at the Lizard, it is possible, even likely, that given the relatively large costs of time and labor to mount such a venture, she viewed it as prohibitive.

Other artistic and literary ventures during this period include twelve black and white illustrations for Edith Lyttelton's 1926 novel, *The Sinclair Family*, which was loosely based on her travels in the Far East and India. Pamela likely met Edith, who was a playwright, translator, and political activist, when they both worked for the War Refugee Relief Fund during WWI. As discussed previously, the Hon. Mrs. Forbes-Sempill's article on Pamela's "music pictures" appeared in *The Illustrated London News* February 12, 1927 and was accompanied by two full pages of black and white illustrations. And for a brief period it appeared that Pamela might be poised for a comeback. However, her 1927 letter to the American art dealer, critic, and author, Martin Birnbaum reveals both how dire her financial situation really was and that her artistic output had slowed considerably. Informing him of Forbes-Sempill's article, she first inquires whether "you know of someone who will buy some drawings?" She soon confides that "I am <u>really</u> in <u>need</u> now—I have a house & 2 acres of ground—poultry &c—and need money <u>badly</u>—to tide things over until I get the work going again."[252] With a note of bitterness that was generally not present in her earlier letters of frustration with publishers, Pamela adds that "People here (in England) are all enthusiastic but have not the <u>brains</u> to see the practical side of handling."[253]

Ellen Terry, Pamela's long-time friend whom she referred to as Gandy, passed away in July 1927. Shortly thereafter, Pamela wrote to Edy, telling her that despite turning a small room in her house into a shop, "I am badly in need of money just now. I have sold *nothing* this year." Pamela asks if Edy could help her sell either some small or large prints of Gandy or even the original signed drawing of Ellen as Mistress Page, which she is willing to part with for ten pounds. It is unknown whether Edy responded or if the two ever met again.

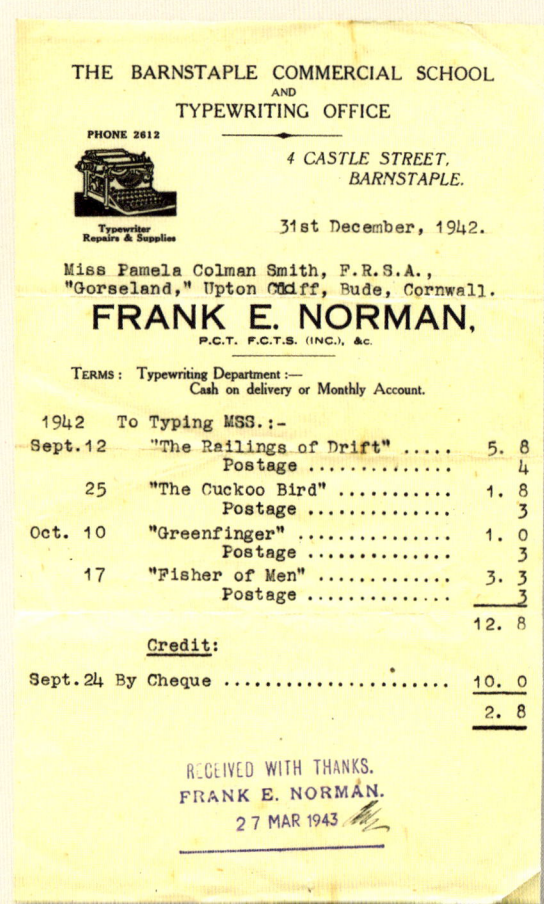

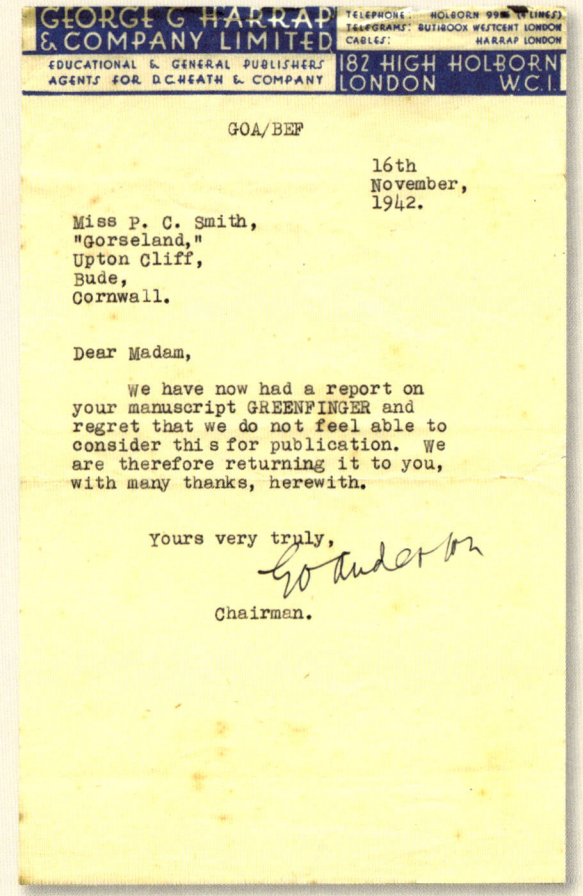

Final Years

PAMELA LEFT PARC GARLAND WITH NORA LAKE IN 1939 AND MOVED FIRST TO EXETER, WHERE Nora had family, and then to Gorseland, at Upton Cliff, just outside Bude, settling there in the early 1940s. In 1939 the *Catholic Who's Who* featured a brief entry on her life and work. After relocating to Bude, Pamela redoubled her efforts at writing and illustrating books. A 1942 receipt shows that she employed a local service to type four manuscripts: *The Railings of Drift*, *The Cuckoo Bird*, *Greenfinger* and *Fisher of Men*. She attempted to place *Greenfinger* with the London publishing firm of George G. Harrap and Co., but it was rejected. Pamela also continued to paint throughout the 1940s. A 1943 watercolor entitled "O' Pines of Sister Pines," was inspired by James Elroy Flecker's poem "Brumana." A 1946 "music picture" entitled, "Duet" was created in response to Stravinsky's *Three Easy Pieces*, depicting a hooded figure slumping beside a denuded tree against a barren landscape. Pamela became a fellow of the Royal Society of the Arts in 1948 and she wrote the letters F.R.S.A. on the backs of all her paintings from this period.

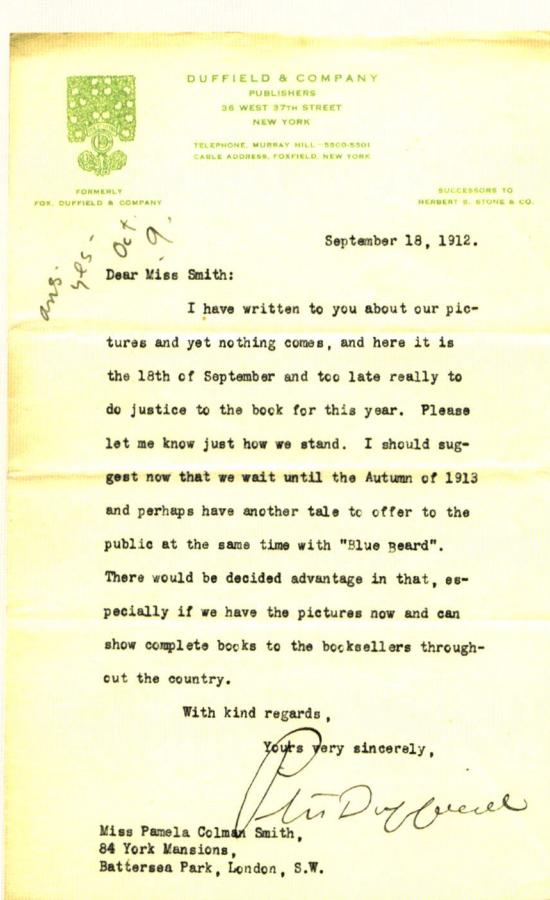

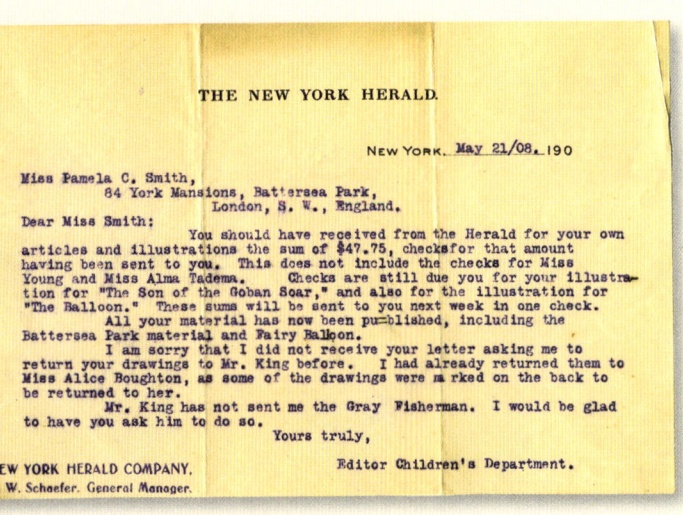

Invoice for typing services dated December 31, 1942; correspondence with Pamela Colman Smith's publishers: George G. Harrap & Company Limited, November 16, 1942; Duffield & Company, September 18, 1912; and *The New York Herald*, May 21, 1908

Opposite: Pamela Colman Smith watercolor on paper entitled "Pines." Illustrates the "sister pines" of the poem "Brumana" by English poet and playwright James Elroy Flecker (1884-1915). Verso is dated December 1943

Pamela died in her apartment on the second floor of Bencoolen House in Bude on September 18, 1951. She was 73. Her friend and neighbor, Elsie T. Bates, who occasionally helped the largely bed-bound Pamela with cleaning and other household tasks, discovered the body. Pamela's will, dated February 23, 1951, left her entire estate "to my friend Nora Lake." Unfortunately, Pamela had many debts, the majority being many years of unpaid income tax, and even after her possessions were auctioned off and proceeds from a trust fund in New York were added into the estate, only approximately 25 percent of her debts were paid. As a result, Pamela's last wish went unheeded and Nora received nothing.

A Catholic until her death, Pamela's Bible and hymnal reveal that she frequently perused these texts, copying down key passages and often doodling images of angels as well as both the crucified and risen Christ. Her death certificate states that her Catholic burial mass was said by the Rev. John de Moulin-Browne, but it does not contain a burial location. As Pamela lacked the financial means necessary at the time of her death to pay for a burial plot and headstone at the closest Catholic cemetery in Launceston, it is highly probable that she was buried in an unmarked grave in St. Michael's Cemetery, the Bude Anglican parish church. However, all the relevant burial records from this period were destroyed in a fire, making it impossible to determine Pamela's final resting place.

Although Pamela was active as an artist until almost the end of her life, her work, which was so highly praised during the early years of her career, had long fallen into obscurity by the time of her passing. Were it not for the continued popularity of her magical imagery on the Rider-Waite Tarot deck, enjoyed by millions of people for more than 100 years, the visionary art of Pamela Colman Smith—her vibrant illustrations and her musical pictures—might be forgotten. This would have truly been a tragic loss since a close examination of her life demonstrates that Pamela certainly achieved much of lasting artistic value. Popular sensibilities underwent a sea change in the aftermath of the Great War, and as a consequence Pamela suffered more than most artists from the vagaries of mass taste. Now at the 140th anniversary of her birth, we can better appreciate her unique creative vision and groundbreaking contributions.

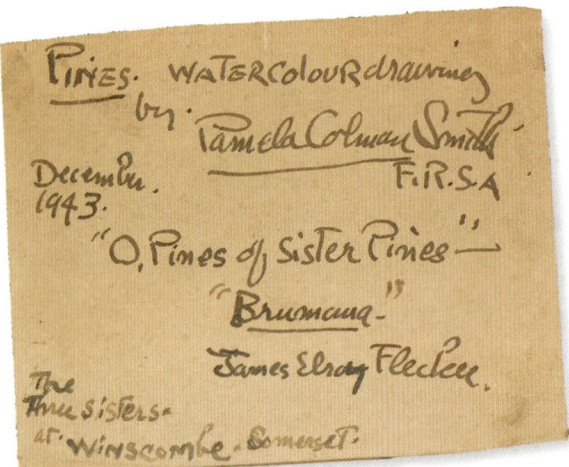

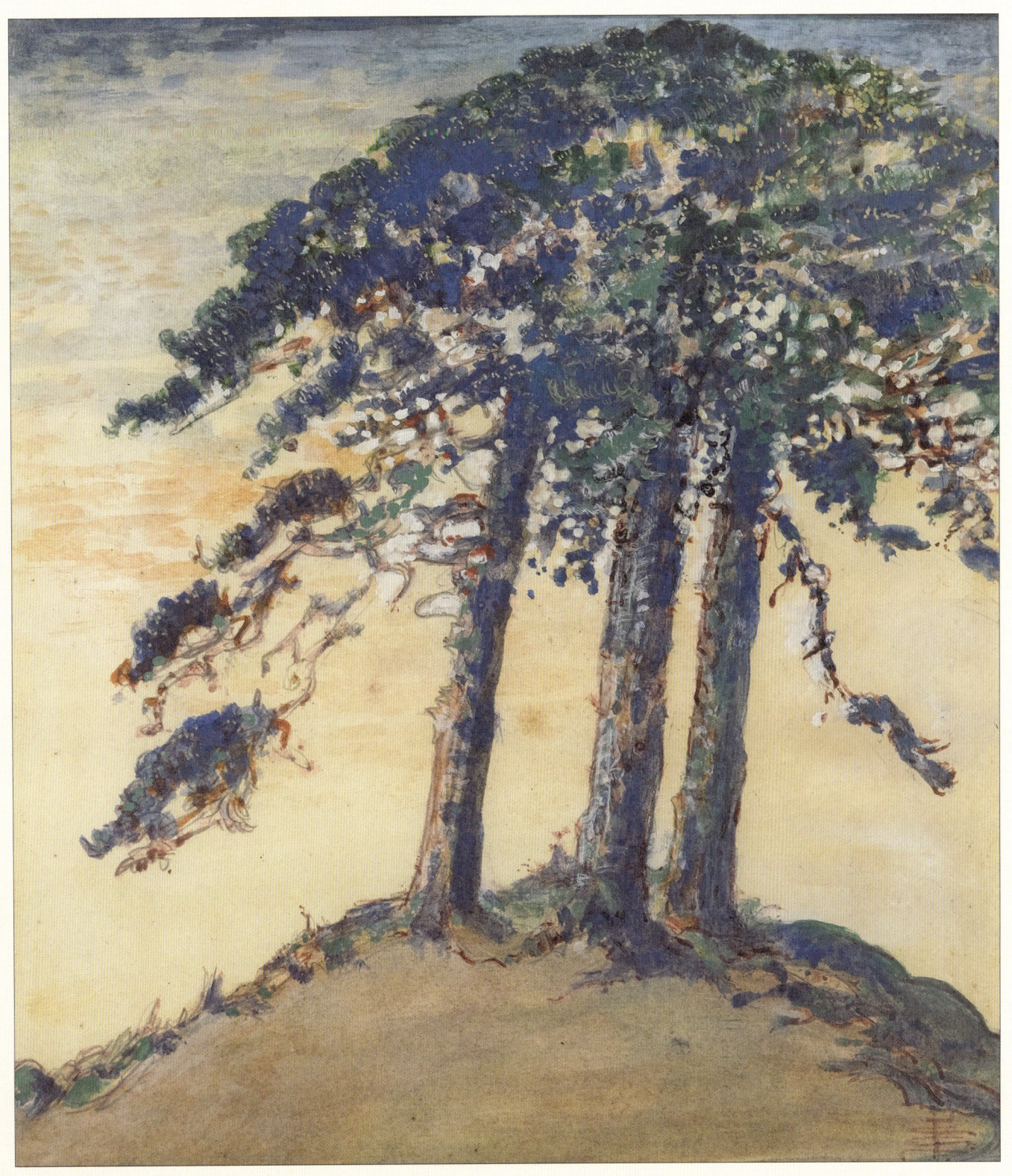

1   March 17, 1901 letter from Pamela Colman Smith to Alfred Bigelow Paine, Huntington Library. AP 1677.
2   J.B. Yeats, *Letters to His Son W.B. Yeats and Others, 1869–1922*, ed. Joseph Hone (New York: E.P. Dutton, 1946), p. 61.
3   Regina Armstrong, "Representative American Women Illustrators: The Decorative Workers," *The Critic*, June 1900, pp. 528-529. See also "Who's Who," *Public Opinion*, volume 28, number 2, p. 768.
4   Unsigned *Brooklyn Daily Eagle* article from Tuesday, November 1, 1904, entitled, "Wins by Witchery in London Drawing Rooms: Remarkable Success of a Heights Girl in Folk-Lore Tales: A Remarkable Personality: Pamela Coleman [sic] Smith, Closely Related to Many Prominent Brooklyn Families, and Her Strange Career," p. 9. Henceforth "Witchery."
5   Joyce Purnick, "A Dig for Artifacts From the Days of Old Bruecklen," *The New York Times*, September 1, 1985, http://www.nytimes.com/1985/09/01/nyregion/a-dig-for-artifacts-from-the-days-of-old-breukelen.html
6   "No More, No More," *The Brooklyn Daily Eagle*, November 16, 1899, p. 8. And "Old Families Ruled in Own Communities," *The Brooklyn Eagle*, April 8, 1934, p. 130.
7   Henry Wood Nevinson, *Changes and Chances*, London: Nisbet & Company, 1923, p. 303.
8   Earnest Elmo Calkins, 'Louder Please': The Autobiography of a Deaf Man, Boston: The Atlantic Monthly Press, 1924, p. 170.
9   Earnest Elmo Calkins, 'Louder Please': The Autobiography of a Deaf Man, Boston: The Atlantic Monthly Press, 1924, p. 170.
10   R.R.G. "Pamela Colman Smith: She Believes in Fairies," *The Delineator*, November 1912, p. 320.
11   R.R.G. "Pamela Colman Smith: She Believes in Fairies," *The Delineator*, November 1912, p. 320.
12   Arthur Ransome, *Bohemia in London*, New York: Dodd, Mead, 1907; pp. 56–57.
13   February 17, 1902 letter from Pamela Colman Smith to George Pollexfen, Stony Brook University, William Butler Yeats Collection, Box 53, 120, 44.
14   Henry T. Tuckerman, *American Artist Life*, New York: G. P. Putnam & Sons, 1867, p. 559.
15   Henry T. Tuckerman, *American Artist Life*, New York: G. P. Putnam & Sons, 1867, p. 559.
16   "Witchery" article in *Brooklyn Daily Eagle*, 1904.
17   Unsigned *Brooklyn Daily Eagle* "Society" entry from January 20, 1900, p. 30 and "Witchery," p. 9.
18   Edward Hooker and Margaret Huntington Hooker, *The Descendants of Rev. Thomas Hooker, Hartford, Connecticut, 1586-1908*, Edited by Margaret Huntington Hooker and published for her at Rochester, NY, 1909. For more on Thomas Hooker see http://connecticuthistory.org/thomas-hooker-connecticuts-founding-father/
19   "A Busy Life Ended: Death of Hon. Cyrus P. Smith," *The New York Times*, February, 14, 1877, p. 5.
20   "A Busy Life Ended: Death of Hon. Cyrus P. Smith," *The New York Times*, February, 14, 1877, p. 5.
21   "Witchery" article in *Brooklyn Daily Eagle*, 1904.
22   "Witchery" article in *Brooklyn Daily Eagle*, 1904.
23   "Charles Edward Smith." *The Brooklyn Daily Eagle*, Saturday, December 2, 1899, p. 18. May 28, 1901 letter from Pamela Colman Smith to Alfred Bigelow Paine, AP1678, Huntington Library.
24   "Witchery" article in *Brooklyn Daily Eagle*, 1904.
25   Pamela Colman Smith's registration card at the Pratt Institute, Stuart R. Kaplan Collection.
26   Arthur W. Dow, "Appreciation," *Pratt Institute Monthly*, volume 7. 1899, p. 62.
27   "Teachers-Students-Things," *Pratt Institute Monthly*, volume 4, June 1896, p. 311.
28   "Teachers-Students-Things," *Pratt Institute Monthly*, volume 4, June 1896, p. 311.
29   September 17, 1896 letter from Pamela Colman Smith to Mary "Bobby" Reed, Special Collections Department, Bryn Mawr College Library, Box 1, folder 2, p. 6.
30   July 25, 1896 letter from Pamela Colman Smith to Mary "Bobby" Reed, Special Collections Department, Bryn Mawr College Library, Box 1, Folder 1, p.1.
31   July 25, 1896 letter from Pamela Colman Smith to Mary "Bobby" Reed, Special Collections Department, Bryn Mawr College Library, Box 1, Folder 1, p. 1.
32   "Our Anancy Stories," *The Daily Gleaner*, February 4, 1898, p. 16.
33   July 25, 1896, letter from Pamela Colman Smith to Mary "Bobby" Reed, Special Collections Department, Bryn Mawr College Library, Box 1, Folder 1, p. 2.
34   September 17, 1896 letter from Pamela Colman Smith to Mary "Bobby" Reed, Special Collections Department, Bryn Mawr College Library, Box 1, Folder 1, p. 4.
35   July 25, 1896 letter from Pamela Colman Smith to Mary "Bobby" Reed, Special Collections

Department, Bryn Mawr College Library, Box 1, Folder 1, p. 4.
36 "Our Anancy Stories," *The Daily Gleaner*, February 4, 1899, p. 16.
37 I.C. Haskell, "The Decorative Work of Miss Pamela Colman Smith," *Pratt Institute Monthly*, vol 6, December 1897, p. 67.
38 "A Jamaica Spider: He is the Hero of Miss Smith's New Book," *Washington Times*, January 15, 1899, p. 17.
39 "A Jamaica Spider: He is the Hero of Miss Smith's New Book," *Washington Times*, January 15, 1899, p. 17.
40 Gardner Teall, "Cleverness, Art, and an Artist," *Brush and Pencil*, volume 6. no. 3., June 1900, p. 140.
41 Stephan Talty, *Empire of Blue Water: Captain Morgan's Great Pirate Army*, New York: Crown Publishers, 2007, pp. 9-19.
42 "School Entertainment at Half-way Trees" in *The Gleaner* (Kingston, Jamaica), December 14, 1896, p. 3.
43 December 8, 1896 letter from Pamela Colman Smith to Mary "Bobby" Reed, Special Collections Department, Bryn Mawr College Library, Box 1, Folder 7, p. 1.
44 December 8, 1896 letter from Pamela Colman Smith to Mary "Bobby" Reed, Special Collections Department, Bryn Mawr College Library, Box 1, Folder 7, p. 3.
45 "School Entertainment at Half-way Trees," in *The Gleaner* (Kingston, Jamaica), December 14, 1896, p. 3.
46 December 15, 1896 letter from Pamela Colman Smith to Mary "Bobby" Reed, Special Collections Department, Bryn Mawr College Library, Box 1, Folder 8, p. 2.
47 "The Pratt Institute," *The Brooklyn Daily Eagle*, December 19, 1897, p. 32.
48 "Teachers-Students-and-Things" *Pratt Institute Monthly*, volume 6, no.4, January 1898, p. 148.
49 "Teachers-Students-and-Things" *Pratt Institute Monthly*, volume 6, no.4, January 1898, p. 148.
50 Earnest Elmo Calkins, 'Louder Please': The Autobiography of a Deaf Man, Boston: The Atlantic Monthly Press, 1924, p. 169. See also Earnest Elmo Calkins, "Advertising Design," *American Printer and Lithographer*, vol. 31, np. 4, December 1900, pp. 243-244.
51 Untitled anonymous article in *The Reader: An Illustrated Monthly Magazine* 2, September 1903, p. 331.
52 For more on Dow see Nancy E. Green "Arthur Wesley Dow, Artist and Educator," in Arthur Wesley Dow and American Arts & Crafts. Eds. Nancy E. Green and Jessie Poesch. New York: The American Federation of the Arts, pp. 55-108, especially p. 66.
53 For a discussion of the influence of Japanese art on Colman Smith's early work see the unsigned review of Colman Smith's *Annancy Stories* and *Widdicombe Fair* in *The Studio: An Illustrated Magazine of Fine & Applied Art* volume 20. number 89, August 1900, p. 199. Dow discusses his design principles in Arthur Wesley Dow, "A New System of Art Teaching," *Pratt Institute Monthly*, volume 6, December 1896, pp. 92-95. See also Arthur Wesley Dow, *Composition: A Series of Exercises in Art Structure for the Use of Students and Teachers*, New York: Baker & Taylor Company, 1899.
54 I.C. Haskell, "The Decorative Work of Miss Pamela Colman Smith," *Pratt Institute Monthly*, volume 6, December 1897, p. 65.
55 Quoted in an unsigned "Teachers-Students-and-Things" column in *Pratt Institute Monthly*, volume 6, no. 5, February 1898, p. 148.
56 "Teachers-Students-and-Things" column in *Pratt Institute Monthly*, volume 6, no. 5, February 1898, p 147.
57 Gardner Teall, "Cleverness, Art, and an Artist." *Brush and Pencil* 6.3, June 1900, p. 135.
58 See untitled anonymous article in *The Reader: An Illustrated Monthly Magazine* volume 2, September 1903, p. 332.
59 Untitled anonymous article in *The Reader: An Illustrated Monthly Magazine* 2 (September 1903): p. 332.
60 Quoted in "Als Ik Kan: Notes: Reviews" *The Craftsman*, volume XI. Number 6, March 1907, p. 770.
61 March 9, 1898, letter from Pamela Colman Smith to Mary "Bobby" Reed, Special Collections Department, Bryn Mawr College Library, Box 1, folder 12, pp. 2-4. See also a September 9, 1898 letter from Pamela Colman Smith to Mary "Bobby" Reed, Special Collections Department, Bryn Mawr College Library, Box 1, folder 14, p. 2.
62 March 9, 1898, letter from Pamela Colman Smith to Mary "Bobby" Reed, Special Collections Department, Bryn Mawr College Library, Box 1, folder 12, pp. 3-4.
63 Christopher Gray, "Apartment Buildings, The Latest in French Ideas," *The New York Times*, July 11, 2013. http://www.nytimes.com/2013/07/14/realestate/apartment-buildings-the-latest-in-french-ideas.html
64 September 9, 1898 letter from Pamela Colman Smith to Mary "Bobby" Reed, Special Collections Department, Bryn Mawr College Library, Box 1, folder 14, p. 2. See also "The Progress of One Student of the Regular Art Class," *Pratt Institute Monthly*, volume 7, no. 3, January 1899, p. 71.
65 "The Progress of One Student of the Regular Art Class," *Pratt Institute Monthly*, volume 7, 1899. p. 71.

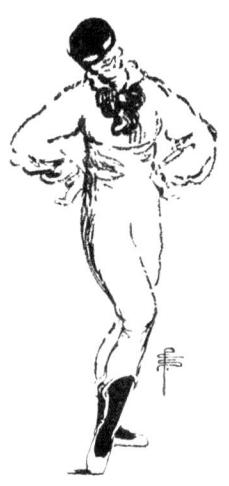

66 "Literature" *Washington Times*, December 25, 1898, p. 15; "Books and Authors," *The New York Times*, December 10, 1898; and "American Studio Talk," *International Studio Magazine*, volume 6, no. 1, January 1899. p. xx.

67 William Shakespeare, *Macbeth*, 1.4.22-23.

68 See Irwin M. MacDonald. The Fairy Faith and Pictured Music of Pamela Colman Smith," *The Craftsman*, XXIII.1 (October 1912)- henceforth 'MacDonald', p. 30.

69 Pamela Colman Smith, *Annancy Stories,"* R.H. Russell, New York, 1899.

70 Thomas Nelson Page, "Introduction" *Annancy Stories* by Pamela Colman Smith, R.H. Russell, 1899; p. 5.

71 "Annancy Stories—A Literary Event," *The New York Herald*, December 11, 1898. This full page spread contained nine black and white drawings by Colman Smith and reproduced the text of three stories: "Bull-Garshananee," "Paarat, Tiger, An' Annancy," and "Mr. Titman." "Ticky-Picky Boom Boom," *New York Herald*, December 25, 1898. "Mother Calbee and Her Cruel Present," *Pittsburgh Daily Post*, December 25, 1898, p. 16.

72 "An American De Monvel," *The Atlanta Constitution*, January 22, 1899; p. 23. The exact same story ran in at least two different papers with different headlines. "A Young Girl Becomes A Brilliant Artist," *The Courier-Journal* (Louisville, Kentucky), January 15, 1899; p. 25 and "An American De Monvel: Flattering Greeting to a Writer of Negro Folk Lore: Rival of Joel Chandler Harris: The Early Life & Later Achievements of Miss Pamela Smith, an American Woman- Brilliant & Original Work," *Omaha Daily Bee*, January 29, 1899; p. 12.

73 Seamus MacManus, *In Chimney Corners* with illustrations by Pamela Colman Smith (Garden City, NY: Doubleday, 1899).

74 Pamela Colman Smith, *Annancy Stories,"* R.H. Russell, New York, 1899, p. 37.

75 Pamela Colman Smith, *Annancy Stories,"* R.H. Russell, New York, 1899, pp. 19, 49, 65, 67, and 73 and Seamus MacManus, *In Chimney Corners: Merry Tales of Irish Folklore,"* illustrated by Pamela Colman Smith, Doubleday McClure Co, 1899, pp. 11, 43 and 113.

76 Seamus MacManus, *In Chimney Corners: Merry Tales of Irish Folklore,"* illustrated by Pamela Colman Smith, Doubleday & McClure Co, 1899, p. 267.

77 See Elizabeth O'Connor, "Pamela Colman Smith's Performative Primitivism" *Caribbean Irish Connections: Interdisciplinary Perspectives*. Eds. Allison Donell, Maria McGarrity, and Evelyn O'Callaghan. Mona: University of the West Indies Press, June, 2015, pp. 157-73.

78 August 7, 1899 letter from Pamela Colman Smith to Albert Bigelow Paine, Huntington Library, p. 2.

79 "The Newest Books," *St. Louis Post-Dispatch*, October 14, 1899, p. 4. The same article appeared in "Literary Notes," *The Washington Times*, October 22, 1899, p. 20; "More Irish Folk Tales," *Brooklyn Life*, November 18, 1899, p. 12; "Children's Gift-Books," *Pall Mall Gazette*, November 28, 1899, p. 9.

80 "Children's Gift-Books," *Pall Mall Gazette*, November 28, 1899, p. 9.

81 "More Irish Folk Tales," *Brooklyn Life*, November 18, 1898, p. 12.

82 "Modern Irish Art," *Dublin Daily Express*, November, 11, 1899, p. 3.

83 Ronald Schuchard, *The Last Minstrels: Yeats and the Revival of the Bardic Arts*, New York: Oxford University Press, 2008, pp. 40-2.

84 Pamela Colman Smith, *The Golden Vanity* and *The Green Bed*. New York: R.H. Russell, 1899.

85 "Guide for the Christmas Book Buyer: Art" *The Critic*, volume 35, December 1899, p. 1145.

86 Pamela Colman Smith, *Widdicombe Fair*, New York: R.H. Russell, 1899.

87 "Reviews," *International Studio*, volume 11, 1900, p. 199.

88 Melinda Boyd Parsons, "Smith, Pamela Colman," *Dictionary of Woman Artists*, Fitzroy Dearborn Publishers, 1997.

89 "Guide for the Christmas Book Buyer: Art" *The Critic*, volume 35, December 1899, p. 1145

90 "Literature," *The Philadelphia Inquirer*, October 22, 1899; p. 46 and "Literature," *The Washington Times*, October 22, 1899, p. 20. See also Pamela Colman Smith letter to Alfred Bigelow Paine, August 23, 1899, AP 1673, Huntington Library.

91 "Literature," *The Philadelphia Inquirer*, October 22, 1899; p. 46 and "Literature," *The Washington Times*, October 22, 1899, p. 20.

92 "Literature," *The Philadelphia Inquirer*, October 22, 1899; p. 46 and "Literature," *The Washington Times*, October 22, 1899, p. 20. The notice also appeared in Anne Pendleton, "About Books & Authors," *The Tennessean*, (Nashville, Tennessee,) November 5, 1899, p. 20.

93 "Here and There," *Brooklyn Life*, February 25, 1899, p. 17; The same notice appeared in "Notes & News: Items

Gathered During This Week's Tour of the Publishing Houses," *The New York Times*, February 25, 1899, p. 17 and "In the Book Room," *The Brooklyn Daily Eagle*, February 25, 1899, p. 7.

94 Pamela Colman Smith, "Sir Henry Irving and Miss Ellen Terry in *Robespierre, Merchant of Venice, The Bells, Nance Oldfield, The Amber Heart,* and *Waterloo,* etc," New York: Doubleday & McClure Co., 1899, unpaginated.

95 "Literary Chat," *The Courier-Journal* (Louisville, Kentucky), November 18, 1899, p. 7. The same notice also appeared in "Literary World," *The Farmer and Mechanic* (Raleigh, North Carolina), November 21, 1899, p. 8; "Theatrical World," *The Record-Union* (Sacramento, California), November 26, 1899, p. 7; "Literary Notes: Interesting News Concerning New Publications," *Virginia-Pilot* (Norfolk, Va) November 26, 1899, p. 11; "Literary Clippings," *The Tennessean* (Nashville, Tennessee), December 3, 1899, p. 20.

96 "Society Continued," *Brooklyn Life*, January 20, 1900, p. 30.

97 *Pamela Colman Smith, William Gillette in Sherlock Holmes: as produced at the Garrick Theatre, New York.* Published with the authorization of Mr. Charles Frohman. New York: R.H. Russell, 1900, unpaginated. See also Anne Pendleton, "About Books and Authors, *The Tennessean* (Nashville, Tennessee), April 22, 1900, p. 20.

98 Heather Campbell Coyle, "The Curious Case of the Stolen Composition, *Illustration History: An Educational Resource and Archive,* September 18, 2015, http://www.illustrationhistory.org/essays/the-curious-case-of-the-stolen-composition.

99 Heather Campbell Coyle, "The Curious Case of the Stolen Composition, *Illustration History: An Educational Resource and Archive,* September 18, 2015, http://www.illustrationhistory.org/essays/the-curious-case-of-the-stolen-composition.

100 For more on Gillette Castle in East Haddam, CT http://www.ct.gov/deep/cwp/view asp?a=2716&q=325204&deepNav_GID=1650%20

101 "In Local Studios," *The Brooklyn Daily Eagle*, April 29, 1900, p. 32.

102 "In Local Studios," *The Brooklyn Daily Eagle*, June 24, 1900, p. 22.

103 "Charles Edward Smith," *The Brooklyn Daily Eagle*, December 2, 1899, p. 18. and "Died," *The New York Times,* December 3, 1899, p. 3.

104 "Charles Edward Smith," *The Brooklyn Daily Eagle*, December 2, 1899, p. 18. and "Died," *The New York Times*, December 3, 1899, p. 3.

105 December 7, 1899 letter from Pamela Colman Smith to Mary "Bobby" Reed, Special Collections Department, Bryn Mawr College Library, Box 1, folder 14, p. 1.

106 December 7, 1899 letter from Pamela Colman Smith to Mary "Bobby" Reed, Special Collections Department, Bryn Mawr College Library, Box 1, folder 14, p. 1.

107 December 7, 1899 letter from Pamela Colman Smith to Mary "Bobby" Reed, Special Collections Department, Bryn Mawr College Library, Box 1, folder 14, p. 1

108 Ellen Terry to Edward Gordon Craig, no. 1067, *The Collected Letters of Ellen Terry, Volume 4* Ed. Katharine Cockin, Taylor & Francis, 2015, p. 88.

109 Ellen Terry to Edward Gordon Craig, no. 1067, *The Collected Letters of Ellen Terry, Volume 4* Ed. Katharine Cockin, Taylor & Francis, 2015, p. 88.

110 February 25, 1900 letter from Pamela Colman Smith to Mary "Bobby" Reed, Special Collections Department, Bryn Mawr College Library, Box 1, folder 15, p. 1.

111 "Ocean Travel," *Brooklyn Life*, May 26, 1900, p. 19.

112 Both portfolios are housed at Smallhythe Place in Tenterdon, Kent, a National Trust site. EC_T10 For more on Edy Craig and Pamela's friendship see Katharine Cockin, *Edith Craig (1869-1947)*, London and Washington: Cassell, 1998, pp. 52-53.

113 December 28, 1900 letter from Pamela Colman Smith to Mary "Bobby" Reed, Special Collections Department, Bryn Mawr College Library, Box 1, folder 17, p. 1.

114 December 13, 1900 letter from Pamela Colman Smith to Alfred Bigelow Paine, AP 1675, Huntington Library.

115 December 13, 1900 letter from Pamela Colman Smith to Alfred Bigelow Paine, AP 1675, Huntington Library.

116 Pamela Colman Smith, "Peg Woffington," *The Kensington*, vol. 2, p. 46; Pamela Colman Smith "Strolling Players" and "Our Adventures," *The Kensington* vol. 4 (June 1901), pp. 97-99; Pamela Colman Smith, "L'Aiglon: Sarah Bernhardt" *The Kensington*, vol. 5 (July 1901), p. 173; Pamela Colman Smith,"The Faithful Wife Dancing Before the Robbers" *The Kensington*, vol. 6 (August 1901), p. 196.

117 May 28, 1901 letter from Pamela Colman Smith to Alfred Bigelow Paine, AP1678, Huntington Library.

118 Pamela Colman Smith, "The Wind," *The Page*, vol. IV. nos. 1 & 2. Edited and published by Edward

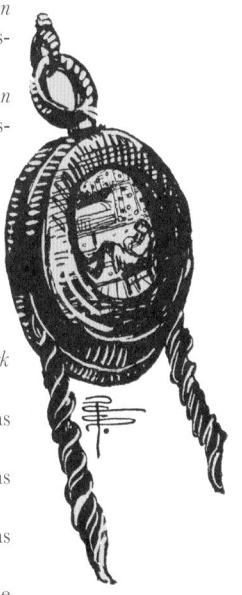

Gordon Craig at the Sign of the Rose, Hackbridge, Carshalton, Surrey, England. 1901. 8vo, unpaginated.

119 Wilbur Macey Stone. *Women Designers of Book-Plates*. New York: Published for the Tryptych by Randolph R. Beam, 1902. 16mo, unpaginated.

120 "Grantham Industrial Exhibition," *Grantham Journal*, January 25, 1902, p. 2.

121 Arthur Ransome, *Bohemia in London*, New York: Dodd, Mead, & Company, 1907, p. 56.

122 Arthur Ransome, *Bohemia in London*, New York: Dodd, Mead, & Company, 1907, pp. 56, 58, 60, 63-65.

123 March 17, 1901 letter from Pamela Colman Smith to Albert Bigelow Paine, AP1677, Huntington Library.

124 Alan Wade, Ed. *The Letters of William Butler Yeats* (London: Hart Davis, 1954), 444. See also Joan Coldwell, "Pamela Colman Smith and the Yeats Family," *The Canadian Journal of Irish Studies*, 3.2, 1977, p. 28-9.

125 Ronald Schuchard, *The Last Minstrels: Yeats and the Revival of the Bardic Arts*, New York: Oxford University Press, 2008, pp. 40, 46, 72, and 124. For brief mention of Pamela lilting at a W.B. Yeats lecture see *The Speaker: The Liberal Review*, Vol 8-16, May 1903.

126 Katharine Cockin, *Edith Craig (1869-1947)*, London and Washington: Cassell, 1998, pp. 28-80.

127 Joan Coldwell, "Pamela Colman Smith and the Yeats Family," *The Canadian Journal of Irish Studies*, 3.2, 1977, p. 29.

128 August 18, 1906 letter from Annie Horniman to Florence Darragh Qtd. In Mary K. Greer, *Women of the Golden Dawn: Rebels and Priestesses*, Rochester, Vermont: Park Street Press, 1995, p. 301.

129 Ronald Schuchard, *The Last Minstrels: Yeats and the Revival of the Bardic Arts*, New York: Oxford University Press, 2008, pp. 101-2, 114-117, 148, and 164-68.

130 Wade, The Letter of William Yeats, 444.

131 January 16, 1901 letter from Pamela Colman Smith to Alfred Bigelow Paine, AP 1676, Huntington Library.

132 March 17, 1901 letter from Pamela Colman Smith to Alfred Bigelow Paine, AP 1677, Huntington Library.

133 August 7, 1899 letter from Pamela Colman Smith to Alfred Bigelow Paine, AP 1671, Huntington Library.

134 March 17, 1901 letter from Pamela Colman Smith to Alfred Bigelow Paine, AP 1677, Huntington Library.

135 May 28, 1901 from Pamela Colman Smith to Alfred Bigelow Paine, AP 1678, Huntington Library. Punctuation in the original.

136 August 1901 letter from Pamela Colman Smith to Alfred Bigelow Paine, AP 1679, Huntington Library.

137 Hilary Pyle, *Jack B. Yeats: A Biography* (London: Routledge & Kegan Paul, 1970); p. 66–67.

138 August 1901 letter from Pamela Colman Smith to Alfred Bigelow Paine, AP1679, Huntington Library.

139 William Michael Murphy, *Family Secrets: William Butler Yeats and His Relatives* (Syracuse, NY: Syracuse University Press, 1995); p. 288.

140 Alan Wade, ed., *The Letters of William Butler Yeats* (London: Hart Davis, 1954); p. 389.

141 This description is on the title page of each of the thirteen issues of Colman Smith's *Green Sheaf*.

142 See Leviticus 23: 10-14

143 "Sheaf" N.5 *Oxford English Dictionary*.

144 See *Martial's Epigrams*, Book 3:82 "To Rufus," Bohn's Classical Library (1897), http://www.tertullian.org/fathers/martial_epigrams_book03.htm

145 Michael Patrick Gillespie, *Oscar Wilde and the Poetics of Ambiguity*. Miami: University of Florida Press, 1996; p. 78.

146 "Advertisements," *The Green Sheaf*, Ed. Pamela Colman Smith, no. 9, London: Pamela Colman Smith, 1904, p. 8.

147 Edward Gordon Craig and Martin Shaw. *Masque of the Harvest Home*. *Green Sheaf*. Ed. Pamela Colman Smith. No. 3. London: Green Sheaf, 1903; pp. 2-3.

148 *The Green Sheaf*, no. 3; p. 4.

149 *The Green Sheaf*, no. 3; p. 5.

150 *The Green Sheaf*, no. 3; pp. 6-7.

151 *The Green Sheaf*, no. 4; p. 9.

152 *The Green Sheaf*, no. 12; p. 5.

153 "Literary Notes" *The Academy and Literature*, volume 66. no. 1657, February 6, 1904, p. 137.

154 "Art Notes," *The Academy and Literature*, volume 66, pp. 1663, p. 307, March 19, 1904.

155 April 25, 1903 letter from Pamela Colman Smith to William Macbeth, Macbeth Gallery Records, Smithsonian Institute Library, NMc11.

156 Ibid.

157 "Miss Pamela Smith's Drawings," (London) *Morning Post*, November 19, 1903, p. 3.

158 Feb. 7, 1904 letter from Pamela Colman Smith to Alfred Bigelow Paine, AP1682, Huntington Library.

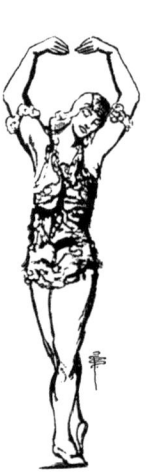

159 February 3, 1904 letter from Pamela Colman Smith to W. B. Yeats, Stony Brook University, William Butler Yeats Collection, Box 53, 120, 115.
160 Ibid.
161 "The Green Sheaf," *The Green Sheaf*, Ed. Pamela Colman Smith, no. 13. London: Pamela Colman Smith; p. 12.
162 Pamela Colman Smith, *Annancy Stories*, R.H. Russell, New York, 1899, p. 52.
163 Brief discussion of the shop in "Art Notes," *Pall Mall Gazette*, December 28, 1905, p. 3.
164 The Hon. Mrs. Forbes-Sempill, "Music Made Visible: An Unmusical Artist's Lightning Impressions Recorded While Listening to Music," *The Illustrated London News*, February 12, 1927, p. 260.
165 February 21, 1908 letter from Pamela Colman Smith to Alfred Stieglitz, Georgia O'Keeffe Collection, Beinecke Library, Yale University, YCAL MSS 85, box 45.
166 The Hon. Mrs. Forbes-Sempill, "Music Made Visible: An Unmusical Artist's Lightning Impressions Recorded While Listening to Music," *The Illustrated London News*, February 12, 1927, p. 260.
167 G. Jean-Aubry, "'Visualised Music" De Miss Pamela Colman Smith," *SIM*, volume 7, February 15, 1911, pp. 44-46.
168 Qtd. In Melinda Boyd Parsons, "Mysticism in London: The 'Golden Dawn,' Synaesthesia, and 'Psychic Automatism' in the Art of Pamela Colman Smith." In *In the Spiritual Image in Modern Art*, edited by Kathleen J. Regier, Wheaton, Ill. Theosophical Publishing House, 1987, p. 99.
169 See Melinda Boyd Parsons, "Theatrical Productionsm Symphonic Music, And the Rise of 'Musical Painting' in the Late Nineteenth Century," *Nineteenth Century Studies* volume1 (1987), pp. 49-72.
170 The Hon. Mrs. Forbes-Sempill, "Music Made Visible: An Unmusical Artist's Lightning Impressions Recorded While Listening to Music," *The Illustrated London News*, February 12, 1927, p. 260.
171 The Hon. Mrs. Forbes-Sempill, "Music Made Visible: An Unmusical Artist's Lightning Impressions Recorded While Listening to Music," *The Illustrated London News*, February 12, 1927, p. 260.
172 "Pictures in Music," *The Strand Magazine*, volume XXXV, no. 210, June 1908, p. 635.
173 "Pictures in Music," *The Strand Magazine*, volume XXXV, no. 210, June 1908, p. 635.
174 "Pictures in Music," *The Strand Magazine*, volume XXXV, no. 210, June 1908, p. 636.
175 "Pictures in Music," *The Strand Magazine*, volume XXXV, no. 210, June 1908, p. 635.
176 M. Irwin Macdonald, "The Fairy Faith and Pictured Music of Pamela Colman Smith," *The Craftsman*, XXIII, no. 1, October 1912, p. 28.
177 The Hon. Mrs. Forbes-Sempill, "Music Made Visible: An Unmusical Artist's Lightning Impressions Recorded While Listening to Music," *The Illustrated London News*, February 12, 1927, p. 260.
178 See Melinda Boyd Parsons, "Pamela Colman Smith and Alfred Stieglitz: Modernism at 291," *History of Photography*, volume 29, no. 4 (Winter 1996) pp. 285-292.
179 James Hueneker, "Some Special Exhibitions," *The New York Sun*, January 15, 1907, p. 6.
180 "Als Ik Kan: Notes: Reviews," *Craftsman*, volume XI, no. 6, March 1907, pp. 769-70.
181 Alfred Stieglitz quoted in Melinda Boyd Parsons, "Pamela Colman Smith and Alfred Stieglitz: Modernism at 291," *History of Photography*, volume 29, no. 4 (Winter 1896), p. 288.
182 "Als Ik Kan: Notes: Reviews," *The Craftsman*, volume XI, no. 6, March 1907, p. 769.
183 April 27, 1907 letter from Pamela Colman Smith to Alfred Stieglitz, Georgia O'Keeffe Collection, Beinecke Library, Yale University, YCAL MSS 85, box 45.
184 April 27, 1907 letter from Pamela Colman Smith to Alfred Stieglitz, Georgia O'Keeffe Collection, Beinecke Library, Yale University, YCAL MSS 85, box 45. See also Giles Edgerton, "Is America Selling Her Birthright in Art for a Mess of Pottage? Significance of this Year's Exhibit at the Pennsylvania Academy," *The Craftsman*, volume XI, no. 6, March 1907, pp. 657-670.
185 November 9, 1907 and December 27, 1907 letters from Pamela Colman Smith to Alfred Stieglitz, Georgia O'Keeffe Collection, Beinecke Library, Yale University, YCAL MSS 85, box 45. See also Giles Edgerton, "Is America Selling Her Birthright in Art for a Mess of Pottage? Significance of this Year's Exhibit at the Pennsylvania Academy," *The Craftsman*, volume XI, no. 6, March 1907, pp. 657-670.
186 Pamela Colman Smith, "A Protest Against Fear," *The Craftsman*, volume XI, no. 6, March 1907, p. 728.
187 February 21, 1908 letter from Pamela Colman Smith to Alfred Stieglitz, Georgia O'Keeffe Collection, Yale University, YCAL MSS, Box 45.
188 March 18, 1908 letter from Pamela Colman Smith to Alfred Stieglitz, Georgia O'Keeffe Collection, Yale University, YCAL MSS, Box 45.

189 "The Photo Secession: Exhibitions," *American Art Annual*, vol. 8, p. 202.
190 Melinda Boyd Parsons, "Pamela Colman Smith and Alfred Stieglitz: Modernism at 291," *History of Photography*, volume 29, no. 4 (Winter 1996) p. 288.
191 "Art Notes Here and There," *The New York Times*, March 21, 1909, p. 56.
192 Benjamin De Casseres, "Pamela Colman Smith," *Camera Work*, July 1909, no. 27, p. 18.
193 Feb. 7, 1904 letter from Pamela Colman Smith to Alfred Bigelow Paine, AP1682, Huntington Library.
194 "London Correspondence," *Sheffield Daily Telegram*, December 19, 1903, p. 6.
195 "West Indian Folklore Stories," *The Winfield Daily Free Press* (Winfield, Kansas), October 21, 1904, p. 3. The same article appeared in *The Columbus Journal* (Columbus, Nebraska), Wednesday, October 26, 1904, p.6; *The Marquette Tribune* (Marquette, Kansas), *October 27, 1904, p.3; The Marshfield News and Wisconsin Hub* (Marshfield, Wisconsin), December 1, 1904, p. 6.
196 "West Indian Folklore Stories," *The Winfield Daily Free Press* (Winfield, Kansas), October 21, 1904, p. 3.
197 "A Pretty Story-Teller," *The Sketch*, March 18, 1908, p. 306.
198 "Café Chantant for Princess Christian's Infant Nursery," January 24, 1904, p. 3.
199 "The League of Mercy," *Morning Post* (London), April 14, 1908, p. 6
200 "Stone: Entertainment" *Bucks Herald* (Buckinghamshire) December 26, 1908, p. 5.
201 "Miss Colman-Smith's Story-Telling," *The Times* (London), February 4, 1908, p. 9.
202 J. T. Grein, "An Afternoon of Folk-Lore," *The Sunday Times* (London), July 15, 1906, p. 6.
203 "Miss Jean Sterling Mackinlay," *Kent & Sussex Courier*, May 31, 1912, p. 7.
204 "Old Songs and Ballads" *Eastbourne Gazette*, January 22, 1913, p. 8.
205 "Italian Officials Guests: Many Prominent Personages Attend Eight Event of Mrs. Hitchcock's Entertainments at the Waldorf," *The Brooklyn Daily Eagle*, January 30, 1907, p. 10.; and "Mayor des Planches Honor Guest: Italian Ambassador Entertained by Entertainment Club at Waldorf," *New-York Tribune*, January 30, 1907, p. 14.
206 "Packer Alumnae At Home," *The Brooklyn Daily Eagle*, February 24, 1907, p. 36.
207 "Packer Alumnae At Home," *The Brooklyn Daily Eagle*, February 24, 1907, p. 36; see also "Pamela Colman Smith to Entertain the Packer Alumnae," *The Brooklyn Daily Eagle*, February 10, 1907, p. 13.
208 "Reading Club Anniversary," *The Brooklyn Daily Eagle*, March 17, 1907, p. 39.
209 "Made Veteran Humorist Laugh," reprinted from the *New York World* in *The Evening Statesman* (Walla Walla, Washington), February 27, 1907, p. 3.
210 "Made Veteran Humorist Laugh," reprinted from the *New York World* in *The Evening Statesman* (Walla Walla, Washington), February 27, 1907, p. 3.
211 "A Lecture on Art: Pamela Colman Smith Talks to Pratt Art Club," *The Brooklyn Daily Eagle*, March 25, 1909, p. 11.
212 "Plays for Children," *The Brooklyn Daily Eagle*, April 3, 1910, p. 33.
213 November 19, 1909 letter from Pamela Colman Smith to Alfred Stieglitz, Georgia O'Keeffe Collection, Yale University, YCAL MSS, Box 45.
214 Mary K. Greer, *Women of the Golden Dawn*, Rochester, Vermont: Park Street Press, 1995, p. 407.
215 A.E. Waite, *Shadows of Life and Thought:* London: Selwyn and Blount, 1938.
216 "History of Sola-Busca Tarot," https://solabuscatarot1998mayer.wordpress.com/history-of-sola-busca-tarot-2/
217 Morton, Tara. (2012) *Changing spaces: art, politics, and identity in the home studios of the Suffrage Atelier. Women's History Review*, volume 21 (No.4). pp. 623-637.
218 Lisa Tickner, *The Spectacle of Women,*: Imagery of the Suffrage Campaign, Chicago: University of Chicago Press, 1988, p. 244.
219 Morton, Tara. (2012) *Changing spaces: art, politics, and identity in the home studios of the Suffrage Atelier. Women's History Review*, volume 21 (No.4). pp. 623-637.
220 Lisa Tickner, *The Spectacle of Women,*: Imagery of the Suffrage Campaign, Chicago: University of Chicago Press, 1988, pp. 30, 35.
221 Lisa Tickner, *The Spectacle of Women,*: Imagery of the Suffrage Campaign, Chicago: University of Chicago Press, 1988, pp. 247-8.
222 Katharine Cockin, *Edith Craig (1869-1947)* London and Washington: Cassell, 1998, pp. 84-85.
223 Katharine Cockin, *Edith Craig (1869-1947)* London and Washington: Cassell, 1998, pp. 96-107.
224 Katharine Cockin, *Edith Craig (1869-1947)* London and Washington: Cassell, 1998, p. 84.

225 Katharine Cockin, *Edith Craig (1869-1947)* London and Washington: Cassell, 1998, pp. 108-32.
226 Katharine Cockin, *Edith Craig (1869-1947)* London and Washington: Cassell, 1998, pp. 118, 128, 139.
227 "Literary Gossip," *Belfast Newsletter*, November 14, 1911, p. 10.
228 Bram Stoker, *The Lair of the White Worm*, London: Rider & Son, 1911, p. 85; Pamela's sketch for *Nicandra* is part of the Ellen Terry archive at Smallhythe Place, Tenterdon, Kent. See also Katharine Cockin, *Edith Craig (1869-1947)* London and Washington: Cassell, 1998, pp. 44-45.
229 Katharine Cockin, *Edith Craig (1869-1947)* London and Washington: Cassell, 1998, p. 45.
230 Pamela Colman Smith, "Susan and the Mermaid" Reprinted by Corinne Kenner, Create Space Publishing, 2010, pp. 16-17.
231 "Pictures for Children," *The Brooklyn Daily Eagle*, November 29, 1913, p. 24.
232 Pamela Colman Smith, *Blue Beard*, New York: Duffield& Co., 1913, p. 4.
233 Pamela Colman Smith, *Blue Beard*, New York: Duffield& Co., 1913, p. 6.
234 Pamela Colman Smith, *Blue Beard*, New York: Duffield& Co., 1913, p. 25.
235 Ellen Terry, *The Russian Ballet*, New York: The Bobbs: Merrill Company, 1913, p. 10.
236 Horace Taylor, "New Books," *The Guardian*, February 21, 1913, p. 5.
237 "The Russian Ballet," *Globe* (London), February 13, 1913, p. 5.

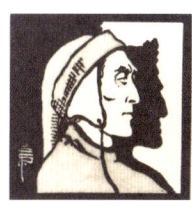

238 "Notes," *The Academy*, volume 86, April 4, 1914, p.428.; "For Every Woman," *Pall Mall Gazette*, March 28, 1914, p. 4.
239 "Books for Young Readers," *The Brooklyn Daily Eagle*, November 21, 1914, p. 21.
240 "Our Catholic Prayers," http://www.ourcatholicprayers.com/litany-of-the-blessed-virgin-mary.html. See also Mary K. Greer, "Pamela Colman Smith 1912—Correspondences," https://marykgreer.com/2015/02/10/pamela-colman-smith-1912-correspondences/
241 "Tableaux at the Savoy Hotel," *The Times* (London), February 9, 1917, p. 3.
242 "The Chelsea Fair," *Chelsea News and General Advertiser*, June 16, 1916, p. 2.
243 "Temple of Mystery," *Pall Mall Gazette*, June 29, 1916, p. 9.
244 "Plymouth," *The Tablet*, December 9, 1899, p. 954.
245 "Plymouth," *The Tablet: The International Catholic News Weekly*, February 10, 1923, p. 32.; See also "Plymouth, *The Tablet: The International Catholic News Weekly*, December 16, 1922, p. 15.
246 "Plymouth," *The Tablet: The International Catholic News Weekly*, February 10, 1923, p. 32.
247 "Plymouth," *The Tablet: The International Catholic News Weekly*, February 10, 1923, p. 32.
248 Pamela Colman Smith, "Producing a Village Play," *Drama*, October 1919, London: Chatto & Windus, p. 47.
249 Pamela Colman Smith, "Producing a Village Play," *Drama*, October 1919, London: Chatto & Windus, p. 47.
250 Pamela Colman Smith, "Producing a Village Play," *Drama*, October 1919, London: Chatto & Windus, p. 49.
251 Pamela Colman Smith, "Producing a Village Play," *Drama*, October 1919, London: Chatto & Windus, pp. 49-50.
252 Undated 1927 letter from Pamela Colman Smith to Martin Birnbaum, Smithsonian Archives of American Art, p. 1.
253 Undated 1927 letter from Pamela Colman Smith to Martin Birnbaum, Smithsonian Archives of American Art, p. 2.

Prior to 1902

1896 — Two Negro Stories from Jamaica

Two Negro Stories from Jamaica. From *Journal of American Folk-Lore*, Oct-Dec 1896

TWO NEGRO STORIES FROM JAMAICA.

ANNANCY AND THE YAM HILLS.

ONE time Annancy libed in a country where the Queen's name was Five, an' she was a witch; an' she say whoeber say five was to fall down dead. It was berry hungry times, and so Annancy go build himself a little house by de side of de riber. An' him make five yam hills. An' when anybody come to get water at de riber he call them an' say: "I beg you tell me how many yam hills I hab here. I can't count berry well." So den dey would come in and say, "One, two, three, four, *five!*" an' fall down dead. Then Annancy take dem an' corn dem in his barrel an' eat dem, an' so he live in hungry times — in plenty. So time go on, an' one day Guinea fowl come dat way, an' Annancy say: "Beg you, Missus, tell me how many yam hills hab I here." So Guinea fowl go an' sit on hill an' say: "One, two, three, four, an' de one I am sittin' on!" "Cho!" say Annancy; "you don't count it right!" An' Guinea fowl mouve to anoder yam hill an' say: "Yes, one, two, three, four, an' de one I am sittin' on!" "He! you don't count right at all!" "How you count, den?" "Why dis way," say Annancy: "One, two, three, four, FIVE!" an' he fell down dead, an' Guinea fowl eat him up!

Dis story show dat "Greedy choak puppy."

DE STORY OF DE MAN AND SIX POACHED EGGS.

Once a man go travellin' an' he get hungry, so he stop at a tavern an' order something to eat, so dey bring him six poached eggs. He eat dem, but he did not hab any money, so he say he would come back an' pay. In six years — or maybe it was more — he come back an' pay sixpence for de eggs. But den de tavern keeper say dat if he had not eaten de six poached eggs dey might hab been chickens, and den de chickens would hab grown up and hatch more chickens, an' dey more — an' more — an' more — an' tell de man he must pay six pounds instead of sixpence. An' de man say he would not. So dey go to de judge. An' while dey was conversin' a boy come in wid a bundle under his arm. An' de judge say: "What you got in de bundle?" and de boy say, "Parch'peas, sa!" "What you goin' do wid dem?" "Plant dem, sa!" "Hi!" say de judge, "you can't plant parch'peas, dey won't grow!" "Well, sa, an' poached eggs won't hatch!" So dey dismiss de man and he neber pay a penny!

Dis story show dat you mus' neber count you' eggs before dey hatch!

Pamela Coleman Smith.

KINGSTON, JAMAICA.

FOLKTALES, ART & POETRY

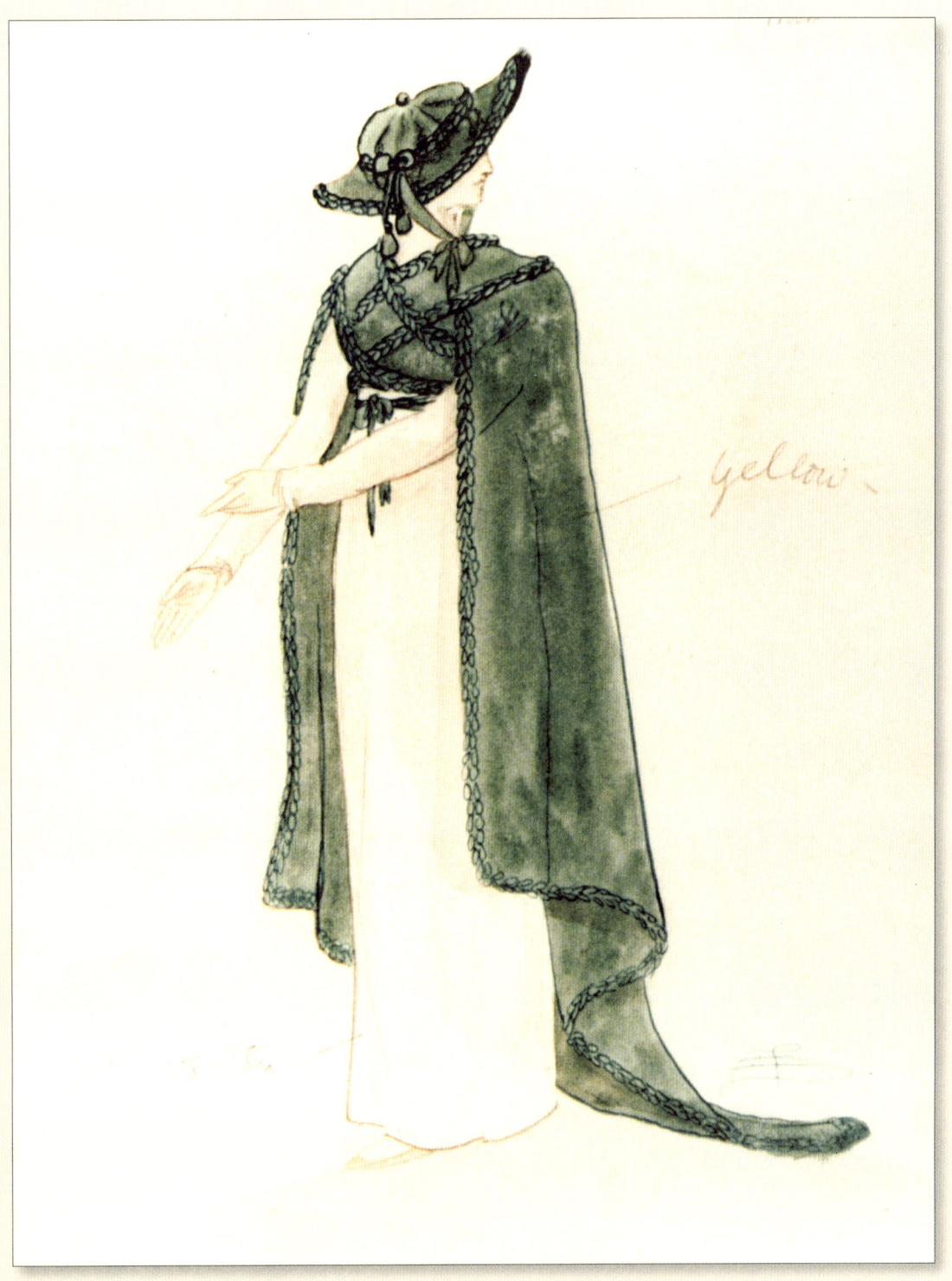

A Christmas Carol

1898

Two illustrations from *A Christmas Carol* by Pamela Colman Smith. Published by R.H. Russell, 1898

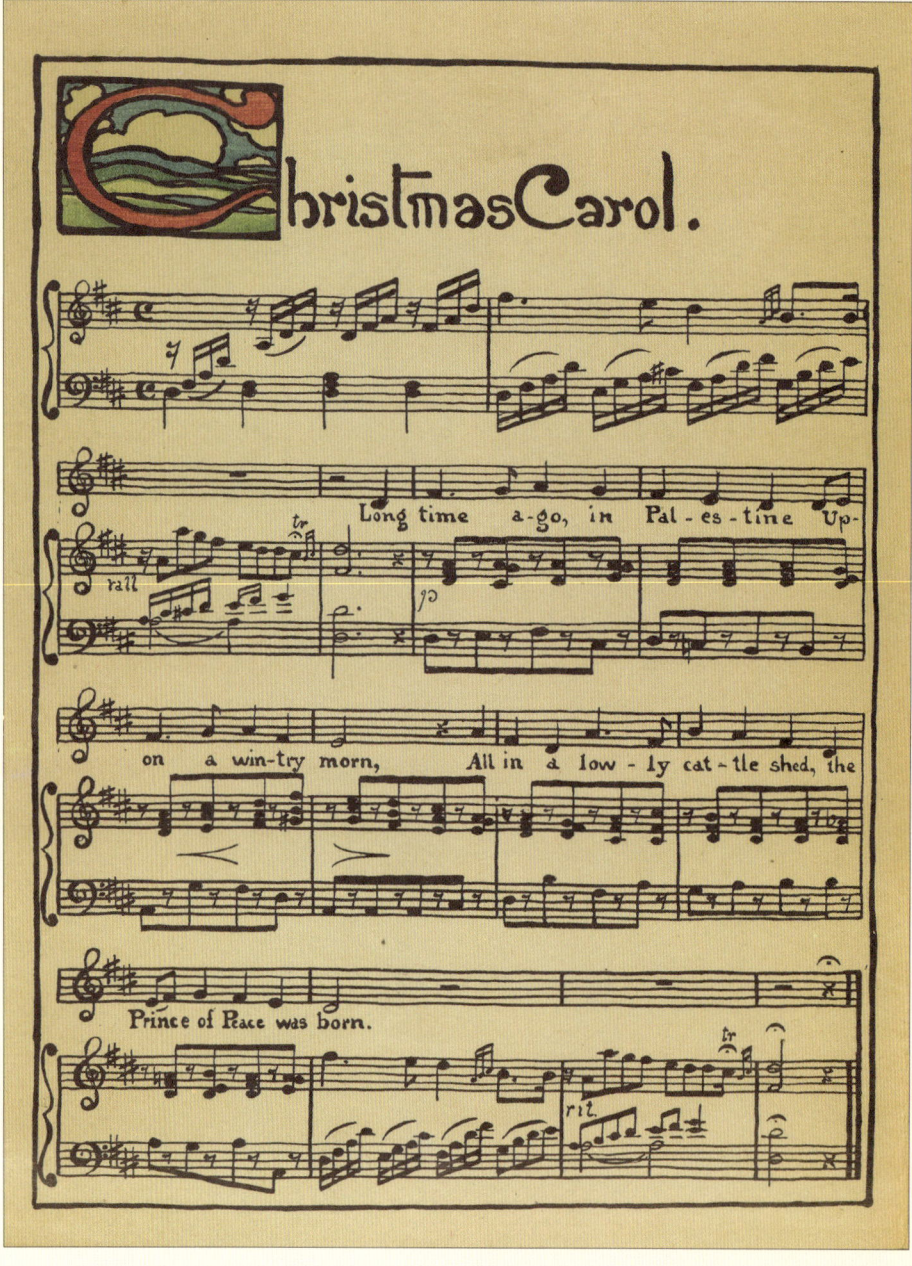

1898

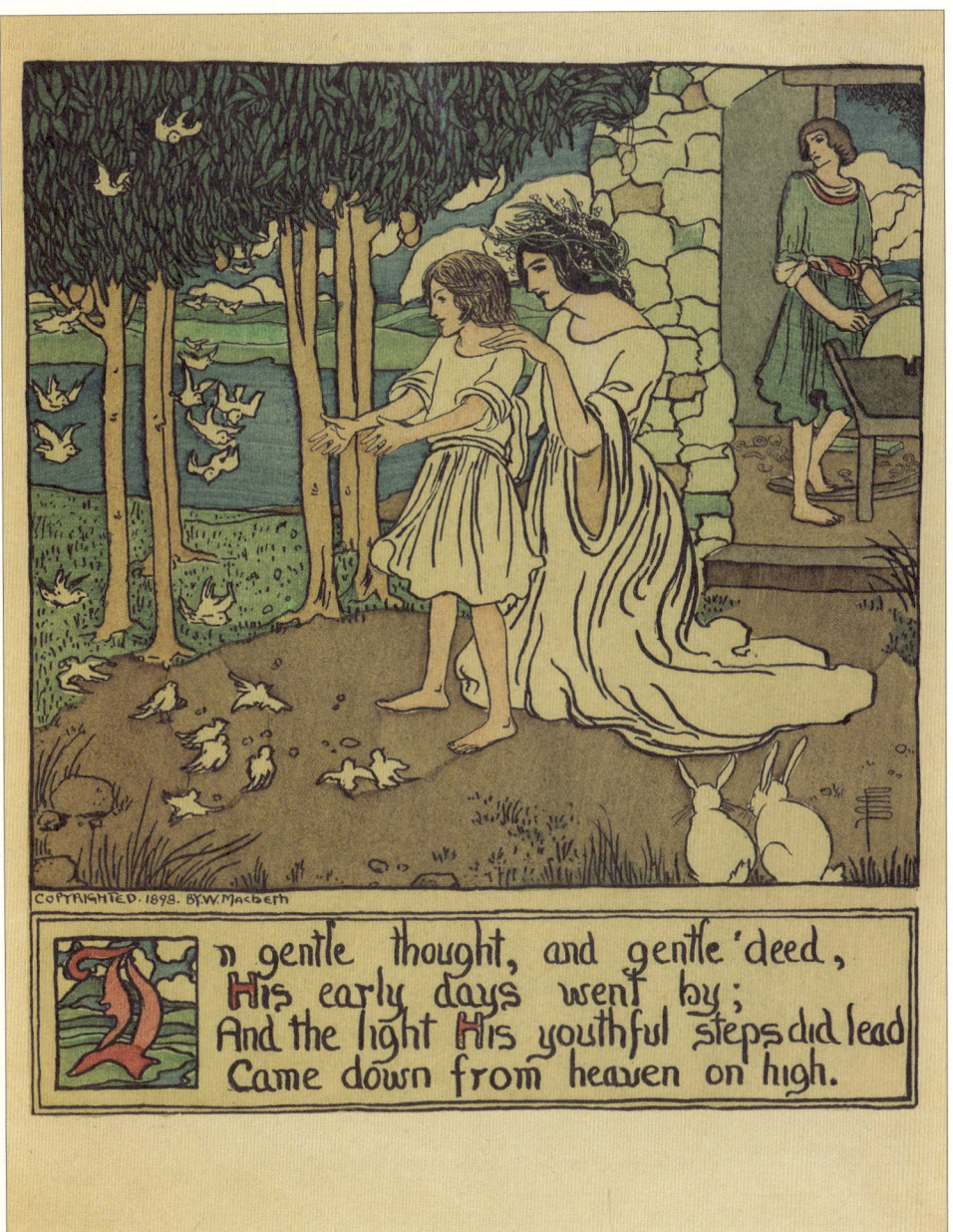

In gentle thought, and gentle deed,
His early days went by;
And the light His youthful steps did lead
Came down from heaven on high.

Sir Henry Irving and Miss Ellen Terry

1899

Cover and illustrations from *Sir Henry Irving and Miss Ellen Terry in Robespierre, Merchant of Venice, The Bells, Nance Oldfield, The Amber Heart, Waterloo, etc.* Published by Doubleday & McClure Co., 1899

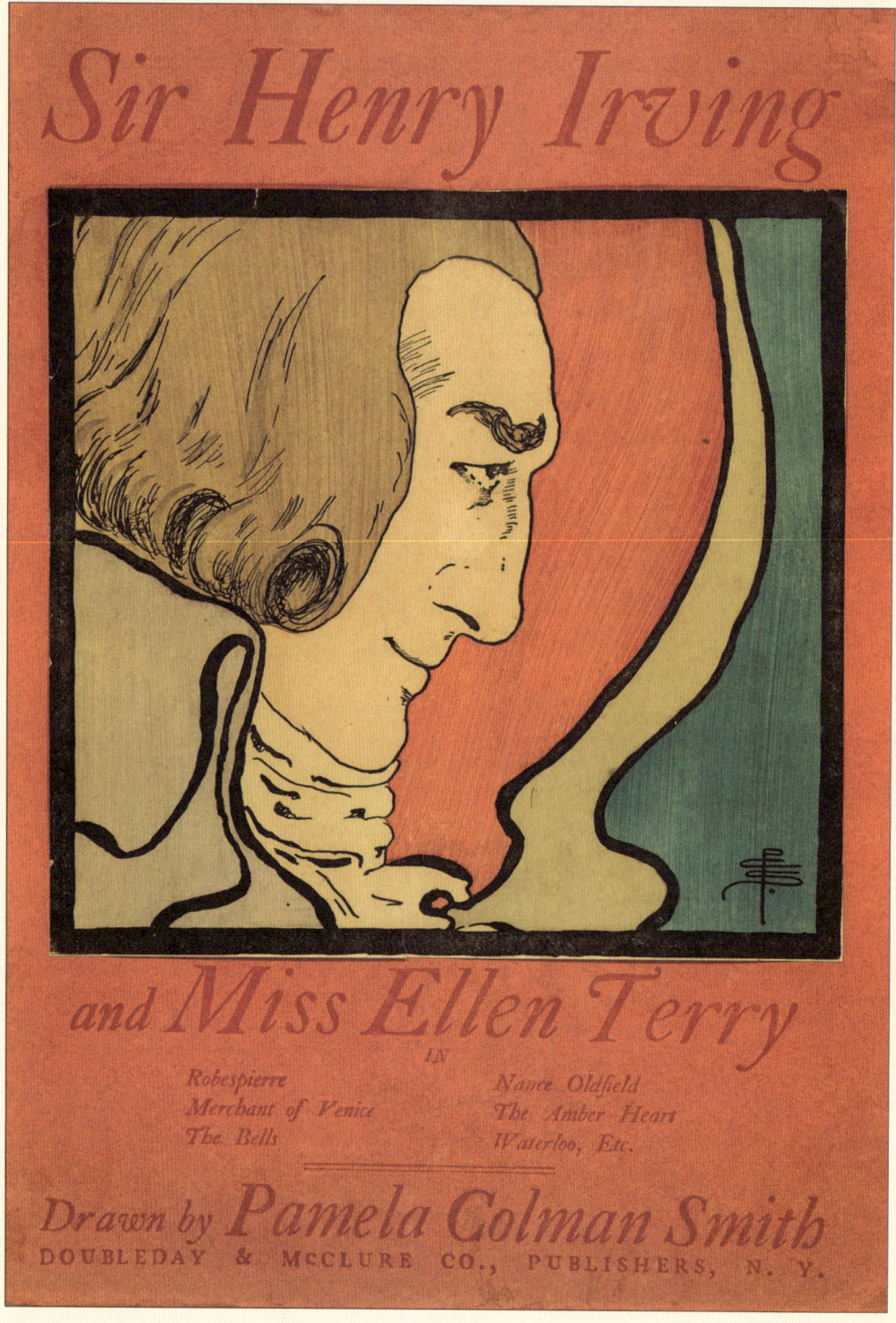

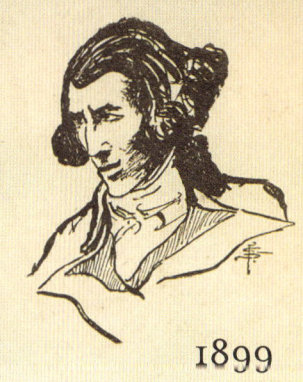

1899

SIR HENRY IRVING

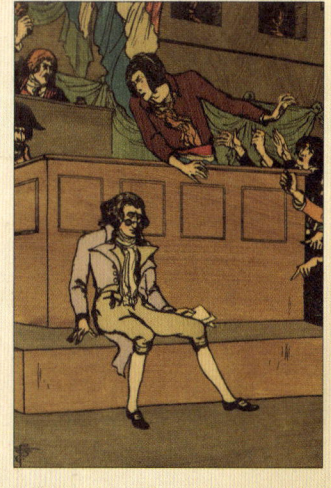

THE practical cause of Henry Irving's success has, after his gifts as an actor, been his constant, unwearied and single-minded devotion to his chosen work. When in 1856, then a boy of eighteen, he took the final plunge from clerkship, which he began at thirteen years of age, into art, he had already behind him several years of steady toil rigourously given in the leisure hours of his daily working life. In those days, as now, the working hours of a London clerk were as long as the work was poorly paid, and it needed a very fixed resolution to keep a young man constant to the self-imposed task of studying an exacting and endless art. Early and late he was at work, studying plays and parts, and half starving himself to pay for the few lessons kindly given to him at an hour in the morning so early as to be inconvenient to himself by an old actor who believed in his future and who predicted for him great

"The traitors machinations are laid bare".
Laurence Irving.

CONVENTION SCENE, "ROBESPIERRE"
(See Frontispiece)

1899

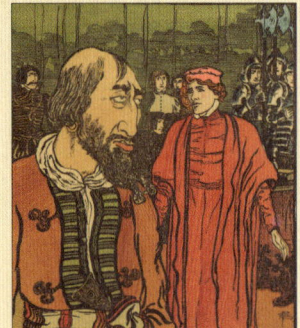

things. This devotion to his aim, however, bore good fruit; and in the earlier years of his stage work at Sunderland and Edinburgh, when the bill was changed so often that it was necessary for a young actor to learn sometimes three or four new parts in a week, he was always able to keep ahead of his work by means of the reserve of some hundred stock parts in which he was in stage language "letter-perfect." This was not only a saving of exhausting labour and a spurning of the prompter's assistance—always a thing to be feared—but it enabled him to give to each part which he undertook something of the necessary care of elaboration. To act a part it is not sufficient to know the words. Dress has to be considered, as well as bearing, manner, intonation, the time suitable to the true setting forth of the phases of the character—in short, all those aids and accessories which go to the convincing of the spectator as to the *vraisemblance* of the character. This artistic exactness, added to his undoubted genius, at once told in his favour, and he began very soon to creep up the ladder of success. Material prosperity is not the measure of a young actor's success. Such, no doubt, follows in due course, but in early days the standard of advancement is in the growing importance of the parts entrusted to him. Young Irving found his possibilities of ultimate success multiplying fast. To-day when the work of the stage is more highly elaborated,

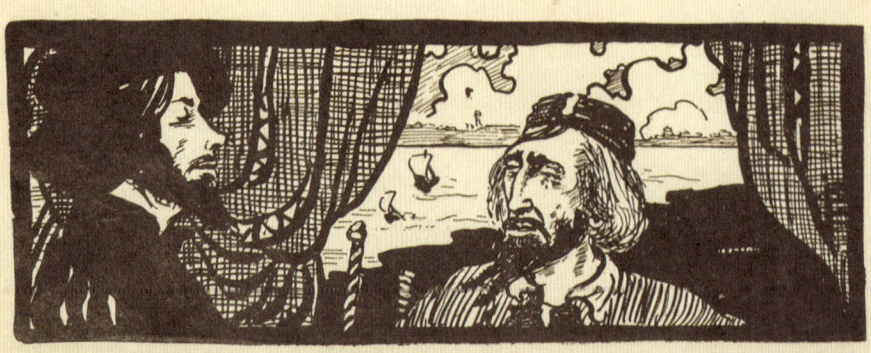

HATH A DOG MONEY?
IS IT POSSIBLE A CUR CAN
LEND THREE THOUSAND
DUCATS?
Merchant of Venice
Act i, Scene iii.

SIR HENRY IRVING

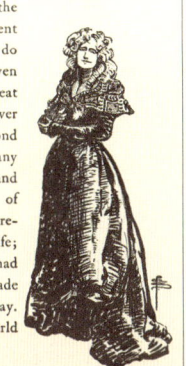

when the length of runs makes a sufficiently lengthy preparation possible and even advisable, when the life of a single drama runs at times into years of continuous existence, when actors are well paid, hold a worthy position in society and have fair prospect of sharing in the good fortune of their time, it is hard to realize the difficulties of a young actor forty years ago. There were then comparatively few theatres in the great cities of Great Britain; none at all in the small ones. In the middle-sized communities the demand for the drama had its only satisfaction in the visits of "Circuit" companies, that moved from place to place in sequence at regular periods of the year. There were few, if any, plays which went touring as the great metropolitan successes do nowadays, with First, Second, Third, or even Fourth Provincial Companies. Though the great actors were received and made much of wherever they went, the small fry had few friends beyond their own circle, and few chances of making any except the chance meetings in lodging-houses and places of refreshment. The meagre salaries of those days were insufficient to allow the recipients to indulge much in the graces of life; and the long vacations, during which they had no opportunity of earning anything at all, made it almost impossible to save against a rainy day. There is a general impression in the great world

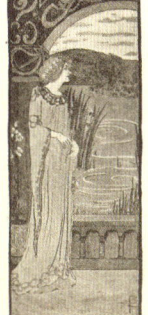

SIR HENRY IRVING

outside the circle of theatrical life that actors are improvident folk. This is entirely erroneous; in no other degree of life are earners of weekly wage more thrifty. Beyond this, in no other degree of life are wage earners so good and helpful toward friends and relatives outside their immediate families.

The class of life in which young Irving found himself was not full of seductive luxuriousness, but it was full of endless and laborious work, of exasperating monotony of daily routine, of anxieties—material and artistic. In such a life it is easy to give way in purpose, to lose ambition, to seek and often to find some duodecimo Capua in which to sink into comparatively luxurious ease. But genius always, if it be true to itself, finds some expression for itself and some way for its manifestation. Irving never faltered, never despaired, never lost hope. Through good times and bad he kept true to his own instinct, always studying. His studies were not merely in the daily routine of the parts he had to learn or which he wished ultimately to play; he took much wider ground than this. As he studied new characters he made himself thoroughly acquainted with all that surrounded them, historically and artistically; so that he came in time to have an instinctive knowledge of the atmosphere and surroundings in which each of his histrionic creations moved. In these days the student who aims high lives in easy places; for everywhere he finds works of

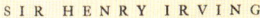

"To doubt is to slip love into the mire"—

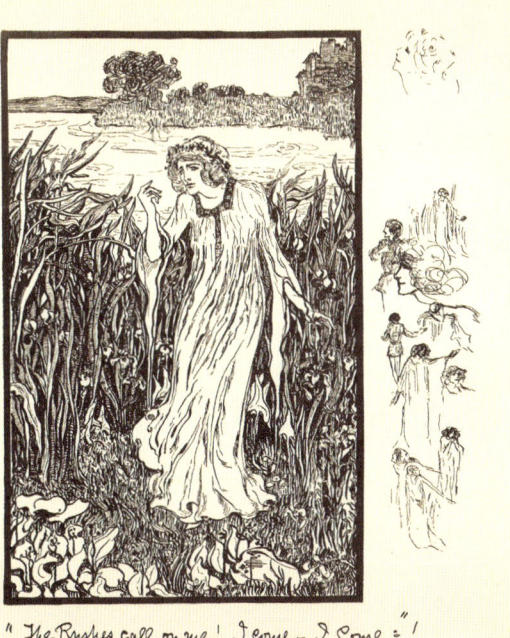

"The Rushes call on me! I come—I come—!"
Ellen Terry = (Amber Hewit)

SIR HENRY IRVING

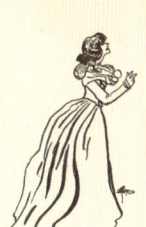

reference in every branch of human thought and endeavour ready to his hand. Forty years ago, however, there were no public libraries in the modern sense. Only in a few of the great cities were there libraries at all; and learning had to be achieved in an uphill manner. Sometimes we hear sneers at self-educated men. Of all baseless scoffing, this is the very worst, for self-education implies not only success already achieved, but an indomitable character exhibited steadfastly in the winning of it. Men who are really learned, who know the value and the difficulty and the rarity of self-culture, are ever the warmest admirers of those who have won such distinction for and by themselves. To-day the very highest of Henry Irving's distinctions is that he has been granted degrees *honoris causa* by three of the greatest universities of the world. In fact, there are few men who hold Doctorships given in such a way by England, Ireland, and Scotland.

Is it any wonder that a man who all his life has exhibited so unfailing a belief in, and a devotion to, his chosen art, who has so wide an experience of its difficulties and its trials, and so thorough an understanding of its possibilities, finds so keen a pleasure in the vast and growing importance of the drama as a factor in national and social life? Whenever he lays the foundation stone of a new theatre—and this is a function which he is often called on to fulfill—he says that he feels it an added joy to life. Life to

SIR HENRY IRVING

him, if it has been full of work, has also been, for now very many years, full of honours and rewards. His portion has indeed been "love and honour and troops of friends," and he has the satisfaction of knowing that all he has has been honestly and honourably won. Two continents have showed him in continuous and in unmistakable manner their full appreciation of his work as an artist, a scholar and a man; and have recognised to the full that he has in his own chosen work upheld the name and fame of his native land. Any man would be proud to carry the honours bestowed on him, all worthily won by hard and earnest work — genius directed skilfully and consistently toward a goodly aim. He is not only a Knight in England, but is a member of the illustrious House Order of Combined Saxe-Coburg Gotha and Saxe Meiningen — for learned and cultured Germany loves to honour genius and great work. He is Doctor of Letters of Dublin University, Doctor of Letters of Cambridge University and Doctor of Laws of the University of Glasgow. This is truly a recognition by scholars of a scholar's work and a tribute to the advancement of his chosen art which he has so nobly furthered. It may truly be said of him with regard to the art of the stage that he "found it brick and made it marble."

For more than twenty years his artistic home at the Lyceum Theatre in London became one of the great centres of thought and art. His work there was

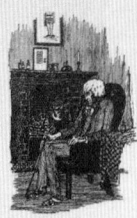

Waterloo.

SIR HENRY IRVING

recognised as a standard by which other players and other managers in his own and other countries were to measure their achievements. Every stranger coming to London could not consider his survey of British life and effort complete without a visit to the Lyceum Theatre. When he was given by Her Majesty the honour of Knighthood, thus winning for the first time in his own or any other country a place for his art in the Court and Governmental purview, the whole of the members of his own craft united in presenting him with a magnificent casket of gold and crystal, in which was a great volume containing an address and all their signatures. Such a thing was alone unique in the history of the stage.

The latest of the many plays which Henry Irving produced at the Lyceum broke in a certain way new ground. For the first time a great French author wrote a play manifestly and ostensibly for an Englishman to act. Irving had for a long time had a wish to portray the character of Robespierre. Victorien Sardou also had a wish that Irving should render some piece of his. The ideas of the two men were exchanged through friends and by letter — for Sardou has never crossed the English channel — and in due time the play was written.

It was a difficult task which the great dramatist had set himself, for the life of Robespierre is so well

SIR HENRY IRVING

known that there were endless limitations to dramatic possibility. The knowledge of the master of stagecraft, however, is very vast on all subjects connected with the French Revolution; and from hints and inferences regarding Robespierre's life and motives he built up a great drama which, when put upon the stage by Irving, has proved to have created an extraordinary interest in two great nations. Of course, as is necessary in all historical plays, certain changes had to be effected. It is not possible

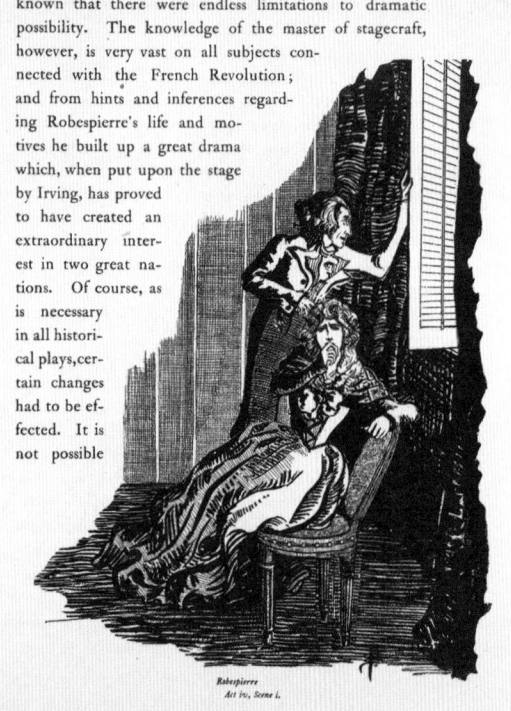

Robespierre
Act iv, Scene i.

SIR HENRY IRVING

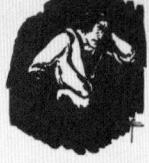

to give in the "two hours traffic of the stage" all the series of events and changes which have led up to great achievements or catastrophes. It is sufficient if the myriad motives of many people are crystallised or concentrated into the motives and purposes and actions of a few. This is the keynote of dramatic excellence, and the master-hand of Sardou has struck it in this great drama which shows in little the mighty upheaval which marked the end of the eighteenth century. In this stormy time there were great men who were heard for only a passing hour and little men who seemed great in their momentary poise amidst the whirling throng. There were great motives which led to terrible results, and little motives which eventually led to magnificent endings. The possibilities for the exhibition of heroic and mean motives are ad-

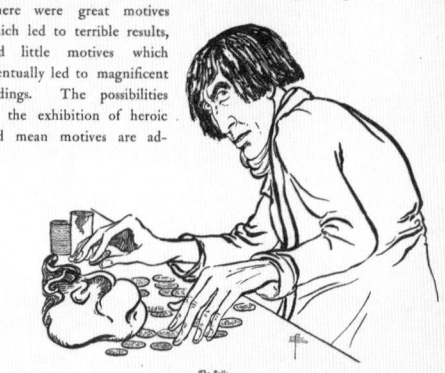

The Bells
Act ii

SIR HENRY IRVING

mirably shown in the prison scene which serves as a background to individual action of the dramatic characters. Here are grouped many moving incidents, every one of which, from the gruesome "game of the guillotine" to the self-sacrifice of friend for friend and stranger for stranger, are recorded in history, though not all taking place at once within the narrow bounds of a single prison within the space of half an hour. The reality or the realism of such scenes shows how great and manifold were the opportunities of one steadfast purpose, though such had not its origin in the loftiest aims, and enables the spectator to realize how it was that such a man as Robespierre could have done so much for good or ill. Through it all—through ambition, pride, vanity, the remorseless logic and action of a pedant—shines the softening touch of nature, which, when it warms the father's heart, brings an irresistible pathos to draw the hearts of the spectators closer to his own. There is a note of pity through all the overwhelming clamour which marks the struggle and downfall of Robespierre in the Convention.

1899

BRAM STOKER.

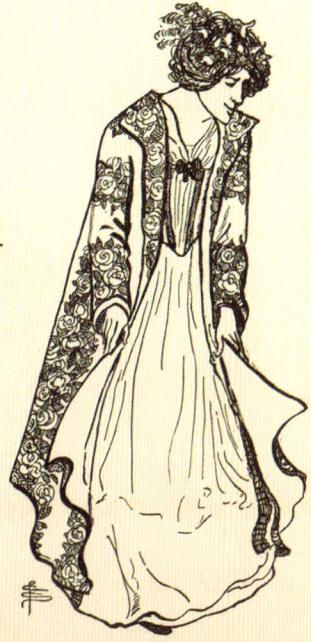

THAT'S WORTH EIGHTEEN
PENCE TO ME
Nance Oldfield

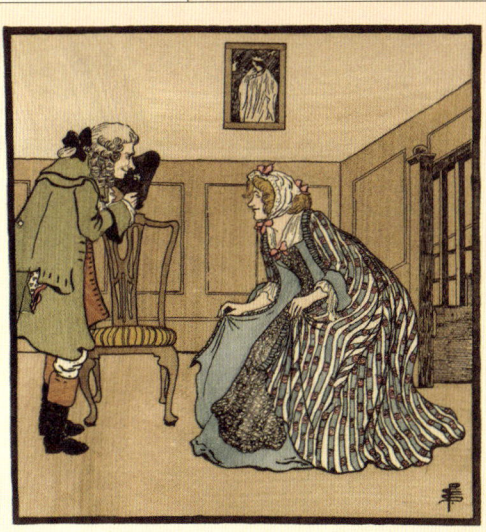

"Mrs Anne Oldfield accepts the apology of
Mr Nathan Oldworthy of Coventry"

In Chimney Corners

1899

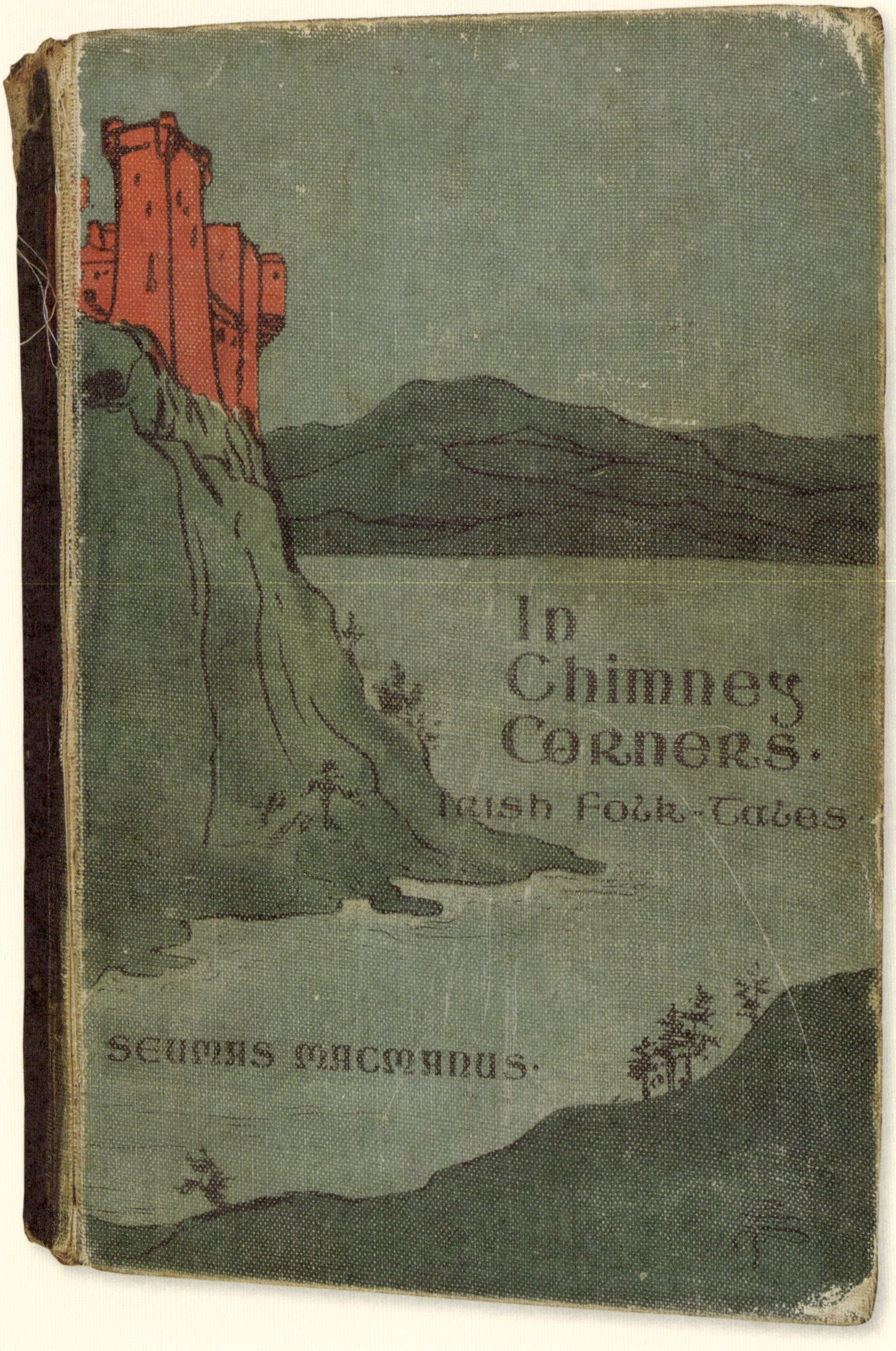

Cover from *In Chimney Corners: Irish Folk-Tales* by Seumas MacManus plus eight illustrations. Published by Doubleday & McClure Co., 1899

1899

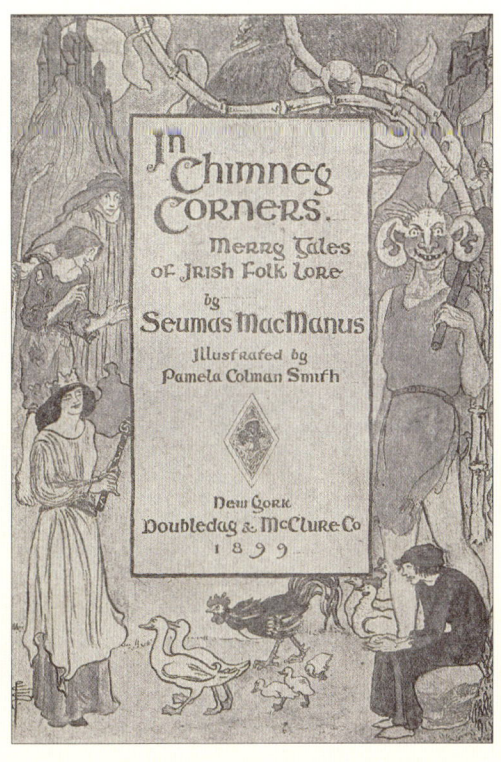
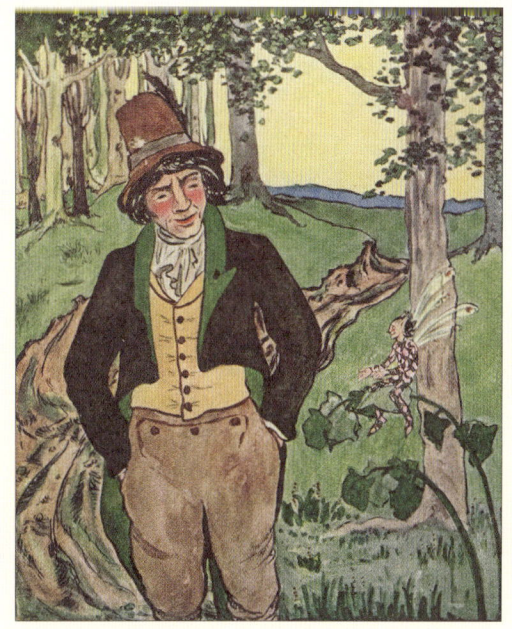
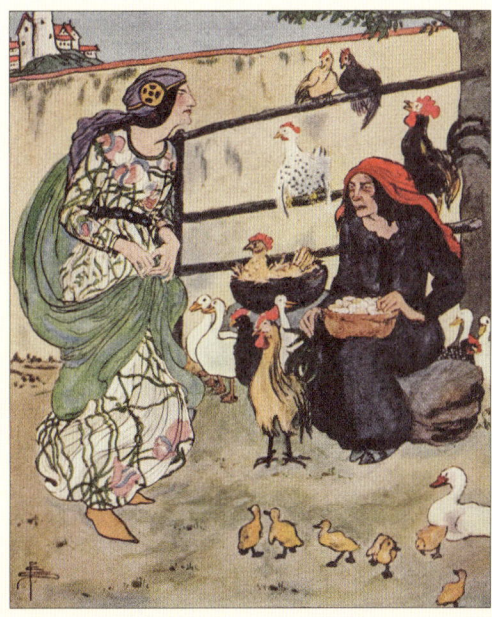
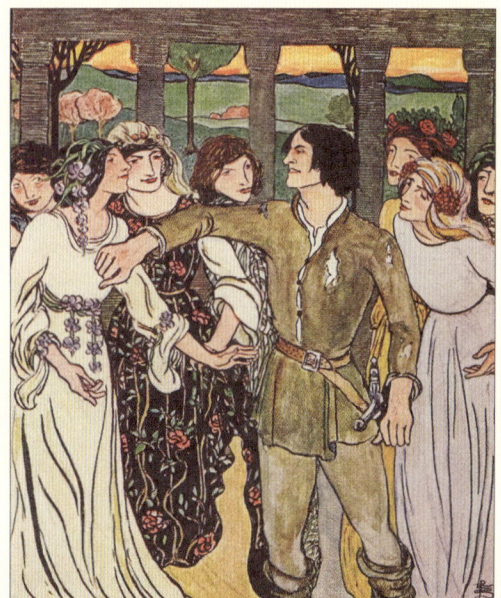

1899

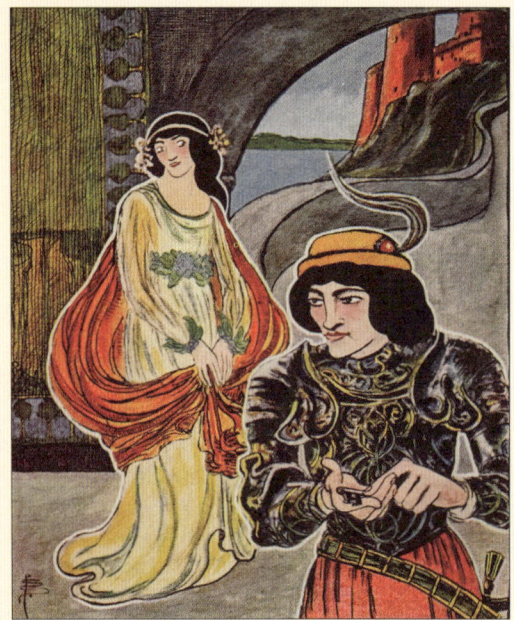
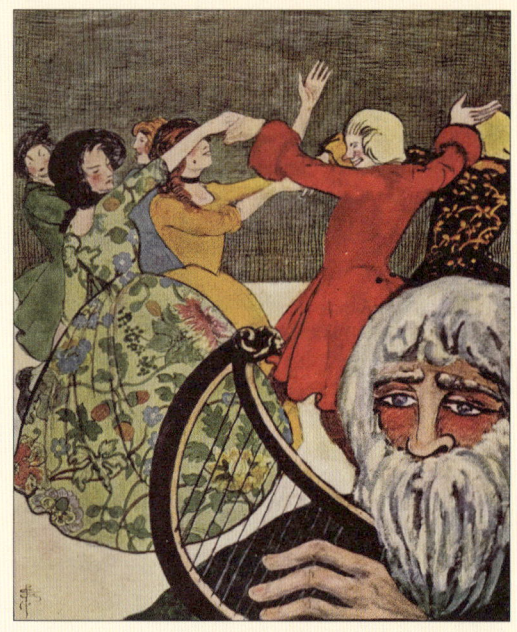
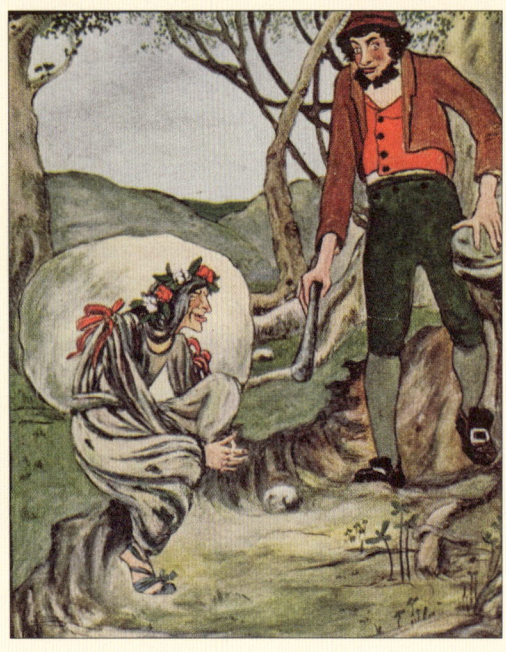
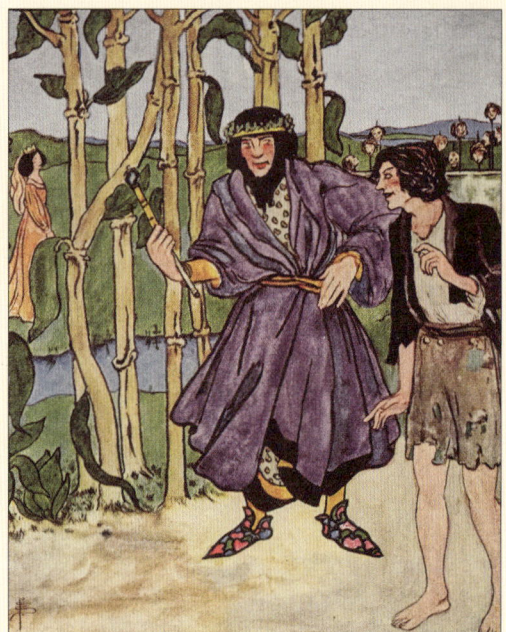
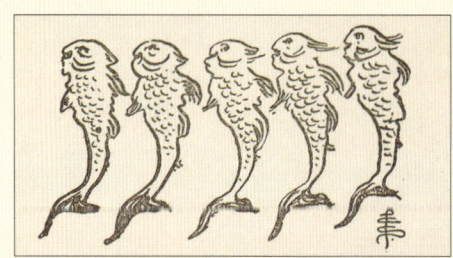

The Golden Vanity and The Green Bed

1899

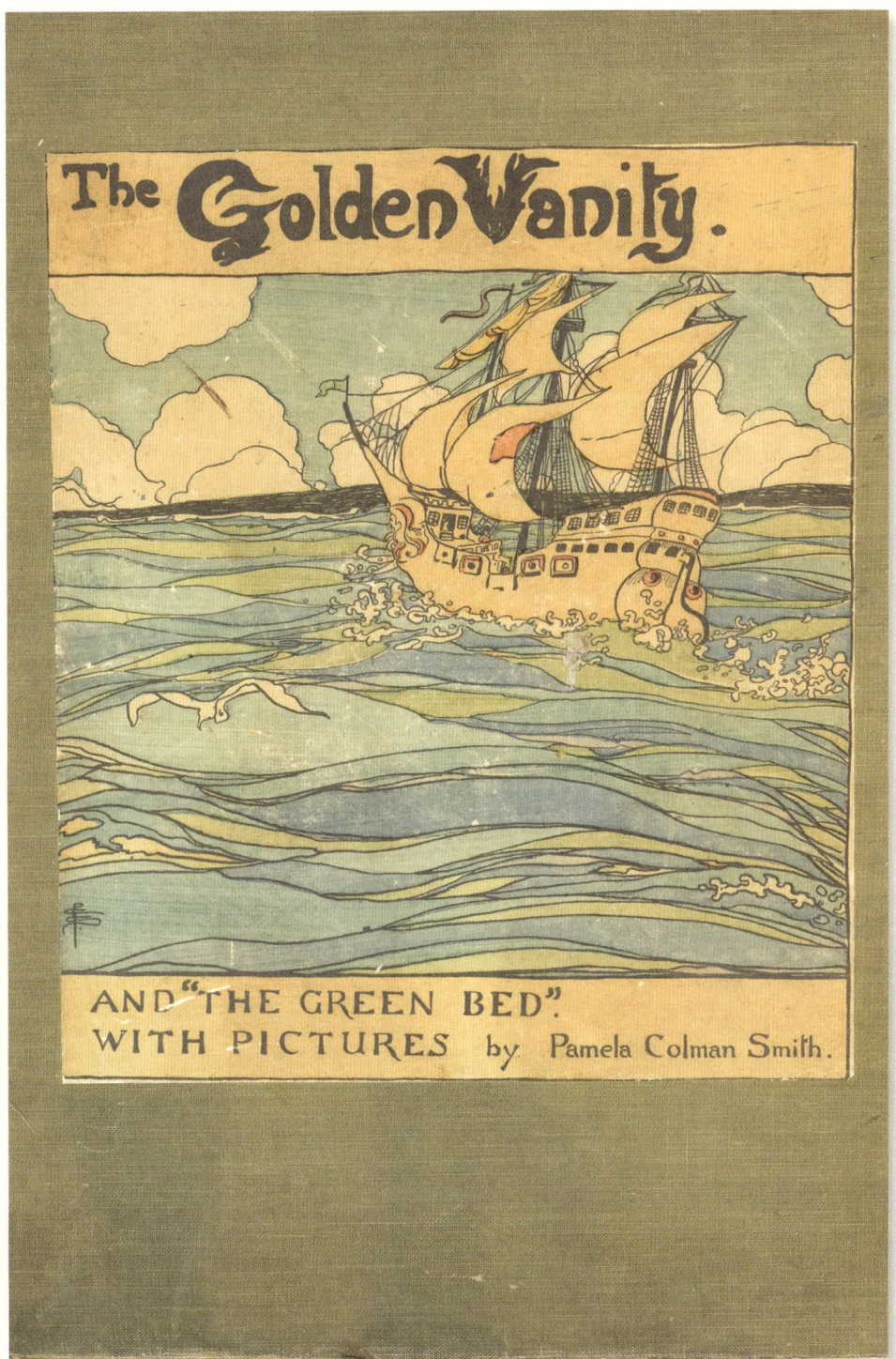

Cover and 12 illustrations from *The Golden Vanity* And *"The Green Bed"* With Pictures

THE GOLDEN VANITY

I

A ship I have got in the North Country
And she goes by the name of the Golden Vanity,
O I fear she'll be taken by a Spanish Ga-la-lie,
    As she sails by the Low-lands low.

II

To the Captain then upspake the little Cabin-boy,
He said, What is my fee, if the galley I destroy?
The Spanish Ga-la-lie, if no more it shall anoy,
    As you sail by the Low-lands low.

III

Of silver and of gold I will give to you a store,
And my pretty little daughter that dwelleth on the shore,
Of treasure and of fee as well, I'll give to thee galore,
    As we sail by the Low-lands low.

IV

Then the boy bared his breast, and straightway leaped in,
And he held all in his hand, an augur sharp and thin,
And he swam until he came to the Spanish galleon,
    As she lay by the Low-lands low.

V

He bored with the augur, he bored once and twice,
And some were playing cards, and some were playing dice,
When the water flowed in it dazzled their eyes,
    And she sank by the Low-lands low.

VI

So the Cabin-boy did swim all to the larboardside,
Saying, Captain! take me in, I am drifting with the tide!
I will shoot you! I will kill you! the cruel Captain cried,
    You may sink by the Low-lands low.

VII

Then the Cabin-boy did swim all to the starboard side,
Saying, Messmates, take me in, I am drifting with the tide!
Then they laid him on the deck, and he closed his eyes and died,
    As they sailed by the Low-lands low.

VIII

They sewed his body up, all in an old cow's hide,
And they cast the gallant cabin-boy over the ship's side,
And left him without more ado adrifting with the tide,
    And to sink by the Low-lands low.

1899

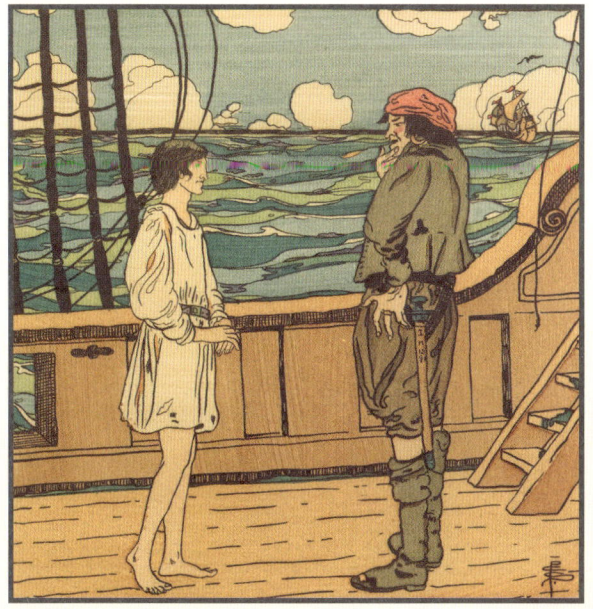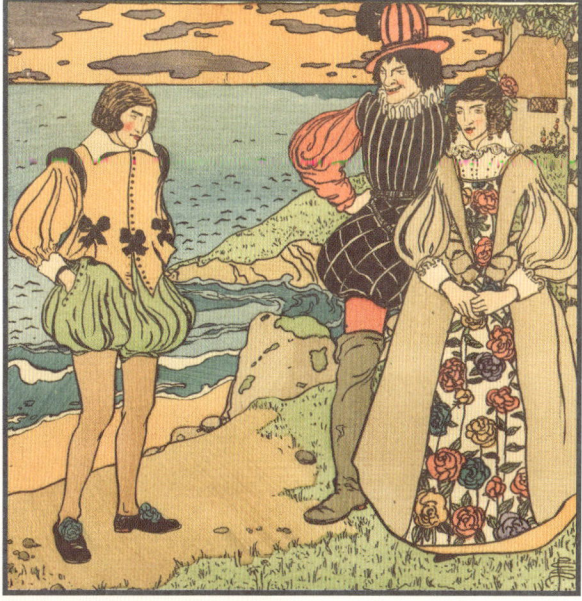

The Golden Vanity
Verses I, II, III & IV

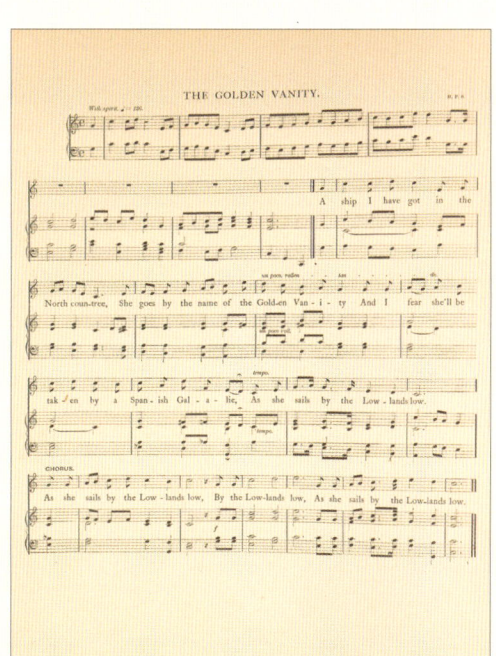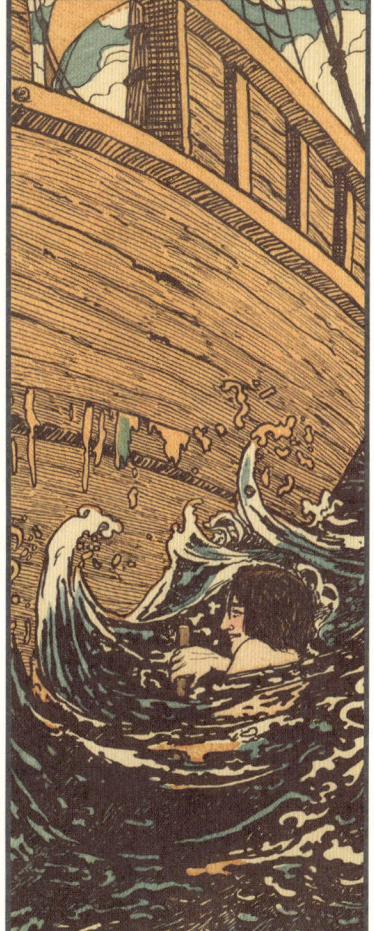

1899

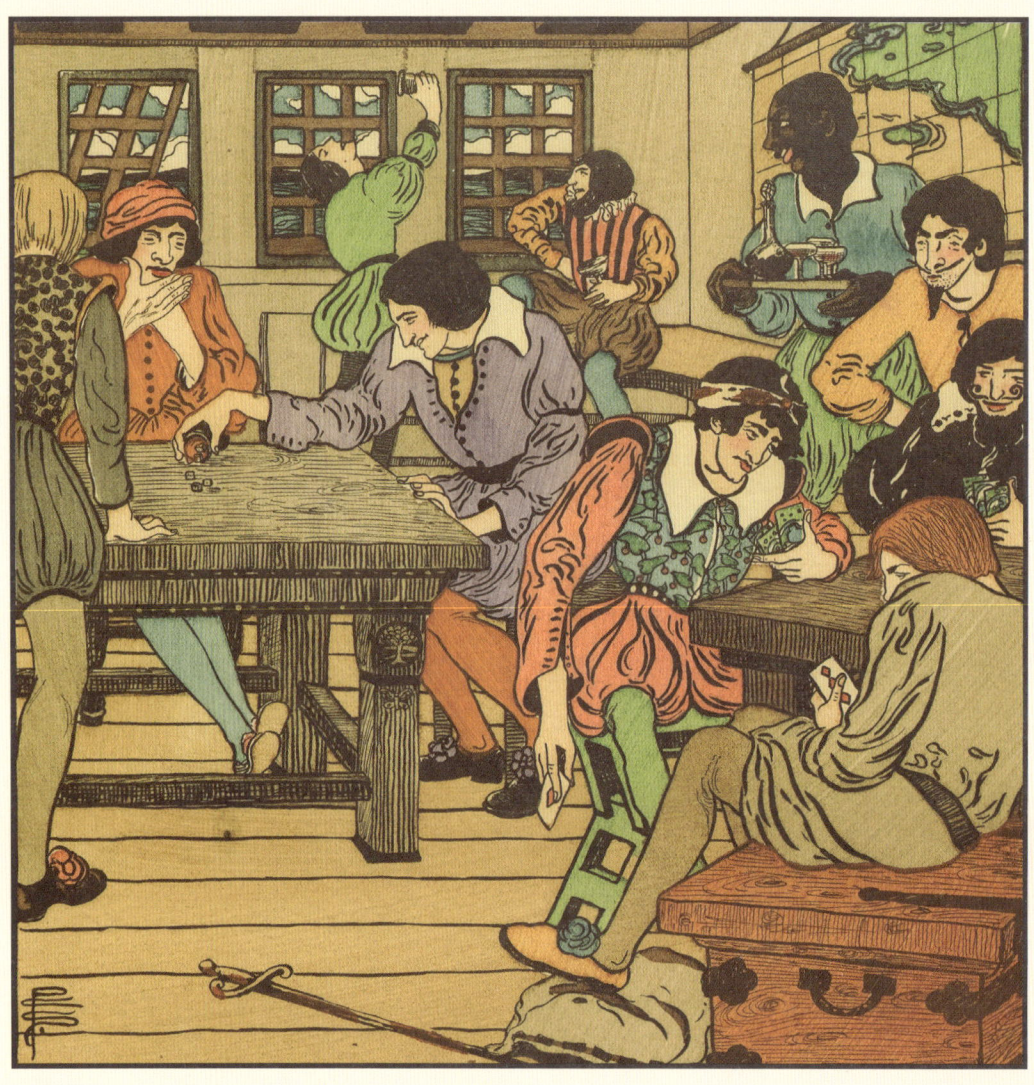

The Golden Vanity Verse V

1899

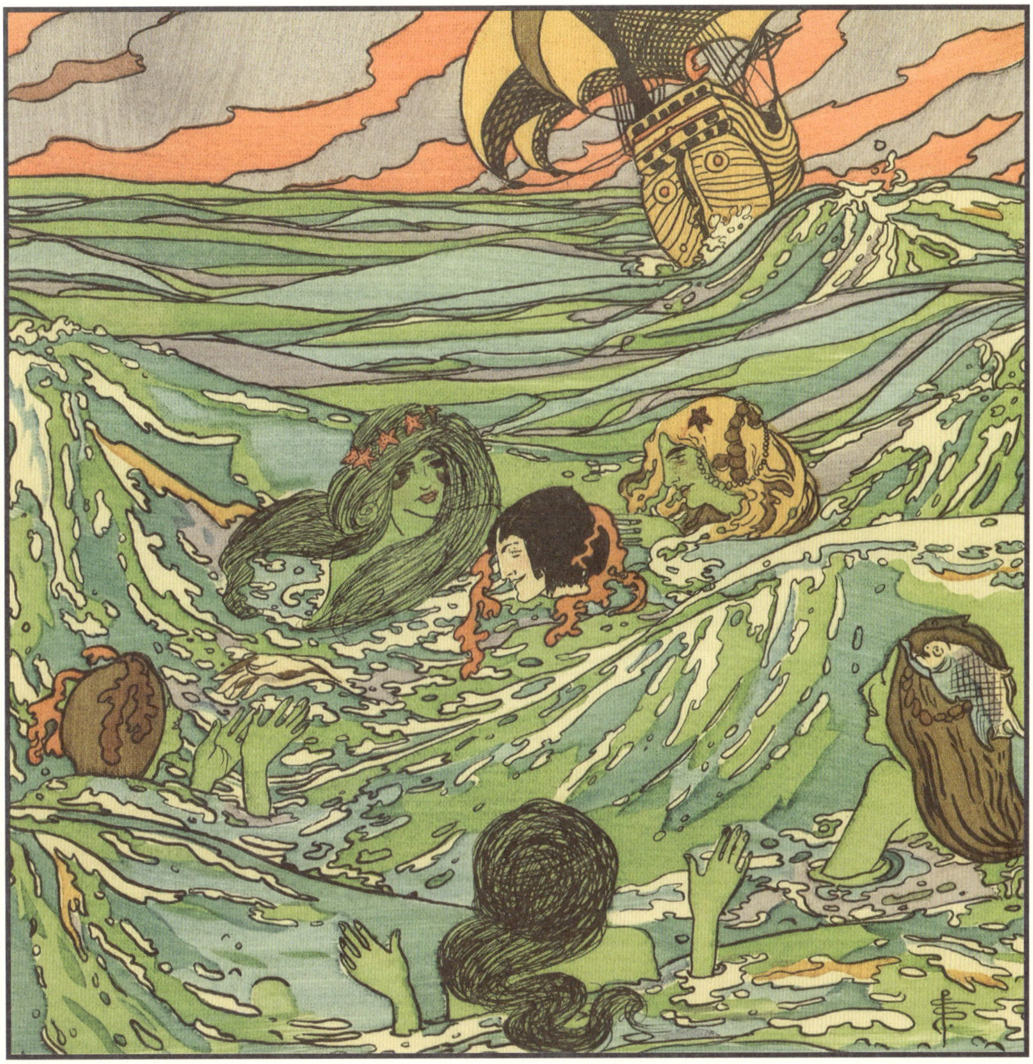

The Golden Vanity Verses VI & VII

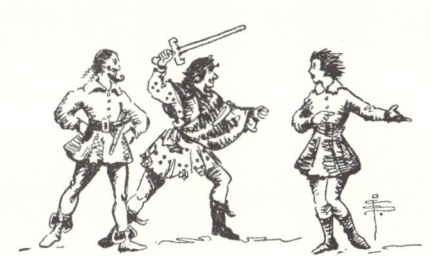

1899

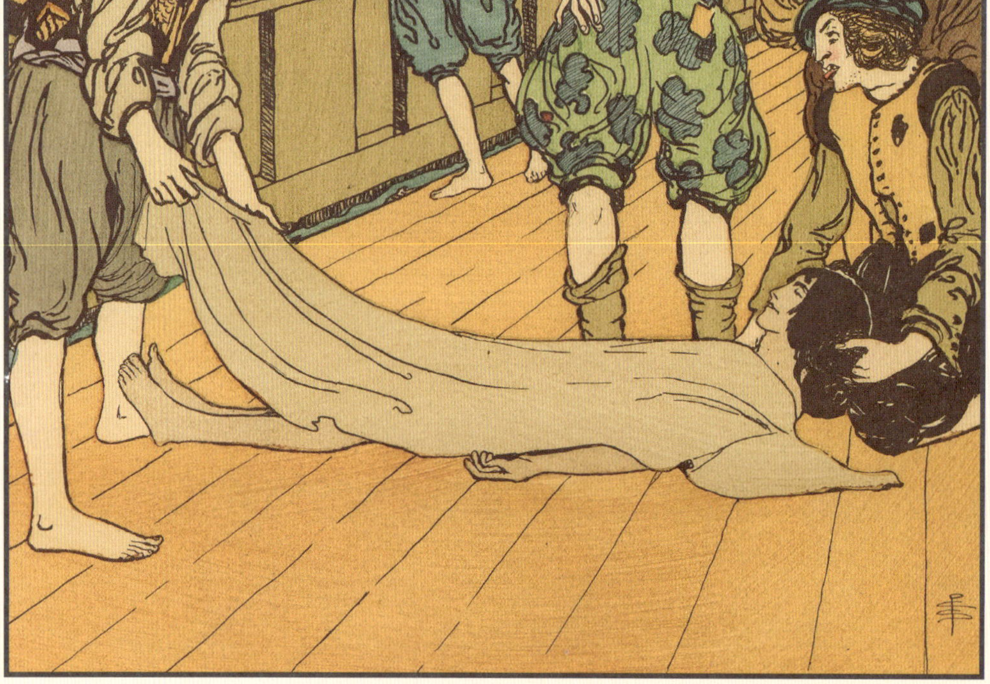

The Golden Vanity Verse VIII

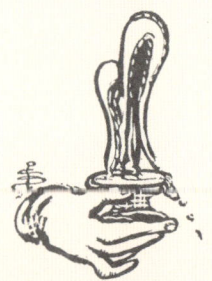

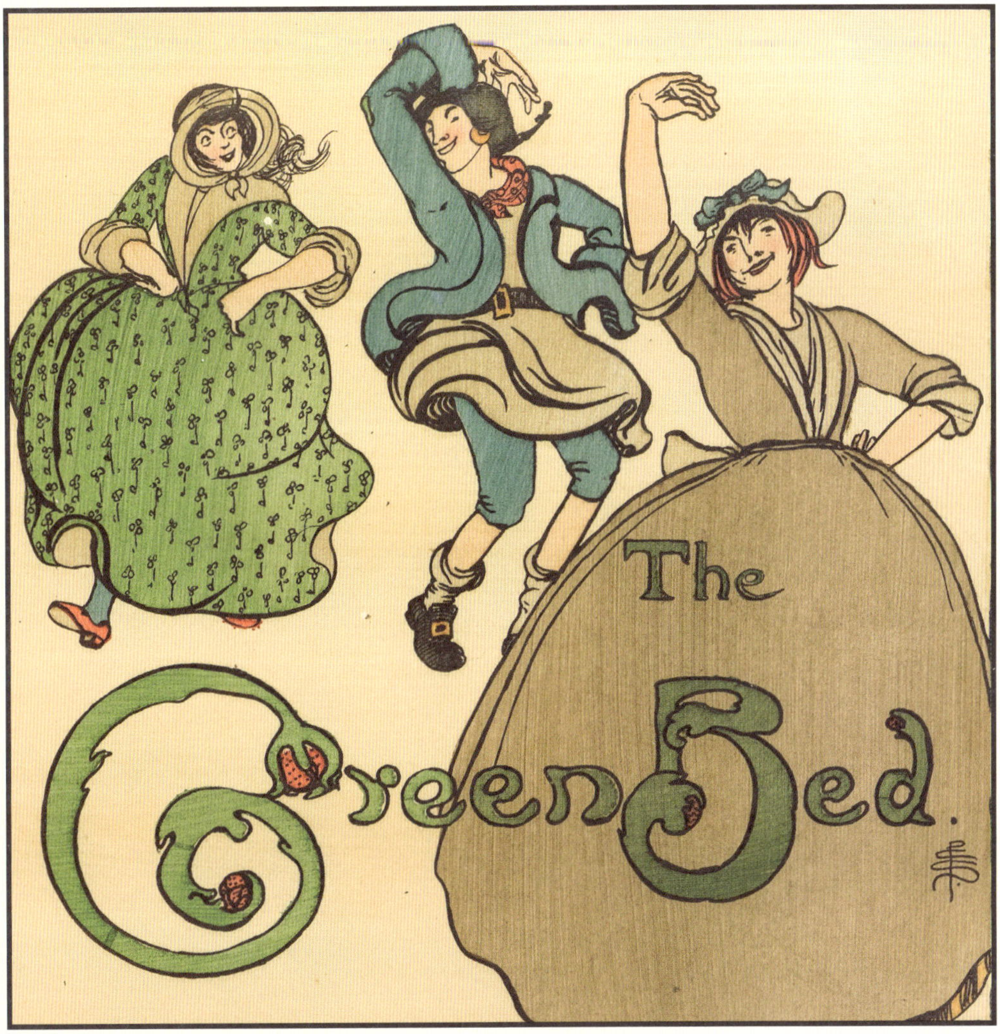

1899

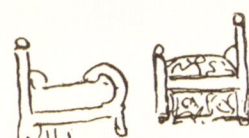

Cover, four illustrations, poem and back cover
design from *The Green Bed*

1899

THE GREEN BED

I

Young Sailor Dick, as he stepped on shore,
    To his quarters of old return'd.
The hostess glad, cries, "Dick, my lad!
    What prize money have you earn'd?"
"Poor luck! poor luck! yet Molly, my duck,
    Your daughter I've come to see:
Get ready some supper, with pipes and grog,
    And the best Green Bed for me."

II

"My daughter, she's gone out for a walk;
    My beds are all bespoken;
My larder's bare, like the rum-keg there,
    And my baccy pipes all are broken."
Says Dick, "I'll steer for another berth,
I fear I have made too bold:
    But I'll pay for the beer that I've just drunk here,"
And he pulled out a handful of gold.

III

"Come down, Molly, quick! here's your sweetheart Dick,
    Has just come back from sea:
He wants his supper, his grog, and a bed,
    The best Green Bed it must be."
"No bed," cries Dick, "no supper, no grog,
    No sweetheart for me, I swear!
You showed me the door when you thought me poor,
    So I'll carry my gold elsewhere."

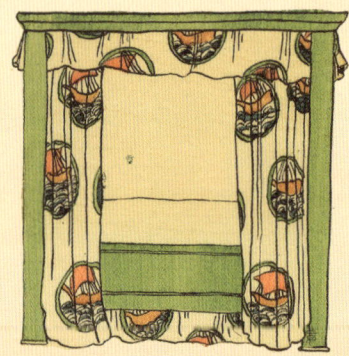

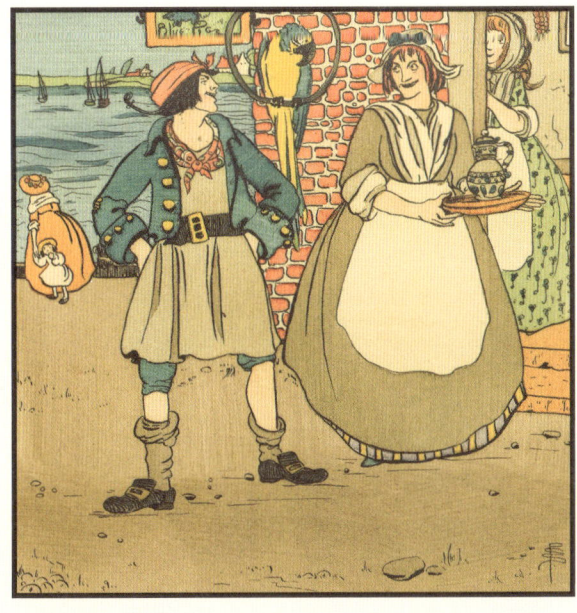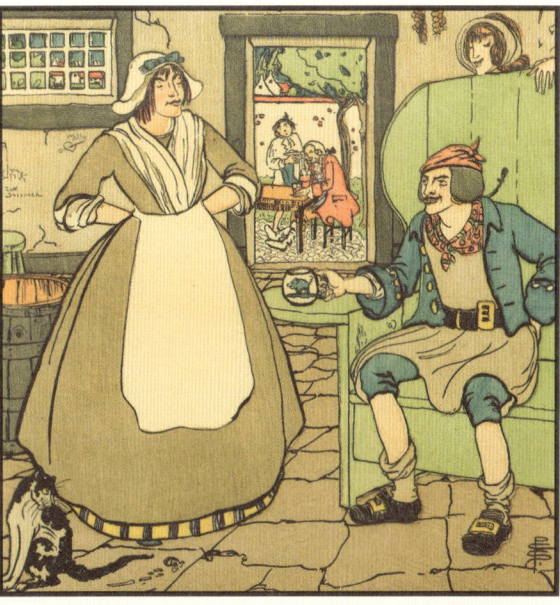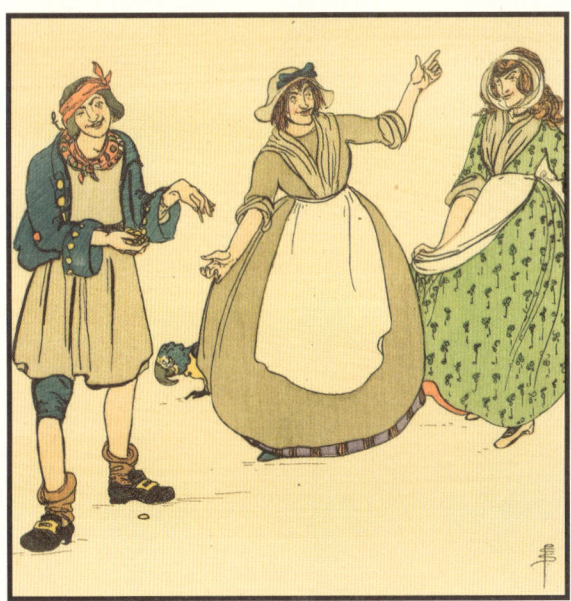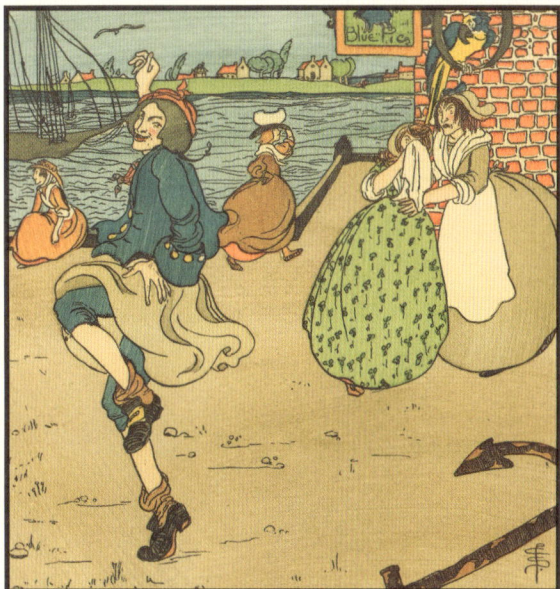

1899

Back cover from *The Golden Vanity and The Green Bed*

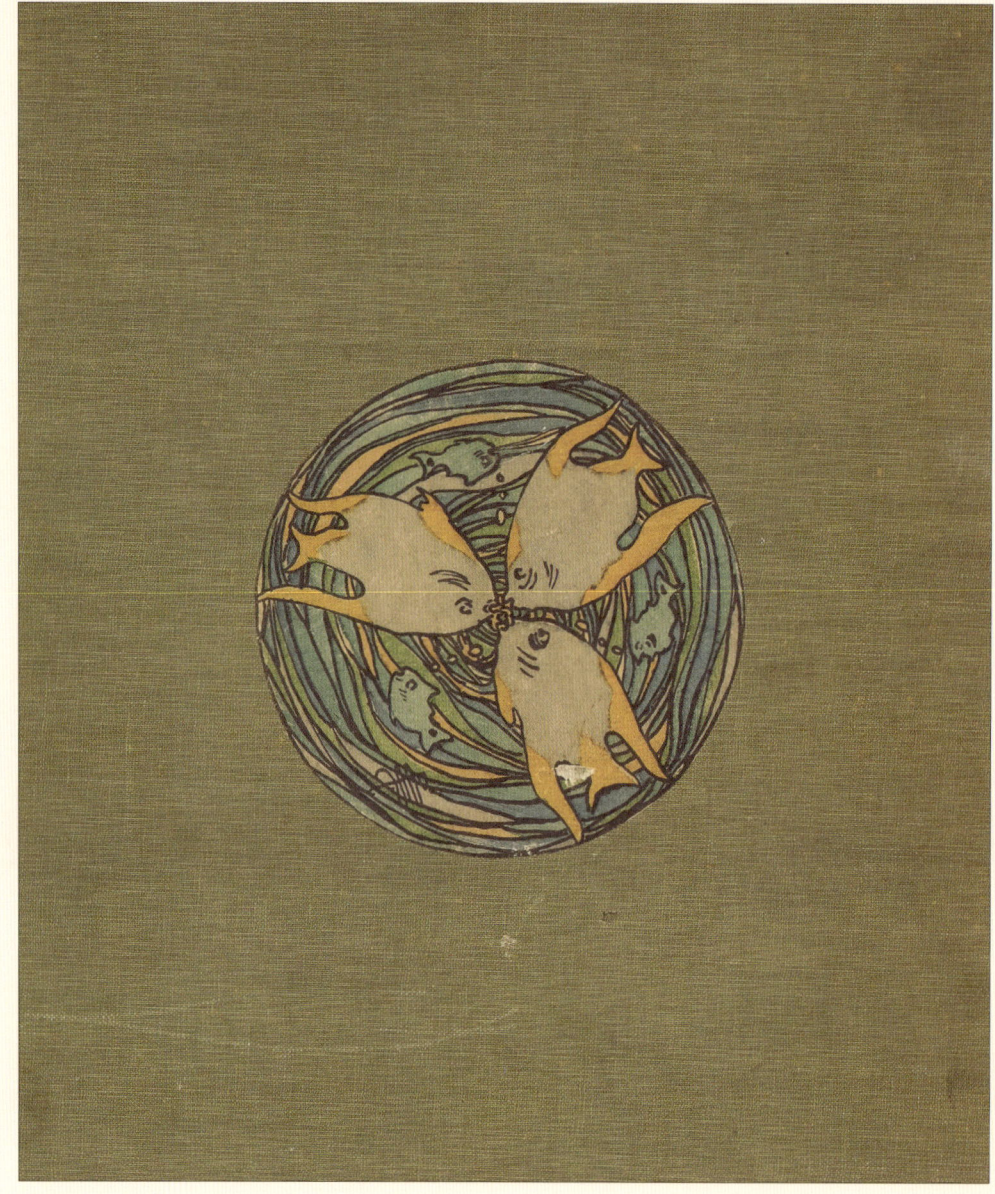

Widdicombe Fair

1899

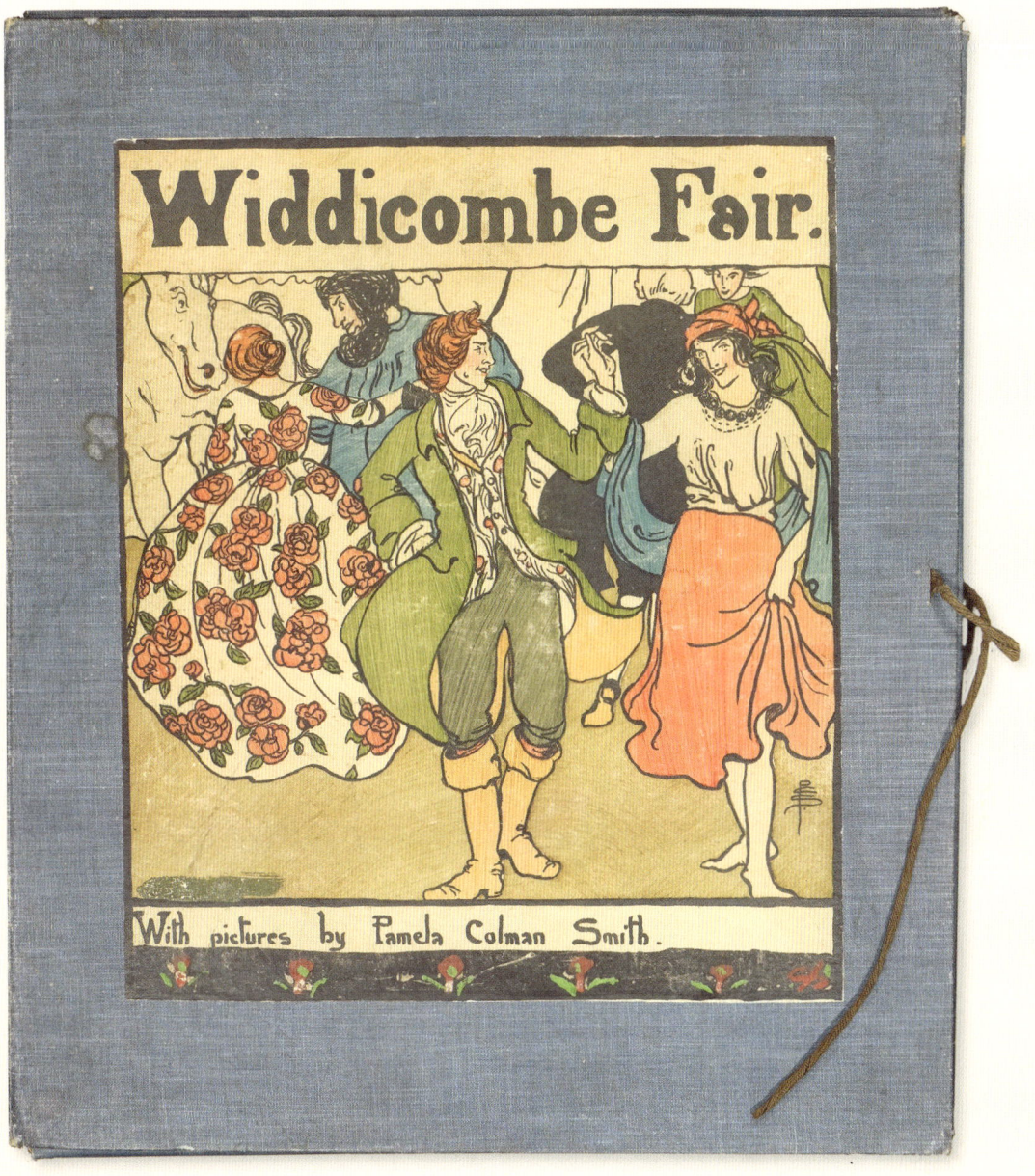

The text of both the words and music in this song is from "Songs of the West," by Rev. S. Baring-Gould and Rev. H. Fleetwood Sheppard (London, 1895). The editors say that "Widdicombe Fair" is "at present the best known and most popular of Devonshire songs. The original Uncle 'Tom Cobleigh' lived in a house near Yeoford Junction. The names in the chorus all belonged to Sticklepath." There have been printed by hand of this edition 500 copies. Each has an original drawing on the inside of the portfolio, and the pictures are all mounted. This is number 264.

WIDDICOMBE FAIR.

1.
"Tom Pearce, Tom Pearce, lend me thy gray mare,
　　All along, down along, out along, lee.
For I want for to go to Widdicombe Fair,
　　Wi' Bill Brewer, Jan Stewer, Peter Gurney, Peter
　　　Davy, Dan'l Whiddon,
　Harry Hawk, old uncle Tom Cobbleigh and all."
　　Chorus.—Old Uncle Tom Cobbleigh and all.

2.
"And when shall I see again my gray mare?"
　All along, down along, out along, lee.
"By Friday soon, or Saturday noon,
　Wi' Bill Brewer," &c.

3.
Then Friday came, and Saturday noon,
　All along, down along, out along, lee.
But Tom Pearce's old mare hath not trotted home,
　Wi' Bill Brewer, &c.

4.
So Tom Pearce he got up to the top o' the hill,
　All along, down along, out along, lee.
And he seed his old mare down a-making her will,
　Wi' Bill Brewer, &c.

5.
So Tom Pearce's old mare, her took sick and die
　All along, down along, out along, lee.
And Tom he sat down on a stone, and he cried,
　Wi' Bill Brewer, &c.

6.
But this isn't the end o' this shocking affair,
　All along, down along, out along, lee.
Nor, though they be dead, of the horrid career
　Of Bill Brewer, &c.

7.
When the wind whistles cold on the moor of a night,
　All along, down along, out along, lee.
Tom Pearce's old mare doth appear gashly white,
　Wi' Bill Brewer, &c.

8.
And all the long night be heard skirling and groans,
　All along, down along, out along, lee,
From Tom Pearce's old mare in her rattling bones,
　And from Bill Brewer, Jan Stewer, Peter Gurney,
　　Peter Davy, Dan'l Whiddon,
　Harry Hawk, old uncle Tom Cobbleigh and all.
　　Chorus.—Old Uncle Tom Cobbleigh and all.

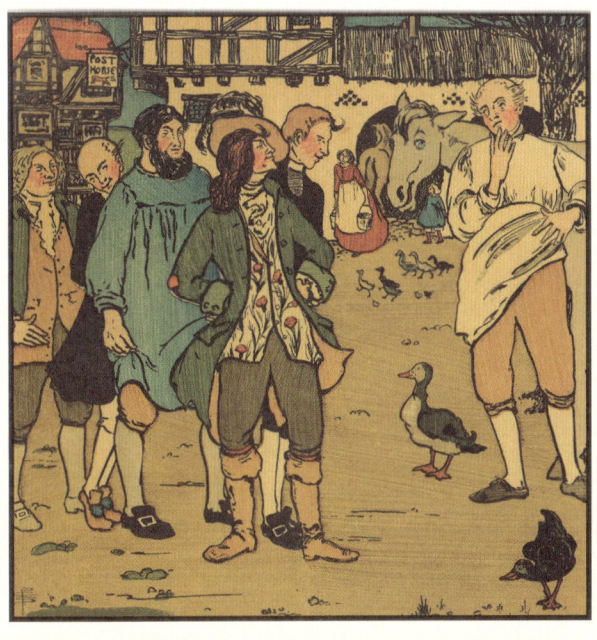
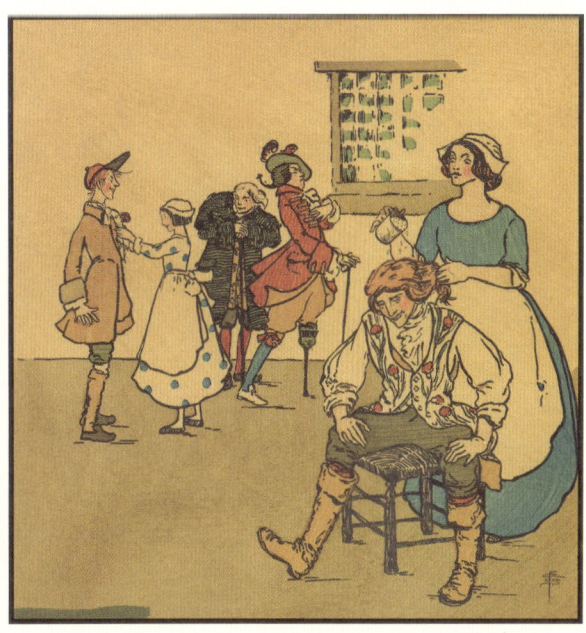
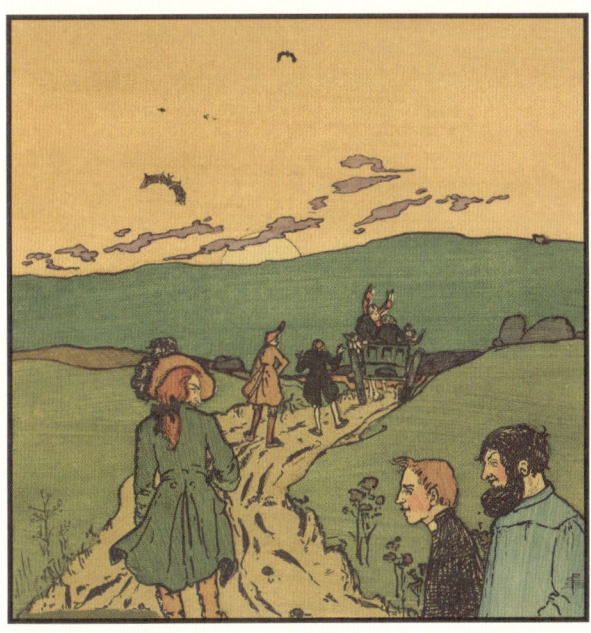
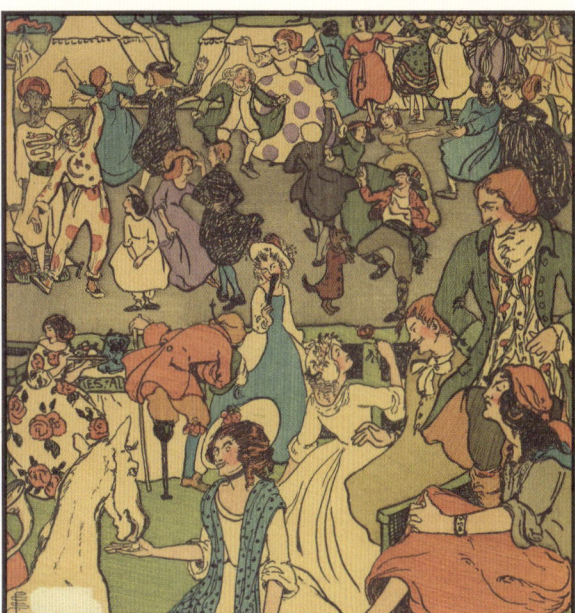

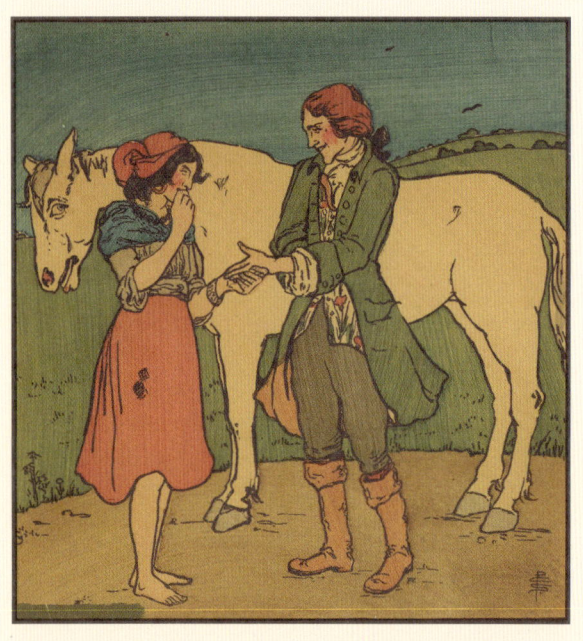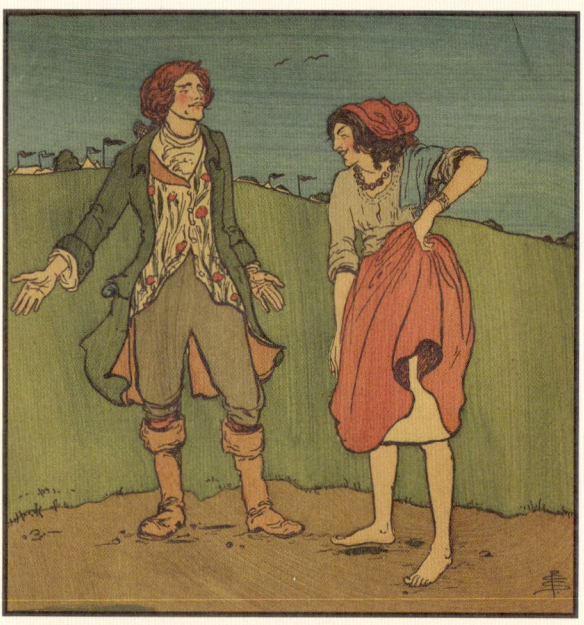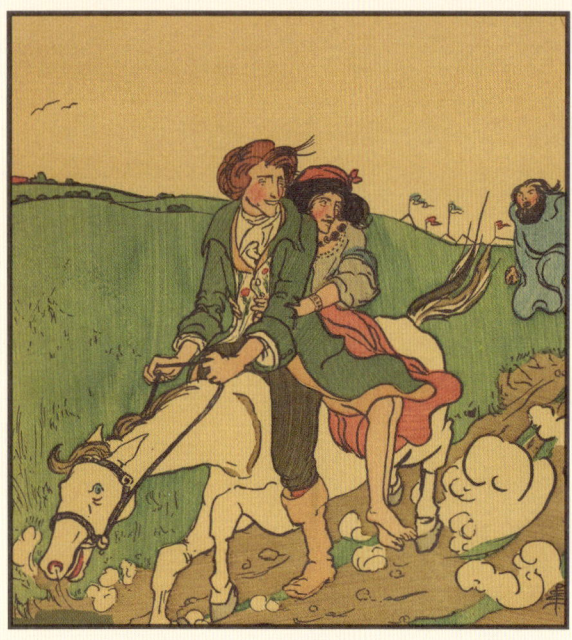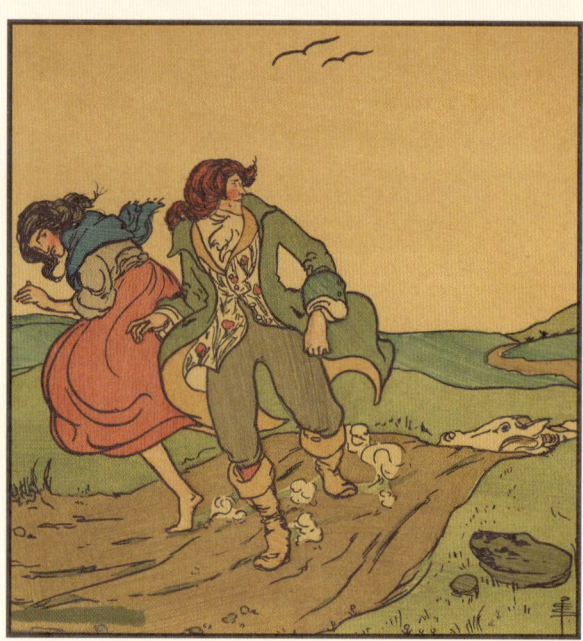

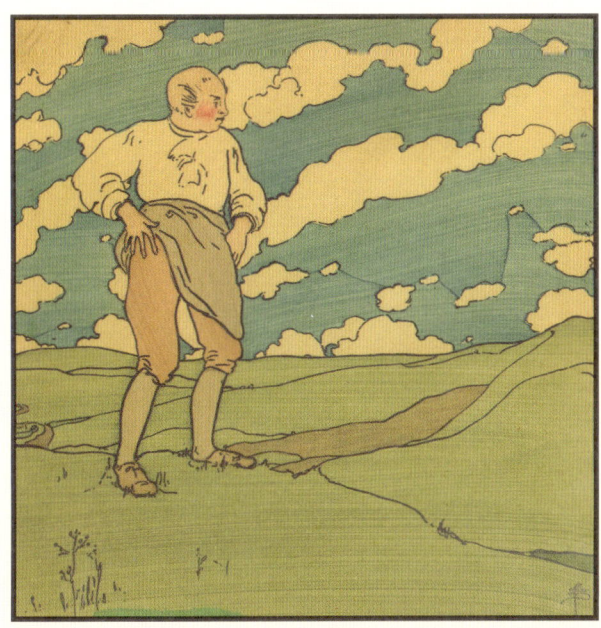
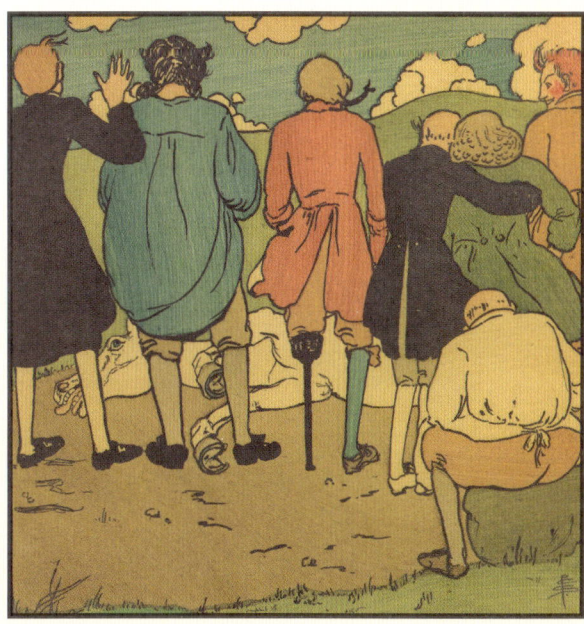
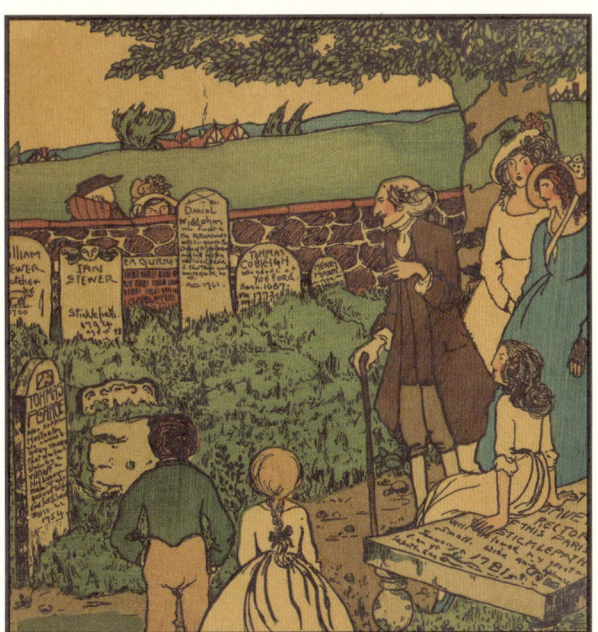
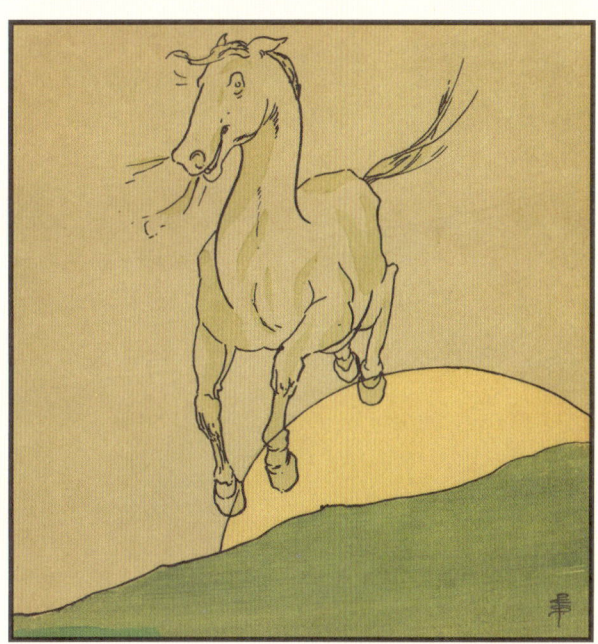

Shakespeare's Heroines

1899

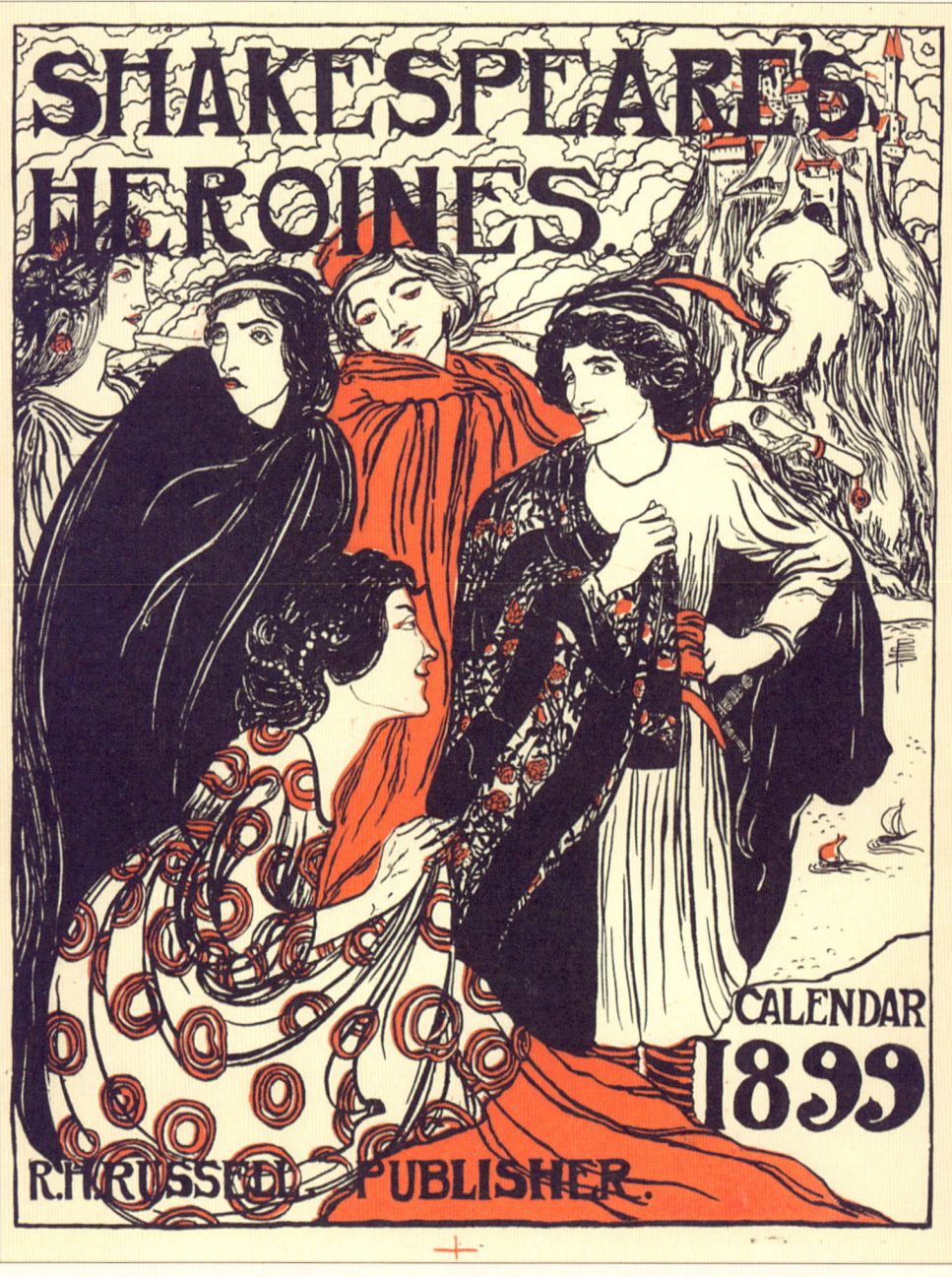

Pamela Colman Smith Shakespeare's Heroines Calendar, 1899. Color Lithograph, (1898). Mark Samuels Lasner Collection, University of Delaware Library

Annancy Stories

1899

Cover from *Annancy Stories* by Pamela Colman Smith. Plus 16 illustrations

1899

INTRODUCTION

THE "Annancy Stories," by Miss Pamela Colman Smith, a young lady who has recently come from Jamaica to live in this country, are perhaps the most original contribution to negro folk-lore literature since the day when "Uncle Remus" gave us his imperishable record of "Brer Rabbit."

These new stories are a contribution from the West Indian Negroes. They belong to the same class with the stories of "Brer Rabbit," which undoubtedly inspired the young authoress to collect them, as they have inspired all other writers of folk-stories, since Mr. Harris's genius blazed the way. The differences form one of the points of interest. Some of the tales bear traces of descent from Æsop; others have the impress of the "Arabian Nights," whilst yet others show marks of the less ancient fairy tale. Whatever their origin, however, "Annancy" will prove of great interest not only to all who may enjoy this class of literature; but to that wider public who recognize the value of sincerity, and read only for entertainment.

The young authoress has been gifted with the power to illustrate her stories in a manner as original as the stories themselves.

Both as narrator and artist she has struck out boldly on new lines and deserves the success which it is hoped her courage and ability may bring her.

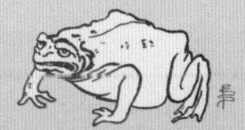

1899

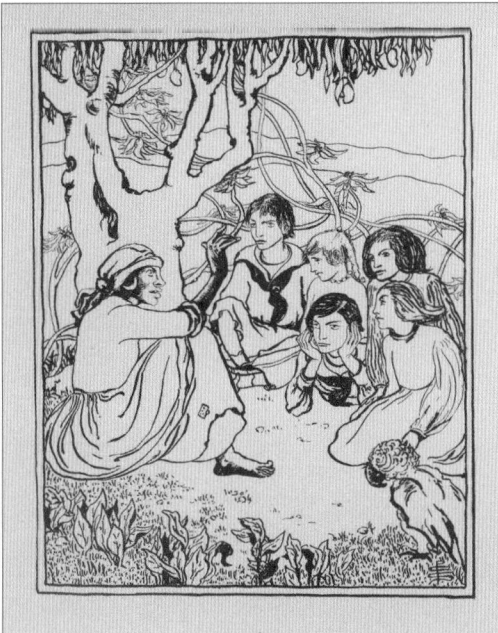 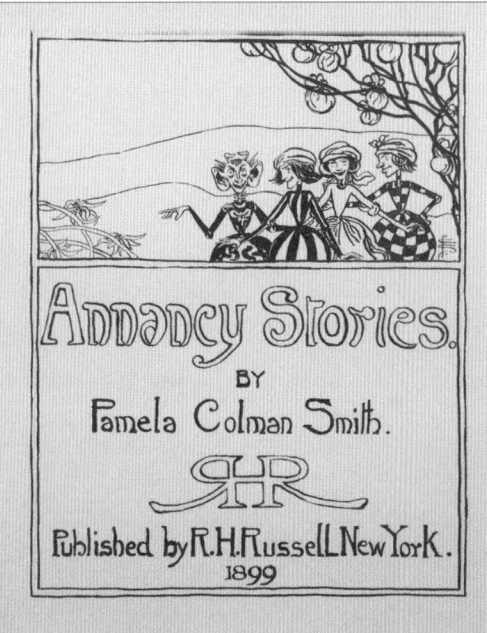

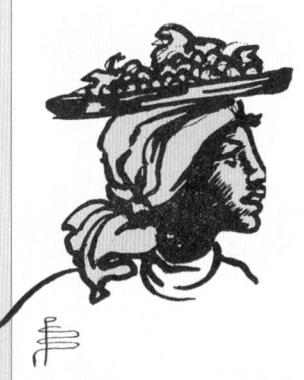

CONTENTS

Annancy and Chim-Chim	9
De Man An' De Six Poach Eggs	12
Why Toad Walk 'Pon Four Leg	14
Annancy An' Tiger Ridin' Horse	17
Mr. Titman	20
Why John Crow Hab Peel Head	25
Candoo	28
Mother Calbee	31
How Annancy Win De Five Dubbloon	35
Morass	38
Annancy And Gingy Fly	41
How Annancy Went To Fish Country	44
Haylefayly An' Pretty Peallope	47
Paarat, Tiger An' Annancy	51
Bull-Garshananee	55
Annancy An' De Nyam Hills	59
Ticky-Picky Boom-Boom	62
De Golden Water, De Singin' Tree An' De Talkin' Bird	65
How Annancy Fooled Death	69
The Three Sisters	72
Annancy And Dry Kull; Or, Why Hog Hab A Long Mouth	75
Dog An' De Duckanoo	78

1899

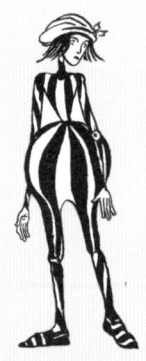

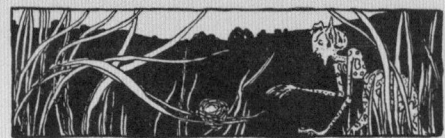

ANNANCY AND CHIM-CHIM

IN a long before time in dis country dere lib Chim-chim Bird, and Chim-chim Bird him buil' him nest on de top of de grass; so dat it blow up an' down wid de wind. An' in de evenin' when de north breeze blow, de nest go up and down and rock Breda Chim-chim Bird to sleep.

Now in dis same country dere lib a bery cleber man call Annancy, an' him sometime make himself big, an' sometime little. A sort o' a jumbe man.

Now dese two, Breda Annancy and Chim-chim, get to know each oder in de bush. An' dey play cyards togeder, and Breda Chim-chim he always win Annancy. Now, before dey play dey agree dat whoefer lose is to pay a fine to de oder one. An' de fine is to be a piece of flesh off de one dat lose. So dey play fe many, many nights, an' Chim-chim he always win. An' each time he take a piece of flesh off Breda Annancy till Annancy get quite thin. So at last one night Breda Annancy say him would only play one time more. So de nex' night dey play, an' Breda Annancy he win! A'en him laugh, him was so please, an' say, "Now, me Breda Chim-chim, you mus' pay you fine." But Chim-chim only laugh an' fly away.

Long time Annancy try to catch Chim-chim all sort of way, by springes, an' caliban an' lime, but all dis time Chim-chim was too cleber fe him.

So at last Breda Annancy go an' tell Breda Tiger about it, an ax him fe help him catch Breda Chim-chim Bird. So Tiger he listen, and when Annancy finish, he t'ink, an' t'ink fe long time, an' at las' him say:—

"I tell you, Breda Annancy what I wi' do. I wi' lie down an' play I dead, an' you get a bell, and you ring de bell all over de town, and say 'Tiger dead!' an' den we wi' see if Chim-chim will come to de funeral."

Den Annancy say:—

"All right, Breda Tiger, an' if I catch Breda Chim-chim Bird I give you a cow."

So it was agree dat if Breda Annancy catch Chim-chim, Tiger would get de cow.

So dey wrote de bargin out.

Nex' market day Breda Chim-chim Bird come to town fe get some salt fish an' yams an' a 'quattie peas. An' as him was goin' troo de town him hear a bell, an' him ax what it is, and de people dey tell him say:—

"De great Massa Tiger is dead!"

So Breda Chim-chim go home an' put on him long-tail-blue coat an' him que-que

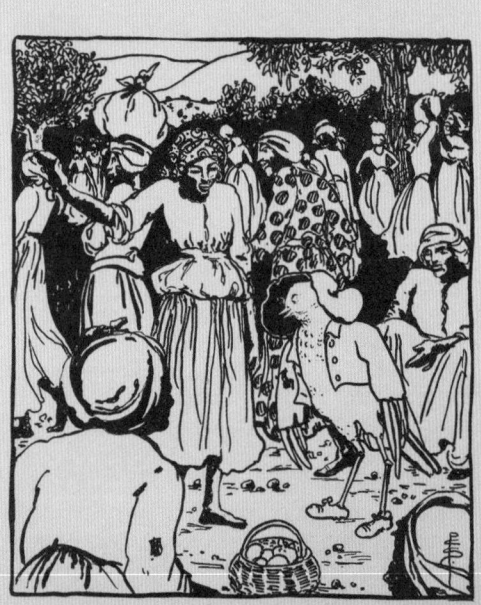

NEX' MARKET DAY BREDA CHIM-CHIM COME TO TOWN.

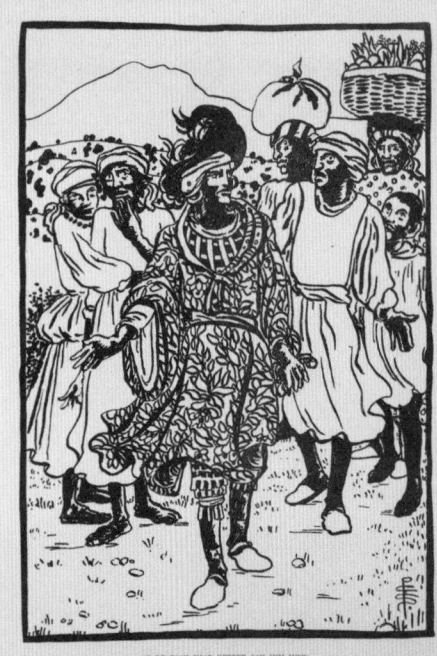

AN' DE COOK SHOP KEEPER SAY HIM MUS'

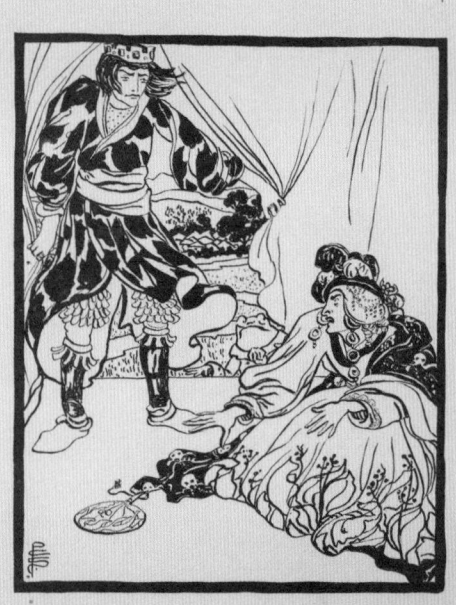

"I KNOW WHAT YOU IS. YOU PLAYIN' TRICK 'PON ME."

132

1899

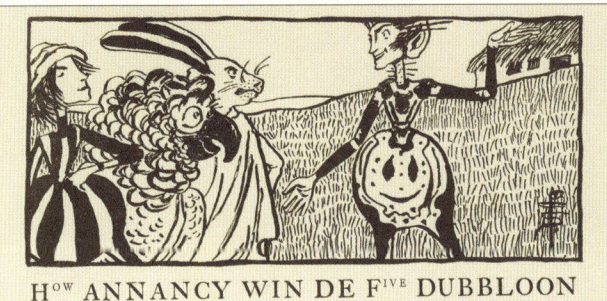
H^{ow} ANNANCY WIN DE F^{ive} DUBBLOON

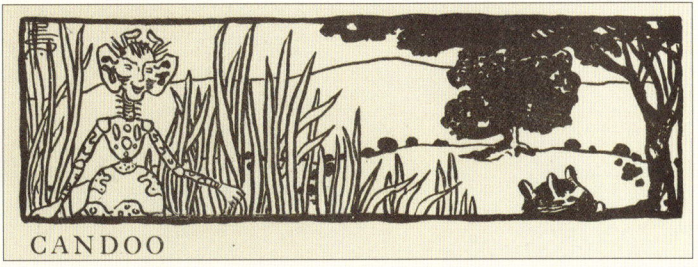
CANDOO

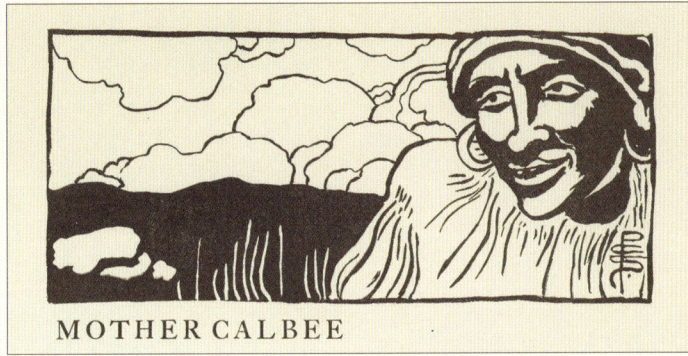
MOTHER CALBEE

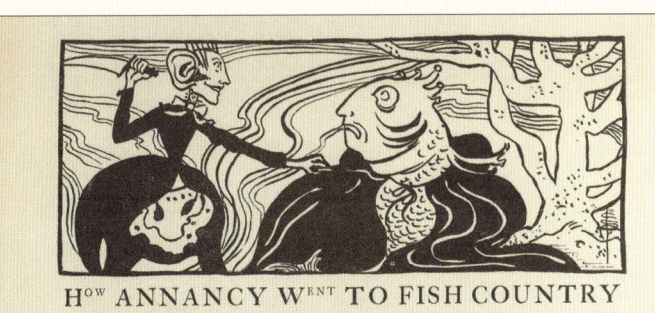
H^{ow} ANNANCY W^{ent} TO FISH COUNTRY

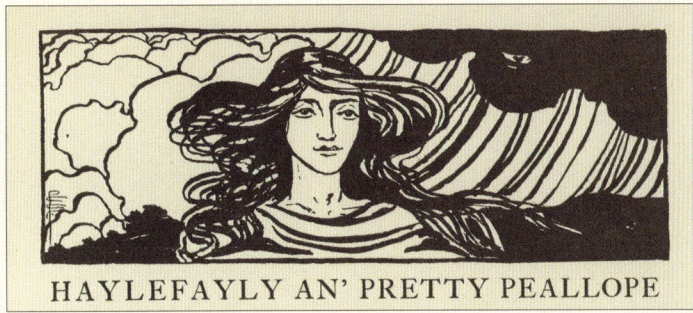
HAYLEFAYLY AN' PRETTY PEALLOPE

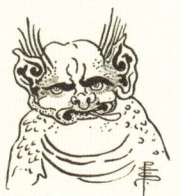

1899

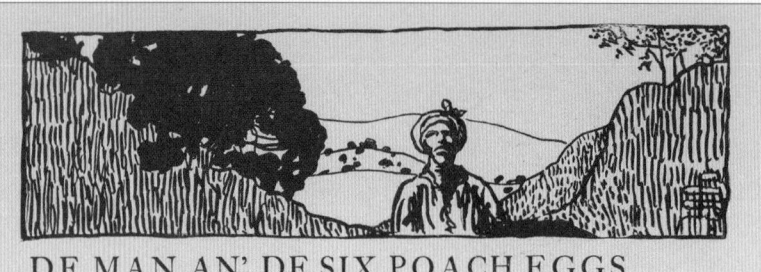
DE MAN AN' DE SIX POACH EGGS

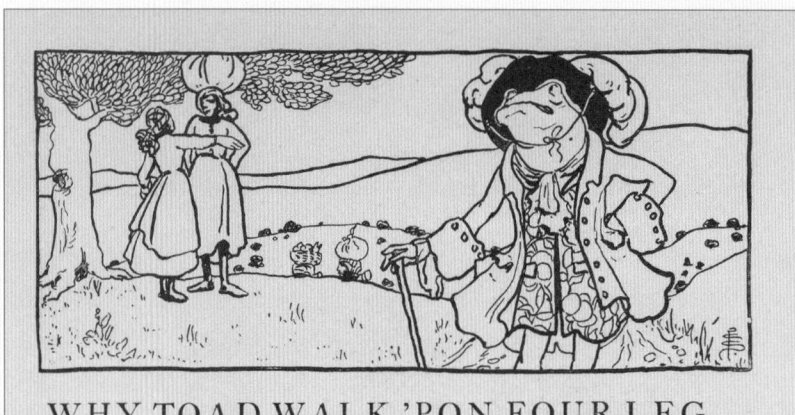
WHY TOAD WALK 'PON FOUR LEG

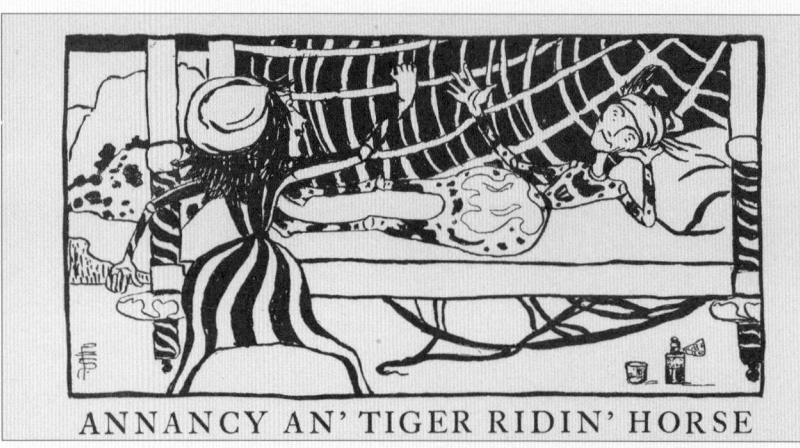
ANNANCY AN' TIGER RIDIN' HORSE

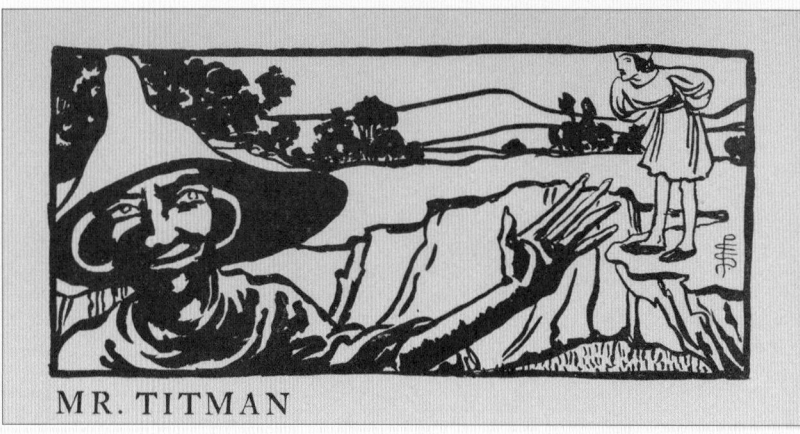
MR. TITMAN

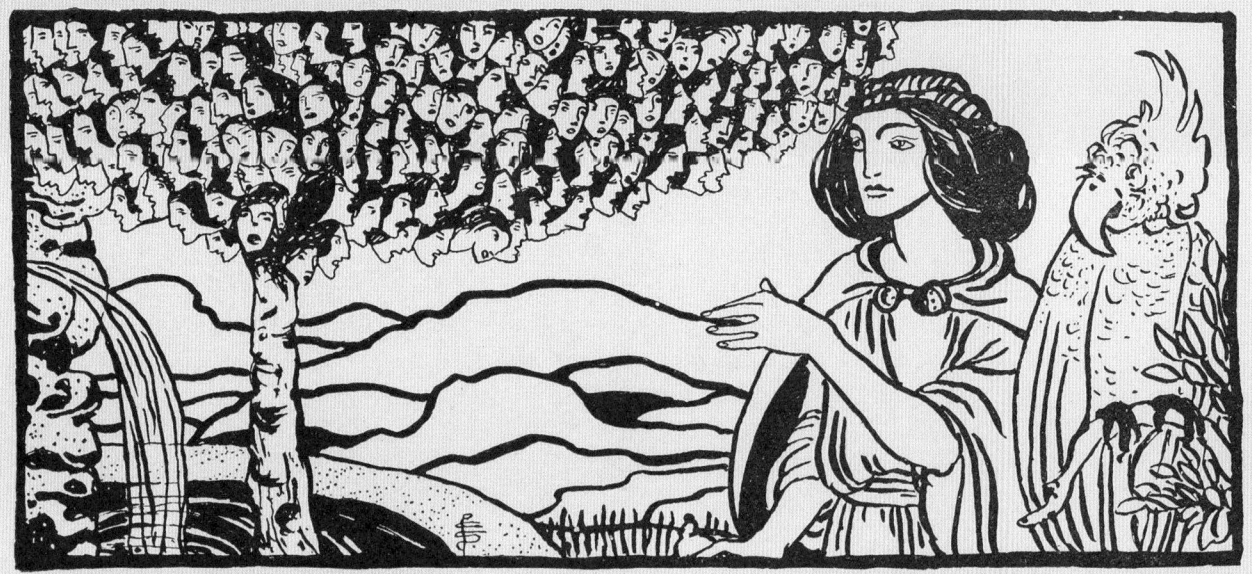

DE GOLDEN WATER, DE SINGIN' TREE AN' DE TALKIN' BIRD

IN a before time dere was t'ree sisters, an' one evenin,, dey was sittin' 'pon de door step—an' de oldes' one say,

"I wish I was de King's chief baker's wife, what nice buns an' cakes I would have to eat!

"An den de nex' one say,

"Oh, how I would like to be de King's chief cook's wife, what nice t'ings I would hab fe eat!"

"An, de las' one she say,

"I wish I was de King's wife, how happy I would be!"

Now who should be goin' by, but de King an' him chief counselor, an' dey hear all dat de t'ree sisters say. But de t'ree sisters did'n know it was de King dat pass by at all. So de nex' day de King him sen' fe dem. An' at firs' dey was frighten' an' didn' want fe go at all. But den dey t'ink dat it may turn out all nice, so dey go. An' de King him ax dem what dey was talkin' about 'pon de door step de night before. An' de oldes' one say she don't remember—an' so den him ax de nex' one—an' she don't remember rightfully—an' so den him ax de younges' one, an' she tell him all about it, an' de King laugh! An' him sen' an' call in de parson an' marry de oldes' gal to de chief baker; an' de nex' one to de chief cook, an' de younges' one him marry himsel'!

Well—So time go on, an' on, an' bum-bye de Queen hab t'ree children. An' de sisters dey was bery jallous, an' one night dey teaf away de t'ree children, an' put dem in a basket, an' trow it in de riber. An' when de King come home from trabblin' him was bery bex, dat him t'ree lubly children was loss. An' him scol' de Queen, but she say she don't know notting of where dey was gone. An' he hab her set up in de yard an' all de dish water trown 'pon her.

De basket float down de riber, an' down de riber, till it come to a sugar mill; an' de water from de riber turn de wheel. An' de book-keeper wife she see de basket on de riber,

65

1899

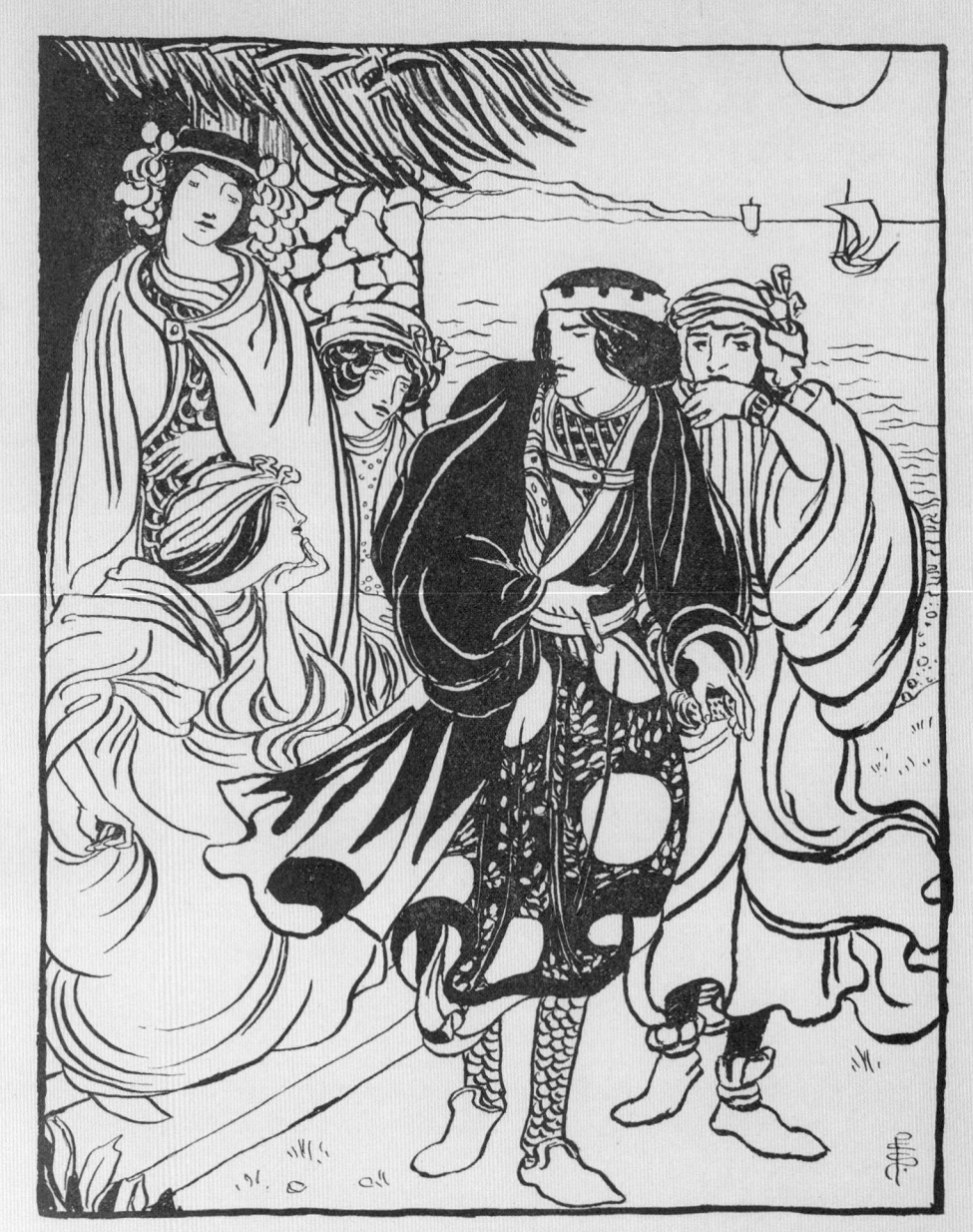

NOW WHO SHOULD BE GOIN' BY, BUT DE KING AN' CHIEF COUNSELOR.

DE GOLDEN WATER, DE SINGIN' TREE AN' DE TALKIN' BIRD

don't see her breddas any where. An' she set out trabblin' home ways. An' bum-bye she come to de foot of de bally.* An' on each side of de road she see a tall rock-a-tone† dat favor like her breddas. An' she 'prinkle, 'prinkle, de rock-a-tones wid de golden water an' dere was her two breddas. So dey all go home togeder.

An' now dere house no' want anyt'ing fe mek it nicer—an' dey fasten up de branch of de singin' tree ober de door; an' de bird he lib in a pretty golden cage, at night, but in de day time, him fly all about, an' find out t'ings! An' dey keep de golden water lock up fe when anybody hab feaver. An' de necklace, de gal she gib her nurse, it stay bright, an' don't turn no oder color but red. An' dey was so please to get back home again!

One day de breddas was out huntin' in de wood an' dey buck up de King. An' de King ax dem to dinner an' dey go, an' den dey ax de King to dere house fe dinner an' him come. An' before him come, de talkin' bird tell de gal to put *him* in de dinin' hall, an' put a dish of pearls 'pon de table. An' de King him come, an' when him see de dish of pearls 'pon de table him was bery surprise. An' him hear de branch of singin' tree sing, an' him was more surprise! An' de talkin' bird say,

"An' you are so surprised at a dish of pearls; what would you t'ink, if you was to know dat dese t'ree children are yours!"

De King him was so delighted! An' him take de t'ree children home wid him. An' him hab dere mumma from where she was in the yard, wid de dish water t'rown 'pon her, an' had her wash wid soap!

An' de two sisters dey was put in a pit, with there arms tie, an' with scorpions, an' snakes, an' centipede, an' lizards; an' Annancy, who eat dem up!

---

*Valley. †Rock-stone.

William Gillette

1900

Five illustrations of William Gillette by Pamela Colman Smith, of which two depict Sherlock Holmes. Used with permission of the Connecticut Department of Energy and Environmental Protection. Chuck 2.0 Landau

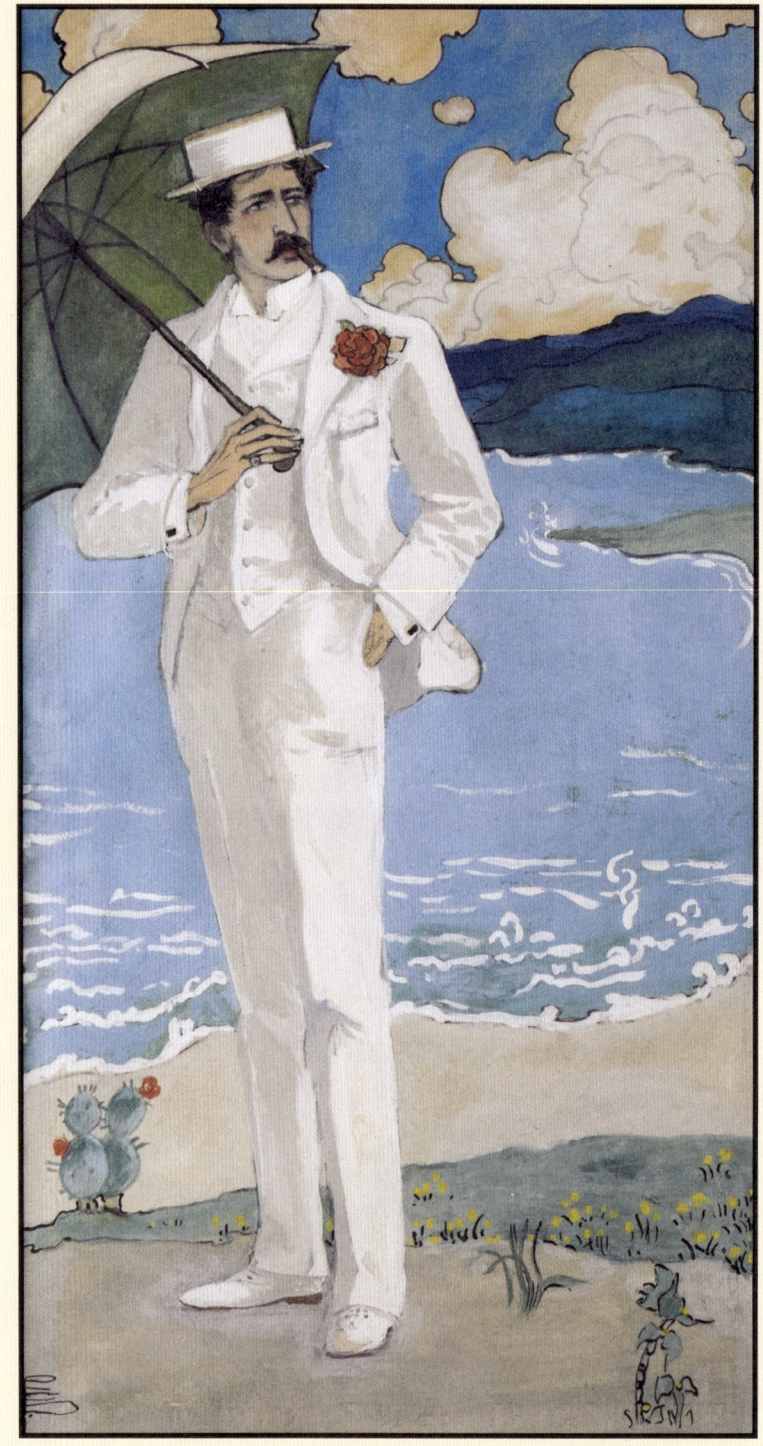

1900

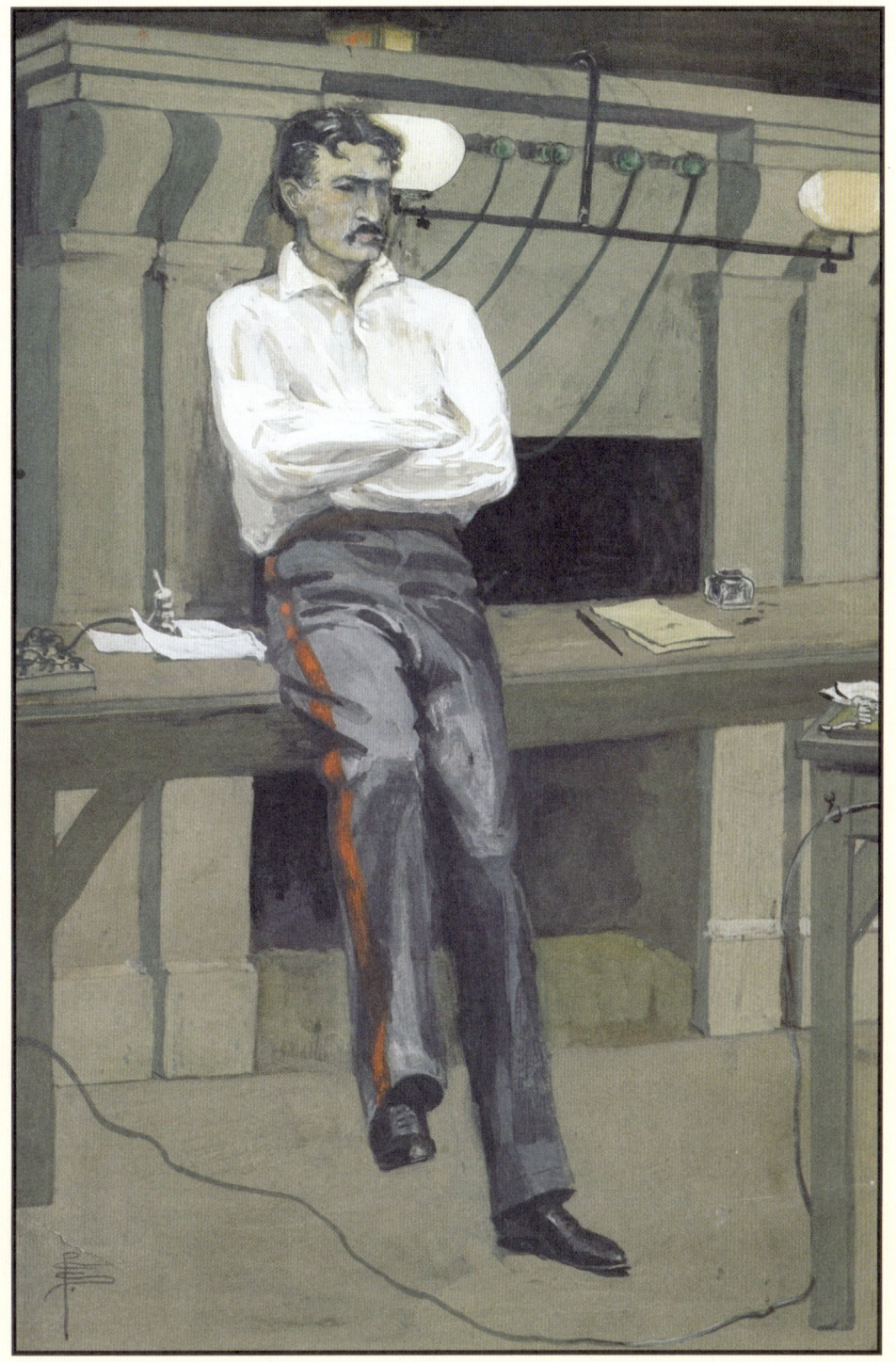

1900

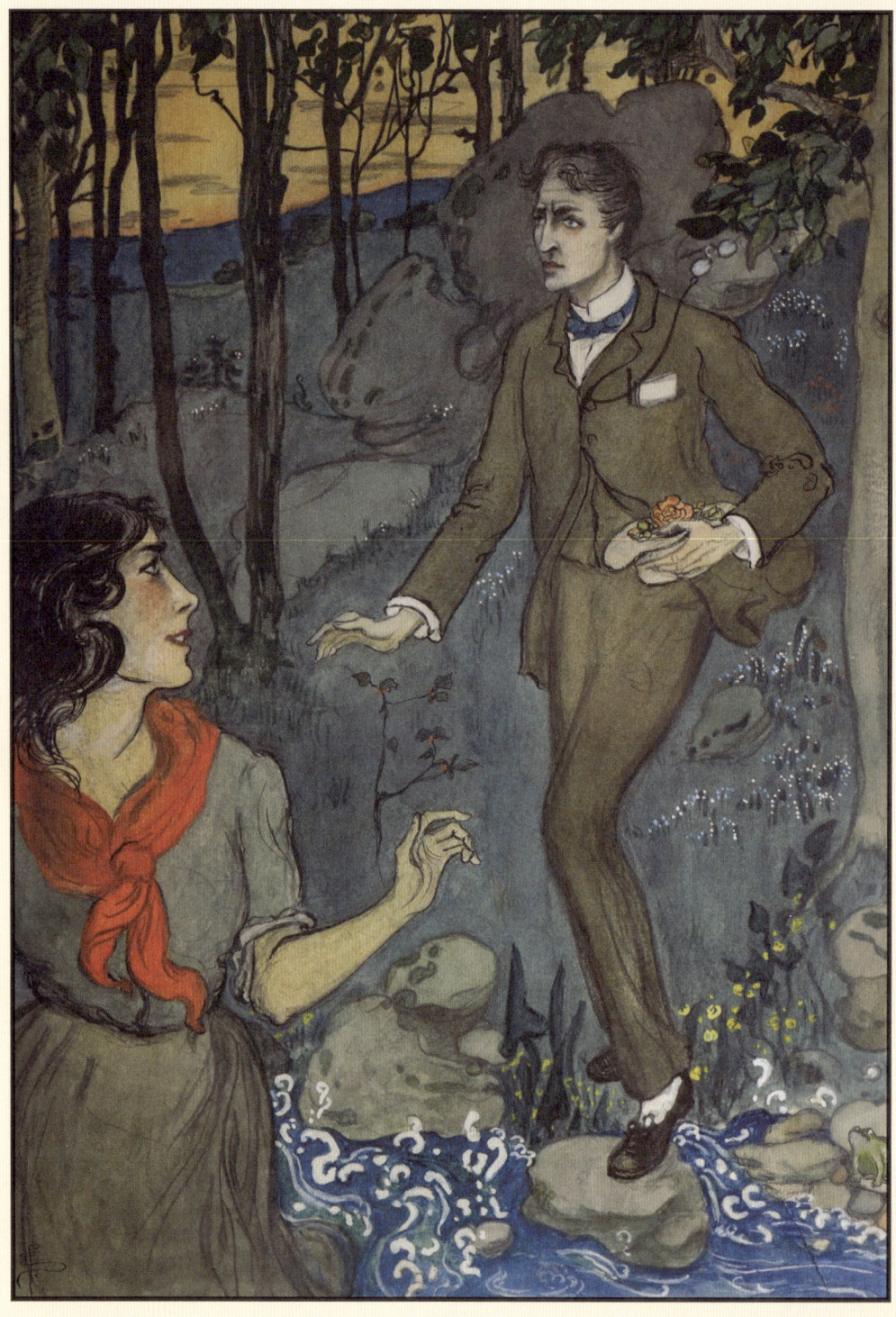

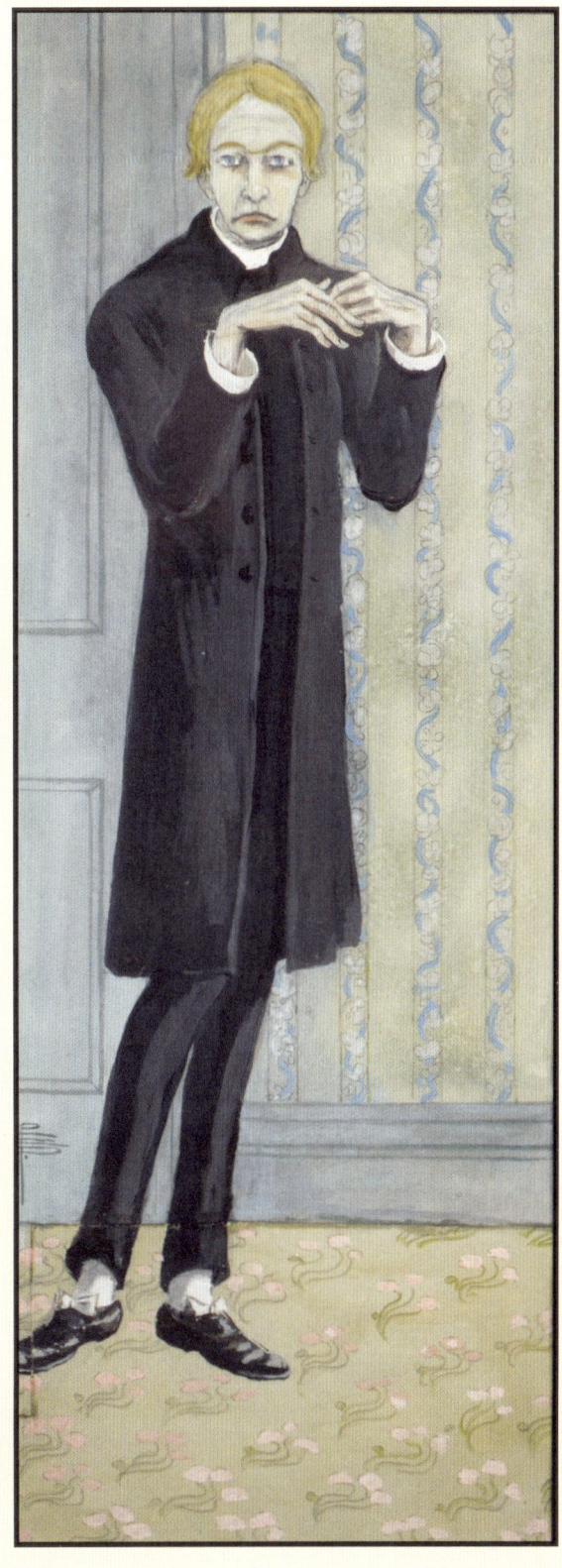

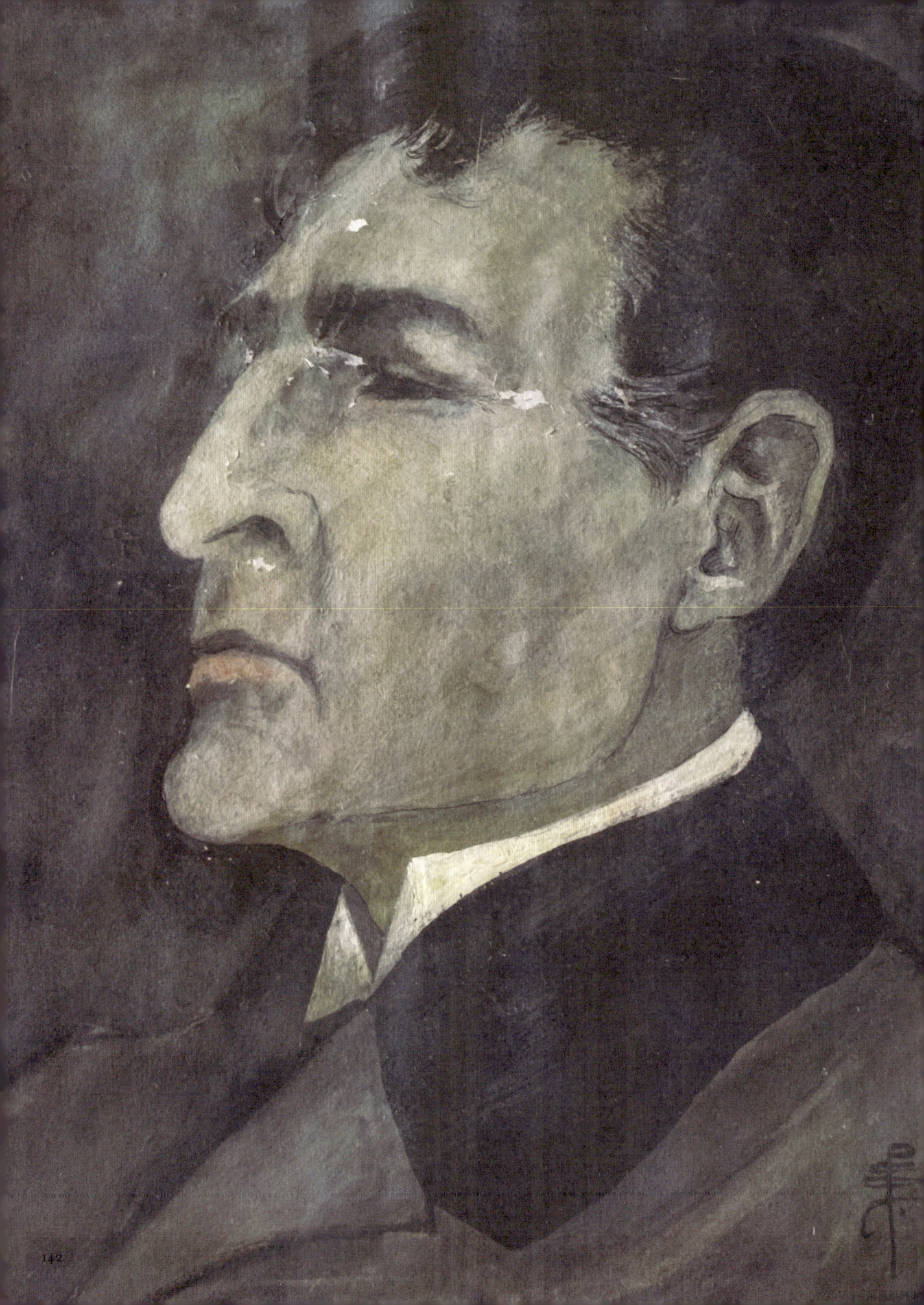

Smallhythe Place, Kent

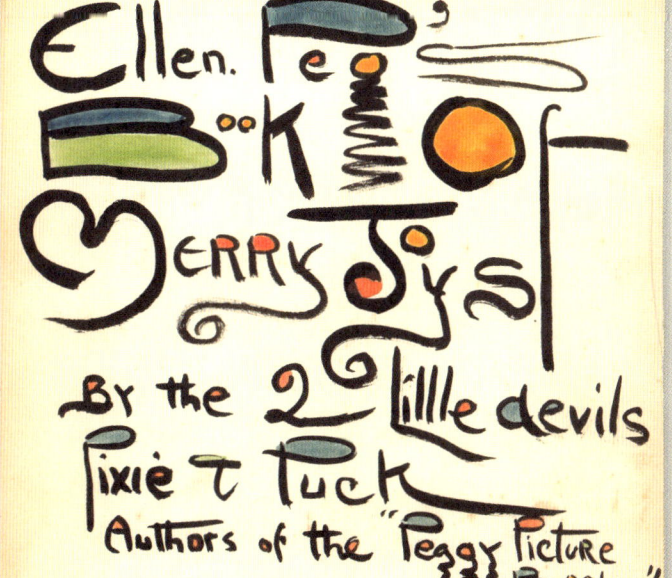

1900

Illustrations by Pamela Colman Smith in this section were drawn during a voyage from New York to Southampton on May 18 to 28, 1900 aboard the S.S. Menominee. Of the 104 passengers on board, over 80 were members of the Lyceum Company. Among the passengers were Henry Irving, Laurence Irving, Bram Stoker and Pamela Colman Smith, who was listed as a single, female artist.

There are two sketchbooks housed at Smallhythe Place, a 16th century cottage formerly owned by Ellen Terry that now contains memorabilia from her life-long career on stage.

"The Ellen Peg" by Pamela Colman Smith. Courtesy © National Trust, UK. "The Ellen Peg" poem by Pamela Colman Smith. Courtesy © National Trust, UK. Special thanks to Susannah Mayor and Alice Hicks for providing these images

1900

Sketch by Pamela Colman Smith depicting Walter Collinson (Henry Irving's personal dresser and valet), Edy Craig, Ellen Terry and Laurence Irving who is holding a stack of books. Courtesy © National Trust, UK

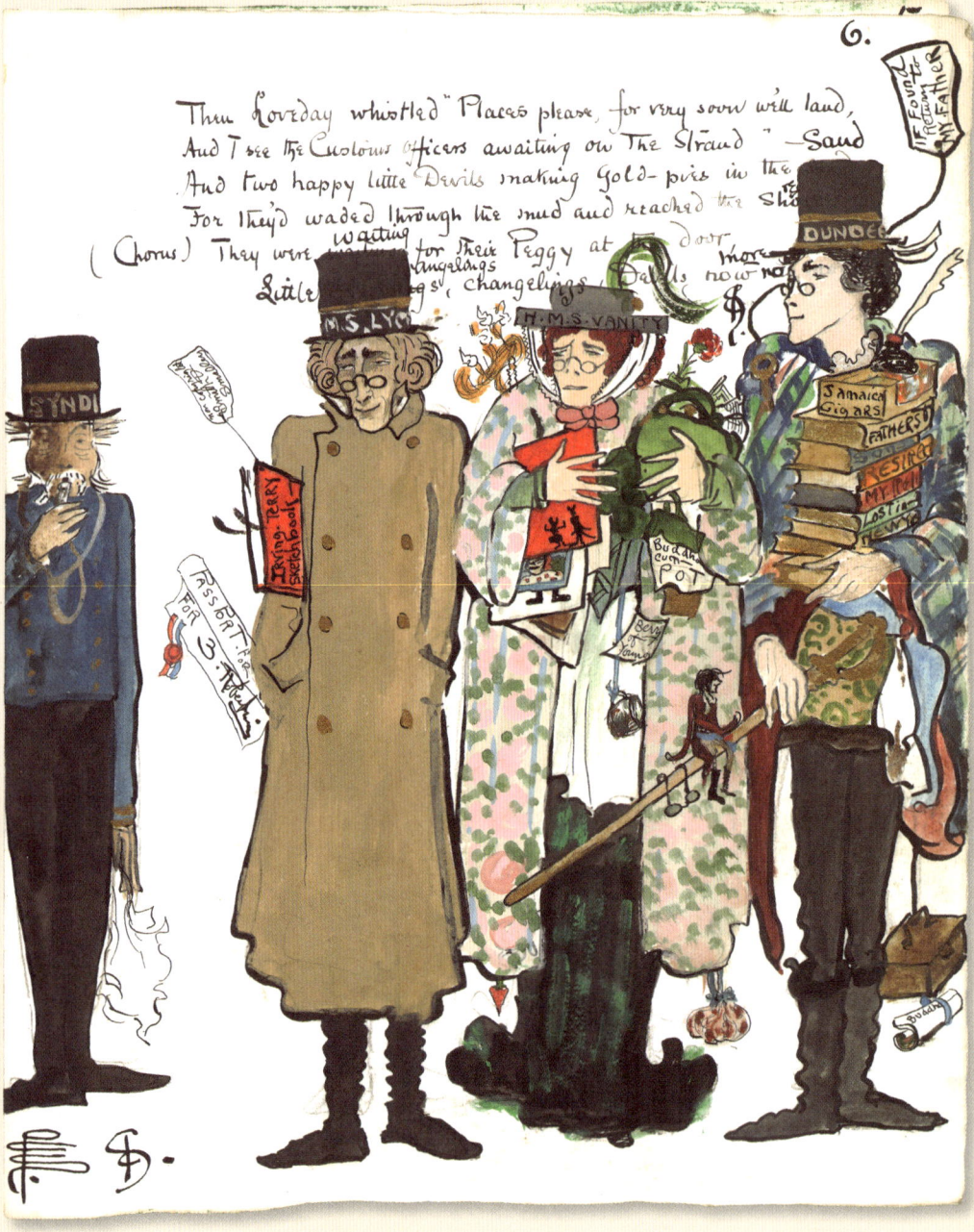

1900

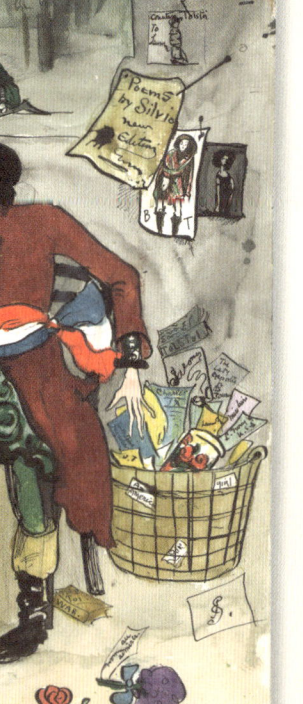

Sketch by Pamela Colman Smith aboard the S.S. Menominee, May 1900. Depicting a seated Laurence Irving looking into a mirror. Courtesy © National Trust, UK

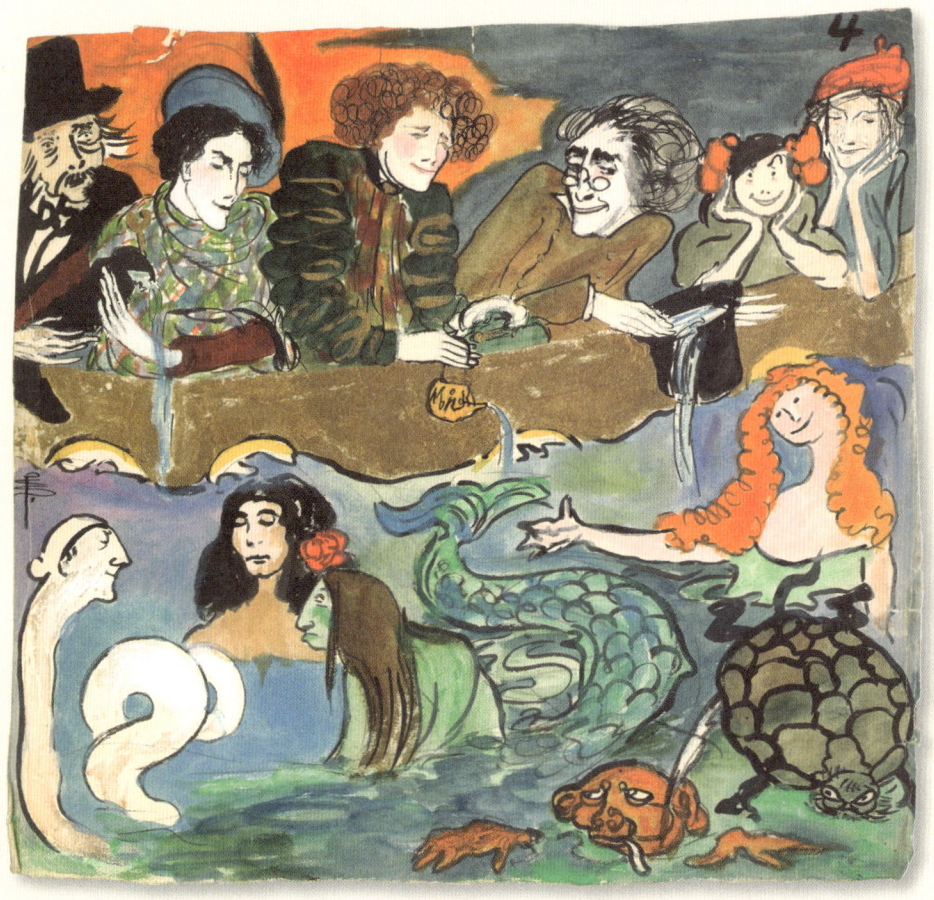

Sketch by Pamela Colman Smith depicting Walter Collinson, unidentified woman, Ellen Terry, Henry Irving, Pamela and Edy Craig. Courtesy © National Trust, UK

1900

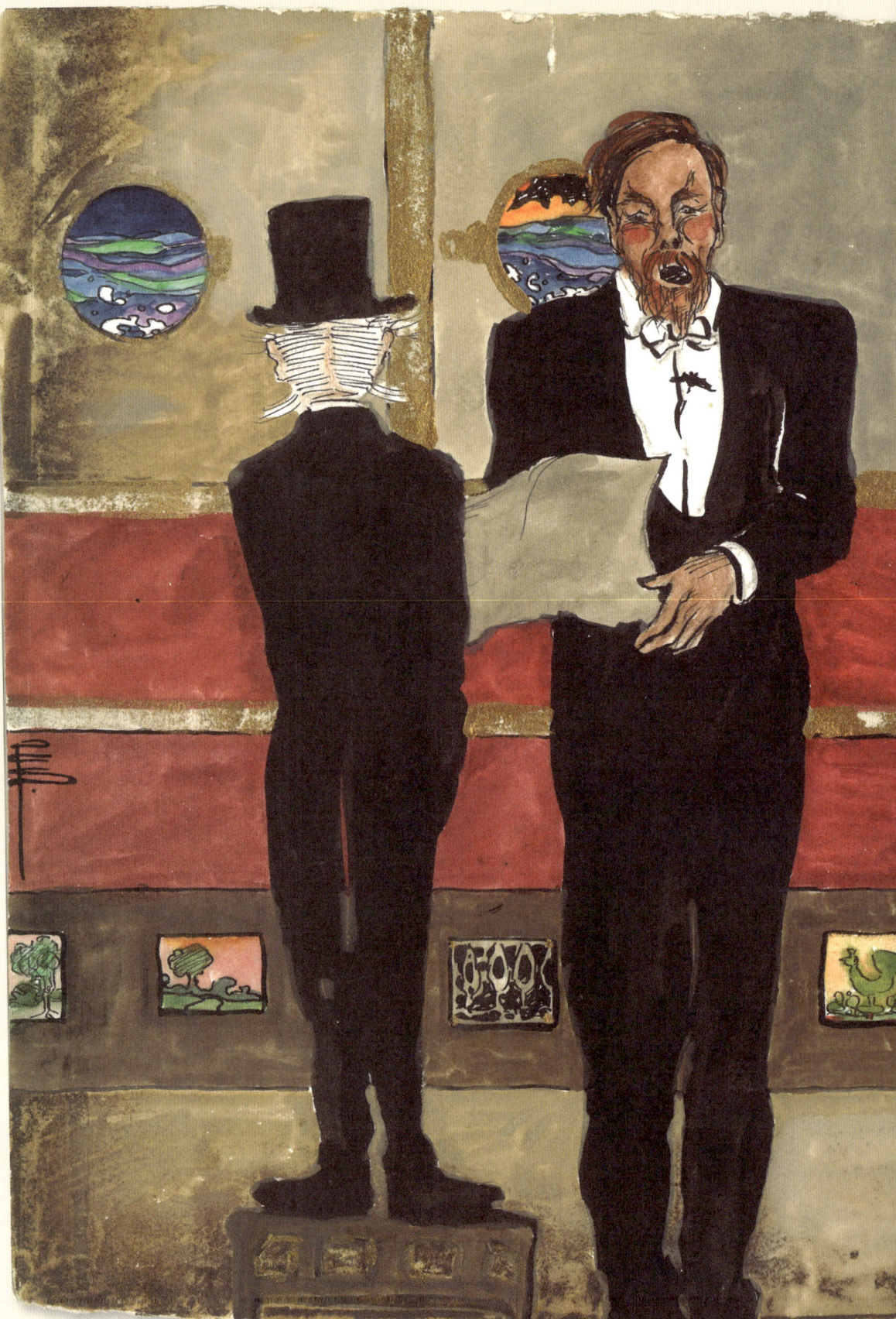

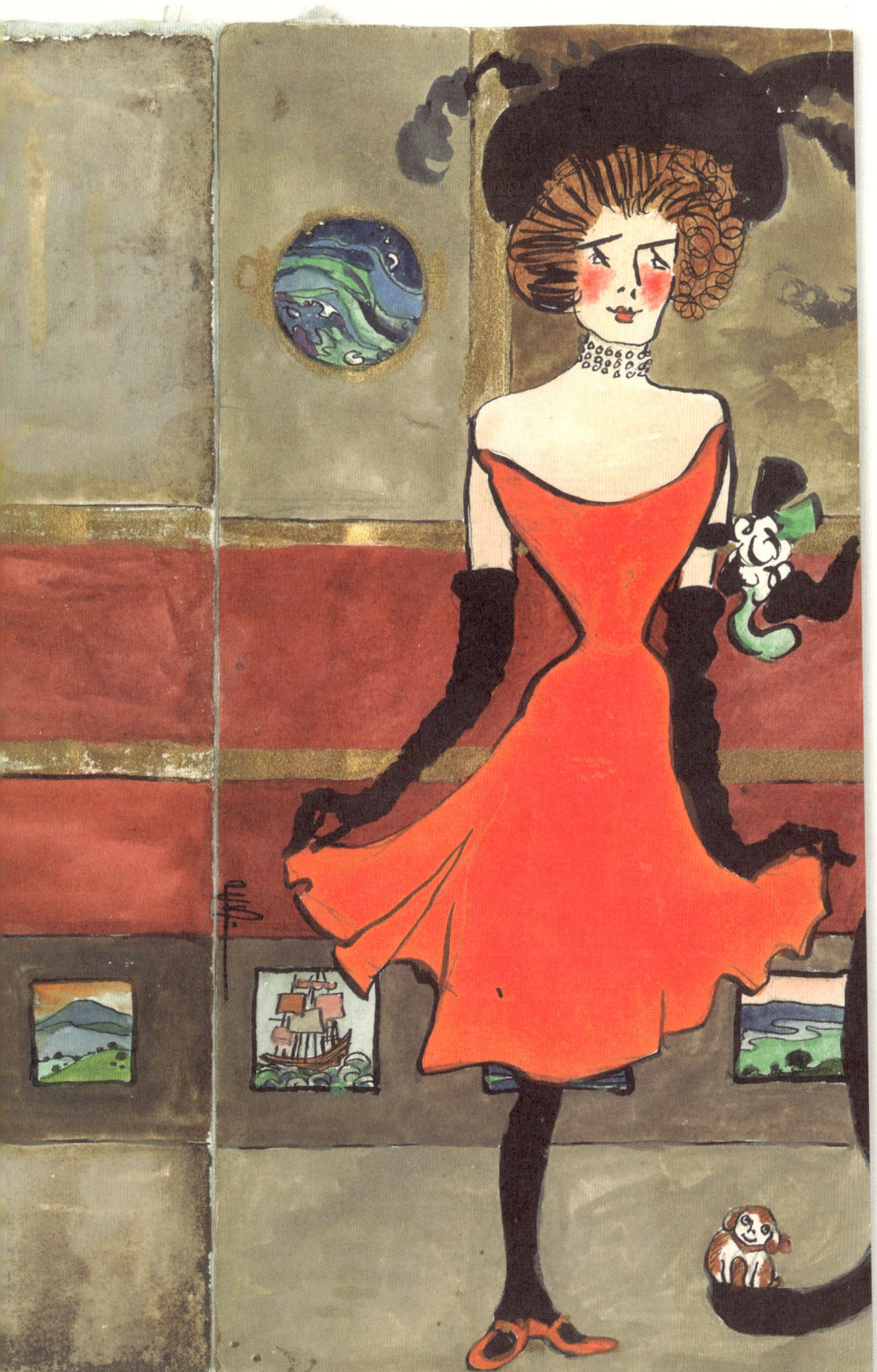

1900

Sketch by
Pamela Colman
Smith depicting
Walter Collinson,
Bram Stoker
and Ellen Terry.
Courtesy ©
National Trust,
UK

1900

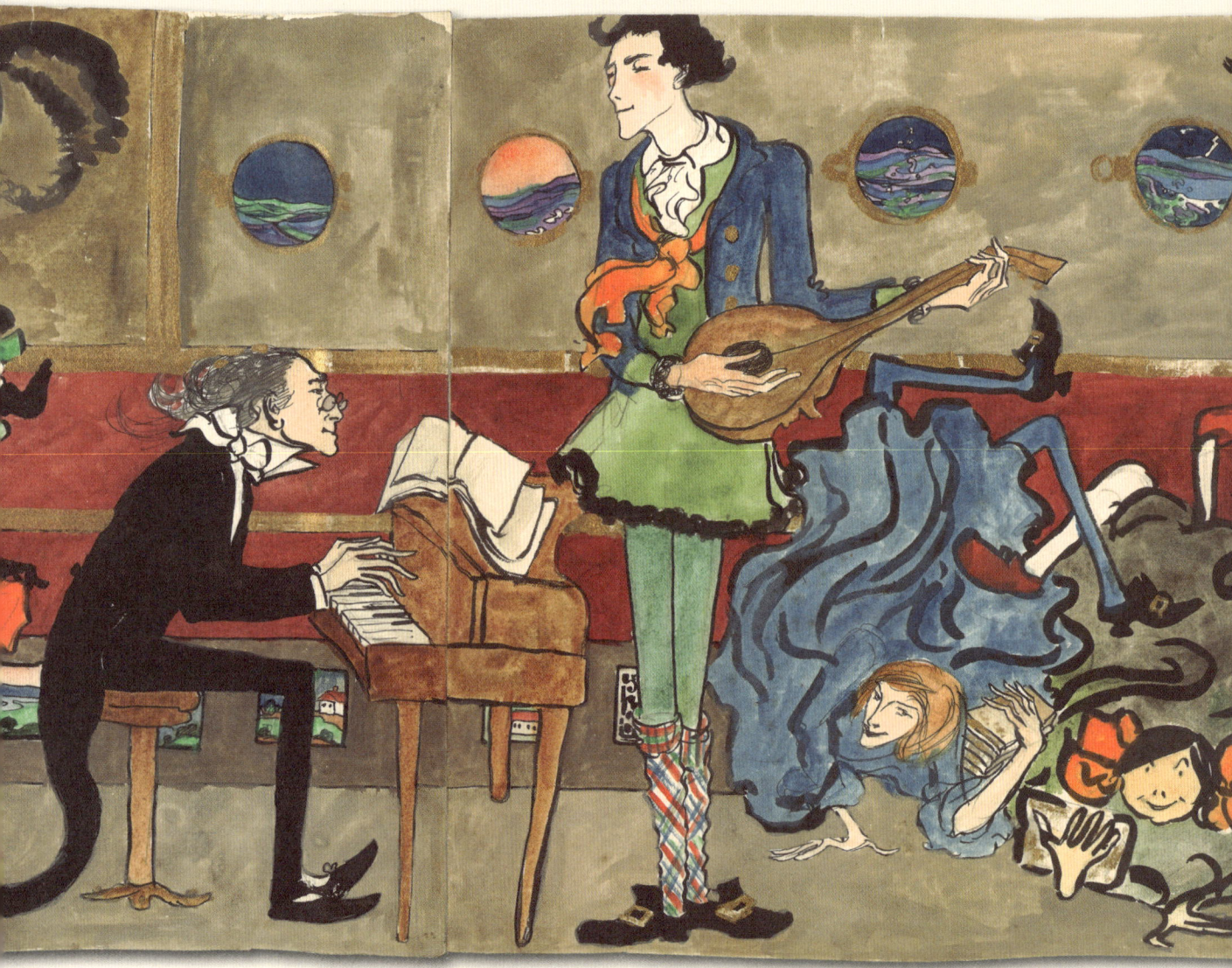

Sketch by Pamela Colman
Smith depicting Henry Irving
at the piano, Laurence Irving,
Edy Craig and Pamela.
Courtesy © National Trust, UK

1901 to 1905
Visitors Book

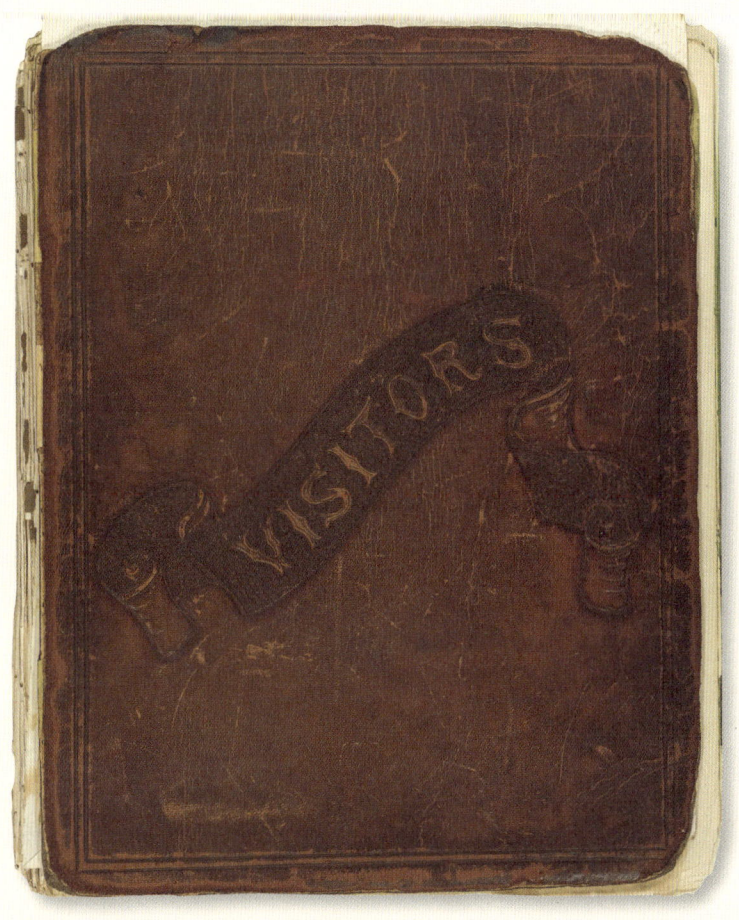

Helena Euthalia	Acebos	
R.	Adams	
L.H.	Alexander	
Claudia A.	Ayton-Lee	Signed the Visitors book "Also English, mixed with Gypsy"
J (John)	Baillie	J and R Baillie are mentioned in The Green Sheaf advertisements as owning a handmade jewelry store/exhibit. Possibly related to Joanna Baillie, a famous early 19th century dramatist
R.	Baillie	
J.M.	Barrie	(1860-1937) Scottish novelist and playwright, creator of Peter Pan
A.M.	Bishop	
Kate	Blackburn	
Margaret	Blanchard	
Gordon	Bottomly	(1874-1948) English poet, playwright and editor. Pamela contributed stage designs for his productions
Albert	Bowner	
Sheila E.	Braisse	Author
Marjorie	Byron	
Audrey Cecil	Campbell	
Sidney	Cargill	
Alphaeus Philemon	Cole	(1876-1988) American artist and engraver. He died at the age of 112, the world's oldest verified living man. His wife was Margaret Cole, who is also listed in the book as Pegotty and sometimes Pegothy or even Peggy Cole

continued on next page

Madge (aka Peggotty)	Cole	Wife of Alphaeus Cole
Edith (Edy, Pealope, Geraldine, Ailsa)	Craig	Ellen Terry's daughter, a stage and costume designer and co-producer of the Pioneer Players. She was Pamela's longtime friend
Claire	de Pratz	English novelist and writer
Arnold	Dolmetsch	(1858-1940) French composer and musical instrument maker
Nicole	Drew	
L. C. (Louis Charles)	Duncombe-Jewell	(1886-1947) Author and founder of the Celtic-Cornish Society, and contributor to The Green Sheaf
Lady Alix	Egerton	English poet, contributor to The Green Sheaf
Hugh (S.R.)	Elliot	Science writer
Bianca	Elliot	Wife of Hugh Elliot
Florence (Beatrice)	Emery	(1860-1917) Married name of Florence Farr, actress and fellow masquer with Pamela. A member of the Golden Dawn
W.E.	Farrow	
Alice	Feilring	
Beatrice	Forbes-Robertson	(1883-1967) Actor, writer and suffragist
Emily	Ford	
Nora	Franco bon Bonadice	
Cecil P.	French	(1879-1953) Illustrator, signed the Visitors book "Fellow of the Masques…Green Sheaf etc etc etc" Also went by the nickname Puffles
William H.	Frothingham	
Ethel P.F.	Fryer-Fortescue	Member of the Golden Dawn
Helen	Graham	
Lady Isabella Augusta	Gregory	(1852-1932) Irish playwright, folklorist, and contributor to The Green Sheaf
Millicent	Hall	
Leslie Price	Hamer	
H	Harvey	
Isabel	Hearn	
James	Hearn	Actor, performed with Ellen Terry
Ethel A. Cade	Hearn	
Pollie	Herman	
Christopher G.	Hope	
W.T.	Horton	(1864-1919) Illustrator, author, mystic, friend of W.B. Yeats, and contributor to The Green Sheaf
W Shafman	Huston	
Beatrice	Irvine	
J. Harry	Irvine	Director and actor
Amy L.	Jackson	
Theresa	Jackson	
Alexander	Jamiesen	(1873-1937) Scottish painter and husband of artist Biddy Macdonald
Lindsay	Jardine	
Fanny	Johnson	
Myrna C.	Jonny	
Tessa L.	Kelso	(1863-1933) American journalist, publicist and head librarian of the Los Angeles Public Library
F (Frederick) A.	King	Well-known literay agent who represented Pamela for a time. Pamela gave King the Visitors book because she "didn't care for people anymore."
Helen	Laird	
Mary (ASL)	Lowndes	(1856-1929) Stained glass designer and suffragist, chair of the Artists' Suffrage League
Frank	Lyons	
Biddy	Macdonald	(1871-1952) English painter and wife of Alexander Jamiesen
Evelyn	Mackenzie	
Eric R.D.	Maclagan	(1879-1951) Director of the Victoria and Albert Museum
Gladys	Major	
Yoshio	Markino	(1874-1956) Japanese author and illustrator who lived in London
Anne	Marshall	
Jenny Owlett	Marshall	
Christabel	Marshall	(1871-1960) Birth name of Christopher St John. Playwright, author and suffragist
John	Masefield	(1878-1967) English poet, novelist and contributor to The Green Sheaf
Editte Elkin	Mathews	Wife of Charles Elkin Mathews
C. Elkin	Mathews	(1851-1921) British publisher and bookseller

Lily M.	Monsell	Possibly related to Elinor Monsell, who designed the title page for Dun Emer Press and was a contributor to The Green Sheaf
Lena	Nelessarse	
Mr and Mrs H	Newcomb	
Pollie	Newman	
Willis L.	Ogden	Brooklyn relatives on Pamela's maternal side
Alice Lydia	Ogden	Brooklyn relatives on Pamela's maternal side
Mary Price	Owen	
Pixie	Pamela	
Euphrosyne Stefan	Pappsajannopoulo	
Dorothy	Reeke	
Arthur J.	Pentz	
Evekyn	Person	
Omar	Ramsden	(1873-1939) English designer and maker of silverware
Arthur M.	Ransome	(1884-1967) Wrote the book Bohemia in London
Mrs W.	Richards	Signed the Visitors book "American Rivals of The Green Sheaf"
Miss A.	Richards	Signed the Visitors book "American Rivals of The Green Sheaf"
Reginald	Rigby	Artist, created colorful posters especially in the 1920s for London Transport, and a contributor to A Broad Sheet and The Green Sheaf
Kessie	Rigby	Probably Reginald Rigby's wife
Grace E.	Roberts	
Nora Murray	Robertson	
Archibald G.B.	Russell	(1879-1955) Archibald George Blomefield Russell, English journalist and art historian
Lily	Salberg	
Pauline	Sant	Someone Pamela knew in Jamaica. Sant's father was a somewhat famous photographer at the time
Poppie	Savin	Friend of Ellen Terry
Helen C.	Semple	(1863-1932) American geographer and author
Martin Edward Fallas	Shaw	(1875-1958) English musician and composer of church music, contributor to The Green Sheaf, and briefly engaged to Edy Craig
Marie L.	Shedlock	
Hilda Robinson	Smith	
Theodore	Smith	Pamela's paternal uncle who later gave her the inheritance with which she bought Parc Garland in The Lizard
Christopher	St John	(1871-1960) Born Christabel Marshall, writer, editor, close friend of Ellen Terry and long-time companion to Terry's daughter Edith Craig, campaigner for women's suffrage
Nona	Stewart	Pamela inscribed Widdicombe Fair Number 89 with a drawing to her
Charles	Thornby	
Scorpana Mary	Vaughan	
Russell	Vaun	Playwright
Blanche Georgiana	Vulliamy	
Dorothy	Walker	Probably wife of Emery Walker. Dorothy was the person who identified Pamela in her passport application on March 24, 1916. She stated that she had known Pamela for 15 years
Emery	Walker	(1851-1933) English engraver and printer
Margaret	Wallace	
Alfred Marcus	Ward	Contributor to The Green Sheaf
D.P. (Dorothy)	Ward	Actress, wife of Alfred Marcus Ward and contributor to The Green Sheaf
William A. Hardcastle	Ward	Irish printer
Frederick J.	Waugh	(1861-1940) American artist
Arthur	Wentz	
Ethel (Rolt)	Wheeler	(1869-1958) Irish poet, author, journalist and suffragette
Beatrice C.	Wilcox	Author and artist
Peggy	Williams	
Duncan	Williams	
E. Harcout	Williams	(1880-1957) Actor and contributor to The Green Sheaf
Hilda	Winkley	
Lily	Yeats	W.B. and Jack Yeats's sister. She ran the Dun Emer and Cuala Press with her sister
W.B.	Yeats	(1865-1939) William Butler Yeats, Irish poet and dramatist, Nobel Prize winner, and contributor to The Green Sheaf
Jack (John)	Yeats	(1871-1957) John Butler (Jack) Yeats, brother of W.B. Yeats, his wife was "Cottie" (Mary Cottenham White). Both Irish artists

1901–1905

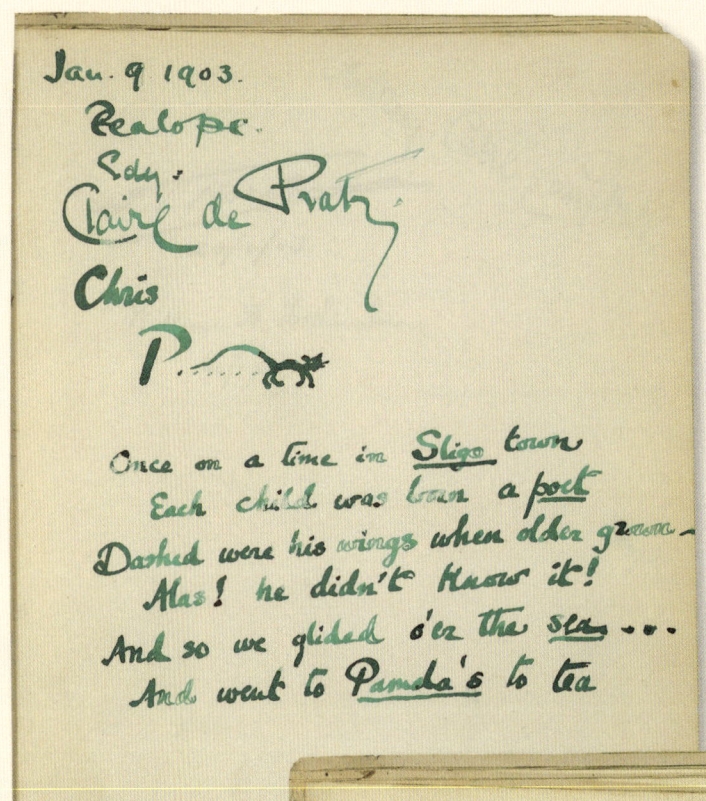

Pamela Colman Smith's Visitors book from 1901 to 1905. Showing 30 of 150 pages. Courtesy of Stuart R. Kaplan library

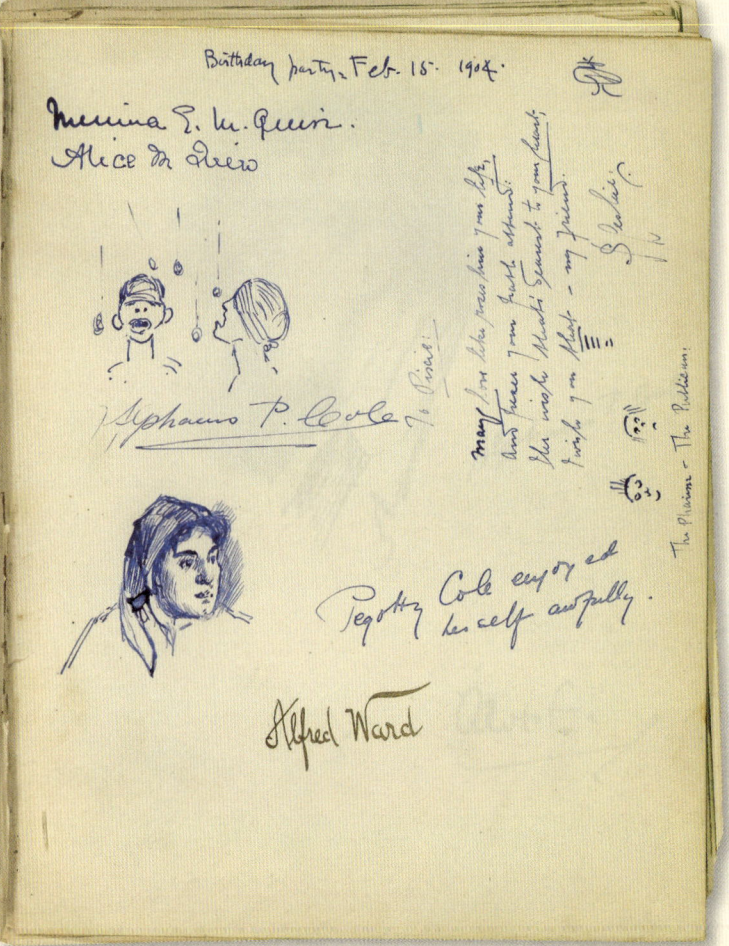

1901–1905

1901–1905

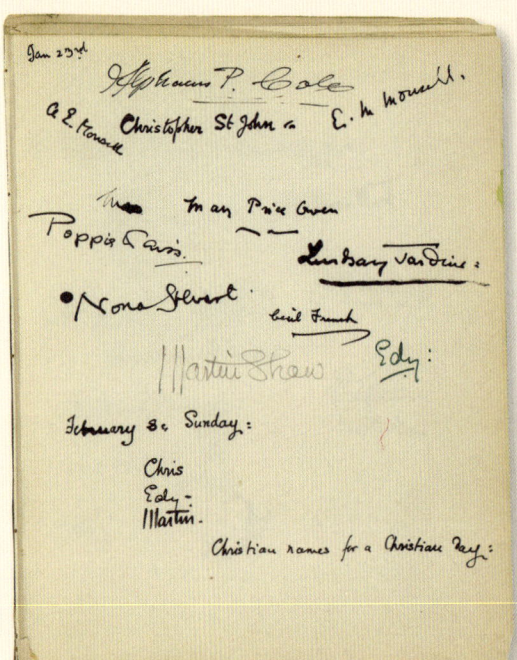

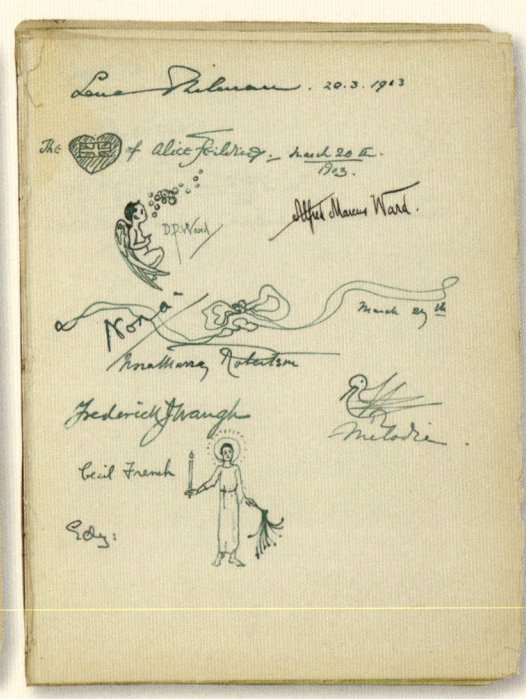

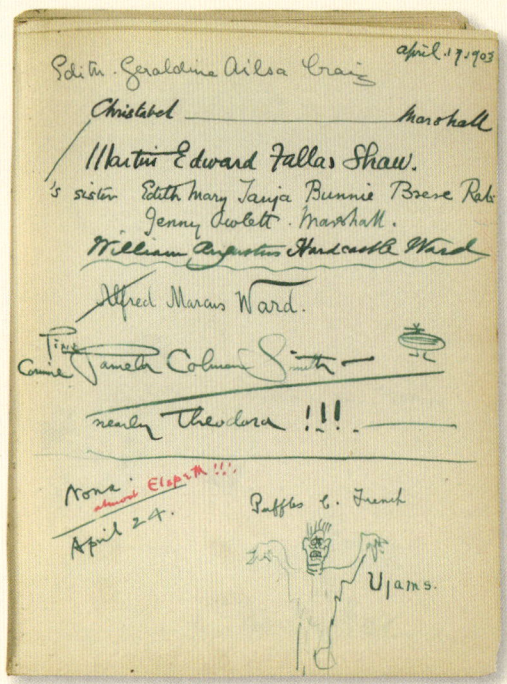

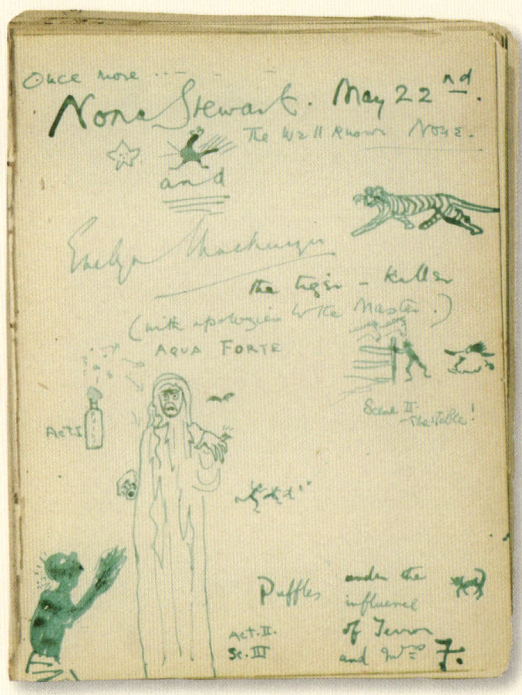

1901–1905

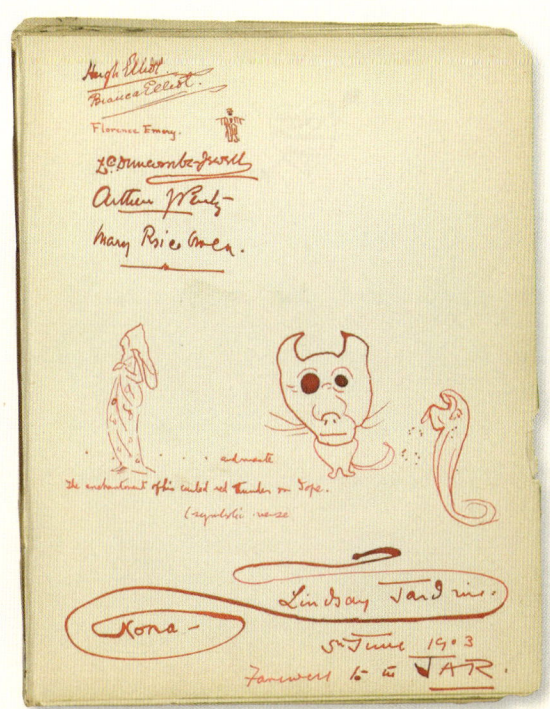
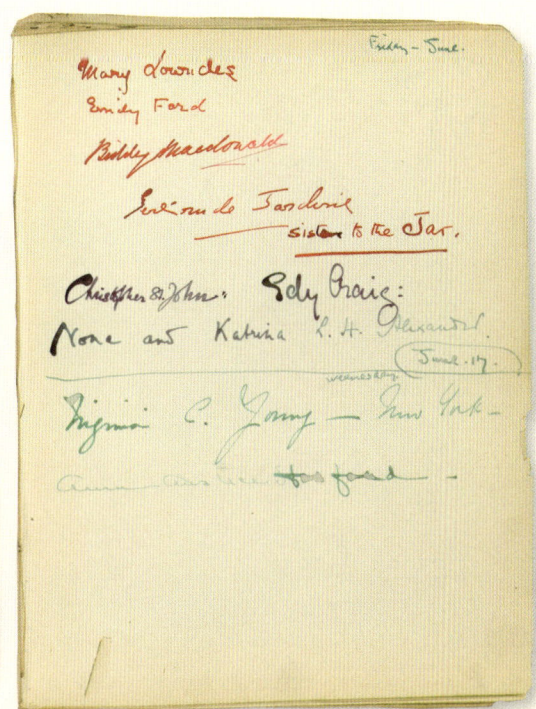
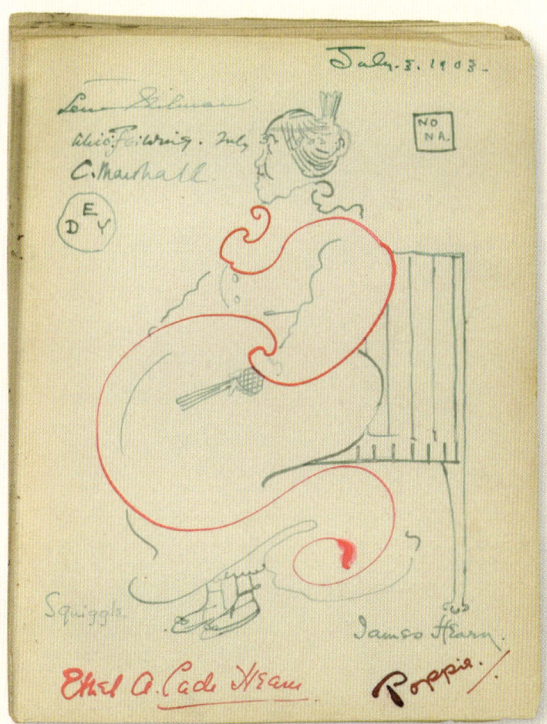
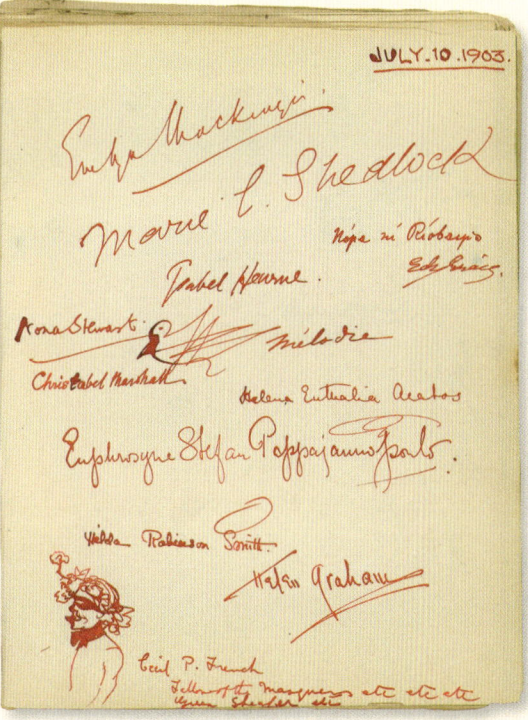

1901–1905

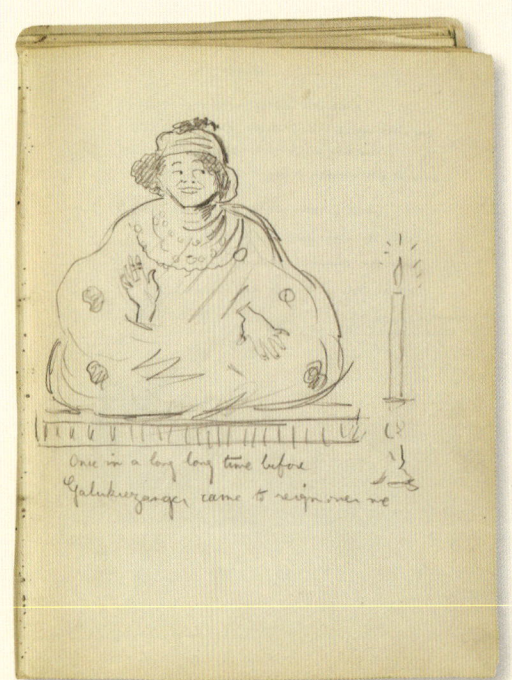

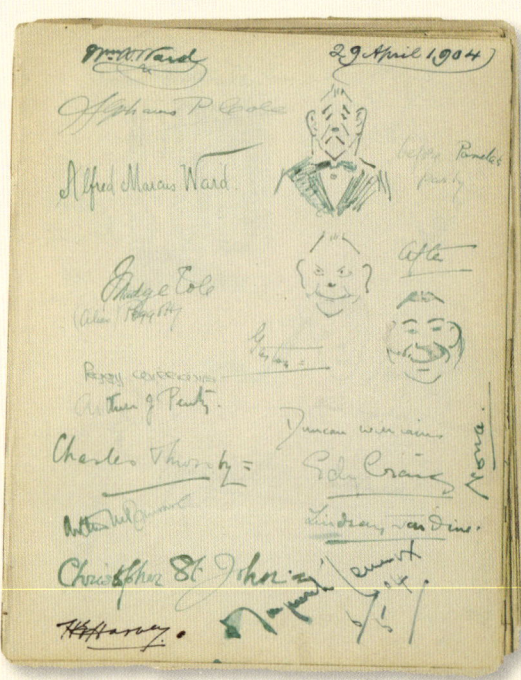

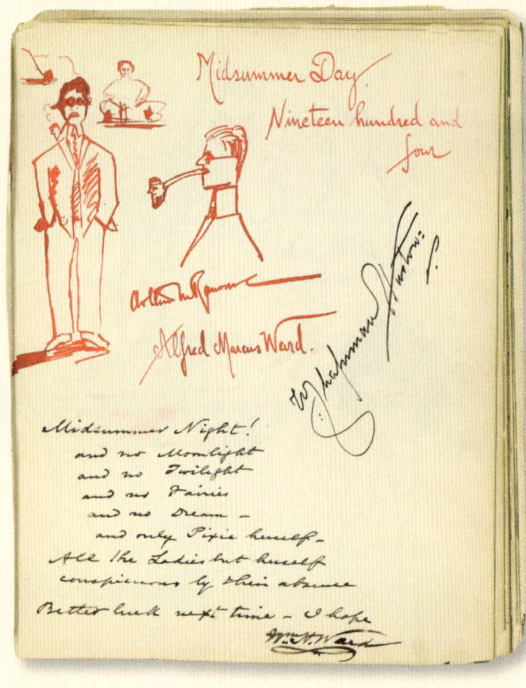

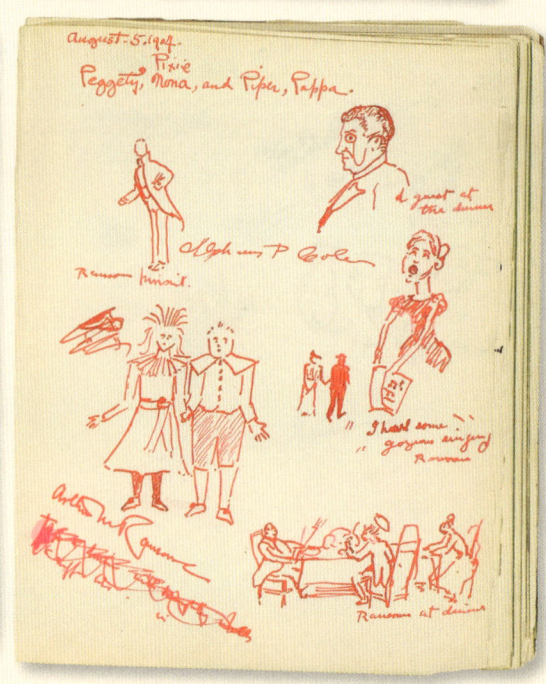

1901–1905

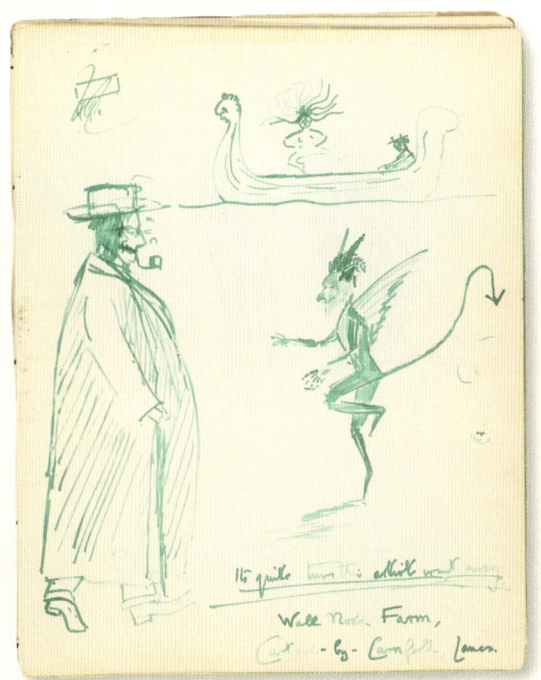
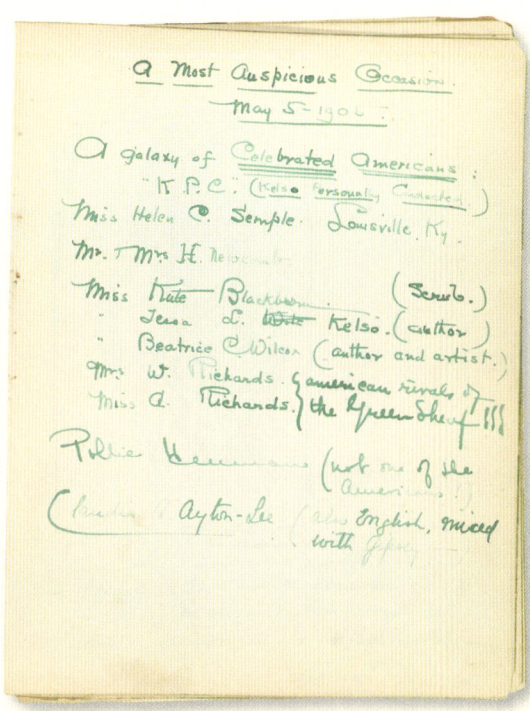
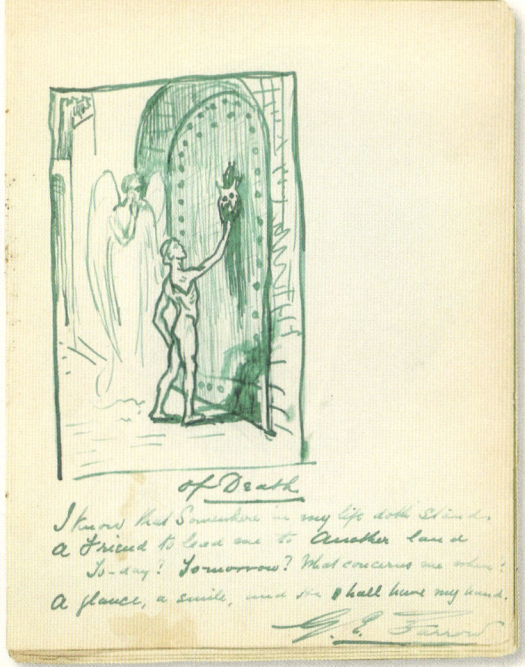
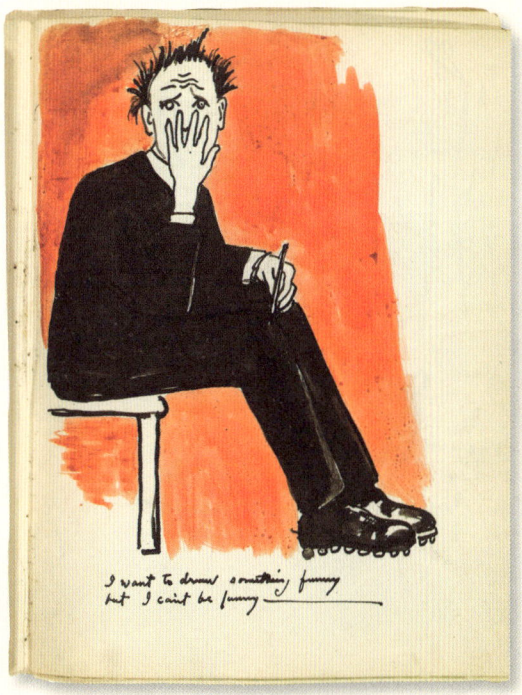

1901–1905

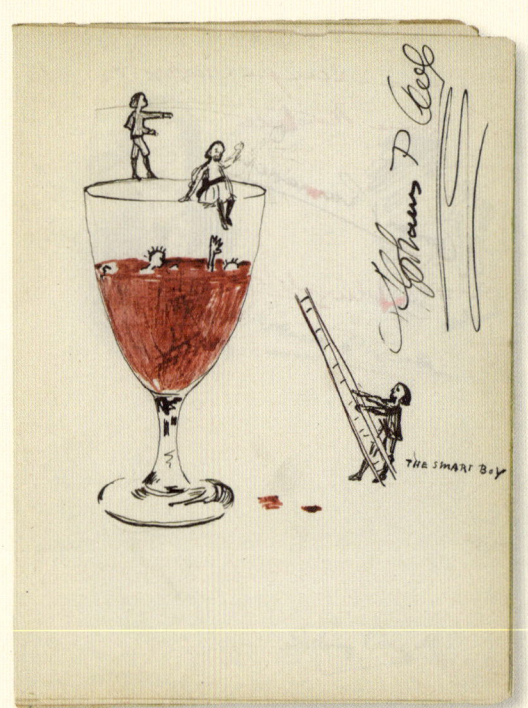
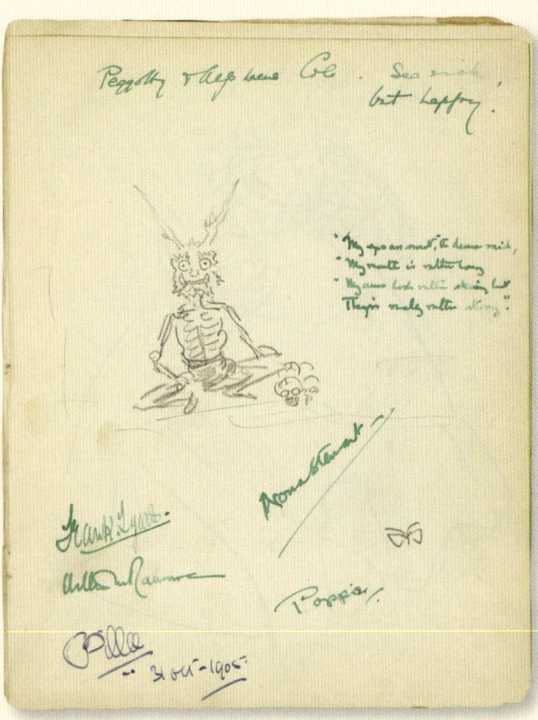
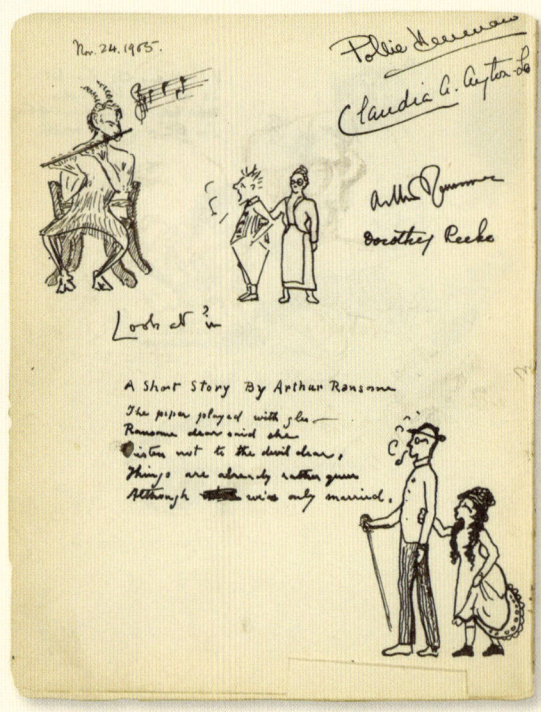
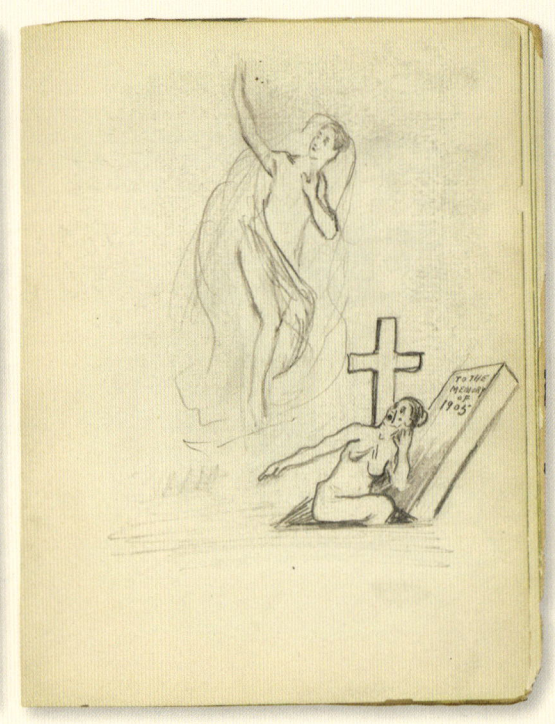

1901–1905

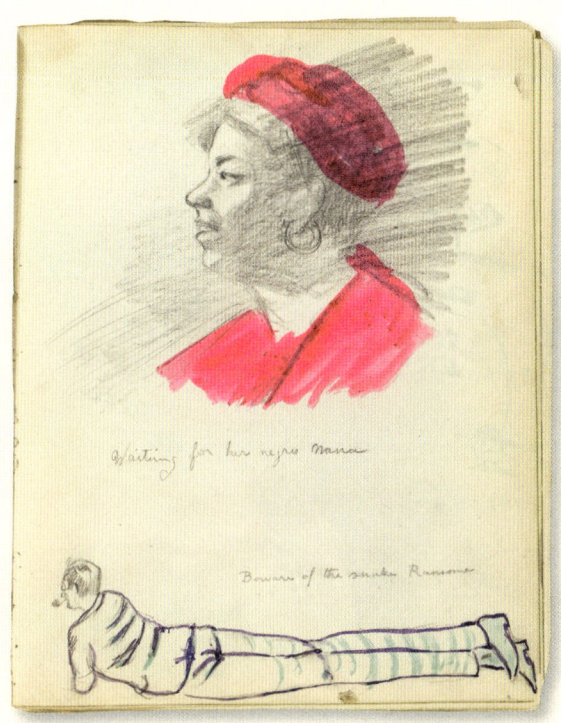
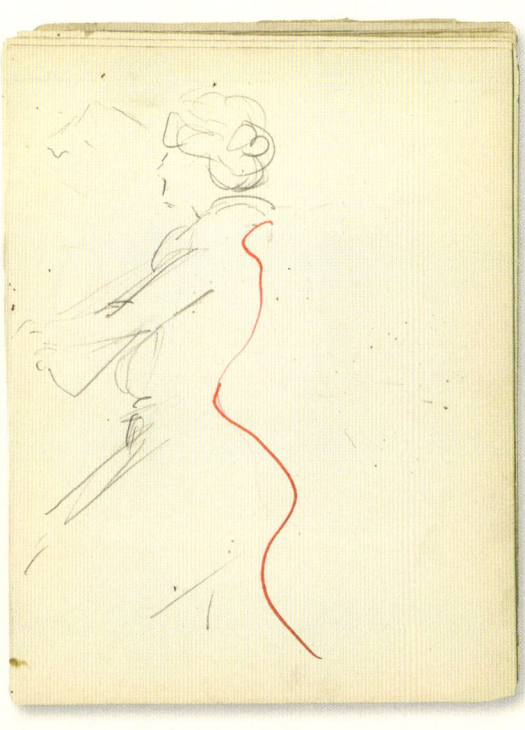
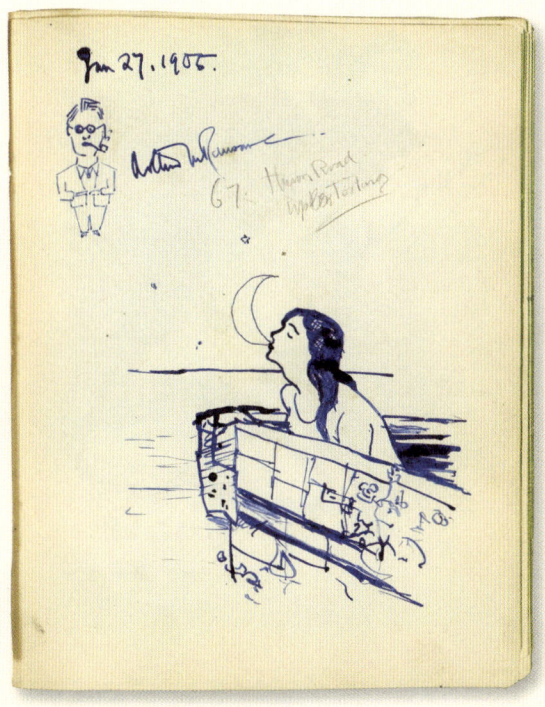
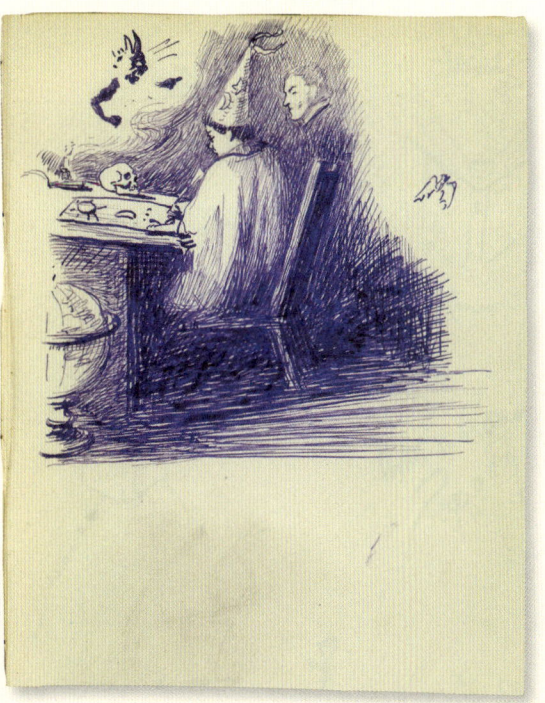

The Basket Maker

1901

"The Basket Maker," from *Little Jack of all Trades*, 1804. Plus illustration by Pamela Colman Smith

THE BASKET MAKER.

FROM the ozier by the brook,
   From the weeping willow's head,
Pliant, drooping boughs I took,
Of my spoils these baskets made.

Plaited, twin'd, and closely wove,
All their diff'rent uses try;
With their price my wants remove,
Gentle friends, my baskets buy.

Angler, this can hold thy fish,
Silk-made flys, and baits, and hooks;
Pretty girl, this to thy wish,
Holds thy dinner, work, and books.

BASKET-MAKING is a very ingenious and useful trade.
The baker, the butcher, the fruiterer, and fishman, and many others, are indebted to the Basket Maker for the convenient work of his hands.

Little Jack of all Trades. 1804.

1901

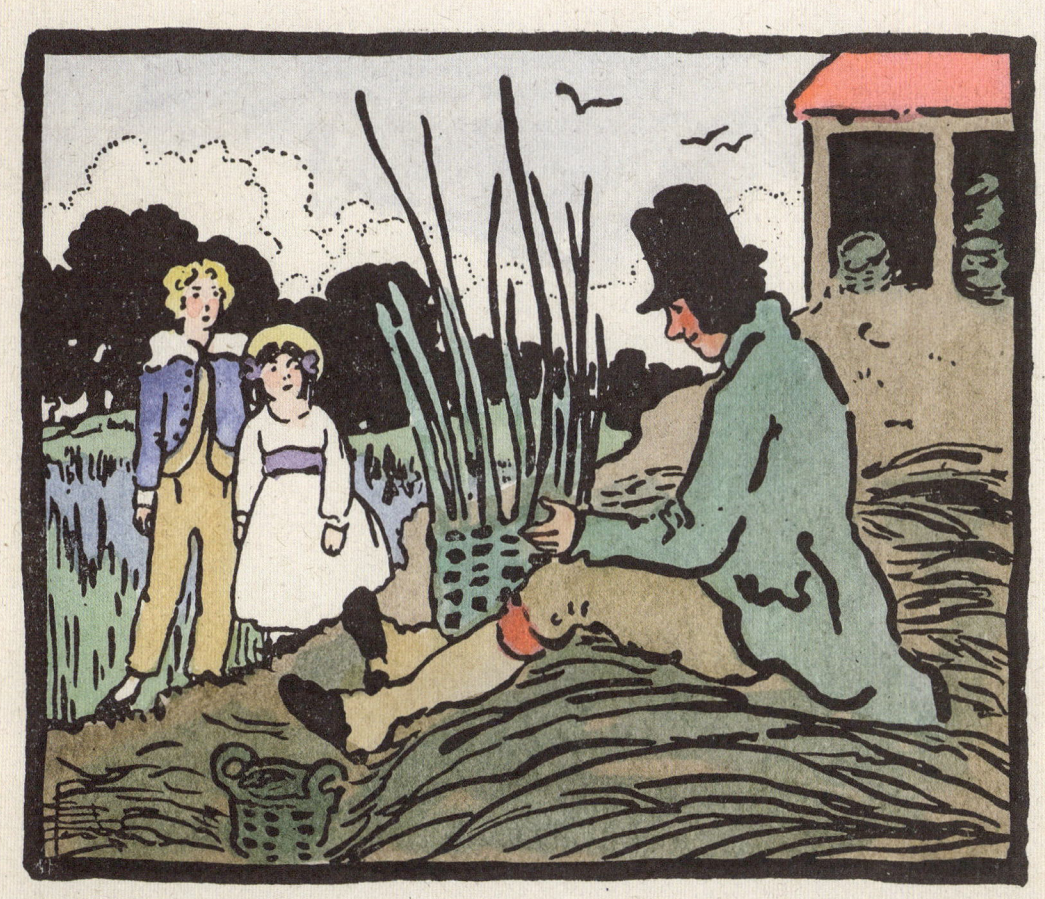

THE BASKET MAKER.   PAMELA COLMAN SMITH.

The Farm House

1901

"The Farmhouse," from *Little Truthes*, 1807. Plus illustration by Pamela Colman Smith

THE FARM HOUSE.

WHAT a fine prospect on this rising ground; Green fields and pleasant plants surround us.
Observe the farmhouse under yon tall tree.
But what makes the top look yellow?
The top of our house looks red.
The top of the farmhouse is thatched—that is, covered with straw, made tight with twigs and wooden pegs.
It looks neat when first done, keeps out wind and water, and comes cheap to the farmer.

Little Truthes. 1807.

1901

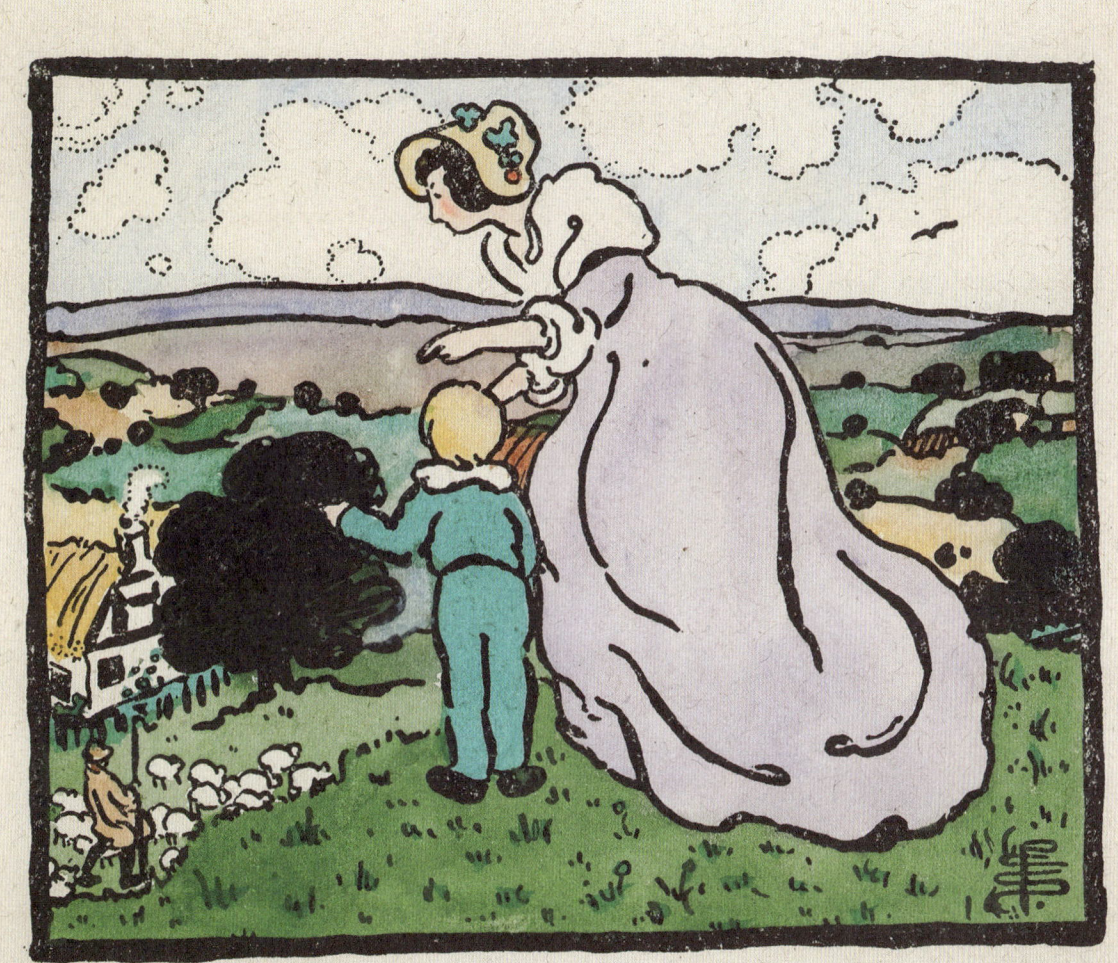

OBSERVE THE FARMHOUSE UNDER YON TALL TREE.   PAMELA COLMAN SMITH

THE WIND

THE wind blows.
   Which way does the wind blow?
   Take out your handkerchief.
Throw it up.
The wind blows this way.
The wind comes from the North.
The wind is North.
It is a cold wind.
The wind was West yesterday, then it was warm.
Rain comes from the clouds.
Look, there are black clouds.
How fast they move along!
Now they have hid the sun.
They have covered up the sun, just as you cover up
Your face when you throw a handkerchief over it.
There is a little bit of blue sky still.
Now there is no blue sky at all; it is all black
With the clouds.
It is very dark, like night.
It will rain soon.

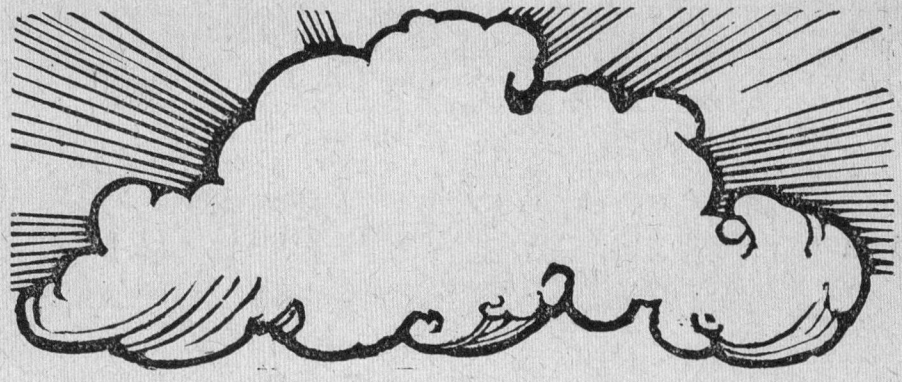

1901

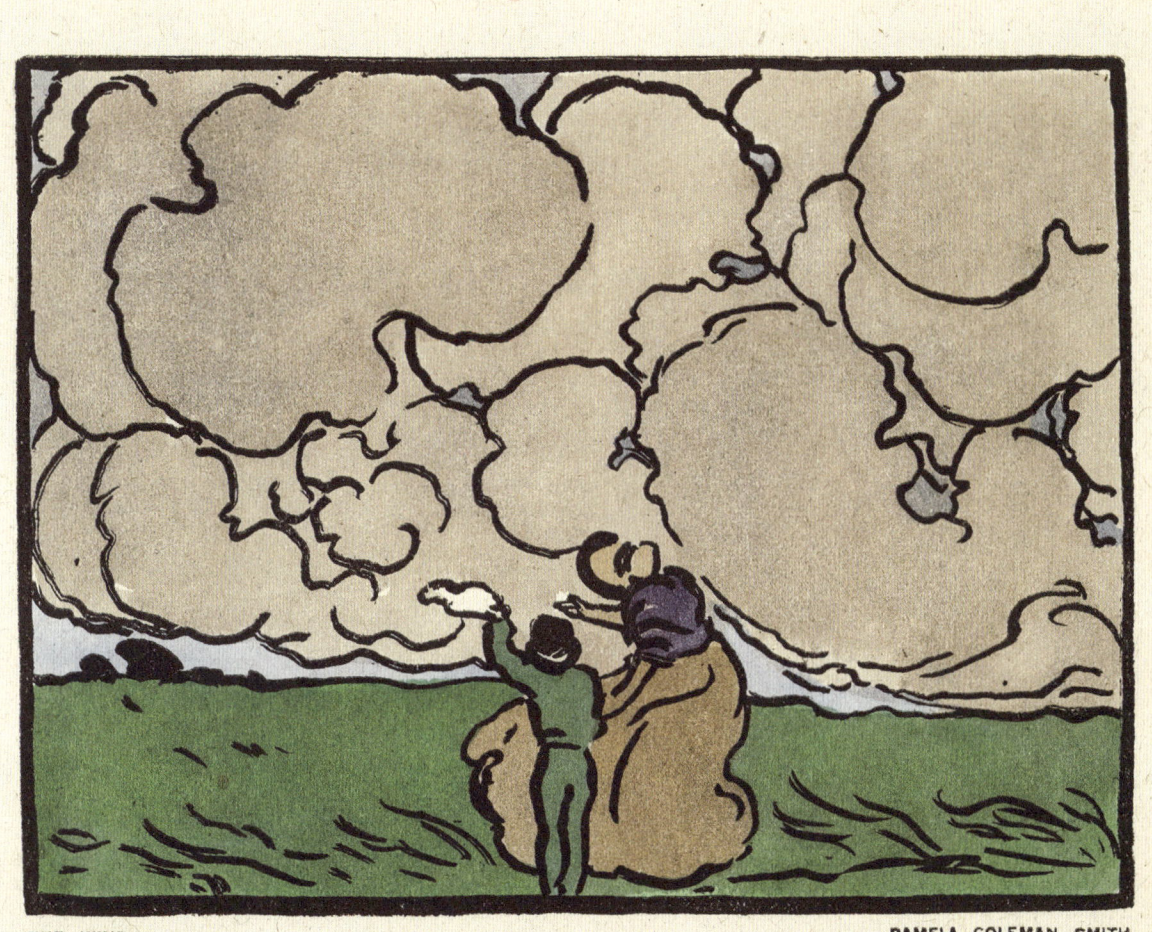

"The Wind" poem plus illustration by
Pamela Colman Smith, circa 1901

1902 to 1904

1902

A Broad Sheet

In 1901, Pamela Colman Smith's most important work was her collaboration with Jack Yeats and others on a monthly illustrated periodical called *A Broad Sheet*, which began its first publication January, 1902. The single sheets measuring 15" x 20" were printed on one side with literature and hand-colored illustrations

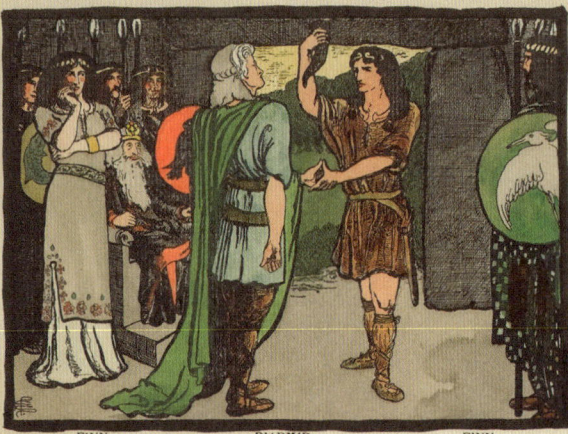

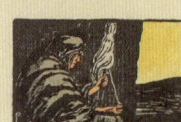

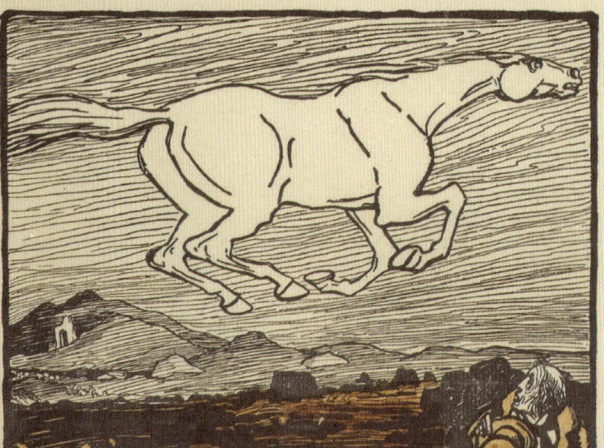

A BROAD SHEET

FEBRUARY, 1902

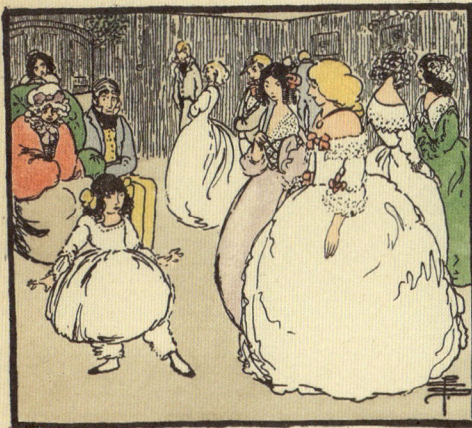

THE RECITATION
Pamela Prettijohn on her birthday reciting "The Brigand's Bride" for Grandmamma and Grandpapa Prettijohn and the assembled family.

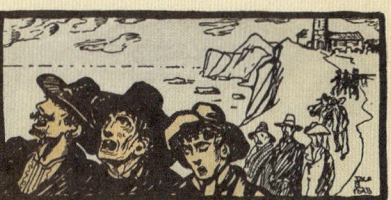

FROM THE FRENCH OF PAUL FORT
Englished by F. YORK POWELL

The pretty maid she died, she died, in love-bed
   as she lay;
They took her to the churchyard: all at the
   break of day;
They laid her all alone there: all in her
   white array;
They laid her all alone there: a-coffin'd in
   the day;
And they came back so merrily: all at the
   dawn of day;
A-singing all so merrily: "The dog must have his
   day!"
The pretty maid is dead, is dead: in love-bed
   as she lay;
And they are off a-field to work: as they do
   every day.

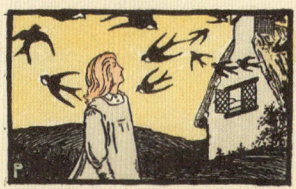

EVENING
By MARIELLA YORK POWELL

The swallows are flying round the
   house,
   The swallows are flying round
     my head;
They say good-night as they fly,
   I say good-night in my bed.

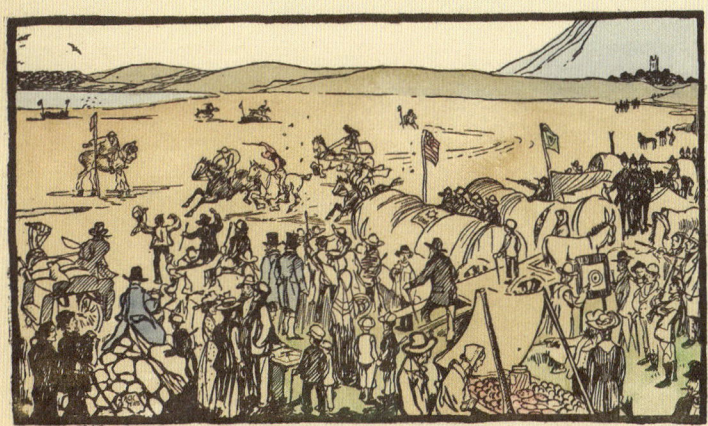

THE BACK STRAND RACES, SLIGO

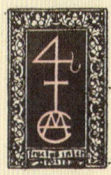

Post free, 12 Shillings a Year. In America, 3 Dollars a Year. A Specimen Copy may be had 13 Pence, post free.
PUBLISHED AND SOLD BY ELKIN MATHEWS, VIGO STREET, LONDON, W.

No. 2   All Rights Reserved   FARNCOMBE & SON, PRINTERS, CROYDON

A BROAD SHEET

MARCH, 1902

1902

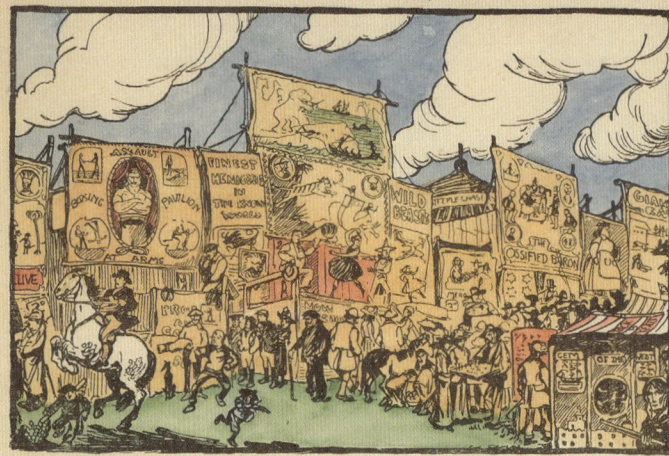

SHOWS AT THE FAIR

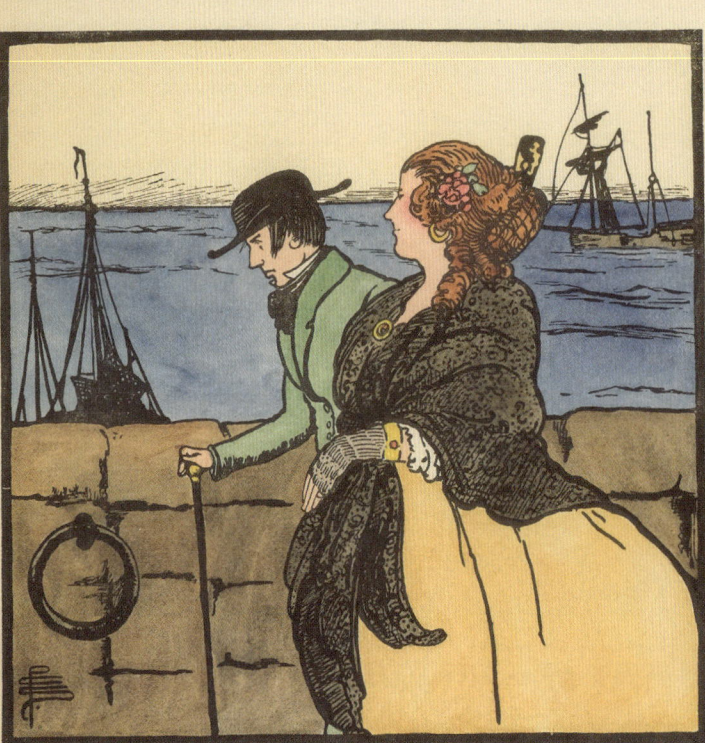

THE BETTER HORSE IS THE OLD GREY MARE, OR MARRIED
TO A PIRATE'S WIDOW

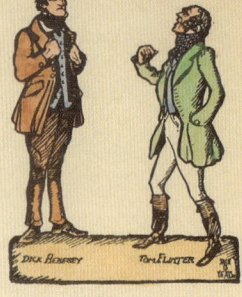

DIALOGUE
between
Tom Flinter and his Man,
by
Ned, the Dog Stealer

TOM FLINTER. **Dick!** said he.
DICK HENESEY. **What?** said he.
TOM FLINTER. **Fetch me my hat,** says he;
For I will go, says he;
To Timahoe, says he;
To buy the Fair, says he;
And all that's there, says he.
DICK HENESEY. *Arrah! Pay what you owe!* said he;
And *then* you may go, says he;
To Timahoe, says he;
To buy the Fair, says he;
And all that's there, says he.
TOM FLINTER. **Well! by this and by that,** said he;
Dick! *Hang up my hat!* says he.

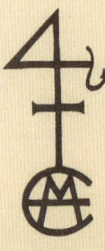

Hand coloured. Post free, 12 Shillings a Year. In America, 3 Dollars a Year. A Specimen Copy may be had
13 Pence, post free.
PUBLISHED AND SOLD BY ELKIN MATHEWS, VIGO STREET, LONDON, W.
No. 3   All Rights Reserved

FARNCOMBE & SON, PRINTERS, CROYDON

A BROAD SHEET

APRIL, 1902

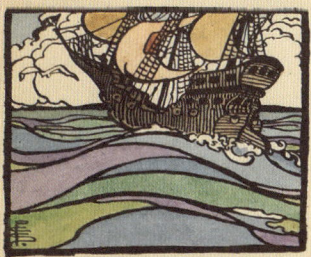

The merry wind,
The rolling sea,
The blazing sun,
The seagulls free.
Henry Morgan,
Thus sailed he.
    P. C. S.

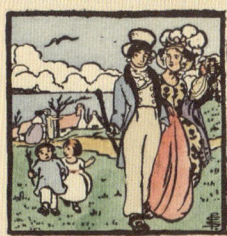

She got a shore tailor
To rig up her sailor
In fine nankeen breeches
And long blue-tailed coat.
He looked like a squire
For all to admire,
With a dimity handkerchief
Tied round his throat.
    "*In Cawsand Bay.*"

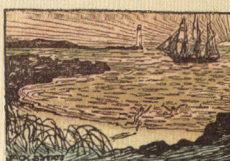

A 1,000 miles to Rosses,
A 1,000 miles away;
A 1,000 miles to Rosses,
Where they keep the old salt say.
    J. B. Y.

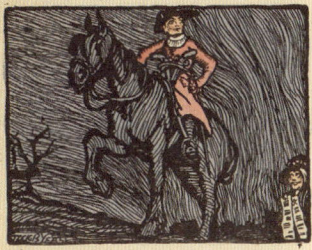

With his long sword, saddle horse, and pistols,
    going thieving O!
Whack-fol-di-riddy-iddy-tiddy-ol-di-ray.
    "*Jack Sheppard.*"

Oh, dear, oh!
The true history of Jack Sheppard I'm
    letting you know.
When Jack got into trouble—that's polite for
    being taken—
And all his amiabilities couldn't save his bacon,
What a pity such a model robber got in such
    a string, sir!
But none can deny in his profession that he
    had his swing, sir.
Oh, dear, oh!
They wasn't very particular them days,
Oh, no!
    "*Jack Sheppard.*"

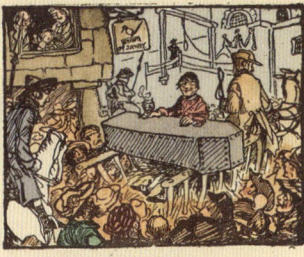

So he went up Holborn Hill—in a cart,
And took a parting gill—in the cart
He went up Holborn Hill,
And he never made no will,
And at Tyburn *Ketch* with skill—did his part.
    "*Jack Sheppard.*"

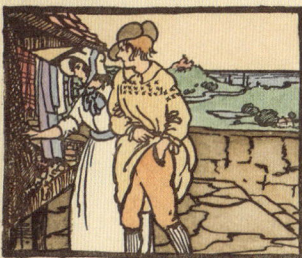

My love, she was good,
And my love, she was kind too,
And many were the happy hours
Between my love and me;
I never could refuse her
Whatever she'd a mind to.
But now she's far away,
Far across the stormy sea.
"*All round my Hat I will wear a Green Willow.*"

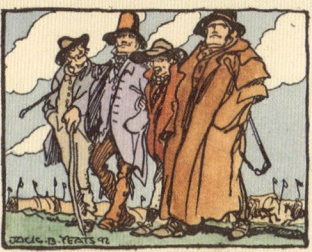

Come gather round, and don't make wry faces,
'Till I tell you a tale of the Cumeen races,
Of Micky Mack and John Devine,
Mulsheen Connor and Gash o' Wine.
    Old Song.

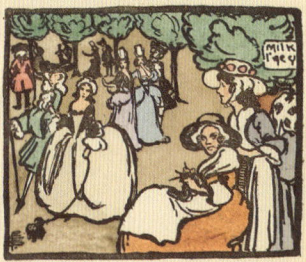

What a fine thing I have seen to-day,
O mother, a hoop!
I pray let me have one, and do not say nay!
O mother, a hoop!
    "*O Mother, a Hoop!*"

Hand coloured. Post free, 12 Shillings a Year. In America, 3 Dollars a Year. A Specimen Copy may be had
13 Pence, post free.

PUBLISHED AND SOLD BY ELKIN MATHEWS, VIGO STREET, LONDON, W.

No. 4   All Rights Reserved   FARNCOMBE & SON, PRINTERS, CROYDON

A BROAD SHEET

MAY, 1902

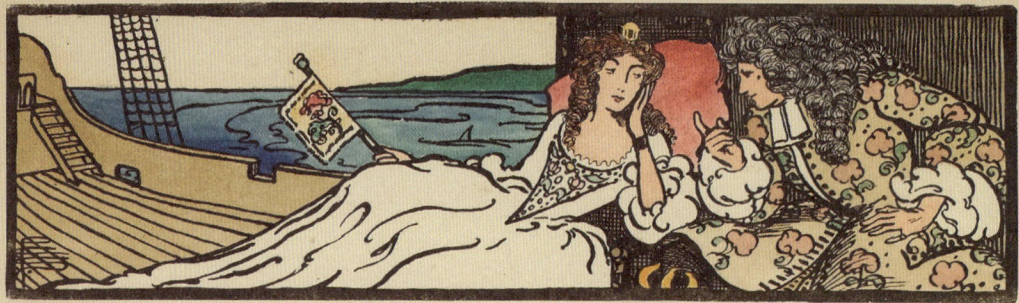

THE SAILOR AND THE SHARK.

A SONG FROM THE FRENCH OF PAUL FORT.   ENGLISHED BY F. YORK POWELL.

All in a good sea-boat, my boys, we fear no wind that blows!

There was a queen that fell in love with a jolly sailor bold,
But he shipped to the Indies, where he would seek for gold.
    All in, &c.

There was a king that had a fleet of ships both tall and tarred;
He carried off this pretty queen, and she jump'd overboard.
    All in, &c.

The queen, the queen is overboard! a shark was cruising round,
He swallowed up this dainty bit alive and safe and sound.
    All in, &c.

Within the belly of this shark it was both dark and cold,
But she was faithful still and true to her jolly sailor bold.
    All in, &c.

This shark was sorry for her, and swam away so fast.
In the Indies, where the camels are, he threw her up at last.
    All in, &c

On one of these same goodly beasts, all in a palanquin,
She spied her own true love again—the Emperor of Tonquin.
    All in, &c.

She called to him, "O stay, my love, your queen is come, my dear."
"Oh I've a thousand queens more fair within my kingdom here."
    All in, &c.

"You smell of the grave so strong, my dear." "I've sailed in a shark," says she.
"It is not of the grave I smell; but I smell of the fish of the sea."
    All in, &c.

"My lady loves they smell so sweet; of rice-powder so fine.
The queen the King of Paris loves no sweeter smells than mine."
    All in, &c.

She got aboard the shark again, and weeping went her way;
The shark swam back again so fast to where the tall ships lay.
    All in, &c.

The king he got the queen again, the shark away he swam.
The queen was merry as could be, and mild as any lamb.
    All in a good sea-boat, my boys, we fear no wind that blows!

Now all you pretty maidens what love a sailor bold,
You'd better ship along with him before his love grows cold.

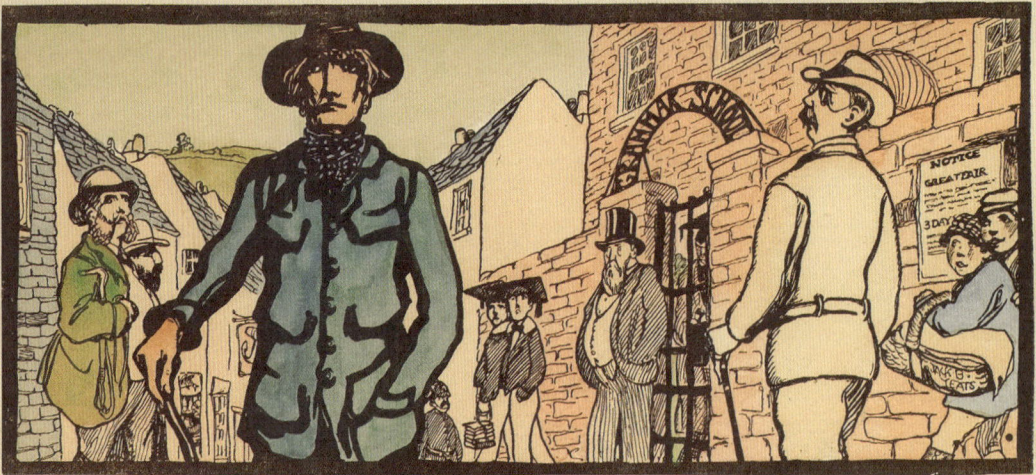

THE GYPSY.

Hand coloured. Post free, 12 Shillings a Year. In America, 3 Dollars a Year. A Specimen Copy may be had 13 Pence, post free.

PUBLISHED AND SOLD BY ELKIN MATHEWS, VIGO STREET, LONDON, W.

No. 5   All Rights Reserved   FARNCOMBE & SON, PRINTERS, CROYDON

A BROAD SHEET

JUNE, 1902

PICTURES BY MISS PAMELA COLMAN SMITH AND JACK B. YEATS.

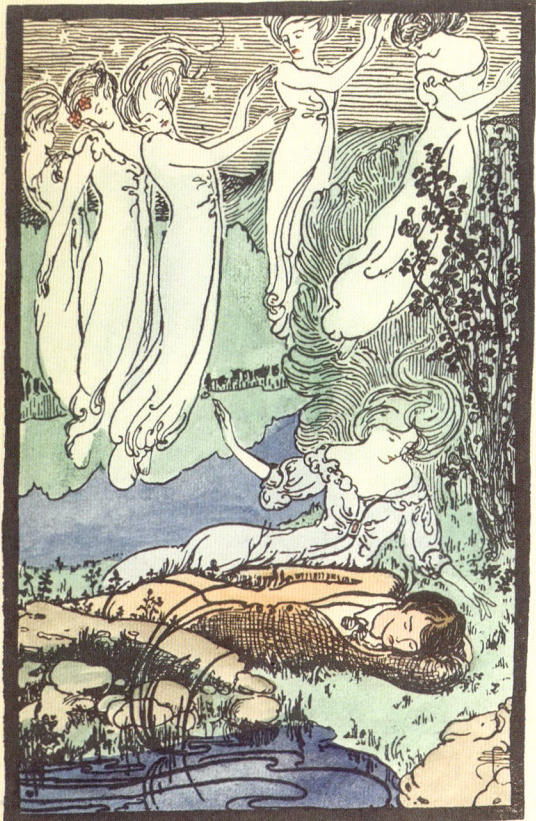

THE GATES OF DREAMLAND.

It's a lonely road through bogland to the lake at Carrowmore,
And a sleeper there lies dreaming, where the water laps the shore.
Though the moth wings of the twilight in their purples are unfurled,
Yet his sleep is filled with music by the masters of the world.

There's a hand is white as silver that is fondling with his hair,
There are glimmering feet of sunshine that are dancing by him there,
And half open lips of faery that were dyed to richest red
In their revels where the Hazel Tree its holy clusters shed.

"Come away," the red lips whisper, "all the world is weary now,
'Tis the twilight of the ages, and it's time to quit the plough.
Oh, the very sunlight's weary ere it lightens up the dew,
And its gold is changed to grey light before it falls to you."

"Though your colleen's heart is tender, a tenderer heart is near;
What's the starlight in her glances when the stars are shining clear?
Who would kiss the fading shadow, when the flower face glows above?
'Tis the Beauty of all Beauty that is calling for your love."

Oh, the mountain gates of dreamland have opened once again,
And the sound of song and dancing falls upon the ears of men;
And the Land of Youth lies gleaming, lit with rainbow light and mirth,
And the old enchantment lingers in the honey heart of earth.

A. E.

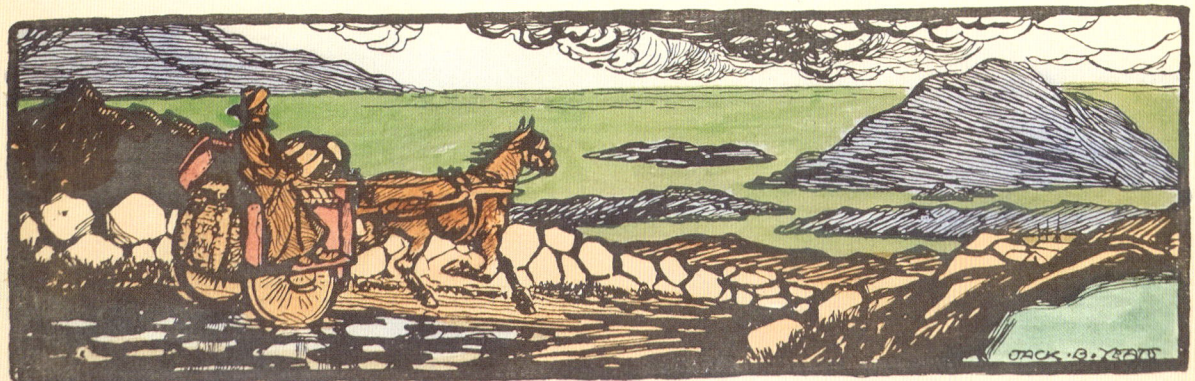

THE MAIL CAR.

A BROAD SHEET

JULY, 1902

PICTURES BY MISS PAMELA COLMAN SMITH AND JACK B. YEATS.

SONG.

Though a wild red star
Fling its traces to the wind,
And unbridled, unconfined,
Into dark unfathomed leap,
Yet the glittering cohorts sweep
With unshaken ranks afar.

Though a wild red soul,
Burning with untamed desire,
Frail as flame and fierce as fire,
Plunge in everlasting night,
Strong white souls with steadfast light,
Star the world from pole to pole.

WILFRID WILSON GIBSON.

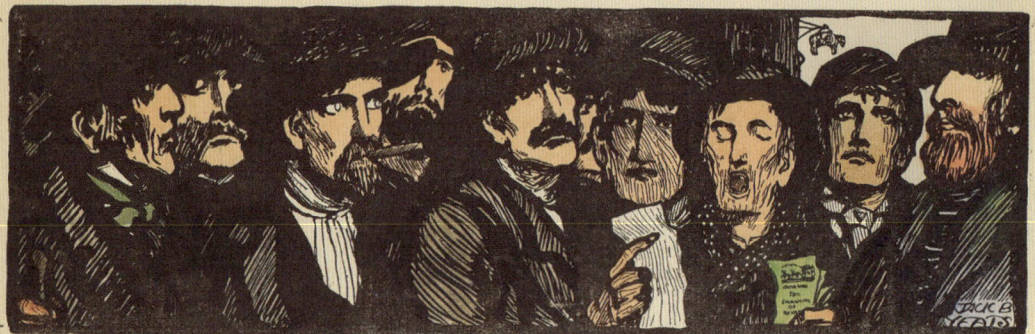

A SLIGO BALLAD SINGER.

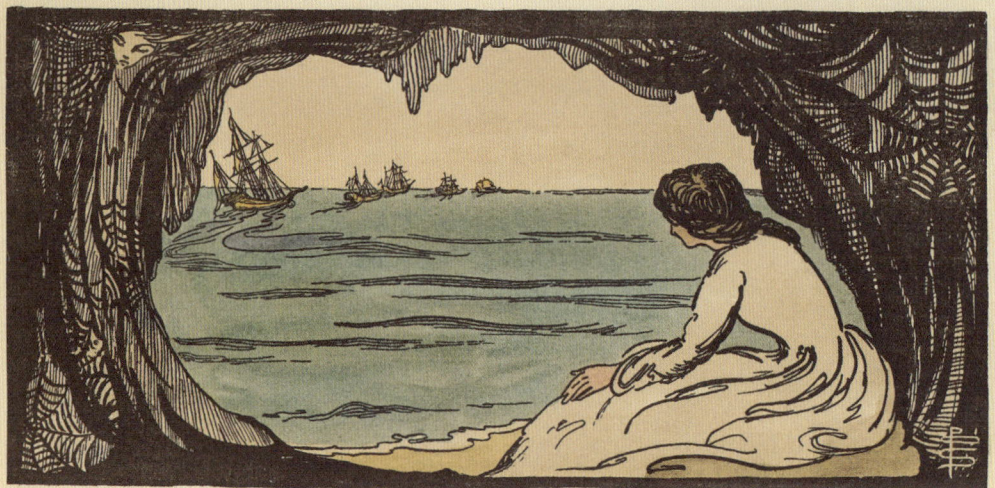

The cobweb cloak of Time has dropped between the world and me,
The Rainbow ships of memory have drifted out to sea.

P. C. S.

Hand coloured. Post free. 12 Shillings a Year. In America, 3 Dollars a Year. A Specimen Copy may be had 13 Pence, post free.

PUBLISHED AND SOLD BY ELKIN MATHEWS, VIGO STREET, LONDON, W.

No. 7   All Rights Reserved

FARNCOMBE & SON, PRINTERS, CROYDON

A BROAD SHEET

AUGUST, 1902
PICTURES BY PAMELA COLMAN SMITH AND JACK B. YEATS.

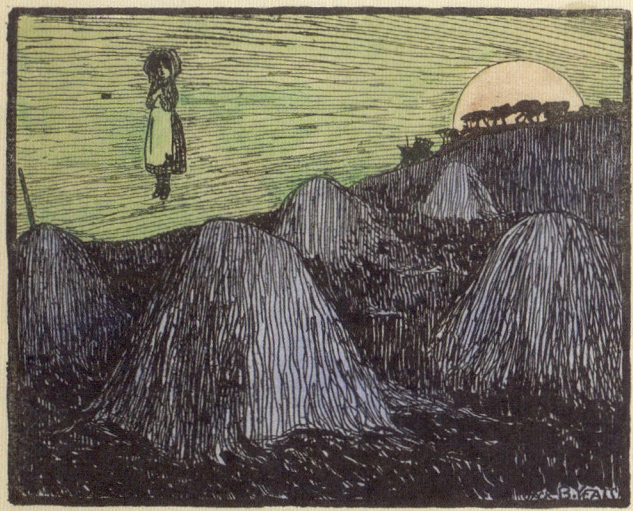

LITTLE LIZA.

Don't you hear me callin', callin' at the fallin' of the May?
I'm the ghost of little Liza, as was smothered in the hay.

    ▸ ▸ ▸ ▸ ▸ ▸

For it fell upon a Sunday, just about this time of day,
I went out with lots of others for to romp among the hay.
We was happy, oh! so happy, we did run and screech and shout,
And we clapper-clawed each other as we flung the hay about.
There was me and Cousin Minnie as was running after Jim,
When he fell across a furrow, and I fell on top of him,
And they heaped a haycock on us; Jim, he was rumbusticall;
Out he wriggled, but I couldn't, 'cause you see I was so small,
And they never thought of Liza as they laughed and tore away,
Never thought of little Liza, as was buried in the hay.
It was just as if a mountain had a fell atop my head,
First I tried to kick and struggle, then I tried to scream instead,
Then at last I grew quite quiet, and a stunning, buzzing sound
Filled my ears, 'twas just as if the field was going round and
   round.
All that night, and early Monday, underneath the pook I lay,
Until father came next morning for to stackle up the hay.
Father'd been abed all Sunday, tired with mowing of the grass,
And I hadn't got no mammy for to wonder where I was.
Then the man as was a tossing of the cocks into the cart,
Sticks his pitchfork in my pinny, then he stops and gives a start,
But he didn't go to hurt me, an' you musn't think he did,
Even father never wondered where his little girl was hid.
So they drove me to the village, with my Sunday pinny torn,
Stretched upon the big hay waggon—dead, against the rising
   morn,
And the clergyman next Sunday told of where all hurts are
   healed,
An' he buried me for nothink, 'cause he said it was *his* field.

    ▸ ▸ ▸ ▸ ▸ ▸

Don't you hear me callin', callin' at the fallin' of the May?
I'm the ghost of little Liza, as was smothered in the hay.
                                                     ANON
By permission of the Editors of "Longman's Magazine."

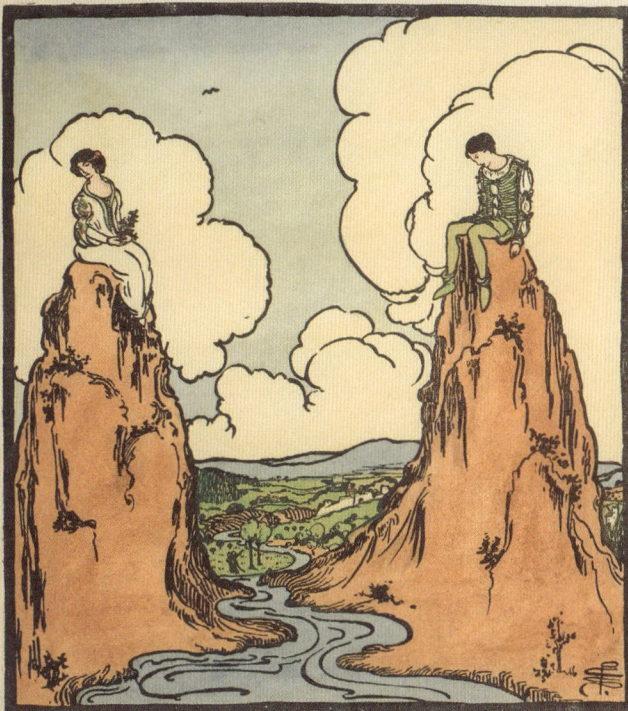

THE MOUNTAIN LOVERS.

Was it for this we loved, O Time, to be
Among Love's deathless through eternity,
Set high on lone divided peaks above,
The sheltered summer valley spreads between?
Was it for this our joy, our grief has been,
Our barren daydreams, dream-deserted nights,
That valley lovers, looking up, might see
How vain is Love among the starry heights,
And loving sigh, "How vain a thing is love"?

O Love, that we had found thee in the shade,
Where all day long the deep leaf-hidden glade
Hears but the moan of some forsaken dove,
Or the clear song of happy nameless streams,
Where all night long the August moonlight gleams
Through warm green dusk, no longer cold and white;
O Love, that we had found thee unafraid
One summer morn and followed thee till night,
As unknown valley lovers follow Love.
                      WILFRID WILSON GIBSON.

Hand coloured. Post free. 12 Shillings a Year. In America, 3 Dollars a Year. A Specimen Copy may be had 13 Pence, post free.

PUBLISHED AND SOLD BY ELKIN MATHEWS, VIGO STREET, LONDON, W.

No. 8   All Rights Reserved   FARNCOMBE & SON, PRINTERS, CROYDON

A BROAD SHEET

SEPTEMBER, 1902

PICTURES BY PAMELA COLMAN SMITH AND JACK B. YEATS.

IT IS SEPTEMBER.

We must gather apples—
No, you cannot go up the ladder;
You must have a little basket,
And pick up apples under the tree.
Shake the tree;
Down they come!
How many have you got?
We will have an apple dumpling.
Come, you must help to carry the apples
   to the apple-chamber.
Apples make cider.
          Mrs. BARBAULD.

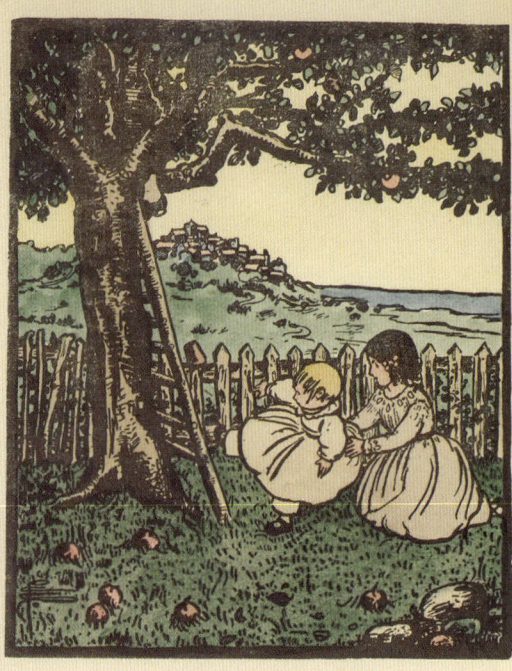

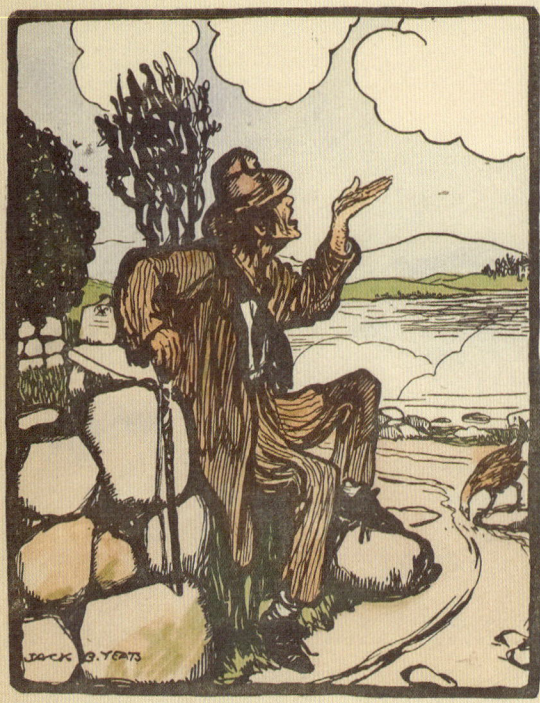

Translated by Lady Gregory from the "Repentance" of Raftery, the Blind Connaught Poet, whose songs are known in every Irish-speaking county of Ireland.

"O King in heaven, I scream to Thee again, and out aloud, for it is Thy grace I am looking for.

"I am in age and my form is withered, it is many a day I have been going astray.

"When I was young my deeds were bad, I delighted greatly in quarrels and rows. It was better to me to be playing or drinking on a Sunday morning than to be going to Mass. I was given to big oaths, and I did not let lust and drunkenness pass me by.

"The day is stolen away, and I have not raised the hedge until the crop Thou didst delight in is destroyed. I am a stake worth nothing in a corner of a hedge, or I am like a boat after losing its rudder, that would be broken against a rock in the sea, and that would be drowned in the cold waves."

Hand coloured. Post free. 12 Shillings a Year. In America, 3 Dollars a Year. A Specimen Copy may be had 13 Pence, post free.

PUBLISHED AND SOLD BY ELKIN MATHEWS, VIGO STREET, LONDON, W.

No. 9   All Rights Reserved   FARNCOMBE & SON, PRINTERS, CROYDON.

A BROAD SHEET

OCTOBER, 1902

PICTURES BY PAMELA COLMAN SMITH AND JACK B. YEATS.

THE LADY OF THE SCARLET SHOES.

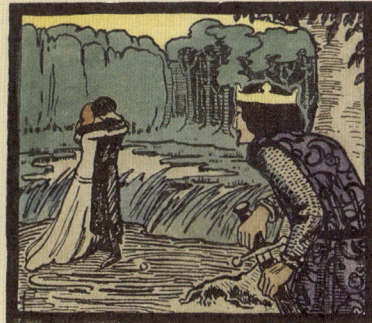

She wound her hair about her head,
  Red as the autumn trees,
While her lips flamed red, and her long eyes
    glowed
  Like amethystine seas;
And she bore herself with the stately grace
  Of a poplar in the breeze.

Over her ashen face she flung
  The white veil of a bride,
And without a pause, or a look, or turn
  Went pacing by his side;
What a king had sold—a king had bought
  (So onward flows the tide).

But as they passed along the aisle
  The king bent down his head,
And he shook like an aspen leaf, and turned
  As pale as do the dead;
Though her dress was white as a bride's should be,
  Her shoes were poppy red.

    *   *   *   *   *

"I saw you start at my scarlet shoes,
  I heard your breath come short;
My soul is his, though my body yours,
  Through the wrong that you have wrought.
I was a chattel to sell," she cried,
  "And you the merchant bought.

"You may remember, on Lammas Eve
  You found us in the wood,
My love and I, with arms entwined,
  As heart to heart we stood;
Your sword was sharp—and his back was turned,
  My feet were bathed in blood.

"Sold by a king, and bought by a king—
  Daughter and bride, a slave;
But the sacrament of blood that binds
  'Twas you alone who gave;
And whether I live as widow or wife,
  Or sleep in an unknown grave,

"I shall reign a queen, my haughty face
  No bleeding heart shall tell;
But the blood and scorn of two lovers wronged
  You shall remember well;
For my feet will be shod with scarlet shoes
  Till we meet again in hell."

    *   *   *   *   *

In an ancient chapel far away
  Among the sculptured dead,
There lies a lady wondrous fair,
  A crown upon her head;
Though her marble form is white as snow
  Her shoes are poppy red.

Alix Egerton.

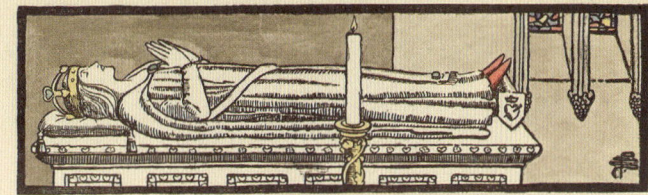

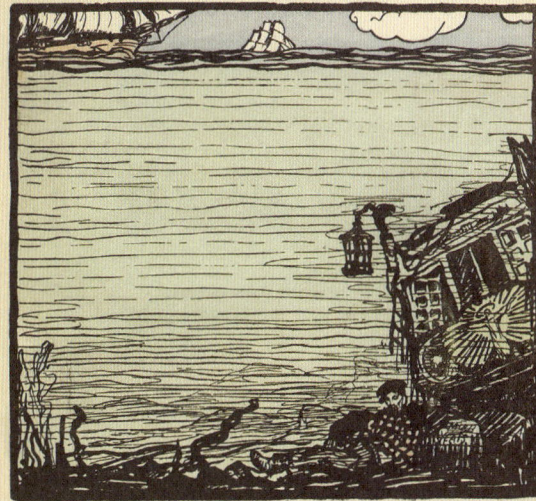

A LAST PRAYER.

"When the last sea is sailed, and the last shallow charted,
  When the last field is reaped, and the last harvest stored,
When the last fire is out, and the last guest departed,
  Grant the last prayer that I shall pray: be good to me, O Lord.

"And let me pass in a night at sea, a night of storm and
    thunder;
  In the loud crying of the wind through rope, and sail, and spar,
Send me a ninth great peaceful wave to whelm and roll me
    under,
  To the cold tunny fishes' home, where the drowned galleons
    are.

"And in the dim green quiet place, far out of sight and hearing,
  Grant I may hear at whiles the wash and thrash of the sea-
    foam
About the fine keen bows of the stately clippers steering
  Towards the bright northern star and the fair ports of home."

John Masefield.

Hand coloured. Post free. 12 Shillings a Year. In America, 3 Dollars a Year. A Specimen Copy may be had 13 Pence, post free.

PORTFOLIOS, to hold 24 copies, may be had, price Two Shillings each, or Two Shillings and Sixpence Post Free.

PUBLISHED AND SOLD BY ELKIN MATHEWS, VIGO STREET, LONDON, W.

No. 10   All Rights Reserved   FARNCOMBE & SON, PRINTERS, CROYDON.

A BROAD SHEET
NOVEMBER, 1902
PICTURES BY PAMELA COLMAN SMITH AND JACK B. YEATS.

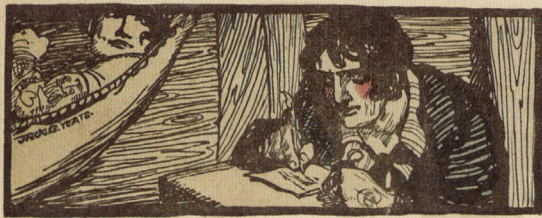

"TO ALL YOU LADIES."

To all you ladies now on land,
 We men at sea indite,
But first would have you understand
 How hard it is to write—
The Muses now, and Neptune,
We now implore to write to you.

For though the Muses should prove kind,
 And fill our empty brain,
Yet if rough Neptune rouse the wind
 To wave the azure main,
Our paper, pen, and ink, and we
Roll up and down our ships at sea.
                    Old Song.

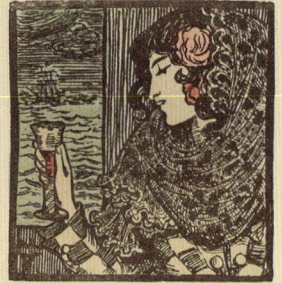

"HEALTH TO THE OUTWARD BOUND."

Fill, fill the sparkling bumper,
 Fill, for the moments fly;
The stars heavy clouds dimmer,
 The moon fades from the sky.
Drink, for the signal flag is up,
 The wind is veering round;
In haste let us drink a parting cup
To the health of the Outward Bound.

Fill high the toast, to-morrow
 No toast or jest shall be,
But a few will meet in sorrow,
 While many plough the sea.
As yet we are glad together,
 Let the glad toast circle round,
"Full sails and prosperous weather,
 And a health to the Outward Bound."
                    Old Song.

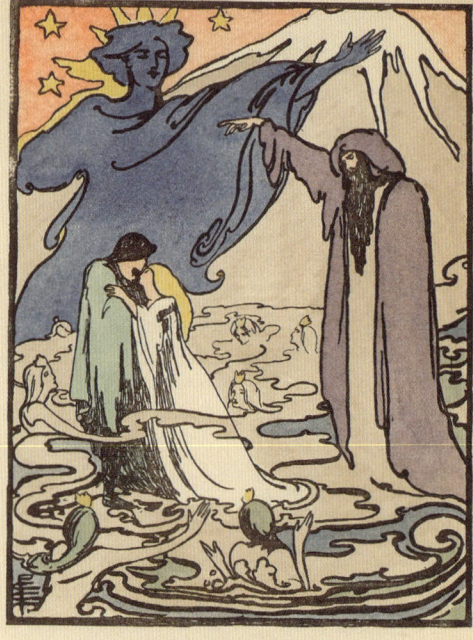

"THE ENCHANTMENT OF CATHVAH."
FROM "DEIRDRE," A PLAY BY A. E.

Cathvah the Druid (without).
 "Let thy waves rise,
 Mananann MacLir.
 Let the earth fall
 Beneath their feet.
 Let thy waves flow over them,
 Mananann,
 Lord of Ocean."

Naisi.
 "Our galley is sinking, and no land in sight. I did not think the end would come so soon. O pale love, take courage. Is death so bitter to thee? We shall go down in each other's arms; our hearts shall beat out their love together; and the last of life we shall know will be our kisses on each other's lips.
 (Ainle and Ardan struggle outside. There is a sound of blows and a low cry.)
 Ainle and Ardan have sunk in the waters! We are alone! Still weeping! My bird, my bird, soon we shall fly together to the bright kingdom in the West, to Hy Brazil amid the opal seas."

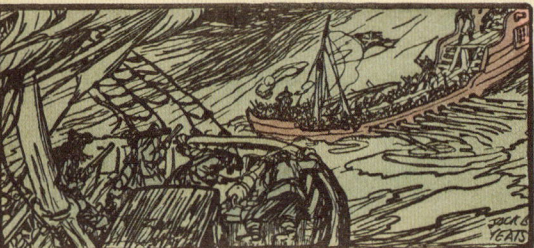

Another lay off Chinese coast for days on fearful tack,
The monsoon blowing in our teeth, the pirates at our back.

Hand coloured. Post free. 12 Shillings a Year. In America, 3 Dollars a Year. A Specimen Copy may be had
13 Pence, post free.
PORTFOLIOS, to hold 24 copies, may be had, price Two Shillings each, or Two Shillings and Sixpence Post Free.

PUBLISHED AND SOLD BY ELKIN MATHEWS, VIGO STREET, LONDON, W.

No. 11   All Rights Reserved   FARNCOMBE & SON, PRINTERS, CROYDON.

A BROAD SHEET

DECEMBER, 1902

PICTURES BY PAMELA COLMAN SMITH AND JACK B. YEATS.

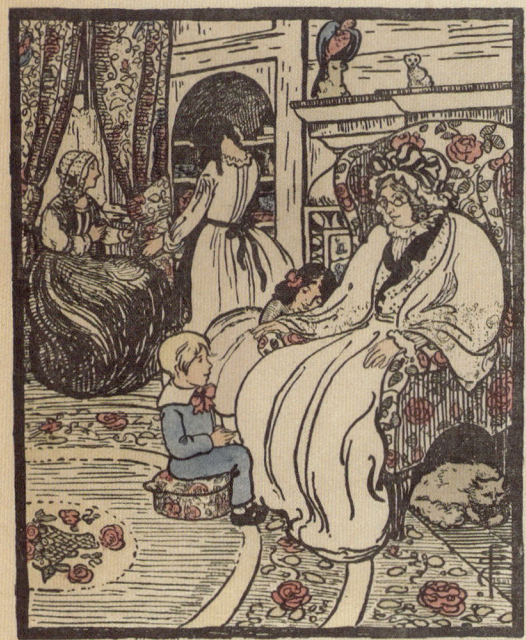

There's sand-bagging and throat-slitting,
   And quiet graves in the sea-slime.
Stabbing, of course, and rum-hitting,
   Dirt and drink and stink and crime.

All the day the wind's blowing
   From the sick swamp below the hills.
All the night the plague's growing,
   And the dawn brings the fever chills.

You get a thirst there's no slaking;
   A parched throat and fever shakes;
Tongue yellow and head aching,
   And then the sleep that never wakes.

And all the year the heat's baking,
   The sea rots and the earth quakes—
      In Spanish Port,
     Fever Port,
Port of Holy Peter.

John Masefield.

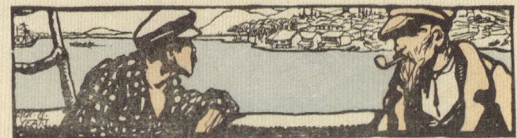

How many legs have fishes?
Fishes have no legs at all.
How do they walk then?
They do not walk;
They swim about in the water;
They live always in the water.
Charles could not live under the water.
No, because Charles is not a fish.
Mrs. Barbauld.

PORT OF HOLY PETER

The blue laguna rots and quivers,
   Dull, gurgling eddies twist and spin;
The climate does for people's livers,
   It's a nasty port to anchor in—
     Is Spanish Port,
    Fever Port,
Port of Holy Peter.

The town begins on the sea-beaches,
   And the town's mad with the stinging flies.
The drinking water's mostly leeches—
   It's a far remove from Paradise.

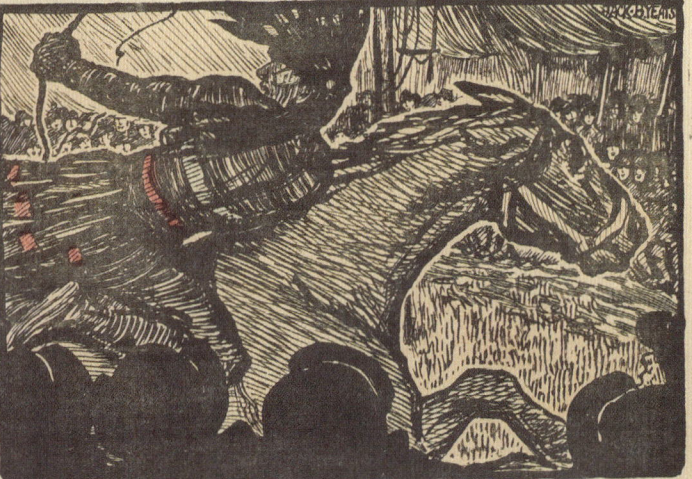

A CIRCUS INDIAN.

Hand coloured. Post free. 12 Shillings a Year. In America, 3 Dollars a Year. A Specimen Copy may be had 13 Pence, post free.

PORTFOLIOS, to hold 24 copies, may be had, price Two Shillings each, or Two Shillings and Sixpence Post Free.

PUBLISHED AND SOLD BY ELKIN MATHEWS, VIGO STREET, LONDON, W.

No. 12   All Rights Reserved   FARNCOMBE & SON PRINTERS, CROYDON.

Mistress Page

1902

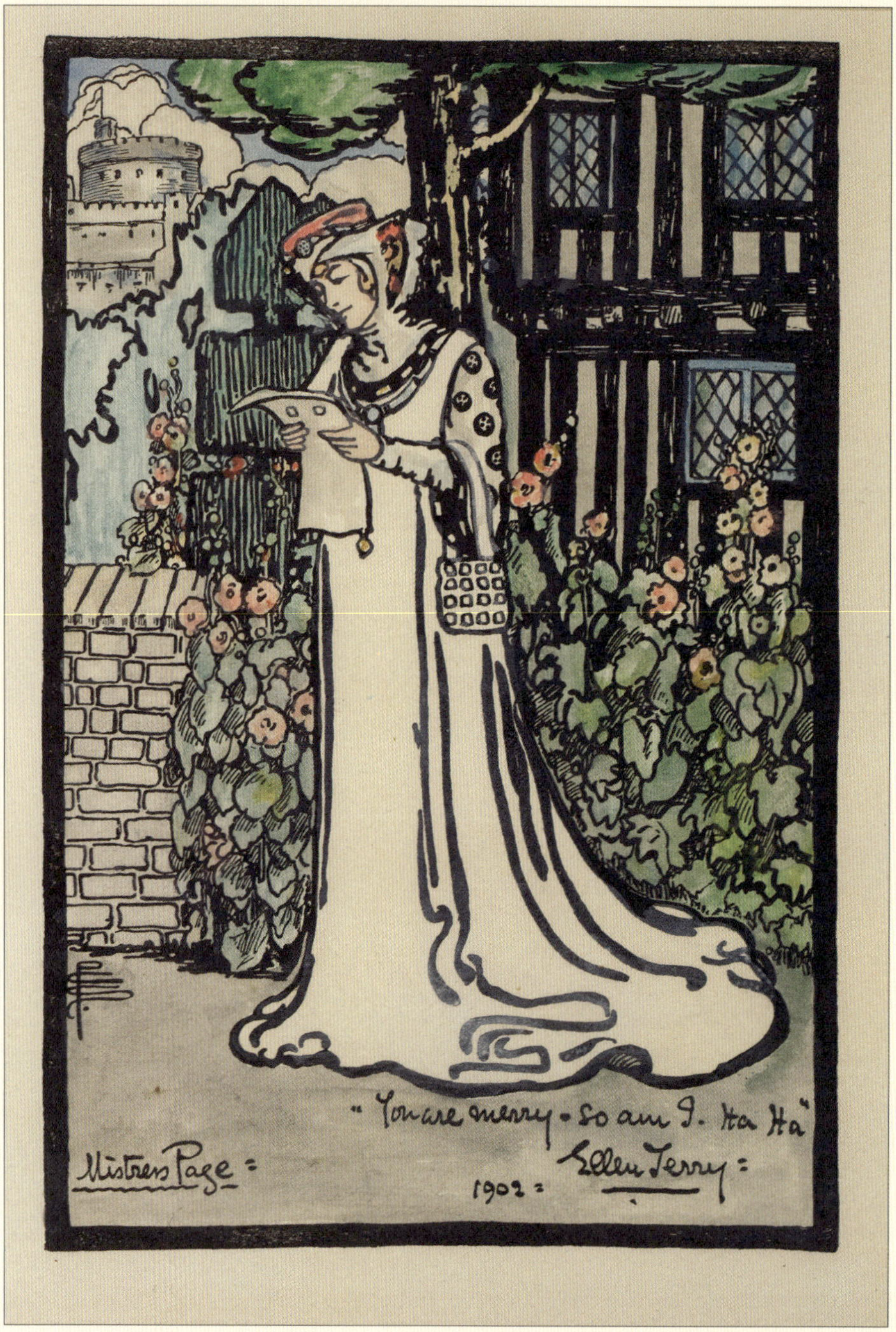

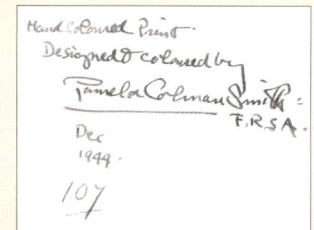

Ladies Reader

1903

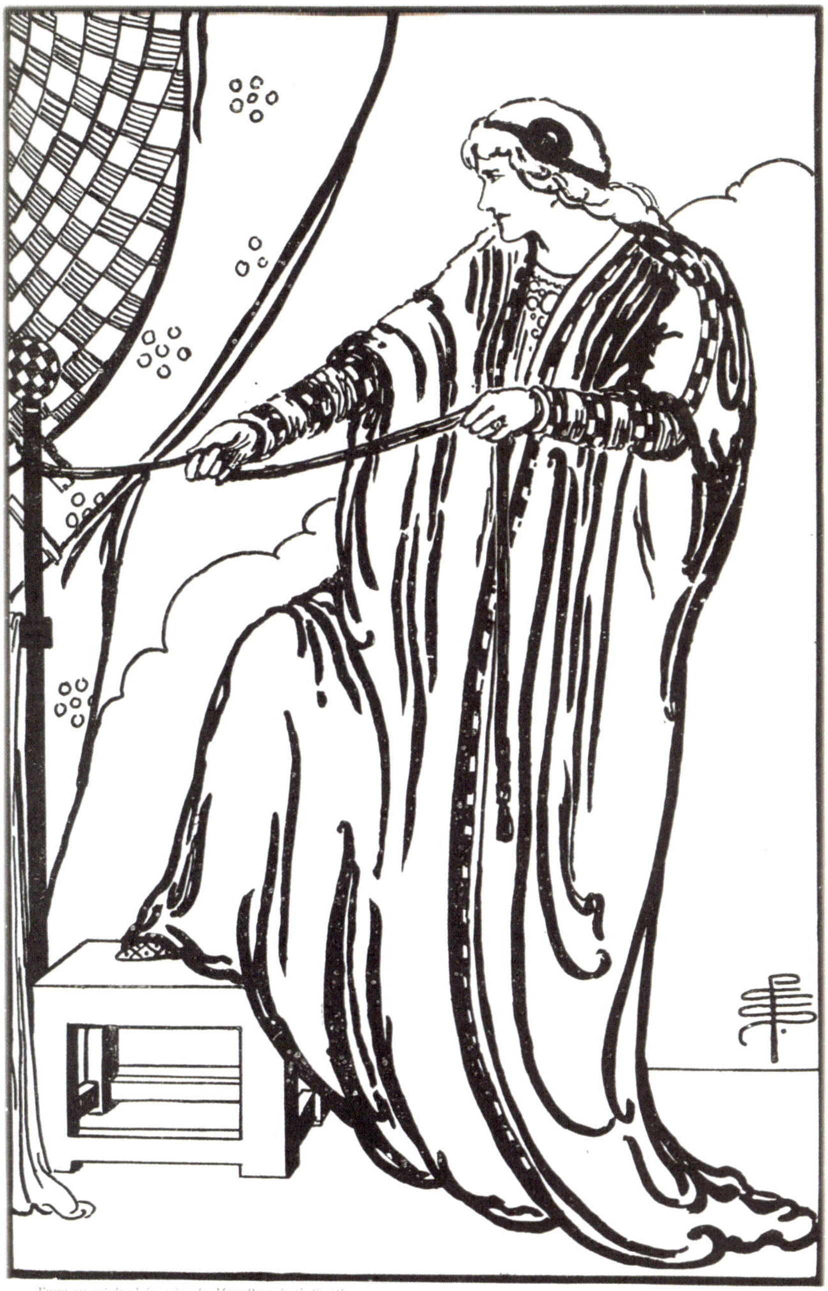

From an original drawing by Miss Pamela C. Smith.

MISS ELLEN TERRY,
As "Hjördis" in Ibsen's play, *The Vikings*.

The Lamp

1903

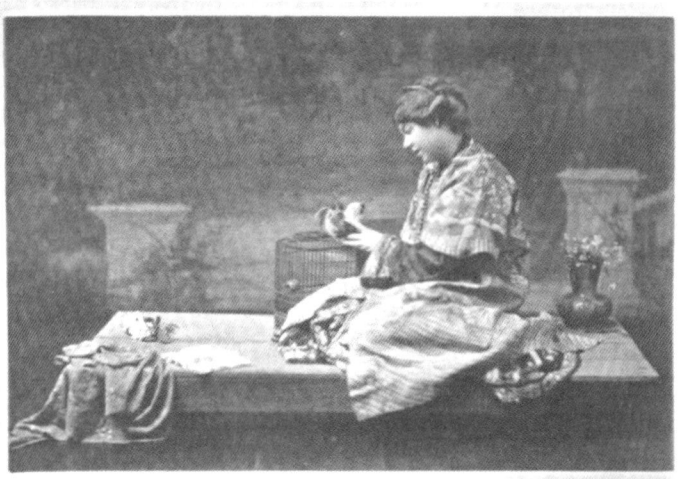

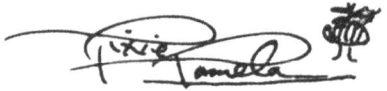

Review from "The Lamp," 1903, Vol. 26

When Pamela Coleman Smith lived in New York a few years ago we were accustomed to see such old-time ballads as "Widdicombe Fair," "The Green Bed," and "The Golden Vanity" pictured in a manner appreciative of their old-time quality. These drawings, with others, like the drawings made for "Macbeth," for W. B. Yeats's "Land of Heart's Desire," and the charming play-time pictures of children, won their way to the appreciative for their vivacity and quaintness in the telling as well as for the freshness of color and directness of design of which this young artist possessed the secret in a notable degree. When she moved to London it became a question whether the new environment would develop or destroy the freshness, the spontaneity, the naïve charm that owed everything to nature and little or nothing to the schools.

Fortunately she seems to have found in London the environment that even better conserves her inherent tendencies; and it is with the peculiar pleasure of finding something unique that one picks up the little publications of which she has been for a year or more the inspiration. Last year "The Broad Sheet" was published in association with Jack B. Yeats, brother of the Irish poet. It consisted of a single sheet showing two or more drawings, colored by hand; the accompanying verses were as brief as possible, scarcely more than captions.

This year Miss Smith brings out alone a folio of a few pages called "The Green Sheaf," and the prospectus sets forth thus the modest and alluring purposes of the editor:

"My *Sheaf* is small . . . but it is green. I will gather into my *Sheaf* all the young, fresh things I can—*pictures, verses, ballads* of *love* and *war;* tales of *pirates* and the *sea.*

"You will find the ballads of the *old world* in my *Sheaf.* Are they not green forever.

"Ripe ears are *good* for *bread,* but green ears are good for *pleasure.*

"I hope you will have my *Sheaf* in your house and like it.

"It will stay *fresh* and *green* then."

Among the contributors to "The Green Sheaf" are names known on this side as associated with the new Irish literary movement, such as Lady Gregory and W. B. Yeats. Besides these there will be verse and prose by Alex Egerton, Christopher St. John, Cecil French, John Masefield, and pictures by Gordon Craig, the Monsells, W. T. Horton, and Dorothy P. Ward.

But the largest contributor is Miss Smith herself.

14, MILBORNE GROVE,
THE BOLTONS,
LONDON, S.W.

You have been kind enough to support "A Broad Sheet," so I think it well to tell you that I have decided to transfer my services to another publication, somewhat of the same nature, to be called "*The Green Sheaf*," and of which I shall be the Editor.

The form of the new publication will be about the size of "Punch," and will consist of eight pages of literary matter, hand-coloured drawings, and wood-cuts.

These are the names of some of the contributors :—

Pictures.	*Letterpress.*
Æ.	A. E.
Gordon Craig.	Alix Egerton.
Cecil French.	Cecil French.
E. Monsell.	Lady Gregory.
J. Monsell.	Christopher St. John.
Pamela Colman Smith.	E. Harcourt Williams.
Dorothy P. Ward.	W. B. Yeats.

There will be thirteen numbers in the year, printed on Hand-made Demy 4to Paper, and the Subscription will be Thirteen Shillings, post free.

The First Number will be published on the 30th January, 1903.

Yours most truly,

Pamela Colman Smith

Æ and A.E were pseudonyms for George William Russell (1867-1935), an Irish nationalist, artist and mystic

Advertisement for The Green Sheaf

Opposite and 13 pages: After *A Broad Sheet* was discontinued, Pamela Colman Smith undertook a publishing venture with W.B. Yeats, initially to be called *The Hour-Glass*, from the title of a play by Yeats. The title of the magazine was changed to *The Green Sheaf* and each issue, starting in January 1903, had on its cover the illustration drawn by Pamela of a sheaf of green-colored papers gathered with a red ribbon

The Green Sheaf.

My *Sheaf* is small . . . but it is green.

I will gather into my *Sheaf* all the young fresh things I can—*pictures*, *verses*, *ballads* of *love* and *war*; tales of *pirates* and the *sea*.

You will find ballads of the *old world* in my *Sheaf*. Are they not green for ever . . .

Ripe ears are *good* for *bread*, but green ears are good for *pleasure*.

I hope you will have my *Sheaf* in your house and like it.

It will stay *fresh* and *green* then.

• • • • • • • • • •

There will be thirteen Numbers in the year, printed on Hand-made paper, and the Subscription will be Thirteen shillings annually, post free. Single Copies may be had at Thirteen pence each.

CONTRIBUTORS.

Pictures.	*Letterpress.*
Æ.	A. E.
GORDON CRAIG.	ALIX EGERTON.
CECIL FRENCH.	CECIL FRENCH.
W. T. HORTON.	LADY GREGORY.
E. MONSELL.	JOHN MASEFIELD.
J. MONSELL.	CHRISTOPHER ST. JOHN.
PAMELA COLMAN SMITH.	E. HARCOURT WILLIAMS.
DOROTHY P. WARD.	W. B. YEATS.

Edited and Published by PAMELA COLMAN SMITH,
14, MILBORNE GROVE, THE BOLTONS, LONDON, S.W.

ALL RIGHTS RESERVED.

The Green Sheaf

1903 to 1904

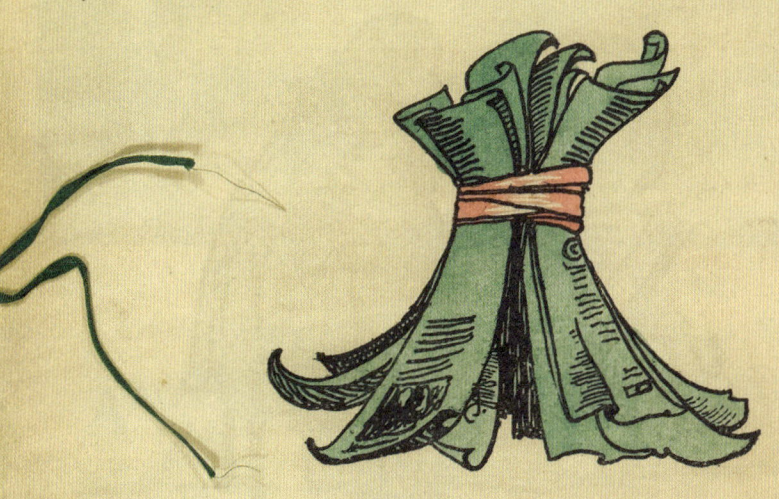

1903-1904

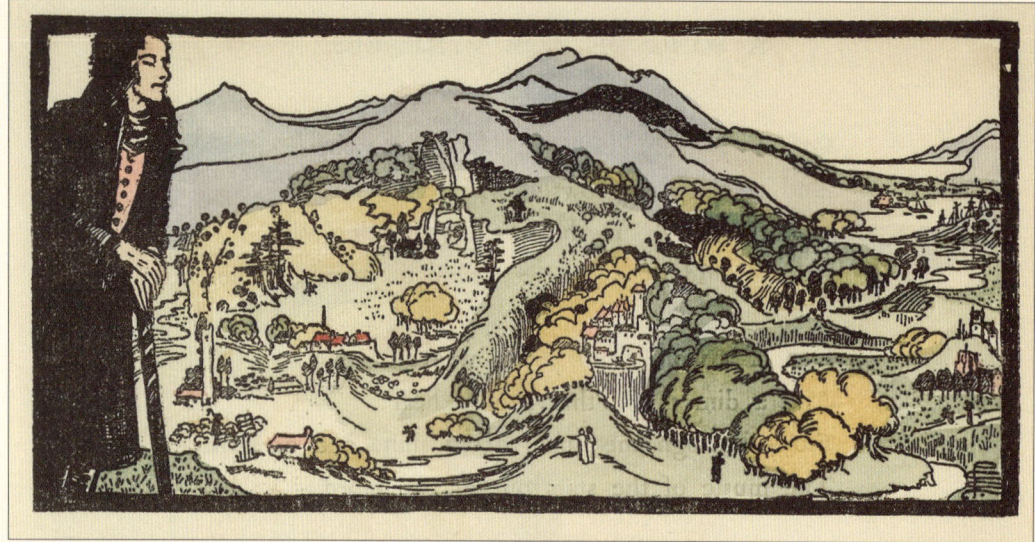

The Hill of Heart's Desire, *The Green Sheaf*, 1903, No. 1; At De Party, *The Green Sheaf*, 1903, No. 2; Spanish Ladies, *The Green Sheaf*, 1903, No. 3; Jan A Dreams, *The Green Sheaf*, 1903, No. 23

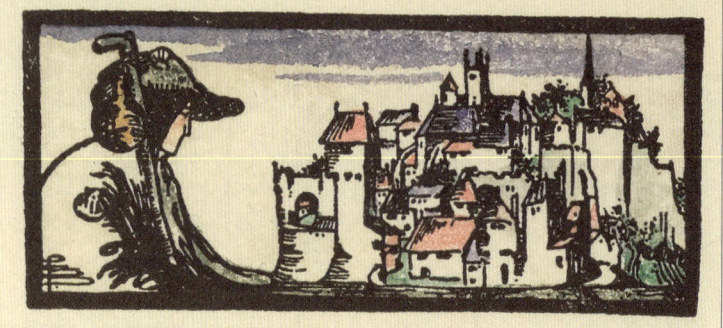

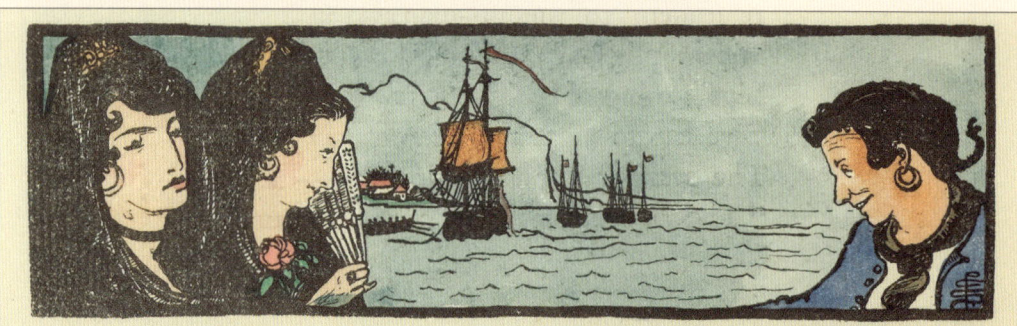

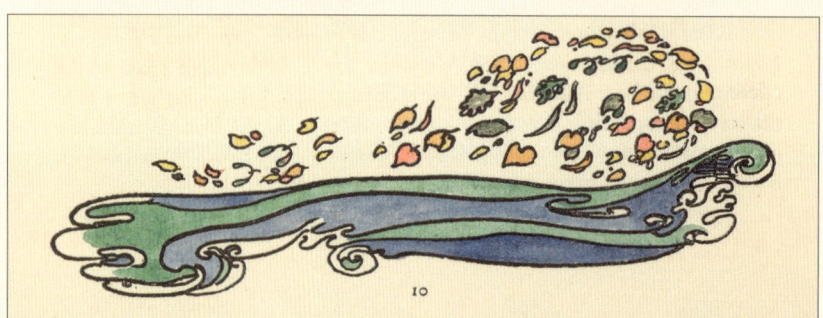

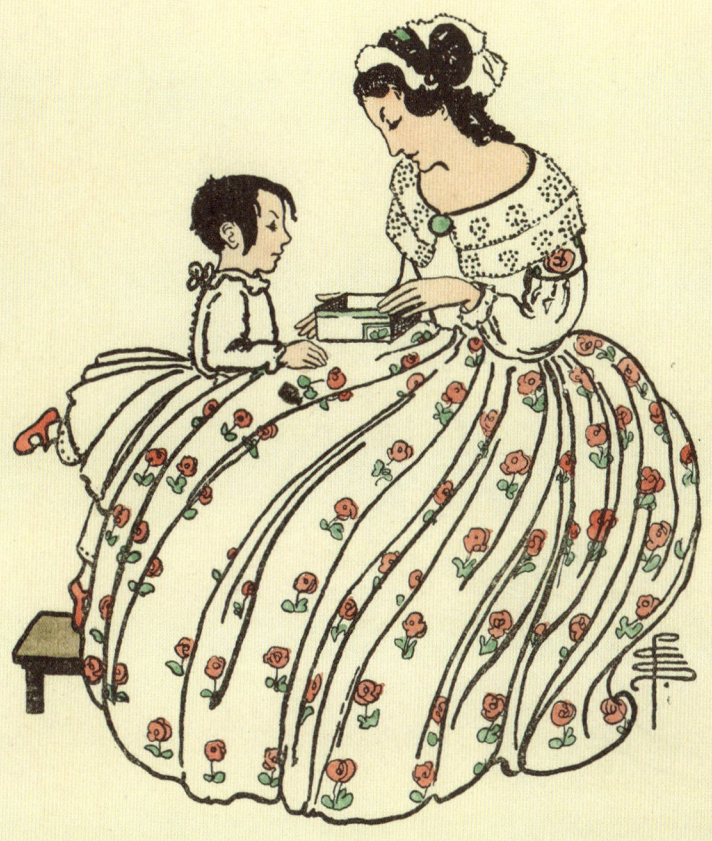

The Green Sheaf

CHARLES, do not you remember the caterpillar we put in a paper box, with some mulberry leaves for it to eat? It is gone—here is no caterpillar—there is something in the box; what is it? I do not know. It is a little ball of yellow stuff. Let us cut it open, perhaps we may find the caterpillar. No, here is nothing but a strange little grub, and it is dead, I believe, for it does not move. Pinch it gently by the tail.

Mrs. Barbauld.

1903-1904

Mrs. Barbauld, *The Green Sheaf,* 1903, No. 4

1903-1904

Mrs. Barbauld, "How Master Constans Went to the North," *The Green Sheaf*, 1903, No. 2; T "A Dream of Angus Oge," *The Green Sheaf*, 1903, No. 4; U "A Deep Sea Yarn," *The Green Sheaf*, 1903, No. 6

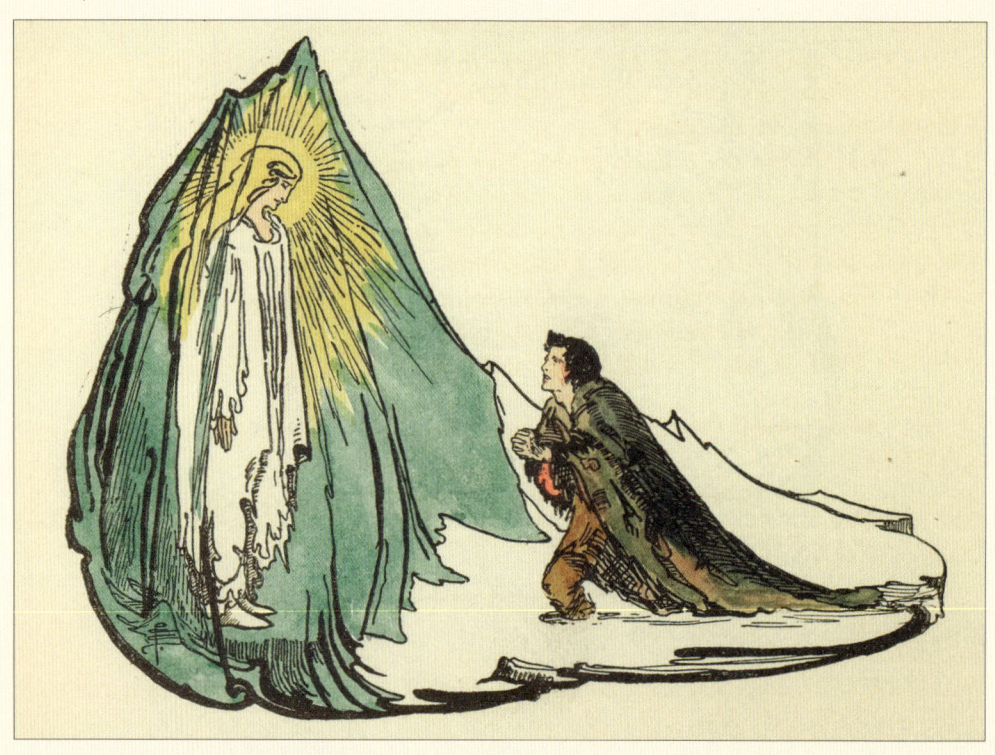

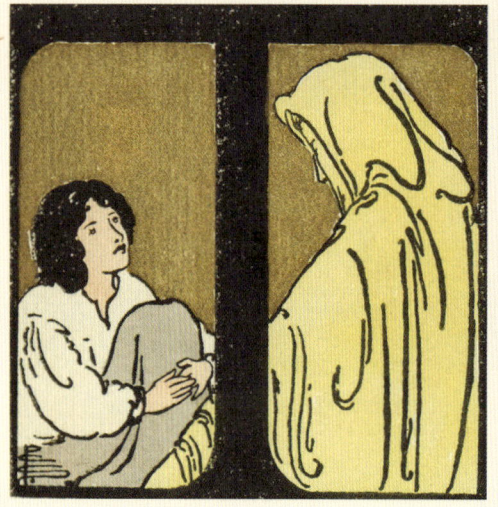

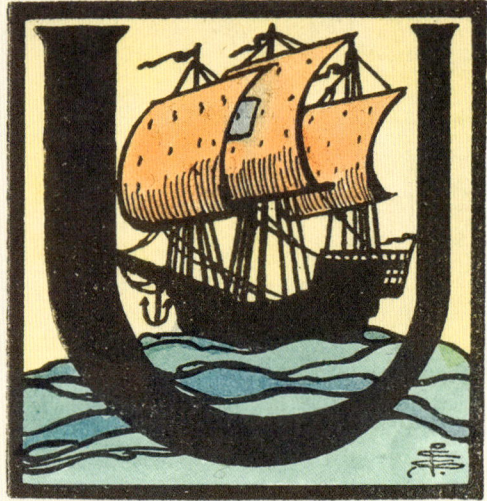

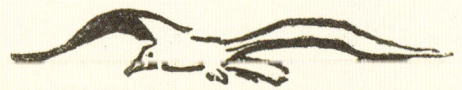

The Green Sheaf

1903-1904

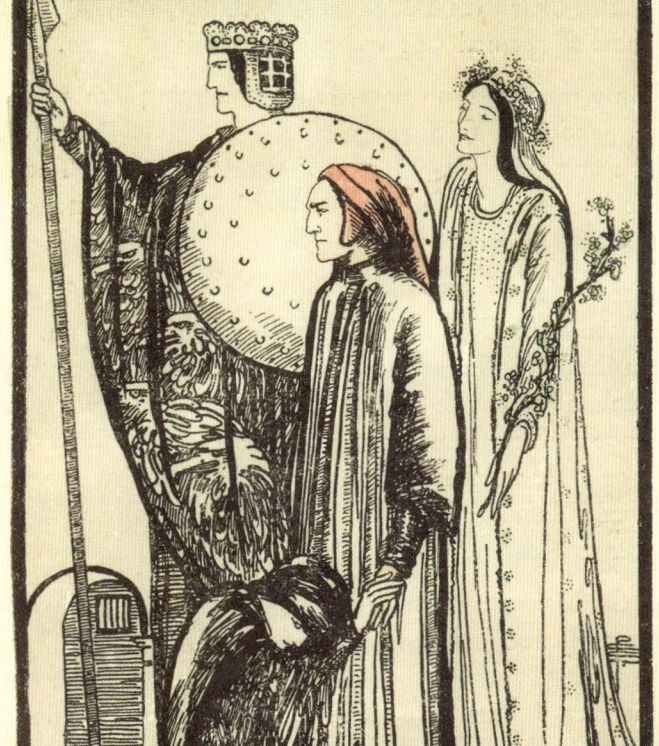

The Lament of a Lyceum Rat, *The Green Sheaf*, 1903, No. 5

trembling, I raced across the stage that was filled with a light subdued but intensely clear, and once more I looked upon Hamlet, Shylock with sweet Portia, Mephistopheles with Margaret and the ill-fated Faust, The Vicar with the Squire and lovely Olivia, incomparable Beatrice and Benedick, the Martyr King with his Queen and Cromwell, Macbeth, Napoleon, the bloodthirsty Louis XI., the tortured Matthias, Robespierre, Richelieu, and countless others. And the old house glowed and breathed

1903–1904

A Pagan Rhyme, *The Green Sheaf*, 1903, No. 3; "Prince Siddartha," *The Green Sheaf*, 1903, No. 3; The Lament of a Lyceum Rat, *The Green Sheaf*, 1903, No. 5; "Juveniles," *The Green Sheaf*, 1903, No. 5

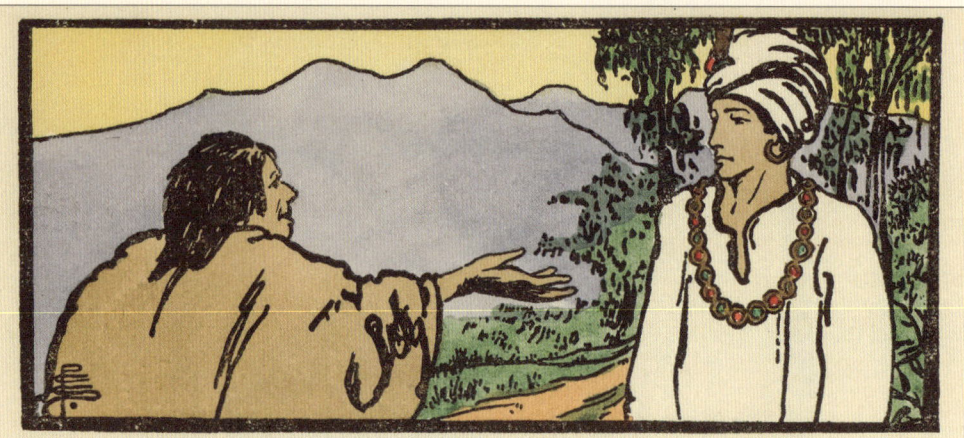
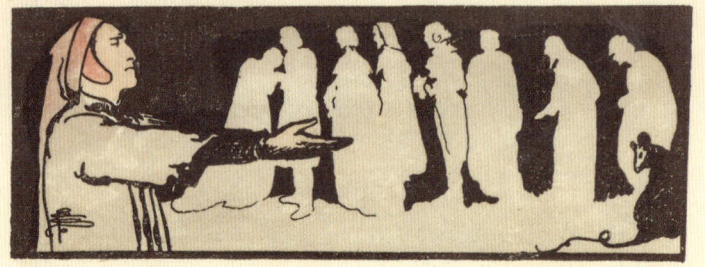
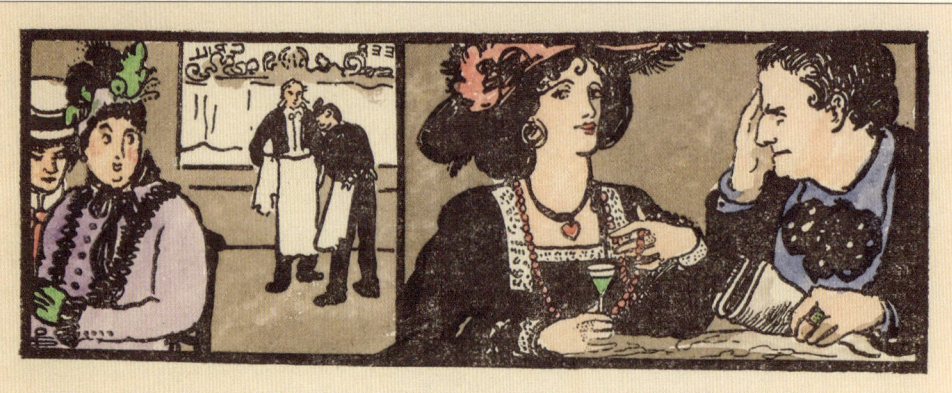

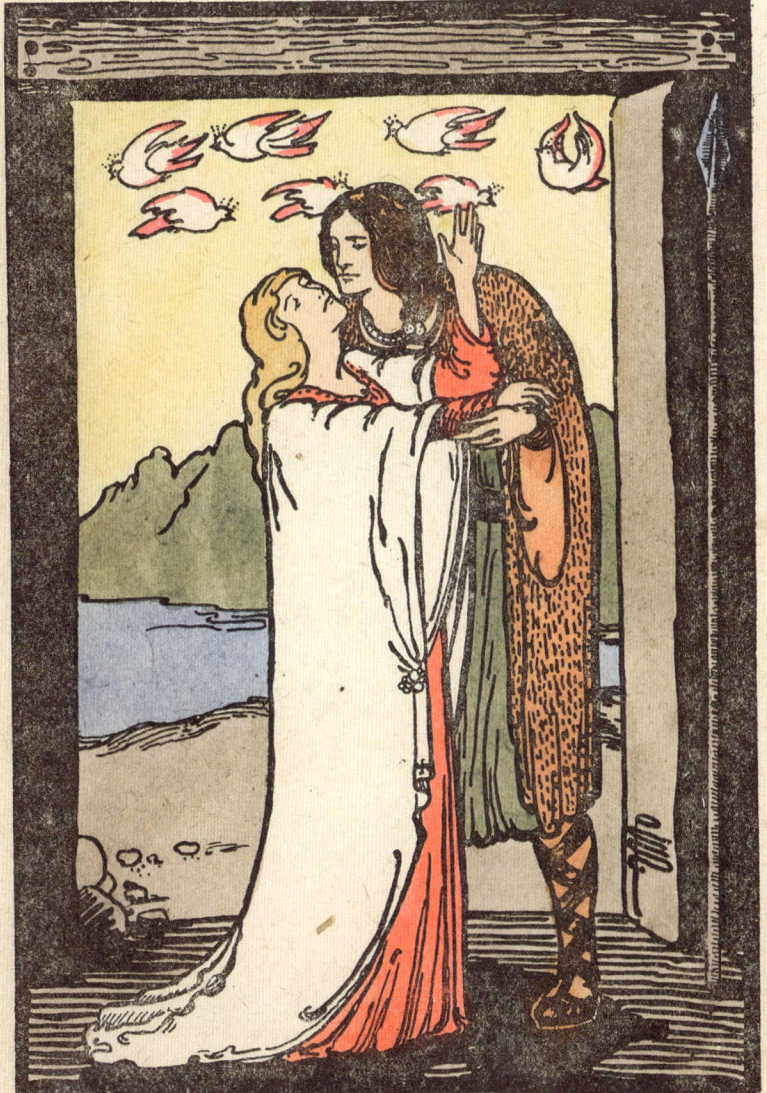

1903-1904

"Do you not see them?" Deirdre, Act II, *The Green Sheaf*, 1903, Supplement to No. 7

1903-1904

A Hymn in Praise of Neptune, *The Green Sheaf*, 1903, No. 6

The Green Sheaf

A HYMN IN PRAISE OF NEPTUNE.

Of Neptune's empire let us sing,
At whose command the waves obey;
To whom the rivers tribute pay,
Down the high mountain sliding;
To whom the scaly nation yields
Homage for the crystal fields.
      Wherein they dwell;
And every sea-god pays a gem
Yearly out of his watery cell,
To deck great Neptune's diadem.

The Tritons dancing in a ring,
Before his palace gates do make
The water with their echoes quake,
Like the great thunder sounding:
The sea-nymphs chant their accents shrill,
And the Syrens taught to kill
      With their sweet voice,
Make every echoing rock reply,
Unto their gentle murmuring noise,
The praise of Neptune's empery.

Thomas Campion.

13

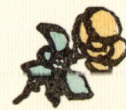

The Green Sheaf

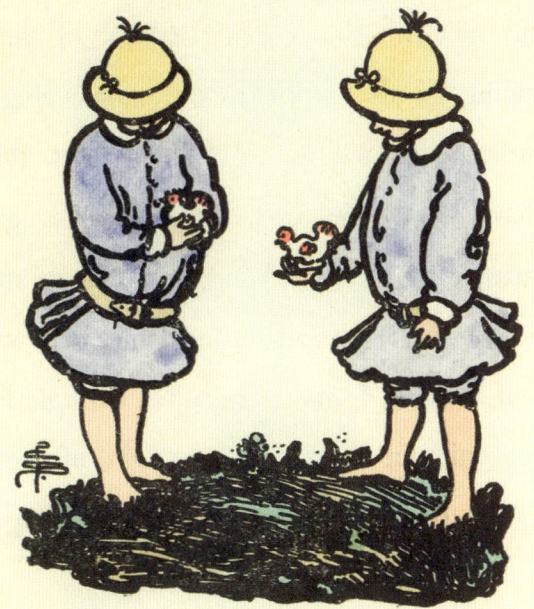

THE CLAY CHICKENS.

1903-1904

The Clay Chickens, *The Green Sheaf*, 1903, No. 8

1903-1904

Mrs. Barbauld, *The Green Sheaf*, 1903, No. 9

The Green Sheaf

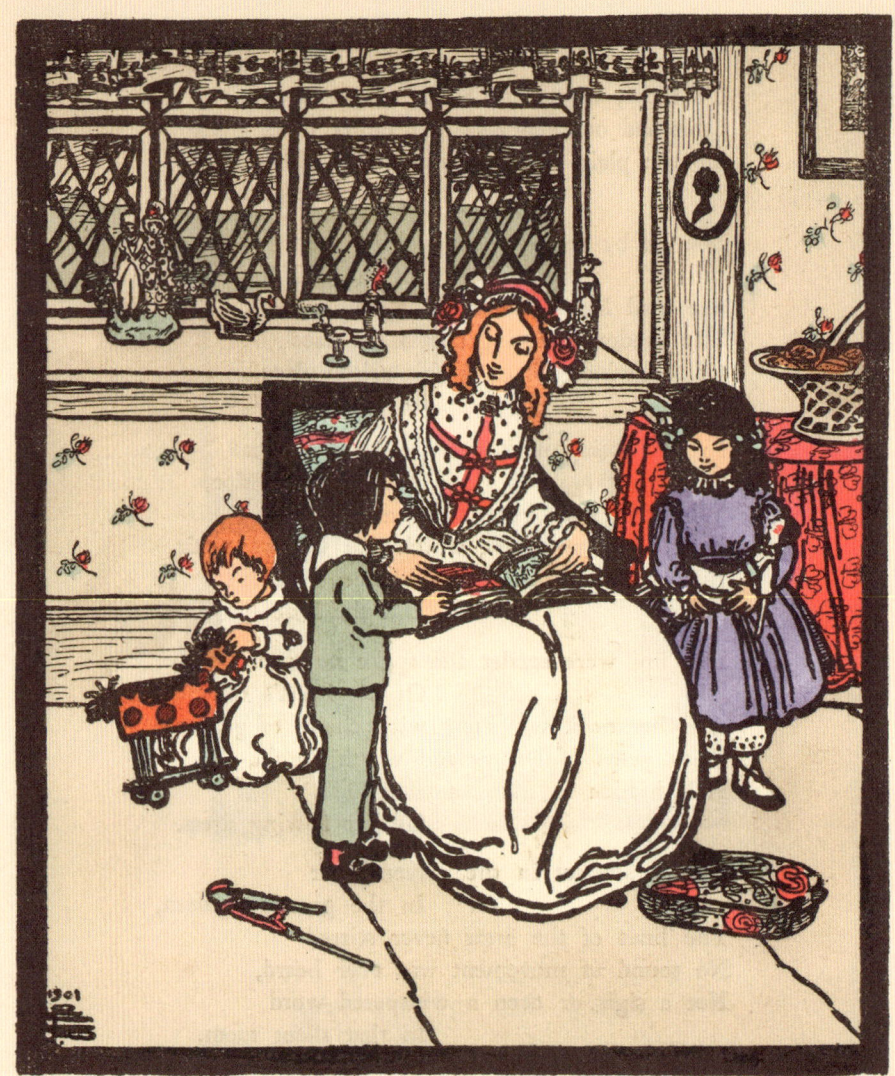

THE sky is very black; the rain pours down. Well, never mind it; we will sit by the fire, and read, and tell stories, and look at pictures. Where is Billy, and Harry, and little Betsey? Now tell me who can spell best. Good boy! There is a clever fellow! Now you shall all have some cake.

Mrs. Barbauld.

6

The Green Sheaf

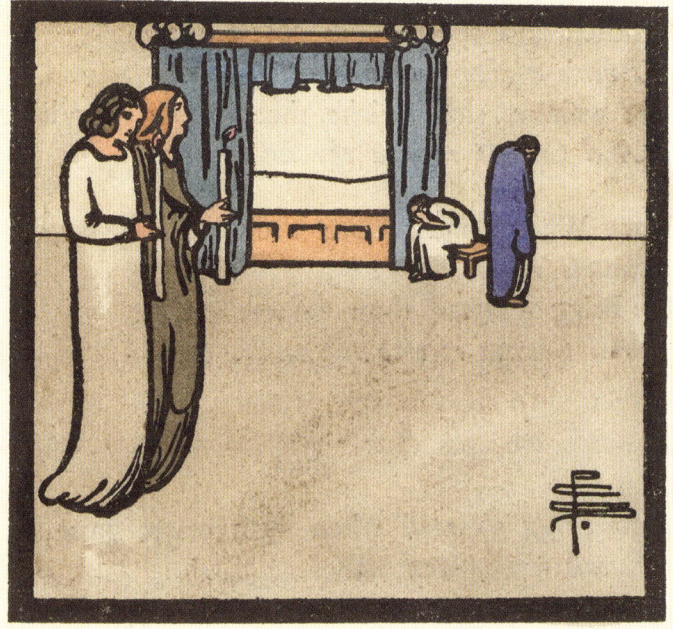

A LYKE-WAKE DIRGE.

This ae nighte, this ae nighte,
   Everie nighte and alle,
Fire, and sleete, and candle-lighte,
   And Christe receive thy saule.

When thou from hence away art past,
   Everie nighte and alle,
To Whinny-muir thou comest at last,
   And Christe receive thy saule.

If ever thou gavest hosen and shoon,
   Everie nighte and alle,
Sit thee down and put them on,
   And Christe receive thy saule.

5

1903-1904

A Lyke-Wake Dirge, *The Green Sheaf*, 1903, No. 11

1903-1904

The Rim of the Sea, *The Green Sheaf*, 1903, No. 6

The Green Sheaf

THE RIM OF THE SEA.

Over the rim of the sea,
Where the sailor sun has set.
Over the rim of the sea,
Where the fisher casts his net.

Over the rim of the sea
The white bird's mournful cry
Over the rim of the sea
The blue waves roll and sigh.

P. C. S.

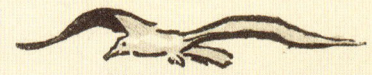

The Green Sheaf

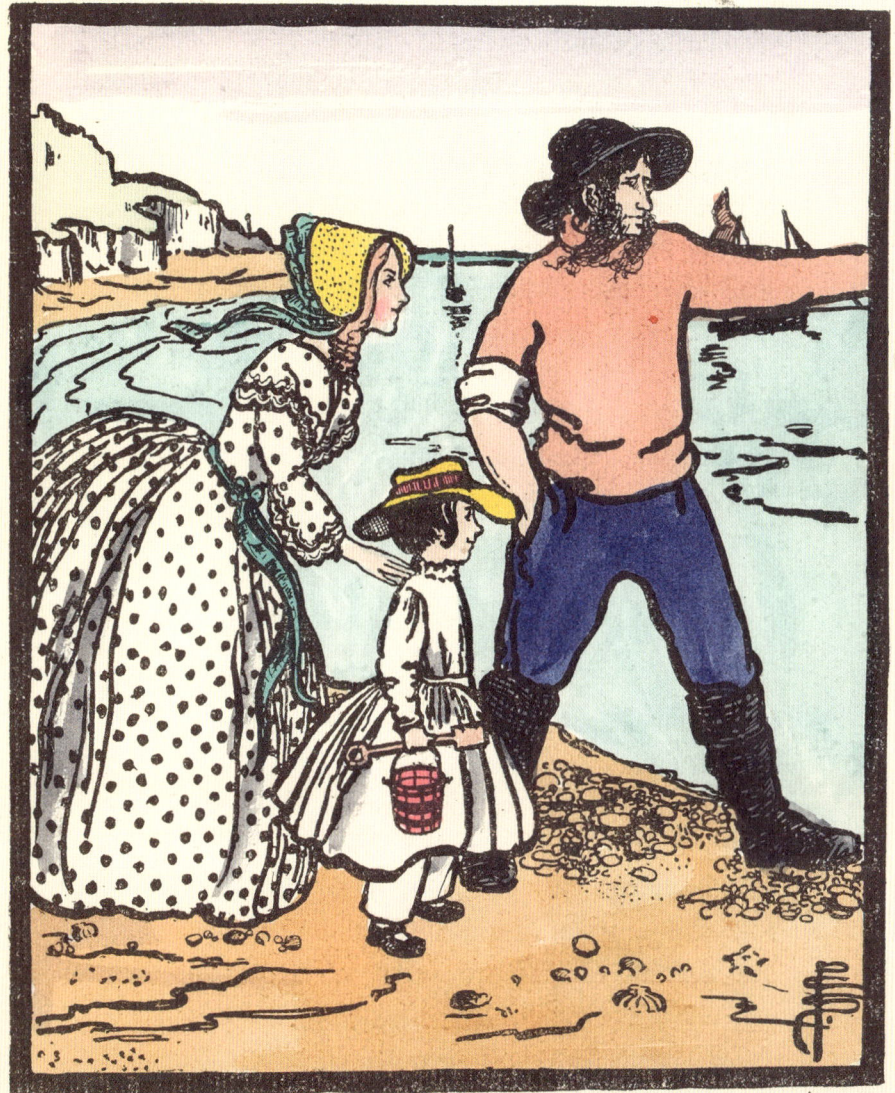

"Pray, Fisherman, what is this great water?"

1903-1904

"Pray, Fisherman, what is this great water?"
The Green Sheaf, 1903, No. 13

A Sheaf of Songs by Alfred C. Calmour, published by the Green Sheaf

Good Bye.

Many a time we have both sat here,
Filled with fond longing and hope and fear;
Lip pressed to lip and hand clasped in hand,
Our hearts keeping time to the waves on the sand—
Which say, " Good-bye, happiness; never again
Will you feel the sweet thrill of this exquisite pain!
Take a last long farewell of your love and your bliss,
You may never again feel the joy of a kiss,
Or meet in the world such deep rapture as this."
But the birds overhead sing of joys yet in store,
And they carol of bliss that shall last evermore;
Singing, " No, not good-bye, just a passing adieu:
No lives can be parted while two hearts beat true!"

Catch Me

1904

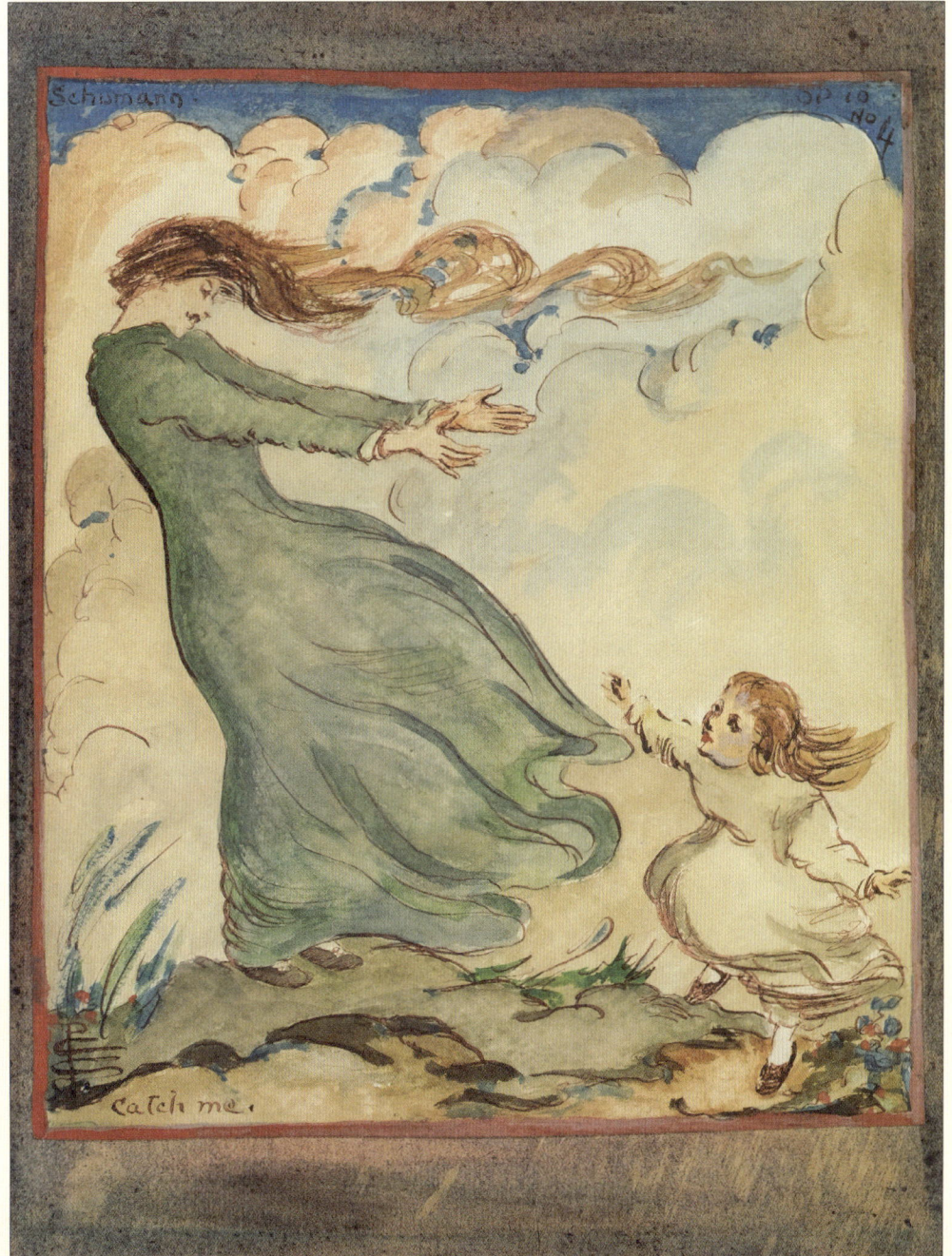

"Catch Me" original watercolor painting by Pamela Colman Smith, circa 1904, painted to Schumann's Opus 10, No. 4

1905 to 1906

The Book of Hours

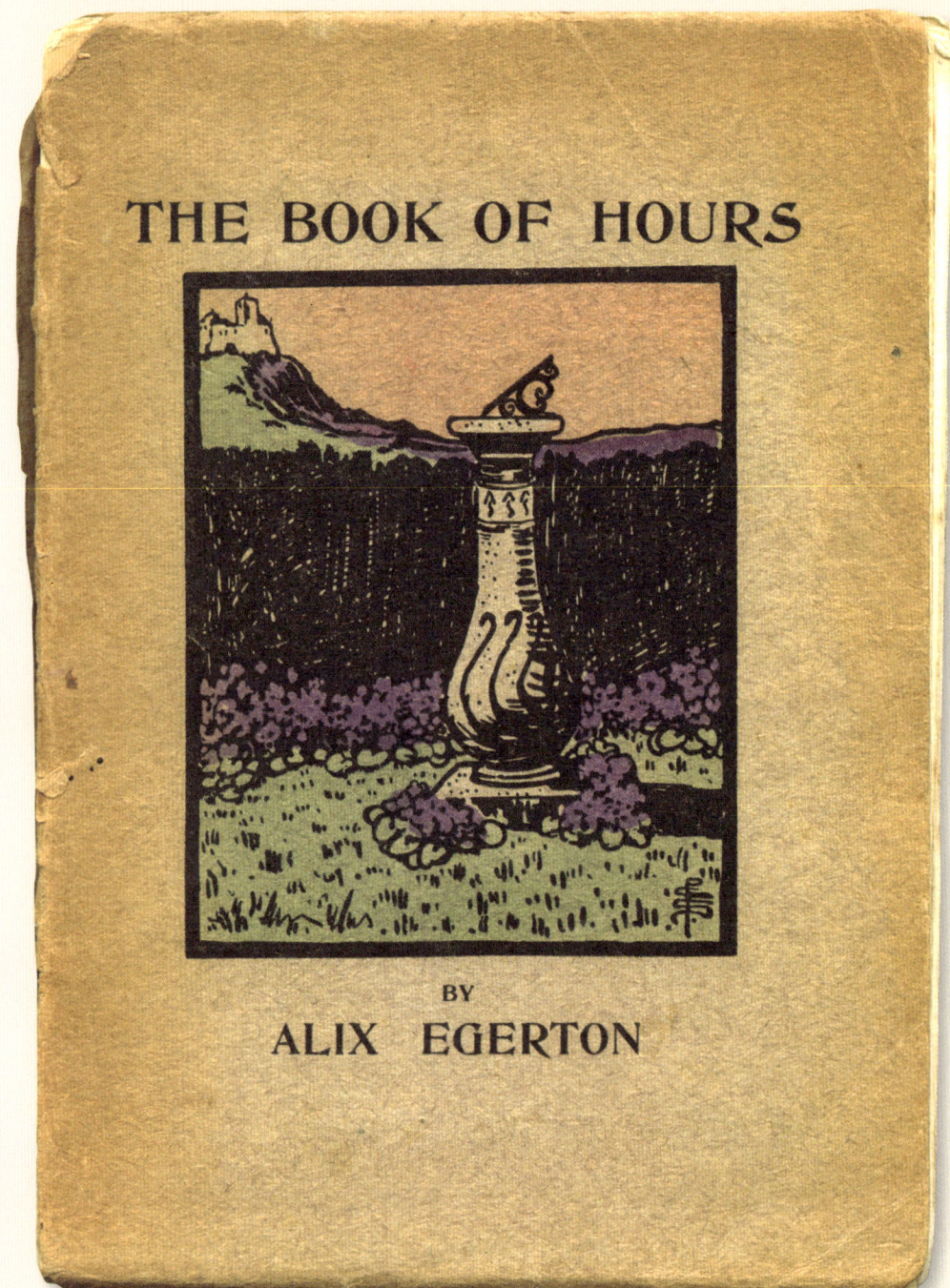

Cover from *The Book of Hours* by Alix Egerton plus frontispiece by Pamela Colman Smith

1905

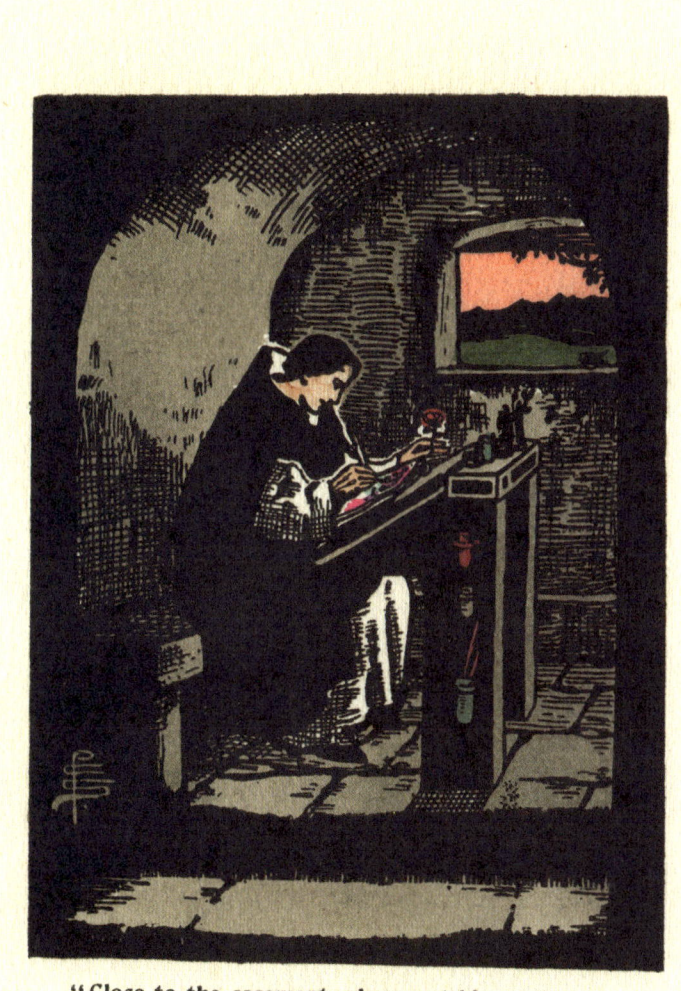

"Close to the casement, always at his work,
The young lay-brother Ambrose sat and toiled."
The Book of Hours.

A Celtic Christmas, The Cold Women

1905

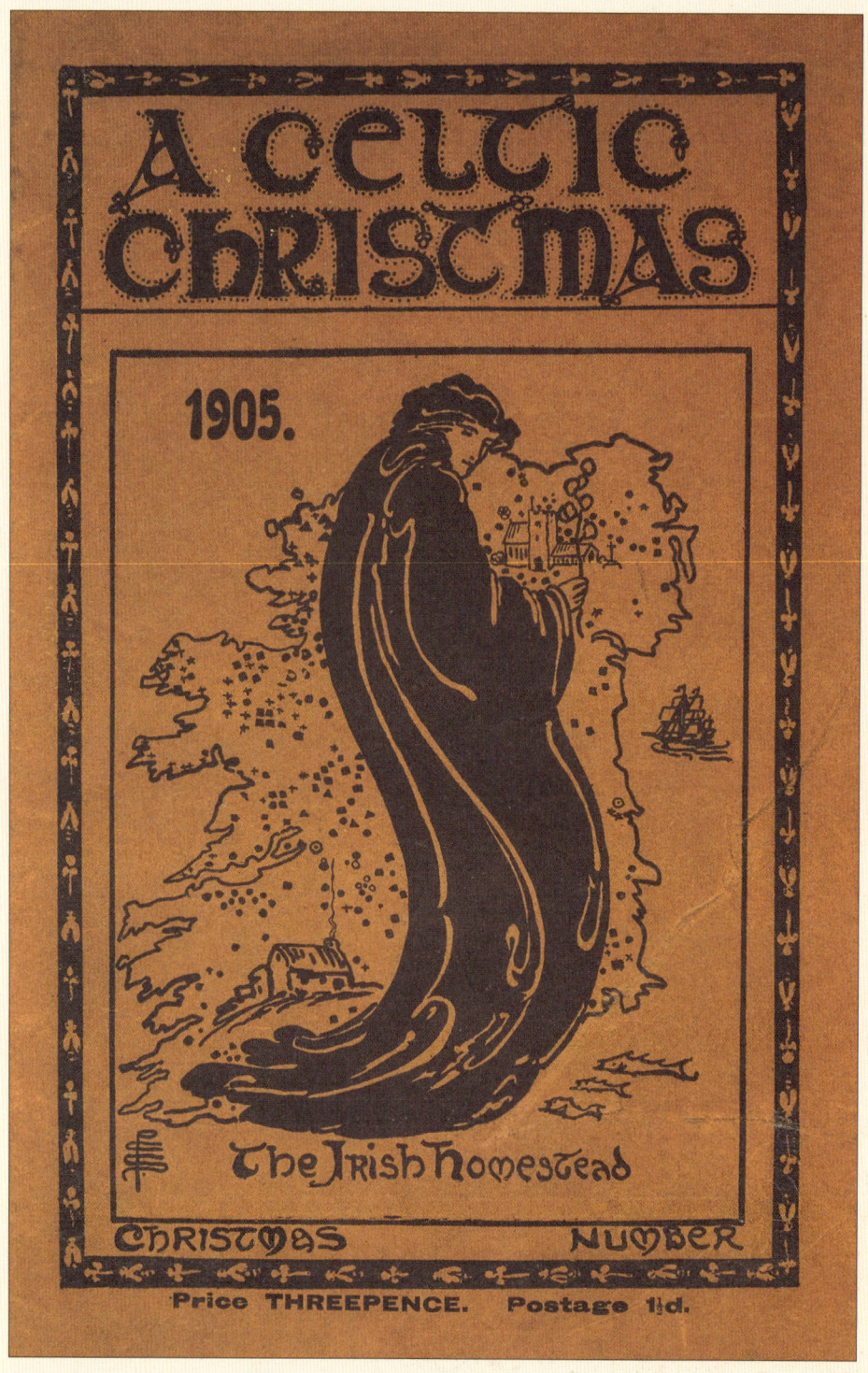

A CELTIC CHRISTMAS.

THE CHRISTMAS NUMBER of the "IRISH HOMESTEAD," December 2nd, 1905.

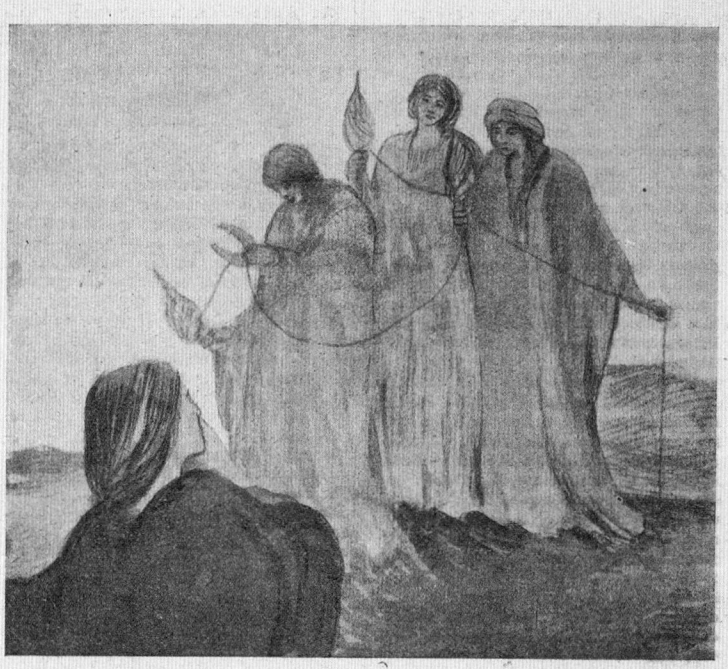

THE COLD WOMEN.

OF three women without pity I have heard the legend say
The old women, the cold women, and sisters three are they.
They three first set to spinning,
When the world was just beginning,
They span the black wool of the night, the red threads of the day.

If you should meet the Cold Women under the morning sun,
Give them no word of greeting lest you should be undone;
But with no backward looking
Pass on with fingers crooking
In the sign against all evil that the spinners may have spun.

If the Cold Women join you, with faces set your way,
You may not hope to eat the fruit whose flower was white in May.
These downward-looking witches,
Have set your shroud's last stitches,
And see you, yet alive and warm, a piece of churchyard clay.

NORA CHESSON.

The First Sorrow of Fergus

1905

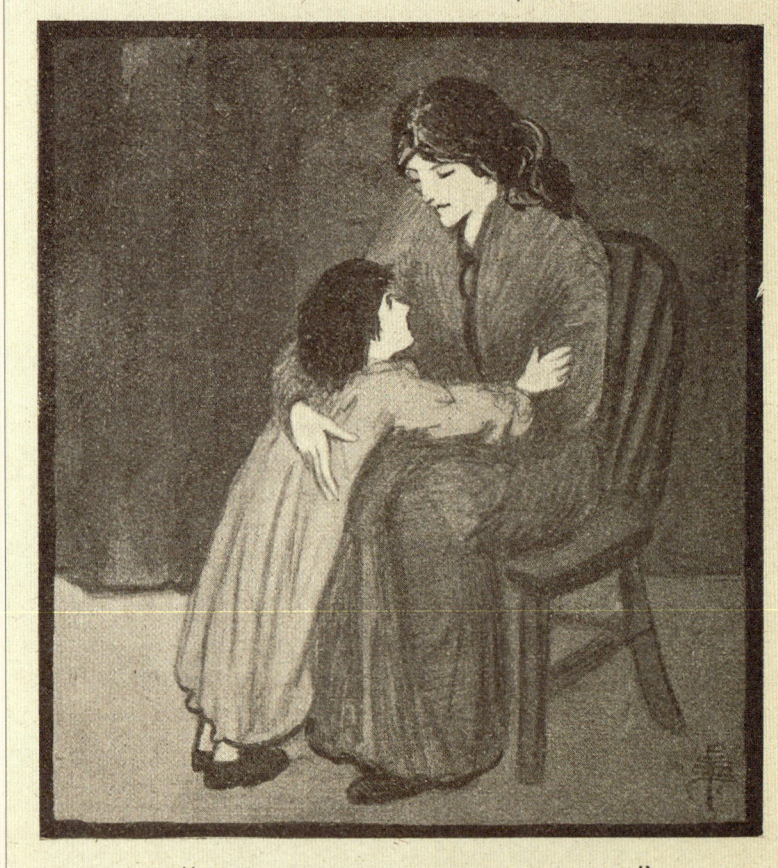

"IT IS WELL FOR THE LITTLE CHILD."

THE FIRST SORROW OF FERGUS.
By Ethel Goddard.

WHEN the twilight falls, and the familiar things of the nursery become grim, unknown giants, it is well for the little child if his mother leads him into that fairyland wherein there is no darkness at all. For the girl, with her young eyes bright with wonder, there are many tales of Deirdre, of Maeve, of Yseult, of Niam, and of Findabair, and of the fairy ladies who met great princes in the enchanted forests, and for the boy whose blood stirs with the battle longing even while he sits wearily leaning a heavy head against his mother's knee, there are marvels done by Hector, by Achilles, by Arthur, Cuchulain, Fionn, and Oisin. These tales will breathe deep dreaming into young hearts, and the little feet never can be too tired to pass within the gates of the land of the ever young. But there was one man who lived in Ireland long ago, and of him no word must be spoken to the little child, and it is not well for those who read his story, for in it is all the sorrow of the world. Those who know all their country's past must write alike of sorrow and of joy, and truly it is needful that all which men have done should be chronicled that the story of life may be fully told. Yet, when this tale is written down, the child should not turn its pages, nor should anyone tell the child what is written therein. It is an enduring truth that he who takes from a little one his dream, his unbroken mirror of life, is, indeed, accursed, and the tale which is written here tells of a man whose trust in his fellows was made a weapon for his stabbing. This is the story of Fergus whose love bought him treachery, whose confidence bought him betrayal. It is written that the old man, when he crouches by the fire, deaf to the familiar voices, blind to the familiar faces, may take the dust-covered book and find upon its pages the sorrow of his own soul. But let not the child read herein, or the young man, or the girl, this is a treasure for him who is old, for here will he meet one who has suffered the uttermost anguish of life.

It was in the spring that love came to Fergus, King of Uladh, and it was for Nessa, the widow of a man of Ireland, that his heart sang its song.

They were together under the shadow of a forest tree, and being closed in by walls of green, they dreamed the world was far from them. So Fergus gazed only on Nessa, as she sat by him on a bank of moss, and his dark face was lighted by the wish of his soul. Then, from where he sat by her, he slid down until he knelt before her on the moss, so that he could look into her eyes. He bowed his head upon her hands. "Nessa, Nessa," he whispered, "I am tired of all life and kingship, unless thou art with me, to be a singing bird in my soul and a sharer of my crown." The leaves rustled, and the birds twittered, but Nessa was silent, her eyes raised over Fergus's bowed head and looking fiercely through the wall of trees. "Nessa, and wilt thou not, and must I be alone?" His head was lifted from her hands; he forced her blue eyes down to look in his. "Nessa, my queen, my fair choice among women. Speak, Nessa." Then, with a sigh, she spoke quickly and low. "Fergus, they call me Nessa, the ungentle, for all my kindliness has been dried up since they did slay my band of faithful teachers. Old men, Fergus, who taught me all their lore, old men who nursed me tenderly and well, and they were killed while I was standing by. Fergus, the good old men were strong to do great things of nobleness, but cruel age had chilled their kindly blood, their eyes were dim, their ears were very tired, and so those devils, strong in no pure thing, killed them and slew my gentleness with them. I am a thorn without sap, I am a fruit never to be ripened; I cannot give love or any tenderness." Nessa's voice died away and Fergus rose to his feet before her.

"Nessa, Nessa, thou art not ungentle to me; see how I stand and plead, and let the pity of thine heart speak for me. Ah, lonely one, dear lonely one, come into the nest I will build for thee. I know thy sorrow, and that tears are lying unshed hidden in thine eyes, and that sad sobs struggle to break the sweetness of thy voice. I know thy sadness, Nessa, let me cheer thee; I know thy coldness, Nessa, let me warm thee, and I will stand between thee and the world; aye, and between thee and the cruel past, and in my arms thou shalt forget thy grief." And Nessa looked up at him where he stood, his eyes lit by his hope. Then she stood straight before him and laid her hands gently upon his shoulders, so that a tremor of great joy ran through him. When she spoke her face, which had been white, was dyed rose-red. "Fergus, nay, I forget myself, King, my heart is a nut that has no kernel at all; my soul is a tree that has been blackened and slain, but I will give myself to thee that thou mayst pour thy love tale in my ears, if thou wilt grant to me the thing I ask."

"Oh, woman, of all women, if it be in my gift the thing thou askest is already thine. But speak not of my love so slightingly. I do not love in any paltry way, as one who shouts to hear his own loud voice. I love that I may sing a tender song into thine ears to bring thee gentle peace."

"I do not deem thy love a paltry thing; but, Fergus, thou art giving for no gain."

"Not so, my store of joy, the gain will come when thy sad heart is cheered. Say now what thou desirest me to do."

"Thou knowest Conchubar, my son? When Conchubar was born my heart was soft awhile."

"Aye, Nessa, and it will be soft again. Sit by me here and say on at thine ease."

Then, as they sat upon the moss, Fergus watched how the sunbeams shone through Nessa's hair, and while he listened to her voice he dreamed of how he would bring joy to her.

"When Conchubar was born the Druid Cathbad made a future for him. He said my son would some day be king. And, Fergus, I did love that foolish dream; but kingship never came towards the boy. I ask this only from thee; give him thy kingship for a little year, so that it may be said his children were king's children. A little year is all I ask." The joy had faded then from Fergus's face, and he saw no more the sun on Nessa's hair. He looked upon the ground and murmured low:

"Nessa, the kingship is not mine to give; it is entrusted to me for my life, and I must guard it as I would mine honour, and serve it day and night. How dare I trust it in a young boy's grasp?"

Then Nessa turned towards Fergus, and she laid her hand upon his arm.

"Foolish, Fergus, how canst thou serve the kingship when thine eyes are dazzled by their first new glimpse of woman? When these strong arms enfold me in their clasp how can they wield the weapon of fierce war? Lend but thy kingship for a little while to one who dreams only of honour's deeds, and then, Fergus, when thou hast tired of me thou canst return and rule in fuller strength."

It was when Fergus heard these words, and thought how in truth, his new joy might assail his kingship that he bowed his head upon Nessa's knees and yielded to her will like a tired child. And while the man spoke in low, burning tones, Nessa looked ever out into the forest, and when she touched his hair in gentleness her thought was far away; and when he said that he could never tire of loving her and serving her in love, she shivered once as though the wind were cold.

A year passed over Fergus and Nessa, and Conchubar sat upon the throne. Then came the chosen day when Fergus was to take his crown again.

He walked with Nessa into the great hall, and whispered to her how she was his queen, and should be while he sat upon the throne, but Nessa's eyes rested on Conchubar where he stood waiting in his robes of kingship, with darting sunbeams glinting on his crown. The warriors were standing near the throne, and Cathbad sat still, like a stony thing.

Then Fergus led Nessa up to the throne, and he stood silently by Conchubar. Then Nessa's eyes rested upon the warriors while Fergus spoke.

"I am come to you again, my people, to wear the kingship, and to bear the burden."

A murmur rose within the hall. "No, no; he is not king." The people looked at Conchubar, who was smiling. A shout broke from their throats. "Conchubar, Conchubar," they cried.

Now Nessa's face looked shamed and sad at that, and all the meanness of the many gifts which she had used to buy the warriors rose up, a grey and gibbering thing before her, when Fergus bent a gentle look upon her, and whispered to her: "Nessa, who is king?"

And Nessa looked away from him in silence. A man strode up then to the throne. "Conchubar is king, for truly Fergus MacRoig has cared but little for us when he could sell us to buy him a wife." Then Fergus saw the forest and the moss, and Nessa and the sunlight through her hair. Thus as he stood with Conchubar and Nessa he saw his crown go from him, and when he saw Nessa crimson and trembling, her eyes running in eagerness over the warriors' faces, his love that once had seemed so young and fair was an old mumbling woman full of sins.

Then he went from them, speaking not a word, and ran into the forest until he found the bank where they had sat. And then he laid his head upon the moss and moaned aloud because of the deceit. When darkness came his heart had found some peace, and he spoke strengthful words beneath the trees, with his white face seared by the day's fierce grief. The wind was still, and as he spoke the night moth fluttered from his heated breath.

"Uladh is more to me, is more to me,
And I must serve it from below the throne,
Because I was not wise upon the throne,
But gave my kingship at a woman's word."

Then Fergus went again to Emain Macha, and he served Conchubar faithfully and bravely, but Nessa was shut out from his sad heart, and when his eyes rested upon her face she knew that she was hideous to him. This, then, was the first great sorrow of Fergus when his love was used to take his kingship from him.

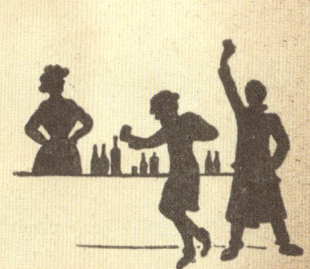

1905

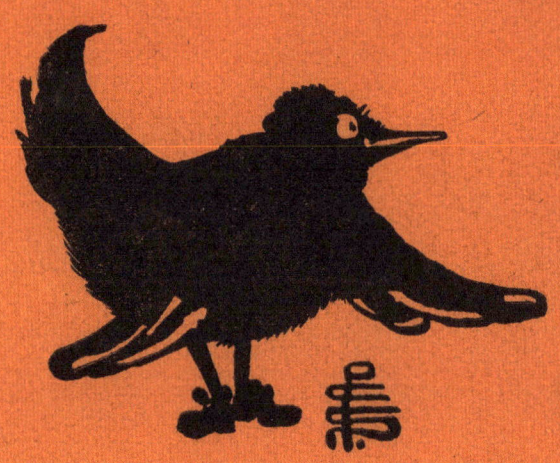

1905

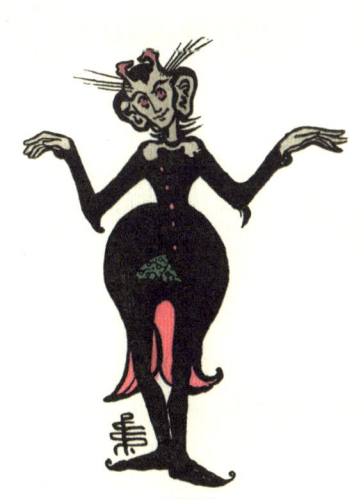

ANNANCY.

CHIM-CHIM

Folk Stories from Jamaica

BY
PAMELA COLMAN SMITH

LONDON:
"THE GREEN SHEAF," 3 PARK MANSIONS ARCADE,
KNIGHTSBRIDGE, S.W.

1905

TURKLE AND PIGEON

ONCE in a long before time before Queen Victoria came to reign over we,

In dis country lib Turkle.

Now Turkle watch de Pigeon dem (dey lib nex to him house) ebery day dey fly off all day round an' round — and Turkle wish him could fly wid dem.

So one time he axe dem if dey can teach him to fly.

An' dey all come together, an' de oldest Pigeon look wise like *kreech-owl, an' say dat dey could!

So each of de Pigeon tek' a feader out of him wing — an' dey stick it in Turkle back, till him stand like a pincushion, all full of feader!

Den dey take hold of Turkle and fly up in de air! —

Bumby dey get to de Debil corn-piece. Ebery dey Pigeon go teaf dere. An' when dey get dere dey each tek' de're own feader out of Turkle back.

* Screech-owl.

28

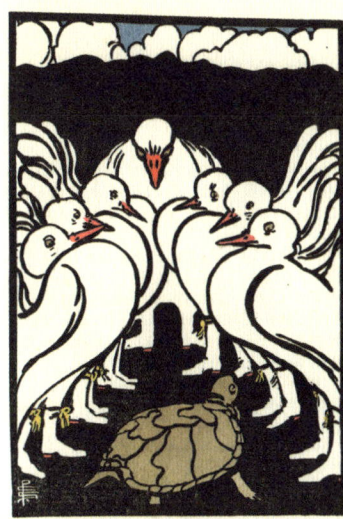

"An' 'dey all come together."

29

Turkle and Pigeon

An' dey gib' Turkle one large bag, an' tell him say him is to pick up corn.

So dey all pick up corn — an' Turkle pick up corn.

Now bumby dey hear a nise!

An' dey all stan' still, an' lif' up dere head!

And den de oldest Pigeon flap him wing an' rise up, an' dey all rise up — and fly away, an' let Turkle all by himself in de corn-piece.

An' now de watchman come — and him find Turkle dere wid' a large bag of corn.

And de watchman say—

"So it is you, sah! who teaf all me Massa Debil corn!"

And Turkle bawl out—

"O me sweet watchman! it no me! it is dem naughty Pigeon!"

An' de watchman say—

"What meke you is here den?"

An' Turkle say—

"O me watchman! Me say me would like to fly, like Pigeon, an' dey lend me feader, an' me come wid dem! — but it no me teaf de corn at all, sah!"

An' watchman say—

"Hi! Me neber see Turkle fly yet! You must come to me Massa Debil."

An' him take Turkle an' put him in pail of water 'pon him head, an' walk off now to de Debil house.

Now Turkle begin sing.

An' him sing so sweet dat de watchman dance an' dance, and spill all de water out of de pail!

An' Turkle bawl out—

"If you let me walk, me will sing so sweet!"

But watchman say—

"No-a!"——

Bumby dey come to Debil house.

And Debil come see Turkle.

An him say de cook was to stew him fe supper —an' him will go out and get all him friend an' relation to come heat him.

So now de cook was mixin' all de onion an' *pimento an' tings together to meke nice flabour.

An' Turkle begin sing.

* Allspice.

Turkle and Pigeon

An' him sing so sweet de cook dance an' dance!

An' Turkle say—

"O me sweet cooky, if you will only put me in de yard, me will sing so sweet!"

So de cook teke up Turkle an' put him in de yard.

An' him sing sweet!

An' de cook dance.

An' all de time Turkle walkin' an' walkin'.

An' bumby Turkle say—

"O me sweet cooky, if you teke me to de riberside and jes' put de tip of me tail in de water — me will sing so sweet!"

An' de cook teke him and put jes' de tip of him tail in de water.

An' Turkle sing sweeter than ever so.

An' de cook dance.

Bumby she no hear any sing!

An' she look down, an' dere at de riber bottom was Turkle!

An' Turkle wave him hand an' swim away.

Now de cook go home back, an' get one goat — an' stew an' stew him, an' meke one lubly stew.

Turkle and Pigeon

Now bumby Debil an' all him friend an' relation come, an' dey bawl out say—

"Where Turkle stew?"

An' de cook bring de goat mutton stew, an' say—

"Here, sah!"

An' dey all eat it, an' dey all say dat Turkle heat bery nice!

An' den de cook come in an' sing de song dat Turkle sing.

Till de Debil an' all him frien' an' relation get up and dance.

An' dance till dey fall down dead!

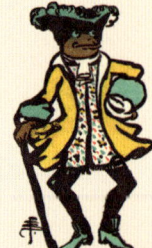

ANNANCY AND DEATH

ONCE in a long before time, before Queen Victoria came to reign over we.

One day Annancy was walkin' out in de bush.

An' bumby him come to a place where dere was sittin' a bery ole, ole man.

And de ole man name Death.

But Annancy no know him name.

An' walk up to him an' say—

"Marnin', Massa!"

An' Death no say noting!

An' bumby Annancy say—

"Marnin', Massa!"

An' Death no say noting!

An' Annancy say—

"Marnin', Massa!—me come fe scraps of food. You got any for me?"

Death no say noting.

An' Annancy say—

"Hi! Him say I can go in de house an' help meself."

Annancy and Death

So Annancy go in an' fill him bag wid all him can find.

An' nex' day Annancy come an' say—

"Marnin', Massa; how you is to-day?"

An' Death say noting, but jes' sit dere, and sit dere.

An Annancy say—

"Me Massa!—me hab' one darter want to go out as cook. Me wi' bring her to you?"

Death no say noting.

An Annancy say—

"Hi! Him say me can bring her, fe be him cook."

An' de nex' day Annancy bring him darter, an' leff' her wid Death.

An' Annancy go home.

Nex' day Annancy come.

Dere was Death sittin'.

An Annancy say—

"Marnin', me Massa! How you like me darter fe cook?"

An' Death no say noting.

Annancy and Death

An' Annancy go in de house and hunt fe him darter — and bumby him find her ring in de oven.

An' him come out to Death an' say—

"Massa! Where me darter?"

An' Death bawl out—

"Me eat her! An' now me will eat you!"

An' him jump 'pon Annancy.

An' Annancy run,

An' Death run.

An' Annancy gallop,

An' Death gallop.

An' Annancy jump,

An' Death jump.

Till bumby dey come near Annancy house. An' Annancy bawl out to him wife Crookie—

"Put de children up pon de rafter, wife!"

An' Crookie bawl out—

"What you say?—You want de bushal basket?"

An Annancy bawl—

"No-a! Me tell you put de children 'pon de rafter!"

1905

Annancy and Death

An' him run into de house an' catch up Crookie an' de children, an' jump up 'pon de rafter wid dem.

An' Death cannot reach dem at all!

An' Death vex!

An' dey hold on de rafter wid dere hands. An bumby de eldis' child bawl out—

", O pappa! Me hand hurt me!"

An' Annancy say—

"Drop, den, drop! Death wi' know what to do wid you!"

An de child drop.

An' Death put him in him bag.

An' bumby anoder child bawl out—

"Pappa! Me hand hurt me!"

An Annancy say—

"Drop, den, drop! Death wi' know what to do wid you!"

An' dat child drop.

An' Death put him in him bag.

An' so all de children drop, and Death put dem in him bag.

44

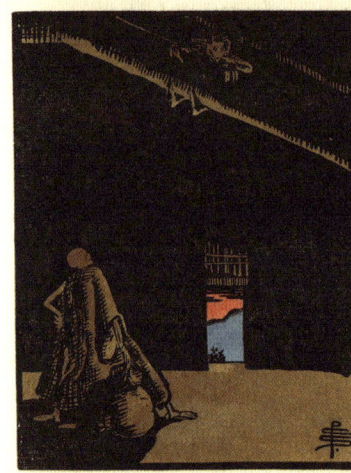

"Annancy is you comin' down?"

45

Annancy and Death

An' at las' Crookie drop.

An' death put her in him bag.

An' Death wait, an' wait, an' Annancy no drop!

An' bumby Death say—

"Annancy, is you comin' down or not?"

An' Annancy say—

"Me good frien', if me drop, me so fat me will pop!—an' if me pop you could not find enough to put in you bag!"

Death say—

"Hi! You is bodersome!"

An' Annancy say—

"Sah! Me tell you! You go a' nex' room, you find one flour barrel. You bring him here, me will drop in it, so me will not mash!"

So Death go an' fetch de flour barrel, an' Annancy say—

"Now, me good frien', see me!"

And him drop, boof! into de barrel of flour, an' all de flour fly up into Death's eye, an' him bawl out, but him can no see Annancy!

An' him rub him eye, an' rub him eye, but while him is rubbin', Annancy run off.

An' Death no catch him to this day!

1905

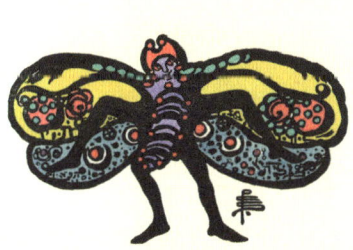

GINGY FLY

Once in a long before time, before Queen Victoria come to reign over we, Annancy live in dis country, an' him hab' a God-mamma an' God-pappa call Raabit. One day Annancy say to himself he wi' go visit dem. So him go out, an walk, an walk, an' bumby him come to dere house, an' 'dere was God-mamma Raabit standin' in de door mout'.

An' Annancy say—

"Marnin', God-mamma."

An' God-mamma say—

Gingy Fly

"Marnin', Annancy."

An' Annancy say—

" I hope you is quite well ? "

An' God-mamma say—

" Tanks, me son, I is quite well."

An' Annancy say—

An' how is God-pappa ? I hope him is quite well."

An' God-mamma say—

" Tanks, me son, him is quite well, him is sittin' down in de house."

An' 'dey go in de house, an' dere was God-pappa sittin' down in 'de house."

An' Annancy say—

"Marnin', God-pappa, I hope you is quite well ! "

An' God-pappa say—

" Tanks, me son, I is quite well."

An' 'dey talk a long time, an' bumby God-mamma say she would go out fetch water at de riberside, an' beg Annancy stay wid God-pappa while she gone. So when she turn her back out de door Annancy tek' him han', box down God-pappa dead ! An' bumby when God-mamma come

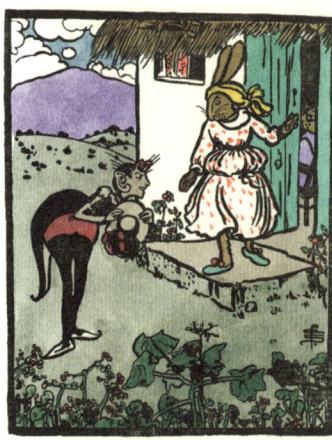

"Marnin'!"

Gingy Fly

home back, Annancy pretended cryin', an' God-mamma say—"Hi! Well, me son, what fe' do? You mus' go bury him."

An' Annancy say—

"Me no can bury him by me self, him is too heaby: an' a' mus' hab' someone help dig de hole!"

So Annancy go out an' get him frien' Gingy-Fly: (dat is a blue-bottle.)

An' Gingy-Fly come.

An' den Annancy an' Gingy-Fly tell God-mamma say—

"We cannot bury God-pappa, till we hab some fry-pan an' lard, an' pepper an' salt, an' knife an' fork, an' a fire pot."

An' den God-mamma gib dem all dese tings an' dey tek' dem, an' dey tek' God-pappa an' dey go to de funeral ground.

An' when dey get to de funeral ground dey build a fire in de fire pot, an' dey put on de fry-pan, an' dey put on de lard, an' dey put on de pepper an' salt, an' dey put on God-pappa, an'

Gingy Fly

dey fry him till him is quite crisp! An' dey heat him up till dem was so full of Raabit dem could'n walk! An' dey lie down 'pon de ground an' go to sleep, tell de evenin' breeze come down from de hills an' wake dem up.

An' when dey was returnin' home back, de moon was shinin' brightly, an' Annancy say to Gingy-Fly—

"Gingy-Fly, what you gwin' tell God-mamma when we get home back, dat we do wid God-pappa?"

An' Gingy-Fly say—

"Hi! Me no will tell her say God-pappa heat very nice!"

An' Annancy say—

"An' how did him agree wid you, Gingy-Fly?"

An' Gingy-Fly say—

"Tanks—him agree wid me nicely!"

An' Annancy say—

"Mek I see you tongue?"

An' Gingy-Fly tik out him tongue.

An' Annancy tek him knife an' cut it off!

Gingy Fly

An' when dey got home back Gingy-Fly can say nottin at all!

An' God-mamma say—

"Hi! What is de matter wi' Gingy-Fly? him can say nottin' at all."

An' Annancy say—

"Him laugh after God-mamma an' God-pappa, an' was struck dumb!"

An' dat is why Gingy-Fly say Vro-Vro-Vro-Vro, to dis day!

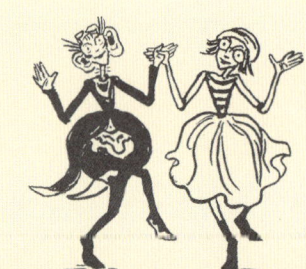

1905

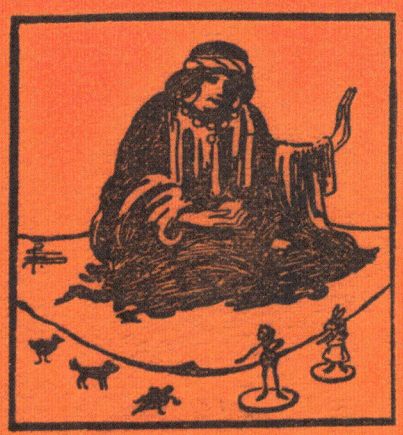

These, and other Annancy Stories are told by the Author at Children's Parties, At Homes, Receptions, Bazaars, &c., with Toys of the characters. 🐏   🐏   🐏   🐏   🐏

For terms apply to *The Green Sheaf*, 3 Park Mansions Arcade, Knightsbridge, London, S.W.

⁂⁂⁂⁂⁂⁂⁂⁂⁂⁂⁂⁂⁂⁂⁂⁂⁂⁂⁂⁂⁂⁂⁂⁂⁂⁂⁂⁂

Orders now taken for Private Christmas and Greeting Cards. Designs on approval. 🐏

Letters from the Beasts to Dina

1905

Letters from the Beasts to Dina
While she was ill with Scarlatina

FROM AUNTIE *(An Introduction)*

SO, my poor dear darling Dina,
You're in bed with scarlatina!
Red all over I suppose,
From your forehead to your toes.

Are you very tired of bed?
Have you got an aching head?
Still, things might be worse by far
Than I think they really are.

LETTERS TO DINA

For you might have twisted toes,
And a blister on your nose;
Or your teeth might always ache
And your head go shaky-shake.

Don't you think you would feel better
If every beast should write a letter—
Scamp, Diogenes and Jan,
And both Canaries, if they can?

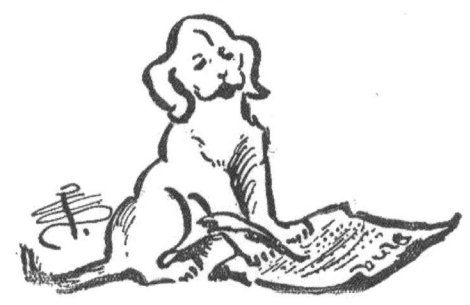

If all your friends in fur and feather
Join to comfort you together,
I feel assured, my little Dina,
You'll soon be rid of scarlatina!

Edith Theobald's "Letters from the Beasts to Dina" from John Baillie's *The Dream Garden: A Children's Annual*, 1905

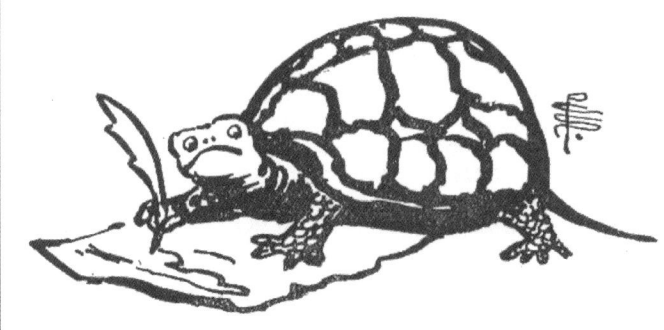

My mouth is rather like a beak,
  I know I shut it very tight;
I never open it to speak,
  Only, in fact, to bite.
I'm quite unlike some folks, I know,
Whose tongues are always on the go.

I fear you think my letter slow,
  It's taken me an age to write;
I was not meant for speed, although
  I've done my best to-night.
Send me a message, Dina, please,
And now good-bye. DIOGENES.

A Celtic Christmas, In Tenebris

1906

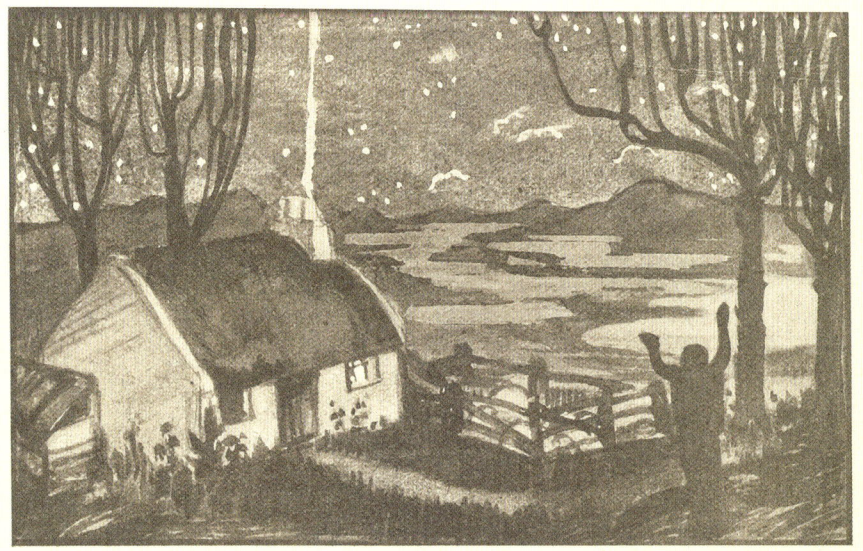

"Who but the Stars that Burn in the Blue."

IN TENEBRIS.

Who are my friends,
   Faithful and true?
Who but the stars
   That burn in the blue.
Who but the sun
   That sinketh so red,
Who but the clay
   That giveth me bread.
Who but the hills,
   Who but the sea,
Who but the flowers
   That fold on the tree.
Who but the moths
   That flutter and pass,
Who but the lambs
   That cry in the grass.
Who but the darkness,
   Who but the rain,
Who but the grave, the grave—
   All else are vain!
       All else are vain!

Seosamh Mac Cathmhaoil.

"In Tenebris" by Seosamh MacCathmhaoil from *A Celtic Christmas*, 1906

In the Valley of Stars

1906

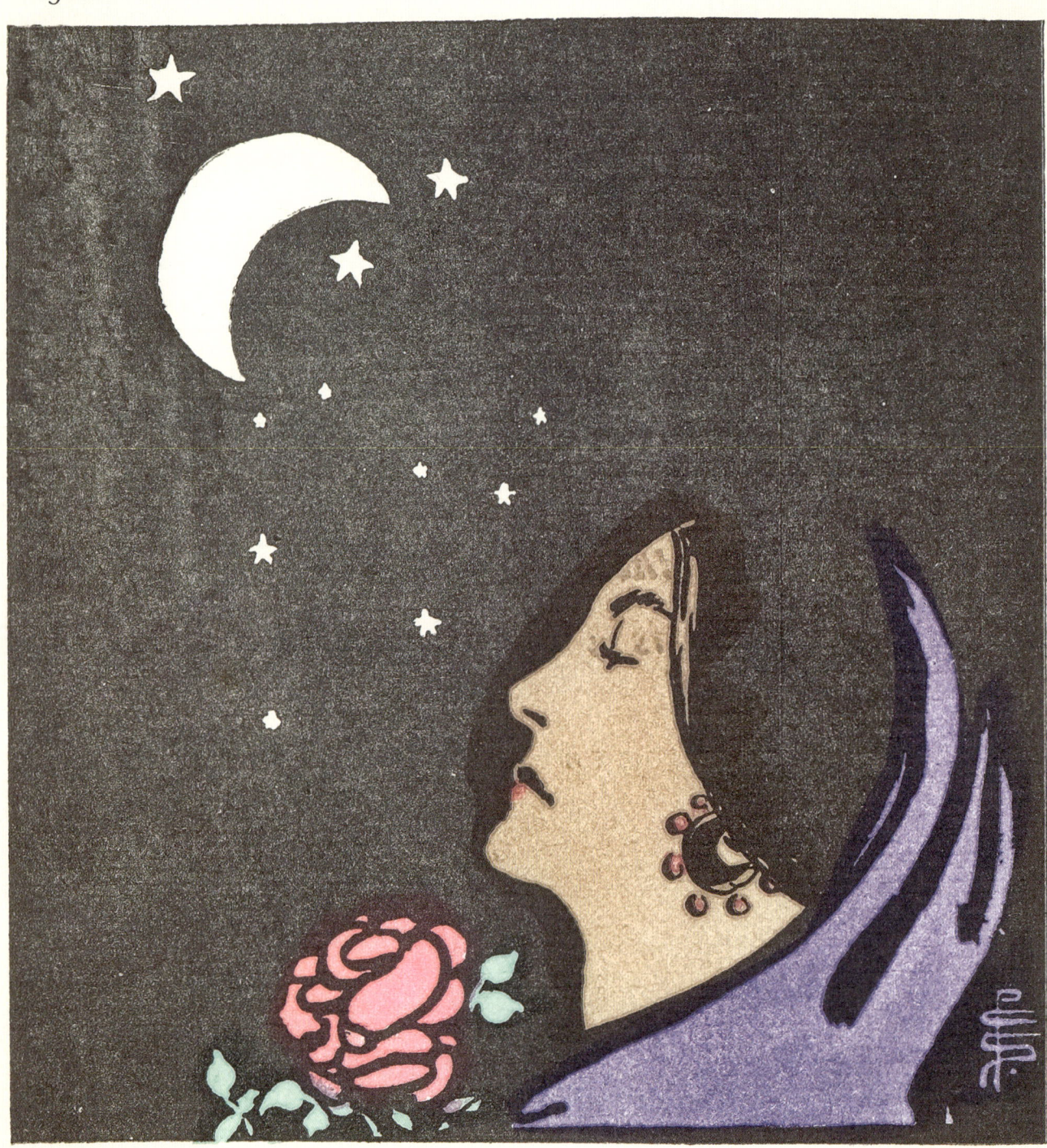

IN THE VALLEY OF STARS THERE IS A TOWER OF SILENCE.

A PERSIAN TRAGEDY.

By SMARA KHAMARA.

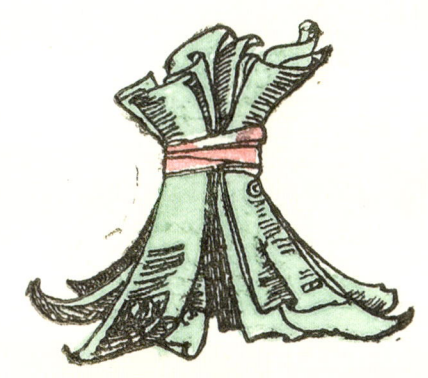

LONDON:
"THE GREEN SHEAF," 3, PARK MANSIONS ARCADE,
KNIGHTSBRIDGE, S.W.
1906.

1907 to 1909

The Craftsman, A Protest Against Fear

A Protest Against Fear

It seems to me that fear has got hold of all this land. Each one has a great fear of himself, a fear to believe, to think, to do, to be, to act.

Who dares to do anything without fear of what some other will think or say? How can a country have a living, growing art when it is so bound down by fear, the most dreadful of all evils?

This marvelous, great country, big in all its feeling and full of energy, and yet producing almost no freedom of thought or work!

You, younger students, who are entering this garden of toil, where flowers are grown by love and patience, why do you not try to be true to your better selves, why do you not try to see the finer, bigger things that are all about you, and to kill in your garden those mawkish weeds of sugar-sweet sentimentality and shallow feeling. Try to feel truly one thought, one scene, and make others feel it as keenly as you do—thus is art born.

— Pamela Colman Smith.

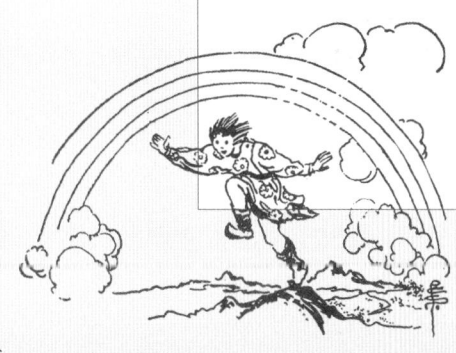

Smithsonian/Egmont   1907

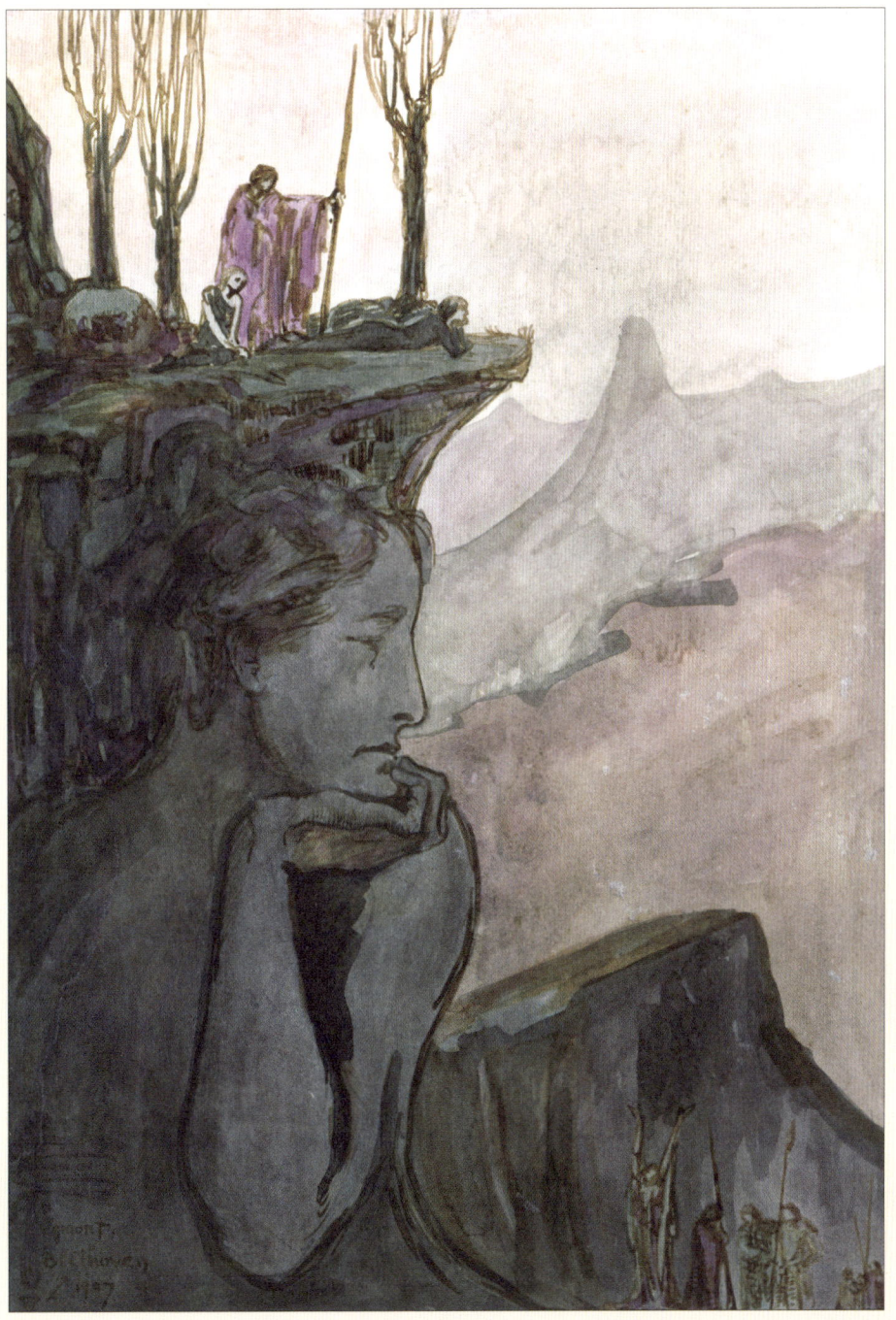

Beethoven, Opus 84, watercolor, brush and ink, and pencil on paper by Pamela Colman Smith. Courtesy of Smithsonian American Art Museum.

George Eastman Museum

1907

Photographic reproduction of untitled artwork by Pamela Colman Smith. Gum bichromate over platinum print by Alvin Langdon Coburn, circa 1907. Courtesy of George Eastman Museum. © The Universal Order

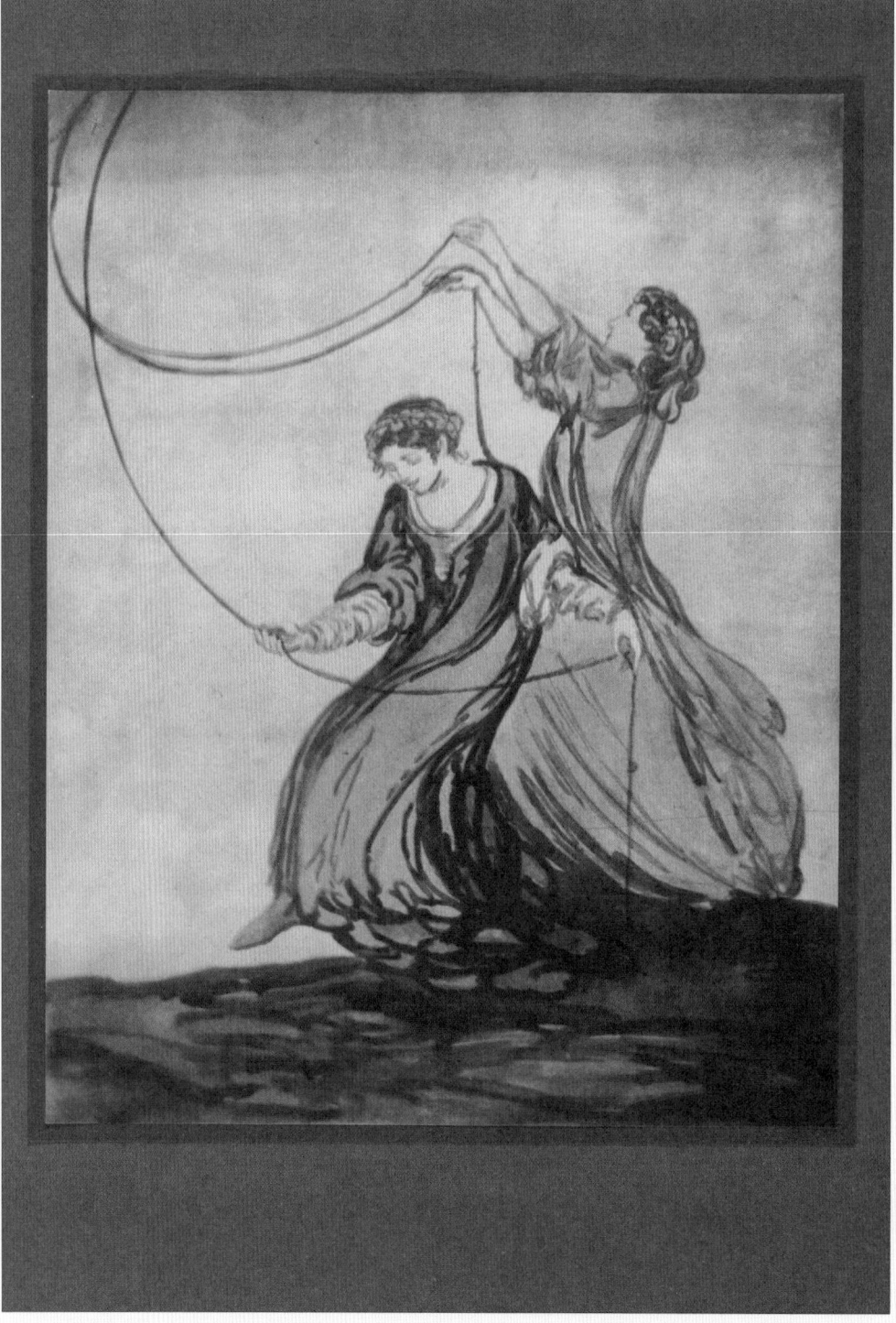

1907

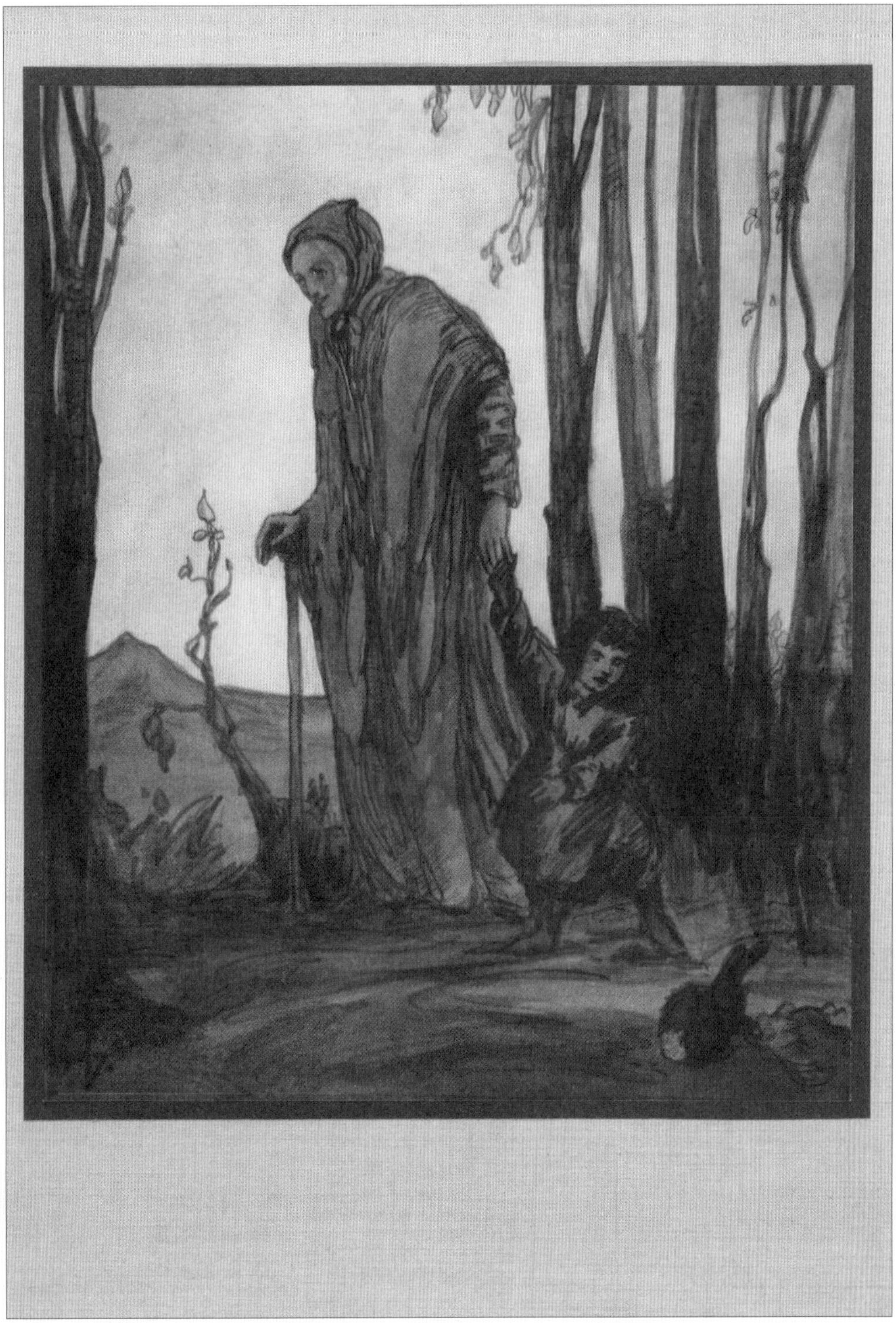

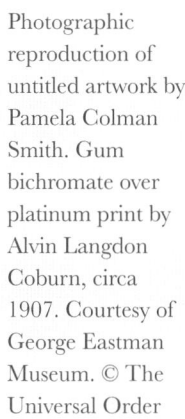

Photographic reproduction of untitled artwork by Pamela Colman Smith. Gum bichromate over platinum print by Alvin Langdon Coburn, circa 1907. Courtesy of George Eastman Museum. © The Universal Order

1907

Photographic reproduction of untitled artwork by Pamela Colman Smith. Gum bichromate over platinum print by Alvin Langdon Coburn, circa 1907. Courtesy of George Eastman Museum. © The Universal Order

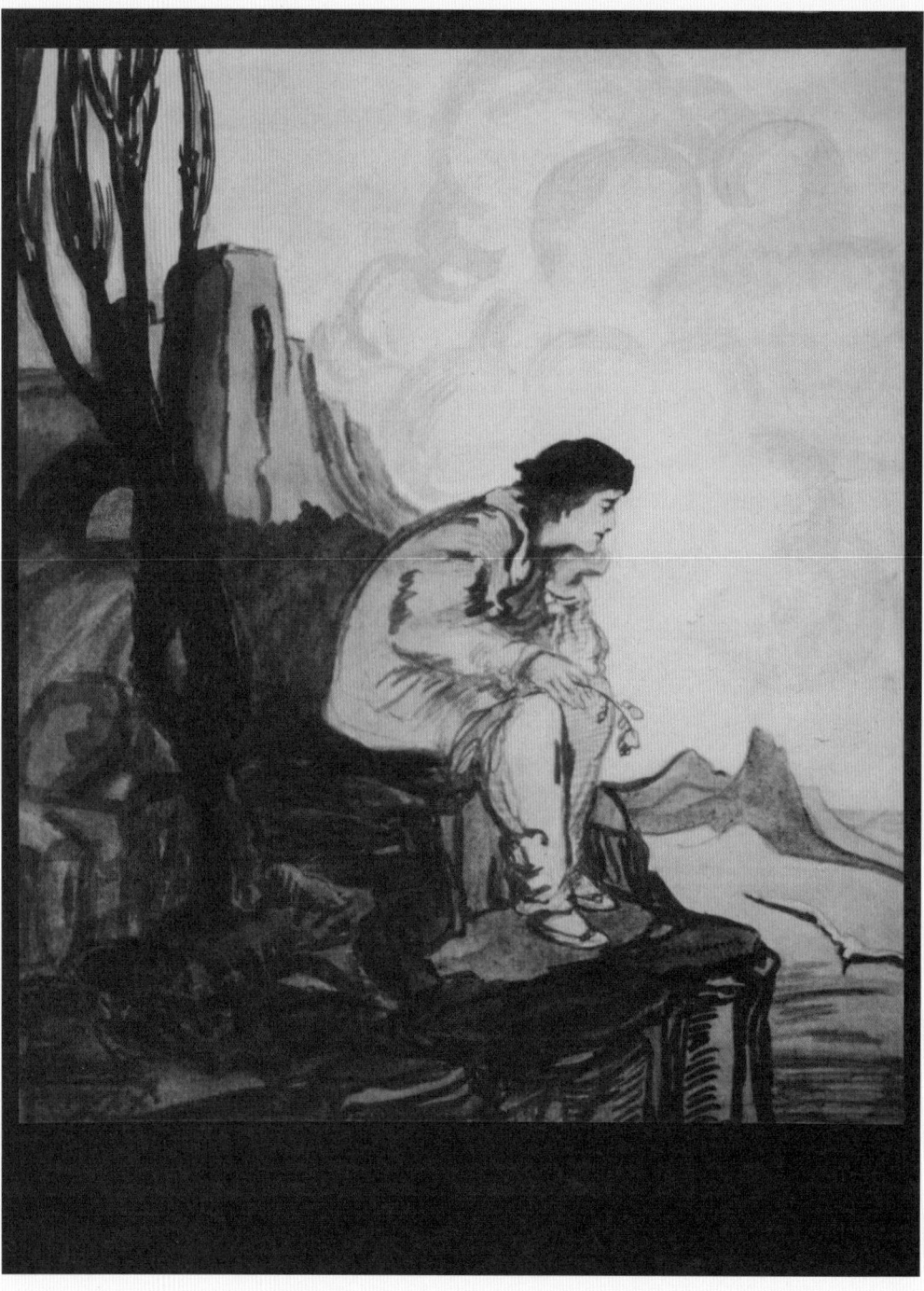

1907

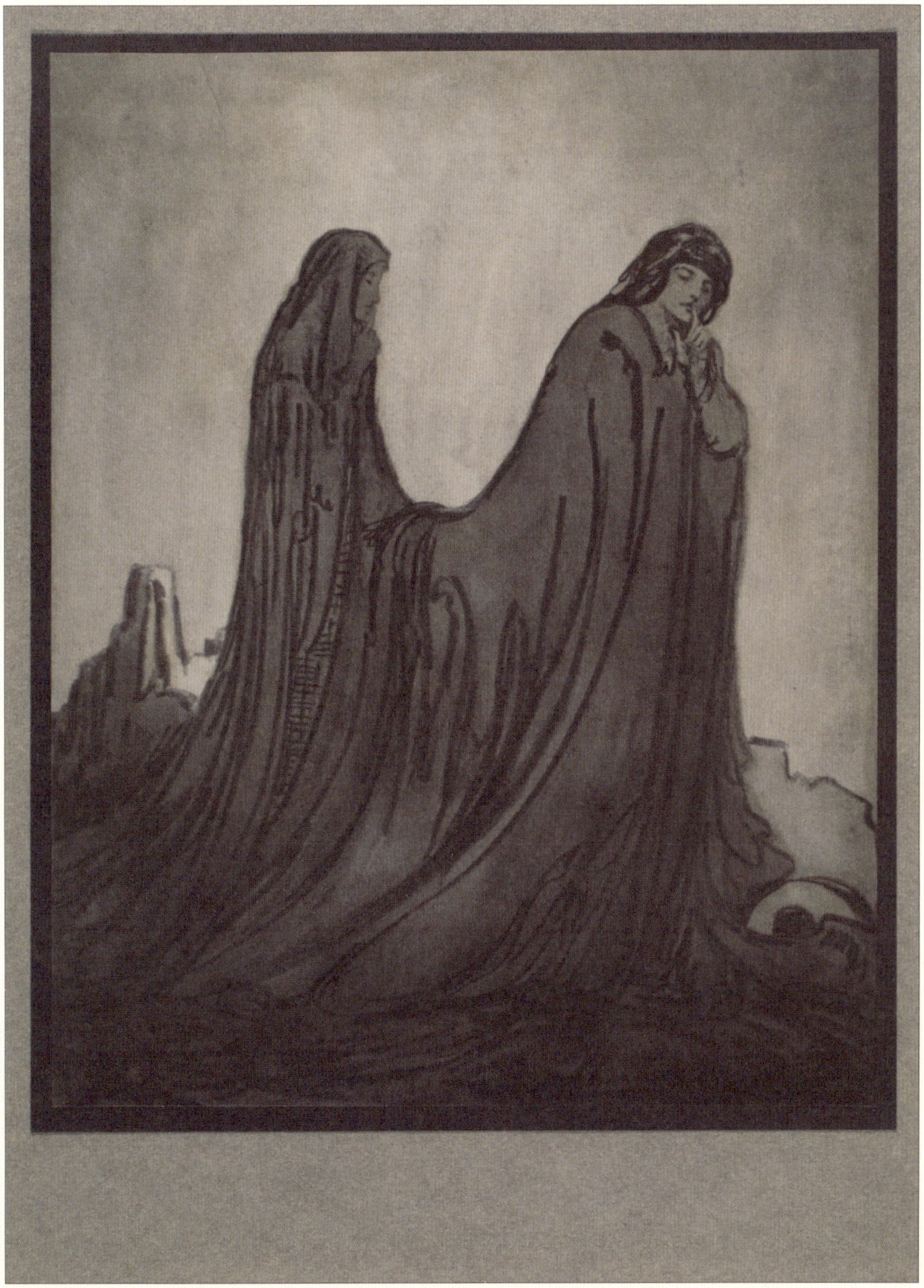

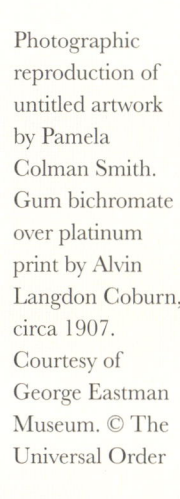

Photographic reproduction of untitled artwork by Pamela Colman Smith. Gum bichromate over platinum print by Alvin Langdon Coburn, circa 1907. Courtesy of George Eastman Museum. © The Universal Order

1907

Photographic reproduction of untitled artwork by Pamela Colman Smith. Gum bichromate over platinum print by Alvin Langdon Coburn, circa 1907. Courtesy of George Eastman Museum. © The Universal Order

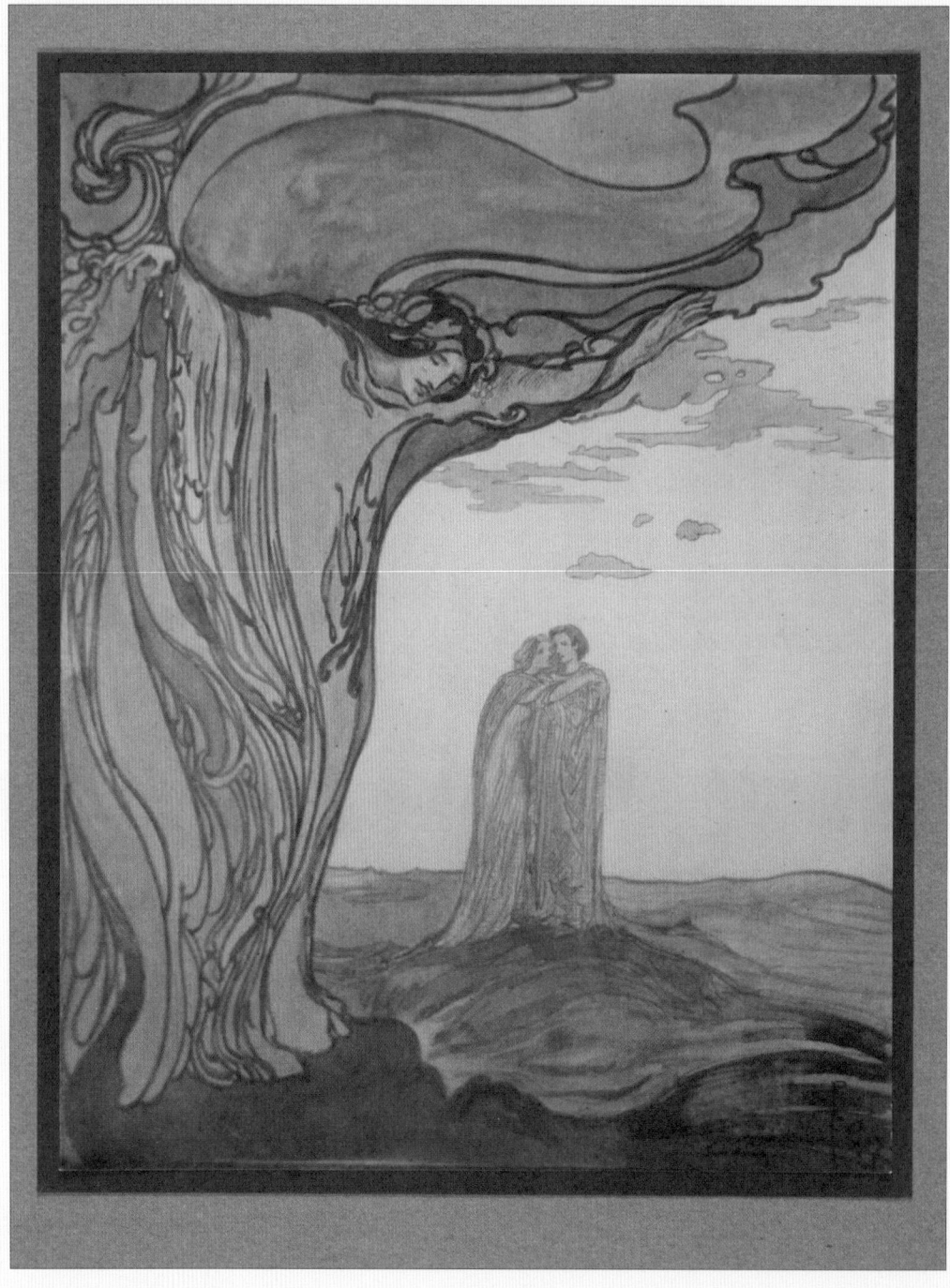

Images from Beinecke/Stieglitz Letters

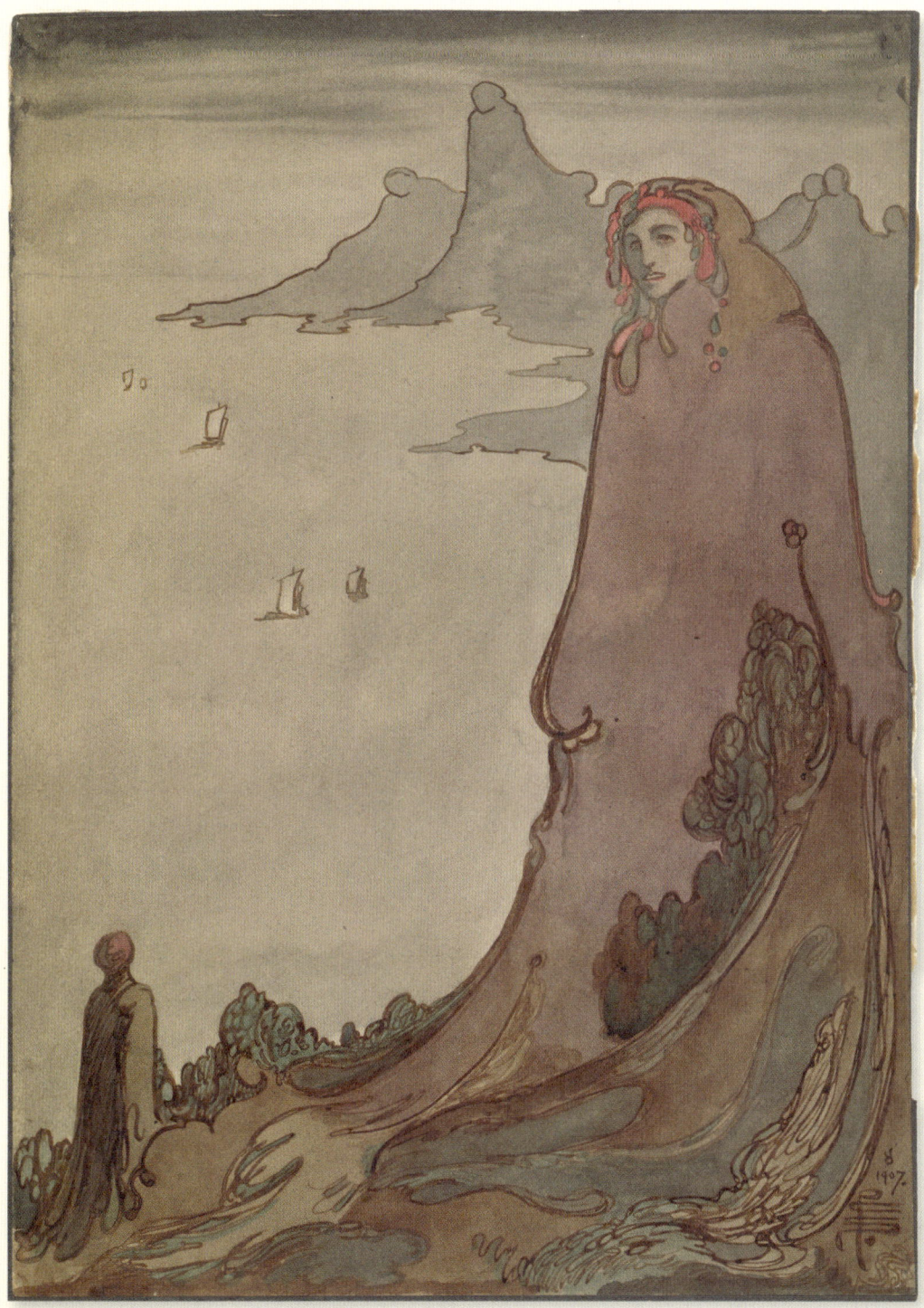

1907

Beethoven, Sonata No. 11, watercolor on paper board by Pamela Colman Smith. Courtesy of The Beinecke Rare Book & Manuscript Library, Yale University

1907

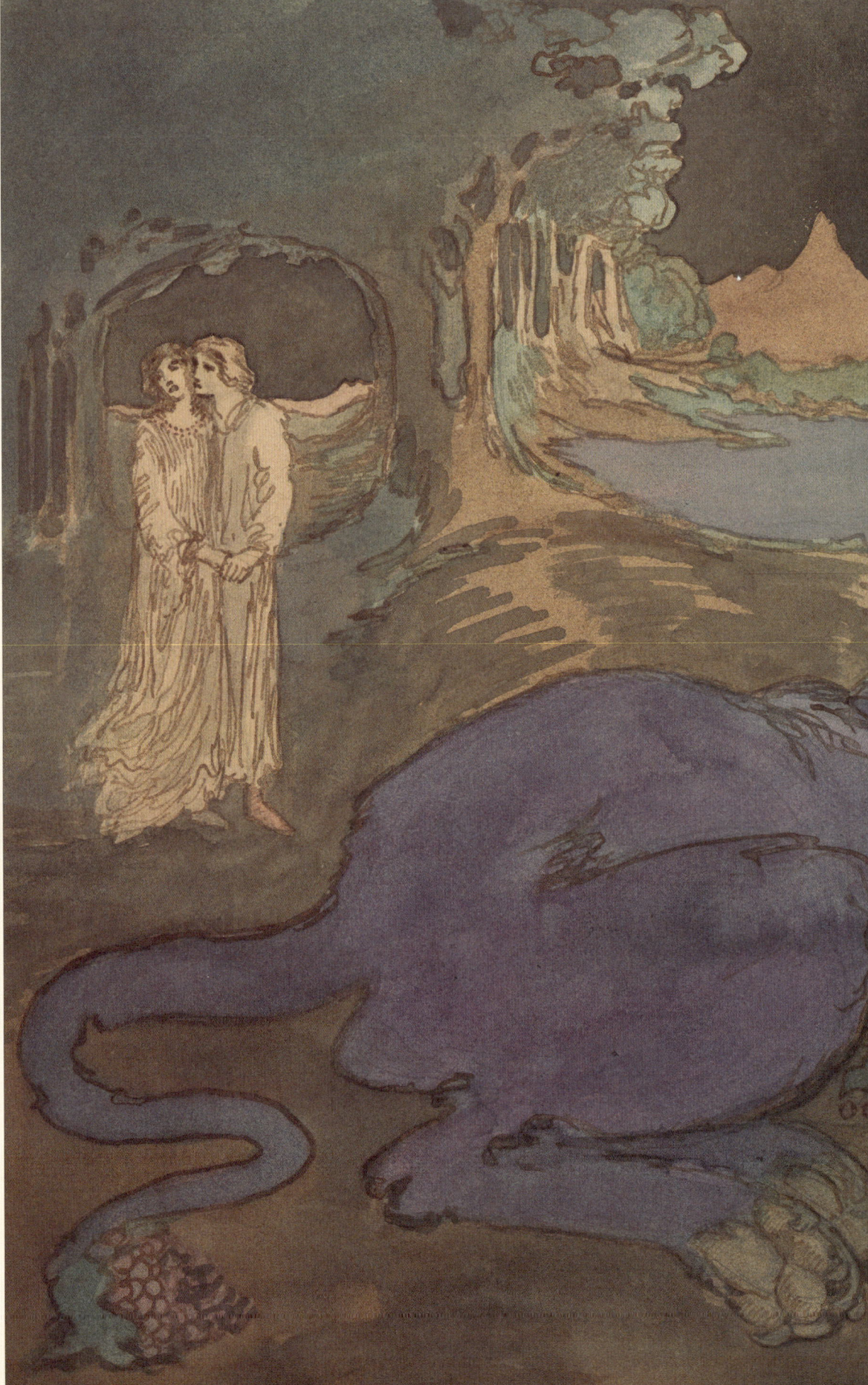

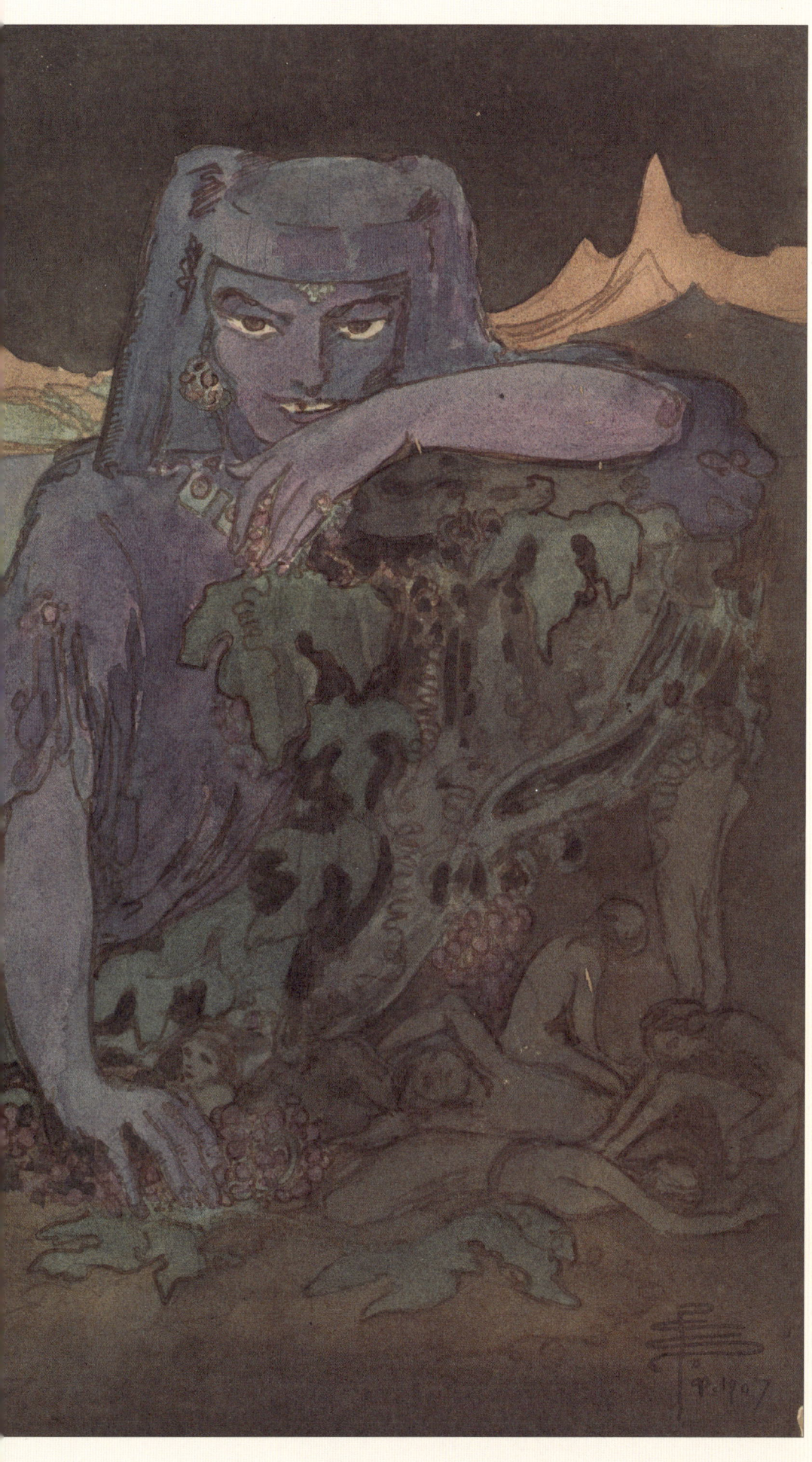

"The Blue Cat," watercolor on paper board by Pamela Colman Smith. Courtesy of The Beinecke Rare Book & Manuscript Library, Yale University

1907

Sketch for glass, watercolor and ink on paper by Pamela Colman Smith. Possibly used for an advertising display at Photo-Secession Exhibition. Courtesy of The Beinecke Rare Book & Manuscript Library, Yale University

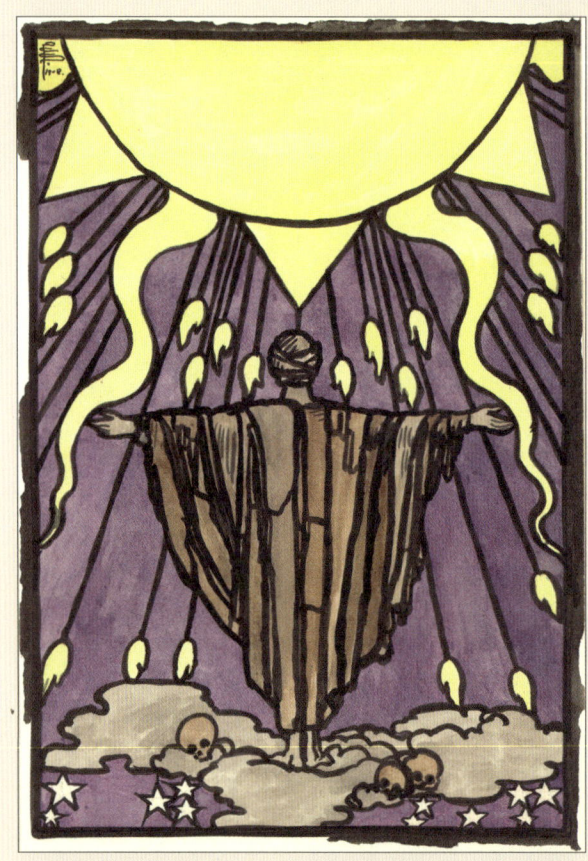

Untitled, possibly an exhibition poster from a street signboard at 291 Fifth Avenue, watercolor and ink on paper by Pamela Colman Smith. Courtesy of The Beinecke Rare Book & Manuscript Library, Yale University

Opposite: Schumann, watercolor on paper board by Pamela Colman Smith. Courtesy of The Beinecke Rare Book & Manuscript Library, Yale University

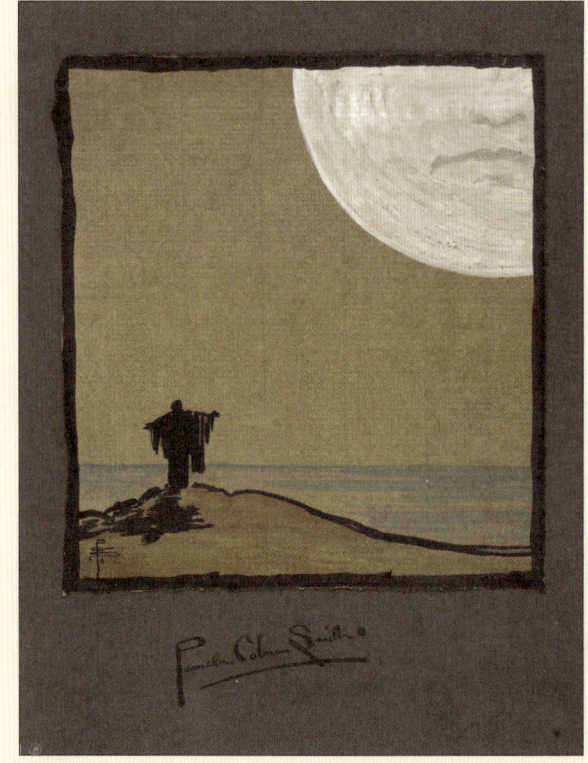

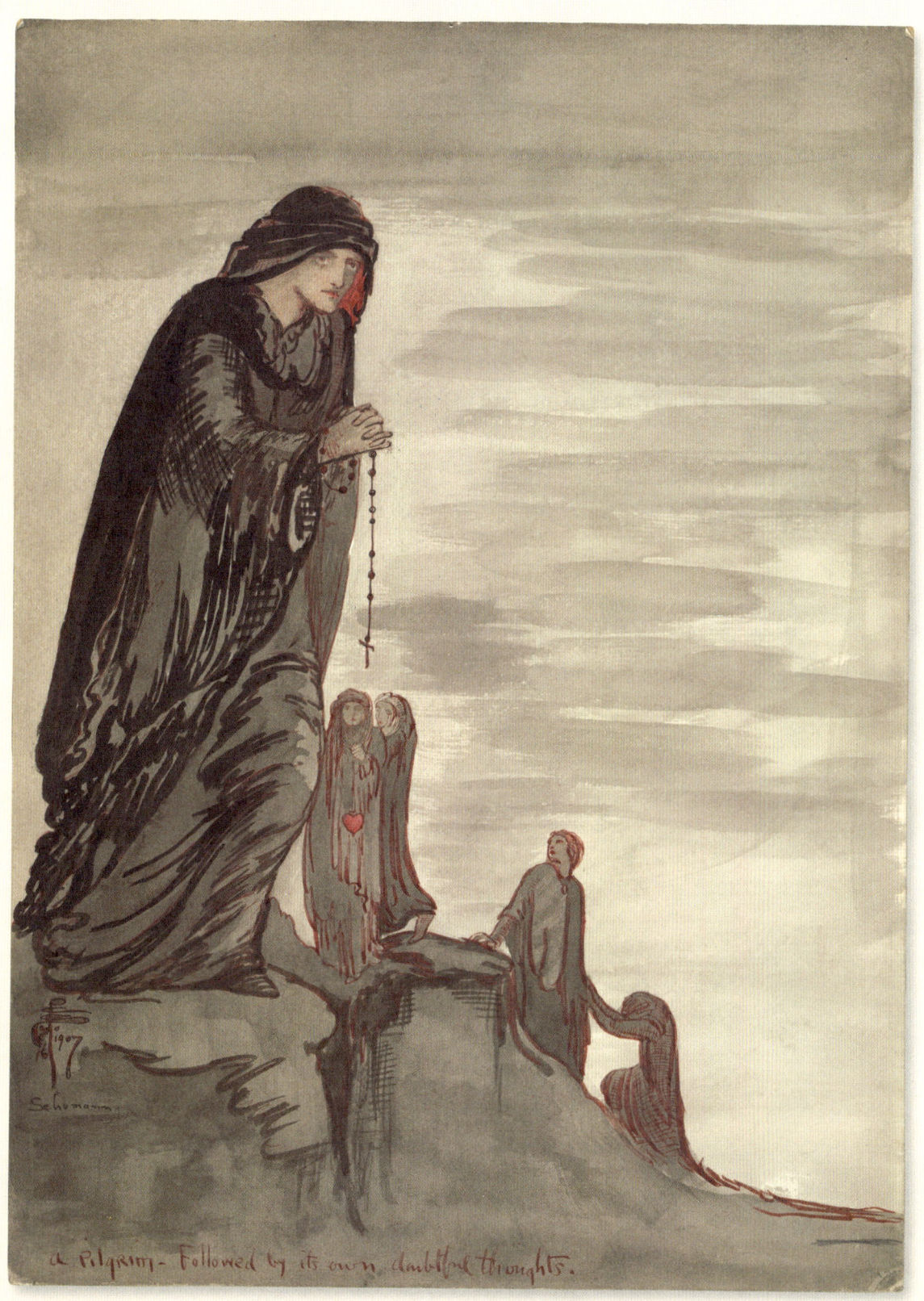

A Pilgrim - Followed by its own doubtful thoughts.

1907

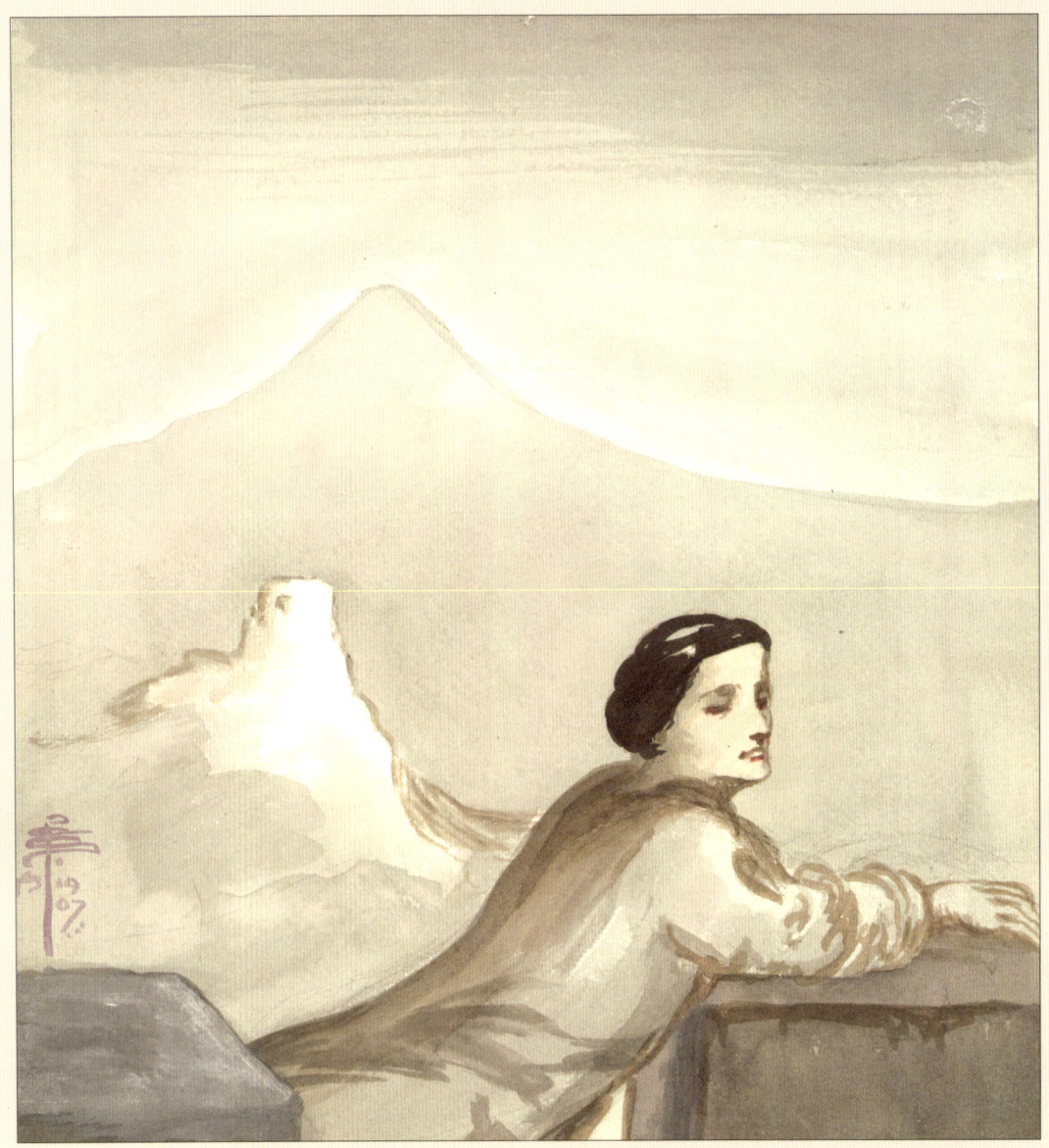

Mozart, Sonata in F Major for Violin and Piano, Second Series Duet, watercolor on paper by Pamela Colman Smith. Courtesy of The Beinecke Rare Book & Manuscript Library, Yale University

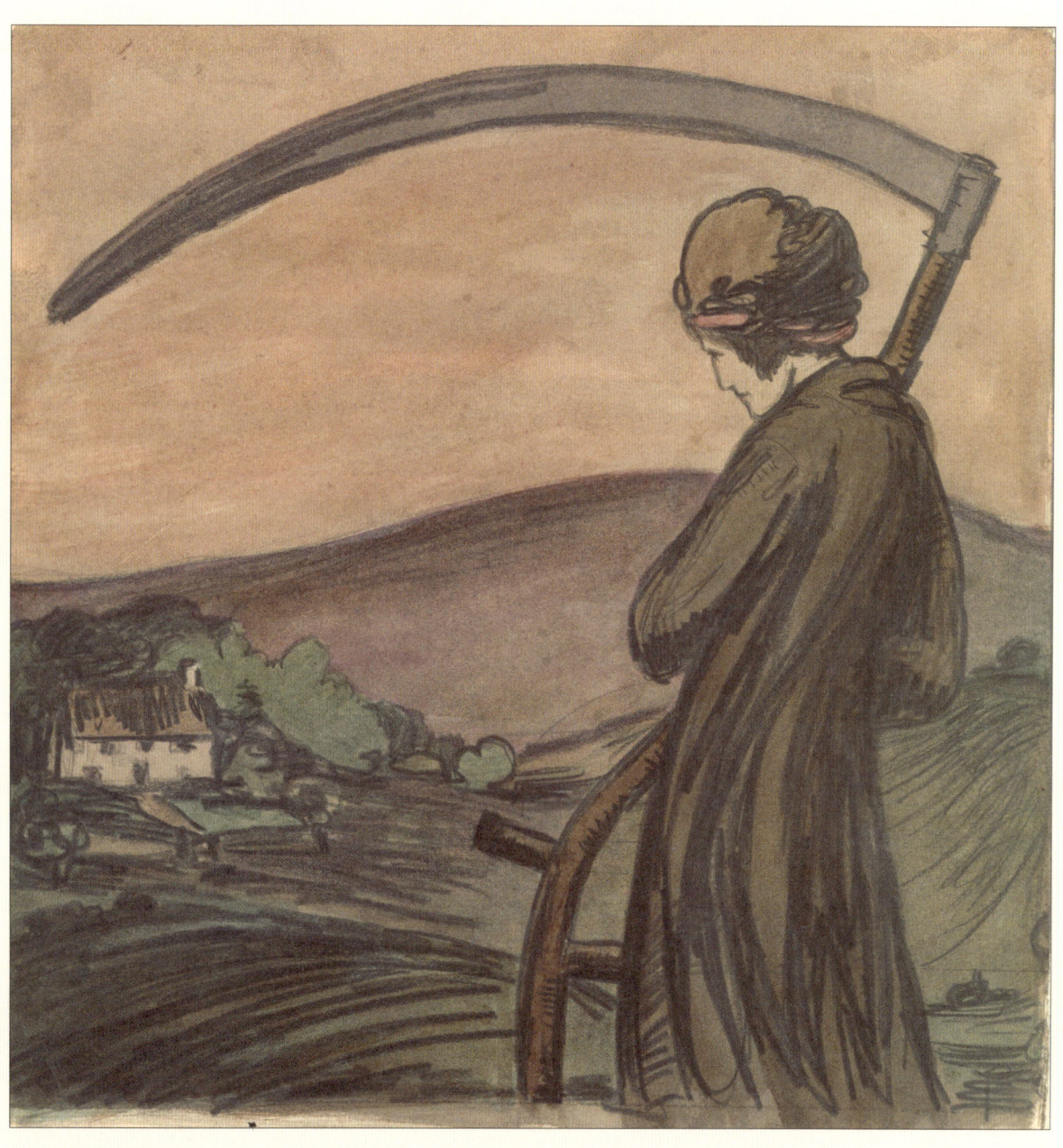

"Time," watercolor and pencil on paper board by Pamela Colman Smith. Courtesy of The Beinecke Rare Book & Manuscript Library, Yale University

1907.

"Red Cloak," watercolor and pencil on paper board by Pamela Colman Smith. Courtesy of The Beinecke Rare Book & Manuscript Library, Yale University

Opposite: "A Dirge," ink and pencil on paper by Pamela Colman Smith. Courtesy of The Beinecke Rare Book & Manuscript Library, Yale University

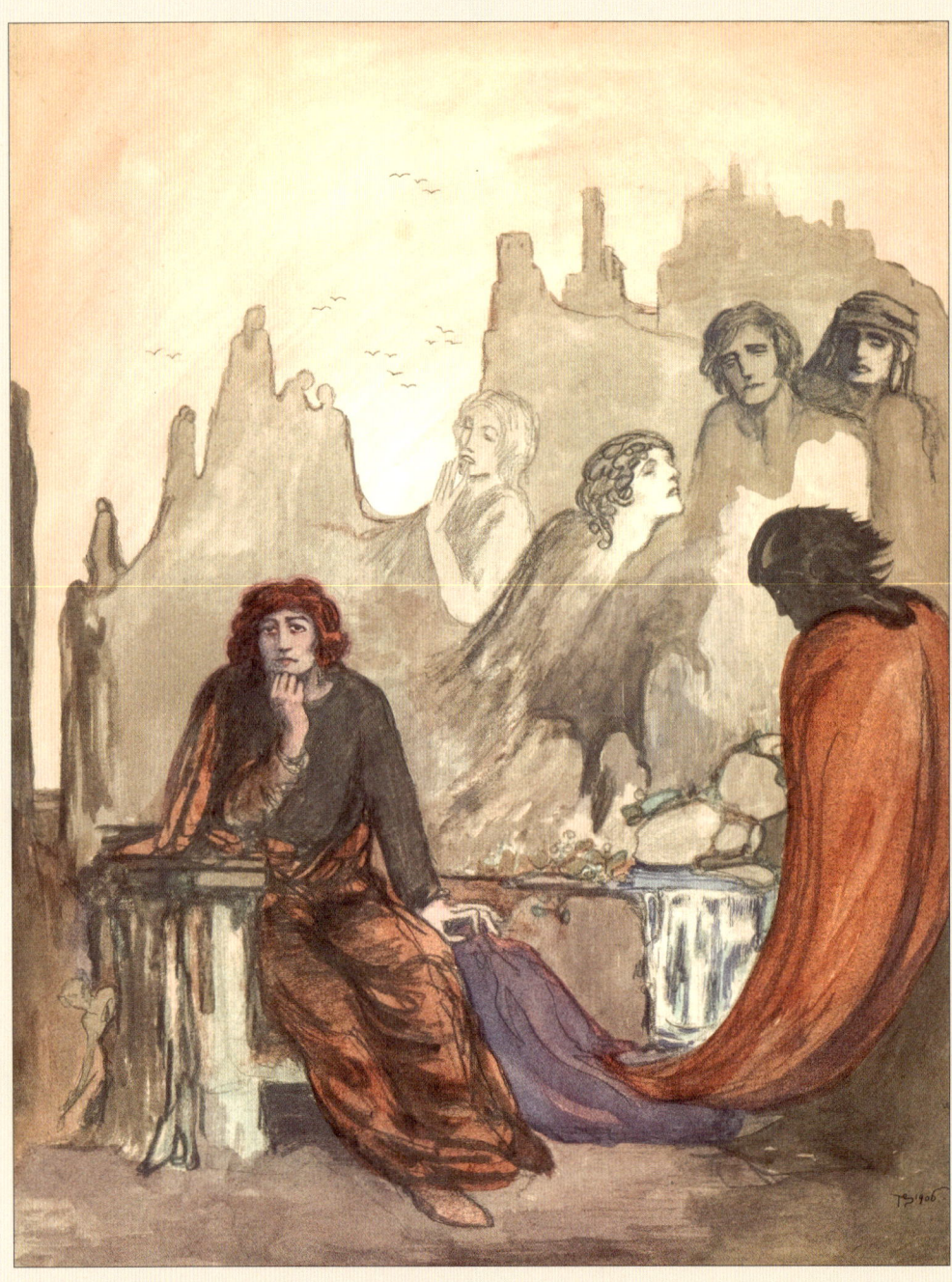

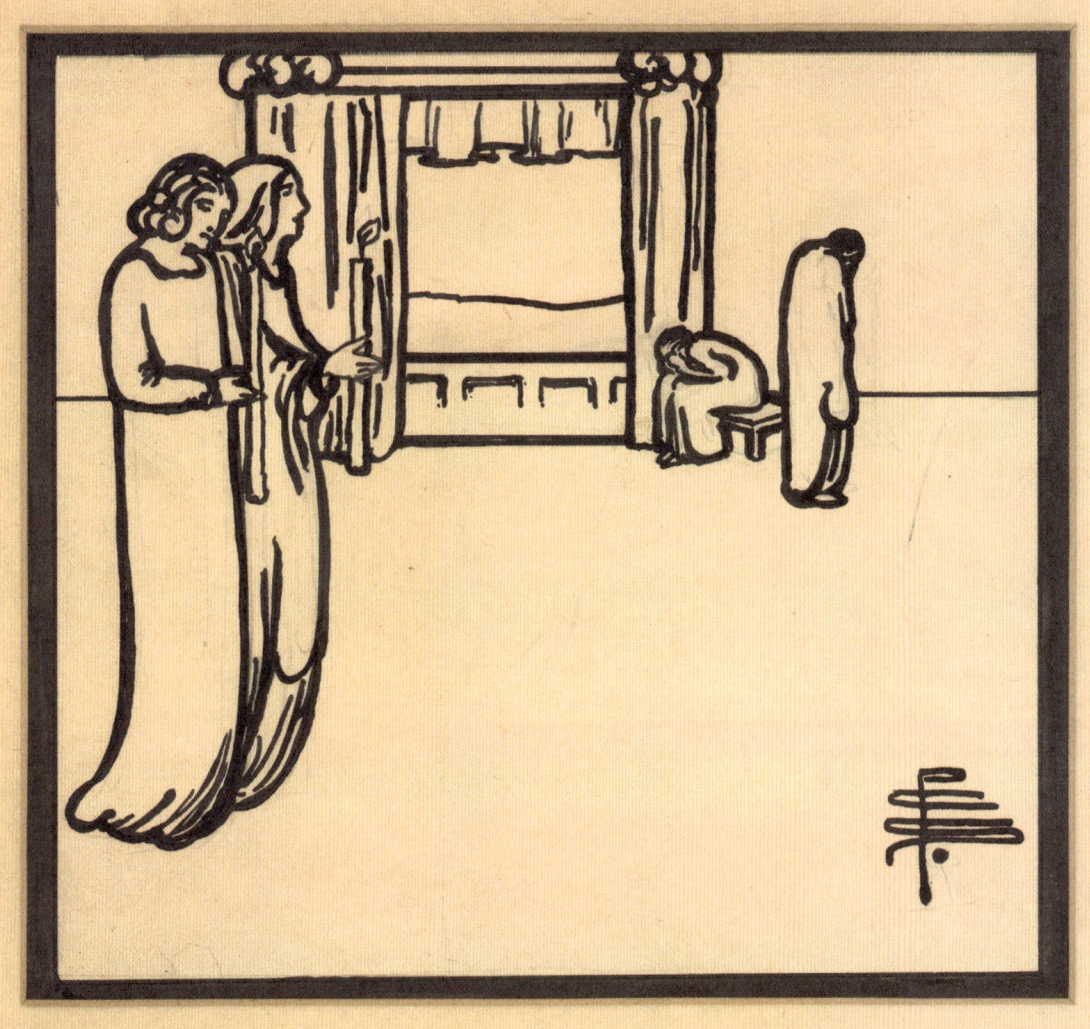

To one who appreciates what this means.
with good wishes
from
Pamela Colman Smith

January 24. 1907.

1907

Right: Letter to Alfred Stieglitz from Pamela Colman Smith dated March 23, 1907 on letterhead S.S. Minnehaha. Courtesy of The Beinecke Rare Book & Manuscript Library, Yale University

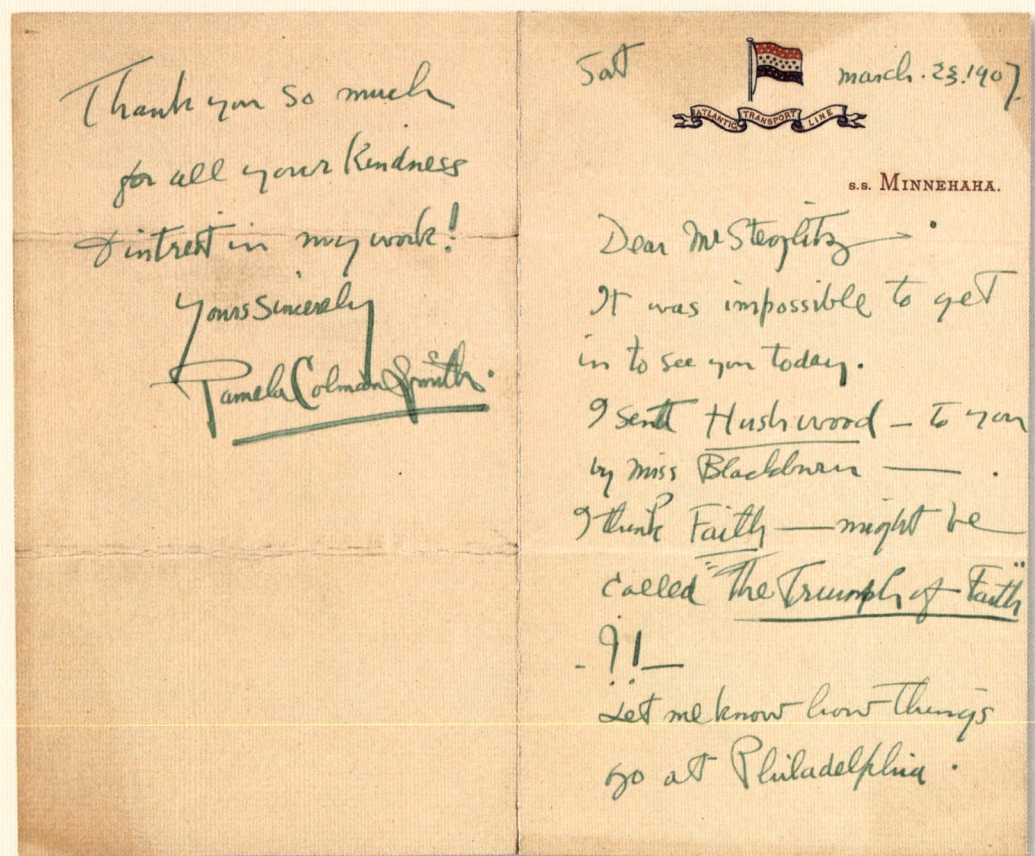

Excerpt of letter to Alfred Stieglitz from Pamela Colman Smith dated November 8, 1907 evidencing her financial difficulties. Courtesy of The Beinecke Rare Book & Manuscript Library, Yale University

December 27. 1907.

84 YORK MANSIONS, BATTERSEA PARK, LONDON, S.W.

TELEPHONE: 276 WESTERN.

Dear Mr Stieglitz — (American Express Co.)

Today I sent you by Express — 13 — drawings and consular certificate — you will find enclosed. I have 10 or 12. more to send. which I will post next Wednesday — also consular certificate

The one for the 13. drawings — is for £ 9-18-0 — I insured for £10 — It goes (they promised me) by tomorrow's ship — & should not be delayed! as it has been marked <u>urgent</u>! The post is much quicker — but some of the things were too large for post! I hope you will like them! I think they are improved! — I am getting another show here ready for a new show all of January. so am very busy! Had a show in Edinburgh — for 2 weeks in December — 3rd to the 15th — I sold 2 drawings & exchanged 1 — (to James Paterson — A.R.S.A) great swell — does ripping things of Scotland! —

Letter to Alfred Stieglitz from Pamela Colman Smith dated December 27, 1907. Courtesy of The Beinecke Rare Book & Manuscript Library, Yale University

Hotel Irving. 26. Gramercy Park. New York.
May. 9. 1909.

Dear Mr Stieglitz.

I have had a cheque from Miss Bird.

Mrs Bush – and Mrs Tatum have still to pay, but I hope to get it tomorrow.

So do not send them a bill till I see you.

It is nice Mr Motman getting 3 more!

We must do the percentage out – as the Secession must have its share.

Thank you so much for all you have done for me.

I appreciate it very much.

Yours sincerely
Pamela Smith

1909

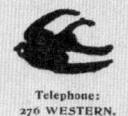

Telephone:
276 WESTERN.

84 YORK MANSIONS,
BATTERSEA PARK,
LONDON, S.W.

November. 19. 1909.

Dear Mr Stieglitz —
 I wonder where you are!! ——— I want some money for Christmas —! — I wonder if you got Mrs Busches money for the "moon"? ——
Can you send it to me? —
 I have 8 or 9 new things — I am sending over next week — You will like them I think —
Perhaps a few people may care for one or two —
They are carefull & nice colour —— & larger than any except the Wave one — I hope you are doing well — & the Little Galleries are still there!
I've just finished a big job for very little cash: a set of designs for a pack of Tarot cards 80 designs.
I shall send some over —— of the original drawings as some people may like them! — I will send you a pack — (printed in colour by lithography) — (probably very badly) as soon as they are ready — by Dec. 1 — I think —
 with goodwishes to you & Mrs Stieglitz & the Secession all of it ——— from yours sincerely
Pamela Colman Smith

Letter to Alfred Stieglitz from Pamela Colman Smith dated November 19, 1909. Courtesy of The Beinecke Rare Book & Manuscript Library, Yale University

Opposite: Letter to Alfred Stieglitz from Pamela Colman Smith dated May 9, 1909. Courtesy of The Beinecke Rare Book & Manuscript Library, Yale University

Smallhythe Place, Kent

1907

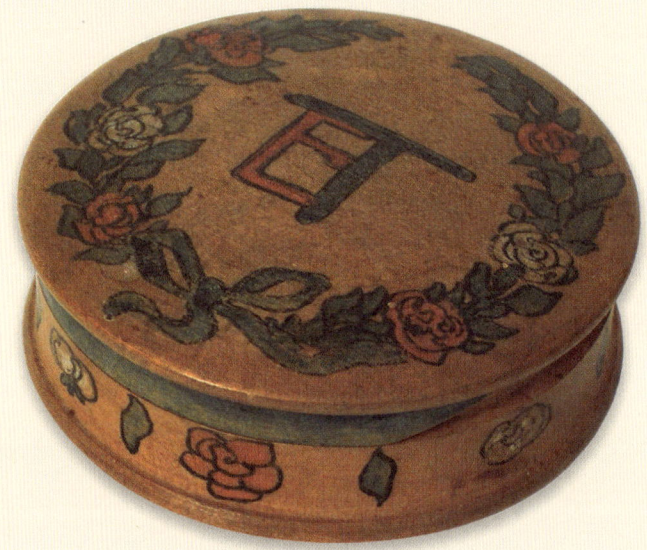

Circular wooden box, natural color, painted with green leaves and red and white roses, and initials "E.T." in center. Design around side. Painted by Pamela Colman Smith, December 16, 1899. Courtesy of Smallhythe Place. © National Trust/Andrew Fetherston

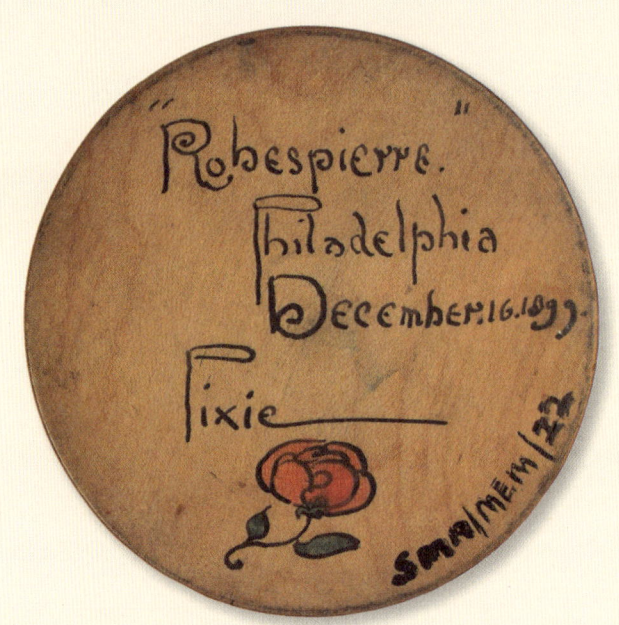

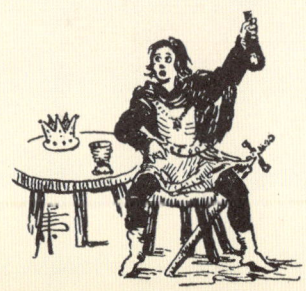

1907

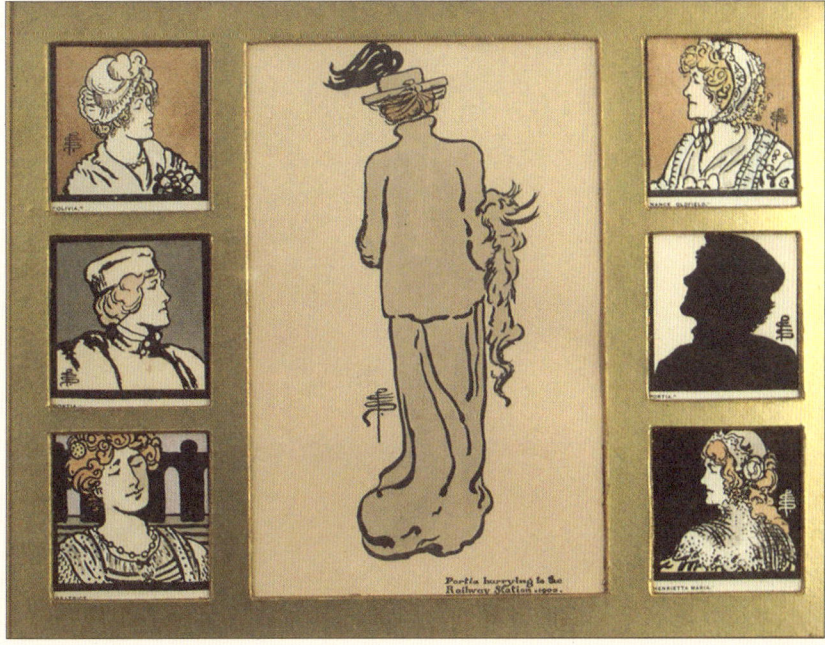

Dame Ellen Terry as "Portia Hurrying to the Railway Station" and other roles with six inset portraits surrounding main image by Pamela Colman Smith, circa 1900. Courtesy of Smallhythe Place.
© National Trust/Andrew Fetherston

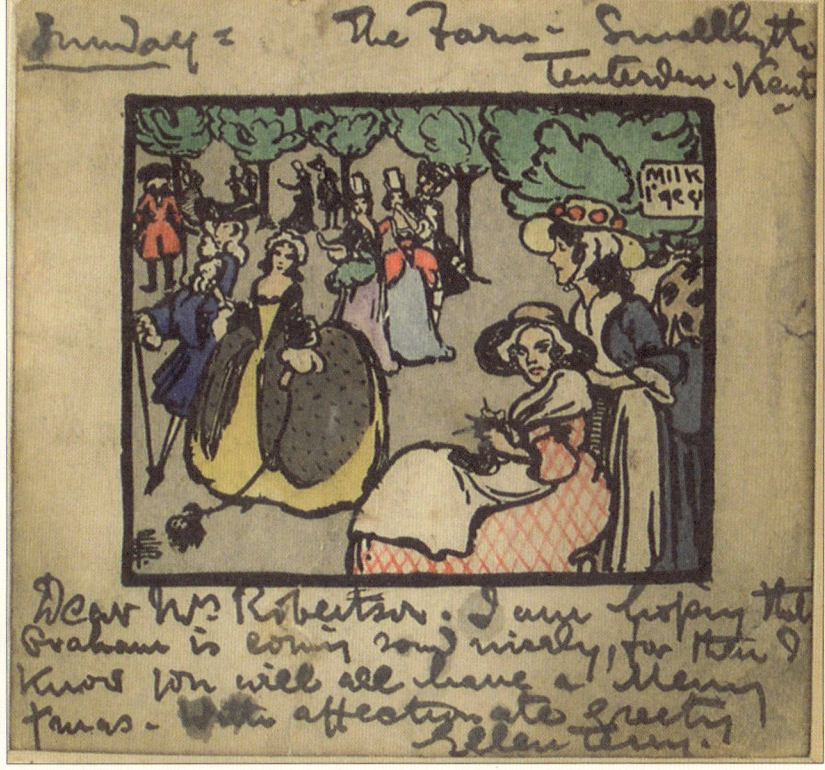

Figures parading before Dame Ellen Terry by Pamela Colman Smith, date unknown. Courtesy of Smallhythe Place.
© National Trust/Andrew Fetherston

1907

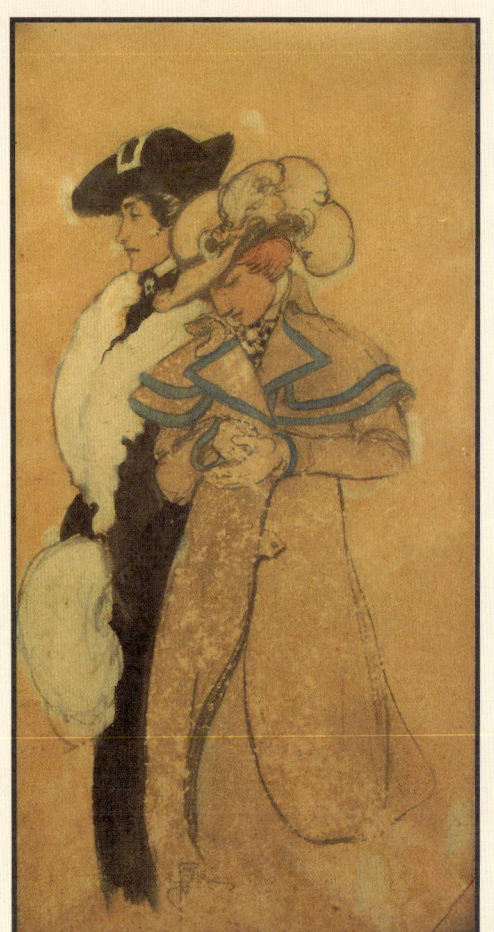

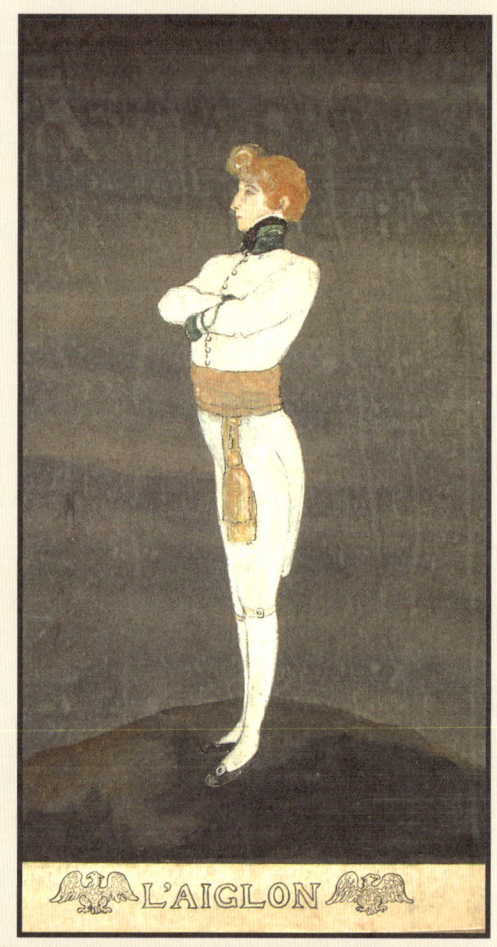

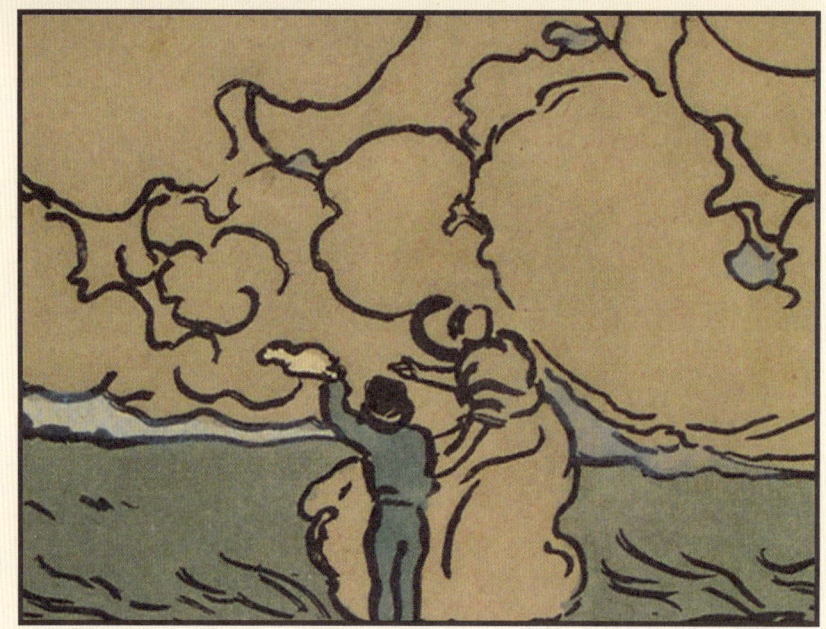

Above left: Dame Ellen Terry and her daughter Edith Ailsa Craig by Pamela Colman Smith, date unknown

Above right: L'Aiglon by Pamela Colman Smith, 1901. Costume for play by Edmond Rostand

At right: "The Wind" by Pamela Colman Smith, date unknown

All images are courtesy of Smallhythe Place. © National Trust/Andrew Fetherston

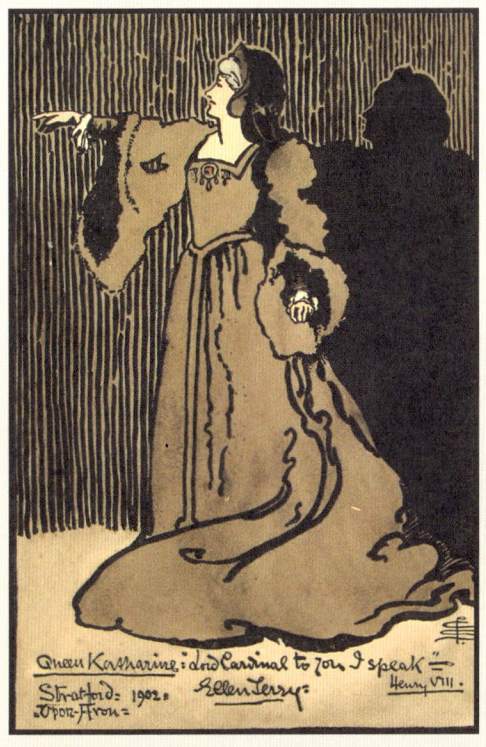
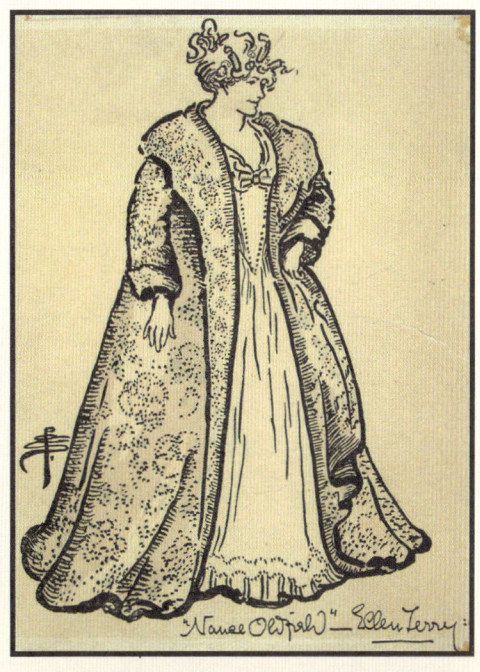
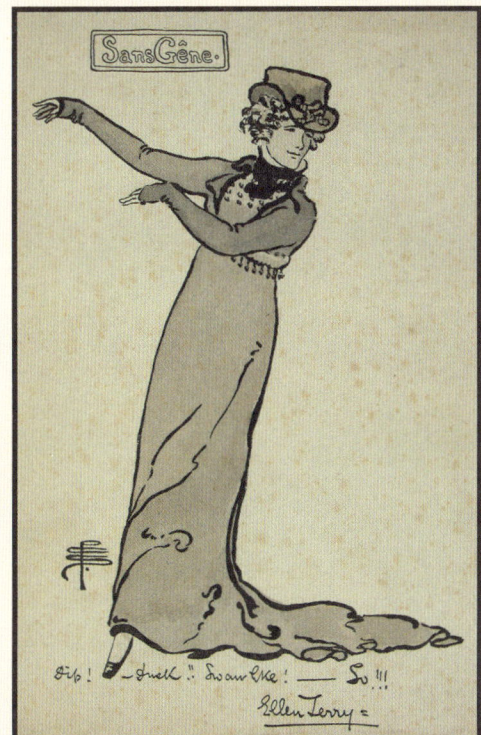
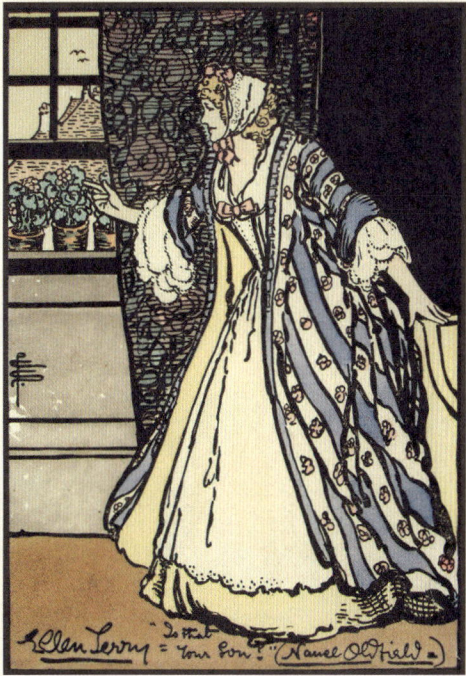

1907

Top left: Dame Ellen Terry as "Queen Katharine" in William Shakespeare's *Henry VIII* by Pamela Colman Smith, 1902. "Lord Cardinal to you I Speak"

Top right: Dame Ellen Terry as "Nance Oldfield" in the comedy "Nance Oldfield" by Charles Reade by Pamela Colman Smith, date unknown

Bottom left: Dame Ellen Terry in the title role of "Madame-sans-Gene" by J. Comyns Carr by Pamela Colman Smith, date unknown

Bottom right: Dame Ellen Terry as "Nance Oldfield" in the comedy "Nance Oldfield" by Charles Reade by Pamela Colman Smith, date unknown

1907

Ellen Terry in "The Good Hope" by Pamela Colman Smith, 1904. Courtesy of Smallhythe Place. © National Trust/Andrew Fetherston

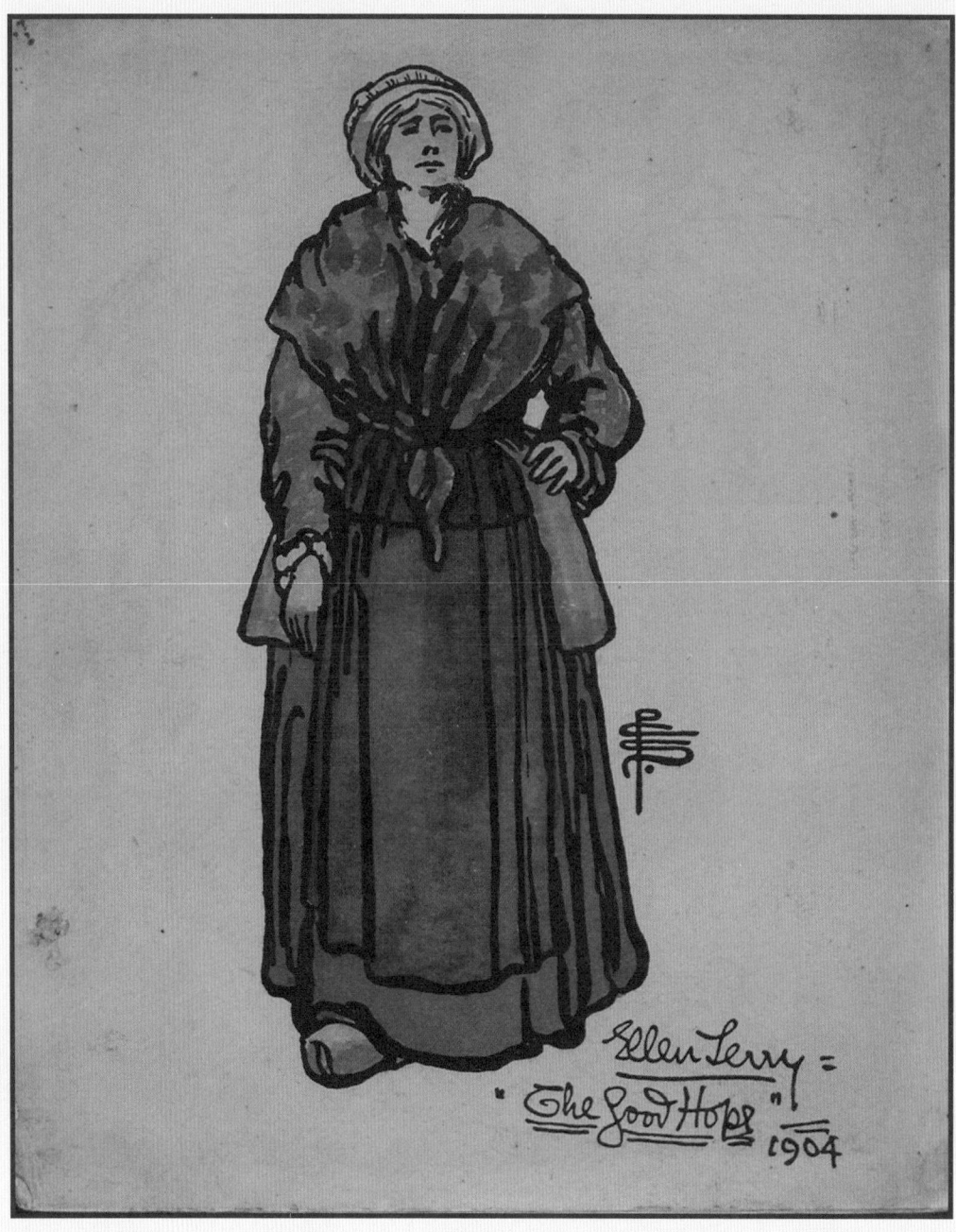

1907

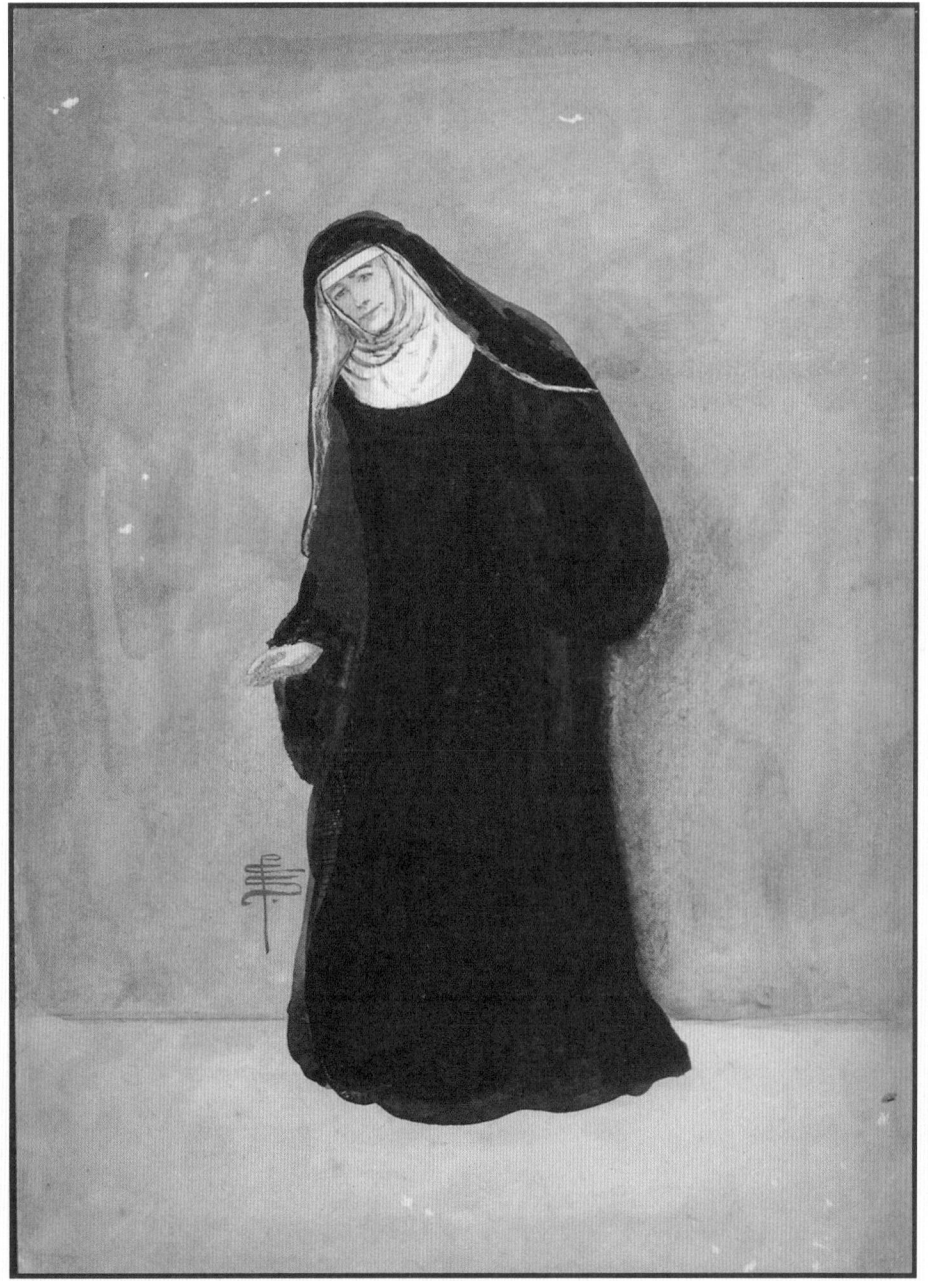

Ellen Terry in "The Good Hope" by Pamela Colman Smith, 1904. Courtesy of Smallhythe Place. © National Trust/Andrew Fetherston

1907

Sir Henry Irving as "Cardinal Wolsey" in William Shakespeare's *Henry VIII* by Pamela Colman Smith, 1904. Courtesy of Smallhythe Place. © National Trust/Andrew Fetherston

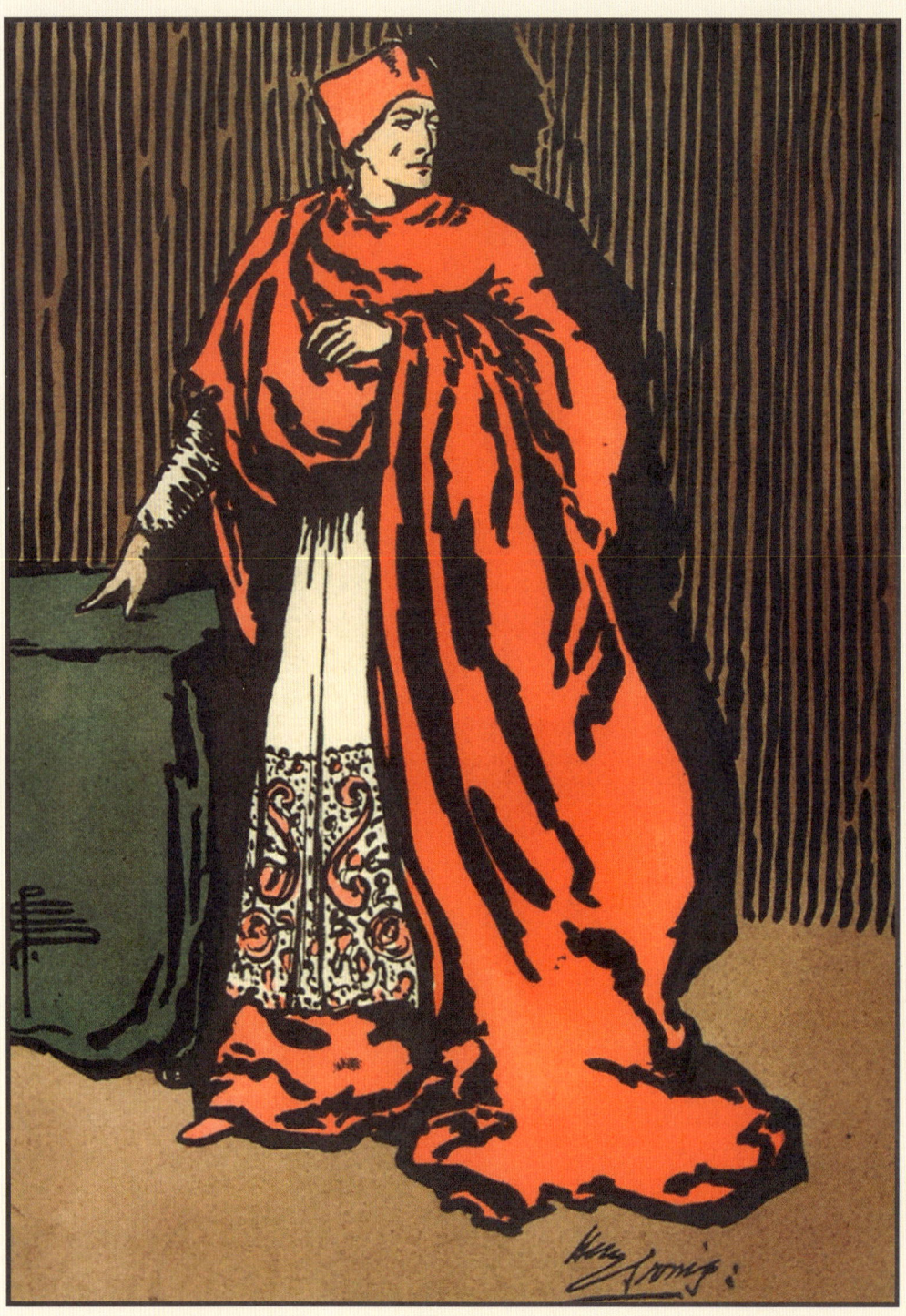

1907

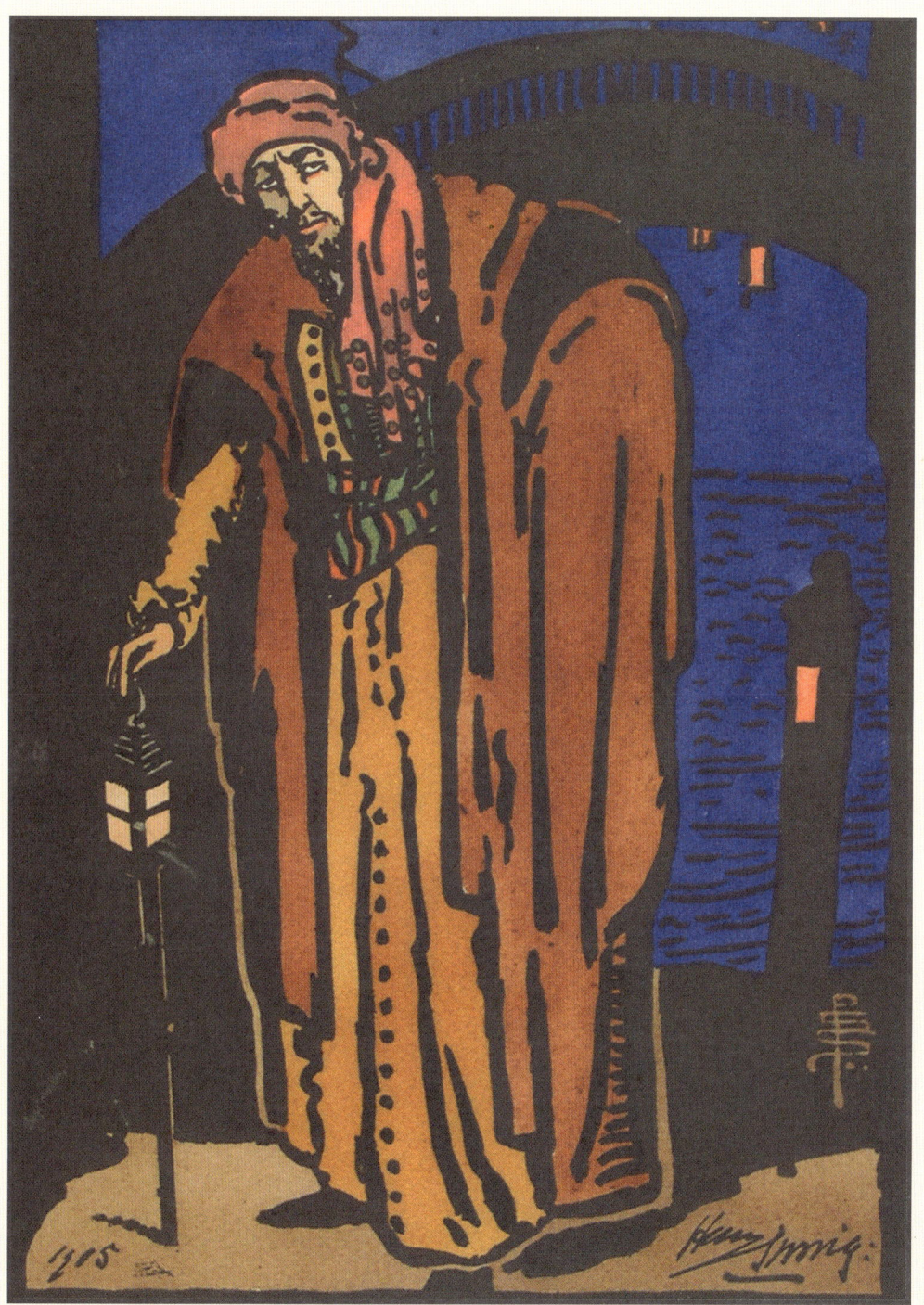

Sir Henry Irving as "Shylock" in William Shakespeare's *The Merchant of Venice* by Pamela Colman Smith, 1905. Courtesy of Smallhythe Place. © National Trust/ Andrew Fetherston

1907

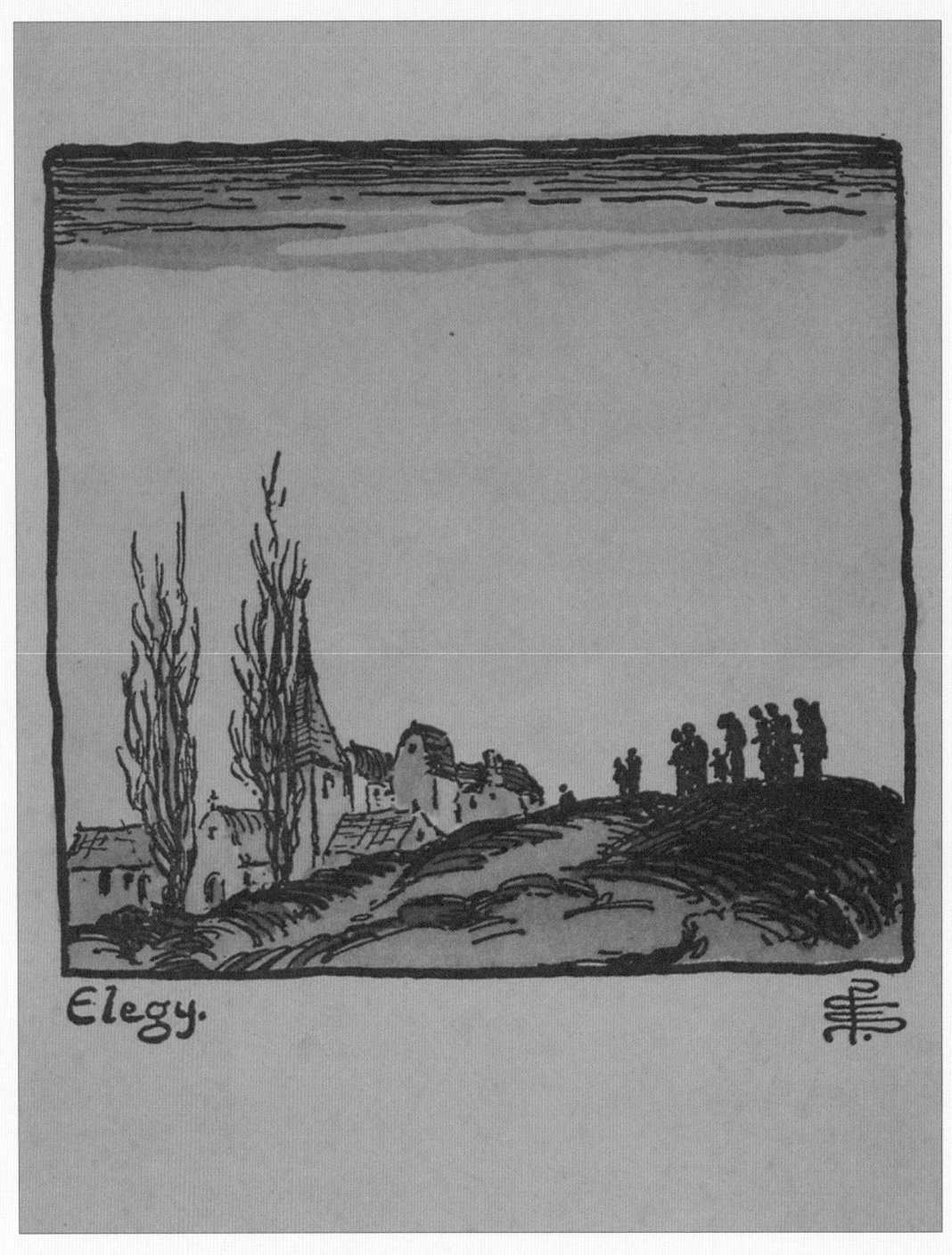

"Elegy" by Pamela Colman Smith, 1928.
Courtesy of Smallhythe Place. © National
Trust/Andrew Fetherston

1907

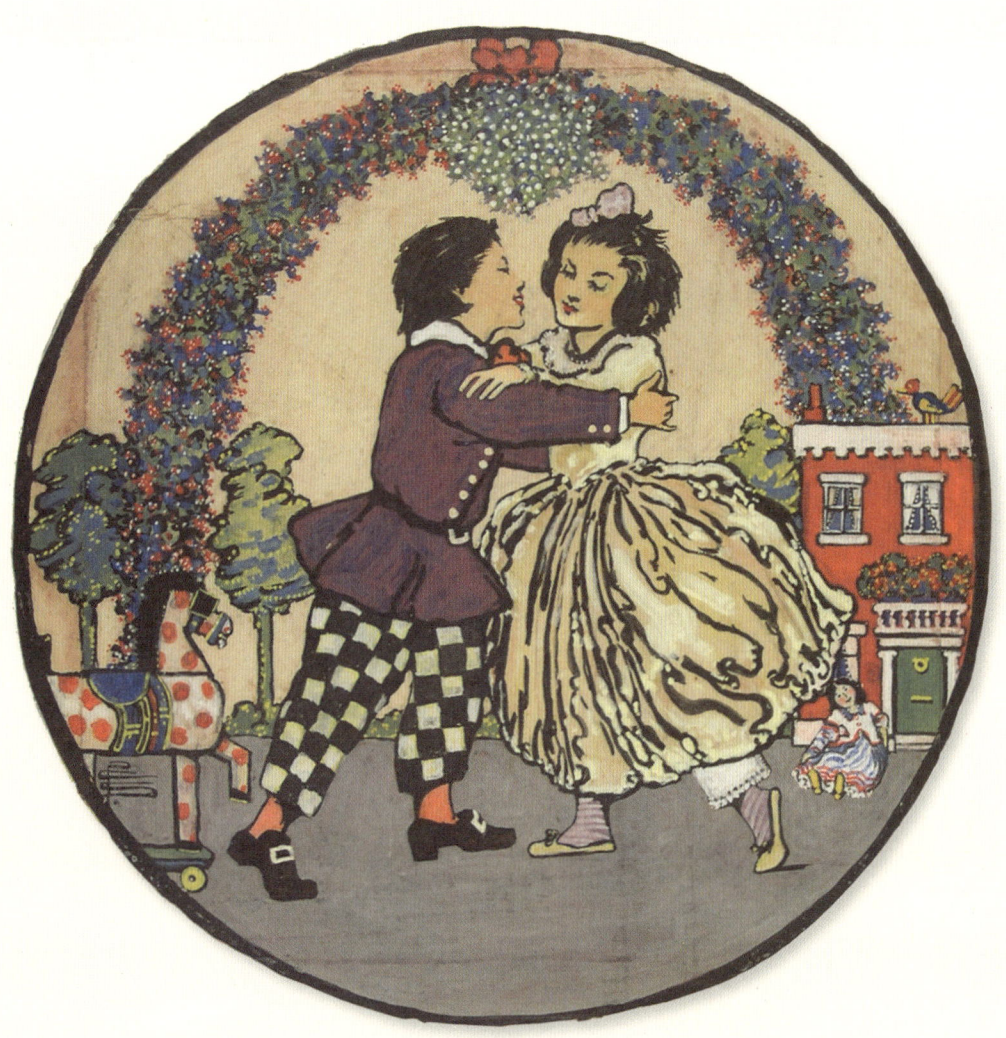

"Two Children" by Pamela Colman Smith, 1913. Round, annotated on back. Courtesy of Smallhythe Place. © National Trust/ Andrew Fetherston

Dearest Peg –

Here is "Alice."

Thank you for signing her

Hope you like it!

Much love from

Your own

Pixie

May 16.
1905.

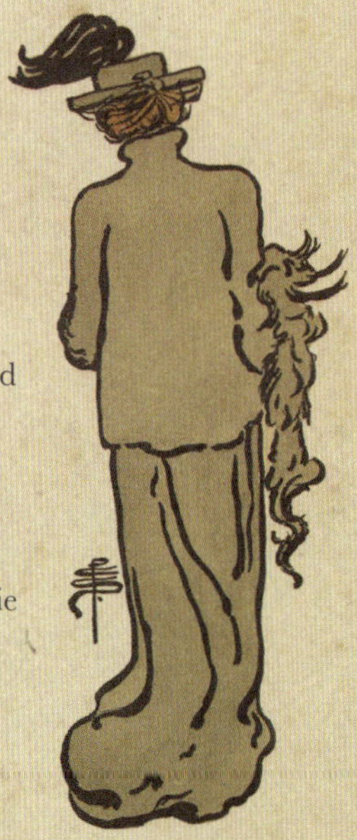

Letter from Pamela Colman Smith to T. Peg (Ellen Terry) dated May 16, 1905. Alice refers to a character in the play *Alice sit by the fire* that J.M. Barrie wrote for Ellen Terry, 1905

"Behold Him Getting Fatty…"

1907

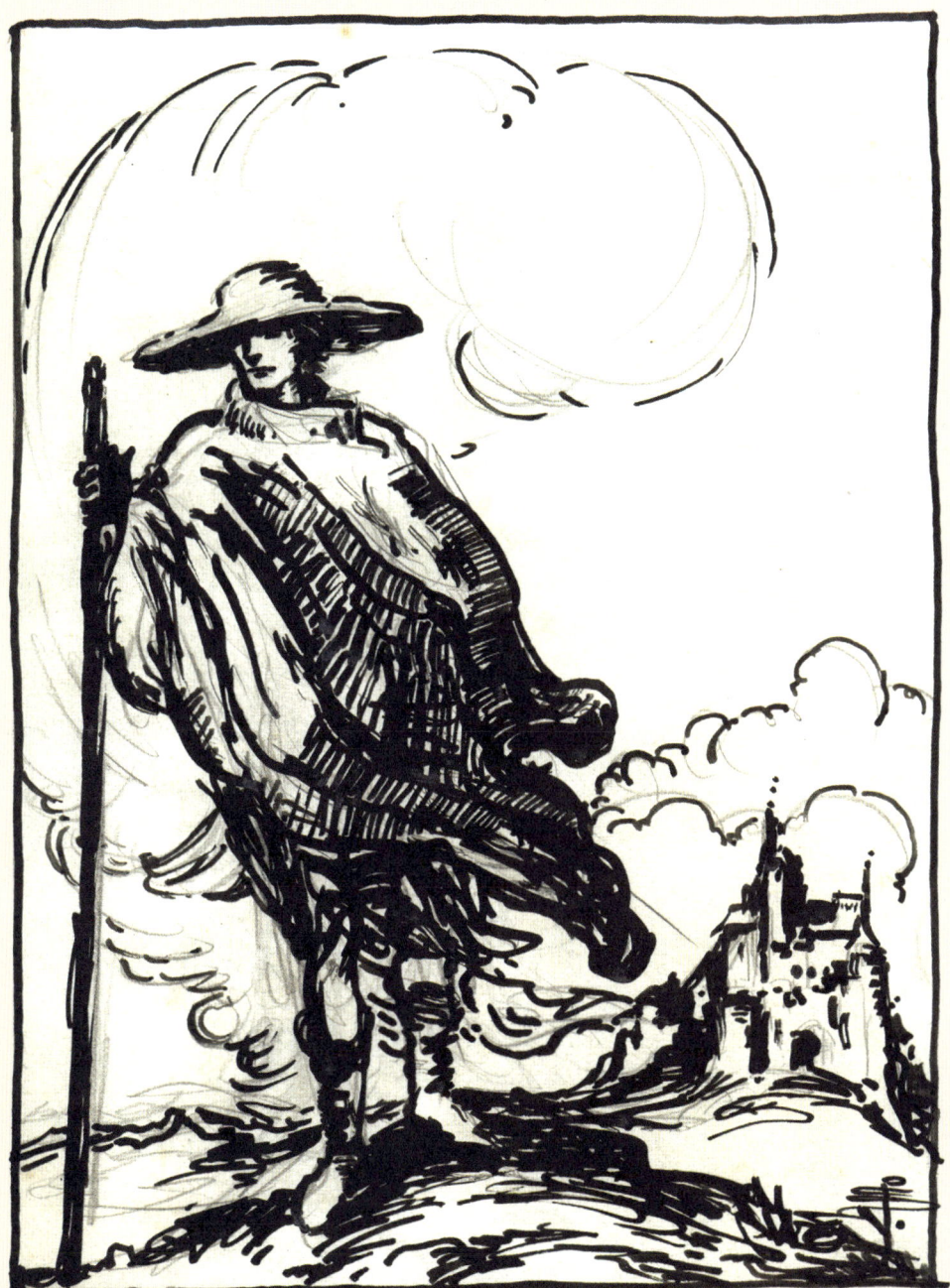

Black and white drawing by Pamela Colman Smith

1907

Reprinted from
Brooklyn Life,
January 12,
1907

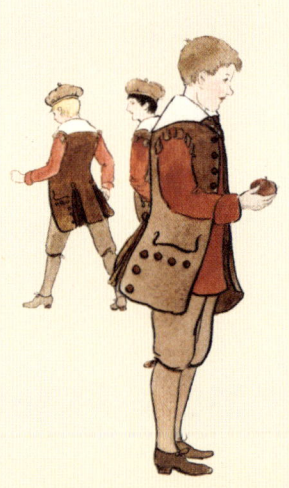

MISS Pamela Colman Smith, some of whose very interesting pictures are now being exhibited across the river, at 291 Fifth avenue, has recently returned to this country, after several years spent in England. Miss Smith had a studio in Chelsea, where she accomplished some quite remarkable work in the color schemes displayed in the late Sir Henry Irving's and Beerbohm Tree's stage settings. Miss Smith is a special protegé of Ellen Terry and she has designed many of the most beautiful costumes worn by that actress. Brooklynites will always have a sort of proprietary claim to this interesting young woman, her parents having lived for many years in this borough. Though she commenced to draw pictures as soon as she could hold a pencil, Miss Smith's artistic career really started at Pratt Institute. Never in the least bound down by the traditions of any conservative master, who was, supposedly, instructing her, she calmly used their studios as convenient workshops. Absolutely original, with a wonderful, almost garish, sense of color, Miss Smith's pictures represent not so much what she sees, as what she feels. After an evening spent at the opera or concert, she will sometimes work all night, not illustrating the music she has heard, so much as the thoughts suggested, and these paintings she calls musical symphonies. In the current exhibition a group of Shakesperean studies is very interesting, but her series of "Impressions of New York"—the huge skyscrapers, the smoky atmosphere, the crowded streets, and the night effects—are the more remarkable. Like many others of an artistic temperament, Miss Smith is too versatile to confine herself to one kind of work. As a sort of side issue, she give recitals of Jamaica folk stories, and old English ballads, dressed in the costume of the people and time she represents. Often in the most gorgeous colors and wearing strings of many hued brilliant beads and astonishing arrangement of head-gear, Miss Smith tells her stories seated flat upon the floor, with candles as footlights. She has been in great demand, both in London and here, especially as an entertainer at children's parties; for all youngsters plainly adore her.

• • •

1907

OVER eighty covers were set for the beautifully appointed dinner given last week Tuesday at the Waldorf-Astoria by the Entertainment Club. It was the twentieth reunion of this association and several hundred additional guests attended the reception following the dinner...

...Possibly the best number on the program—certainly the greatest novelty—was furnished by Miss Pamela Colman Smith, who gave Jamaica folk stories. Having passed many years on that island, Miss Smith is conversant with the correct Jamaican costume and has acquired a capital West Indian dialect. Gowned in old rose cashmere, with deep black fringe, and wearing beads about her neck and chiffon twined about her head to represent a kerchief, Miss Smith sat flat upon a small round table with her feet tucked beneath her gown and a row of half a dozen short fat candles at her knees to represent footlights. An artist of quite exceptional brilliancy and absolute originality, Miss Smith knows the value of every gesture, every smile and every inflection. The Entertainment Club, nearing its majority, can surely be congratulated upon its twentieth celebration.

Reprinted from *Brooklyn Life*, February 9, 1907

* * *

ONE successful young woman leading almost too strenuous a life for this chronicler to keep tab on, is Pamela Colman Smith. She has not only given recitations at the Fine Arts Club, Pratt Institute, the Pen & Brush, and Mrs. Hitchcock's Entertainment Club, but has appeared at numberless private houses, both here and in Boston, was at the Brooklyn Barnard Club on Tuesday, and will tell her Jamaica Folk Stories before the Associate Alumnae of Packer, within the next fortnight. Even with the prestige of English approval, Miss Smith's instant success here is a bit unusual. I think it is largely due to her absence of all pose; queer, unexpected, absolutely original as Miss Smith is, one realizes her quite unmistakable genuineness as well as appreciates her talents. She is a gentlewoman, presenting an odd type of thoroughly unconventional femininity—therein lies her greatest charm.

Reprinted from *Brooklyn Life*, February 16, 1907

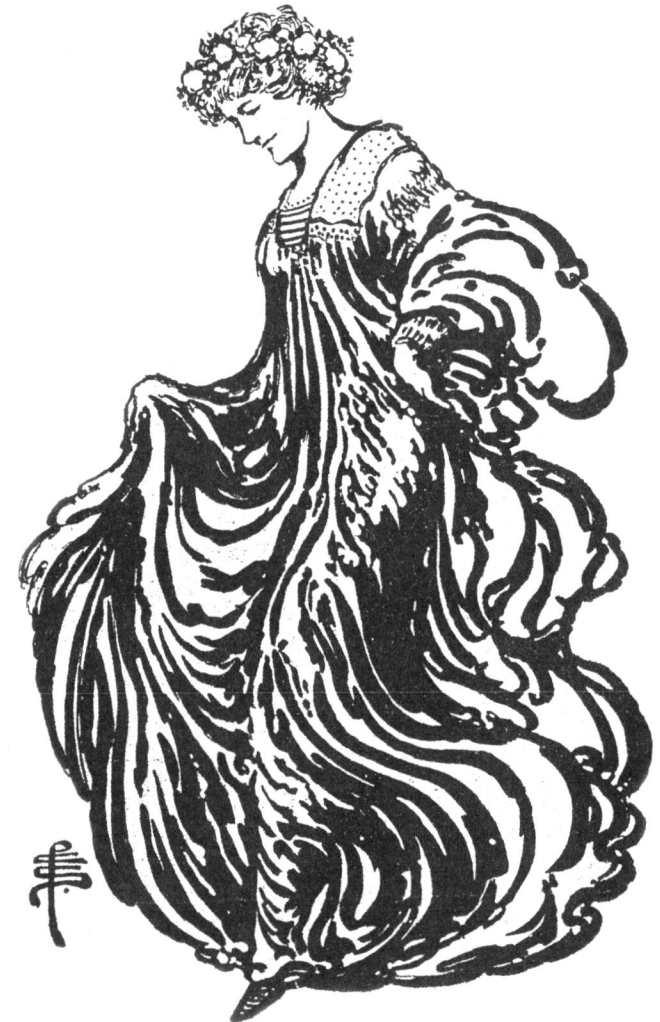

Ellen Terry

1856   1907

BY E. HARCOURT WILLIAMS
ILLUSTRATED BY PAMELA SMITH

" A star danced and under that I was born "

A STAR, they say, her coming did proclaim
  And gaily tripped a measure o'er the earth
  In joyous welcome of her precious birth.
O happy star, I would I knew thy name
That thou mightst share the glory of her fame,
  As we have shared the treasures of her mirth
  And known the anguish of those tears, the worth
Of ringing voice 'neath angry eyes aflame;
  For fifty years she's held the old world's heart
Nor frees it yet from such a sweet embrace,
  But triumph after triumph, part on part,
Swells that fair galaxy of wit and grace

Photo-Secession

1907

Photo-Secession Galleries, Exhibition of Drawings by Pamela Colman Smith, January 5 to January 15, 1907. From the Collection of Dorothy Norman, 1997. Courtesy of Philadelphia Museum of Art

**PHOTO-SECESSION GALLERIES
EXHIBITION OF DRAWINGS
BY PAMELA COLMAN SMITH
JANUARY FIFTH TO JANUARY
FIFTEENTH, MDCCCCVII ✠ ✠ ✠**

1. THE REEDS
   (Loaned by Miss Mildred Howells)
2. MAMMA'S BIRTHDAY
3. TRÄUMEREI (SCHUMANN)
4. GOOD-NIGHT
5. QUEEN OF THE TIDES
6. THE CORSE
7. WEEPING WAVE
8. FUGITIVE (CHOPIN)
9. IN A GARDEN
10. FOREST AND HILL
11. DOUBT (SCHUMANN)
12. SPIRITS OF PAIN
13. THE CASTLE OF PAIN
14. ARLEQUIN
15. CHIARINA
16. SPHYNXES
17. PIERROT ⎫
18. FLORESTAN ⎬ SCHUMANN'S CARNIVAL
19. COLUMBINE AND PANTALOON ⎭
20. COQUETTE
21. SISTERS
22. BENEDICTUS
23. MUSIC
24. THE NARROW WAY
25. FOLLY
26. TRIUMPH OF LAUGHTER
27. THE WAVE
28. WATER
29. EARTH (LOT'S WIFE)
30. DEATH IN THE HOUSE
31. SEVEN PRINCESSES (MAETERLINCK)
32. SCENE FROM AN UNWRITTEN PLAY
33. SLEEP
34. INCANTATION
35. ANGELS AT A WELL
36. MAY
37. LYKE WAKE DIRGE
38. WIDDICOMBE FAIR
39. PLAGUE
40. JUNE
41. ANNANCY AND GUINEA FOWL
42. FISHERMAN AND GENII
43. CLOUD
44. MOUNTAINS
45. CLOUD CHOIR
46. A SCOTCH FARM
47. THE WATCHERS
48. PETER PAN
49. A SUN GOD
50. NEW YORK—STEAM
51. RAIN
52. SUNSET (CORELLI)
53. HUMORESQUE (DVORAK)

SHAKESPEARE SERIES—1898

54. MACBETH
55. TOUCHSTONE
56. LAUNCELOT AND GOBBO
57. QUEEN MARGARET
58. VIOLA
59. LEAR
60. JOHN OF GAUNT
61. RICHARD II
62. ARIEL
63. CALIBAN
64. HOTSPUR
65. THE SHREW
66. IACHIAMO
67. BUCKINGHAM
68. REGAN
69. FLUELLEN AND HENRY V
70. YORICK
71. HAMLET, 1906
72. FAITH

PRICES UPON APPLICATION

Philadelphia Museum of Art/ Stieglitz Platinum Prints

1907

Untitled drawing by Pamela Colman Smith. From the collection of Dorothy Norman, 1997. Courtesy of Philadelphia Museum of Art

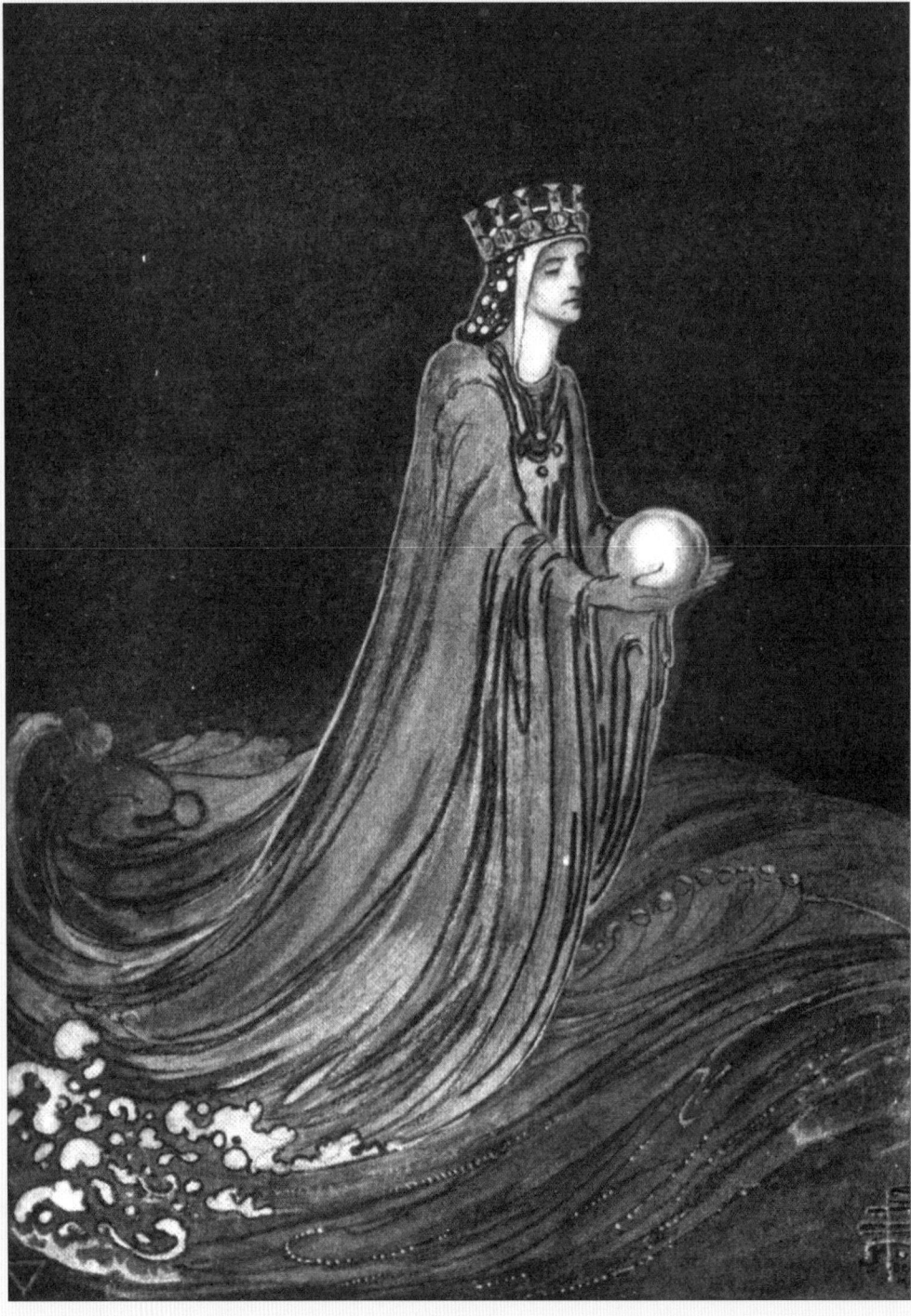

1907

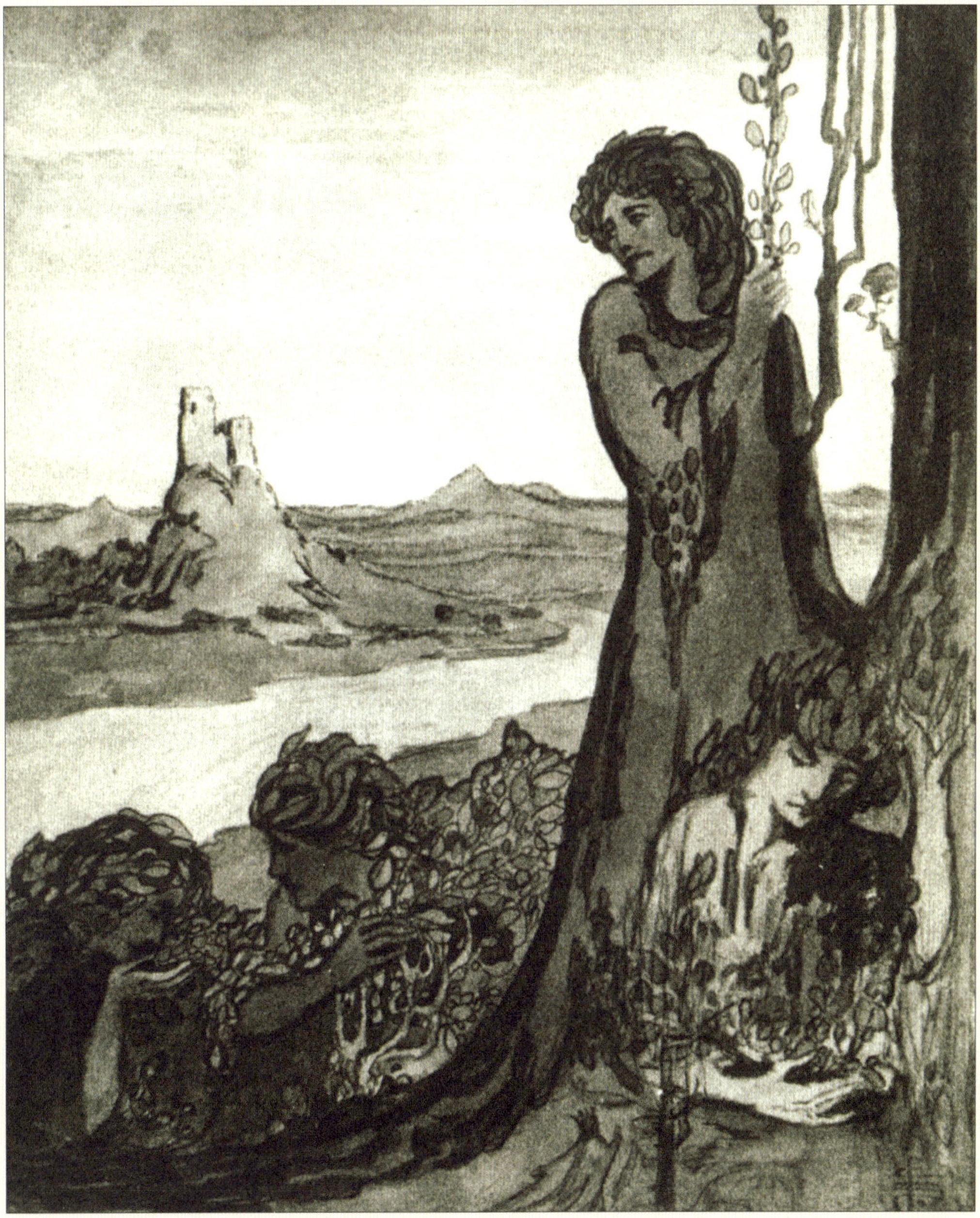

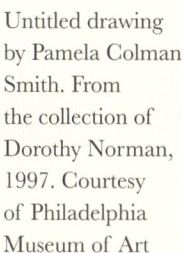

Untitled drawing by Pamela Colman Smith. From the collection of Dorothy Norman, 1997. Courtesy of Philadelphia Museum of Art

1907

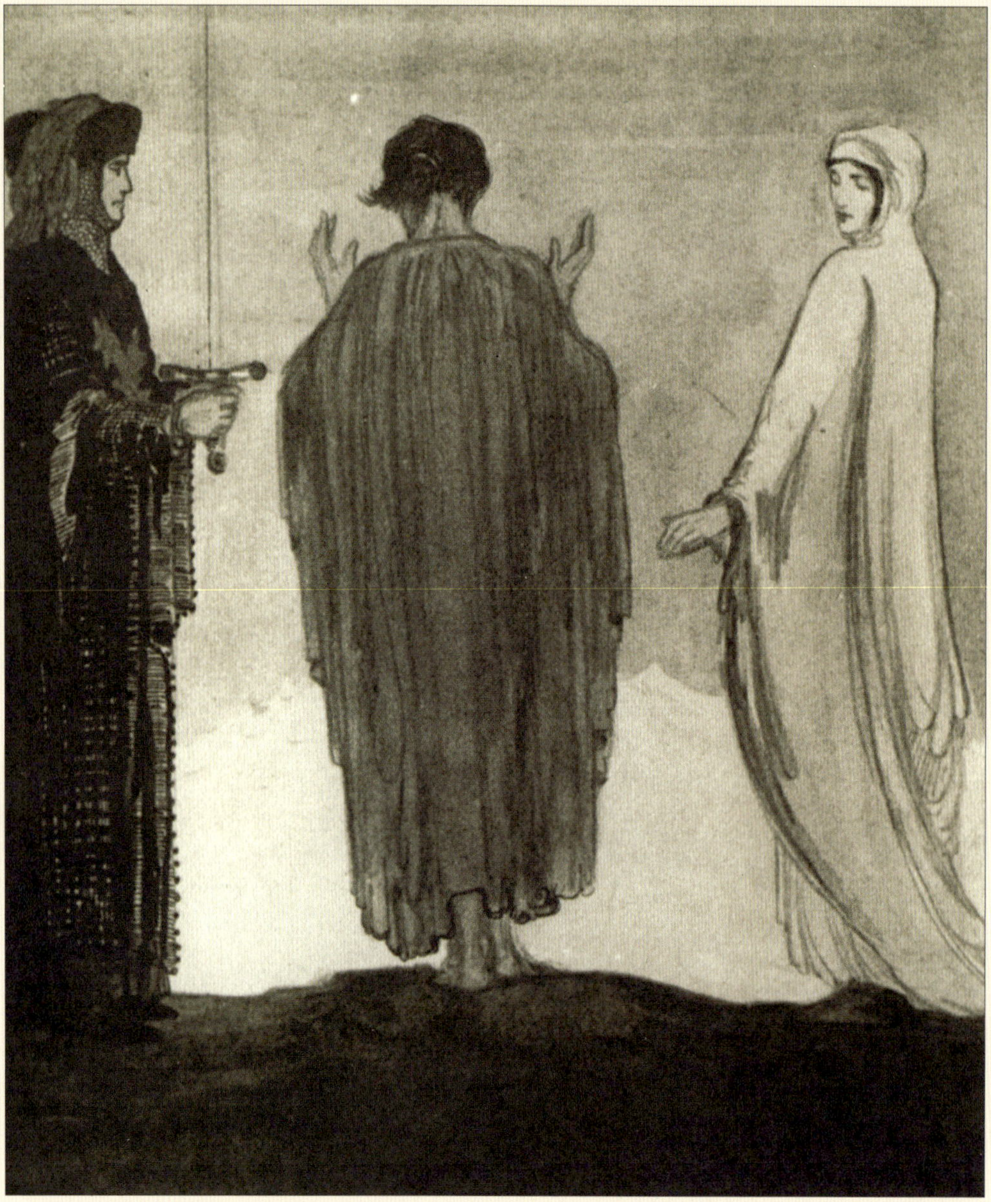

Untitled drawing by Pamela Colman Smith. From the collection of Dorothy Norman, 1997. Courtesy of Philadelphia Museum of Art

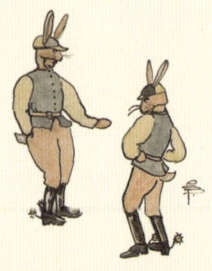

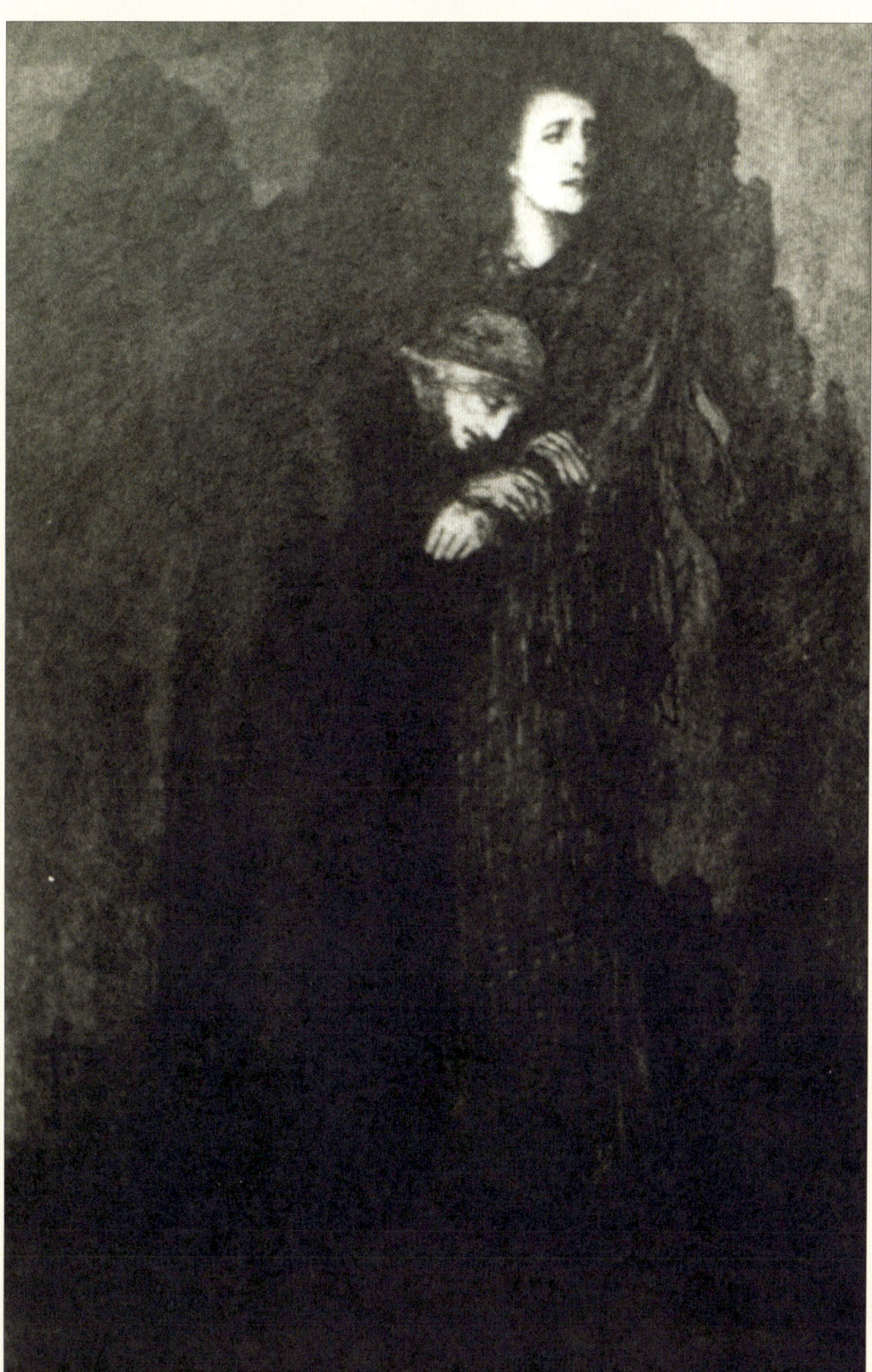

1907

Untitled drawing by Pamela Colman Smith. From the collection of Dorothy Norman, 1997. Courtesy of Philadelphia Museum of Art

1907

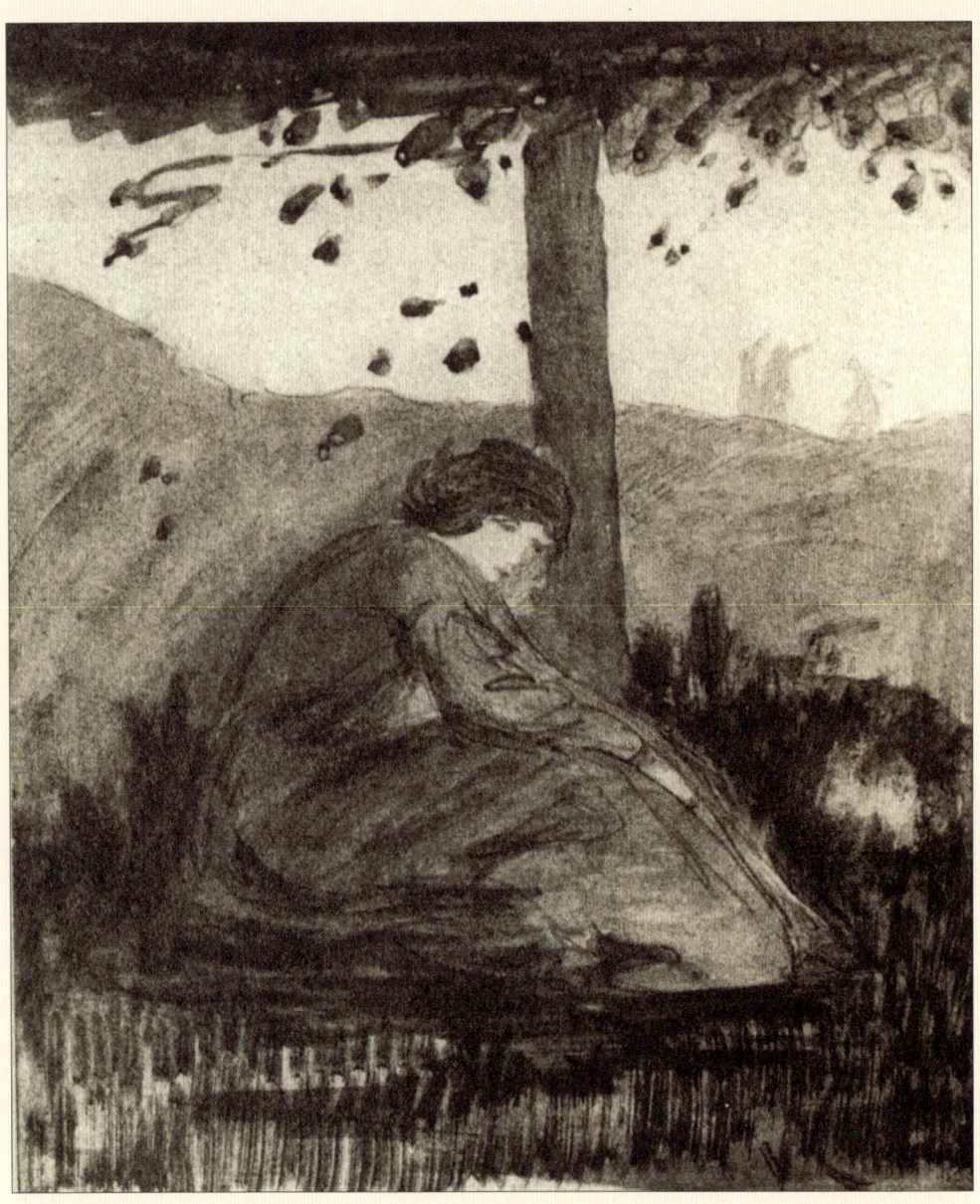

Untitled drawing by Pamela Colman Smith. From the collection of Dorothy Norman, 1997. Courtesy of Philadelphia Museum of Art

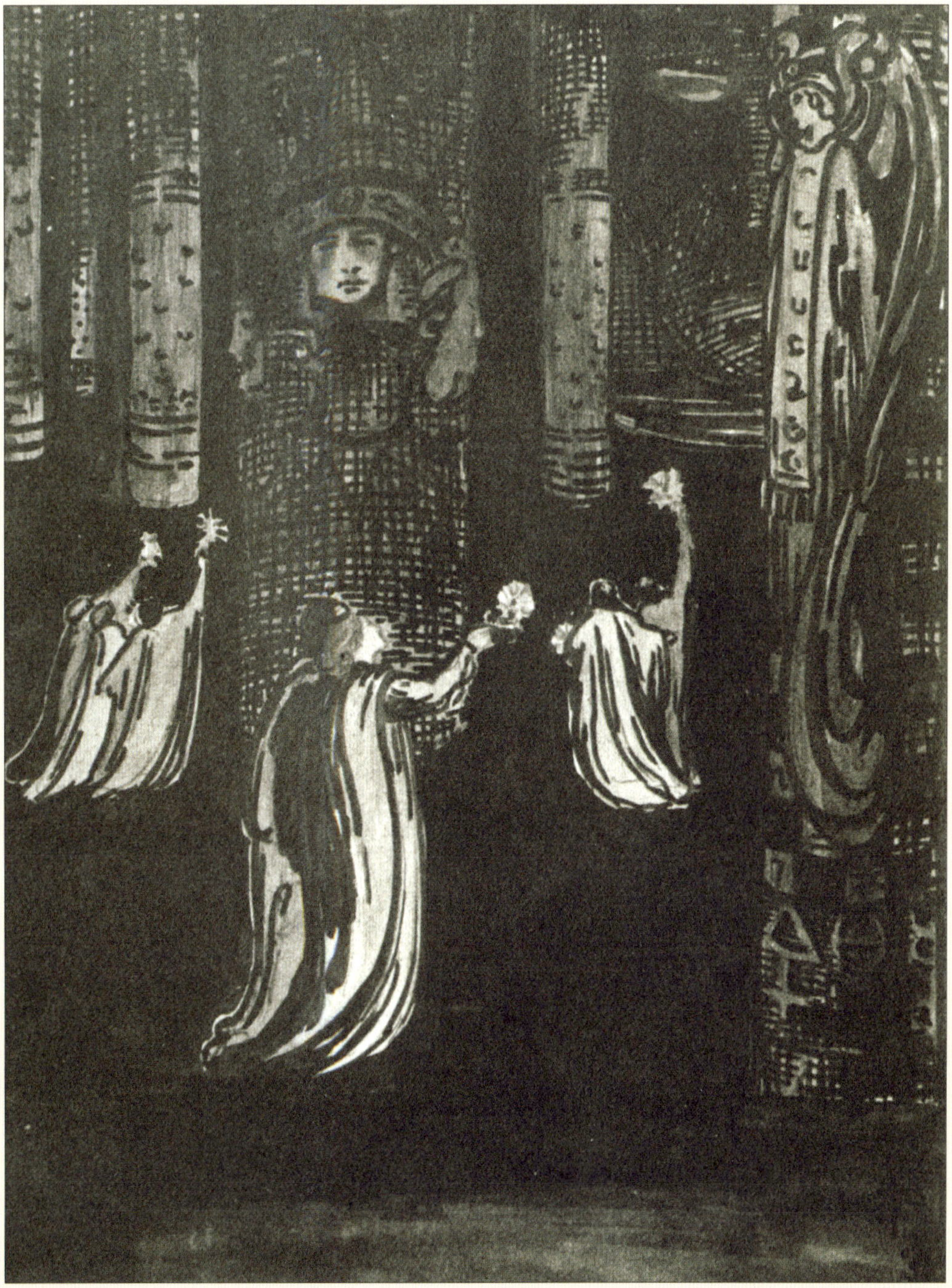

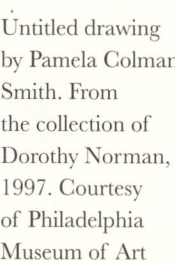

1907

Untitled drawing
by Pamela Colman
Smith. From
the collection of
Dorothy Norman,
1997. Courtesy
of Philadelphia
Museum of Art

1907

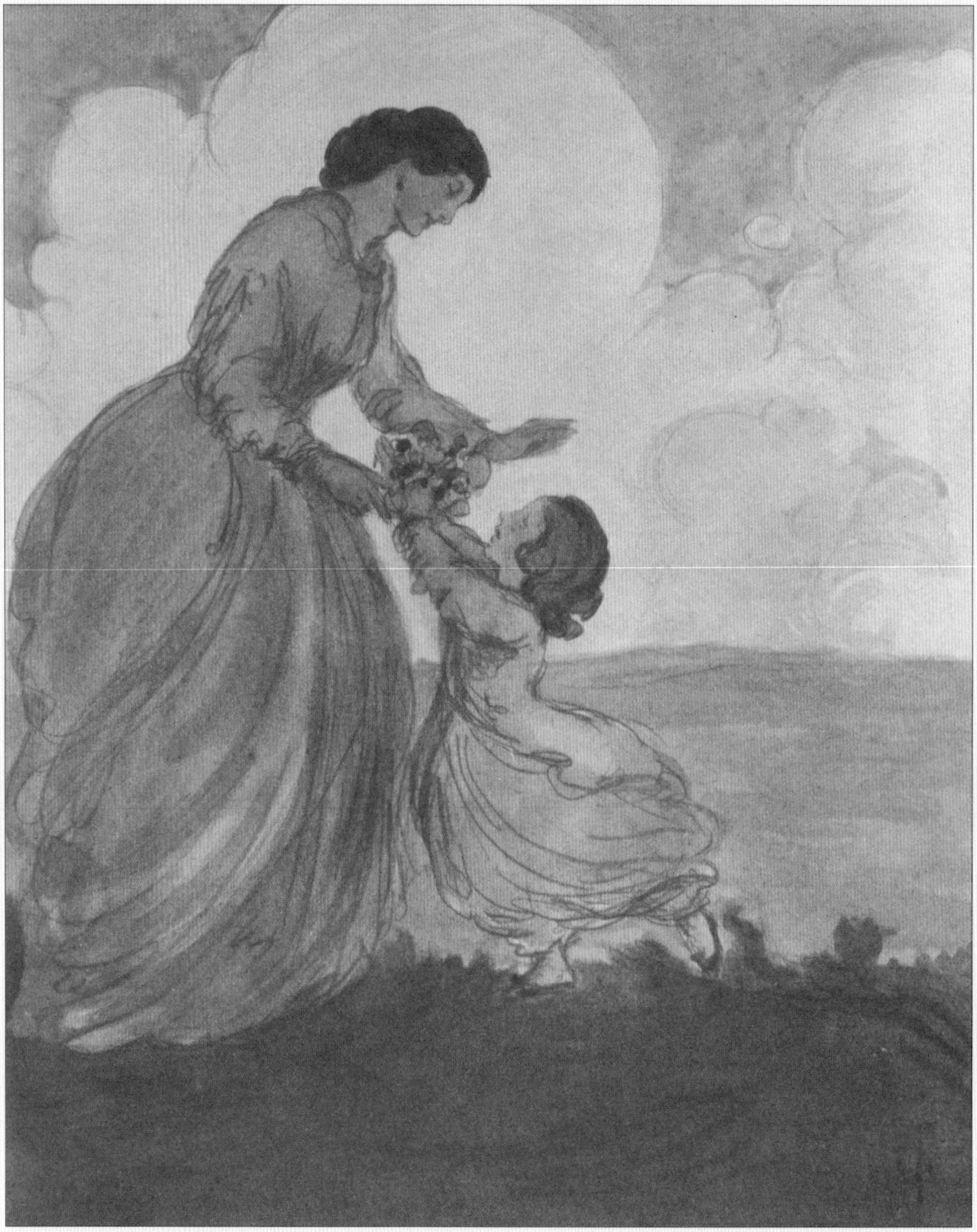

Untitled drawing by Pamela Colman Smith. From the collection of Dorothy Norman, 1997. Courtesy of Philadelphia Museum of Art

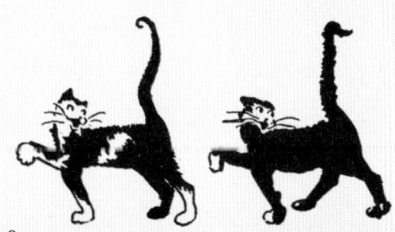

1907

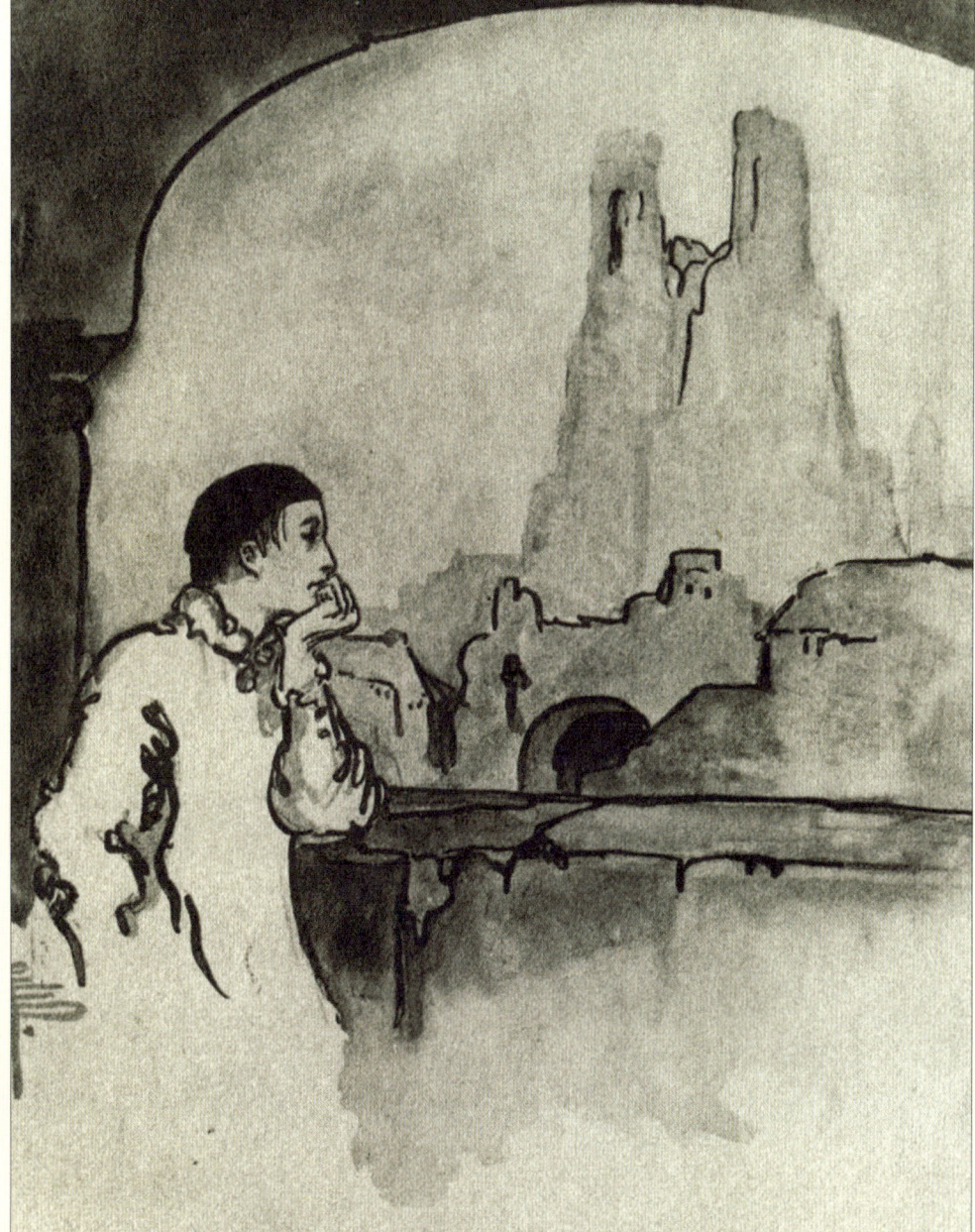

Untitled drawing by Pamela Colman Smith. From the collection of Dorothy Norman, 1997. Courtesy of Philadelphia Museum of Art

1907

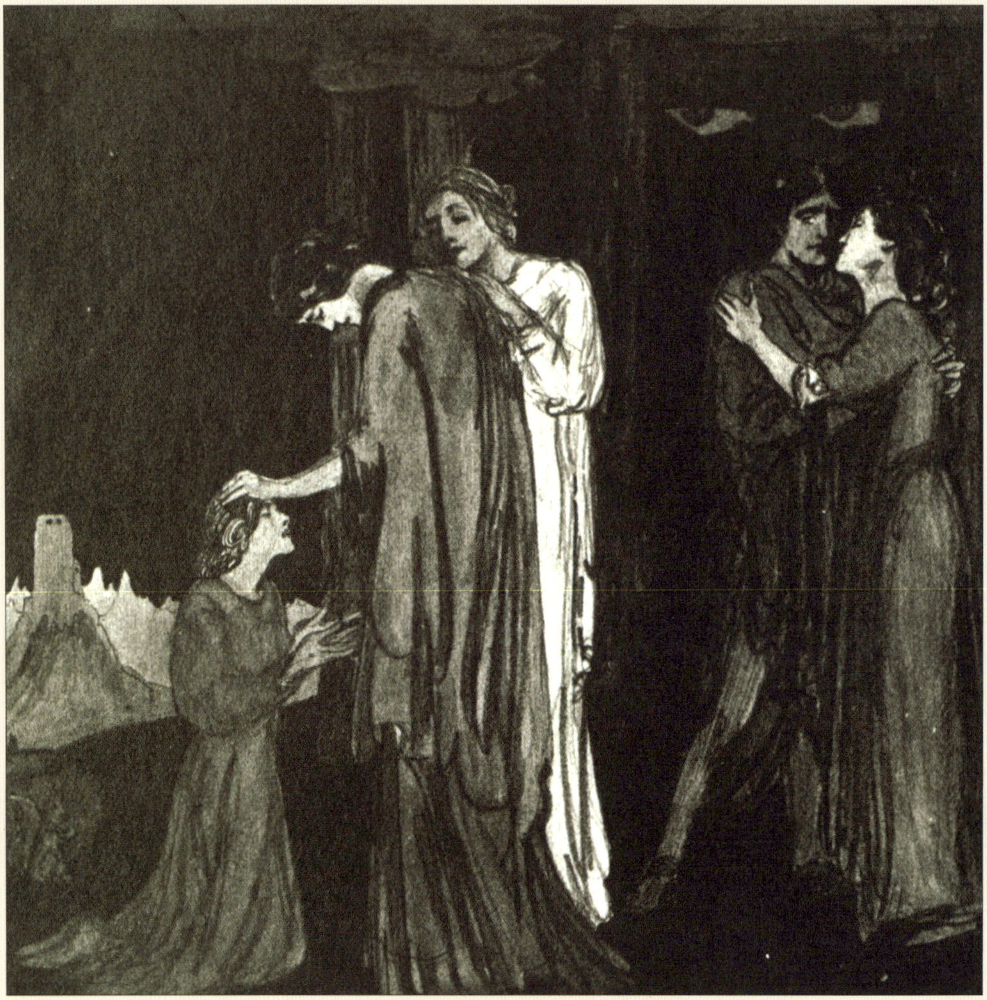

Untitled drawing by Pamela Colman Smith. From the collection of Dorothy Norman, 1997. Courtesy of Philadelphia Museum of Art

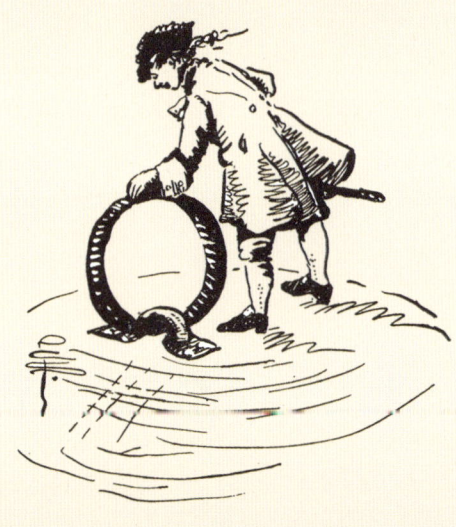

1907

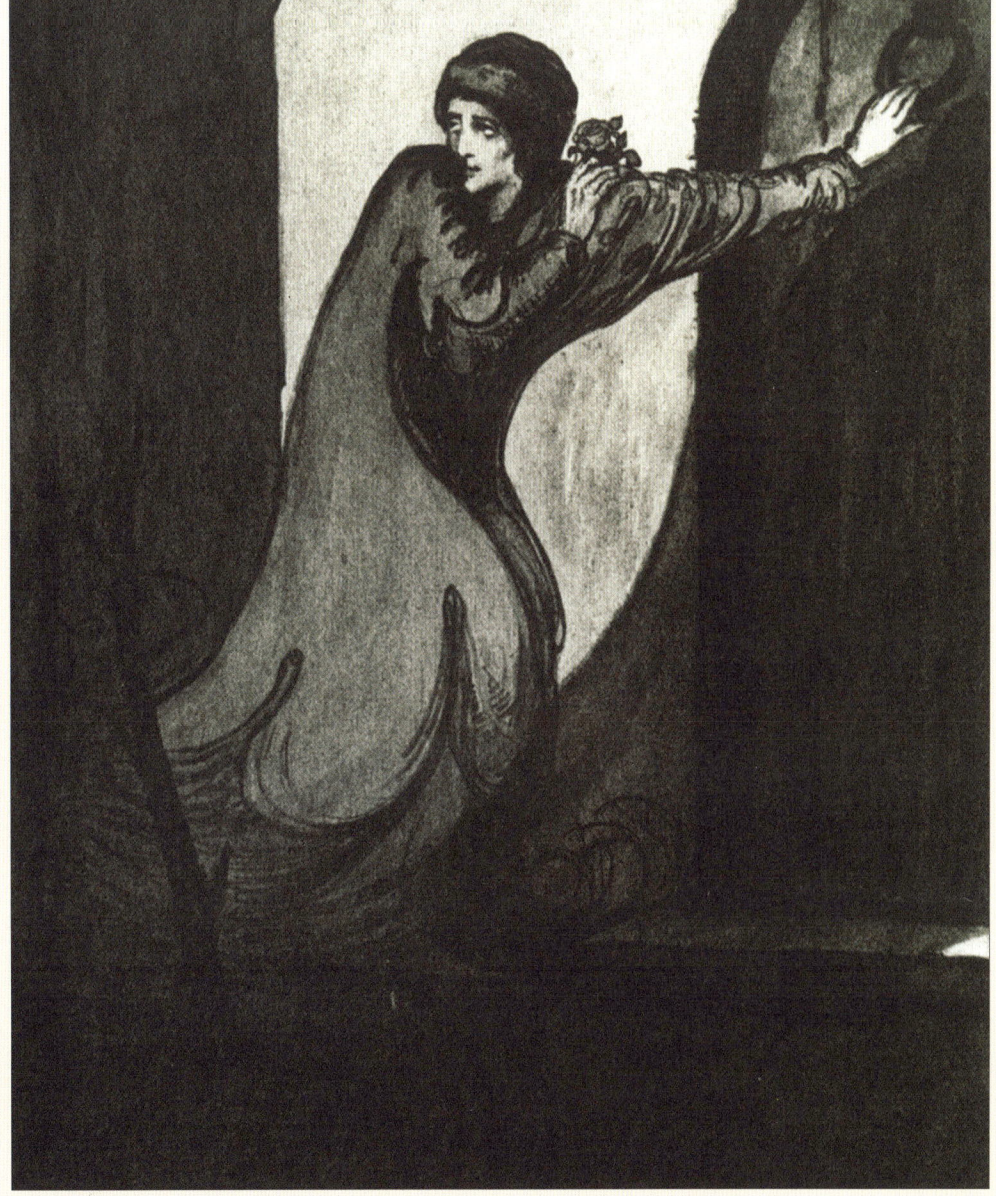

Untitled drawing by Pamela Colman Smith. From the collection of Dorothy Norman, 1997. Courtesy of Philadelphia Museum of Art

1907

Untitled drawing by Pamela Colman Smith. From the collection of Dorothy Norman, 1997. Courtesy of Philadelphia Museum of Art

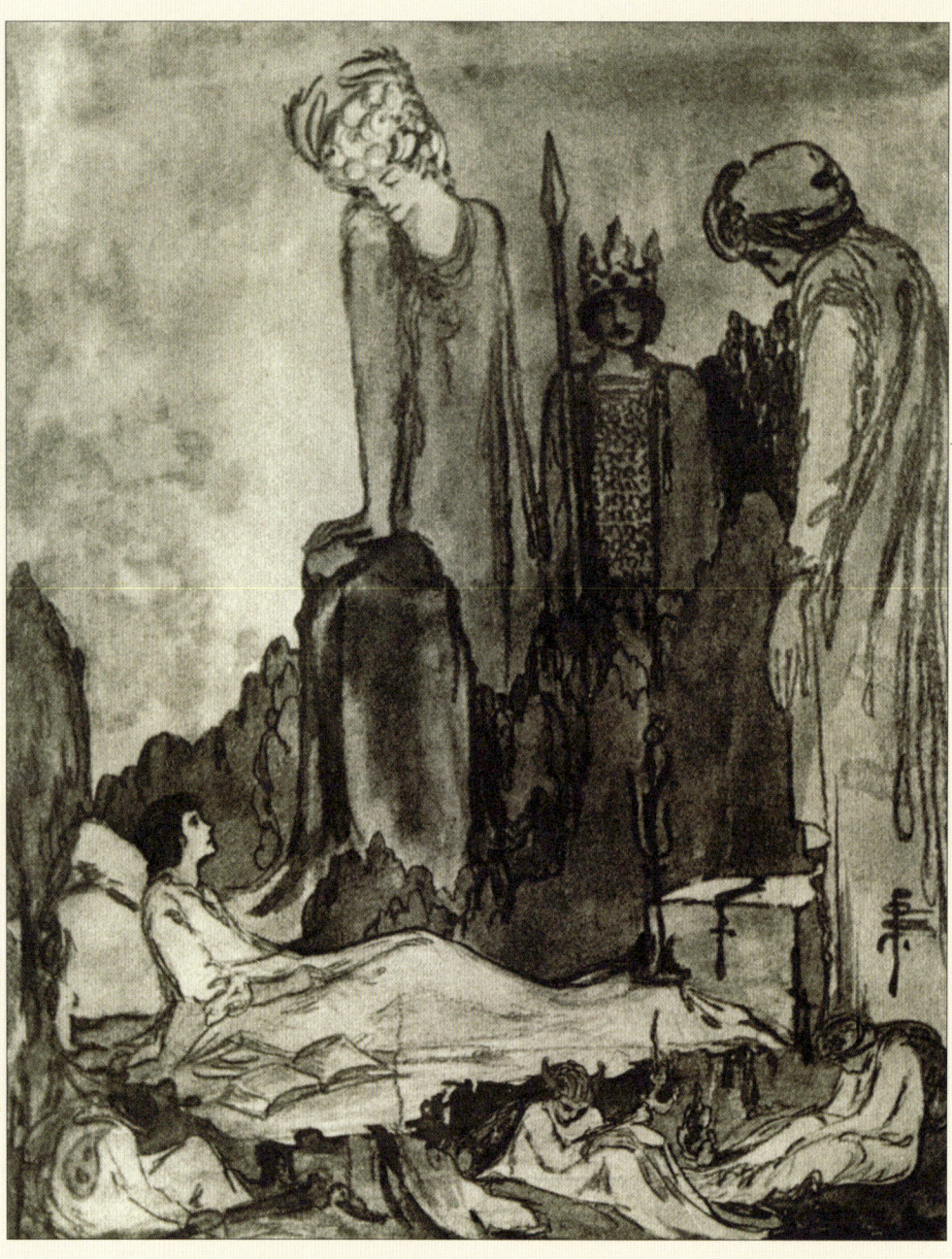

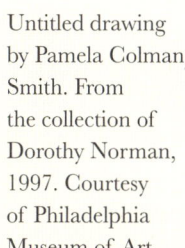

1907

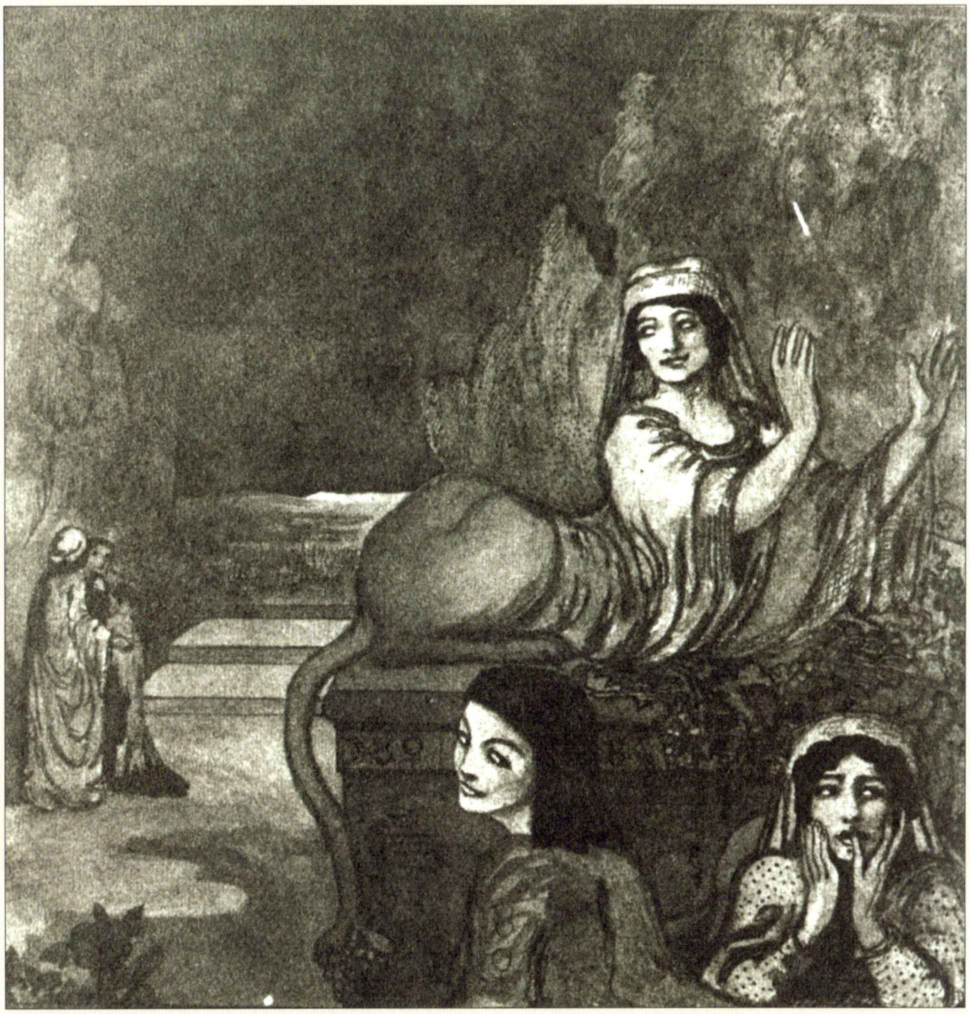

Untitled drawing by Pamela Colman Smith. From the collection of Dorothy Norman, 1997. Courtesy of Philadelphia Museum of Art

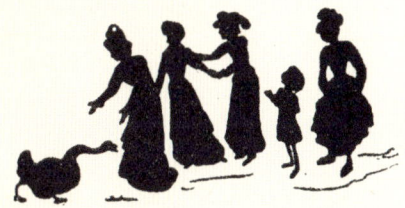

1907

Untitled drawing by Pamela Colman Smith. From the collection of Dorothy Norman, 1997. Courtesy of Philadelphia Museum of Art

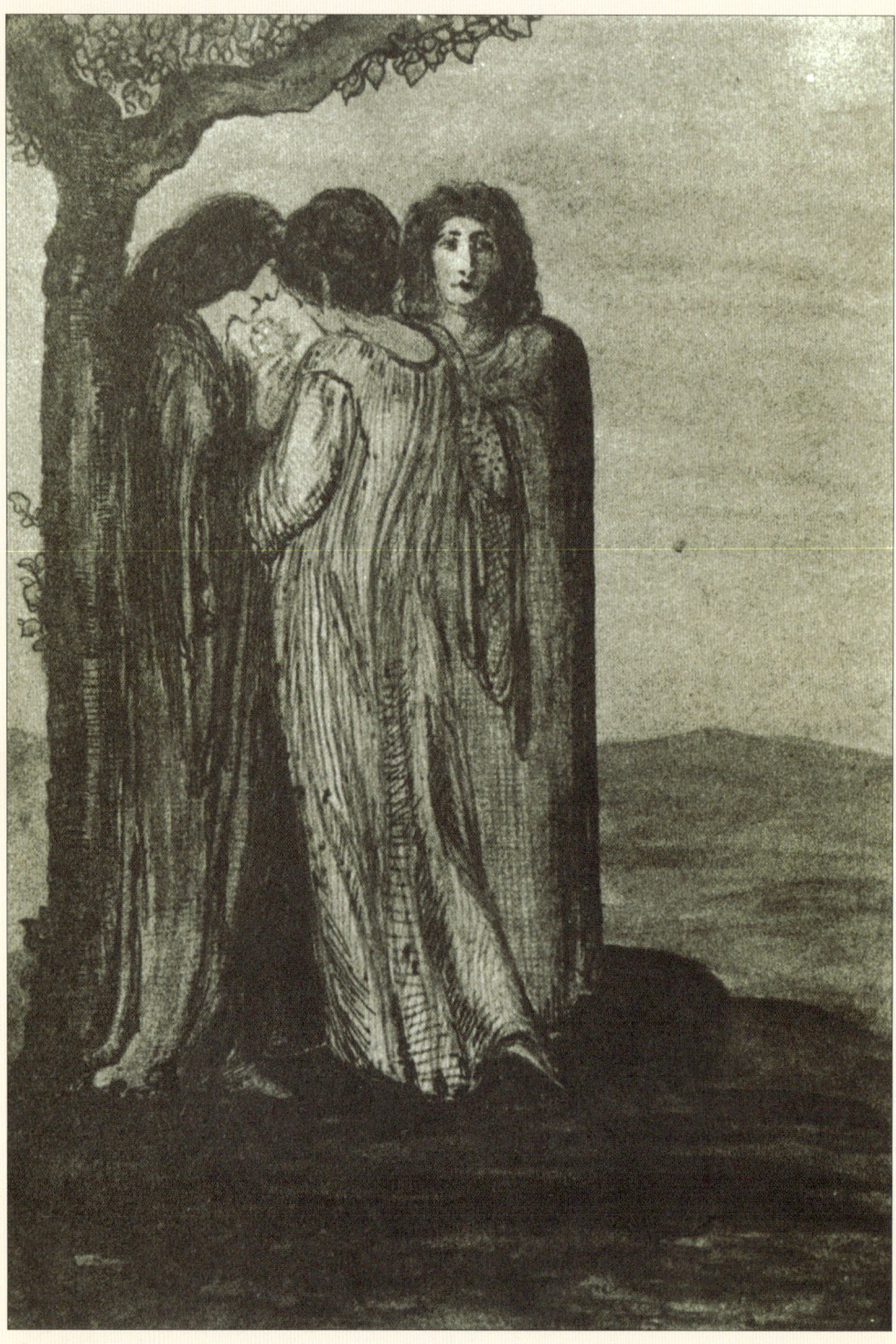

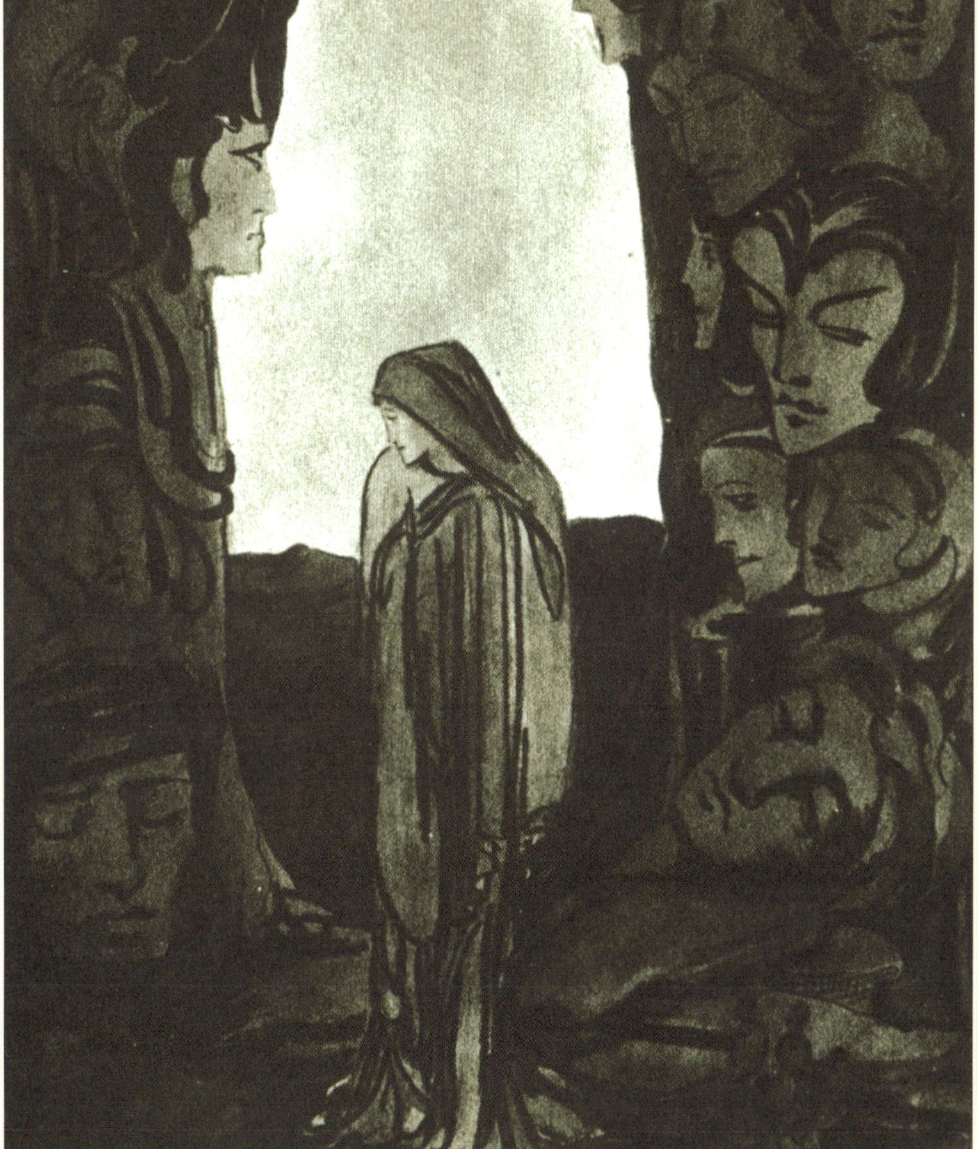

1907

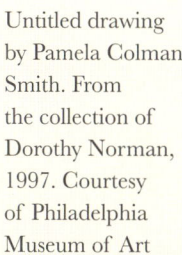

Untitled drawing by Pamela Colman Smith. From the collection of Dorothy Norman, 1997. Courtesy of Philadelphia Museum of Art

1907

Untitled drawing by Pamela Colman Smith. From the collection of Dorothy Norman, 1997. Courtesy of Philadelphia Museum of Art

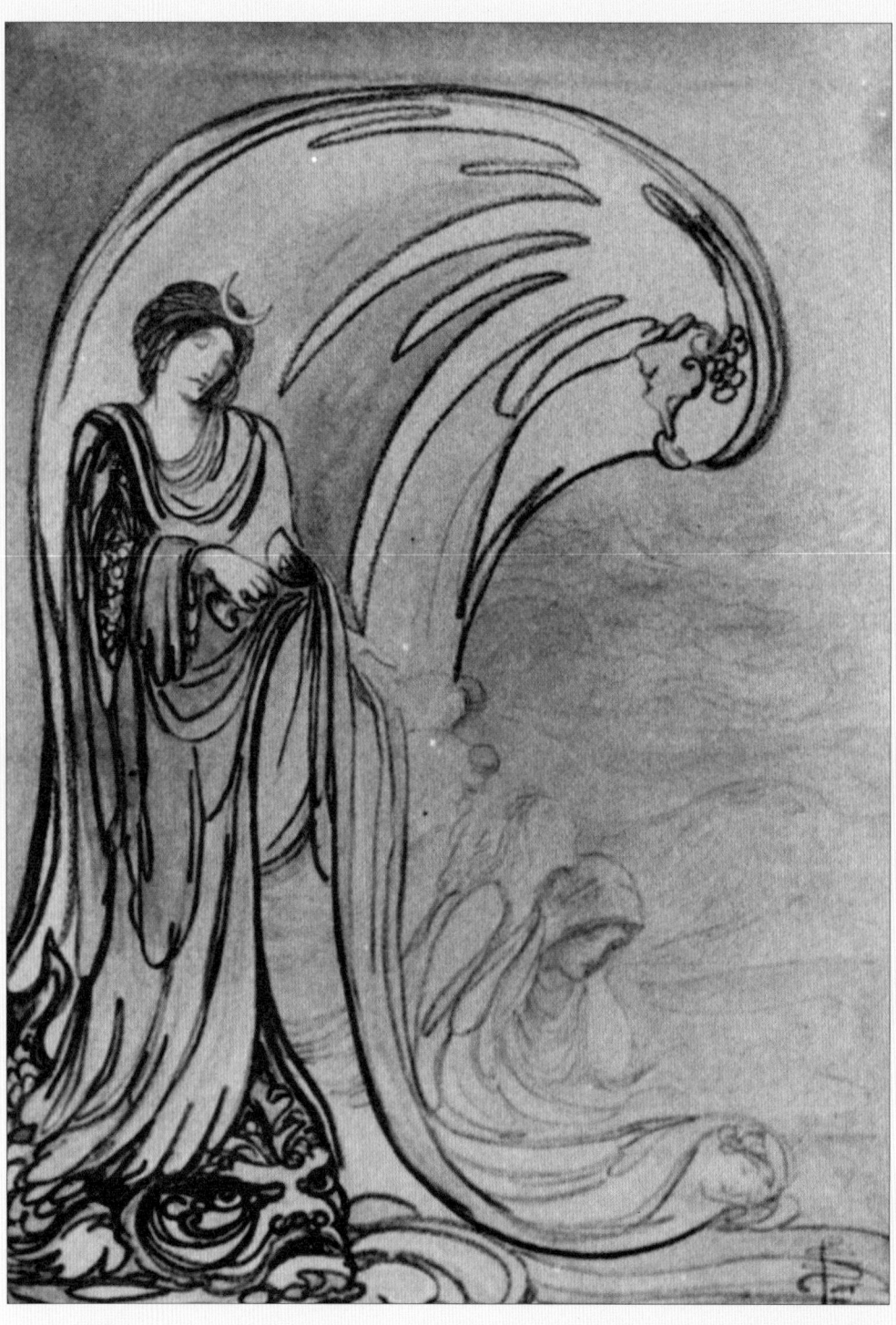

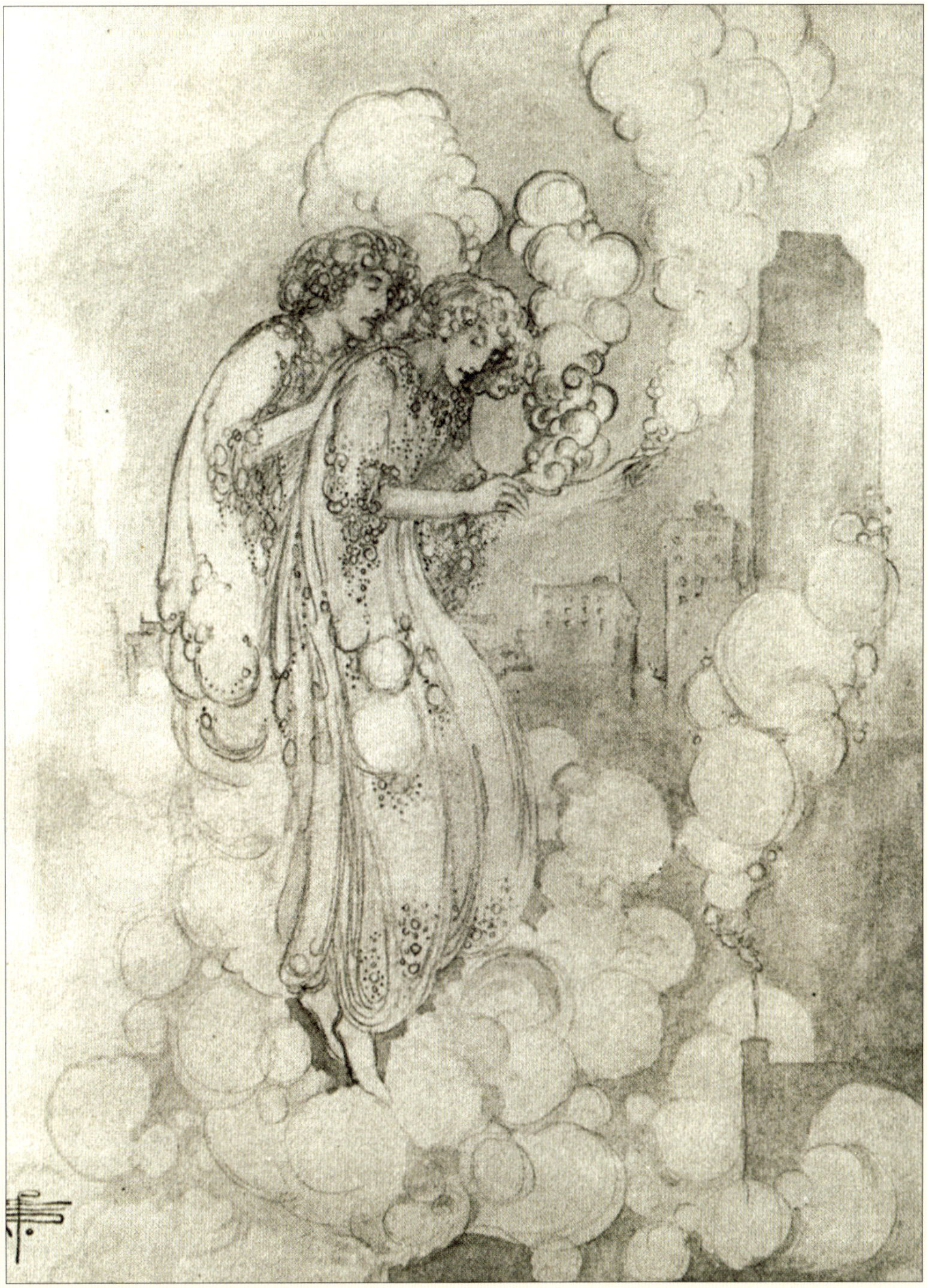

1907

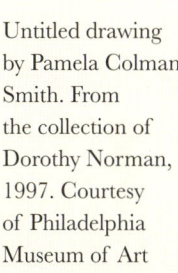

Untitled drawing
by Pamela Colman
Smith. From
the collection of
Dorothy Norman,
1997. Courtesy
of Philadelphia
Museum of Art

1907

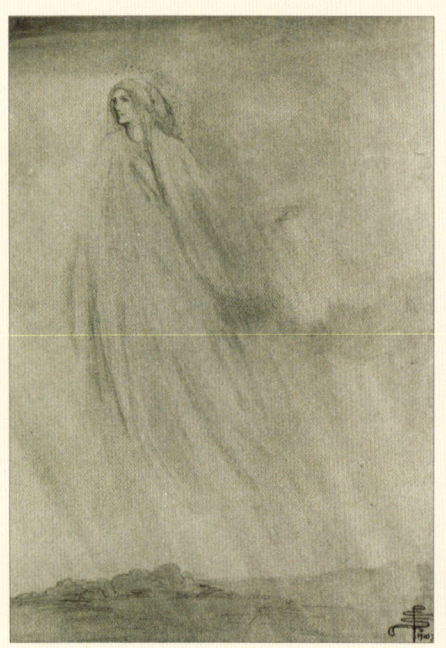

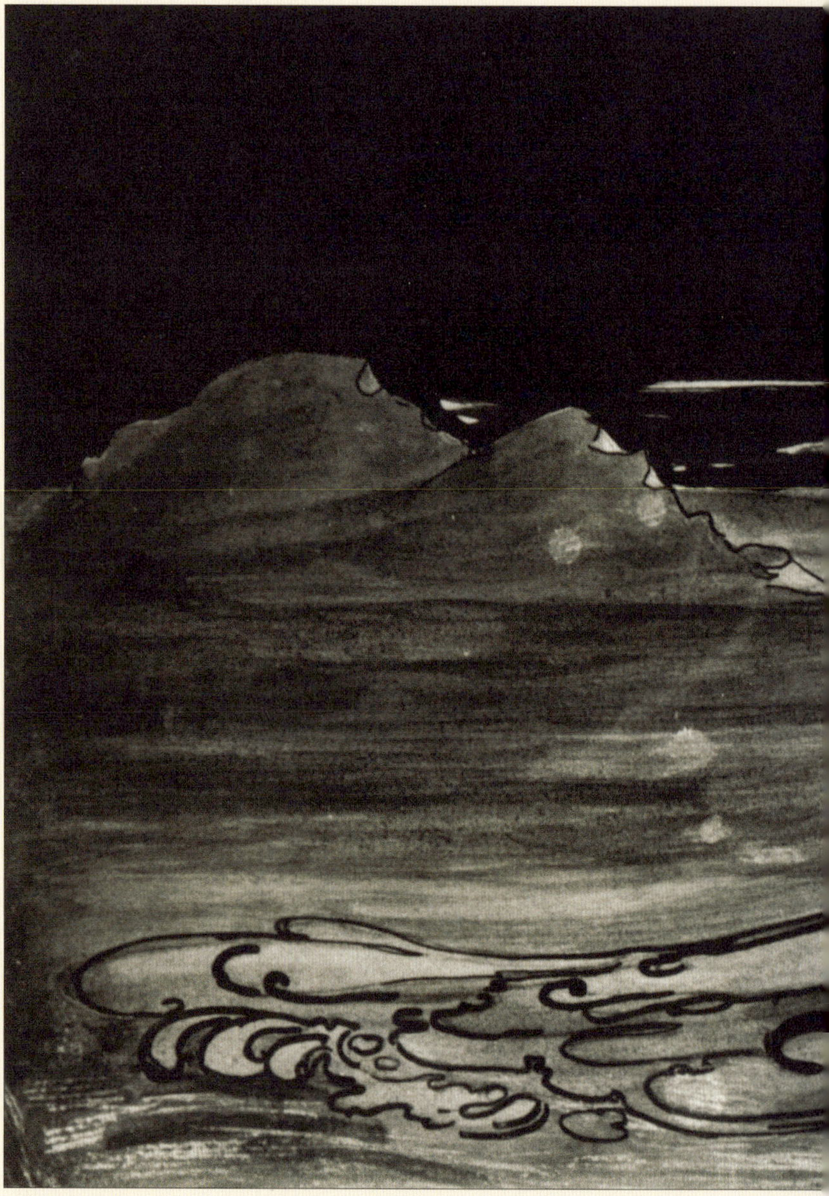

Untitled drawing by Pamela Colman Smith. From the collection of Dorothy Norman, 1997. Courtesy of Philadelphia Museum of Art

1907

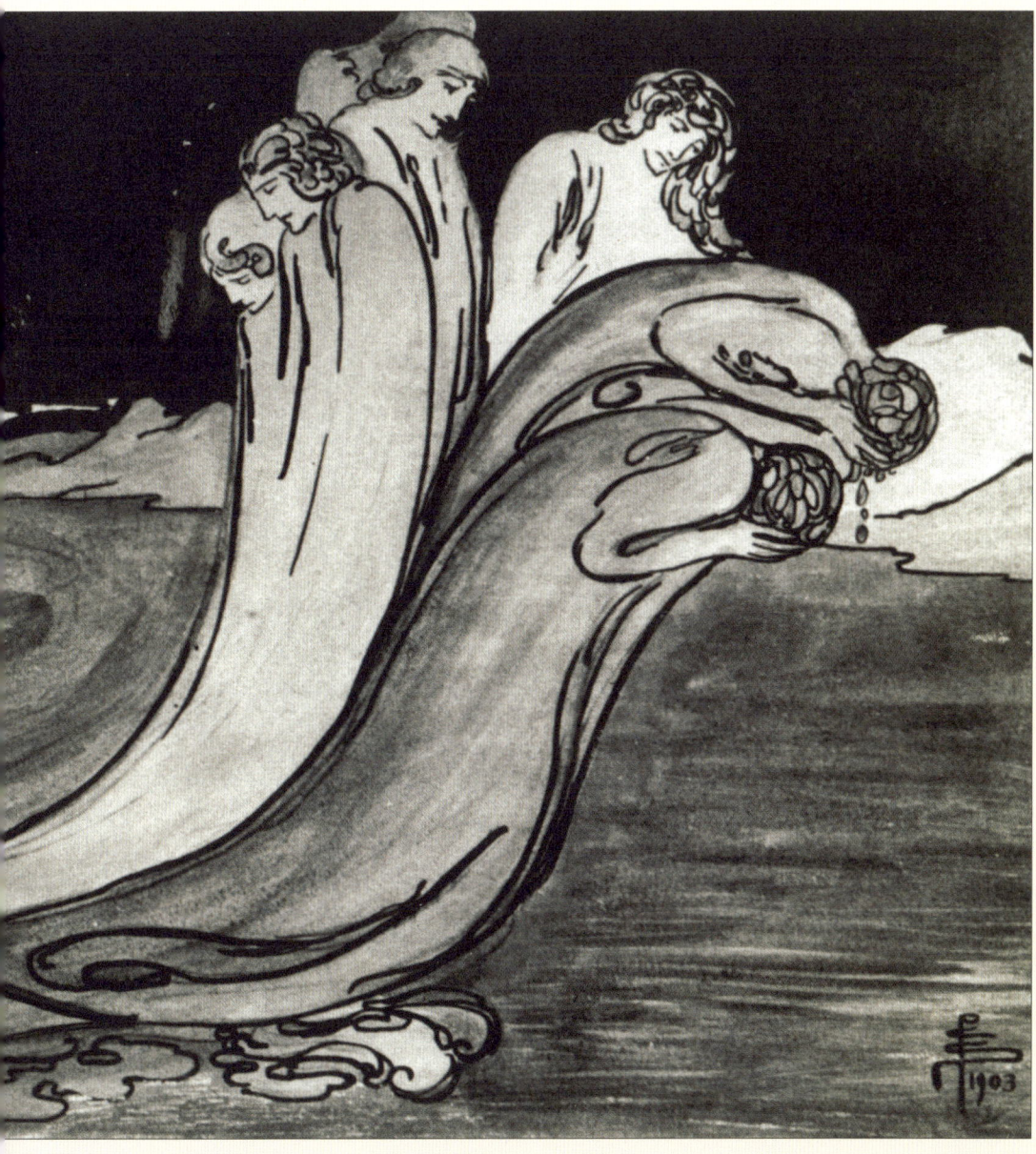

"The Wave," watercolor by Pamela Colman Smith, 1903. Courtesy of Whitney Museum of American Art, New York; Gift of Mrs. Sidney N. Heller

1907

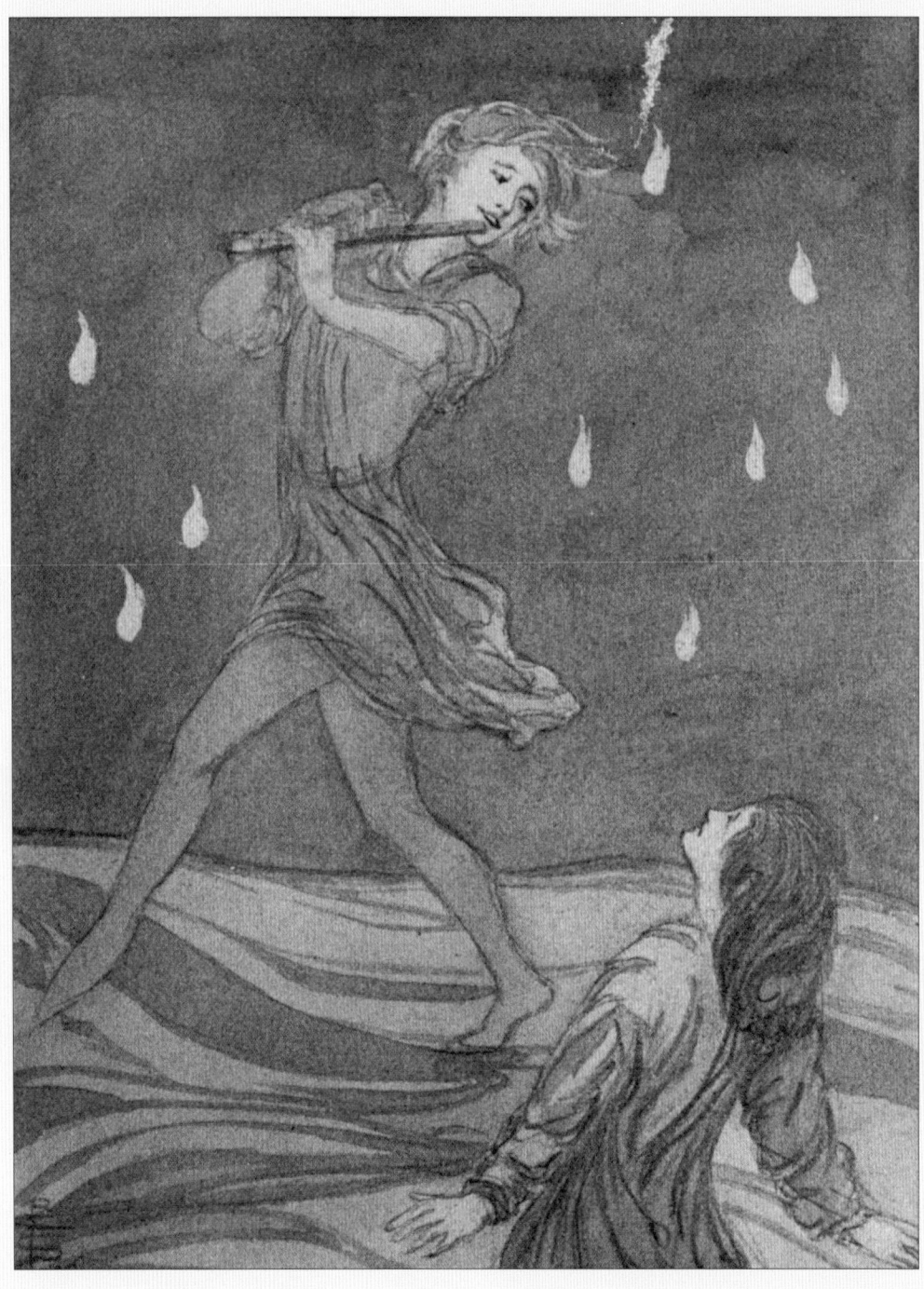

Untitled drawing by Pamela Colman Smith. From the collection of Dorothy Norman, 1997. Courtesy of Philadelphia Museum of Art

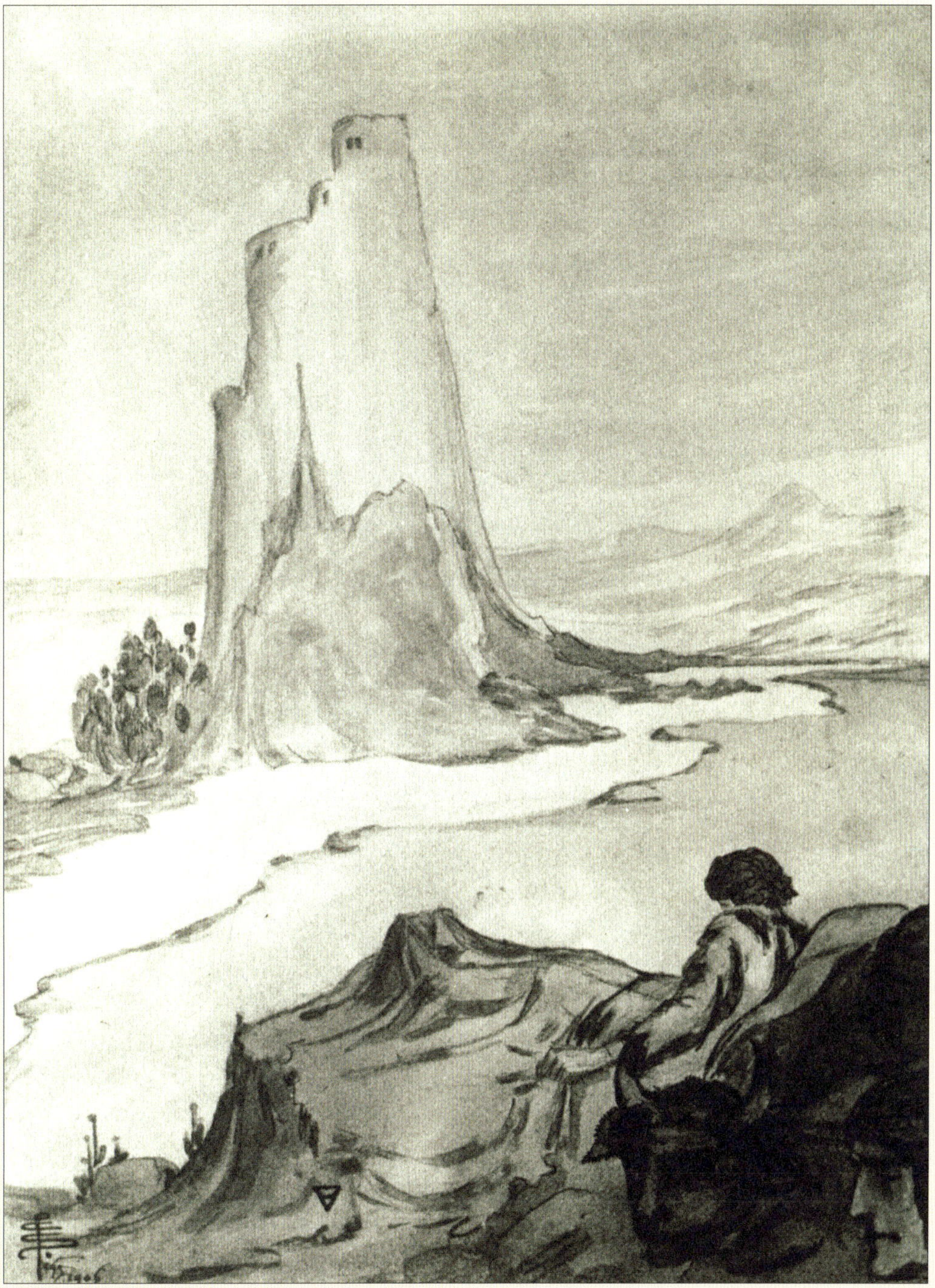

1907

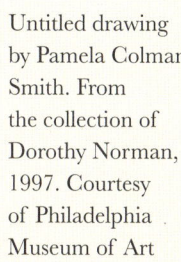

Untitled drawing by Pamela Colman Smith. From the collection of Dorothy Norman, 1997. Courtesy of Philadelphia Museum of Art

1907

Untitled drawing by Pamela Colman Smith. From the collection of Dorothy Norman, 1997. Courtesy of Philadelphia Museum of Art

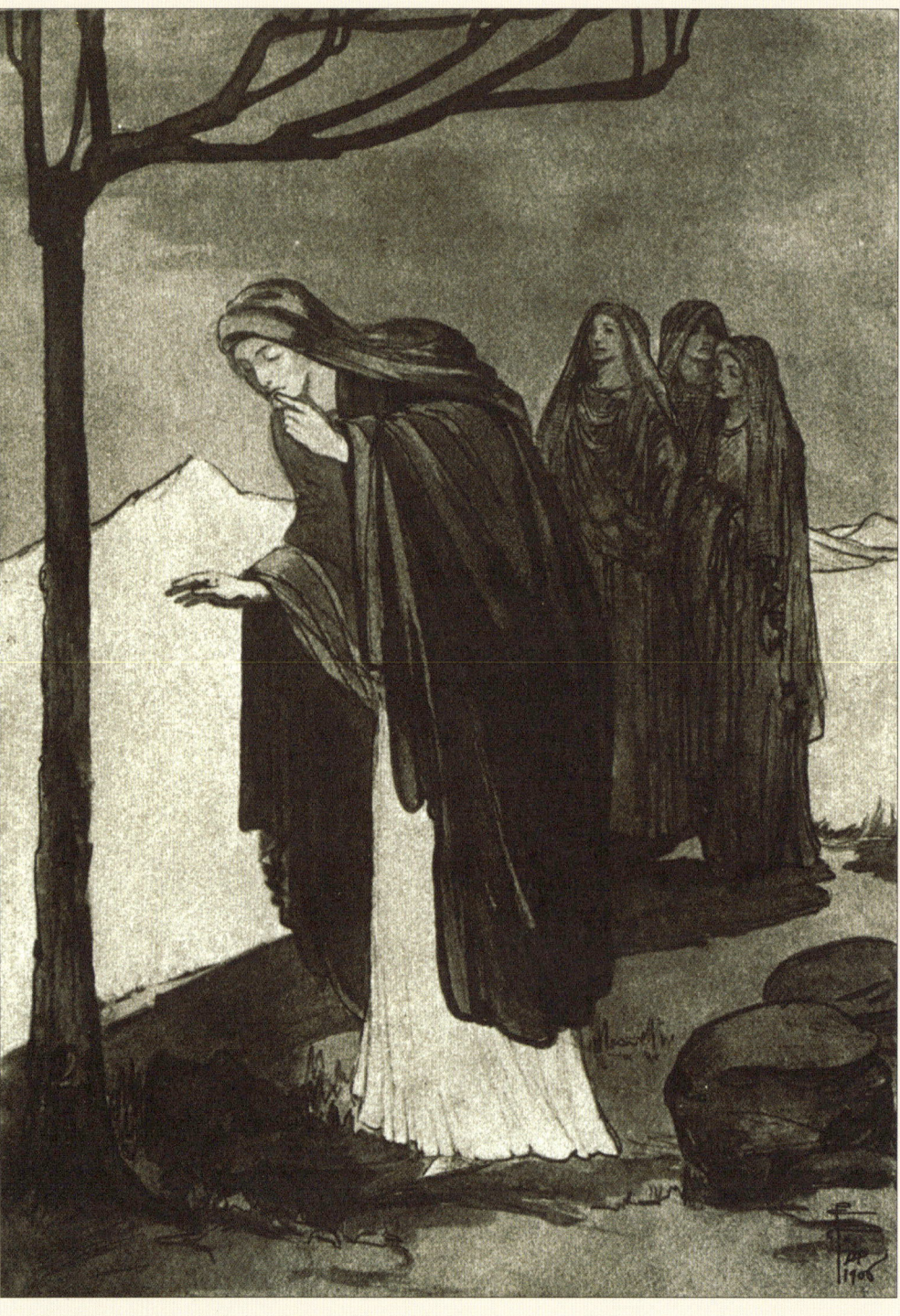

1907

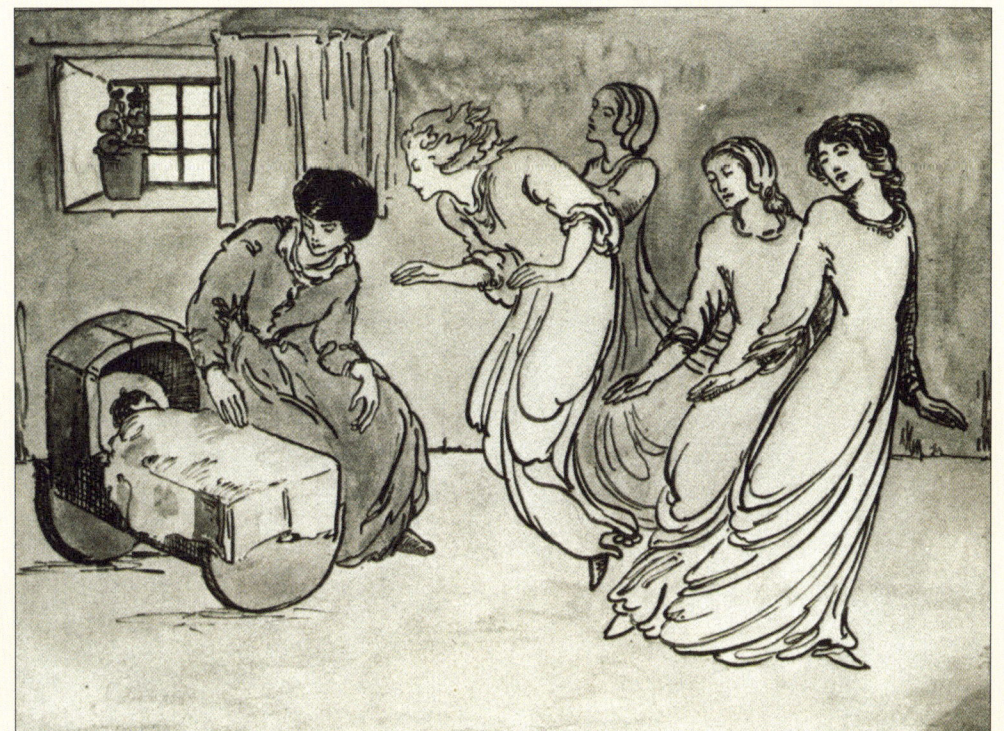

Untitled drawing by Pamela Colman Smith. From the collection of Dorothy Norman, 1997. Courtesy of Philadelphia Museum of Art

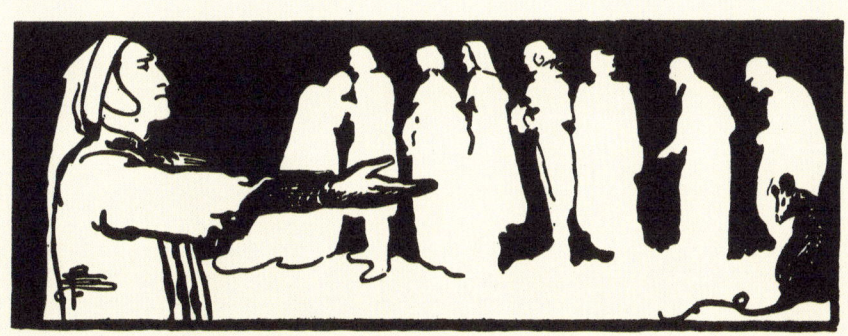

1907

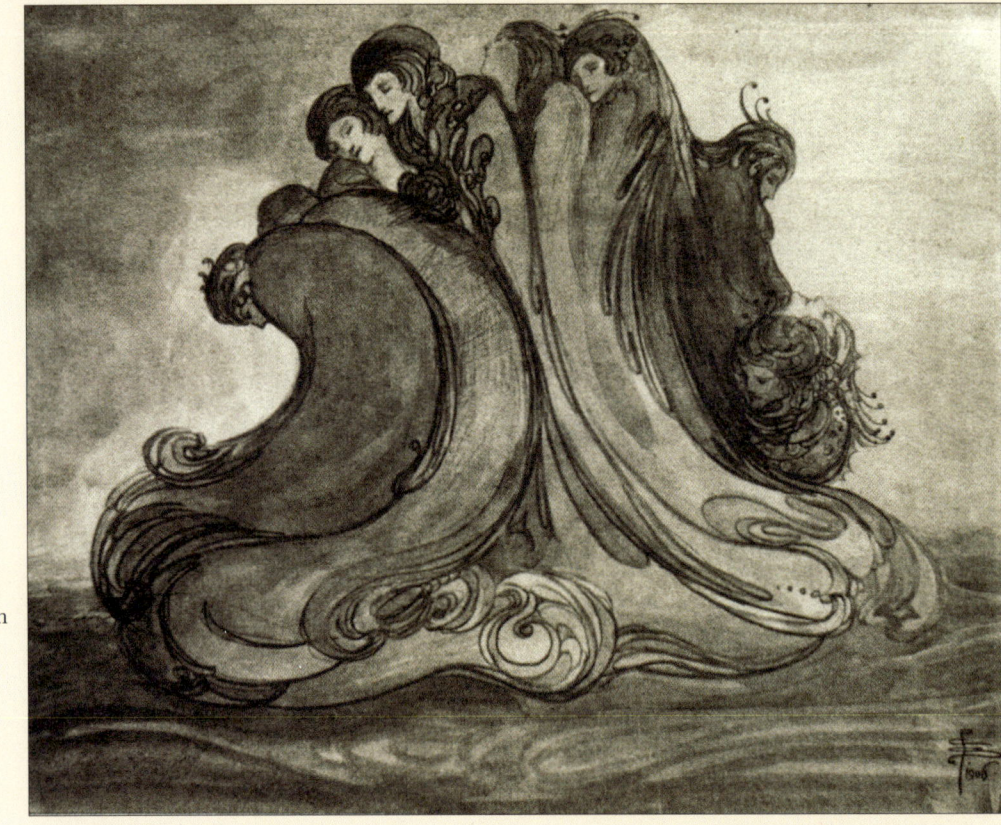

Untitled drawings by Pamela Colman Smith. From the collection of Dorothy Norman, 1997. Courtesy of Philadelphia Museum of Art

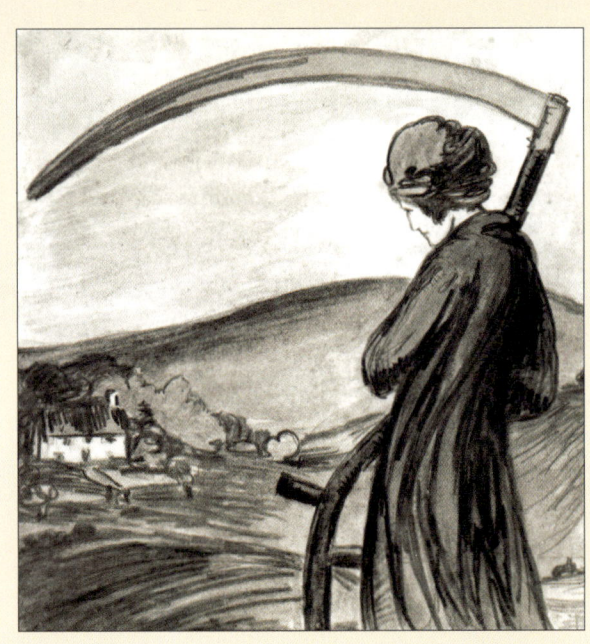

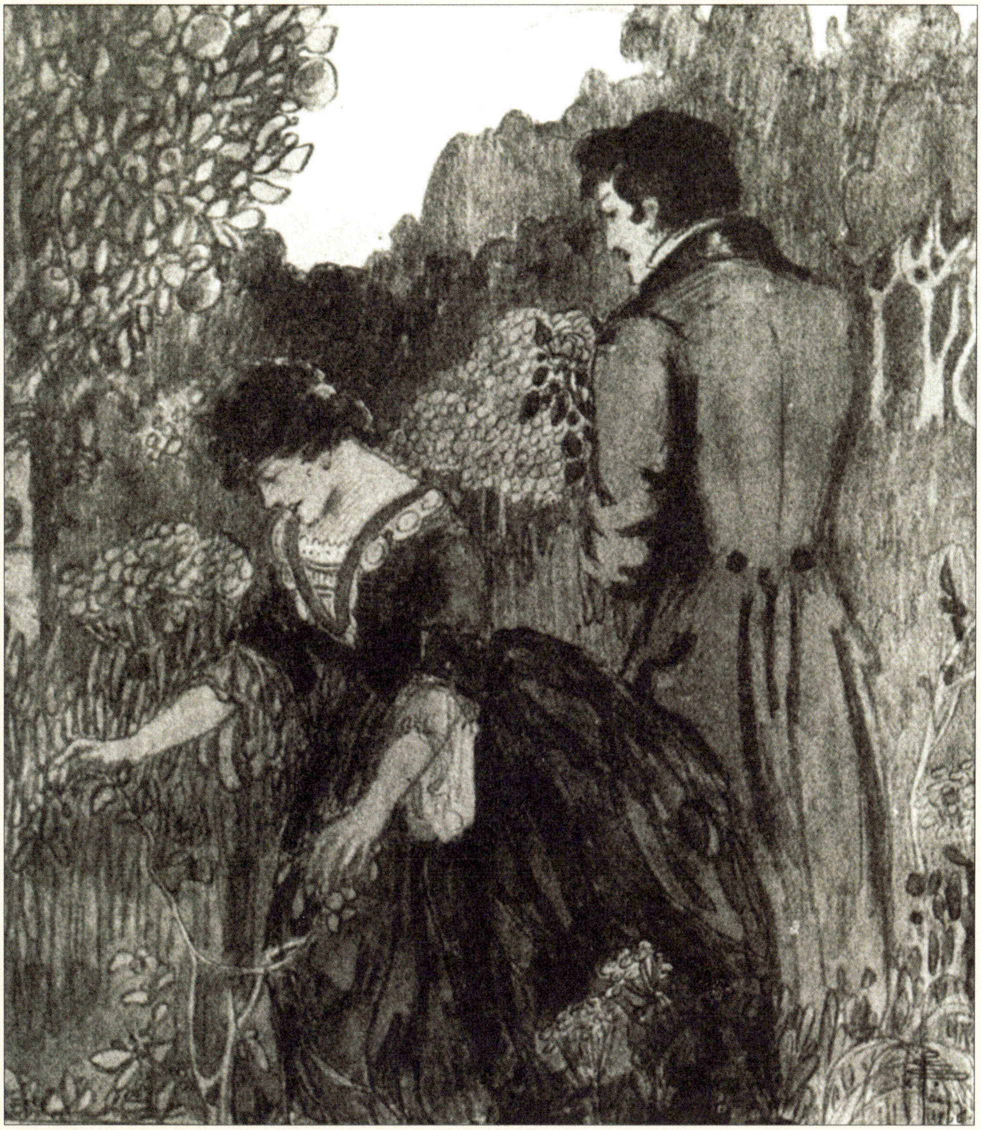

1907

Untitled drawing by Pamela Colman Smith. From the collection of Dorothy Norman, 1997. Courtesy of Philadelphia Museum of Art

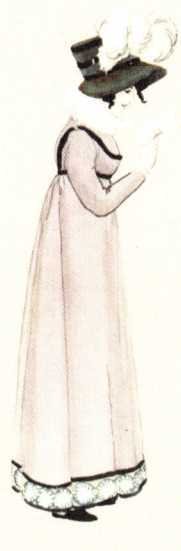

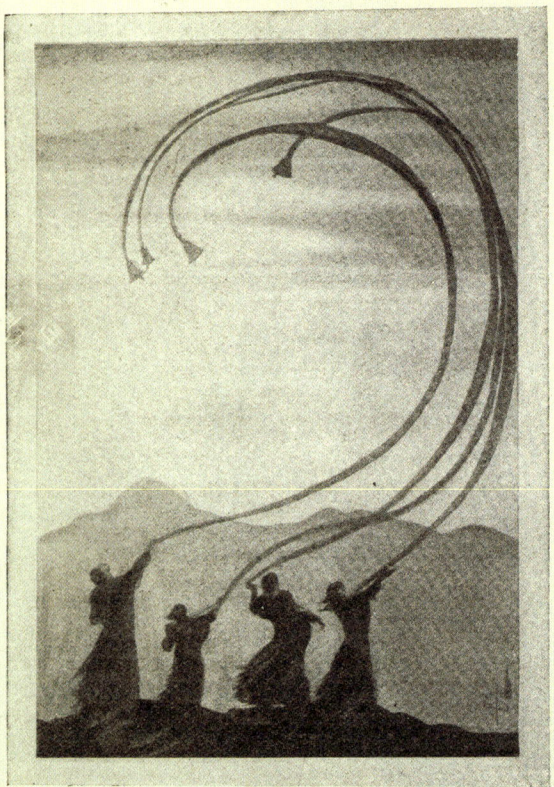

CHROMATIC FANTASY—BACH.
"Often when hearing Bach I hear bells ringing in the sky, rung by whirling cords held in the hands of maidens dressed in brown."

PICTURES IN MUSIC.

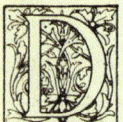O you see pictures in music? When you hear a Beethoven symphony or a sonata by Schumann, do mystic human figures and landscapes float before your eyes?

It is by no means new or uncommon for a composer to have a distinct picture in his mind when he sets himself to create a work. Schumann saw children at play in an embowered wood, dancing merrily until, lo! the sudden advent of a satyr sent them shrieking to their homes.

Few, however, have been able to delineate their hallucinations born of music. Mendelssohn, who was no mean draughtsman, was often asked to do so, but always refused. "It is like asking a sculptor to paint a portrait of his statue," he once said. "All art is one, just as the human body is one, but each of the members has its functions. It is the function of music to hear, not to see." Nevertheless, it is highly interesting to see music translated in the terms of a sister art, and this is what a clever artist, Miss Pamela Colman Smith, has done, in pictures which are published now for the first time in THE STRAND MAGAZINE.

Many of the compositions selected by the artist will instantly be recognised as

PICTURES IN MUSIC.

conveying, in quite a surprising way, a vivid idea of the music as a whole. Every reader can ascertain for himself whether he possesses this peculiar psychic gift—this power of conjuring up music pictures. When you next hear a famous sonata, close your eyes and see what, if any, "pictures" pass before the eye of your brain. Under the magical influence of music the soul has glimpses of wondrous shapes, lit by the light that never was on sea or land.

"You ask me how these pictures are evolved," said Miss Colman Smith. "They are not pictures of the music theme—pictures of the flying notes—not conscious illustrations of the name given to a piece of music, but just what I see when I hear music—thoughts loosened and set free by the spell of sound.

"When I take a brush in hand and the music begins, it is like unlocking the door into a beautiful country. There, stretched far away, are plains and mountains and the billowy sea, and as the music forms a net of sound the people who dwell there enter the scene; tall, slow-moving, stately queens, with jewelled crowns and garments gay or sad, who walk on mountain-tops or stand beside the shore, watching the water-people. These water-folk are passionless, and sway or fall with little heed of time; they toss the spray and, bending down, dive headlong through the deep.

"There are the dwellers, too, of the great plain, who sit and brood, made of stone and motionless; the trees, which slumber till some elf goes by with magic spear and wakes the green to life; towers, white and tall, standing against the darkening sky—

Those tall white towers that one sees afar,
Topping the mountain crests like crowns of snow.
Their silence hangs so heavy in the air
That thoughts are stifled.

"Then huddling crowds, who carry spears, hasten across the changing scene. Sunsets fade from rose to grey, and clouds scud across the sky.

"For a long time the land I saw when hearing Beethoven was unpeopled; hills, plains, ruined towers, churches by the sea. After a time I saw far off a little company of spearmen ride away across the plain. But now the clanging sea is strong with the salt of the lashing spray and full of elemental life; the riders of the waves, the Queen of Tides, who carries in her hand the pearl-like moon, and bubbles gleaming on the inky wave.

"Often when hearing Bach I hear bells ringing in the sky, rung by whirling cords held in the hands of maidens dressed in brown. There is a rare freshness in the air, like morning on a mountain-top, with opal-coloured mists that chase each other fast across the scene.

"Chopin brings night; gardens where mystery and dread lurk under every bush, but joy and passion throb within the air, and the cold moon bewitches all the scene. There is a garden that I often see, with moonlight glistening on the vine-leaves, and drooping roses with pale petals fluttering down, tall, misty trees and purple sky, and lovers wandering there.

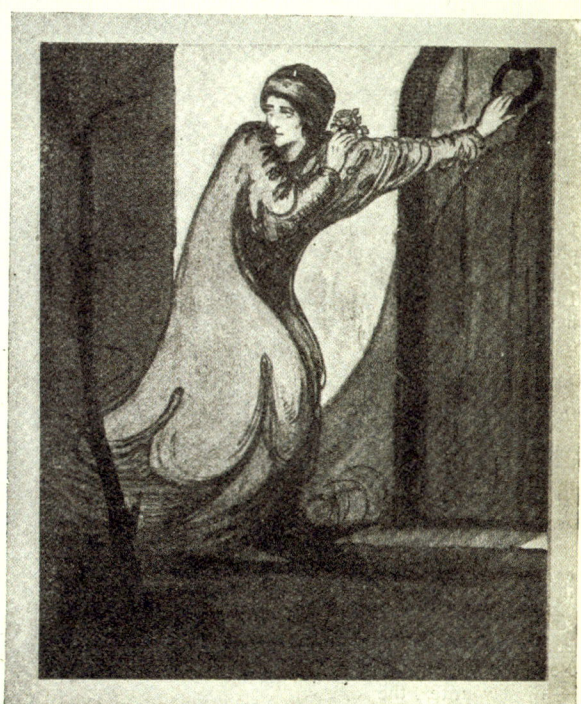

BALLADE No. 1, OP. 23, IN G MINOR—CHOPIN.
"Chopin brings night; gardens where mystery and dread lurk under every bush, but joy and passion throb within the air." The artist calls this picture "The Fugitive."

over which dragon-flies hover, where nymphs bathe hand in hand."

One of the most sensitive of music-lovers was Heine, who tells us that as he listened the world around would disappear, and in its place strange phantom forms, mystic scenes, and figures born of melody would glide before his rapturous vision. Few things in literature are more impressive than his description of Paganini playing:—

"As for me, you already know my musical second-sight, my gift of seeing at each tone a figure equivalent to the sound, and so Paganini, with each stroke of the bow, brought visible forms and situations before my eyes; he told me in melodious hieroglyphics all kinds of brilliant tales; he, as it were, made a magic-lantern play its coloured antics before me, he himself being chief actor. At the first stroke of his bow the stage scenery around

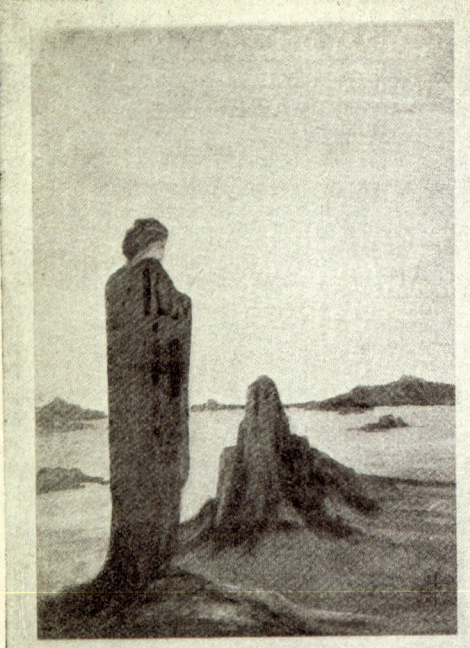

SONATA PATHETIQUE—BEETHOVEN.
"Tall, slow-moving, stately queens, with jewelled crowns and garments gay or sad, who walk on mountain-tops or stand beside the shore."

"A drawing of that garden I have shown to several people and asked them if they could play the music that I heard when I drew it. They have all, without any hesitation, played the same. I do not know the name, but—well, I know the music of that place."

It is interesting to compare with these experiences the words of great artists and writers who have been endowed with the same gift.

"When I listen to music," wrote the great Meissonier, "it takes shape in my inner soul, it conjures up form and landscapes. For instance, Beethoven's Symphony in A—my favourite, the one I adore—always shows me a Greek landscape smiling in the sunlight, with clear water

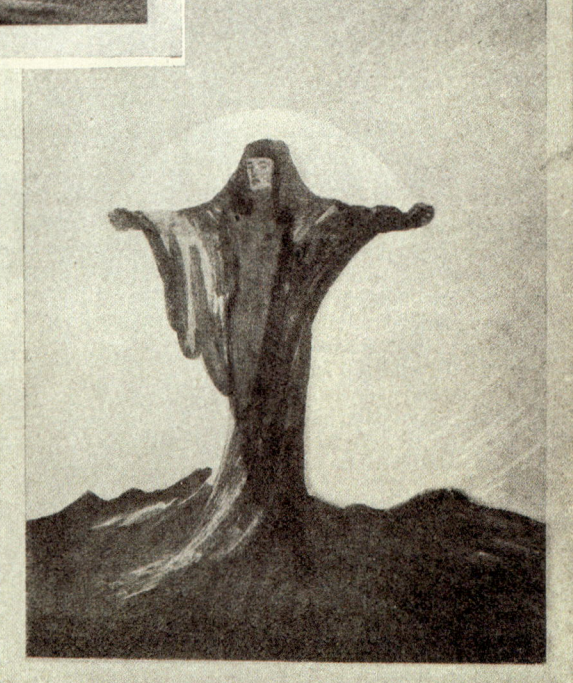

SYMPHONY No. 5 IN C MINOR—BEETHOVEN.
"But now the clanging sea is strong with the salt of the lashing spray and full of elemental life; the riders of the waves, the Queen of Tides, who carries in her hand the pearl-like moon."

him had changed; he suddenly stood with his music-desk in a cheerful room, decorated in a gay irregular way after the Pompadour style; everywhere little mirrors, gilded Cupids, Chinese porcelain, a delightful chaos of ribbons, garlands of flowers, white gloves, torn lace, false pearls, diadems of gold leaf and spangles—such tinsel as one finds in the room of a *prima donna*. Paganini's outward appearance had also changed, and certainly most advantageously; he wore short breeches of lily-coloured satin, a white waistcoat embroidered with silver, and a coat of bright blue velvet with gold buttons; the hair in little carefully-curled locks bordered his face, which was young and rosy, and gleamed with sweet tenderness as he ogled the pretty young lady who stood near him at the music-desk while he played the violin."

At other times when Paganini began to play a gloom came before the listener's eyes. The sounds were not transformed into bright forms and colours; the master's form was clothed in gloomy shades, out of the darkness of which his music moaned in the most piercing tones of lamentation. Only at times, when a little lamp that hung above cast its sorrowful light over him, could Heine catch a glimpse of his pale countenance, on which the youth was not yet extinguished. His costume was singular, in two colours, yellow and red. Heavy chains weighed upon his feet. Behind him moved a face whose physiognomy indicated a lusty goat-nature. And he saw at times long, hairy hands seize assistingly the strings of the violin on which Paganini was playing.

"Then a rush of agonizing sounds came from the violin, and a fearful groan, and a sob such as was never heard upon the earth before, nor will perhaps be heard on earth again; unless in the Valley of Jehoshaphat, when the colossal trumpets of doom shall ring out and the naked corpses shall crawl forth from the grave to abide their fate. But the agonized violinist suddenly made one stroke of the bow, such a mad, despairing stroke that his chains fell rattling from him, and his mysterious assistant and the other foul mocking forms vanished."

Again the master musician and his surroundings seemed suddenly changed. He could scarcely be recognised in the monk's

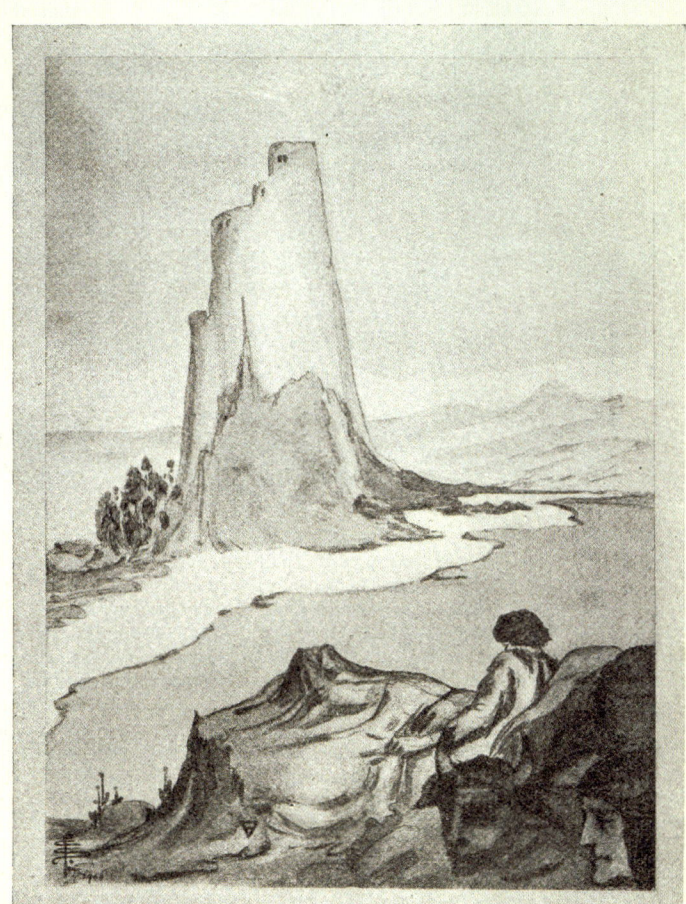

CONCERTO IN A MINOR, "CASTLE OF PAIN"—SCHUMANN.
When hearing Schumann's Concerto in A minor the artist sees a castle, grim and solitary, and peopled with despairing human souls. She calls it the "Castle of Pain."

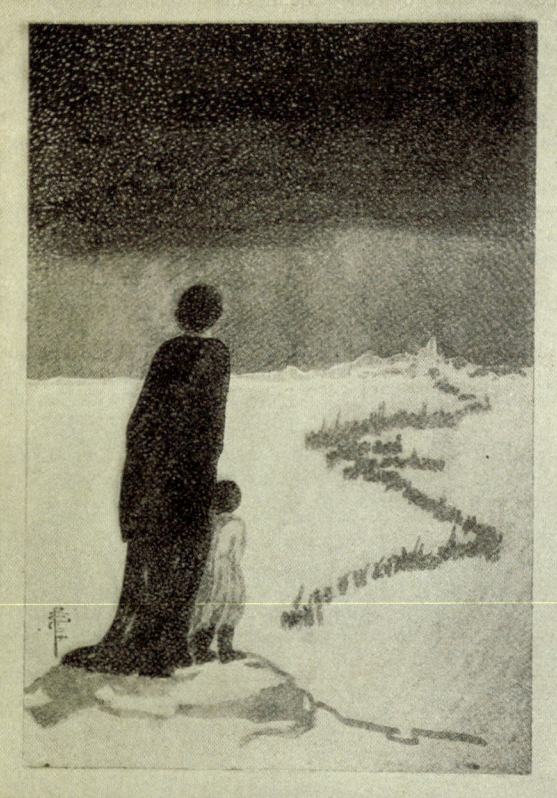

OVERTURE "1812"—TSCHAIKOVSKY.

Tschaikovsky's famous overture, "1812," was written in a fervour of Russian patriotism to commemorate his country's achievements during that fateful year. In the above picture we see Napoleon's army in the midst of their disastrous retreat from Moscow. A widow and her child gaze sadly from an eminence across the snow-clad plains which were destined to become the grave of so many thousands.

brown dress, which concealed rather than clothed him. With savage countenance half hid by the cowl, waist girt with a cord, and bare feet, Paganini stood, a solitary, defiant figure, on a rocky prominence by the sea, and played his violin. But the sea became red and redder, and the sky grew paler, till at last the surging water looked like bright scarlet blood, and the sky above became of a ghastly corpse-like colour, and the stars came out large and threatening; and those stars were black, black as glooming coal. But the tones of the violin grew ever more stormy and defiant, and the eyes of the terrible player sparkled with such a scornful lust of destruction, and his thin lips moved with such a horrible haste, that it seemed as if he murmured some old accursed charms to conjure the storm and loose the evil spirits that lie imprisoned in the abysses of the sea. Often when he stretched his long, thin arms from the broad monk's sleeve, and swept the air with his bow, he seemed like some sorcérer who commands the elements with his magic wand; and then there was a wild wailing from the depth of the sea, and the horrible waves of blood sprang up so fiercely that they almost besprinkled the pale sky and the black stars with their red foam. There was a wailing and a shrieking and a crashing as if the world was falling into fragments, and ever more stubbornly the monk played his violin. He seemed as if, by the power of violent will, he wished to break the seven seals wherewith Solomon sealed the iron vessels in which he had shut up those vanquished demons. The wise king sank those vessels in the sea, and Heine seemed to hear the voices of the imprisoned spirits while Paganini's violin growled in its most wrathful bass. But at last he thought he heard the jubilee of deliverance, and out of the red billows of blood emerged the heads of the fettered demons: monsters of legendary horror, crocodiles with bats' wings, snakes with stags' horns, monkeys with shells on their heads, seals with long patriarchal beards, women's faces with breasts in place of cheeks, green camels' heads, hermaphrodites of impossible combination—all staring with cold, crafty eyes, and with long, fin-like claws grasping at the fiddling monk. From the latter, however, in the furious zeal of his conjuration the cowl fell back, and the curly hair, fluttering in the wind, fell round his head in ringlets like black snakes.

Madame Knowledge

1907

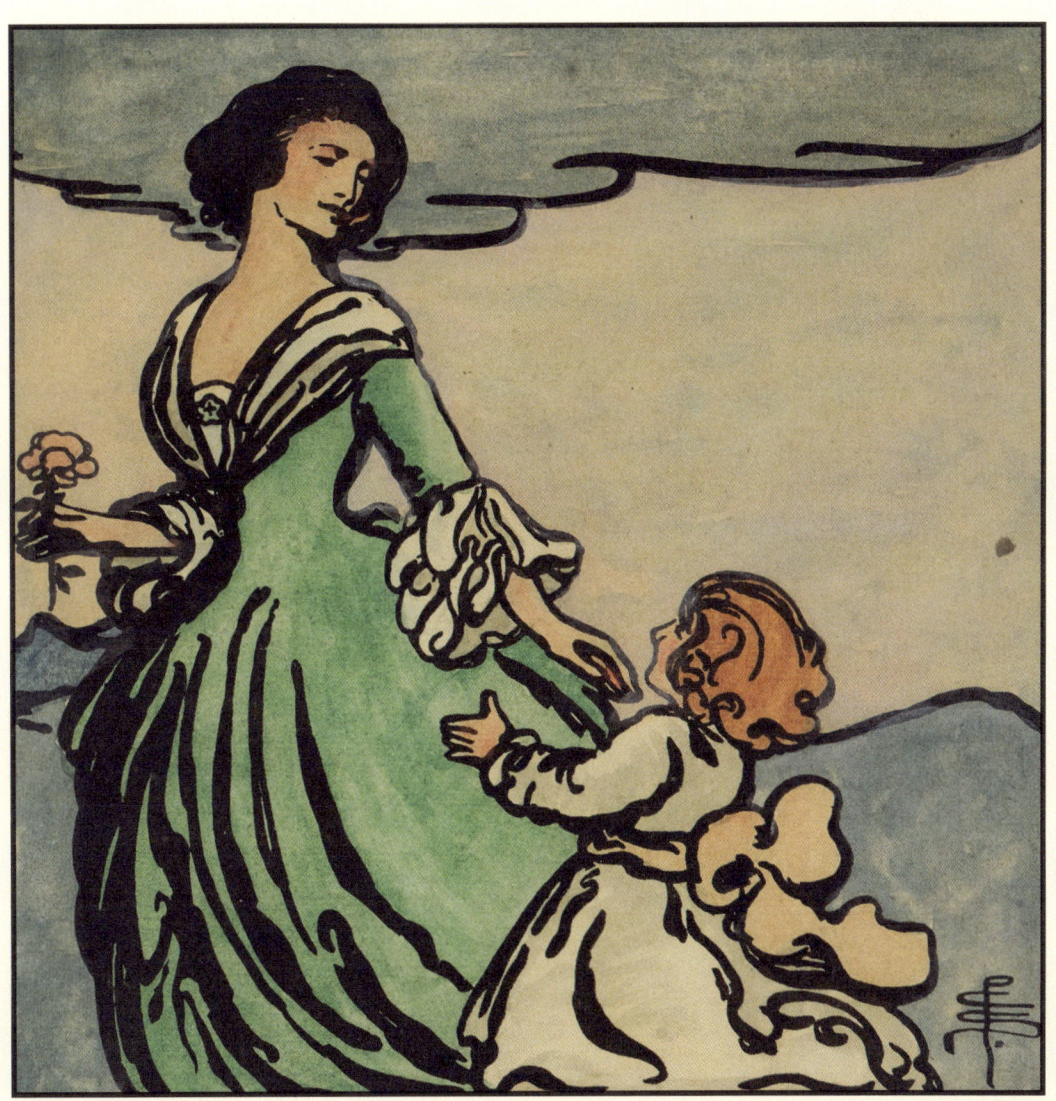

"Madame Knowledge," watercolor
on paper by Pamela Colman Smith

1907

List of drawings and Prices. [12/21/07]

84 YORK MANSIONS, BATTERSEA PARK, LONDON, S.W.
TELEPHONE: 276 WESTERN.

A. Overture - "King Stephen" - Beethoven
   London price.   £ 12.12.0
  Suggested - N.Y. " $ 75.00

B. Symphony no 5. in C.   Beethoven -
46   London price   £ 12-12-0
   N.Y. " $ 50.00

53 C. Sonata. no 11. op 22.   Beethoven
   London price   £. 7-7-0
   N.Y. " $ 35.00

D. Sonata - Grieg —
   London price — £. 6-6-0 9
   N.Y. " $. 25.00.

E. Spring Song - Grieg —
   London price — £ 5-5-0
   N.Y. " $ 25-00.
         R 20-00.

F. Overture - "Manfred" Schumann.
   London price. £ 5.5.0
   N.Y. "   25-00

1907

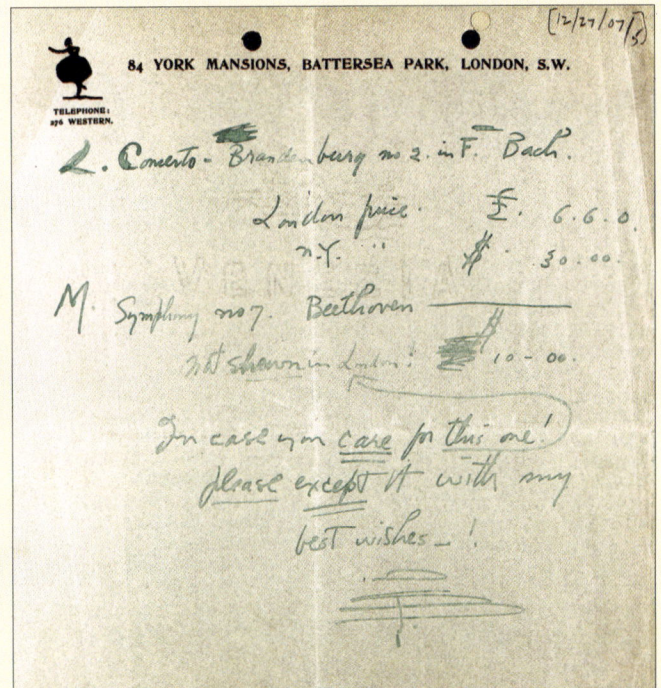

Letter from Pamela Colman Smith to Alfred Stieglitz dated December 27, 1907 listing 13 drawings to music with suggested prices. Courtesy of The Beinecke Rare Book & Manuscript Library, Yale University

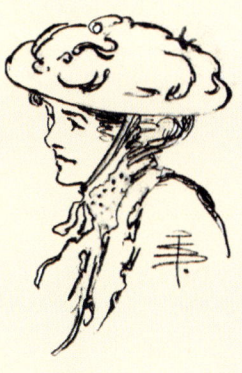

1907

UNDER the auspices of the Pratt Art Club, Miss Pamela Colman Smith gave an extremely interesting recital at the Institute last Saturday evening. While telling her Jamaica folk stories, Miss Smith sat upon a low platform with her feet tucked under her, and a row of half-dozen big fat candles before her to serve as footlights. The room was darkened and the young narrator presented a very picturesque figure gowned in a loose robe of flame colored silk, with an arrangement of tulle and beads bound about her head like a kerchief. Her capital West Indian dialect rendered the stories all the more piquant. In a charming recital of old English ballads, this clever artist dressed the part in soft gray and white with a quaint cap; while in her tragical odd lilting of a group of poems by William B. Yeats, Miss Smith again showed her rare knowledge of dramatic values by wearing a long dark green cloak with hood drawn close about her face, and only one nervous hand visible. Miss Kate Simmons, president of the Art Club, introduced Miss Smith very gracefully. This association, by the way, has delightful meeting rooms at 296 Lafayette avenue, where tea is served Friday afternoons and all former students are made as welcome as the more recent art pupils. It is rapidly becoming a popular, informal rendezvous and is by no means an Adamless Eden either; for Mr. Warren F. Wheelock is vice-president of this club of which Miss Maud L. Calkins and Miss Fannie J. Cooke are secretary and treasurer.

Pamela Colman Smith is a young woman with that quality rare in either sex—imagination. She is exhibiting at the galleries of the Photo-Secession, 291 Fifth avenue, a collection of seventy-two drawings, colored and black and white. There is a Shakespeare series, and illustrations to Schumann's "Carnival." You read the titles and dream of Blake, of Fantin-Latour, of the Japanese, of De Groux, of James Ensor, of Beardsley, of Edvard Munch, of Maeterlinck and of Chopin. But your eyes tell you that Miss Smith is in every design, many of them mere memoranda of a spiritual exaltation, of the soul under the influence of music, or haunted by some sinister imagining. "Death in the House" is absolutely nerve shuddering. Yet it is not concerned with the familiar symbols of the grewsome. There is little statement, much suggestion. Munch, himself a master magician of the terrible, could not have succeeded better in arousing a profound disquiet, that is at once the play of the nerves and the inner images of our common destiny. Morbid? Yes, perhaps; but so is Chopin, so is Schumann morbid. The Schumann set is very effective. To the lover of this exotic *cahier* of pianoforte music, miniature poems all, Miss Smith's interpretation of "Sphinxes" will be startling.

Top left, Pratt Art Club Recital. Reprinted from *The Sun (NY)*, January 15, 1907.
Top right, review of Exhibition at Photo-Secession Galleries. Reprinted from *Brooklyn Life (NY)*, January 26, 1907.
Right, Story Telling at John Baillie Gallery. Reprinted from *The Times (London)*, February 4, 1908

MISS COLMAN-SMITH'S STORY-TELLING.—A charmingly unconventional little entertainment was given last night at the John Baillie Gallery in Baker-street by Miss Pamela Colman-Smith, who told a series of Jamaican folk-stories collected by her on the spot. They were told with delightful gusto and spirit, and dealt for the most part with the doings of a remarkably unscrupulous spider, named Annancy, some of whose adventures have come before the members of the Folk-Lore Society before now. The incidents, like that of Daniel in the lions' den—related in a curiously homely fashion—took place "once in a long-before time before Queen Victoria come to reign over we," and, if any one wished a perfect object-lesson in the meaning and application of the much-abused word "conviction," he has only to hear Miss Colman-Smith's delivery of the tales, in which she seems to believe with all her heart. She also sang some ballads, such as "Little Sir William" and the forgotten "All Round My Hat," in the true folk-song manner. On the walls of the gallery, among other drawings, are shown some most interesting and very clever imaginative drawings by Miss Colman-Smith herself, conceived and in part executed during the performance of well-known musical compositions, in which it is remarkable to see how the same composer inspires her with the same class of desires

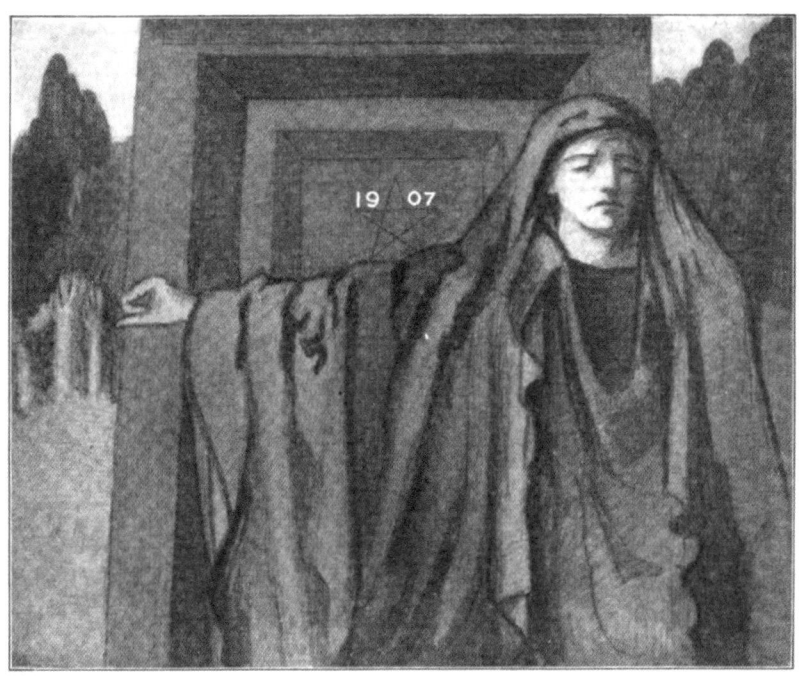

LET NO MAN'S SOUL DESPAIR!

BY ROBERT BURNS WILSON

DRAWING BY PAMELA COLEMAN SMITH

LET no man's soul despair!
　　The same eternal powers, for good or ill,
　　　The same unslumbering care
　Which lived of old, are quick and potent still
　And bend, obedient to the dauntless will
　　　Of souls that do and dare.

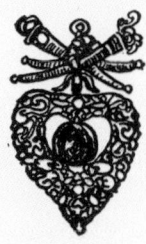

Ellen Terry's Story of My Life

1908

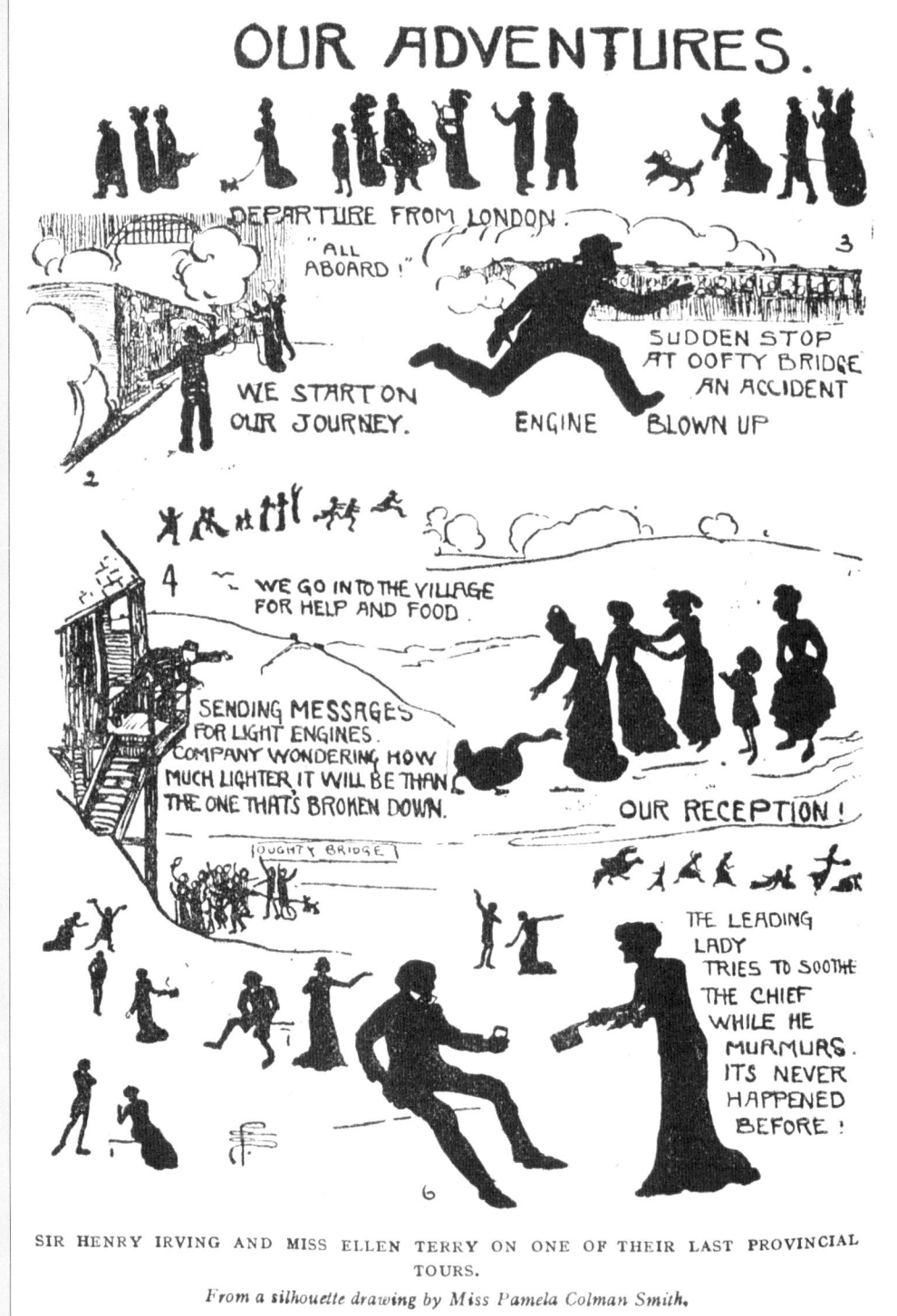

SIR HENRY IRVING AND MISS ELLEN TERRY ON ONE OF THEIR LAST PROVINCIAL TOURS.
From a silhouette drawing by Miss Pamela Colman Smith.

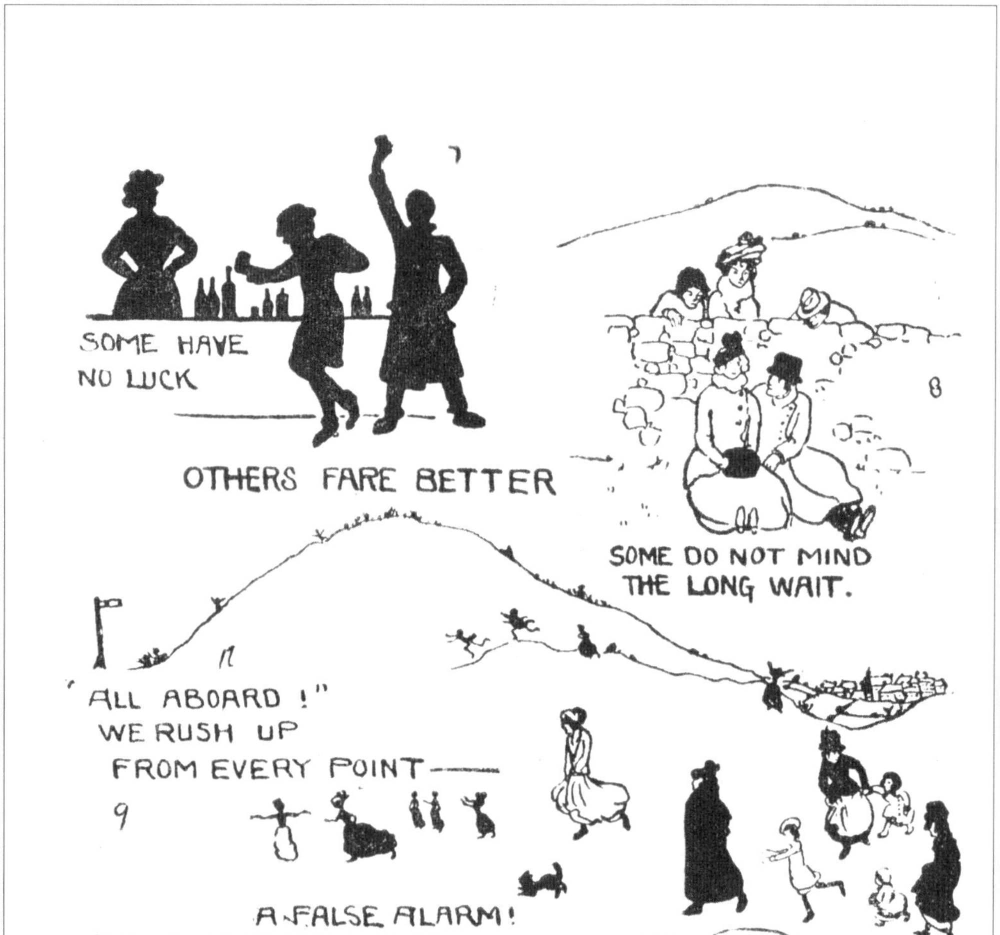

1910 to 1951

1910 — Supplement to the New Age

Appropriate Stage Decoration.
By Pamela Coleman Smith.

About us is the glowing beauty of the world, with its leaves and flowers, rags, gold and purple. Kings on thrones of iron, beggars on beds of clay, laughing, weeping, dreaming.

And this pageant of life moves before us, intensified, in the theatre.

People go, most of them, to the play to be amused, and in spite of themselves, are often tricked into a mode of thinking quite contrary to their usual habit of thought. That is why the theatre is the place where all beauty of thought, of sound, of colour, and of high teaching, comes to be of use.

All arts are branches of one tree.

There in the theatre, unconsciously, the onlooker is moved, or interested, and finds himself agreeing or disagreeing with the playwright; and every time he enters a theatre he comes out with a little more knowledge than when he went in. Agreeing or disagreeing, it brings uppermost in his mind some thought which crystallises and becomes a new intelligence.

Theatre-going is a habit, where one cultivates a new kind of observation, a new pair of eyes and ears.

What strikes one most, when thinking of the theatre as a whole, is the lack of beauty, the formlessness, as regards costumes, scenery and properties; those things which are next in importance to the play, players, and producer.

The large playhouses are kaleidoscopes of meaningless colour and over-elaboration. The great bulk of stage-production is unbeautiful, elaborate and vulgar. There is a glut of technical ability with an inability of mind to perceive beauty, or to apply it.

The perfection of art is when one does not see the artifice. "Ars est celare artem."

Good acting appears so easy that we overlook the fact that it is the result of fine technique, and of genius in some cases. Fine technique is visible in all the arts at the present day, but it is a shallow and empty mask, a self-conscious sham, without sincerity and meaning.

On the one side is vulgar display, on the other, affected simplicity, while in the middle Realism panders to the sensation-loving Ignorant, by the introduction of real animals, real trees, real water, on the stage.

Those in power have not remembered that Illusion is the aim of the theatre. It is a great game of pretence that recalls the time when, as children, we baked stones in the sun for cakes, and feared the dragon that lurked behind the garden wall, or by the pond. A remnant of that imaginative life we re-live in beholding a play set forth before our eyes.

If the illusion is good, we follow it more easily, and illusion to be good need not be realistic. *Realism is not Art.* It is the essence that is necessary, to give a semblance of the real thing.

Absolute correctness in dress or scene does not necessarily give the illusion. Everything must be exaggerated in order that it may be visible across the footlights.

There are conventions in the form of a theatre, such as the proscenium, the stage, the wings and flat backcloths, which should be an aid to the designer, not a hindrance.

An artist should use the conventions that are to his hand and make them subject to his skill, trying to simplify rather than elaborate.

From the first he must be able to see in his mind the whole production complete.

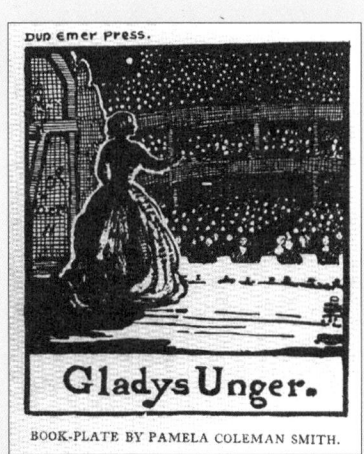

BOOK-PLATE BY PAMELA COLEMAN SMITH.

Certainly a knowledge of the working of a theatre is as necessary to a costume-designer as it is to a playwright. A designer of patterns for fabrics, or a painter of portraits who is asked to make a set of costumes for a stage play, is apt to do so without the knowledge of the technical working of a theatre, the difficulties and conventions of lighting, and the host of details which make up the component parts of a modern playhouse; and so, too often, their well-intentioned efforts, though possibly correct in historic detail, are more or less lacking in effectiveness and suitability for dramatic purposes.

A coat of curious cut should not be made *less* fantastic than the original, but more so. For the use of costume on the stage, cut is more important than material. The textiles now used in the dressing of costume plays are far too expensive and ineffective. Cotton stuffs and woollens can be used with greater effect, in many cases, than silks, satins and cloth of gold.

The most important part of costume is the wearing of it, and is the greatest difficulty met by the designer. How few players know how to put on, and wear, their clothes with an air of distinction! One sometimes wonders whether the fear of seeming ridiculous to the people "in front" is the reason why many an actor finds it beneath his dignity to wear a fantastic coat which he does not like, or understand.

I have often noticed the unsuitability of dress worn by some actresses. Their dresses would appear to be provided according to the length of their salaries, or their parts.

If players would only realise the importance of dressing their heads correctly, not leaving it to facial make-up! It has caused me much annoyance to see ladies-in-waiting in a Shakespearean play with their hair done exactly as they wear it at a party, but with the addition of a string of pearls! This on top of a good Elizabethan dress.

The wardrobe mistress, or whoever is in charge, should see that the clothes are worn correctly. It is most distressing to a designer to see some detail which has cost much anxious thought, worn incorrectly, or repaired in such a manner as to have lost all its primary significance.

The great need in a theatre is a person who will supervise for the designer. After production, there is often a lamentable want of care in the wearing and repairing of clothes. The Supervisor should be able to help the designer by bringing into use a practical knowledge of stage effects, and, after production, should be responsible for the wearing and repairing of the costumes throughout the run of the play.

Scenery is far too elaborate at present. A cleverly painted scene gets a round of applause, from the same people who admire a Royal Academy landscape. Costume is more important than scenery, which should be simple and in harmony with the dresses. How can a designer know how his dresses will look in a realistic wood, lit by glaring electric light? The scene-painter and designer of dresses should work in harmony, so that the work of one may not jar upon the colour scheme of the other, and both should read the play, before setting out to design a background for it.

At present, a designer does not see the lighting or scenery until the dress-rehearsal, when it is too late to alter any important dress.

Colours are forces but little understood. Strong colour is disliked, and perhaps the fear and hatred of strong, clean colour is due to ignorance. People think they like "sweetly pretty" soft and "art" colours, muddy, dirty and wishy-washy tones. Yet did they but know it, grey is the admixture of pure colours, as we observe in the work of the French impressionist painters, who use red, blue and yellow side by side to get the effect of light and atmosphere. Is it the fear of the dreaded accusation of vulgarity? I believe the public would prefer the effect got by the use of strong primitive colour, if they saw it.

A reform need not always necessarily take the form of savage force, but by gentle ways and patient insistence the truth may be inserted and the public pleased.

The designer must insist on the balance being kept, and work in harmony with, and not be ruled by, the producer or stage manager. Of course the producer must have confidence in the designer to complete his work.

Let us see what happens now.

A costume play is to be produced. The present course is simply to hire from a costumier a set of costumes considered suitable for the play. These possibly have neither beauty nor historical accuracy, and quite often are merely in the tradition of the part, the model having done duty in many revivals. How is it possible that these dresses should bear any relation to their setting, or to each other?

Or, supposing the manager wishes to do the thing handsomely, he calls in a designer. Judging by the results, it is left by the designer to the costumier, who cuts the dresses by the traditional pattern, softening down the characteristic points to please the wearer. The designer may see the dresses tried on two or three times, and, should he make a suggestion that the cut should be more exaggerated, he is told by the costumier that it is impossible, "it is always done this way."

How rarely does one see an entire production welded together into a thing of beauty by artist hands?

"Supers" are most important. Where ten men, if skilfully used, could represent an army, there are now perhaps fifty or so, unintelligently-trained supers who only represent a muddle, and are an unnecessary expense. The money paid to extra supers could be saved, and young members of the company might thus learn their craft, with one or two good actors scattered among them to play crowds and soldiers. This is actually the case in some provincial Shakespearean repertory companies.

What a useful thing a dramatic library would be. In such a place students of the drama, actors, producers, designers, and others, could easily refer to valuable material. At present it takes endless trouble and time to find what is wanted in a library or museum not intended for this particular study.

Take a case in point. Where would one look for the dress of a Jewish woman in England in the year 1185? I think that would baffle most people! There *is* the material to go on, given the knowledge of where to find it. The much-talked-of National Theatre should include a carefully classified and arranged library, to which donors could give prints and scrap-books of value for the study of historical and international costume.

Supplement to the New Age, June 2, 1910

The Lair of the White Worm

1911

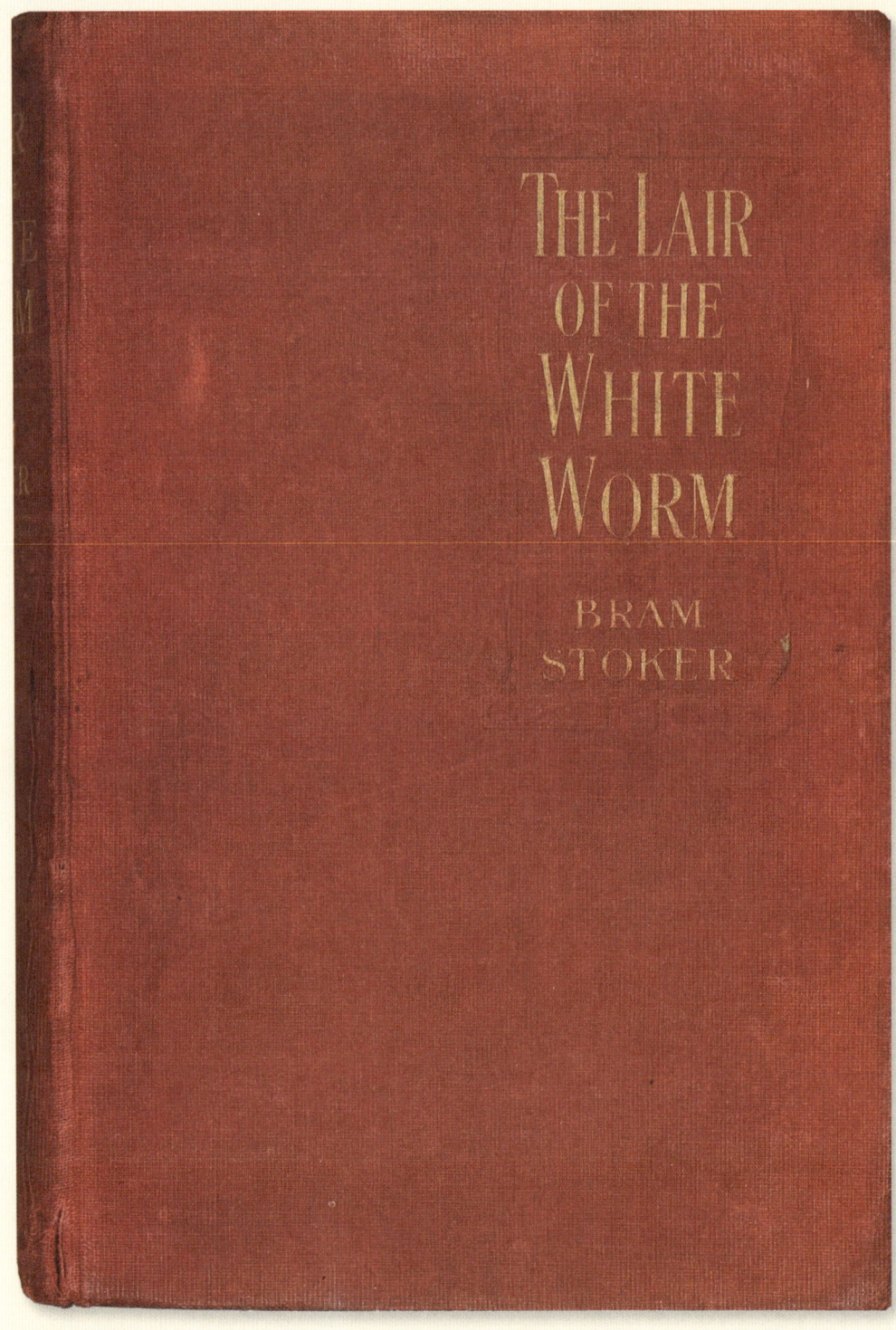

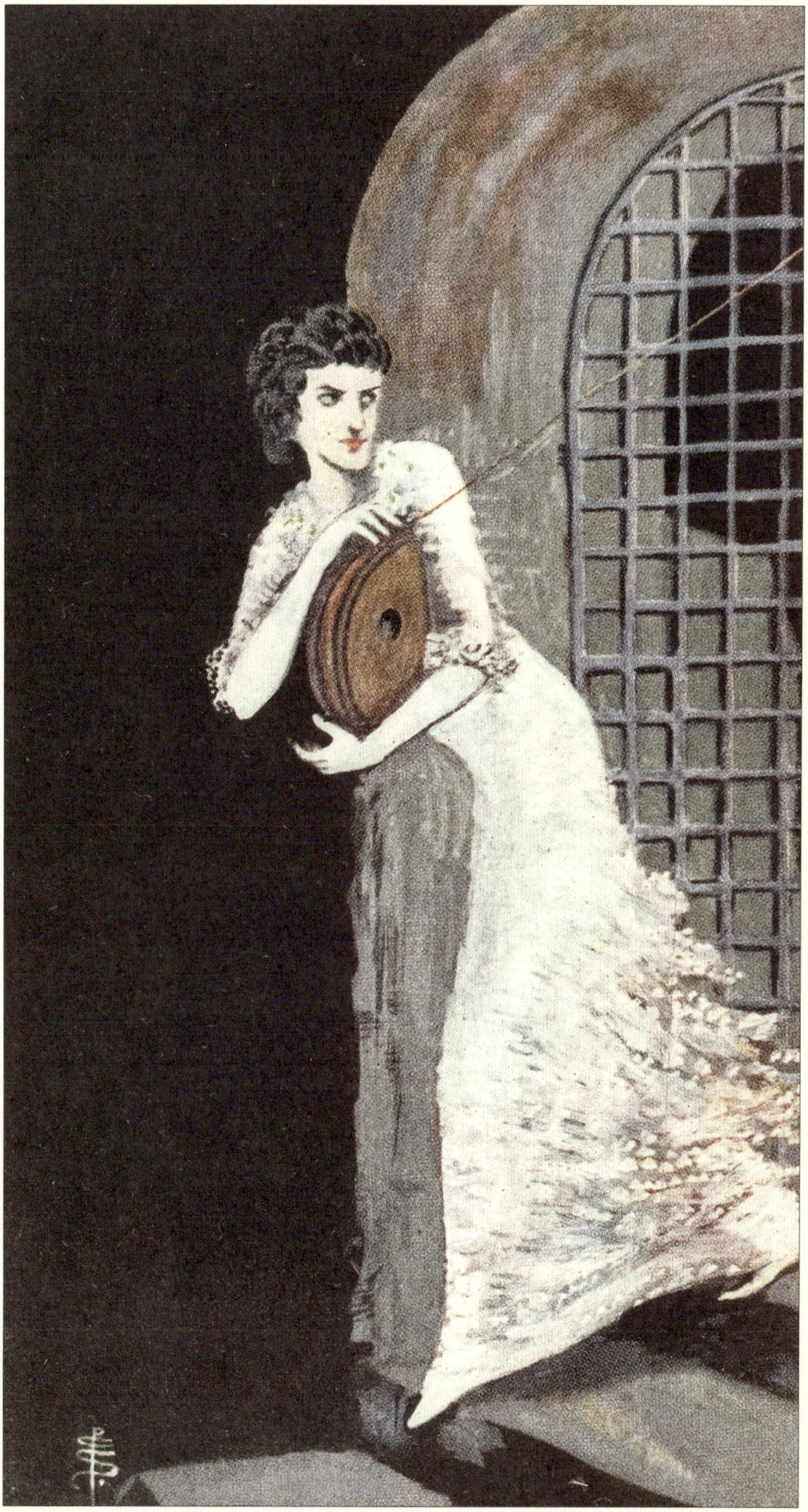

"Down the turret stair she flew quickly"

1911

"He kept his eyes fixed on Lilla"

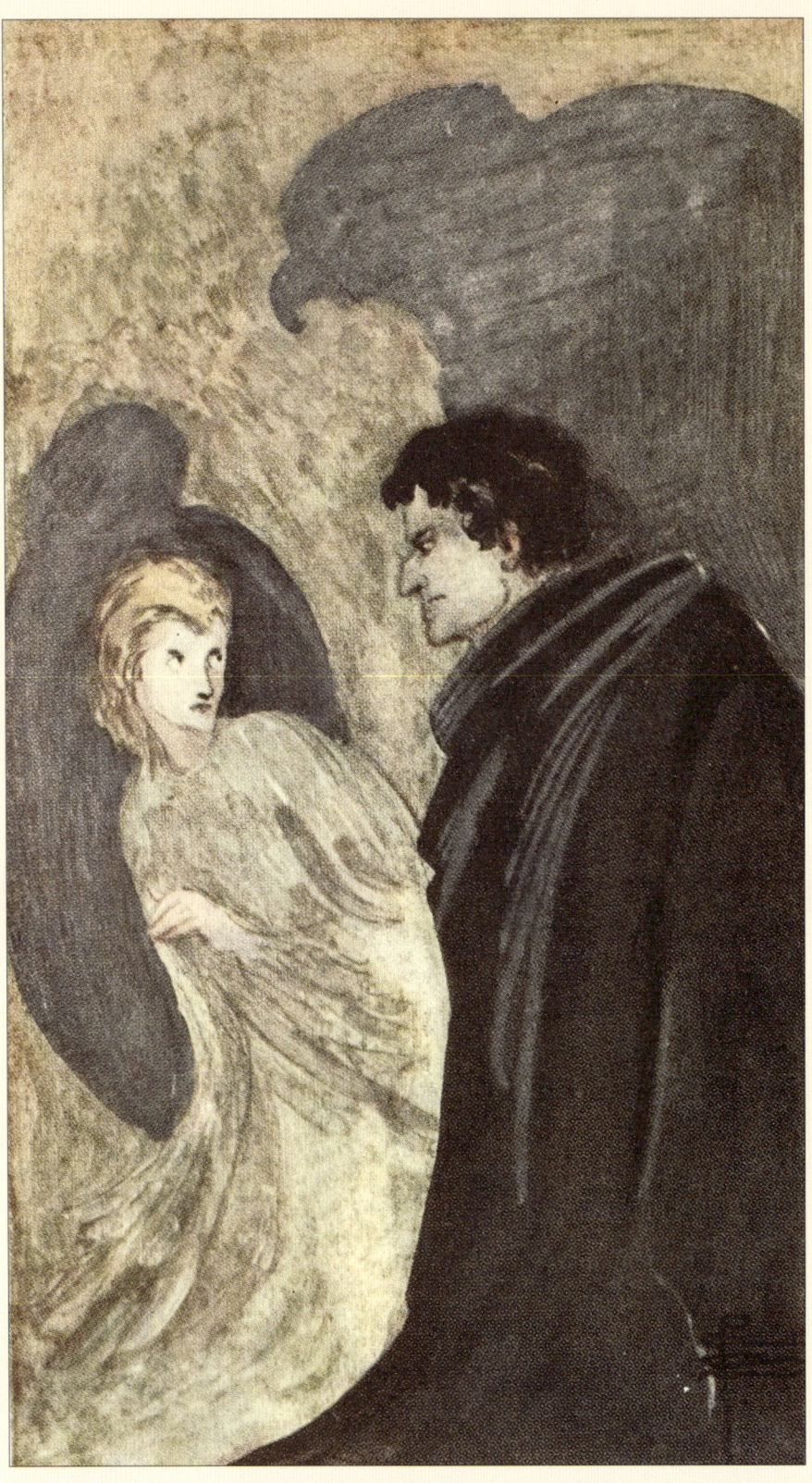

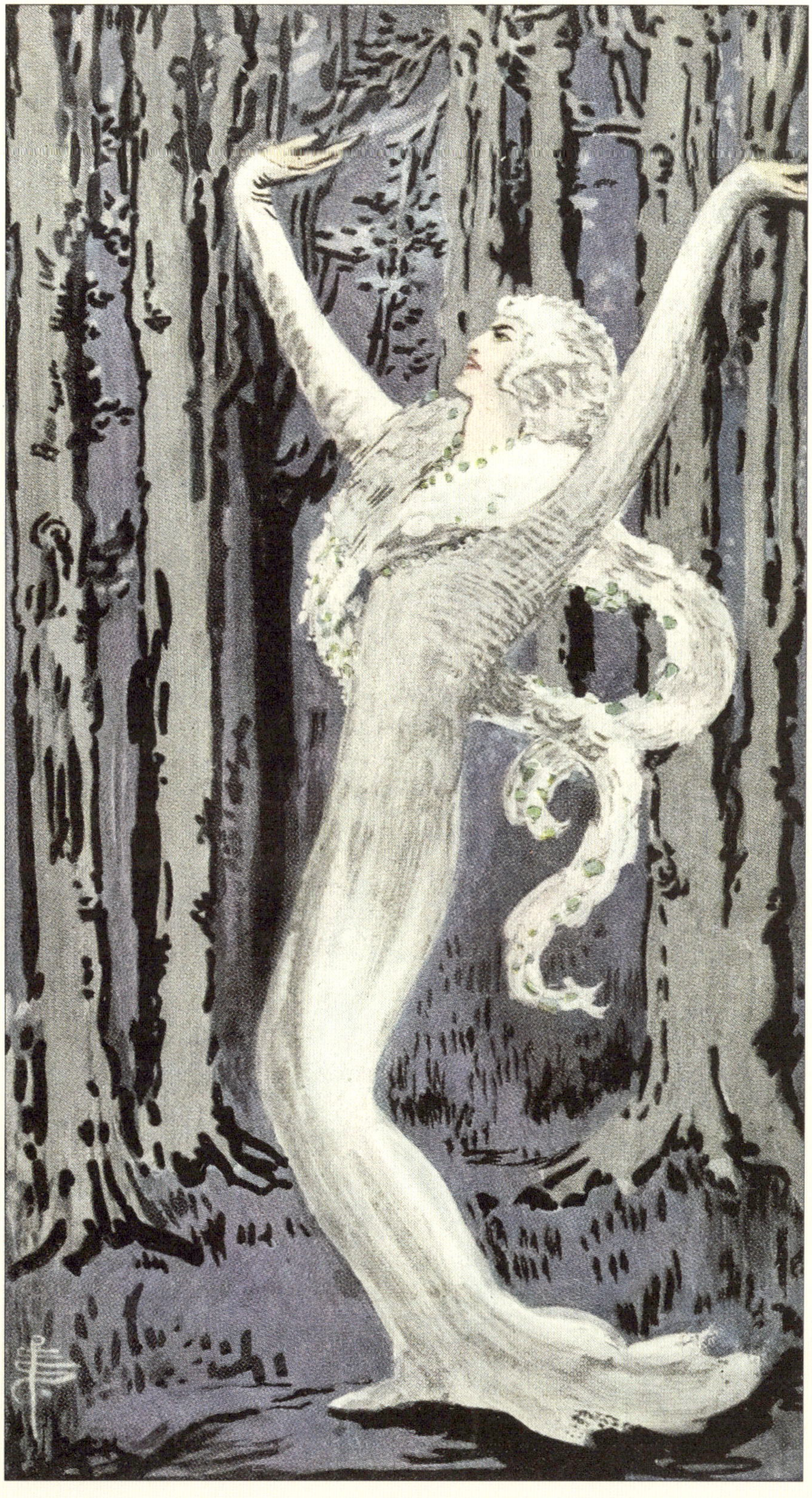

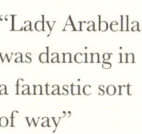

"Lady Arabella was dancing in a fantastic sort of way"

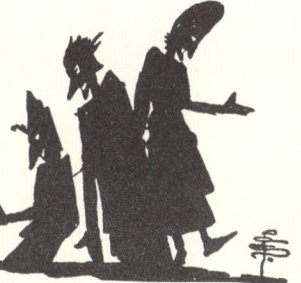

1911

"The kite was shaped like a great hawk"

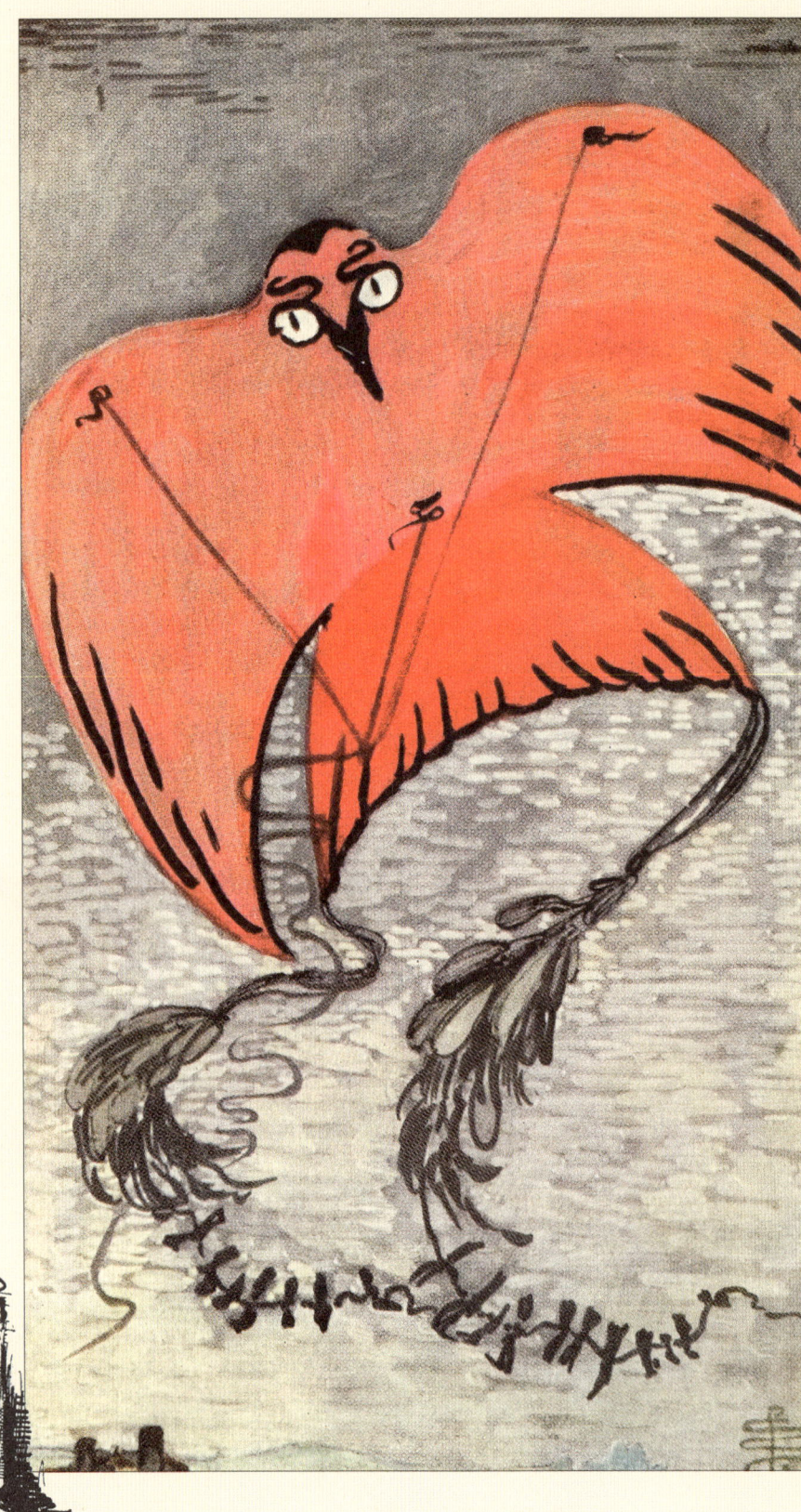

1911

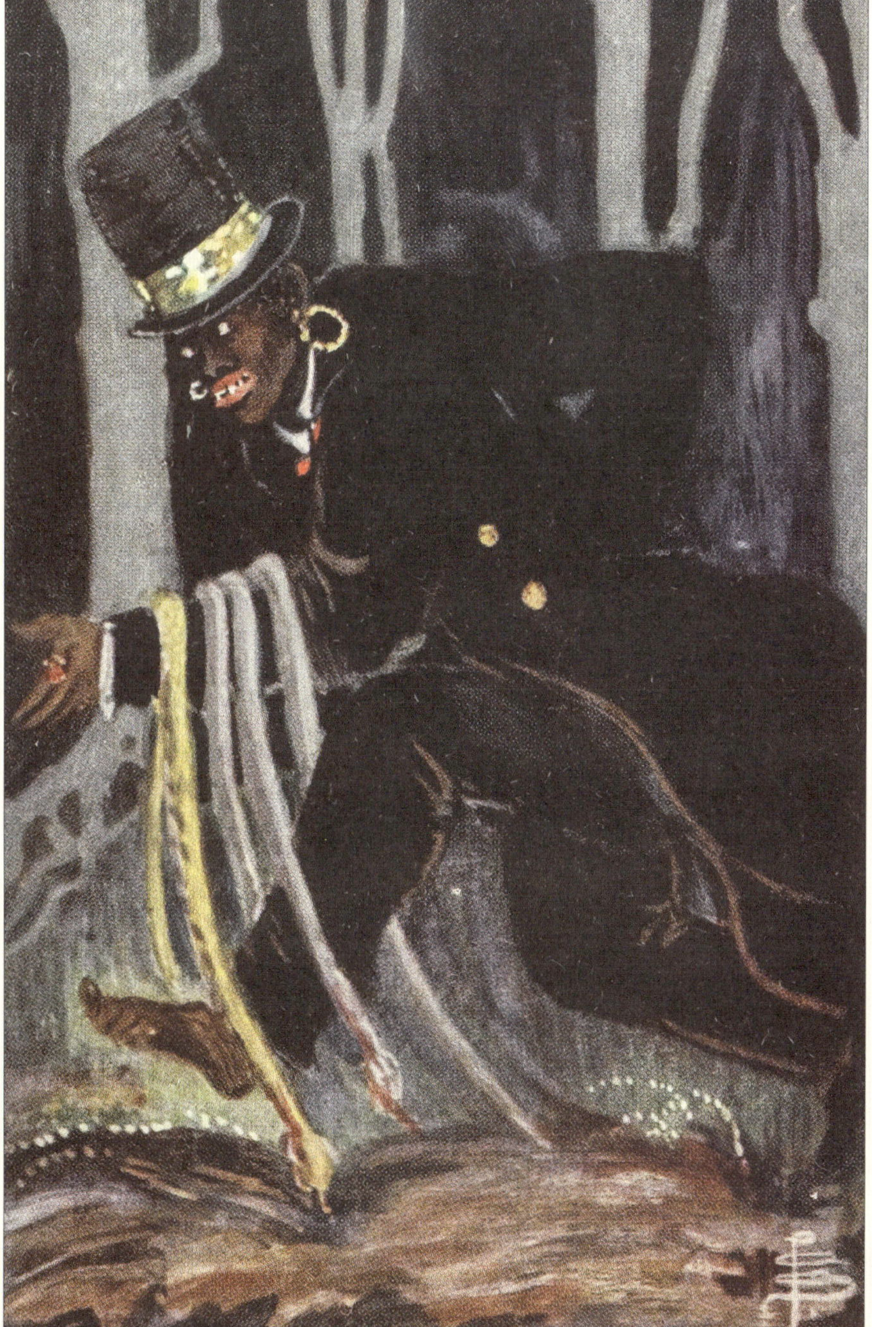

"Oolanga's black face…peering out from a clump of evergreens"

1911

"They could follow the tall white shaft"

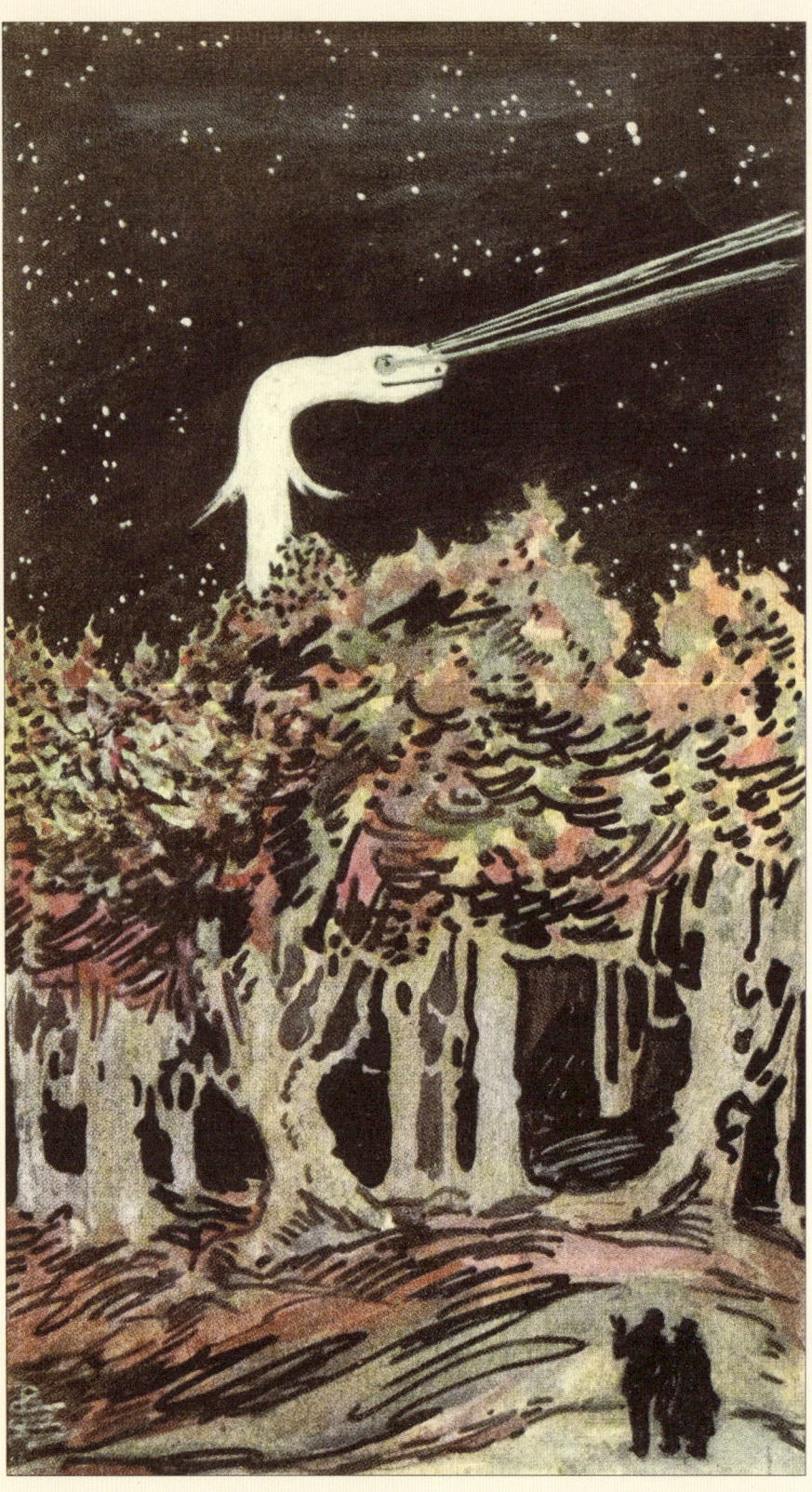

A Strange Sanctuary

1911

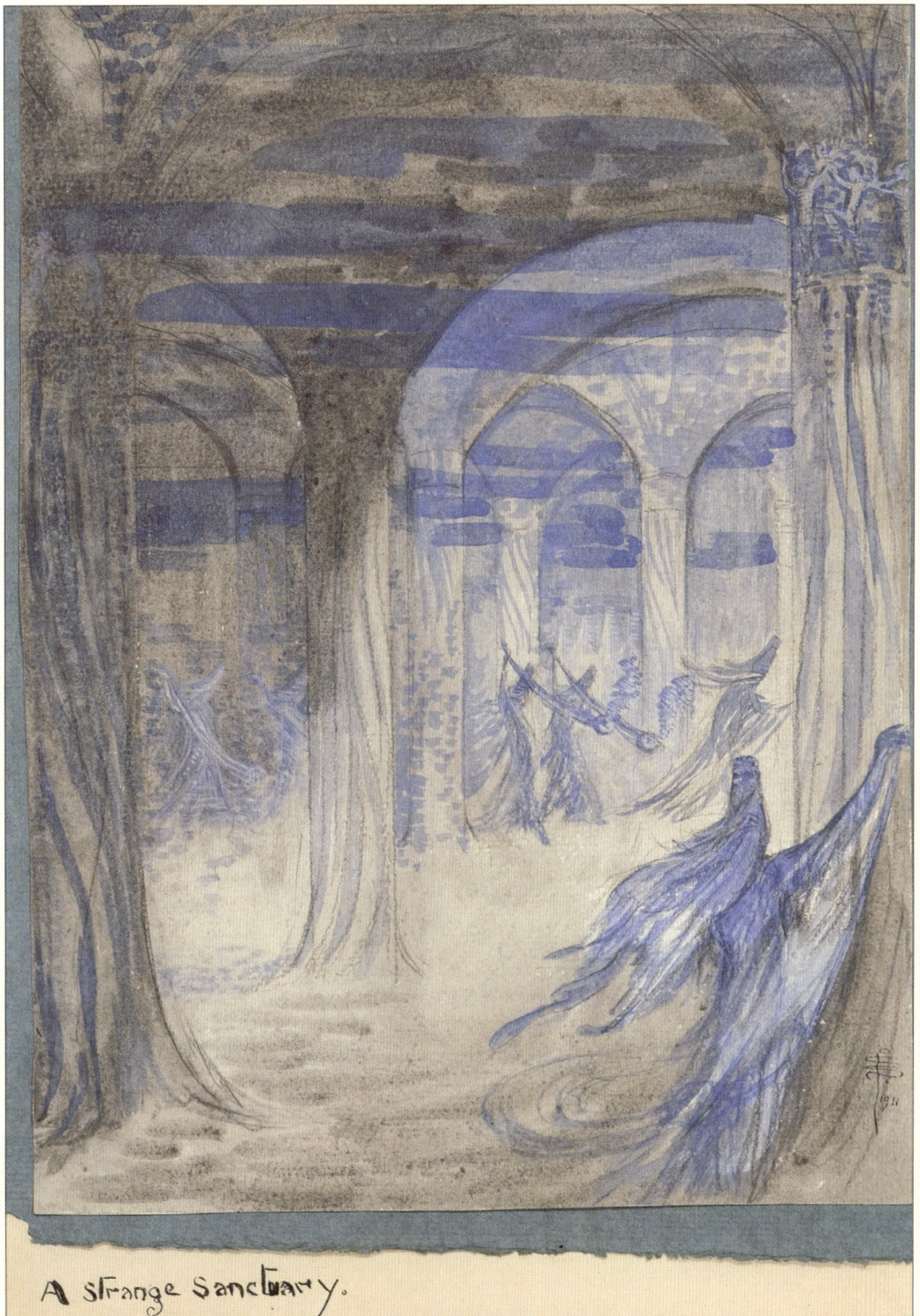

A Strange Sanctuary.

"A Strange Sanctuary" by Pamela Colman Smith. Watercolor painting of diaphanous figures as they flit in a vaulted crypt. Two figures in the center hold oversized smoking pipes or censers on chains. On the capital of a column, in the right foreground, elfin creatures frolic, while at the base of the column two large figures rise effortlessly.

Beethoven's Symphony No. 5 in C

1912

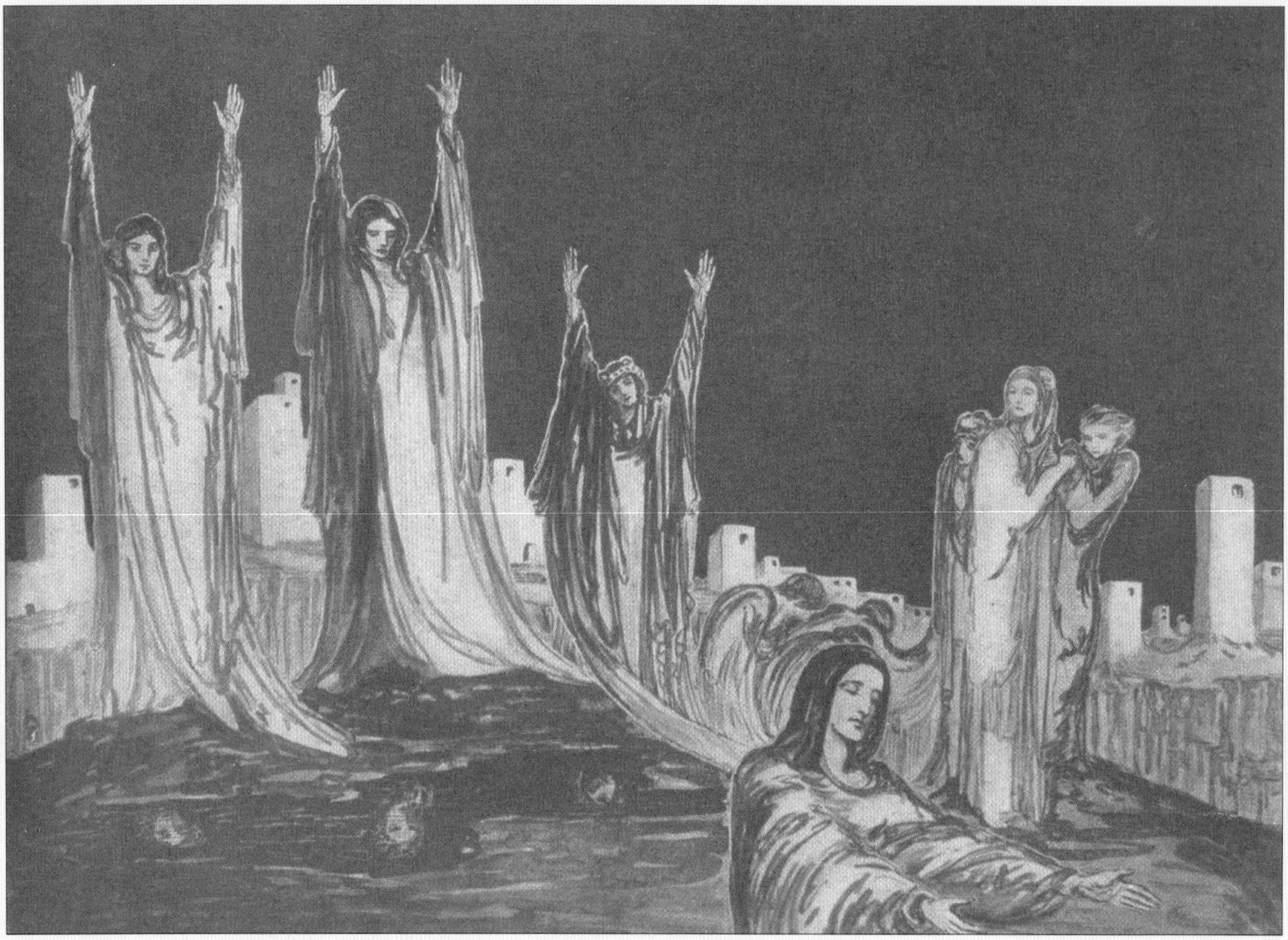

Above: From a drawing by Pamela Colman Smith. Inspired by Beethoven's Symphony No. 5 in C. From *The Craftsman*, October 1912

Right: From a drawing by Pamela Colman Smith. God save you merry gentlemen may nothing you dismay. From *The Craftsman*, October 1912

Both items courtesy of Art & Architecture Collection, Miriam and Ira D. Wallach Division of Art, Prints and Photographs. The New York Public Library, Astor, Lenox and Tilden Foundations

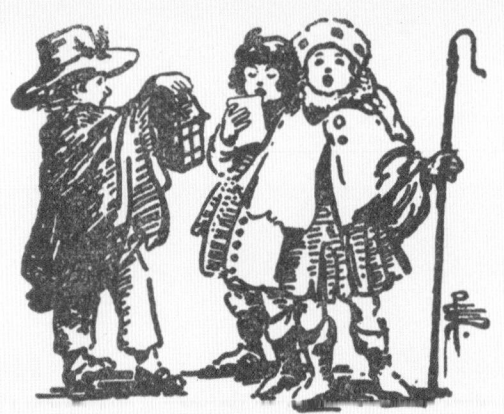

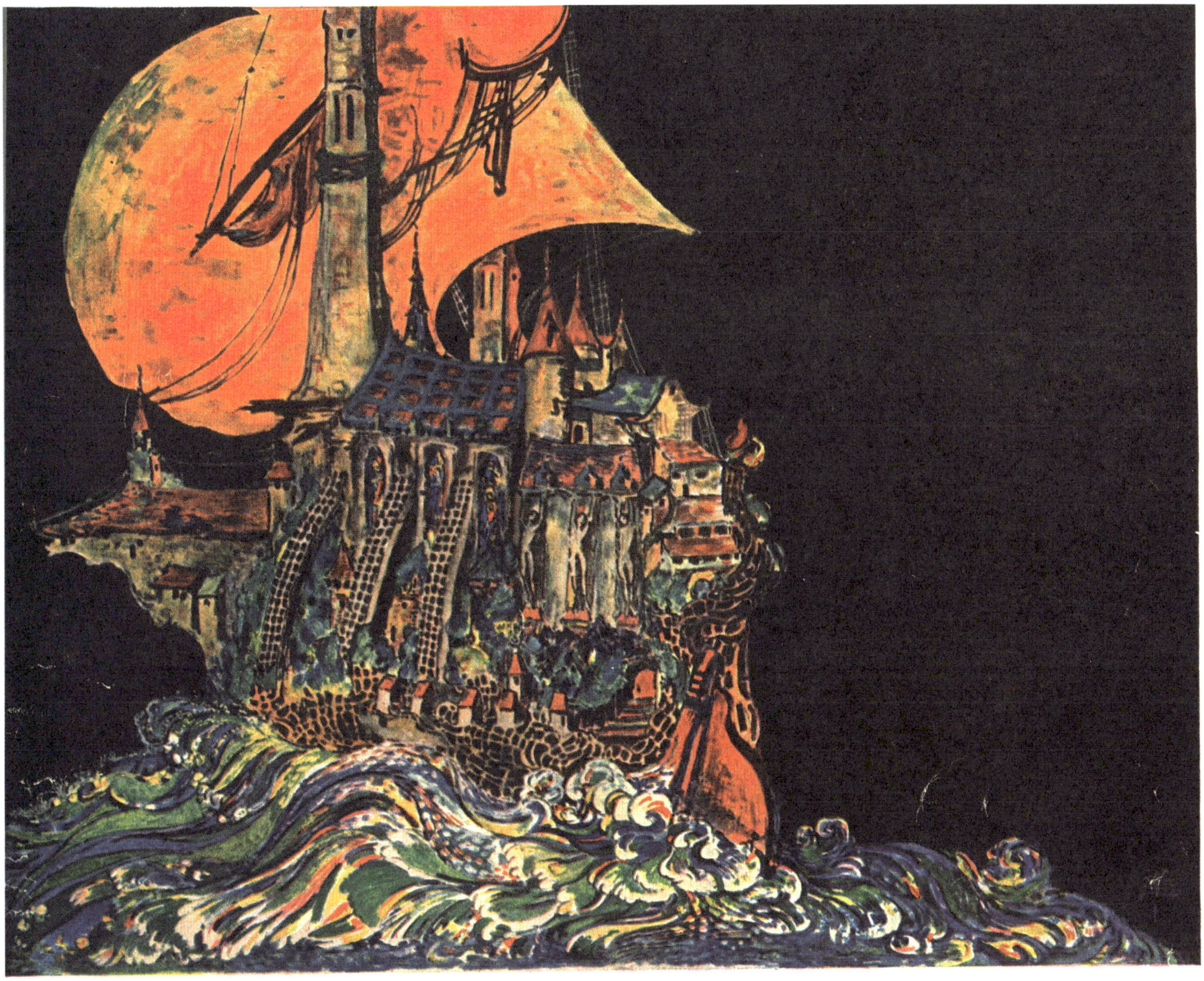

The Ship of Dreams

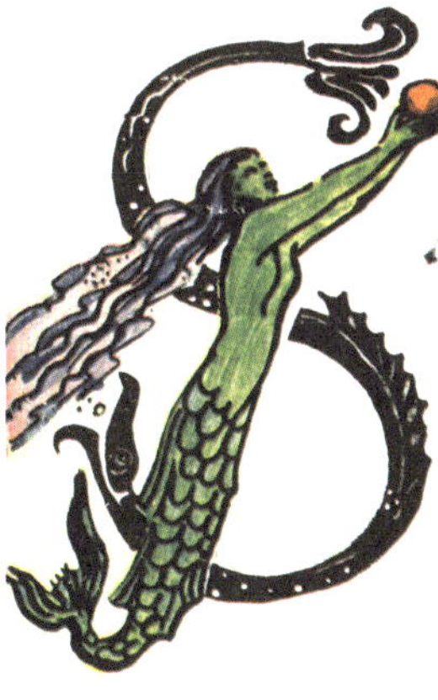

Susan and the Mermaid
Told and Pictured by Pamela Colman Smith

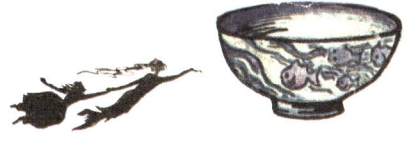

GRANDMAMA sat by the fire knitting. Outside the wind blew the yellow-beech leaves in clouds across the lawn, and the rain tapped on the window-panes. Susan sat on a hassock at Grandmama's knee.

It had rained since early morning and Susan had not been allowed out. She was tired of being indoors all day, not being able to visit her friends, the brown owl Diogenes, and the goldfish in the fountain. There was no one in the house to play with. Grandmama had read her all her favorite fairy stories.

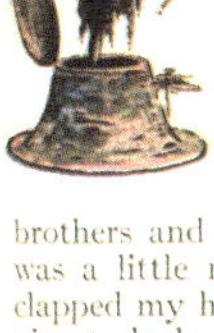

"Did you ever see a fairy?" asked Susan suddenly. "I was thinking of them this morning at lessons, and did wish one would come out of the ink-pot."

"Yes, Susan, I remember seeing one when I was small. I was walking along a country road with my brothers and my cousin Matilda, and on the top of a high wall was a little man dressed in yellow leaves. I danced about and clapped my hands, calling to the others, but when they came running to look—he was gone! And once, by the seashore, I was sitting on a rock looking down into a little pool where there were starfish and crabs and tufts of red seaweed. The sand at the bottom of the pool was golden, and from under some seaweed swam a tiny mermaid, with a tail like a fish. She was all green, with blue hair, and a string of red-coral beads round her neck. She was not longer than my finger. As she rose to the top of the water she held out her hand, and in it was a large pearl. She called out to me in a high, silvery voice: 'This is for you, O mortal, a gift from the sea!' And she gave me this pearl. It was made into a ring by a wise man with horn spectacles.

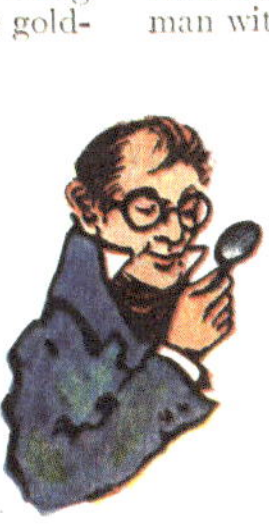

"I wonder if we can bring the little mermaid here for you to see! We must have a bowl of water. Run and ask Jenkins to give you that one with fish on it from the cupboard shelf. I had it for bread and milk when I was a little girl."

When Susan came back with the bowl, Grandmama was sitting in her great armchair, looking so wise in her tortoise-shell spectacles. Susan thought of the wise man who made the ring.

Grandmama took the bowl from Susan, and slipping the ring from her finger, she dropped it into the water. Susan leaned over the bowl, and as the ring touched the bottom the water clouded over, and turned green, and then blue, and then rose-color; little waves began to lap against the sides of the bowl, the water became clear once more, and in the place of the pearl a little mermaid was standing on the very tip of her tail, holding out her hand

PAGE 422 THE DELINEATOR FOR DECEMBER 1912

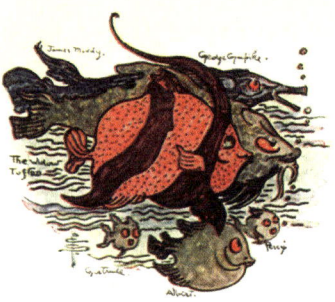

The rude fish who stared

to Susan, who took it.

There was chiming of silver bells, and the crash of waves, and sinking through the water and the bottom of the bowl Susan saw the wise face with horn spectacles growing dimmer and dimmer, and found herself swimming hand in hand with the green mermaid who had blue hair and a string of red beads round her neck.

"Has she grown large, or have I grown small?" thought Susan to herself, for she and the mermaid were both the same size.

They swam along a great avenue of coral-trees.

"Much easier than walking on land," said Susan.

"I thought you would find it so," replied the mermaid

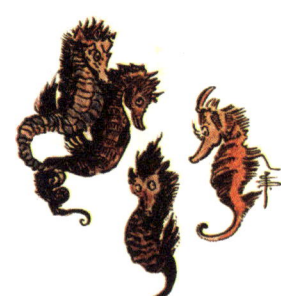

So on they swam through the forests, and over fields of sand, and by pastures full of colts and sea-horses, over long bare tracts of rock, and came to a mountain covered with red seaweed bushes. Very like the hill behind Grandmama's house, Susan thought.

They swam up the side of the mountain and could see far-stretching valleys and hills and flat fields, and at last they came out of the water, and on the beach of a little island.

They sat there awhile, and the mermaid said:

"This is a reef, Susan—you have no doubt read in your geography book how they are formed. It is the best place in the world to see a royal procession. It is never overcrowded, as the fish find the air too strong for them, so we mer-people have it to ourselves, but most of us are busy and have little time for sightseeing."

("I wonder what they are busy about," thought Susan.)

Just then they heard shouts of laughter and splashing, and three nice mer-children with their Governess and a pugfish emerged from the water. The pugfish saw Susan and began to bark angrily. The Governess cried: "Oh, Toby, you must not bark at the little girl!"

But Toby only barked more and more.

"If you are not quiet," she went on, "I shall put you on the lead—you ought to know better!"

So Toby subsided.

The mer-children were very smartly dressed: they had hats made of shells, and reefer jackets, and their fins neatly combed and brushed. They carried bunches of wild flowers from the coral fields.

From over the water came the sound of clanging bells.

"She is coming!" shouted the children.

They saw little tides rise in rows of waves, and between them came a pompous-looking officer on a dolphin followed by a troop of fishguards, with long plumes of spray in their mother-of-pearl helmets.

The Queen of the Tides

"My father the Colonel," whispered the mermaid as they passed.

Coming along the way lined with tides was a tall figure in a long spreading cloak, fringed with drops of crystal and pearls, and trimmed with foam. In her right hand she carried a jeweled scepter, and in her left a full moon, and on her head was a silver crown.

"Her Majesty, the Queen of Tides," whispered the mermaid as they all courtesied low.

When Susan raised her head again, the tides bowed and fell into the water head first, and a cloud of mist was speed-

politely. Fat fish with glowing eyes swam in and out between the tree-trunks.

"I fear you find the behavior of these common fish rather disconcerting. Please remember they have not the least education, and can not possibly know how rude it is to stare at strangers!"

So saying the mermaid drew Susan aside onto a coral branch. Down the waterway came a company of spearfish with a captain looking very smart, with waxed mustache and an eye-glass, his Highland bonnet much over his left ear.

"Going to meet her majesty," said the mermaid. "She has been on a visit to her sister, the Empress of the Underseas, and is returning with a large treasure from the tribes of the hidden valleys, deep down in the black water. Let us hurry to the reef—we may see her pass by there, the tides bowing before her, ringing their bells."

So they started swimming along the waterway. And the mermaid continued:

"The Queen sometimes rides in a polished shell coach, drawn by forty swift-swimming fish. She arranges all the storms and the fine weather. Storms are kept in strong boxes made of shell, and are carried with great care, and let loose at the top of the water. Fine weather is kept in bags of seaweed woven closely, and opened only when the order is given. Sun-rays caught in golden nets and wrapped in mist to keep them bright are put in the bags with the fine weather."

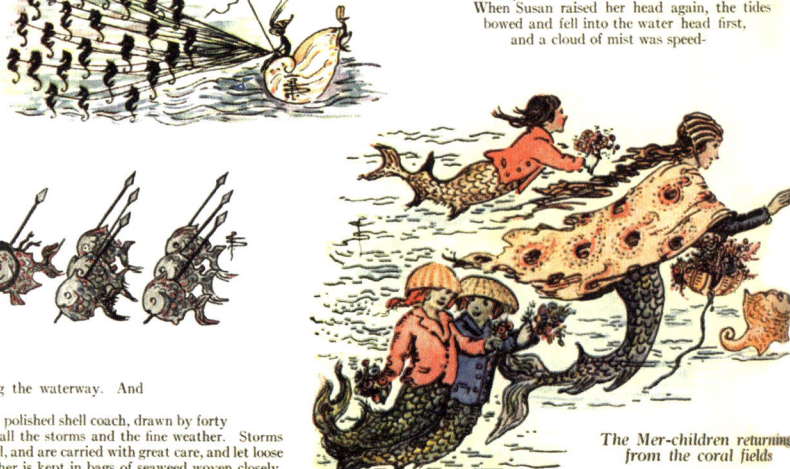

The Mer-children returning from the coral fields

ing gently away over the sea.

"That was very nice," said Susan. "I should like to know where she lives."

"Her Majesty lives where a good monarch always should, in the midst of her people—the city of coral," said the mermaid in a reproving voice.

"We will go there now, if you think you can swim so far."

"I am not in the least tired, thank you," said Susan.

So bidding the mer-children and their Governess good-by, and patting the pugfish, who by this time was quite friendly, they slipped into the water on the other side of the island.

Down the hillside blue with anemones they swam. They passed an orchard of sea-apples and saw a poet sitting reading under a tree, and a garden where a mer-lady was picking gooseberries; until in the distance they saw the gleaming towers of the city, its domes and palaces and its waving turrets, twisted like tulip stems, full of windows with boxes of flowers and hanging gardens.

The Mer-lady taking the little girl to a party

"No stairs, you know," remarked the mermaid. "You just swim in and out as you like. It saves a deal of trouble."

Susan thought it would be lovely if it would only rain very hard for days and days, and weeks and weeks, and months and months, and years and years! It might fill up all the country with water except the hill-tops, and then it would be so delightful to go to church on Sunday in the family shell coach, drawn by fat fish—only if it rained as hard as that, all the dates would be washed off the almanac and no one would know when it was Sunday.

In a garden near the royal palace they saw a mer-lady drying her hair, and three girls with a puss-fish. They saw the bank of ocean guarded by spearfish, and met a mer-lady taking a little mer-girl to a party, and a Duchess driving her own twenty-four-in-hand with a footman perched on the back of her dog-shell.

They swam aside to let a parcels-post shell go by, with a large, high-swimming, black sea-horse.

They went all over the city, and saw great galleries of pictures, and the national theater, and a large concert-hall with notes painted outside, that played themselves when you looked at them.

Suddenly it grew dark, and the mermaid hastily dragged Susan under an overhanging roof.

"That is a large giant fish going by. We must keep very still, so he will not hear us; they are stupid and dull-sighted, but they do eat us when they can."

He passed overhead without seeing them.

By this time it was really dark, and the starfish were being lighted by lamplighters.

"I shall have to

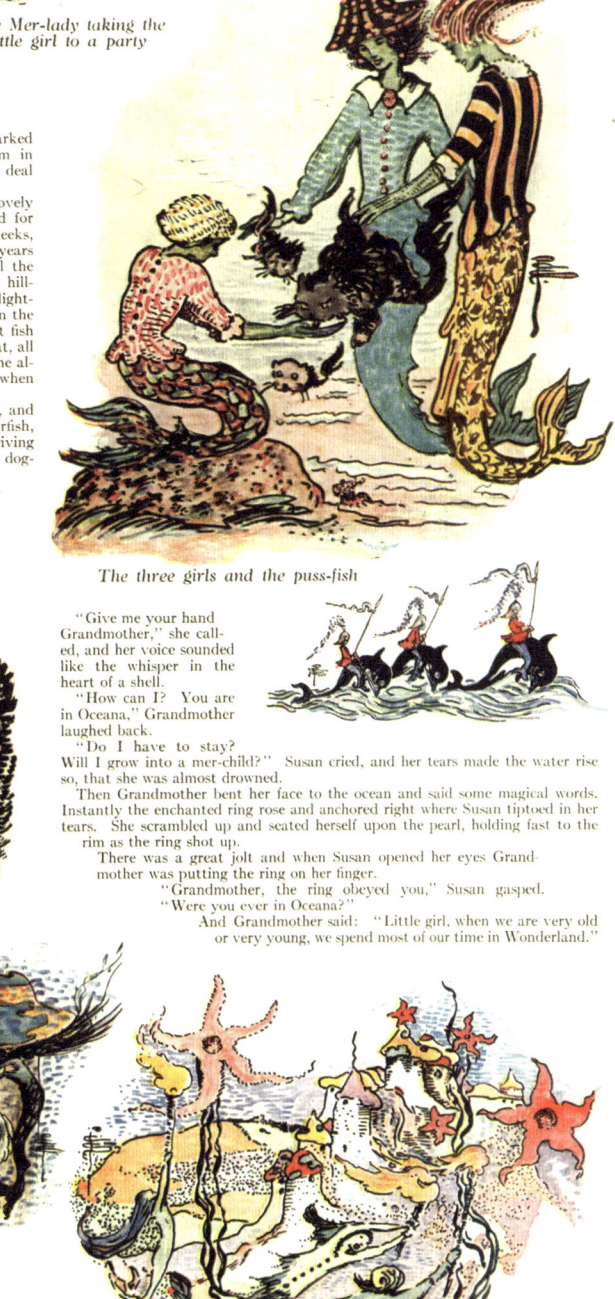

The three girls and the puss-fish

"Give me your hand Grandmother," she called, and her voice sounded like the whisper in the heart of a shell.

"How can I? You are in Oceana," Grandmother laughed back.

"Do I have to stay? Will I grow into a mer-child?" Susan cried, and her tears made the water rise so, that she was almost drowned.

Then Grandmother bent her face to the ocean and said some magical words. Instantly the enchanted ring rose and anchored right where Susan tiptoed in her tears. She scrambled up and seated herself upon the pearl, holding fast to the rim as the ring shot up.

There was a great jolt and when Susan opened her eyes Grandmother was putting the ring on her finger.

"Grandmother, the ring obeyed you," Susan gasped.

"Were you ever in Oceana?"

And Grandmother said: "Little girl, when we are very old or very young, we spend most of our time in Wonderland."

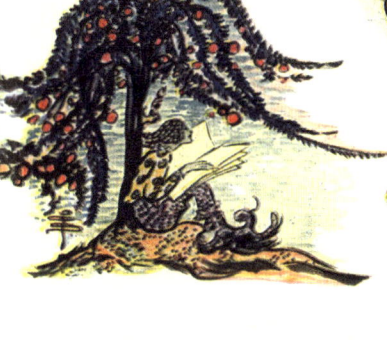

Lighting the starfish

leave you now," said the mermaid. "Father will be wanting his dinner, and I am the only one at home; he so hates coming back to an empty house. Good-by; come again one day. So pleased to meet you, little Susan." And she turned on her tail and disappeared through a gaping door.

"How does she think I am to get home?" thought Susan. Just in front of her she saw two lights with black rims, that reminded her of Grandmama's tortoise-shell spectacles.

"I wonder where Grandmama is," she said as she rubbed her eyes.

"Here I am," said Grandmama, smiling wisely at Susan through her tortoise-shell spectacles.

But she seemed a great way off as if miles of blue sea separated them. Susan began to feel very queer.

"Ship O Dreams"

1912

Partially colored drawing by Pamela Colman Smith

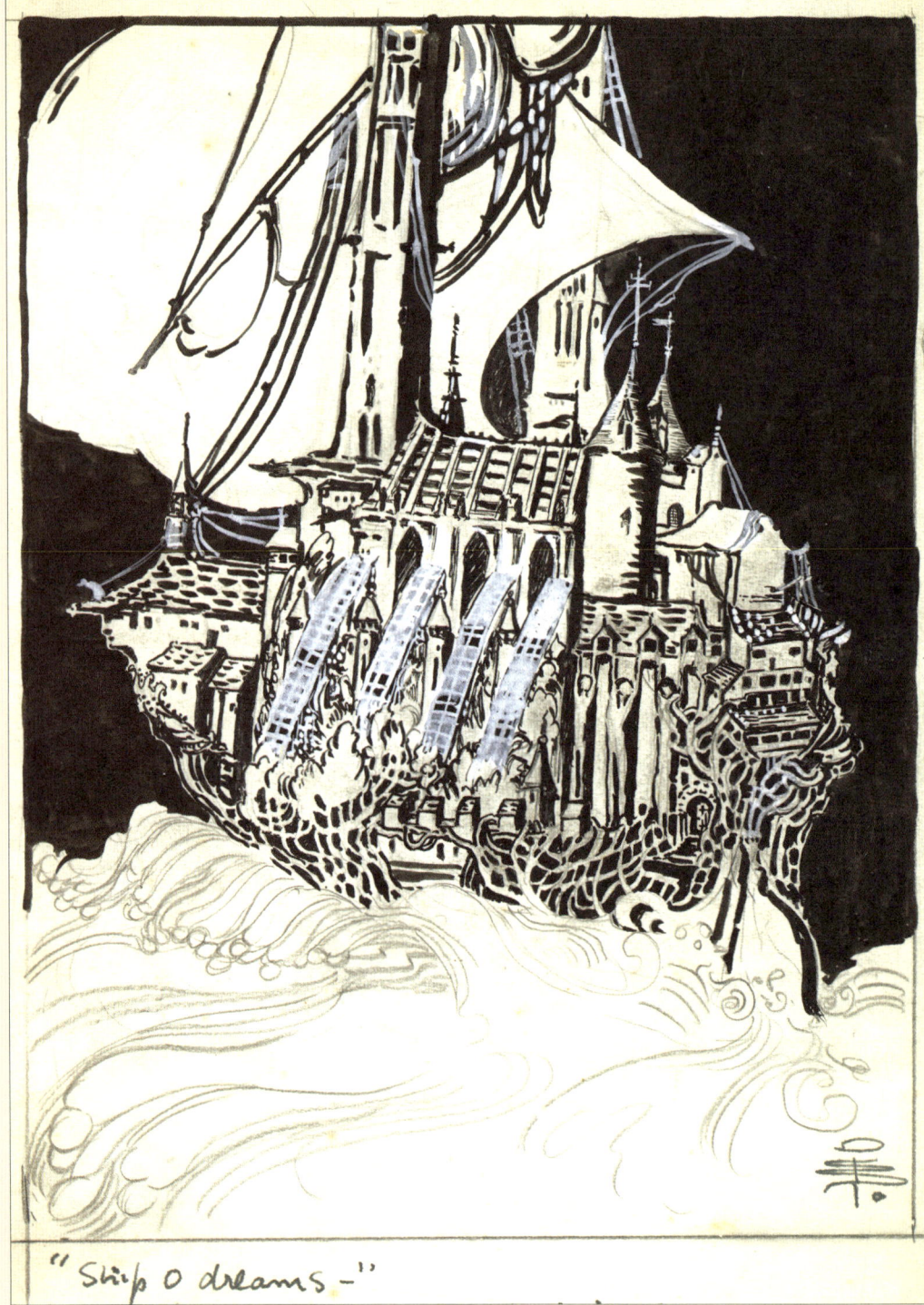

"Ship O dreams—"

Blue Beard

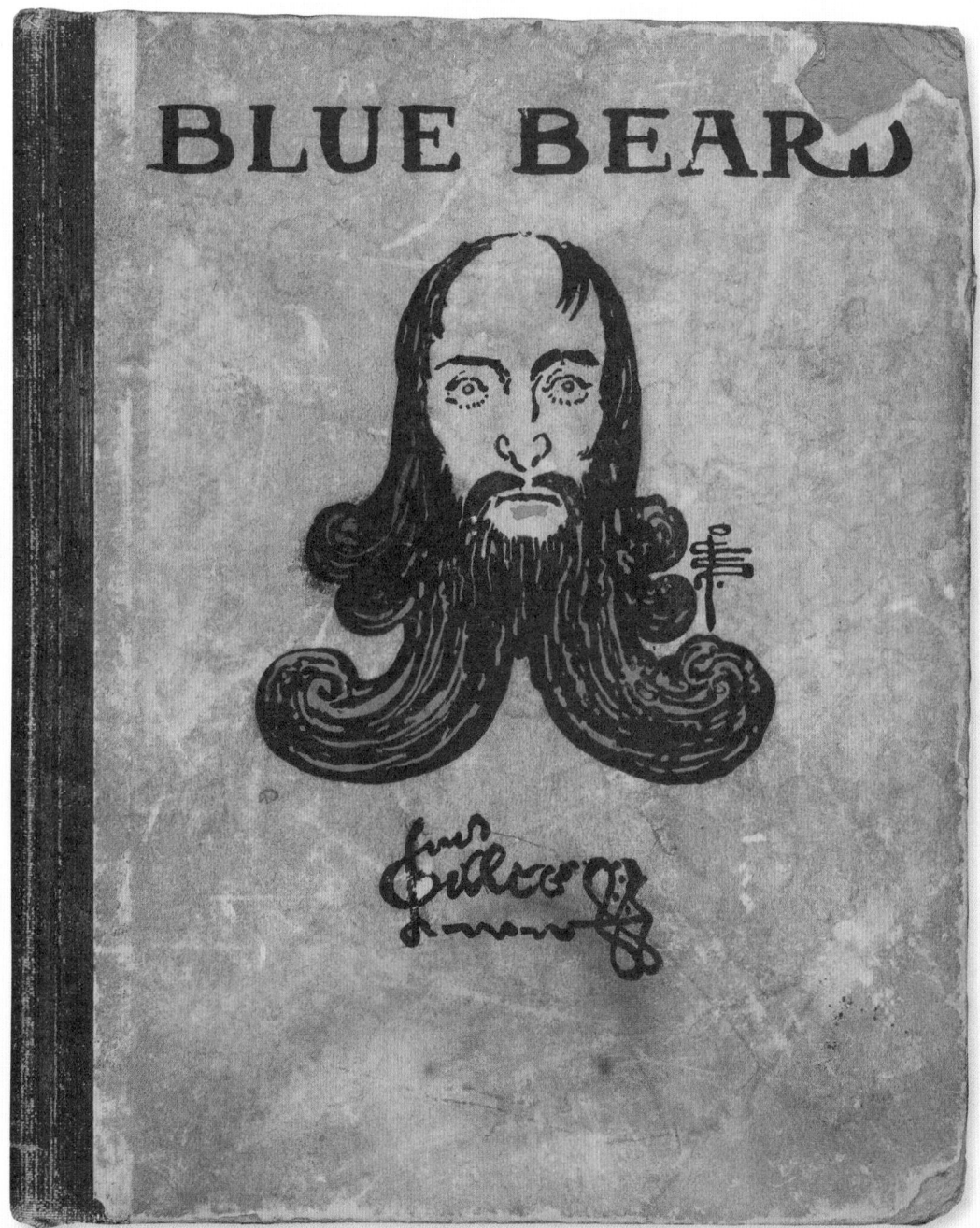

1913

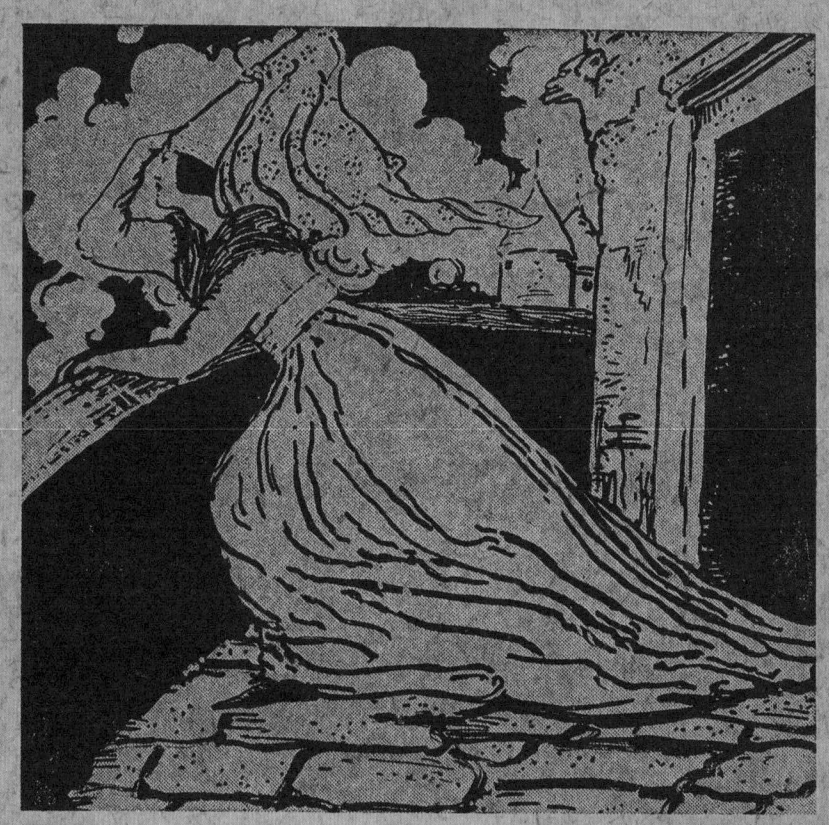

"'Anne, Sister Anne, do you see any one coming?'"

Blue Beard

Pictures by
Pamela Colman Smith

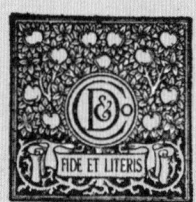

New York
Duffield & Company
1913

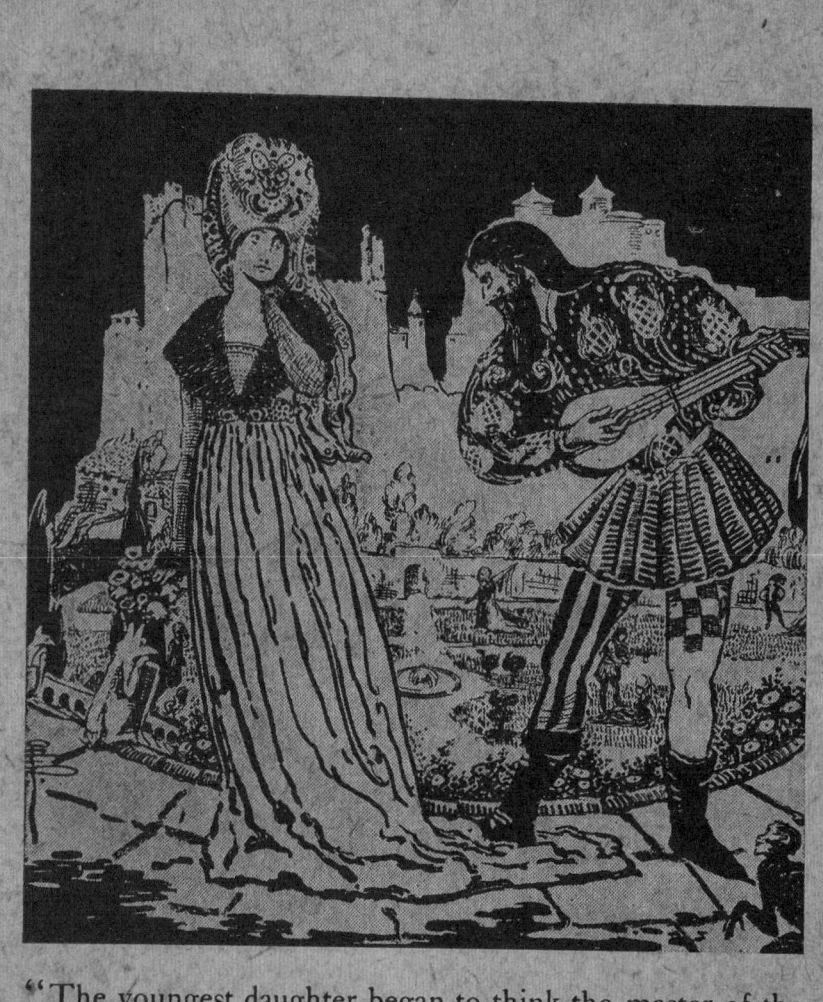

"The youngest daughter began to think the master of the house a very civil gentleman."

BLUE BEARD

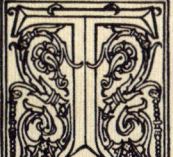HERE was a man who had fine houses, both in town and country, a deal of silver and gold plate, embroidered furniture, and coaches gilded all over with gold. But this man was so unlucky as to have a blue beard, which made him so frightfully ugly that all the women and girls ran away from him.

One of his neighbours, a lady of quality, had two daughters who were perfect beauties. He desired of her one of them in marriage, leaving to her choice which of the two she would bestow on him. They would neither of them have him, and sent him backward and forward from one another, not being able to bear the thoughts of marrying a man who had a blue beard, and what besides gave them disgust and aversion was his having already been married to several wives, and nobody ever knew what became of them.

1913

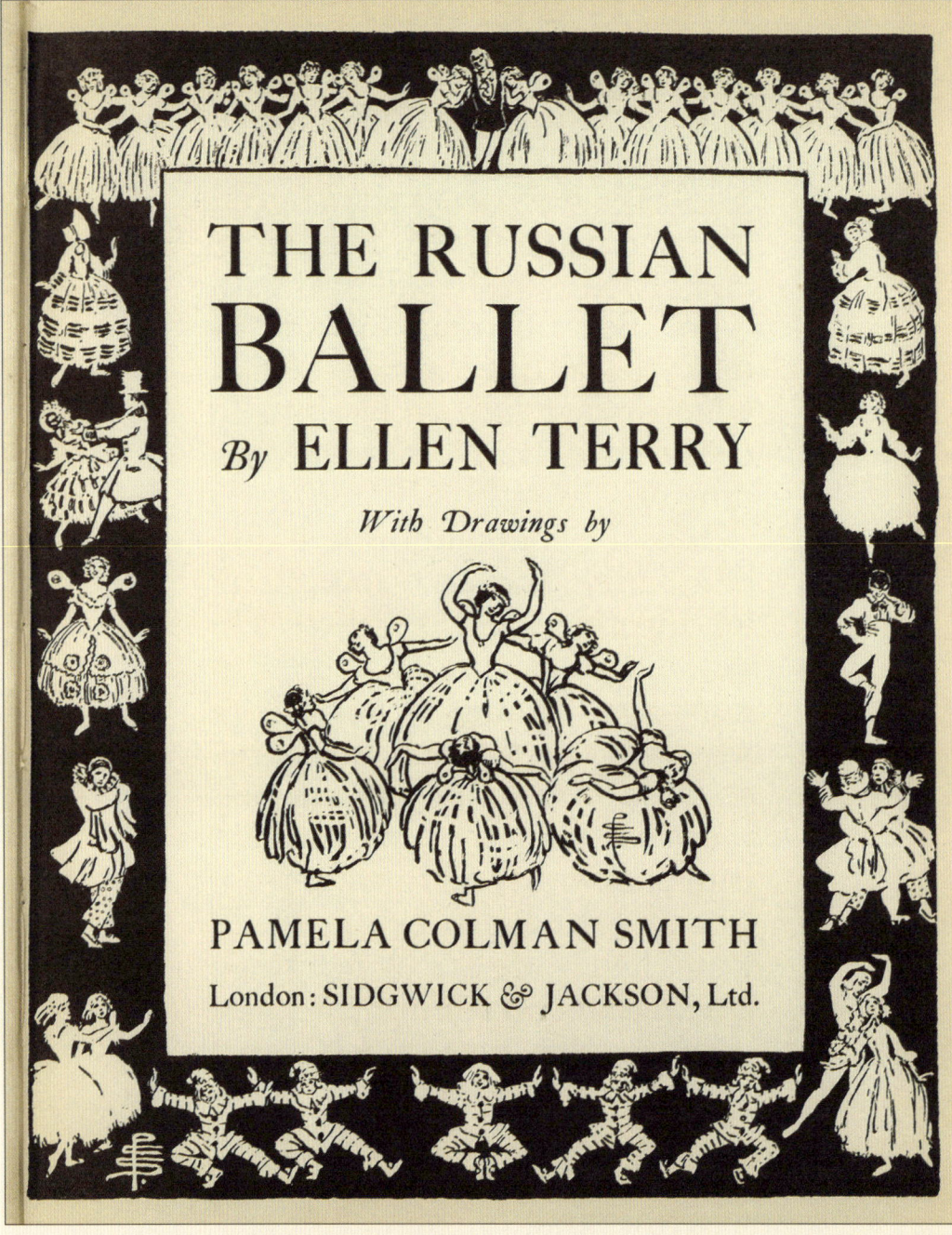

LIST of ILLUSTRATIONS

1913

TITLE-PAGE: Border and Design	Page v
SCHEHERAZADE	3
HEADPIECE: "Les Sylphides"	5
SPECTRE DE LA ROSE	7
PAVILLON D'ARMIDE	11
TAILPIECE: "Le Carnaval"	12
TAILPIECE: "Spectre de la Rose"	17
LE CARNAVAL	19
LE CARNAVAL	21
LE CARNAVAL	23
LES SYLPHIDES	25
LES SYLPHIDES	27
LES SYLPHIDES	29
LE CARNAVAL	31
LE CARNAVAL	33
TAILPIECE: "Le Carnaval"	34
LE CARNAVAL	35
SPECTRE DE LA ROSE	37
SPECTRE DE LA ROSE	39
SCHEHERAZADE	41
SCHEHERAZADE	43

vii

LIST of ILLUSTRATIONS (continued)

TAILPIECE: "Scheherazade"	Page 44
SCHEHERAZADE	45
TAMAR	47
PRINCE IGOR	49
LES BOUFFONS ("Pavillon d'Armide")	51
NARCISSE	53

1913

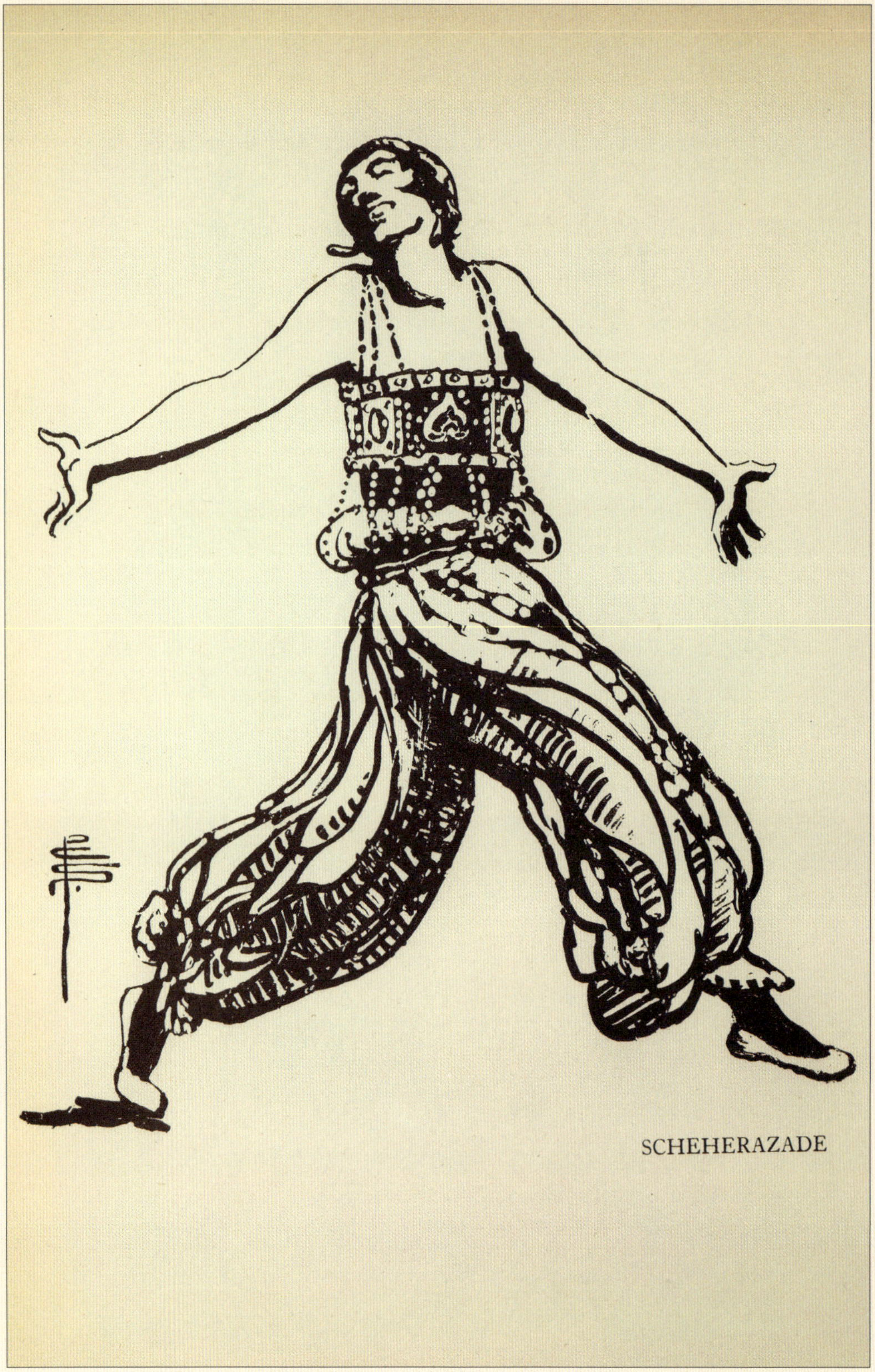

SCHEHERAZADE

1913

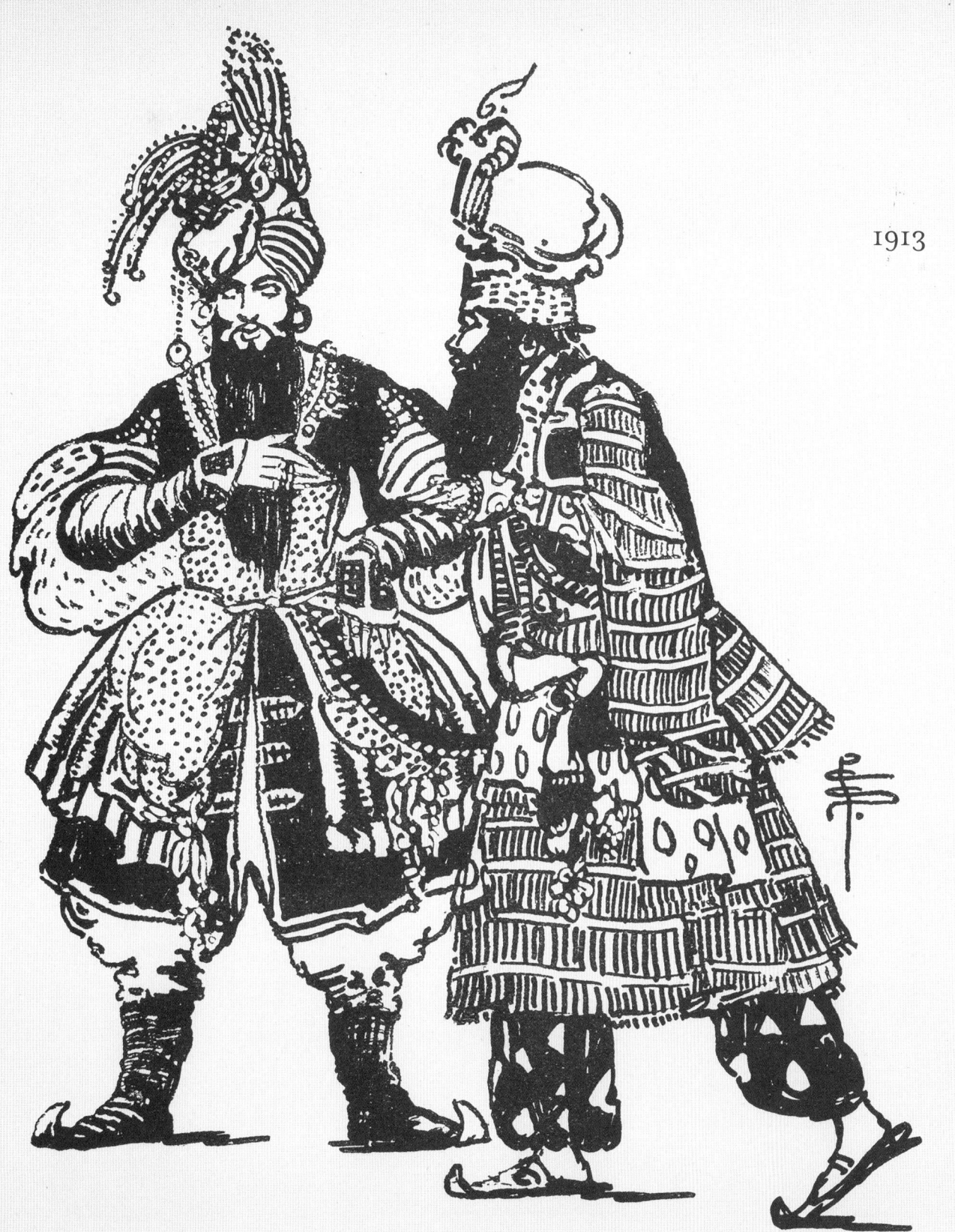

SCHEHERAZADE

1913

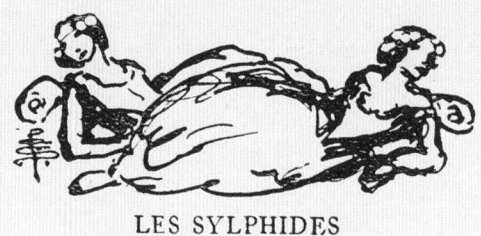
LES SYLPHIDES

Dancing in General

WHAT is dancing? The Russians have done much to show us that it is something more than *sauterie*, although they can *sauter* with the best. As an actress I salute dancers with the reverence of a man for his ancestors. The dancer is certainly the parent of my own art, but he has other children. All arts, of which the special attribute is movement, descend from the dancer. The Greek word "chorus" means dance, and the Greek choruses were originally dances. It can be proved that dancing movements formed the first metres of true poetry. Why do we speak of "feet" if not because the feet of the body used to mark the rhythm of inspired utterance?

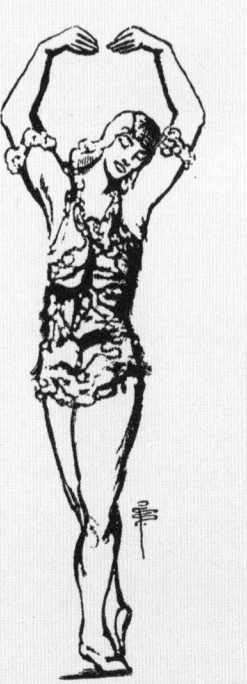
SPECTRE DE LA ROSE

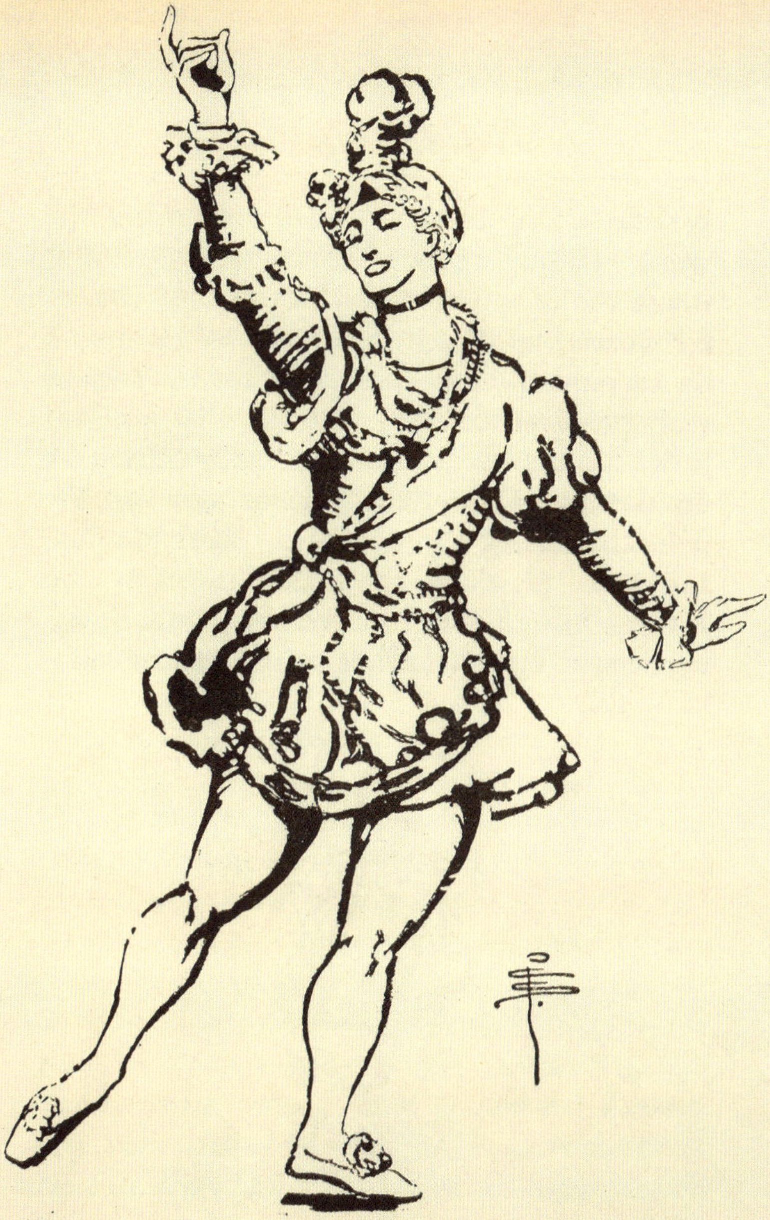

1913

PAVILLON D'ARMIDE

1913

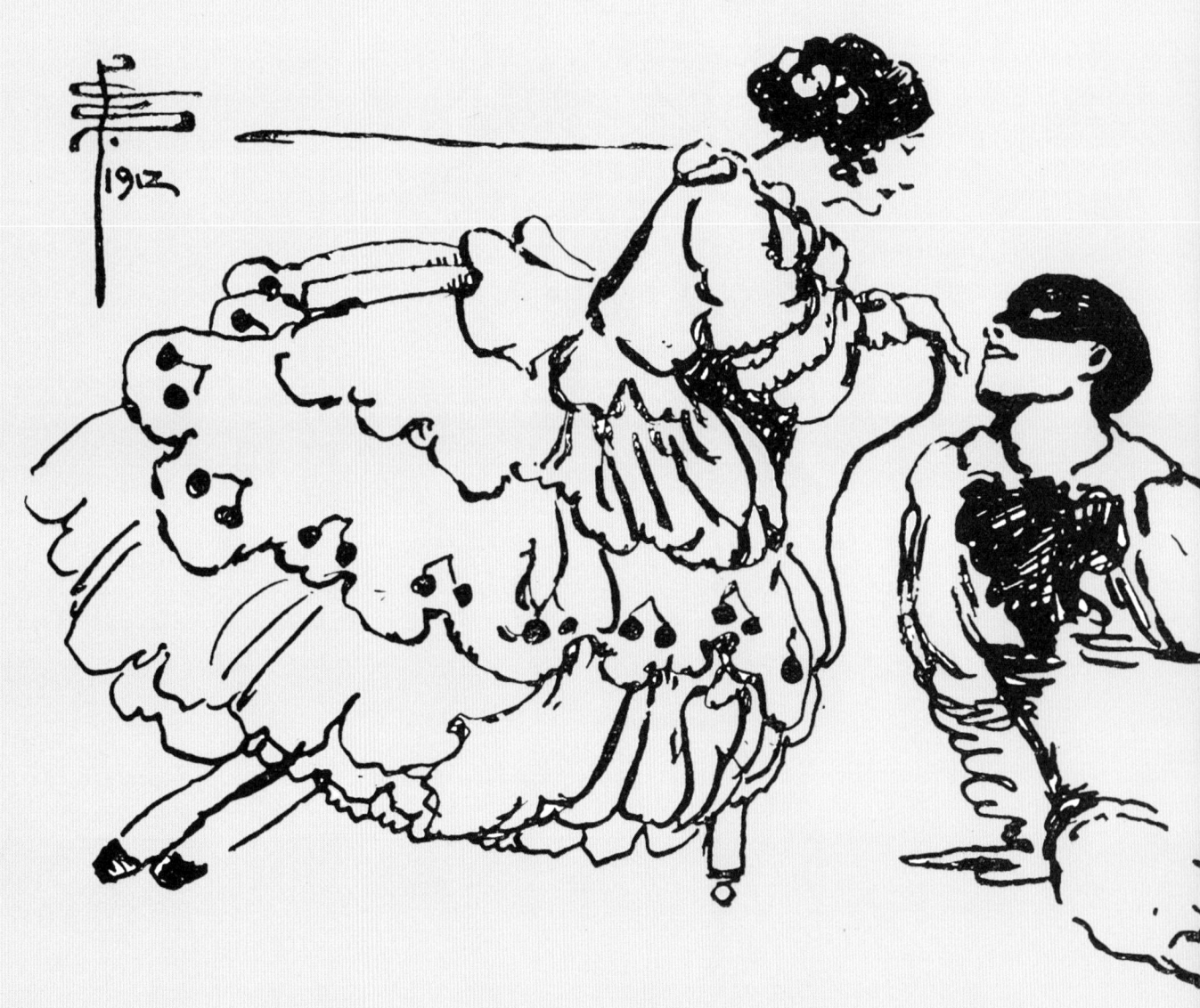

1913

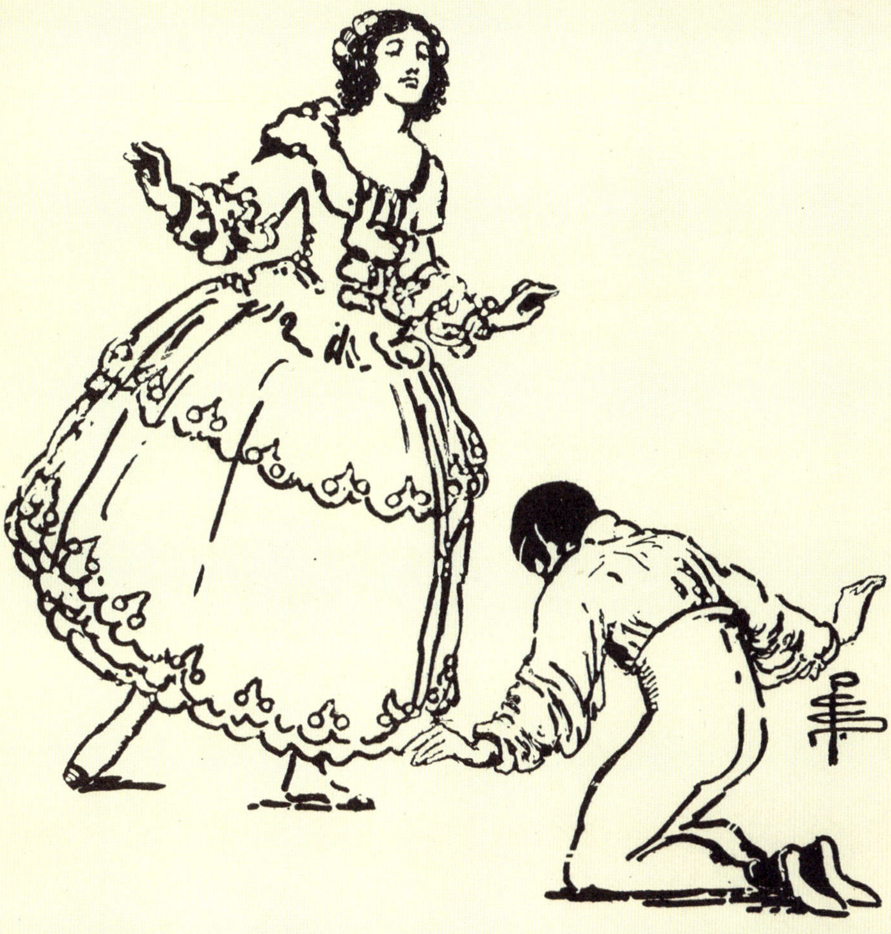

LE CARNAVAL

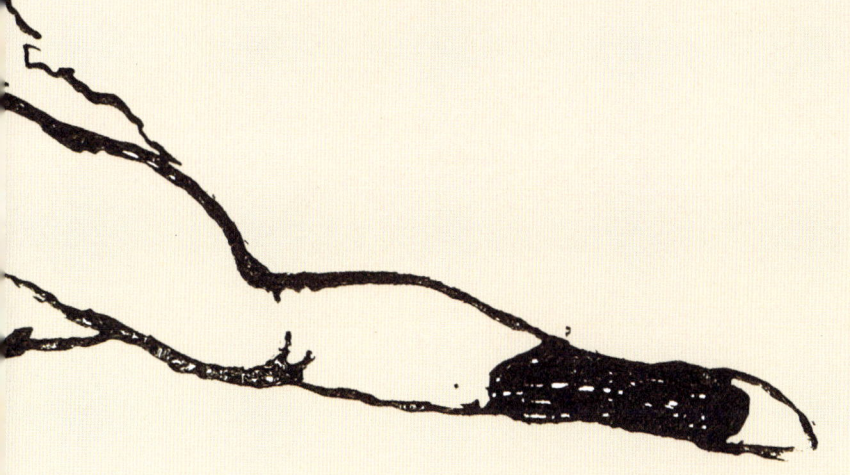

1913

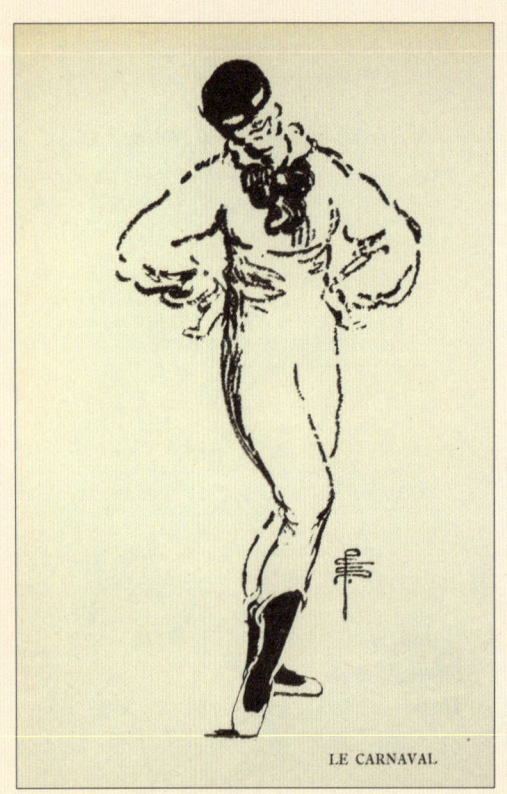
LE CARNAVAL

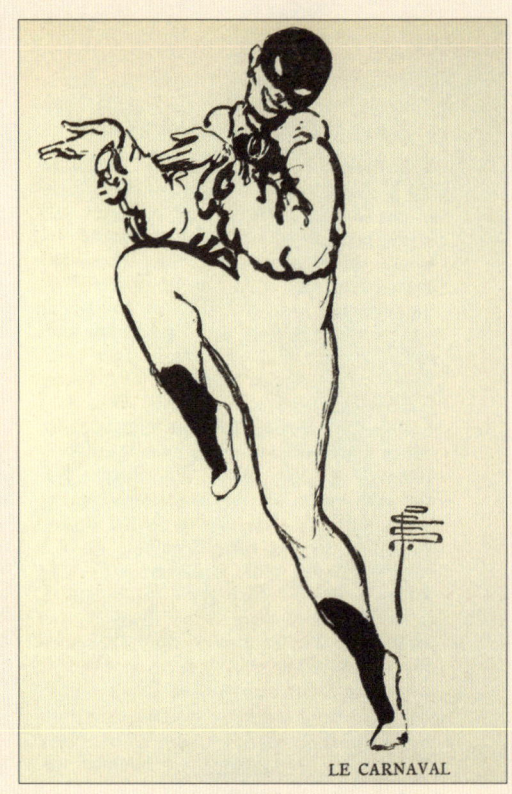
LE CARNAVAL

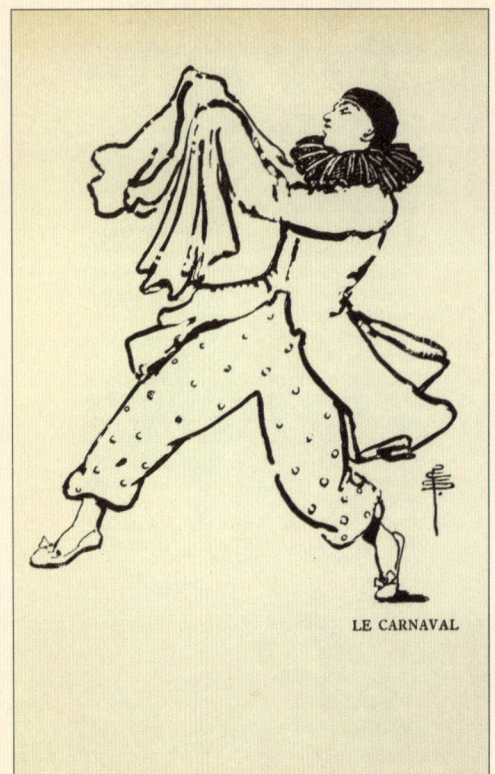
LE CARNAVAL

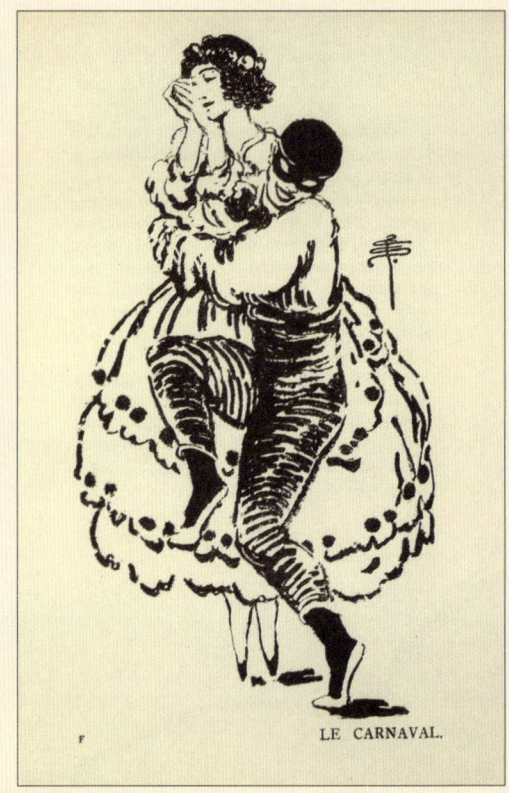
LE CARNAVAL.

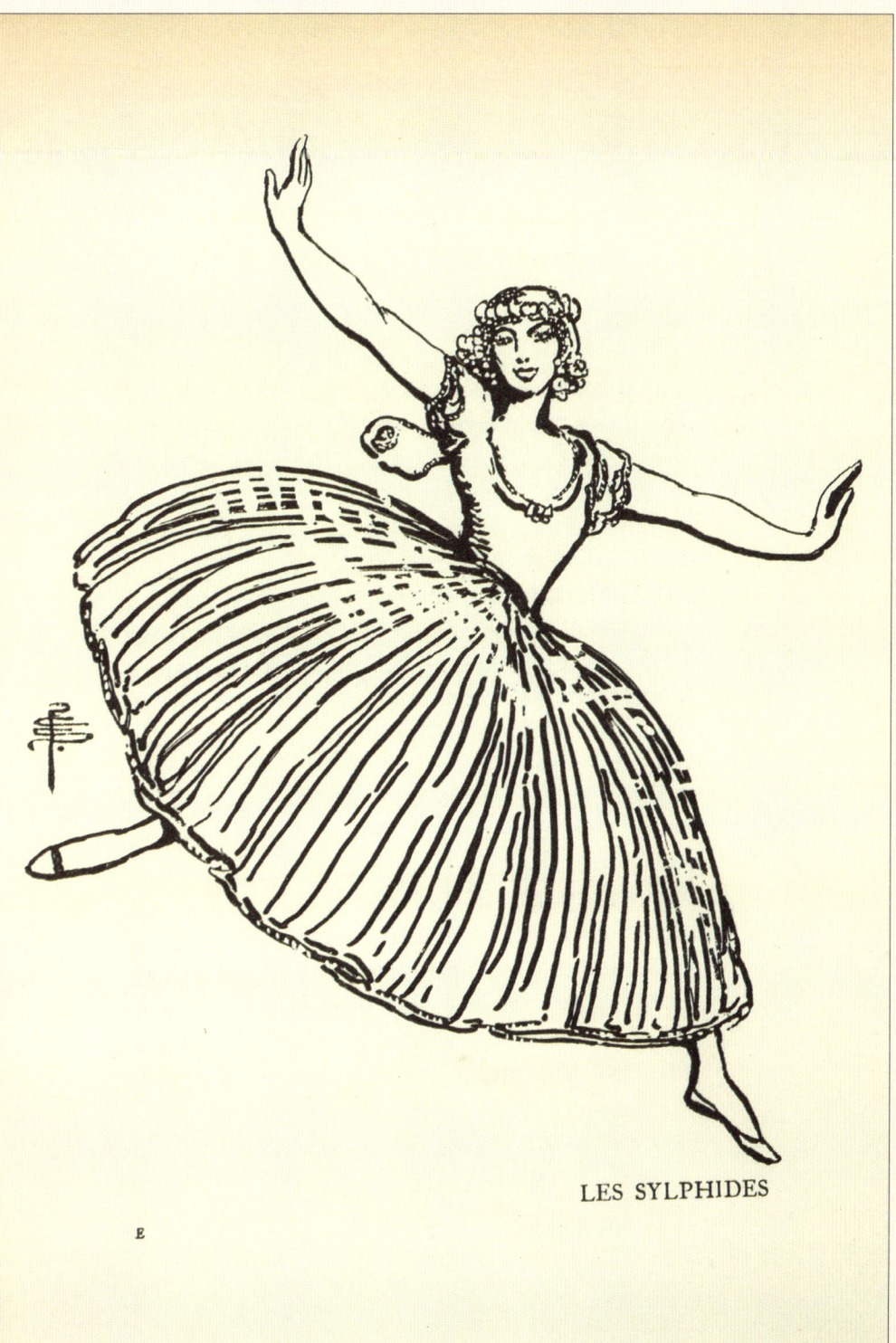

LES SYLPHIDES

1913

The Corps de Ballet

I NOTICED in "Carnaval" the individual work done by each individual of the *corps de ballet*, yet always done in such a way as to contribute to the harmonious effect of the whole. The Pierrot (Bolm), the Harlequin (Nijinsky), the Columbine (Karsavina), played the leading parts incomparably, but that was not surprising. It was far more surprising to see in every member of the ballet the talent of a "star." They were not there just to wear their 1860 costumes well and to form themselves into mechanical groups. The entire *corps* vibrated with life, did their full share in the dancing and miming. They never appeared to be waiting for an opportunity for distinction; they were content to distinguish themselves.

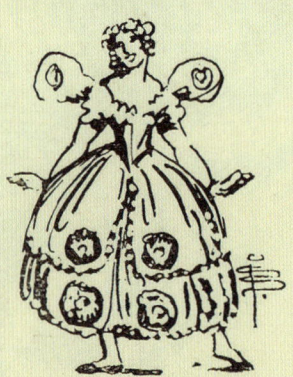

LE CARNAVAL

1913

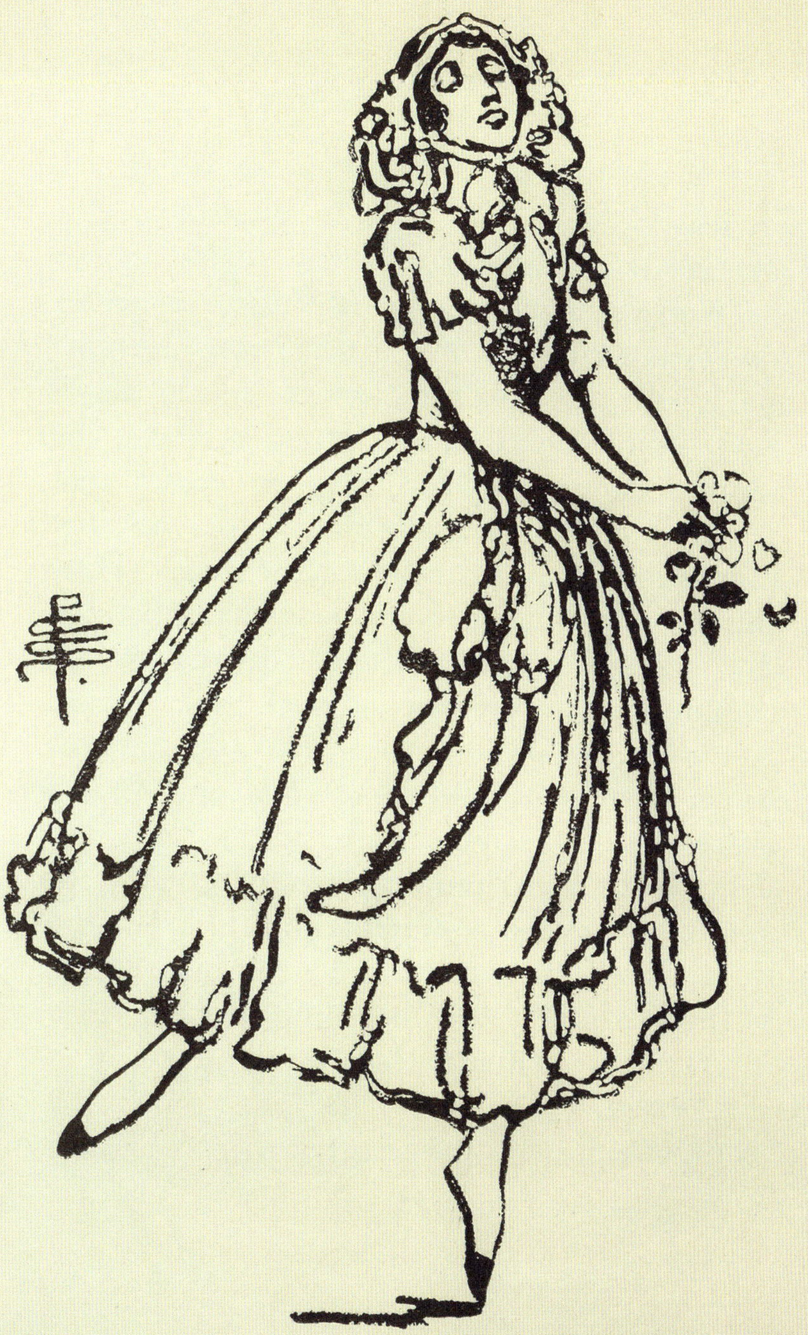

SPECTRE DE LA ROSE

1913

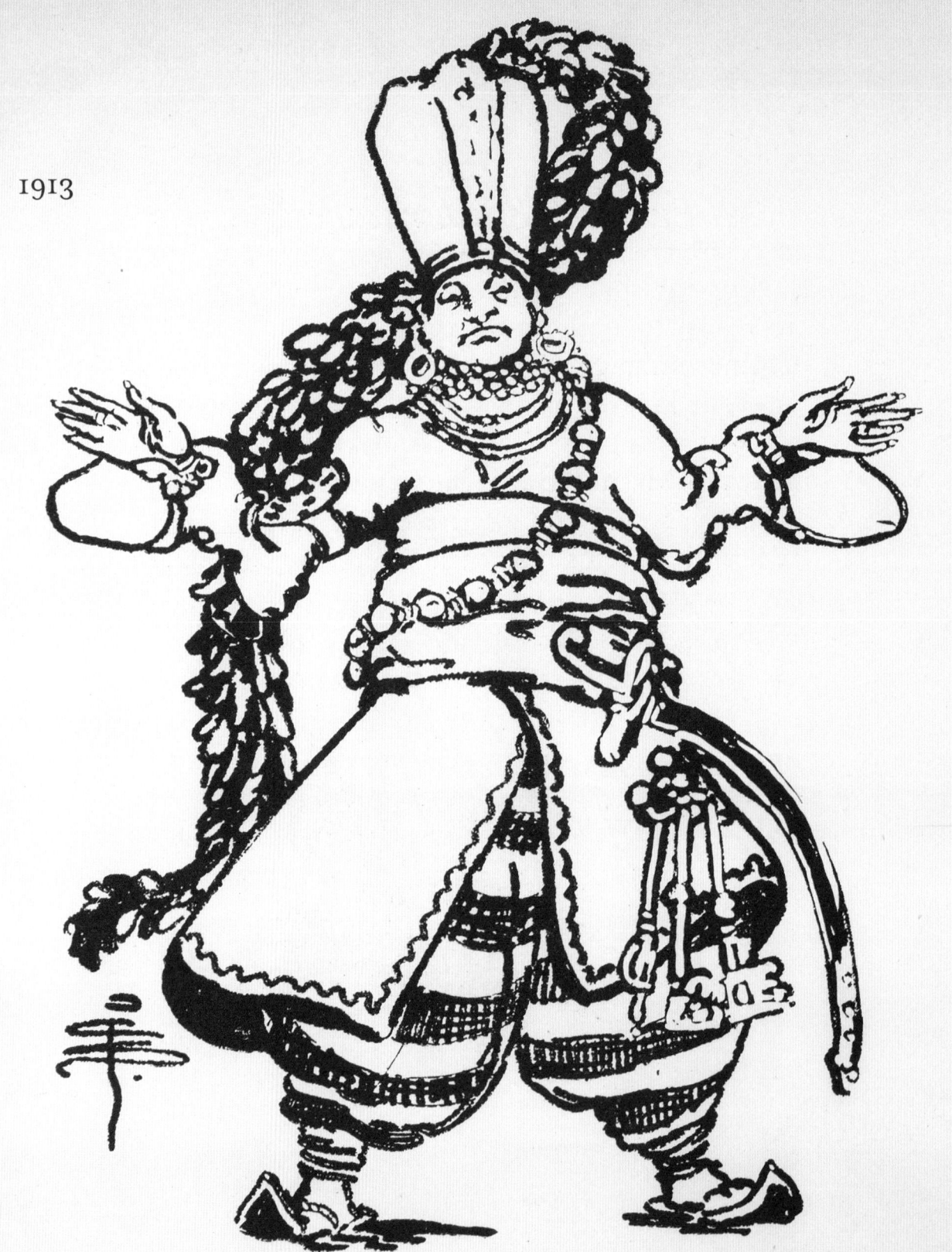

SCHEHERAZADE

1913

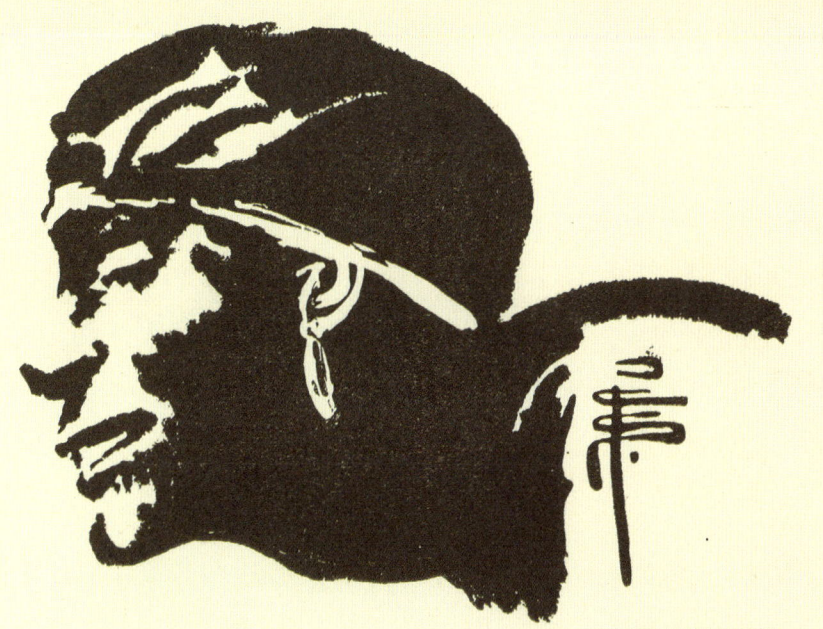

SCHEHERAZADE

Strauss after a plain-song hymn, or Wagner after Mozart, could not be a greater shock to the system. Everything in "Scheherazade" suggests violence and horror. Bakst's palace was built for dreadful deeds; no one, I am sure, could ever feel safe in it. Its colour makes it vibrate on its foundations, if indeed it has any foundations. There are bad dreams as well as good ones, and the dream quality, on which I have insisted, so far, as the special

1913 Brutal "Scheherazade"

waving invisible garlands in the serene air, are ready to coil round their prey in a serpentine embrace. The lips which gave the innocent kiss of naïve youth are now twisted in the spasms of desire." Nijinsky in "Scheherazade" is not the incarnation of evil, but its spirit. . . . His ghastly pallor is terrible. Really he seems to turn white under his black skin.

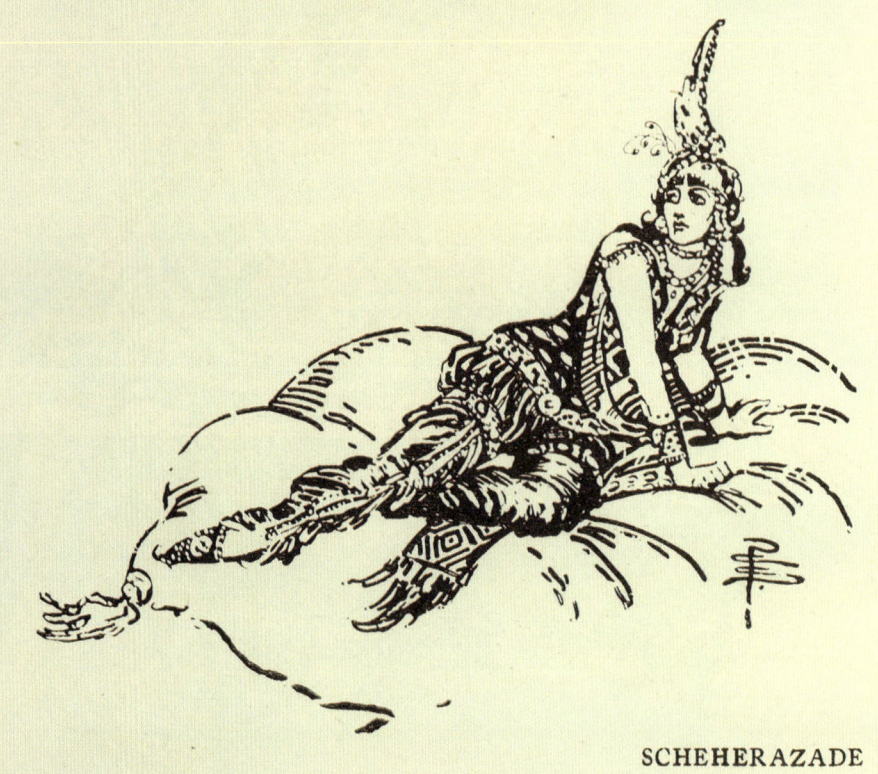

SCHEHERAZADE

1913

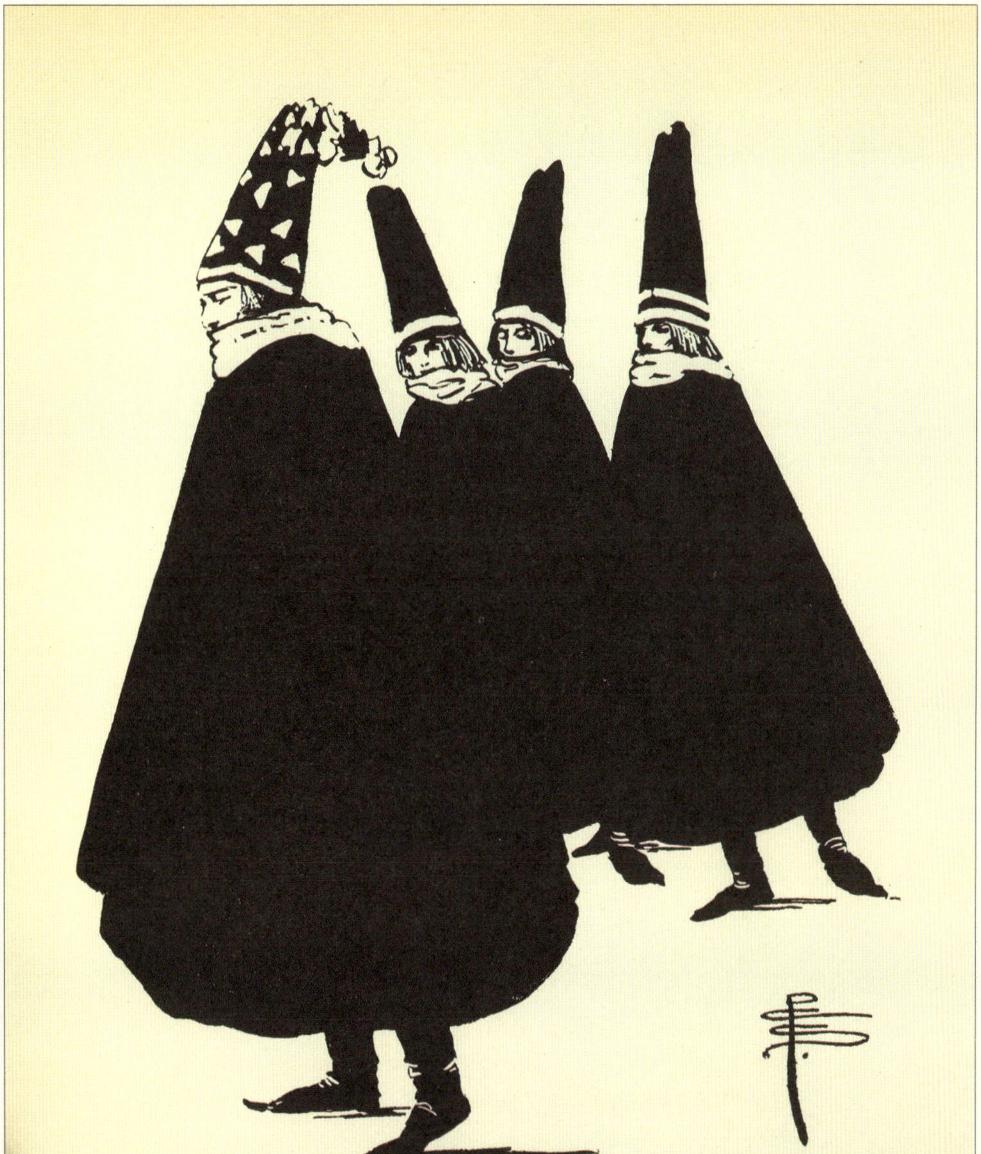

TAMAR

1913

Opposite page including 13 illustrations. Costume design in pencil, ink and watercolor on paper inscribed with names of characters and detailed instructions for the making of costumes for a children's play by Mabel Dearmer with music by Martin Shaw produced at the Little Theatre in London, April, 1914. Two illustrations originally had fabric samples attached. Courtesy of the University of Delaware Library. Special thanks to Mark Lasner and Rachel Olsen for providing these images.

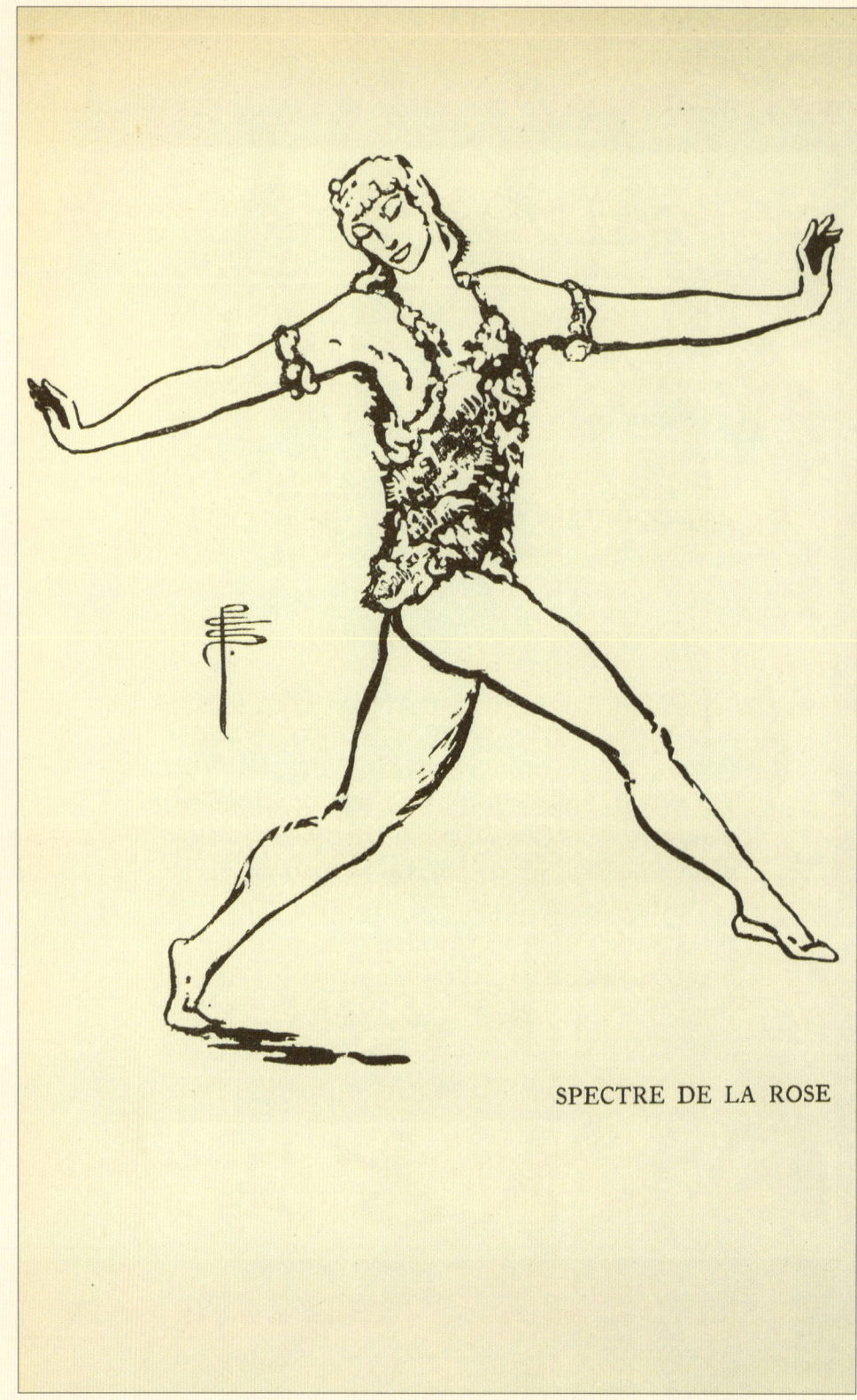

SPECTRE DE LA ROSE

Brer Rabbit and Mr. Fox

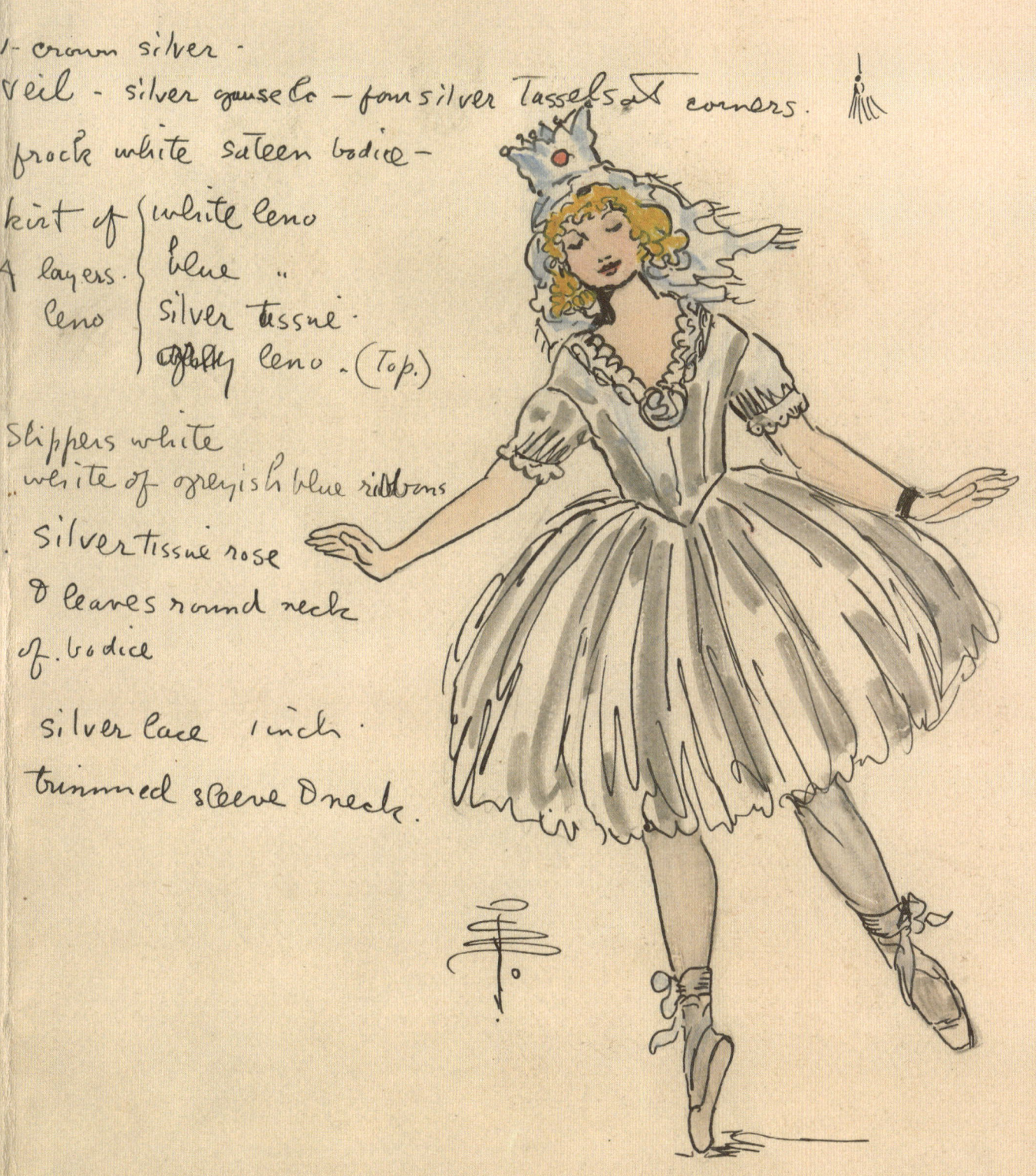

1 - crown silver -
veil - silver gauze Co - four silver Tassels at corners.
frock white sateen bodice -
skirt of { white leno
4 layers. { blue ..
leno { silver tissue.
{ ~~softly~~ leno . (Top.)

Slippers white
.. white or greyish blue ribbons

silver tissue rose
& leaves round neck
of bodice

silver lace 1 inch.
trimmed sleeve & neck.

King Deer's daughter :

1914

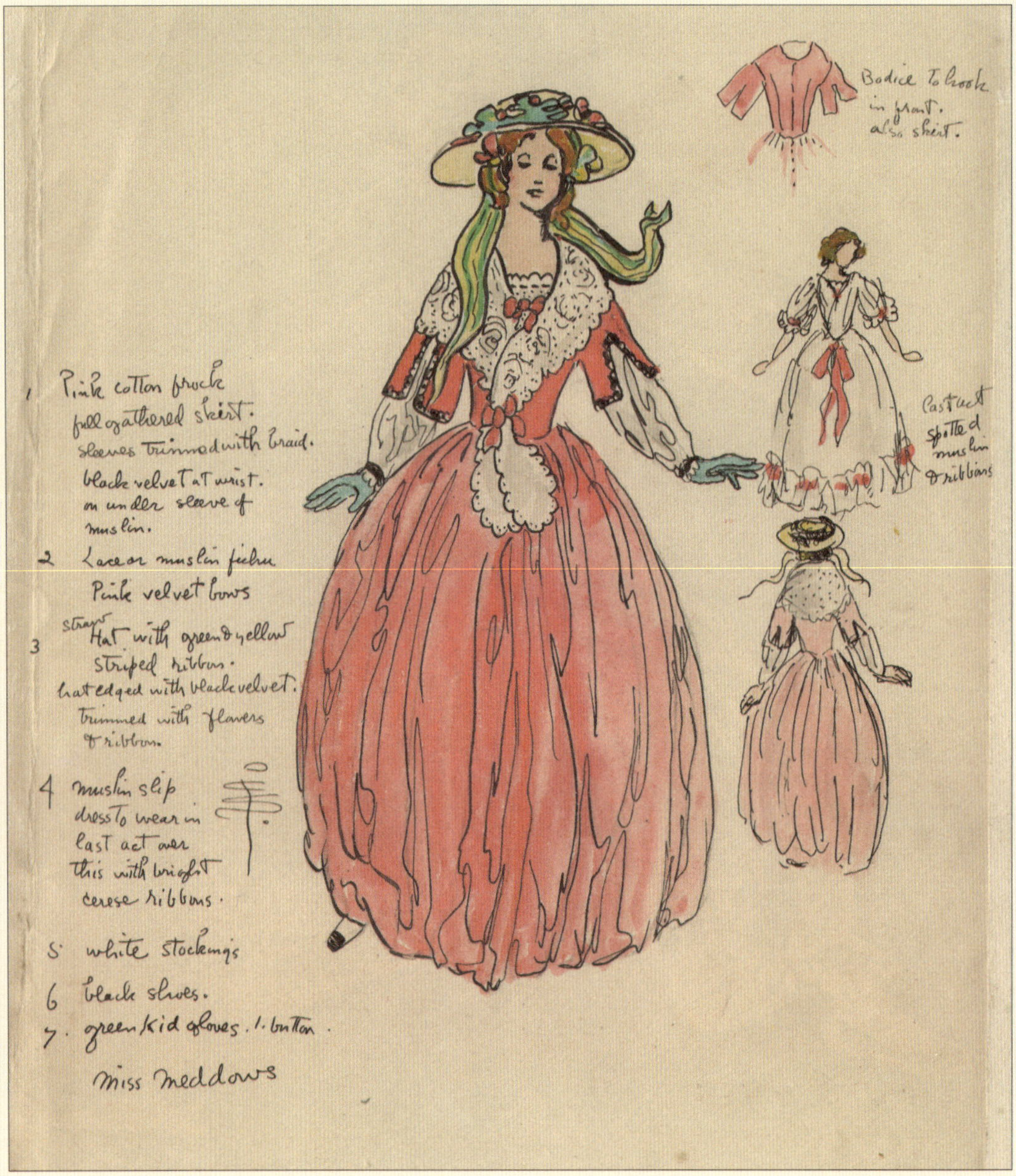

1. Pink cotton frock full gathered skirt. sleeves trimmed with braid. black velvet at waist. an under sleeve of muslin.
2. Lace or muslin fichu. Pink velvet bows
3. straw Hat with green & yellow striped ribbons. hat edged with black velvet. trimmed with flowers & ribbon.
4. muslin slip dress to wear in last act over this with bright cerese ribbons.
5. white stockings
6. black shoes.
7. green kid gloves. 1. button.

Miss Meddows

Bodice to hook in front. also skirt.

Last act spotted muslin & ribbons

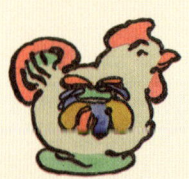

1914

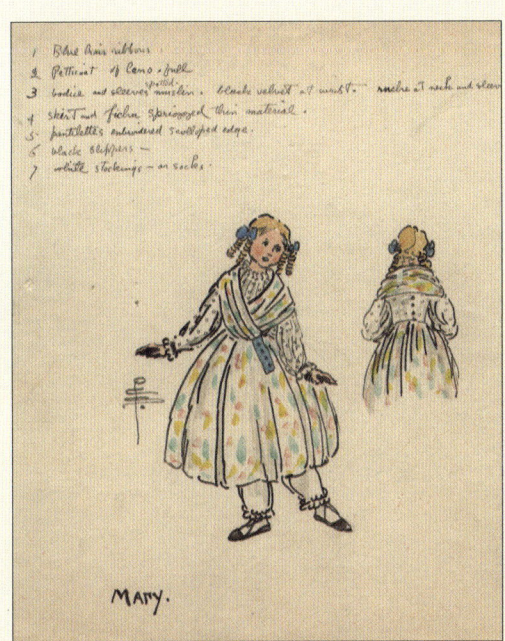
Mary.

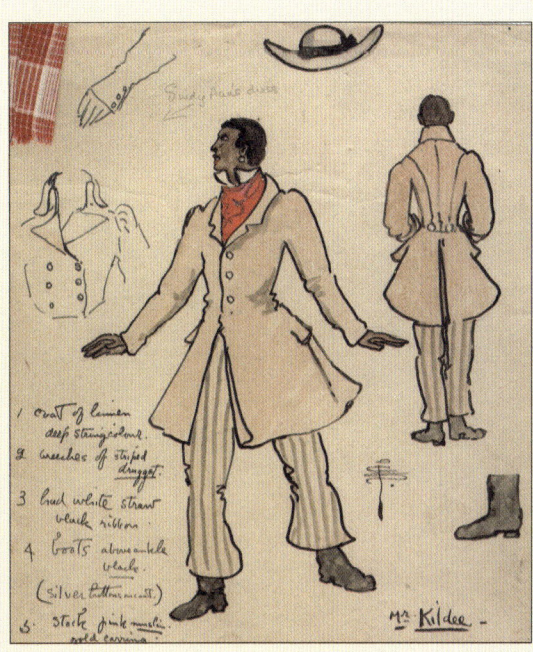
Mr Kildee.

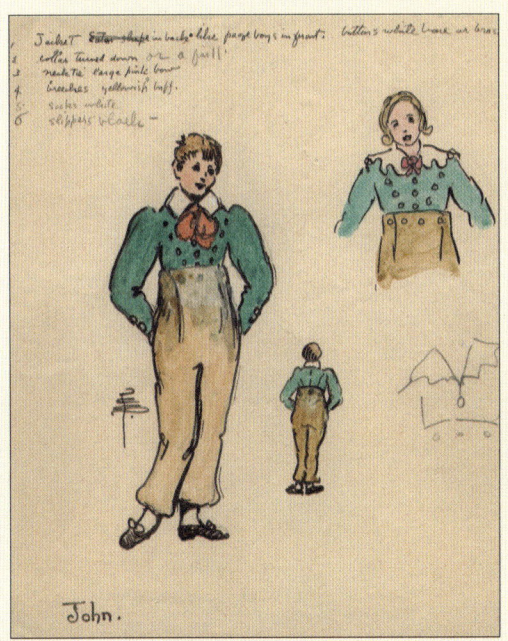
John.

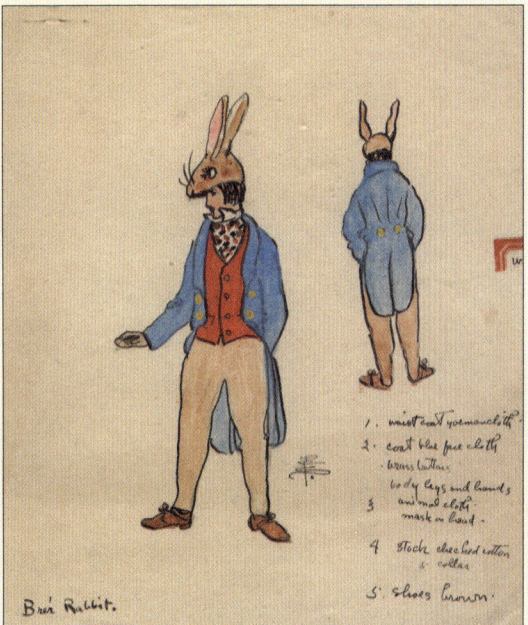
Br'er Rabbit.

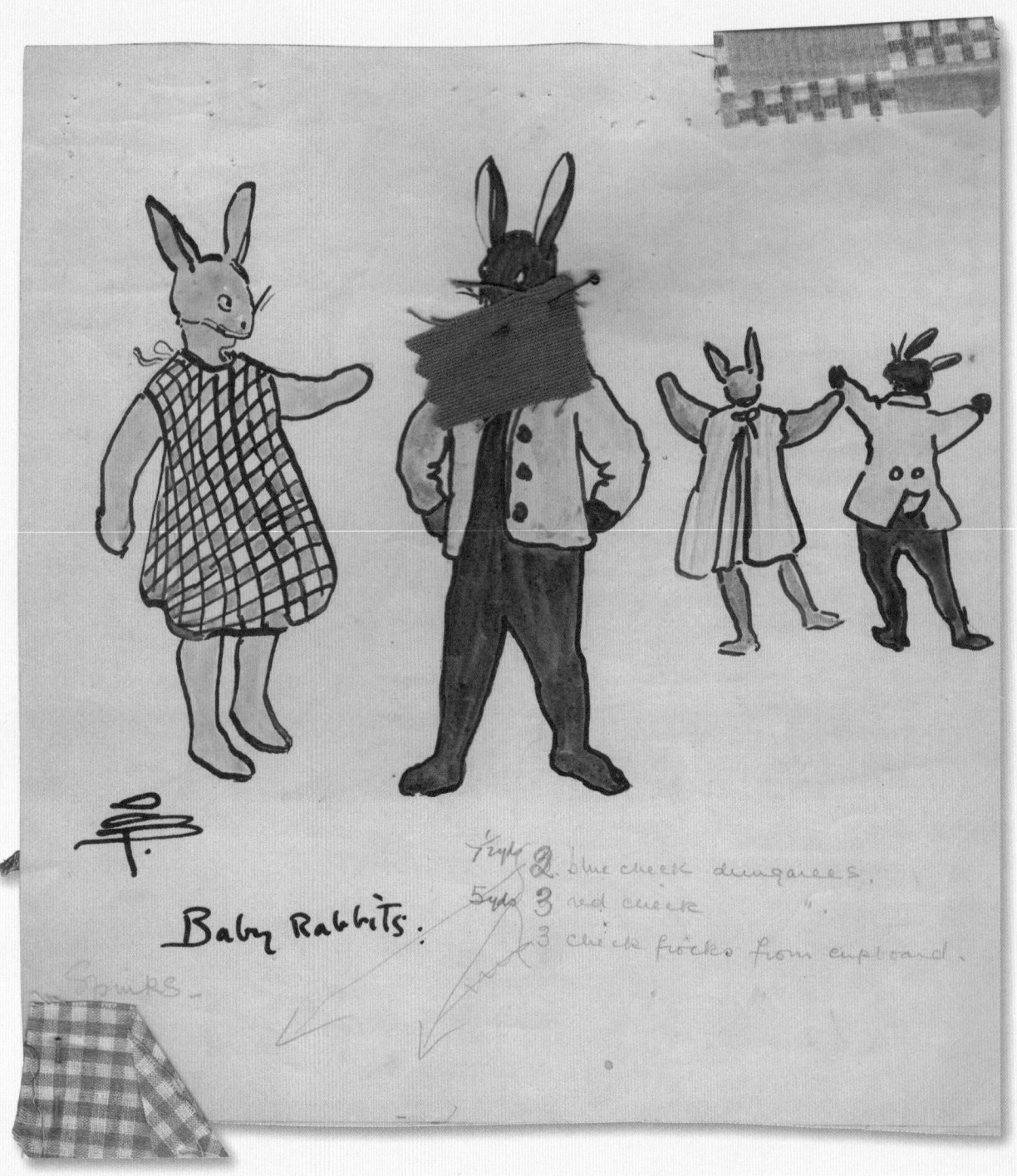

Baby Rabbits.

2 blue check dungarees
3 red check "
3 check frocks from cupboard.

1914

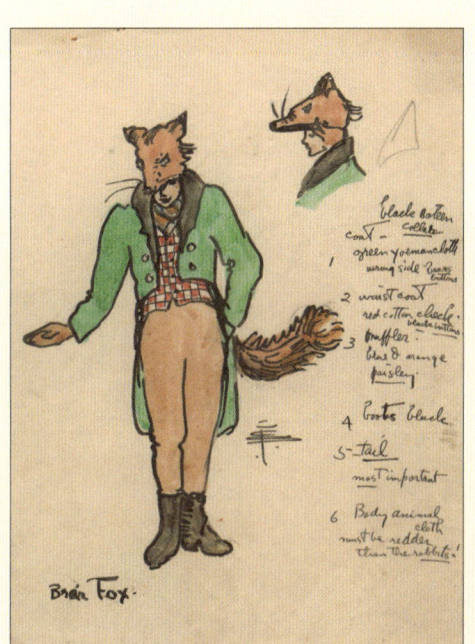
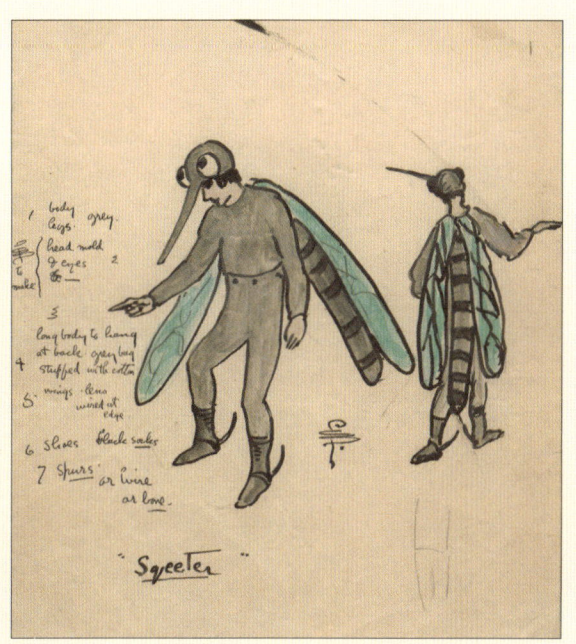
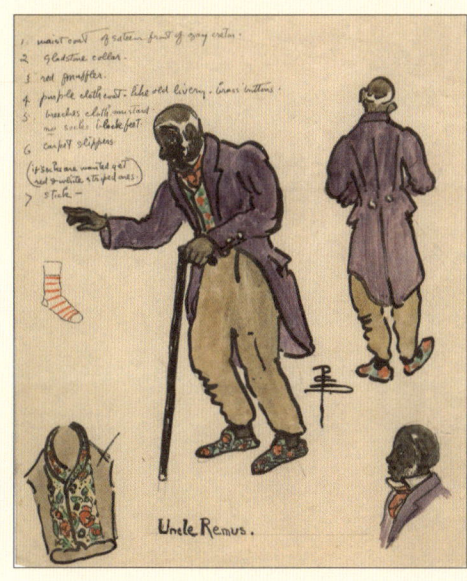
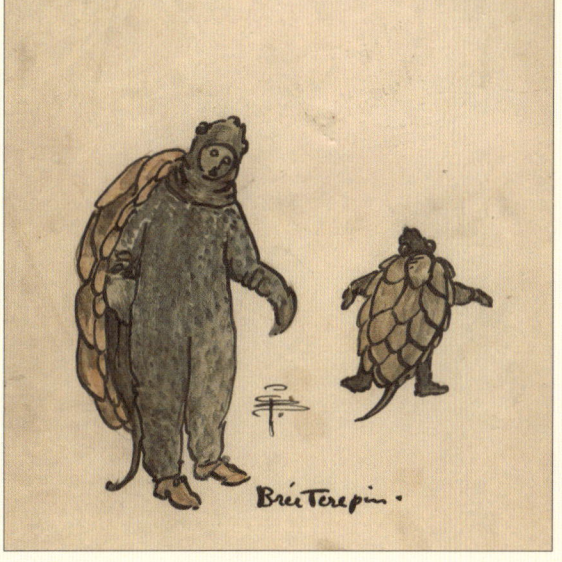

1914

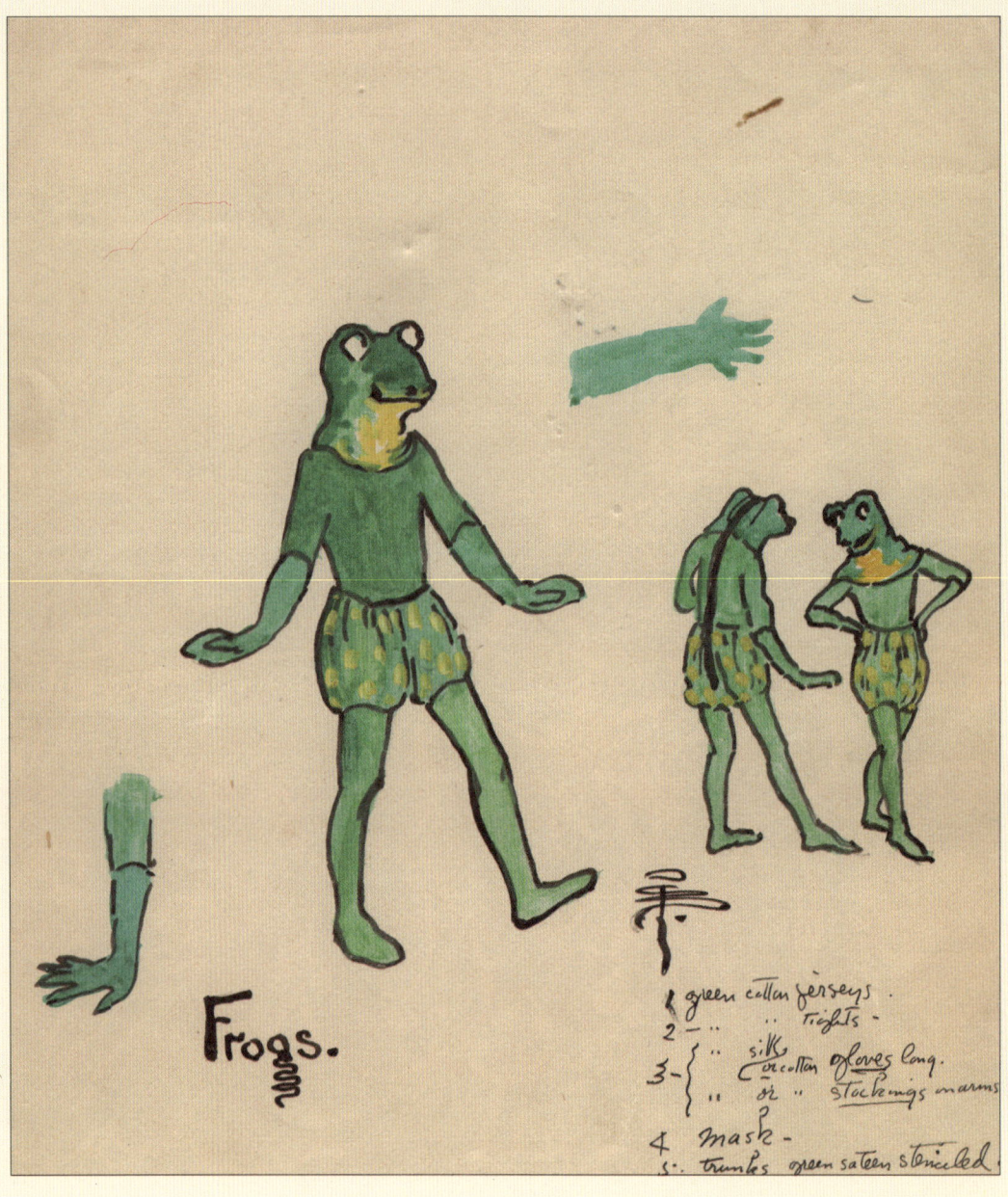

1914

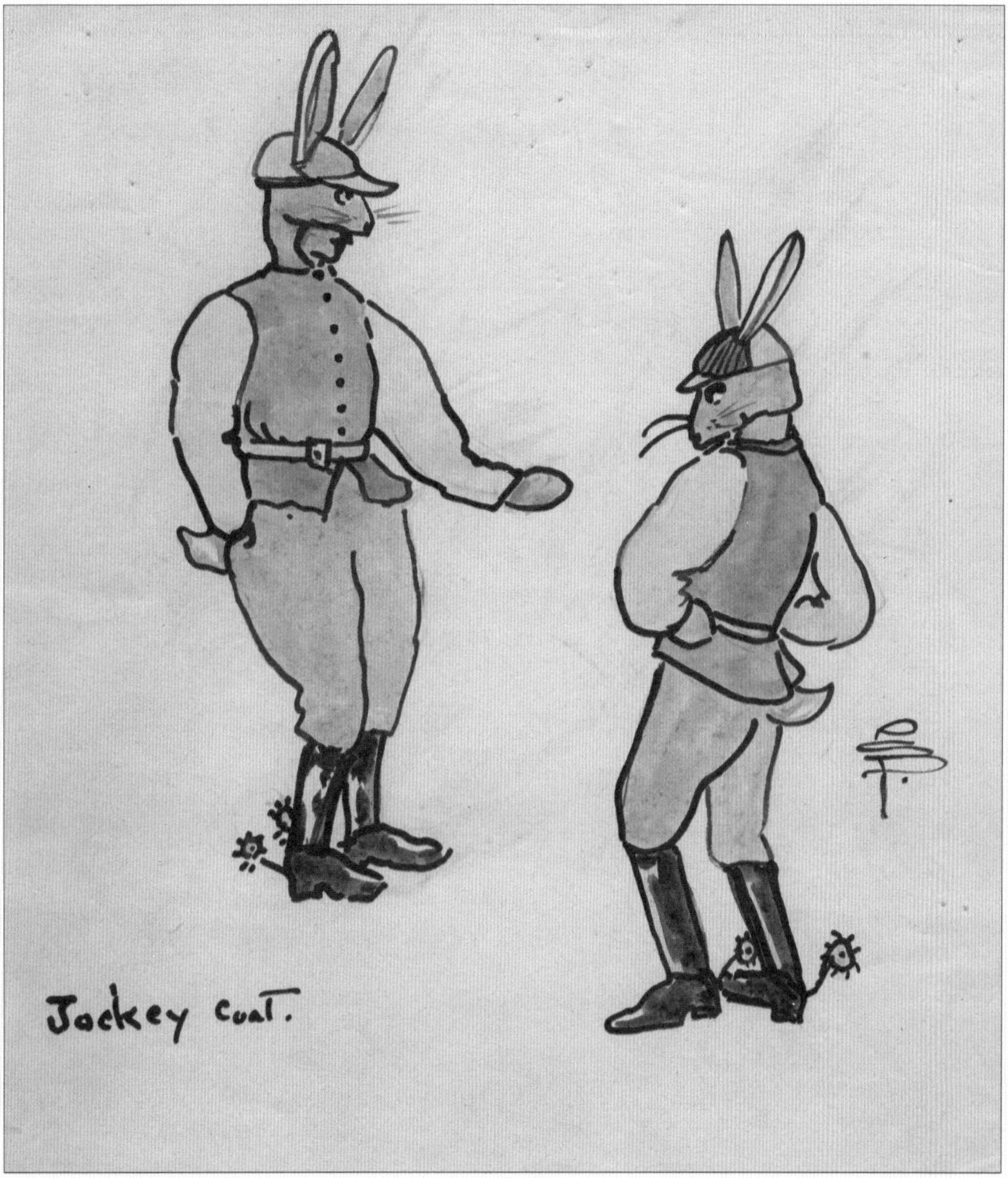

Jockey coat.

The Book of Friendly Giants

1914

Cover and ten illustrations from *The Book of Friendly Giants*

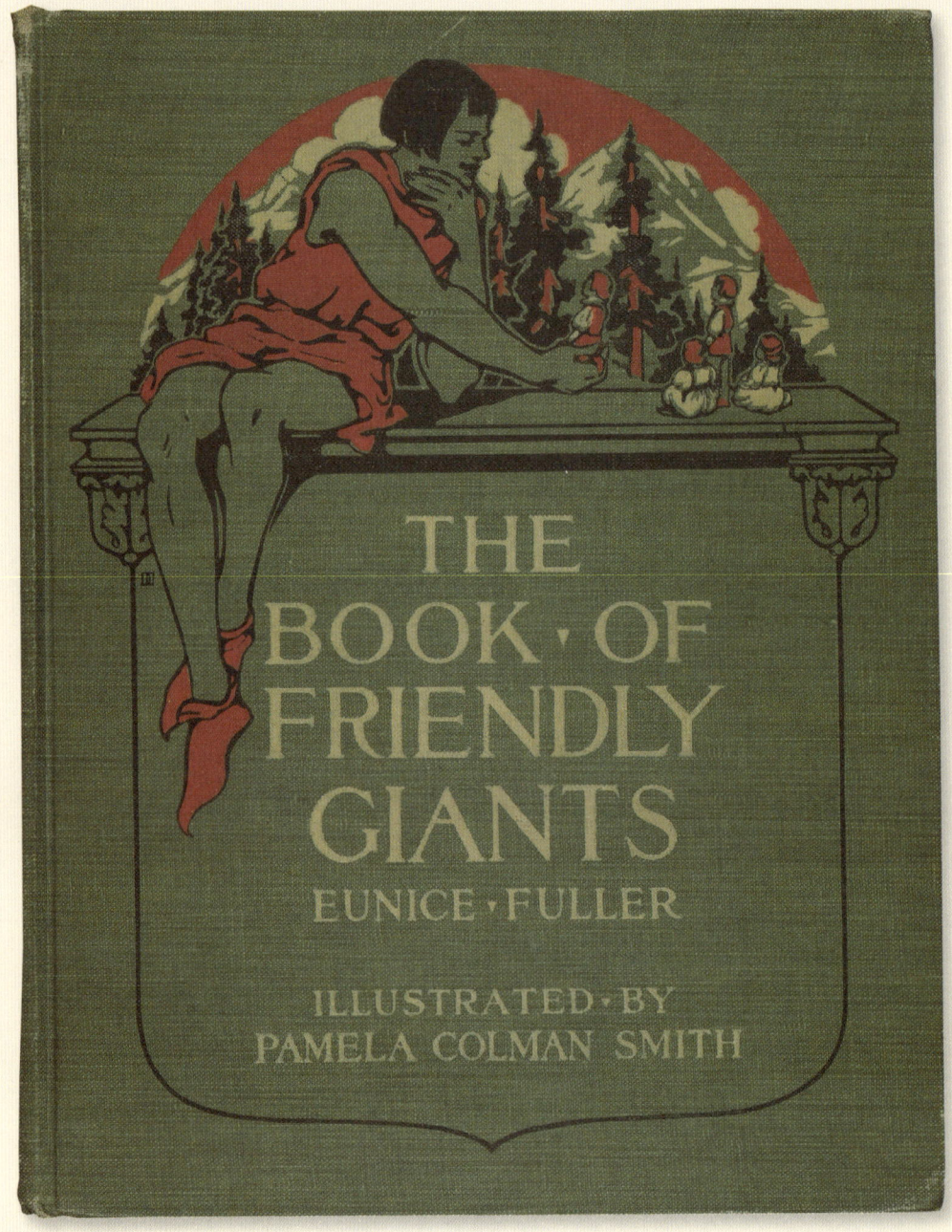

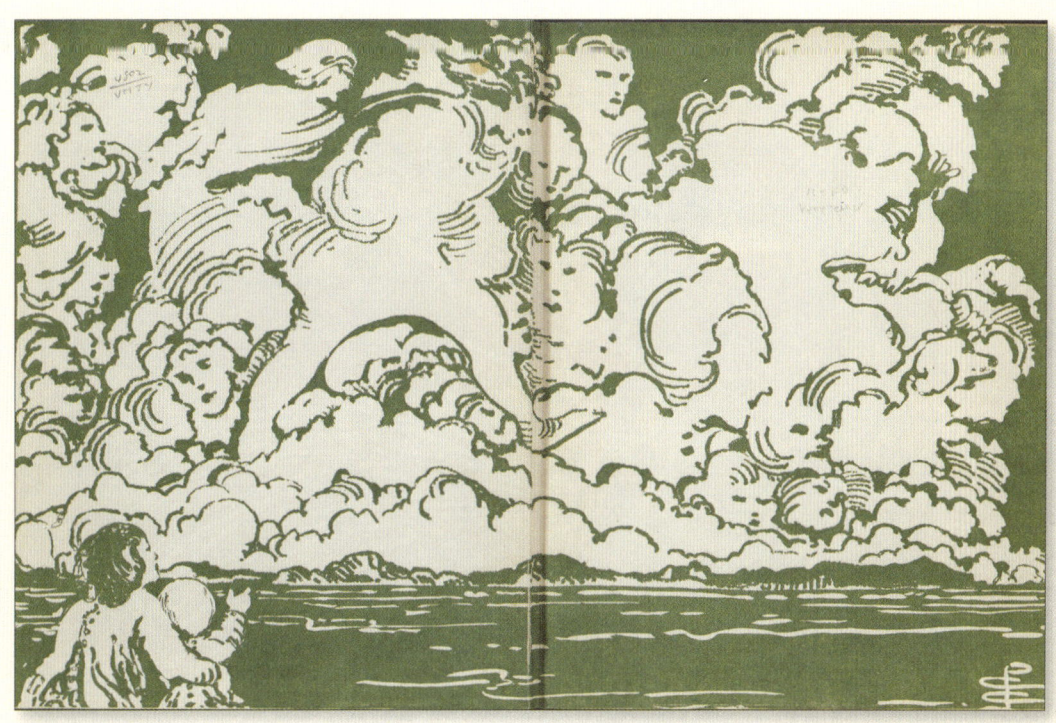

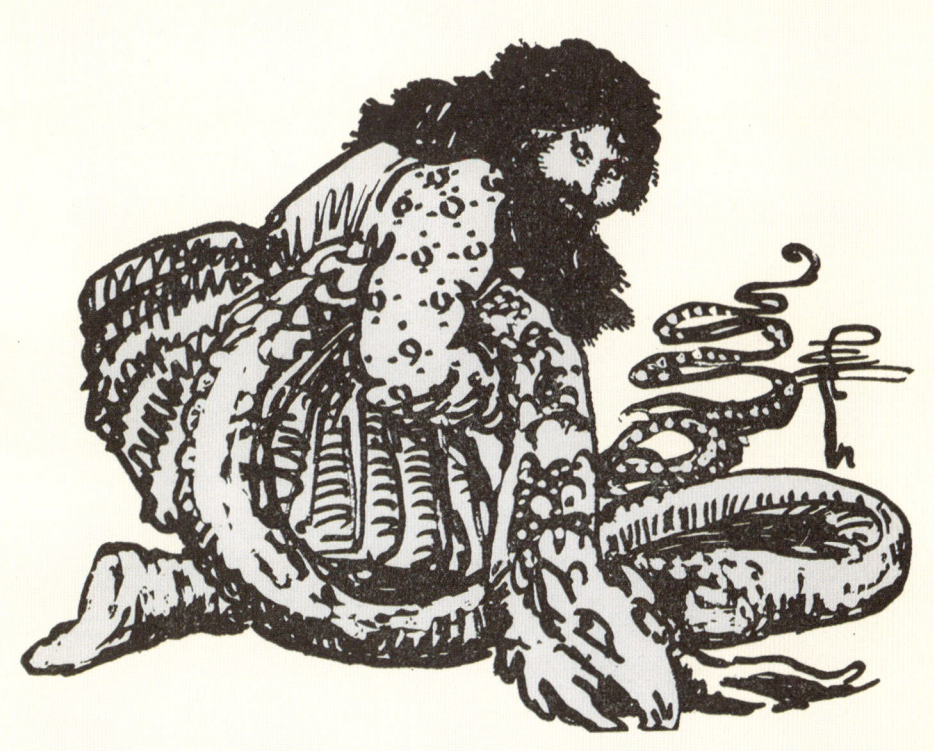

1914

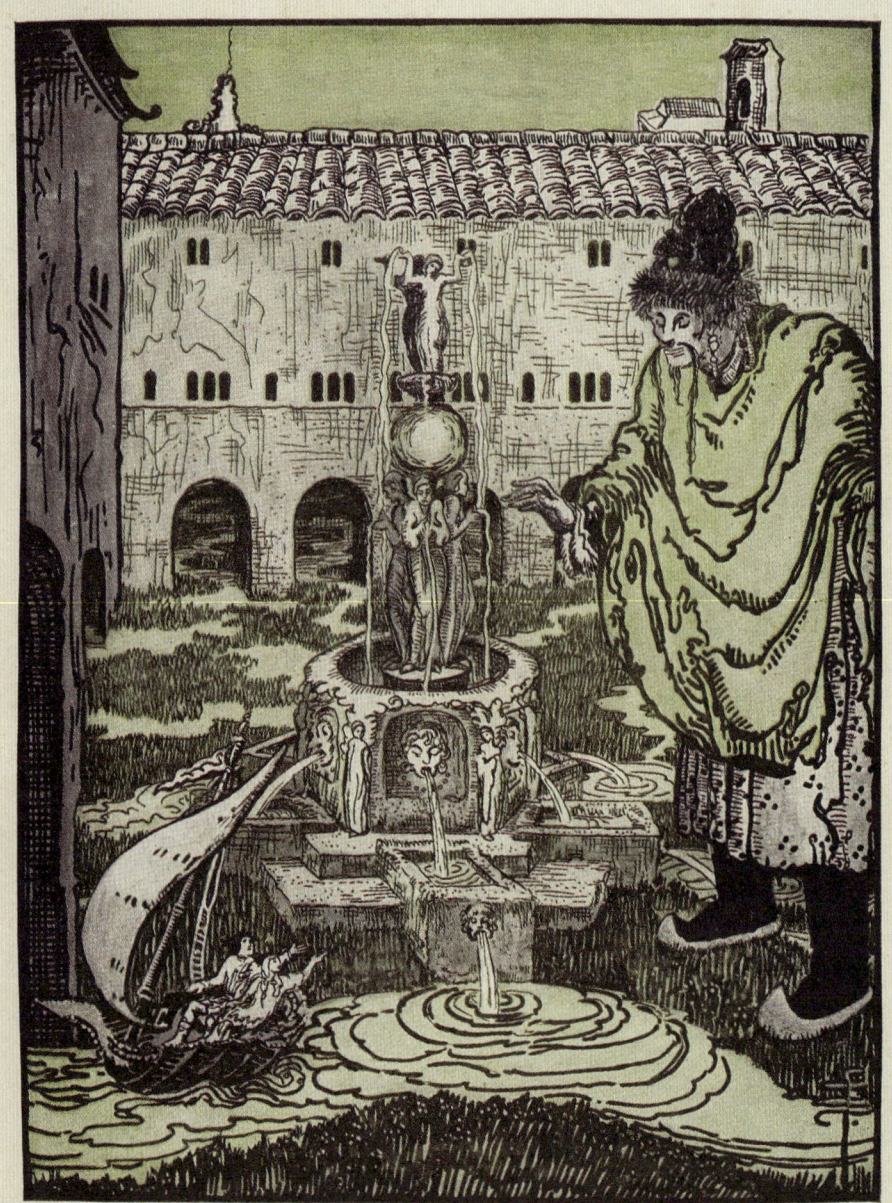

"Good-bye," he roared. "And don't forget the giant Riverrath"

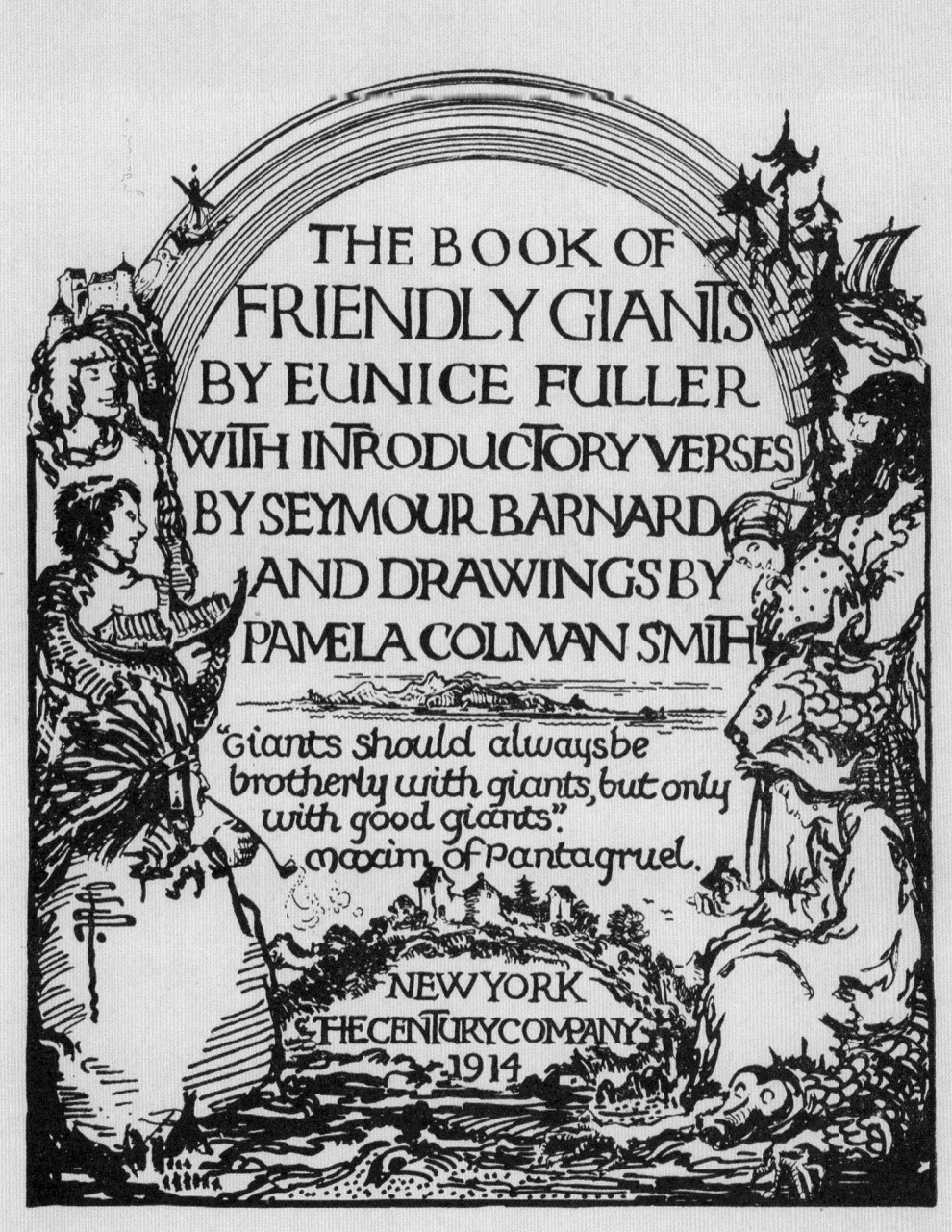

1914

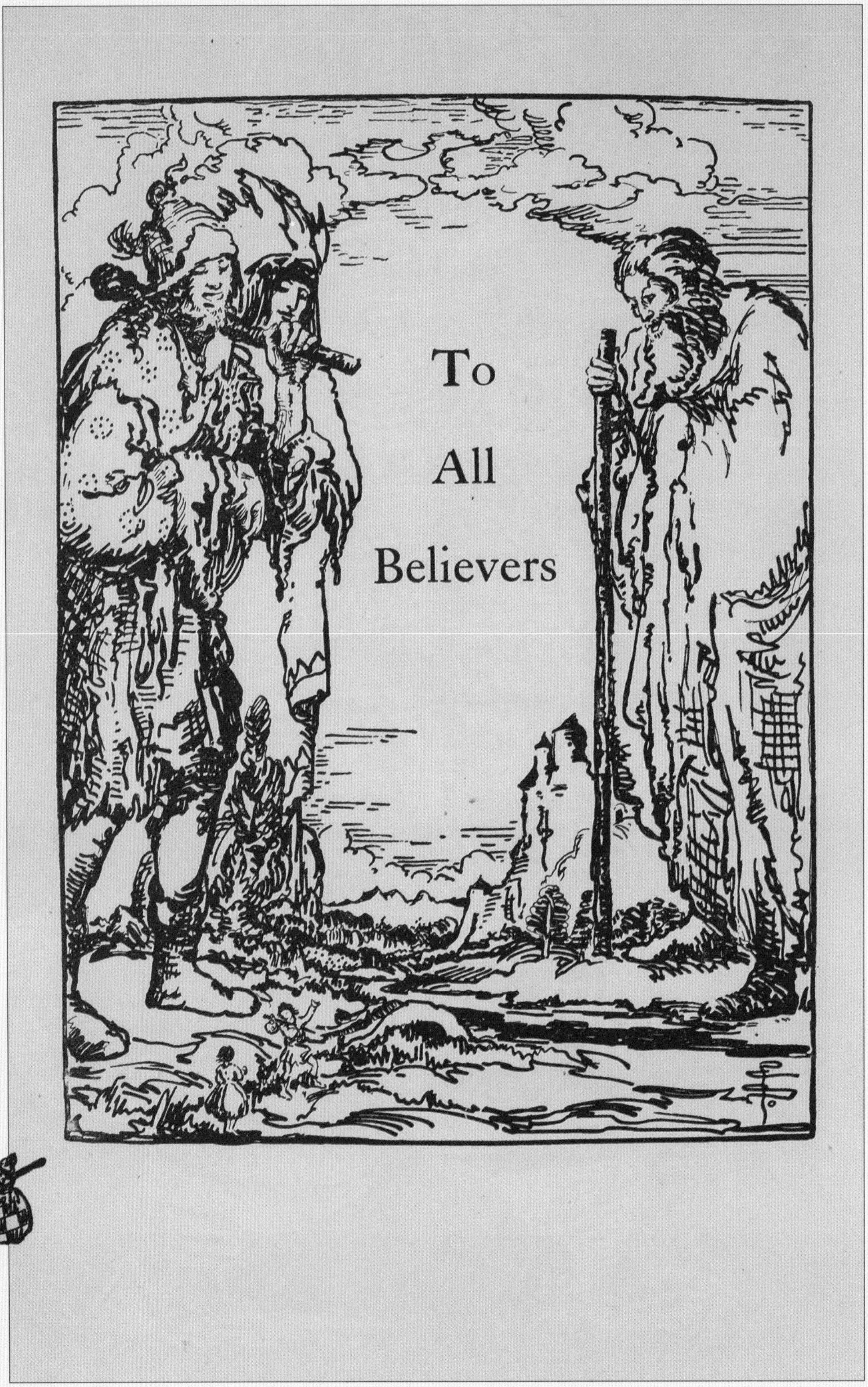

To
All
Believers

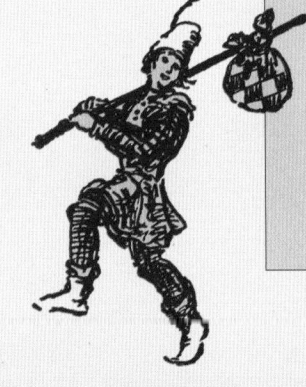

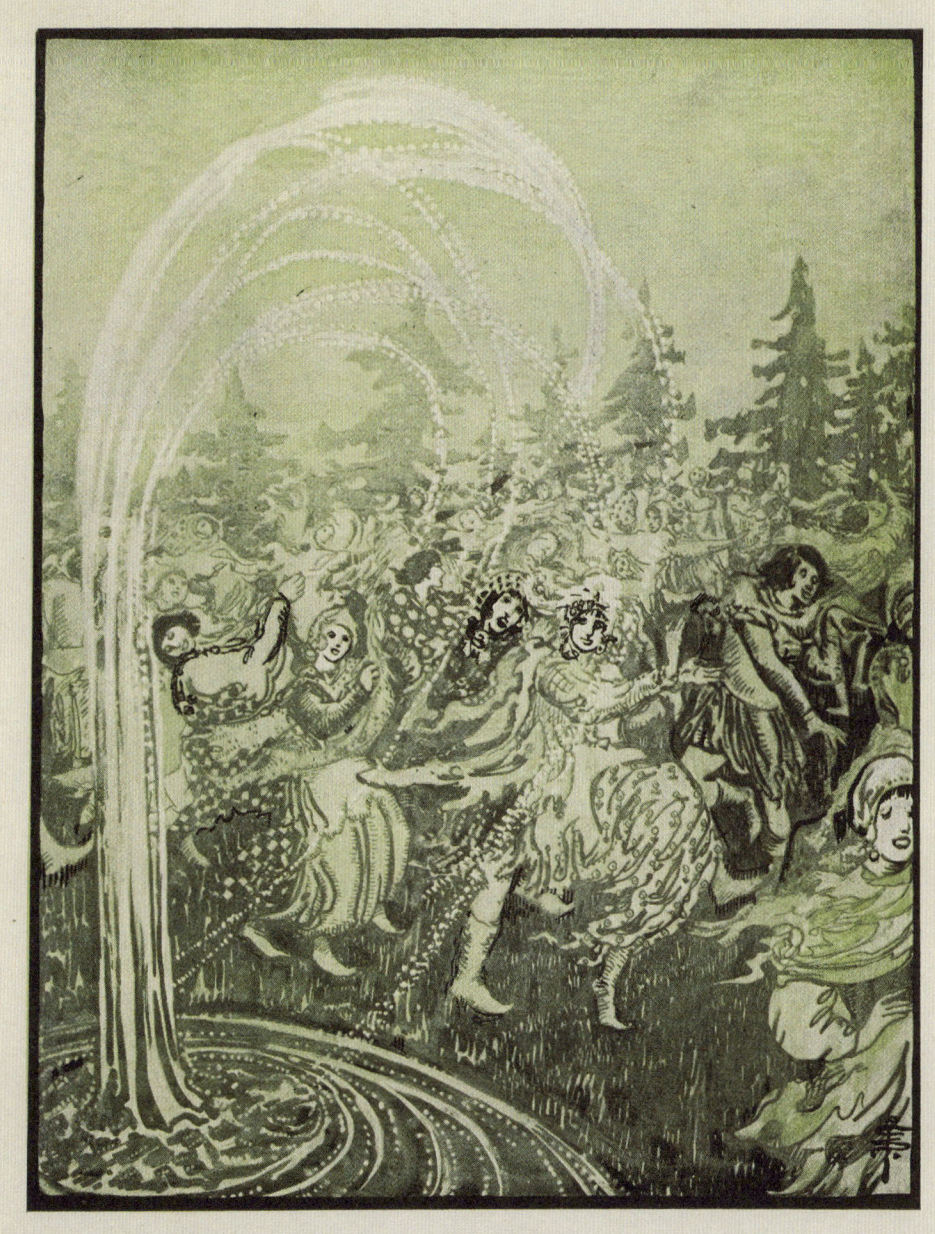

A fountain that shot up in a silver torrent

1914

1914

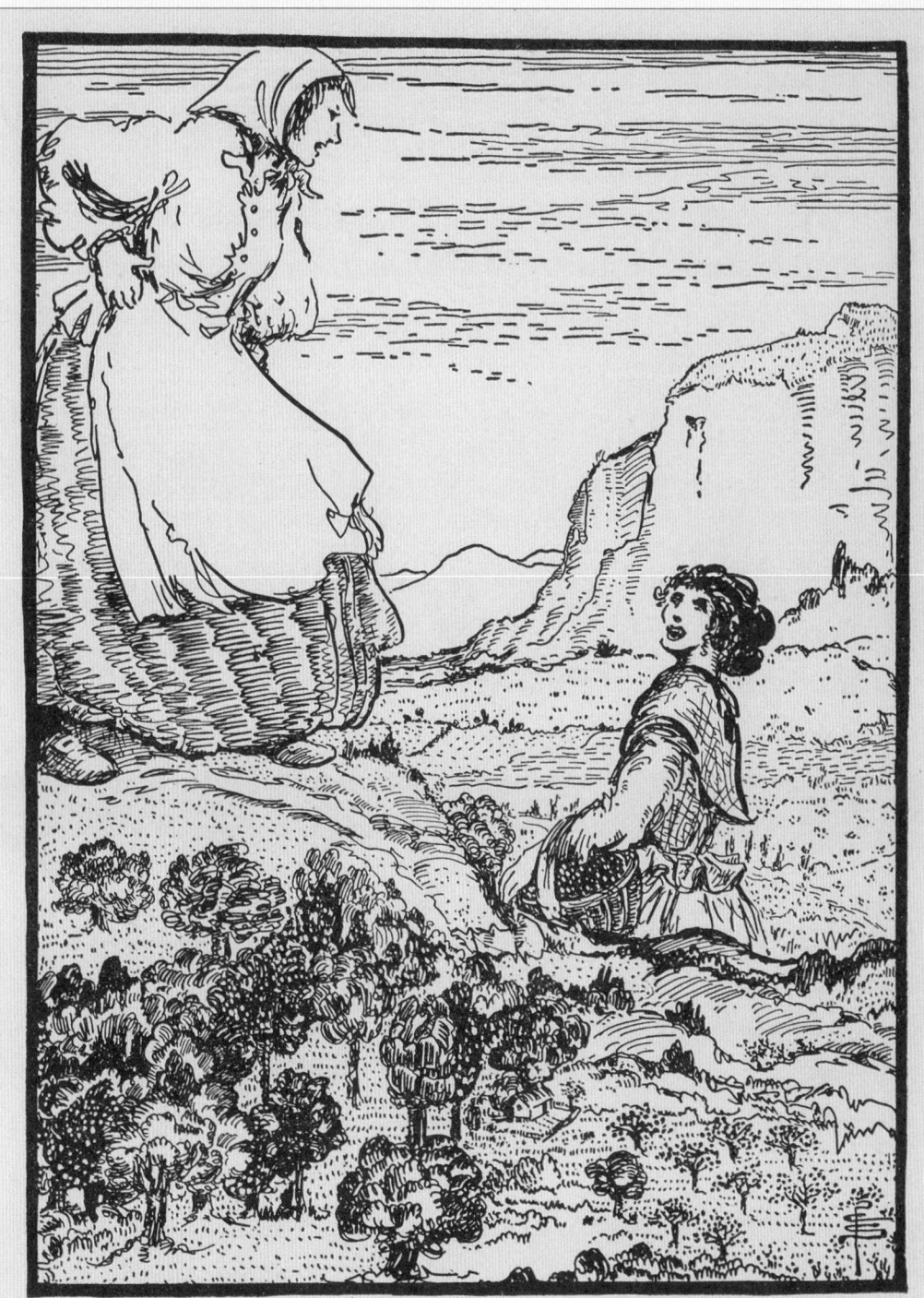

"No," said Granua, "I'm down in the valley, picking bilberries"

1914

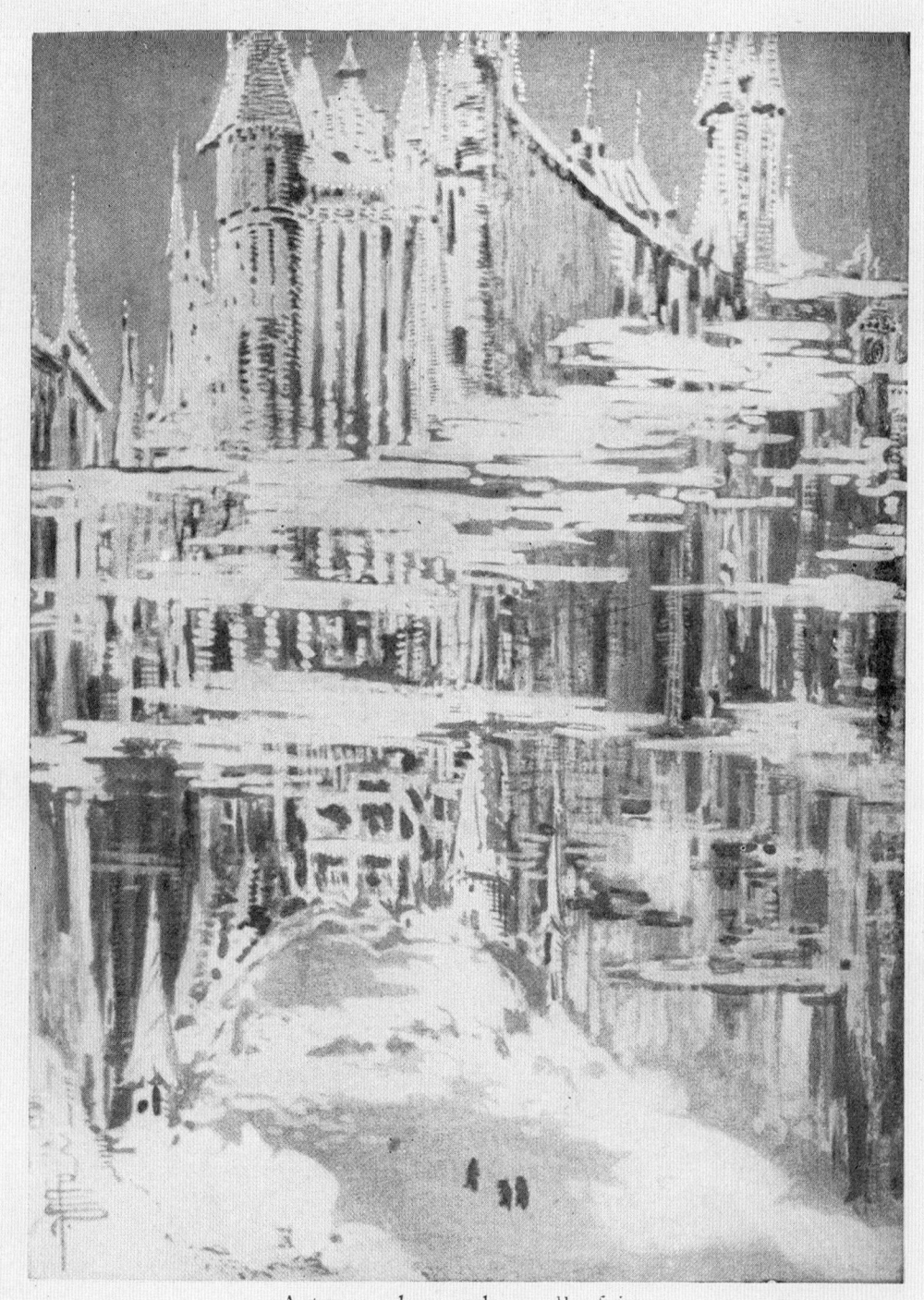

A tremendous palace, all of ice

The Giant Who Rode on the Ark

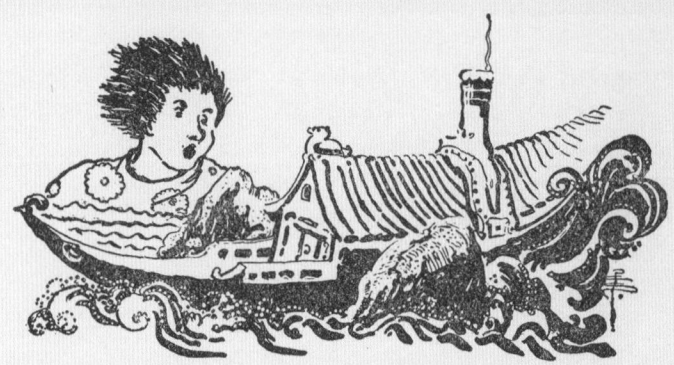

There, stuck on the rocks, was a tremendous wooden box

ing over into the water. Then wearily he opened his mouth and snored to high heaven.

All of a sudden, Hurtali awoke. Somewhere there was a noise that disturbed him. It was the queerest noise anyway. It seemed to be made up of a hundred small sounds. It was a twittering, a rustling, a chirping, and a tiny screaming all at once.

"Just my luck!" thought Hurtali sleepily. "I've gone and laid my head in a whole colony of eagles' nests."

Then he rubbed his eyes open. It was morning, and what felt so cold around his neck was water. It had risen until it had covered him up in the night.

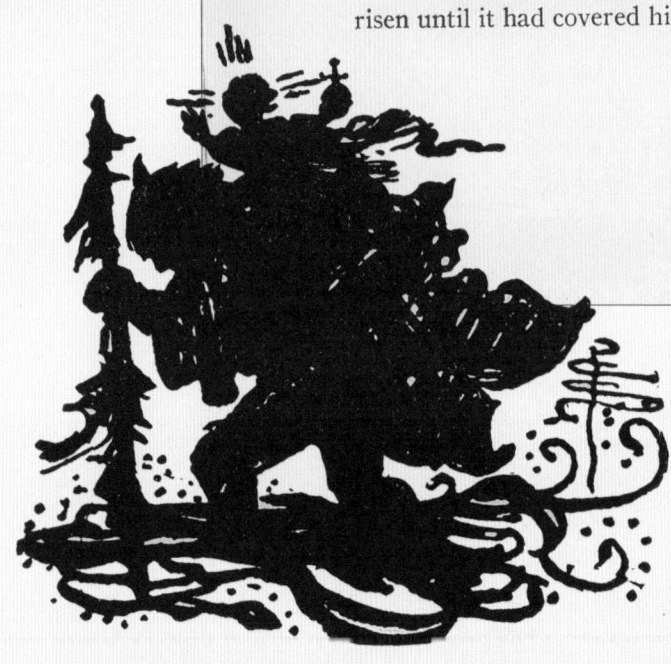

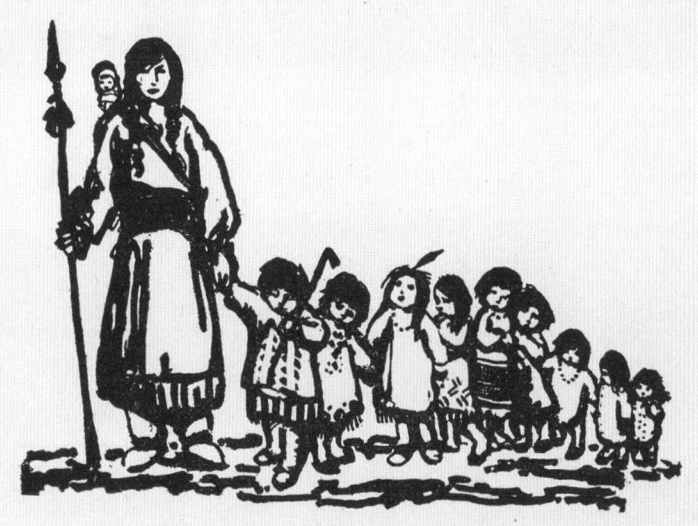

He had a wife and ten children

VIII

The Wigwam Giants

ONCE upon a time, in the not-so-very-long-ago, an Indian had his wigwam on the shore of a cold north sea. The Indian's name was Pulo-wech, and he had a wife and ten children. But for all

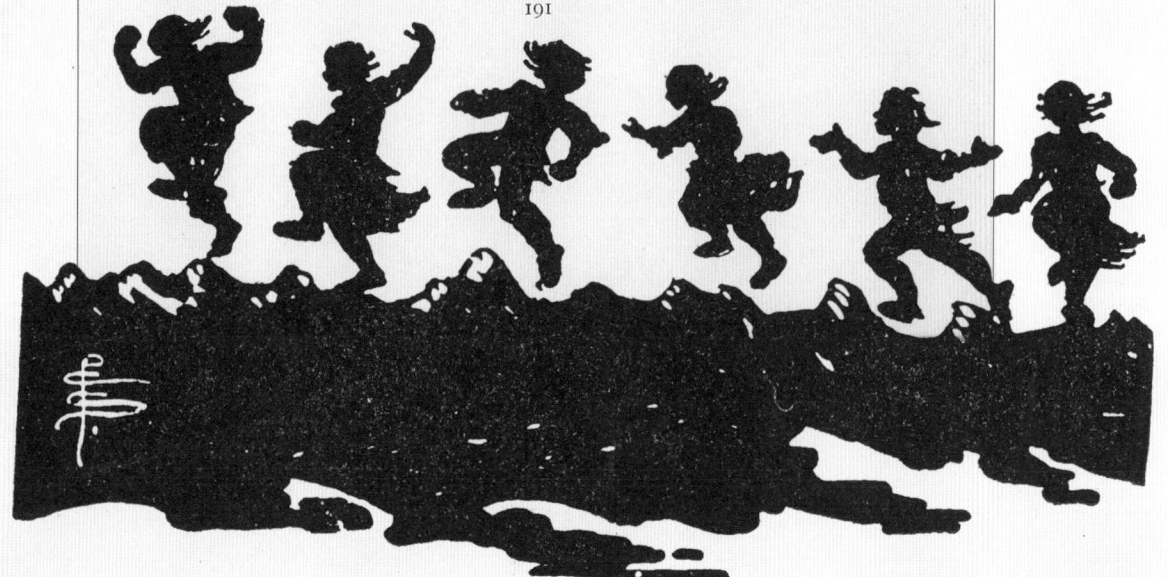

Debussy's Submerged Cathedral

1916

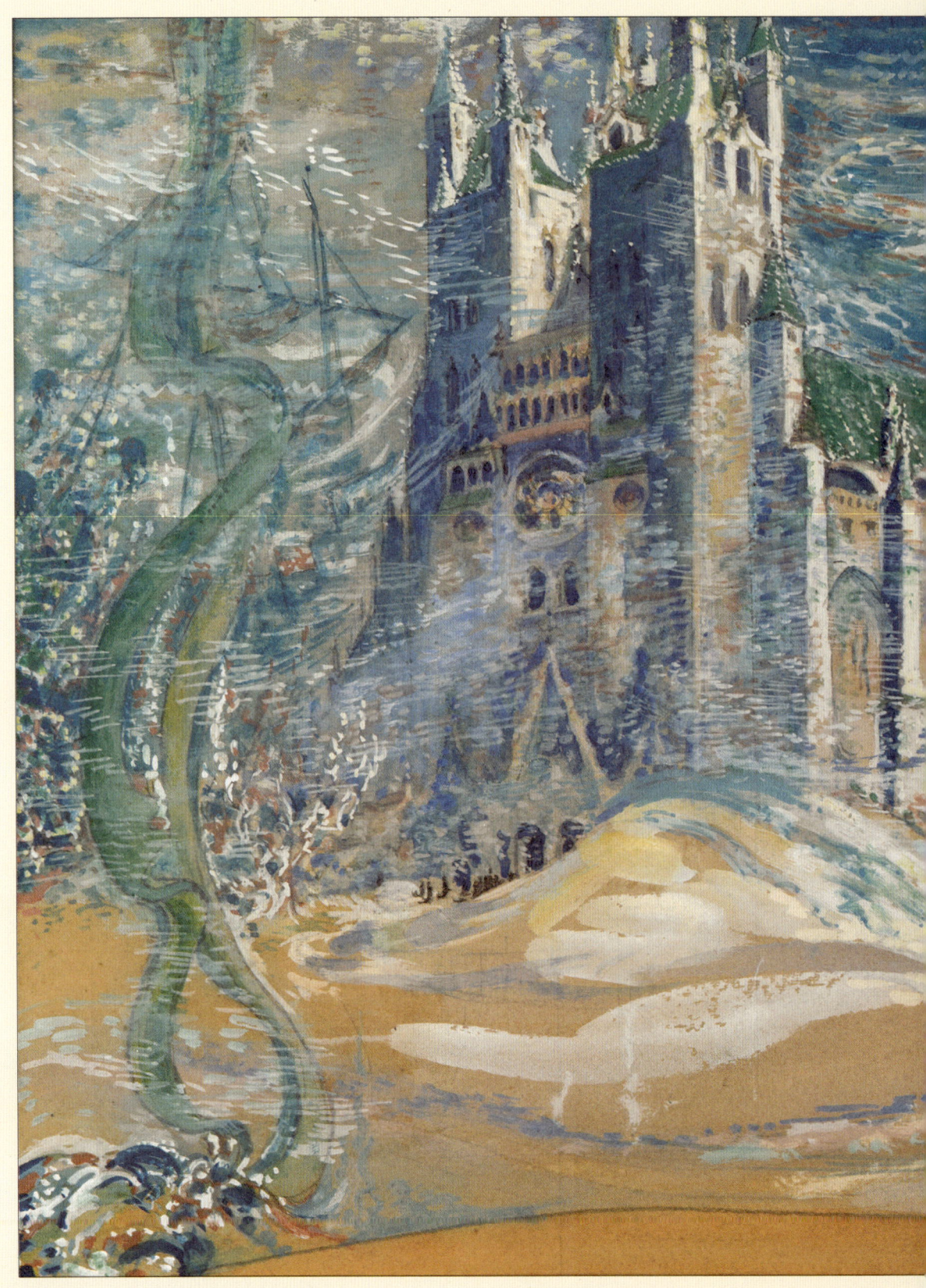

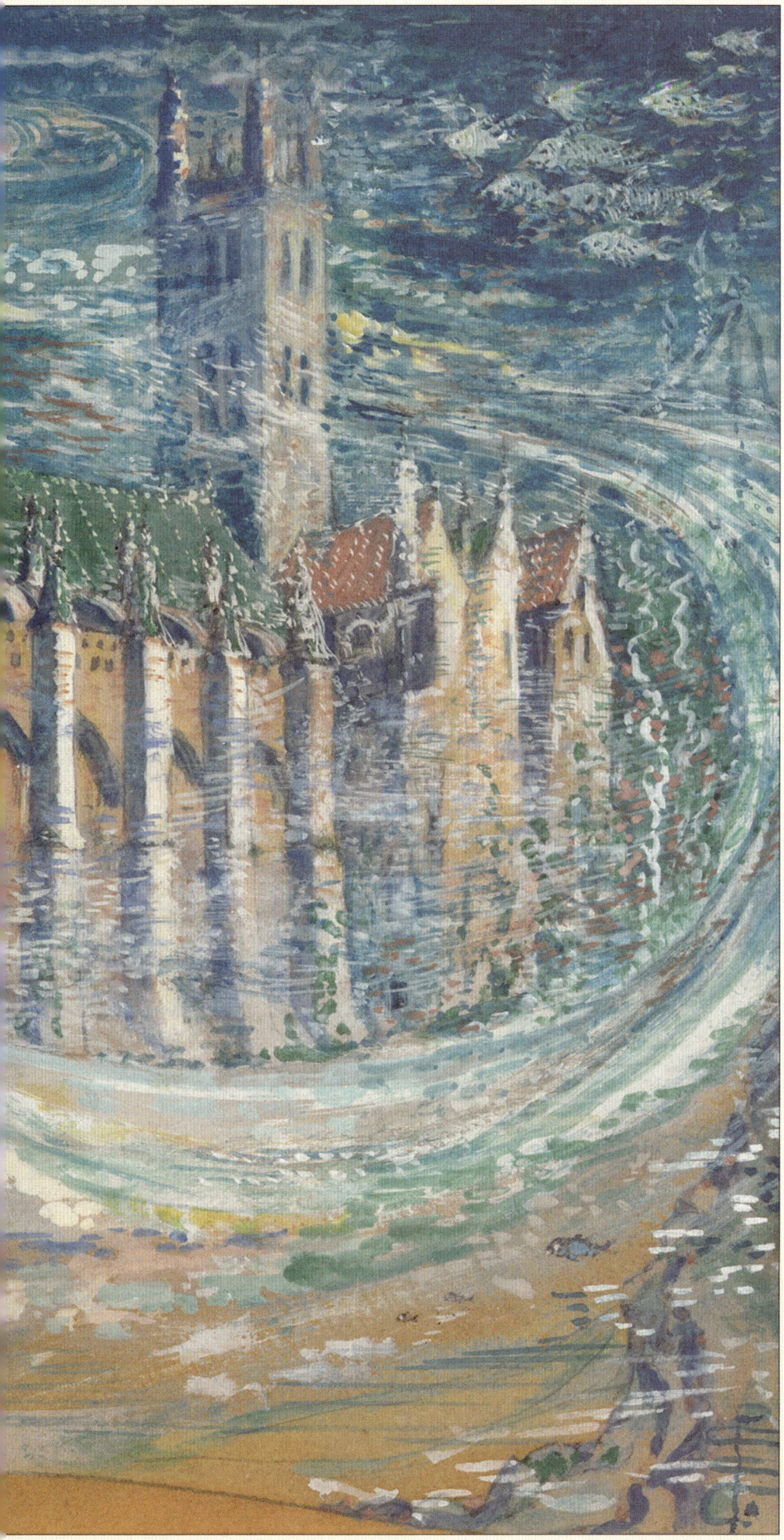

"The water is profoundly deep. At first no form or outline is visible, as down and down, deeper and deeper you sink, without a ripple or a bubble to mark your descent. The watery green medium becomes opalescent and is troubled. A little light grows, and very far away comes the sound of a formal Tone, but heard only for a moment. In front of you the cloudiness of the water is being rolled up, as if by a wind of the underwater world. It ripples, it flows, it rushes, whilst bells peal distinctly through it. Vaguely a form appears. The bells peal louder. Then the Sunken Cathedral in its Close of green weed is outlined clearly, the huge arches and the waving pinnacles. The Tone is heard again. But the pulsing of the sound gives way to a movement of the water in which the image once more grows vague and indistinct. The Cathedral remains almost till the end, when the opalescence and shimmering of the water turns to opacity and the green coolness again supervenes, while one tall strand of weed occupies the place where once the Cathedral was seen." From *The Living Age*, "Art After the War," by Thomas J. Gerrard, March 18, 1916, quoting from an unpublished volume *"Music Drawings"* by Rowland Thurnam

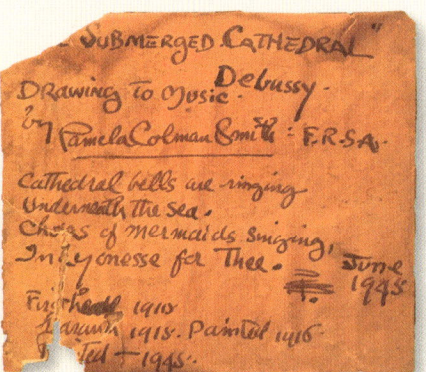

*Debussy's Submerged Cathedral.
Courtesy © Caroline Wise*

343

Way of the Cross

1917

Passion illustration VI by Pamela Colman Smith in *Way of the Cross from the French of Paul Claudel* by Rowland Thurnam

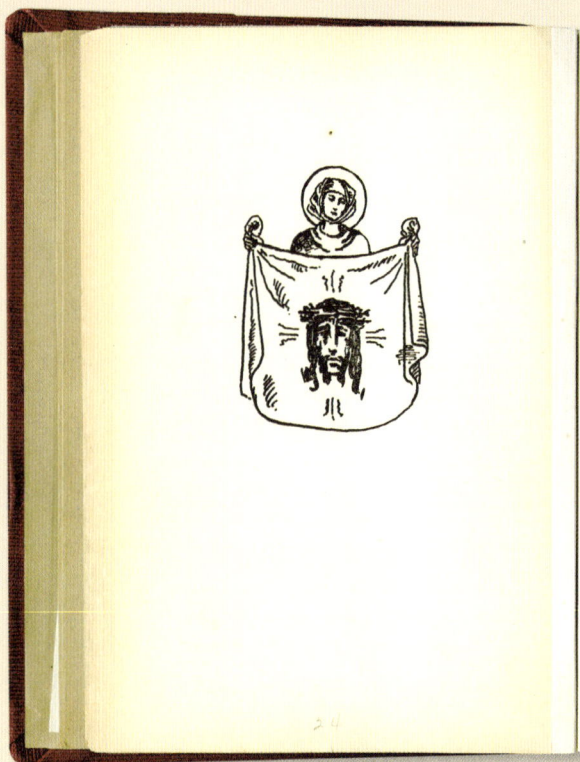

To be returned not later than September 1st, 1938

The Catholic Who's Who, 1939
With a Preface by LORD CLONMORE

(Over 500 pages, 5¾ in. by 4½ in., cloth 6s.)

The CATHOLIC WHO'S WHO, 1939, will be the thirty-second annual volume.

The publishers will be grateful if you will kindly return this form, with any alterations or additions, at your earliest convenience to the Editor, CATHOLIC WHO'S WHO, 43–45 Newgate Street, London, E.C.1.

The details specially requested for inclusion are : name and present title ; year of birth ; parents ; where educated ; career ; marriage and number of children ; published works ; address.

Suggestions of names which could be considered for inclusion in the CATHOLIC WHO'S WHO are cordially invited. The aim of the publishers is to include all Catholics of distinction in every part of the British Commonwealth.

Smith, Miss C. Pamela Colman— b. London 1878, dau. of Chas Edwd Smith and Corinne Colman, of Brooklyn, New York, U.S.A.; art studies at Pratt Institute, Brooklyn, under Fenelosa and Arthur Dow; specialised in book illustration; exhibited at the Internatl Exhbn and Arts and Crafts, London; also at Ghent, Paris, and Leipzig. Recd into the Church at Farm Street 1911: Parc Garland, The Lizard, Cornwall.

The Sinclair Family

1926

Illustrations by Pamela Colman Smith in *The Sinclair Family* by Edith Lyttelton. An account of the author's travels in the Far East and India

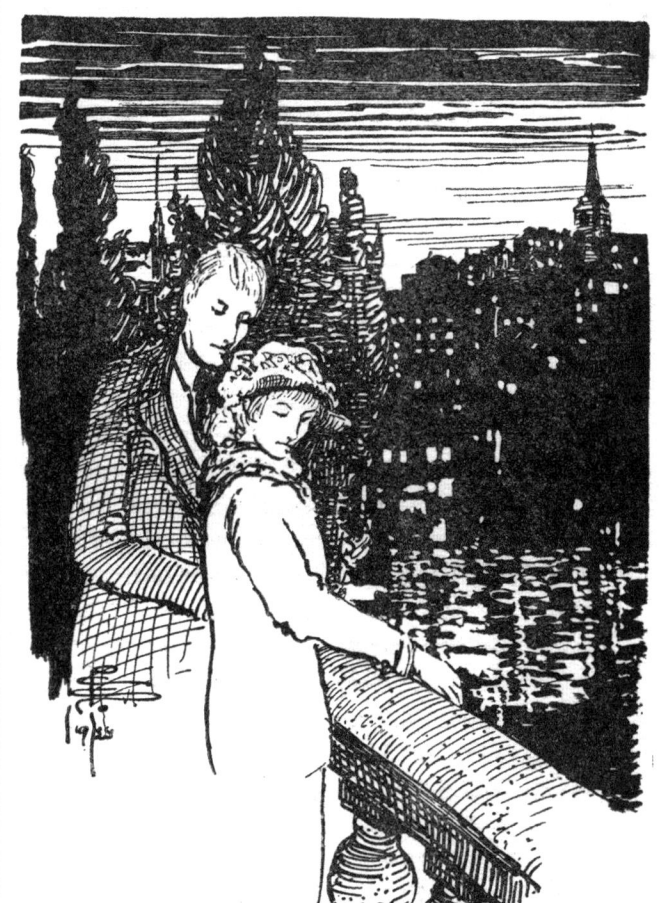

"PETER AND ANN IN STOCKHOLM"

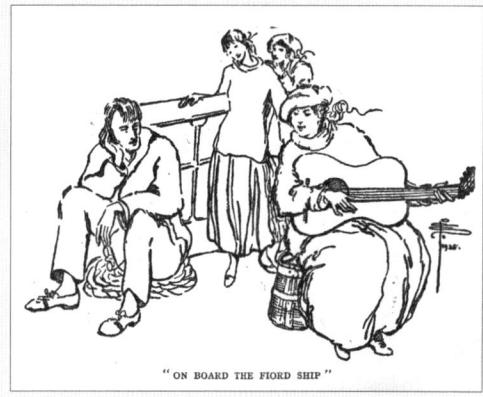

"ON BOARD THE FIORD SHIP"

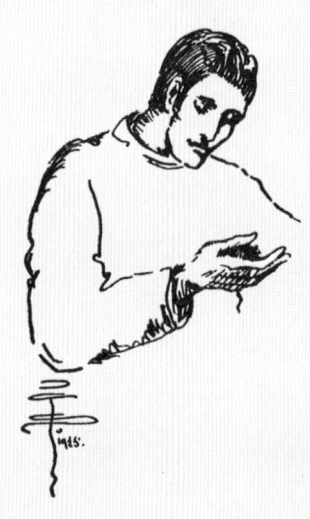

"STRAGGLING WOODEN HOUSES"

1927

Reproduction of "Music Made Visible" by Mrs. Forbes Sempill from *The Illustrated London News*, February 12, 1927 with illustrations by Pamela Colman Smith. Courtesy of Mary Evans Picture Library Ltd.

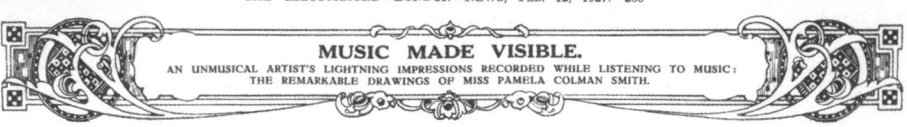

MUSIC MADE VISIBLE.

AN UNMUSICAL ARTIST'S LIGHTNING IMPRESSIONS RECORDED WHILE LISTENING TO MUSIC: THE REMARKABLE DRAWINGS OF MISS PAMELA COLMAN SMITH.

By the HON. MRS. FORBES-SEMPILL. (See Illustrations on two Preceeding Pages.)

"There is a certain border of the mind where all sound becomes visible."
WILLIAM JAMES.—"Varieties of Religious Experience."

Few minds, perhaps, have reached this border, and fewer have the power of reproducing what they see beyond, still less of conveying it to others. Miss Colman Smith is probably unique, for not only does she actually *see* music while it is being played, but, being an exceptionally talented artist, she is able to set down instantly the strange and exquisite pictures that appear before her as she listens. She is not a musician—in fact, she knows nothing whatever about music, nor does she play upon any musical instrument—but she *feels* music so intensely that the sounds really take shape before her eyes. She does not think this is unusual, as she has met and talked with many people who see pictures when hearing music, but they are unable to set them down.

It was on Christmas afternoon, 1900, at the house of Dame Ellen Terry, that Miss Colman Smith did her first drawing to music. Mr. Gordon Craig was playing some Bach, when suddenly, to use her own words, " a shutter clicked back and left a hole in the air about an inch square, and through it I saw a bank and broken ground, the smooth trunks of trees with dark leaves ; across from left to right came dancing and frolicking little elfin people, with the wind blowing through their hair and billowing their dresses. The picture was very vivid and clear, and of beautiful colour, with bluish mist behind the tree trunks. I drew an outline in pencil of what I saw on the edge of a newspaper, and as I finished—in perhaps a minute—the shutter clicked back again." After this, Miss Colman Smith apparently did no more drawings to music for about two years. Then she went to a series of concerts by Arnold Dolmetsch, and again saw the same type of tiny moving pictures. She also began making larger drawings at Queen's Hall concerts ; but some people in the audience objected to the scratching of her pencil, so she took to using a brush. Sometimes she would do as many as twenty or thirty drawings at one concert, and at other times only two or three. She often sees these pictures in colours, and would, of course, prefer to reproduce them so ; but, as the music usually lasts only a very few minutes, there is not time, and she has to content herself using sepia, blue, or black ; and afterwards, if it is something that has appealed to her very much, she does a larger and more finished picture in colour from her original sketch.

Her impressions do not always come in the same way. Sometimes the picture appears and grows in colour and form upon the paper as she draws, and

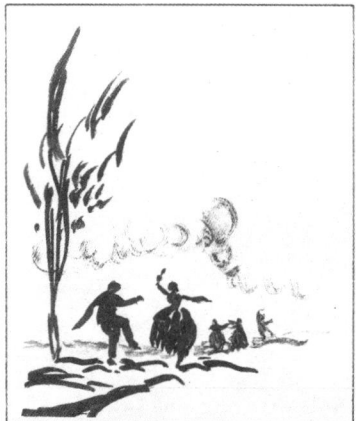

WHAT THE ARTIST SAW DURING A RENDERING OF SCHUBERT'S "MOMENT MUSICAL" (OP. 94, NO. 3): A DRAWING BY MISS PAMELA COLMAN SMITH, MADE DURING THE PERFORMANCE.

she seems just to trace over it with her brush. At other times it is a living and moving picture that she sees before her in a frame as already described : this is the most usual way. She does not seek to analyse these impressions at the time, as this would interfere with the subconscious action ; she is absolutely sincere, and sets down only what she sees, holding her imagination well in check. In fact, she says that, if she ever alters her drawing in the least detail from what she sees, the picture instantly breaks up and disappears. She feels quite detached from these drawings, and is immensely interested in them, viewing them as an outsider who has never seen them before ; but she is perfectly conscious all the time she is drawing, and puts into her work all the skill of which she is master. Each is a perfectly complete picture, and, although done with the rapidity of a lightning artist, is finished in every detail ; usually as the last notes of music die away, her brush is putting the finishing strokes to the picture. She nearly always begins at the lower left-hand corner of the paper, and works upwards with big, sweeping strokes, and never pauses or hesitates for an instant, unless the music does not appeal to her ; then she either draws nothing at all or leaves a half-finished sketch.

The music of some composers moves her more strongly than that of others, and in such cases her drawings are more satisfactory and complete. For instance, her drawings to Bach, Beethoven, César Franck, and Debussy are usually better and more interesting than those to Chopin, Mendelssohn, or Brahms, although she has done many lovely drawings to these also. There is one only one composer whose music always disturbs and affects her adversely, and that is Wagner. It sends her mad with irritation and fury, and she cannot draw to it, as she sees nothing but the obvious material fact, which does not inspire her. She senses nothing behind it. It is perhaps better to describe in her own words what she feels when listening to Wagner music : " Scratchy little brown fir-trees rising through a brown fog ; my scalp tingles and my hair pricks ; I feel so full of rage that I want to crack the heads of people together like nuts. When it is played in a room, thick curtains of brown spiders' webs appear, sticky and evil-smelling. I have come into a room after Wagner music had been played and found that sickly, sweet, evil smell clinging to everything. I have had to leave a concert when Wagner music was being played." This is quite genuine, I know, for I have tried experiments myself with Miss Colman Smith on many occasions.

The music of Debussy seems to her more natural than that of any other composer, to have more in common with the sounds in nature—not the ordinary singing or chirruping of birds, but sounds like bells in the wind, and a curious pulsing under-rhythm, beating and throbbing—like the breathing of living things and the sap running in the trees. The composer told her once that he always heard music in the trees and upon the hills, and often composed his music out in the woods. She has done some really weird and wonderful drawings to Debussy's music—some to the composer's own playing. The first time she heard any was in 1908. To " L'Après-Midi d'un Faune " she drew a faun asleep in a tangle of under-growth in a wood, with nymphs and hamadryads around him. She had no idea of the title of the music ; as a matter of fact, she hardly ever remembers the titles, even when she has been told them, unless she hears the same piece continually, and, even if she does sometimes remember it, she does not always do the same drawing to it. Perhaps the most strange and inexplicable fact about these drawings is the consistency of the ideas in some pictures and the utter inconsistency in others. To " La Lune descend " she did several drawings at different times (1908-1909-1910) and they hardly varied. It was the same with " Granada " and " Jardins sous la Pluie." Debussy was delighted with her drawings when she showed them to him in 1910, and told her that they developed and carried on his own idea in many cases.

When she first heard Beethoven's music she saw only an open plain, dun-colour, dried and burnt with the sun, with hills around and a river winding in the middle distance. A few months later she saw the same plain, but this time it was a greyish-green colour, and still empty. Then, suddenly, she heard the beating of drums, and, with banners flying and spears glinting, an army came rushing across the plain from afar off, then coming nearer ; behind the hills were great rounded clouds tipped with rose-colour, against a deep blue sky. But I could describe hundreds of these drawings which I have seen. Each one has its own particular attraction, and they are all obviously the work of an artist, and, as such, will be appreciated, apart from a certain psychological value which cannot but appeal to those interested in this absorbing subject.

Miss Colman Smith's drawings were described by Lewis Hind in 1912 as : " Sign-posts on a bye-path to the art of the future." Perhaps many may be interested in them from the artistic as well as from the psychological point of view. Many also may try to explain them, and find it difficult to arrive at any logical or satisfactory explanation ; but the fact will remain that " There are more things in heaven and earth Than are dreamt of in our philosophy."

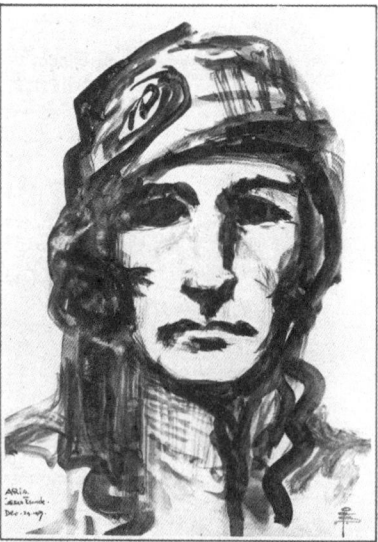

THE IMAGE EVOKED IN THE ARTIST'S MIND, AND RECORDED WHILE LISTENING TO CÉSAR FRANCK'S "ARIA": A DRAWING BY MISS COLMAN SMITH, MADE ON DECEMBER 24, 1917.

A note by the artist mentions that this drawing was much admired by Dr. John G. Vance, who recently drew attention to the psychological interest of her pictorial impressions of music. Other examples are illustrated on pages 258 and 259.

Drawings by Courtesy of the Artist. (Copyright Reserved.)

THE "SHAPES" OF FAMOUS MUSIC—AS SEEN BY AN ARTIST.

Drawings by Miss Pamela Colman Smith. By Courtesy of the Artist. (Artist's Copyright Reserved.)

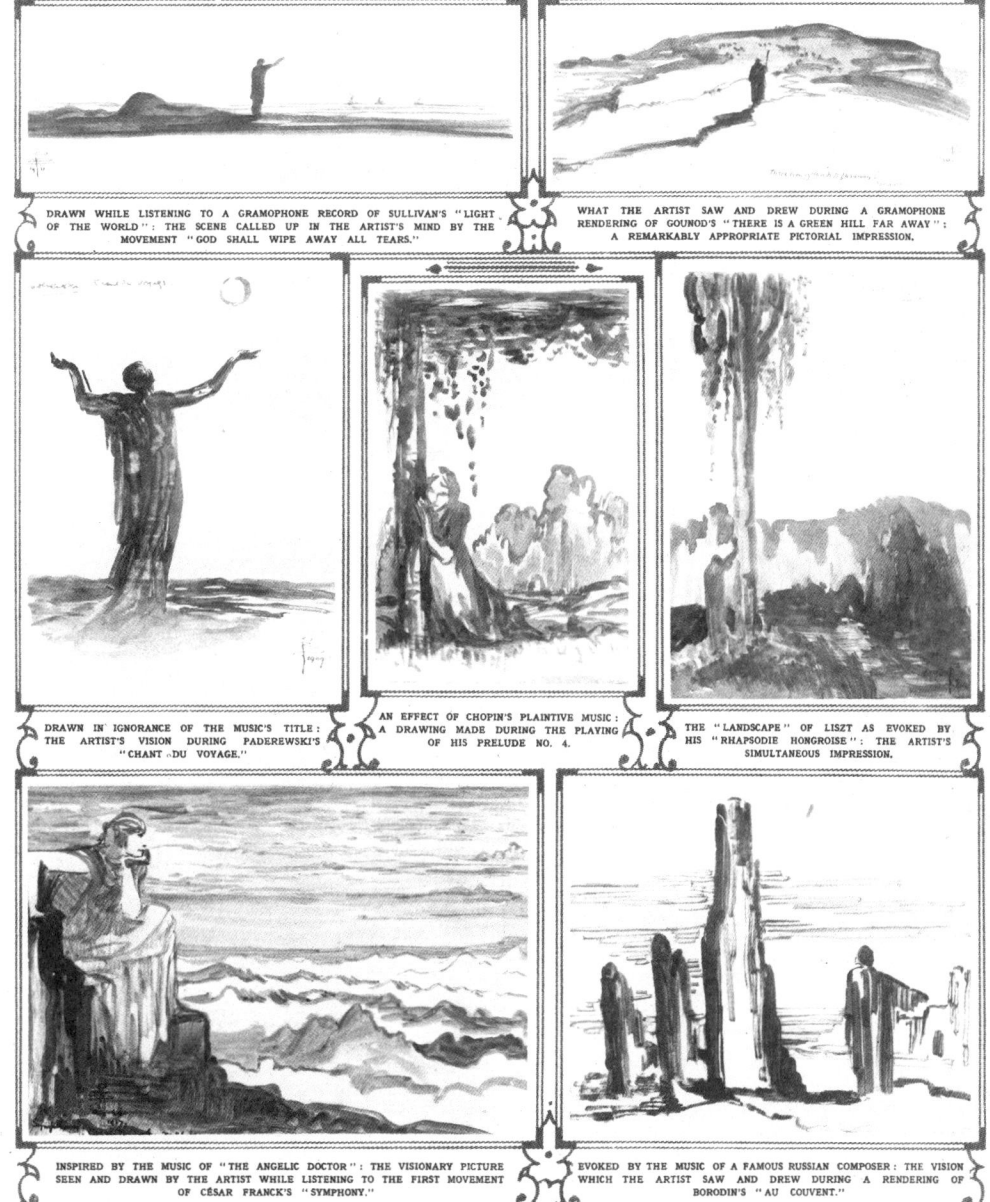

DRAWN WHILE LISTENING TO A GRAMOPHONE RECORD OF SULLIVAN'S "LIGHT OF THE WORLD": THE SCENE CALLED UP IN THE ARTIST'S MIND BY THE MOVEMENT "GOD SHALL WIPE AWAY ALL TEARS."

WHAT THE ARTIST SAW AND DREW DURING A GRAMOPHONE RENDERING OF GOUNOD'S "THERE IS A GREEN HILL FAR AWAY": A REMARKABLY APPROPRIATE PICTORIAL IMPRESSION.

DRAWN IN IGNORANCE OF THE MUSIC'S TITLE: THE ARTIST'S VISION DURING PADEREWSKI'S "CHANT DU VOYAGE."

AN EFFECT OF CHOPIN'S PLAINTIVE MUSIC: A DRAWING MADE DURING THE PLAYING OF HIS PRELUDE NO. 4.

THE "LANDSCAPE" OF LISZT AS EVOKED BY HIS "RHAPSODIE HONGROISE": THE ARTIST'S SIMULTANEOUS IMPRESSION.

INSPIRED BY THE MUSIC OF "THE ANGELIC DOCTOR": THE VISIONARY PICTURE SEEN AND DRAWN BY THE ARTIST WHILE LISTENING TO THE FIRST MOVEMENT OF CÉSAR FRANCK'S "SYMPHONY."

EVOKED BY THE MUSIC OF A FAMOUS RUSSIAN COMPOSER: THE VISION WHICH THE ARTIST SAW AND DREW DURING A RENDERING OF BORODIN'S "AU COUVENT."

We reproduce here (and on the opposite page) remarkable interpretative drawings of music which are discussed in the article on page 260 by the Hon. Mrs. Forbes-Sempill, daughter of Sir John Lavery. They were also mentioned, not long ago, in a letter to the "Times" by the Very Rev. Dr. John G. Vance, Professor of Philosophy at St. Edmund's College, Ware, who is the author of a thesis on the experimental psychology of recognition. "This extraordinary gift of translating from the realm of sounds into pictorial imagery," he writes, "has been practised for about twenty-six years by Miss Pamela Colman Smith, now at the Lizard, Cornwall. The lady is an artist of distinction, and whilst the music is actually being played gives a brush drawing of what she sees. We have tested her on many occasions with new and unknown music, and have been surprised at the beauty of her drawings, and above all at the accuracy of the delineation of the music and its title. Her hand works feverishly whilst the music lasts. When it ceases, the brush falls from her hand, as she *sees* no more. It is to her as if the sun had suddenly been totally obscured as she watched some landscape. It seems almost as if she *sees* sound; so rapid is the translation, and so strangely vivid and varied the impression." Dr. Vance also referred to an exhibition of pictures suggested by music by another artist, Miss Juliet Williams.

THE ILLUSTRATED LONDON NEWS, FEB. 12, 1927.—259

REMARKABLE "VISIONS" OF MUSIC: "AUTOMATIC" IMPRESSIONS.

DRAWINGS BY MISS PAMELA COLMAN SMITH. BY COURTESY OF THE ARTIST. (ARTIST'S COPYRIGHT RESERVED.)

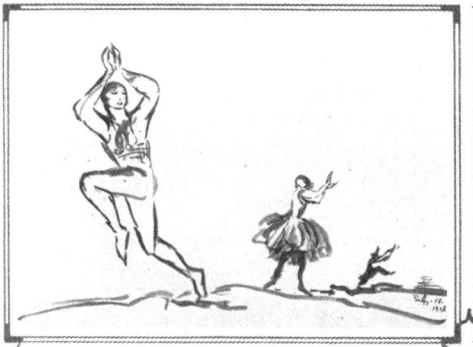

A PICTORIAL INTERPRETATION OF SCHUMANN'S KINDERSCENEN NO. 3—"CATCH ME": A DRAWING MADE WITHOUT KNOWLEDGE OF THE TITLE WHILE THE PIECE WAS BEING PLAYED.

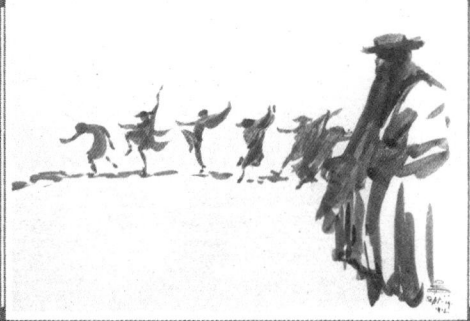

DRAWN DURING THE PLAYING OF MODERN SPANISH MUSIC BY AN ARTIST WITHOUT KNOWLEDGE OF ITS TITLE OR OF THE COMPOSER: A SPANISH DANCE VISUALISED WHILE LISTENING TO ALBENIZ.

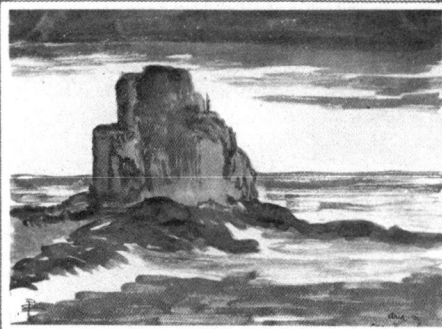

BY AN ARTIST WHO HAS BEEN INTERPRETING MUSIC PICTORIALLY DURING PERFORMANCE FOR SOME TWENTY-SIX YEARS: MISS COLMAN SMITH'S VISION DURING CÉSAR FRANCK'S "ARIA."

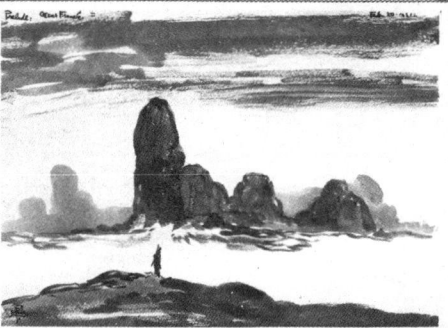

TYPICAL OF THE PICTURES SEEN BY THE ARTIST, IN COLOUR AND THROUGH "A HOLE IN THE AIR," WHILE MUSIC IS PLAYED: A PICTORIAL INTERPRETATION OF CÉSAR FRANCK'S "PRELUDE."

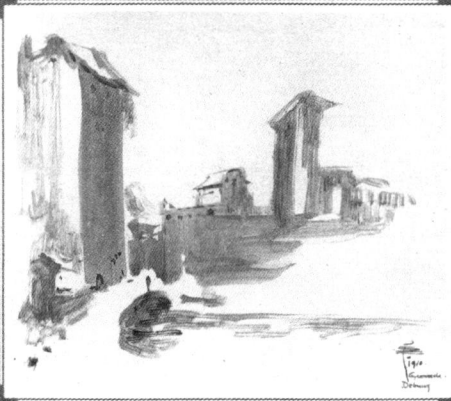

ADMIRED BY THE COMPOSER AS DEVELOPING HIS OWN IDEA: ONE OF SEVERAL DRAWINGS MADE BY MISS COLMAN SMITH AT VARIOUS TIMES, BUT ALL SIMILAR, DURING THE PLAYING OF DEBUSSY'S "GRANADA."

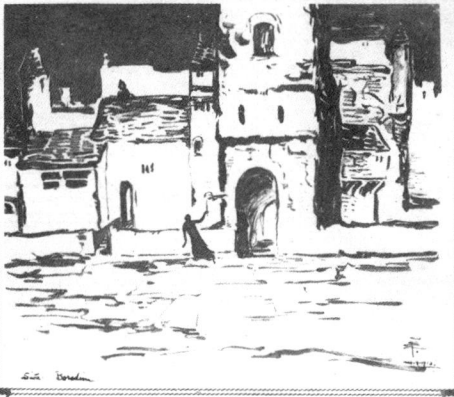

VISUALISED BY THE ARTIST AS "A LIVING AND MOVING PICTURE IN A FRAME ABOUT AN INCH SQUARE": A SCENE DRAWN WHILE BORODIN'S "SUITE" WAS BEING PLAYED.

It is a fascinating question whether music can be interpreted in terms of pictorial art. Many musical works purport to express aspects of nature, and some even have geographical titles, while musical critics frequently talk of "colour." Whether there is any definite connection between certain sounds and certain forms is a matter for scientific investigation. Very interesting evidence of such a connection is afforded by the remarkable drawings of Miss Pamela Colman Smith, described by Lewis Hind as "sign-posts on a bye-path to the art of the future." Examples are given above and on pages 258 and 260, with an article on her work by the Hon. Mrs. Forbes-Sempill. "The music of Debussy," we read, "seems to her more natural than that of any other composer.... She has done some really weird and wonderful drawings to Debussy's music—some to the composer's own playing.... Perhaps the most strange and inexplicable fact about these drawings is the consistency of the ideas in some pictures, and the utter inconsistency in others. To 'La Lune Descend' she did several drawings at different times (1908-9-10), and they hardly varied. It was the same with 'Granada.' Debussy was delighted with her drawings when she showed them to him, and told her that they developed his own idea in many cases." She always sees her pictures in colours, as it were through "a hole in the air about an inch square."

Duet

1946

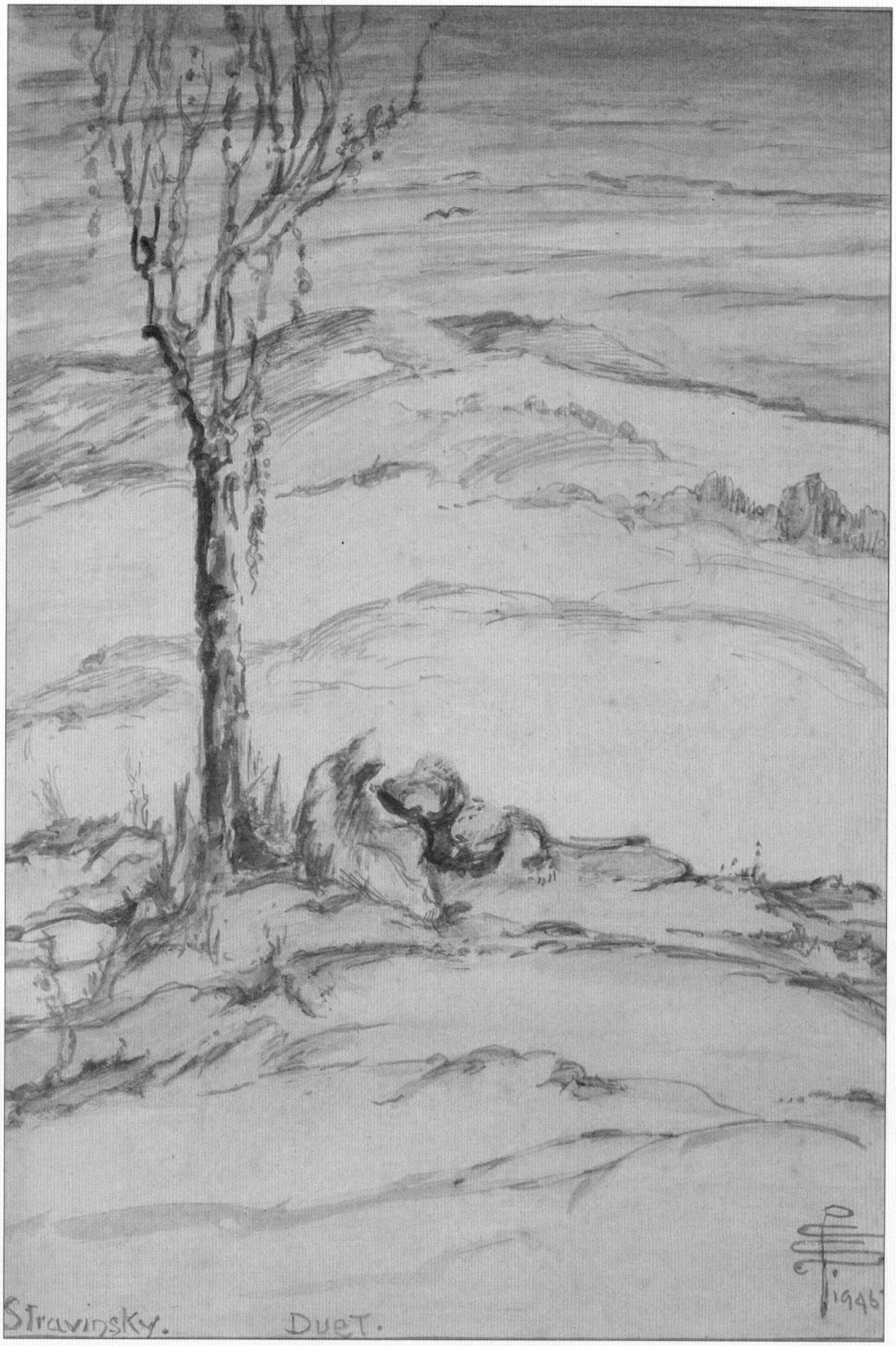

Drawing by Pamela Colman Smith, watercolor on paper, inspired by Stravinsky's Duet

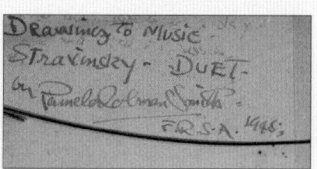

INFLUENCES AND EXPRESSION IN THE RIDER-WAITE TAROT DECK

"All arts are branches of one tree."
Pamela Colman Smith, 1910

Introduction

THIS CHAPTER EXPLORES SOME OF THE SYMBOLISM IN THE RIDER-WAITE TAROT DECK, AND the ways Pamela Colman Smith drew inspiration from her own life, beliefs, interests and friends at the time she created the cards.

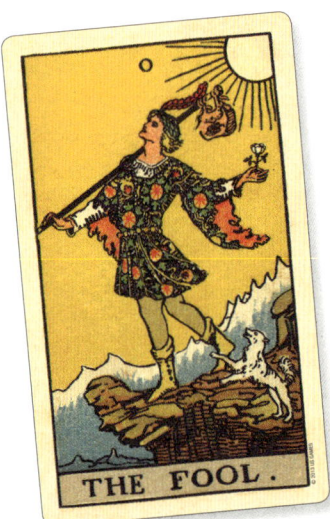
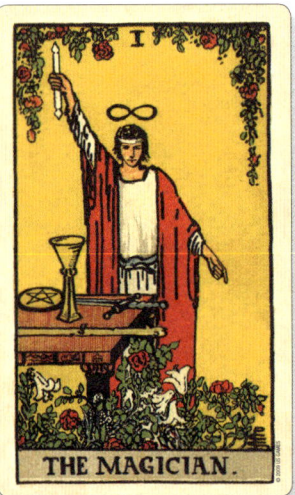

There are two groups of cards in the tarot deck. First are the 22 Trump cards (also called the Major Arcana), which are the most tradition-bound, dating back to 15th century Renaissance cards that were used in card games. These cards are numbered and have names and illustrations, for example, The Fool or The Magician, but they do not correspond to any suits, nor do they have parallels in the traditional playing card deck. Second are the 56 Minor Arcana cards, which have suits similar to those in today's playing cards that correspond to Cups (Hearts), Pentacles (Diamonds), Wands (Clubs), and Swords (Spades). Additionally, each suit relates to one of the four basic elements—earth (Pentacles), air (Swords), fire (Wands) and water (Cups). What's fascinating is how much the four elements—earth, air, fire and water—dominate the imagery in Pamela's visionary paintings, a characteristic that not surprisingly carries over into her tarot designs.

There are four court cards—Page, Knight, Queen, King—in each suit.[1] The court cards display medieval-style military or crusader figures—the Page and Knight—and royalty—Queen and King—in each suit. According to tarot scholar Mary Greer, the court cards were based on designs by one of the founders of the Golden Dawn and somewhat resemble the very popular photographic postcards (called cabinet cards) of Victorian actors in costume. Pamela Colman Smith drew several of the court cards in the Rider-Waite Tarot as representations of Victorian and Edwardian actors in costume. They were, in fact, actor friends of hers whom she knew well and admired.

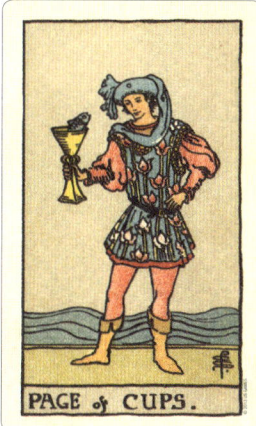 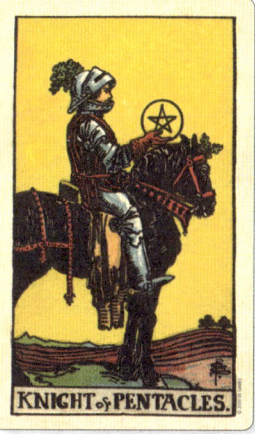 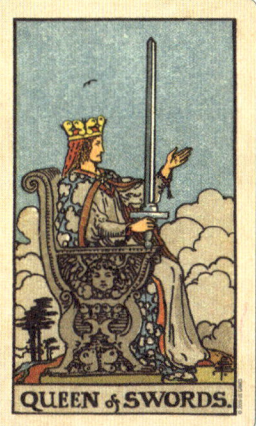 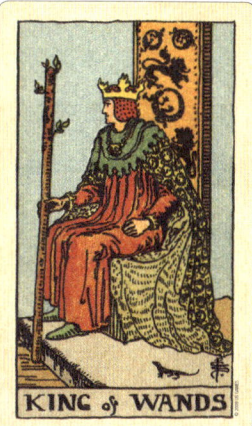

In addition to the court cards in each suit, there are numbered cards from One to Ten, also called "pip" cards.

To tarot historians, what is particularly interesting about the Rider-Waite deck is that it was the first modern deck to have pictorial scenes on every numbered pip card in each suit. Pamela's detailed artwork is what makes the tarot deck more accessible and easier to use. The pictorial scenes enable tarot readers to view each card and project themselves into the scene and to identify with those actions and meanings. The Rider-Waite deck also helps indicate Pamela Colman Smith's own concerns at the time, as she was largely responsible for creating it. Waite's descriptions of the Minor Arcana cards in *The Pictorial Key to the*

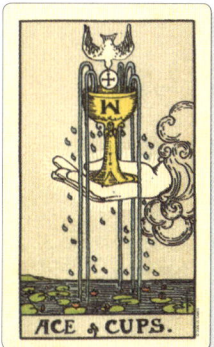 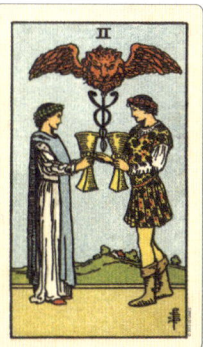 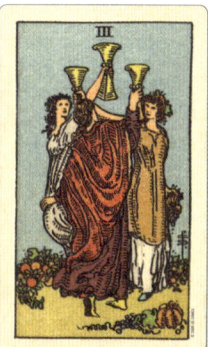 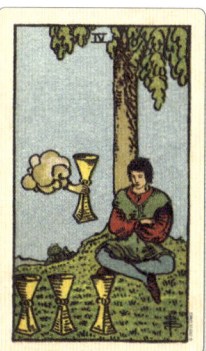 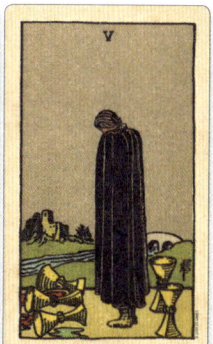

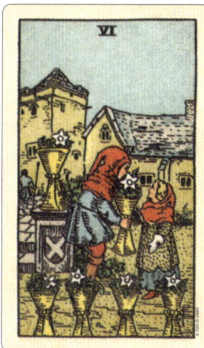 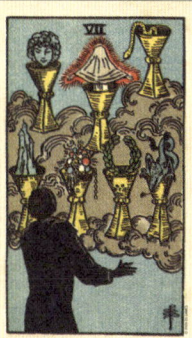 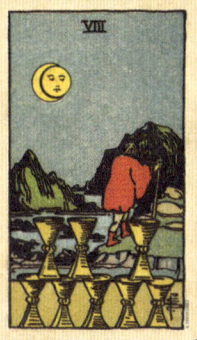 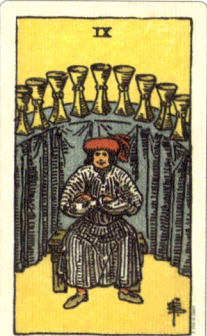 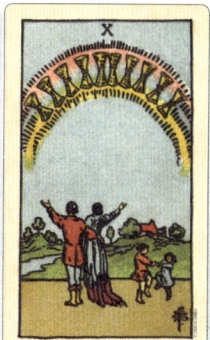

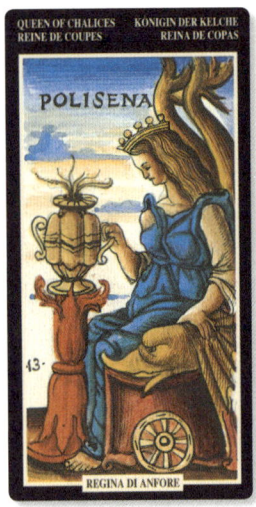 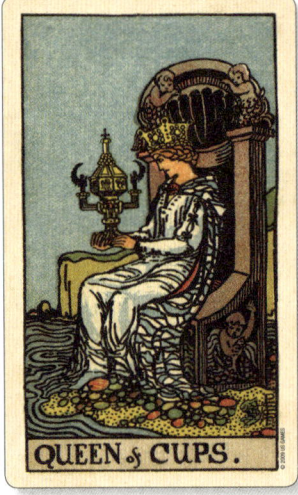

Tarot are considerably briefer than his discussion of the Major Arcana. Therefore, it's impossible to know now whose idea it was originally to illustrate the numbered cards. There were photographs of the Renaissance Sola-Busca Tarot, the only earlier deck that had full illustrations on the numbered cards, on display at the British Museum from 1907 on. Waite's knowledge of the Sola-Busca cards—or lack thereof—is unknown. Pamela, the artist and art historian, certainly was familiar with the deck, as she used a few of the Minor Arcana cards as sources for several of her own pip cards and court cards.

The Sola-Busca and Rider-Waite Queen of Cups

Pamela Colman Smith and Arthur Edward Waite

How and why did Waite and Pamela come together to create the Rider-Waite Tarot? In 1901, just after Pamela said she had her first vision to music, she joined London's Isis-Urania Temple of the Hermetic Order of the Golden Dawn, a secret group devoted to the practice of magic, occultism, religious studies and mysticism. Disagreements among members led to a schism in 1903. Those interested in magic and occultism followed William Butler Yeats into his branch, while Pamela and others interested in Judeo-Christian mysticism went with Arthur Waite.

As Waite came to know Pamela better, he realized she had mystic and visionary qualities. Not only did he regard her as psychic, but he was pleased she already knew something of tarot.[2] So she was the perfect person to create a "rectified" tarot deck, that is, one based on Judeo-Christian mysteries rather than occult magic. Waite had been Catholic but left the church, while Pamela converted to Catholicism a little over a year after she drew the tarot. As Waite said:

> I…have interested a very skilful and original artist in the proposal to design a set [of tarot cards]. Miss Pamela Coleman [sic] Smith, in addition to her obvious gifts, has some knowledge of the Tarot values; she has lent a sympathetic ear to my proposal to rectify the symbolism by reference to channels of knowledge which are not in the open day, and we have had help from one who is deeply versed in the subject. The result…is a marriage of art and symbolism for…a true Tarot under one of its aspects.[3]

Much of Waite's writing is obscure and often purposely misleading perhaps to protect the public from ideas Waite found "dangerous," an attitude recalling the Greek philosopher Pythagoras and his secret "Pythagorean Brotherhood."[4] And Pamela, because she kept her Golden Dawn vow of secrecy, never discussed anything about possible meanings in her cards. Without evidence to the contrary, we can surmise that whatever other ideas Pamela may have brought to her interpretation of the images, her views on tarot were essentially compatible with Waite's. Those ideas were mystical to the extent that mysticism can be expressed in words or pictures.

For Waite, the tarot was a vessel for meanings with both obvious and esoteric aspects. Less attention has been paid to the possibility that Pamela Colman Smith may have placed her own hidden meanings and symbols in the cards. We cannot know today how much of Waite's thinking about the tarot's hidden aspects he shared with Pamela, nor which aspects of her ideas about the images she shared with him. Clearly they were "sympathetic," though, as tarot scholar Gertrude Moakley wrote in 1959:

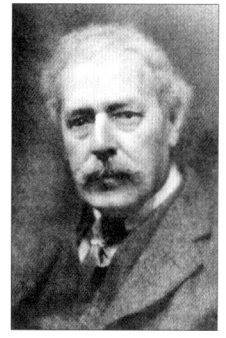

Arthur Edward Waite

> This set of mystical Tarot cards…seemed at the time a mere trifle to both of them, compared with their more ambitious projects. Yet their Tarot is one of the few published works by either of them that has remained almost continuously in print for nearly fifty years. Toward the end of his life, Waite did come to realize that of all his monumental works, all his multitudinous activities…, this little Tarot was one of the most fruitful. Yet at the time he was doing the actual work, it was little more than a delightful avocation…. How often this happens! The little thing which is just 'tossed off' turns out to be the epitome of all its author stood for, still alive and fresh when all the rest of his work has begun to smell of dried lavender. And when a brilliant man and woman like Waite and Pamela Smith work together, his masculinity and her femininity are sometimes flint and steel to produce new brilliance.[5]

The Secret Tradition

FOR WAITE, THE TAROT'S TRUMP CARDS WERE CARRIERS OF WHAT HE CALLED THE "SECRET Tradition" in Western Christian mysticism, an idea he emphasized strongly in *The Pictorial Key to the Tarot* and elsewhere. In part, this inclination grew from Waite's interest in the story of the Holy Grail, which he wrote about in *The Hidden Church of the Holy Graal*, a book published in 1909 while he and Pamela were working together on their tarot cards.[6] In the Arthurian Grail cycle, the four objects associated with Christ's Passion are the Grail, the Lance, the Sword and the Dish. These objects correspond to the tarot's four suits of Cups, Staves (Wands), Swords and Pentacles respectively. Undoubtedly, Pamela felt comfortable with this Arthurian interpretation, given her interest in Arthurian legend, suggested by her increasing attraction to Catholicism. Her letters to Mary Reed also evince a strong interest in the legend, especially as a subject for her art. In August 1899, with her father, Pamela visited Tintagel, the romantic ruins of a castle on the north coast of Cornwall where King Arthur was conceived, according to Malory in *Le Morte d'Arthur*. On this trip, Pamela also met with Henry Irving.[7]

While he derived some of his tarot symbolism from Western literary and religious sources, Waite thought that it was only surface meanings that were specific to particular cultures and periods. He believed that the "meaning behind meaning" i.e, the Secret Tradition, was universal. He insisted that the "ultimate and highest meaning" of the trump cards "lies deeper than the common language of picture or hieroglyph." Yet he felt that all the cards—even the pip cards—had a "meaning beyond meaning;" a surface meaning and a deeper meaning that couldn't be put into words.[8] So the surface interpretation of the images, which most people could see, was a pictorial expression of some aspect of mysticism in the physical world. Such double levels of meaning are much like Pamela's mysterious paintings to music, which are almost impossible to interpret definitively.

Waite's belief in this universal tarot meaning is clear in comments he published with the Rider-Waite Tarot: "The Tarot is, of course, allegorical—that is…it is symbolism—but allegory and symbol are catholic [universal]—of all countries, nations and times; they are not more Egyptian than Mexican; they are of Europe and Cathay, of Tibet beyond the Himalayas and of the London gutters."[9] Likewise, Pamela believed the "musical" character of her art gave it a universal appeal, an idea she had absorbed at Pratt from Arthur Dow and his mentor, the eminent Japanologist Ernest Fenollosa, who lectured at Pratt periodically. The similarity between Waite's comments, above, and Fenollosa's celebration of spirituality embedded in the material world (the "meaning behind meaning") is truly remarkable:

> "We express, but it is not a matter of indifference what we express. Thought, sentiment, analogy, symbolism, the interpenetration of meaning, plane behind plane…the organic union of parts, the intrinsic beauty of life…, even the spiritual significance of trees and rocks, and mountains, and water;… all these like so many glintings of prismatic color refracted from the facets of matter, an elemental harmony which the Master Artist has woven into the substance of the world."[10]

It's probably at least partly for this reason—the notion that Spirit is embedded in nature—that Pamela created elaborate scenes in her tarot drawings, especially in the pip cards, and why almost all of the cards are set in nature. Similar perceptions of the divine in the ordinary aspects of nature had been communicated to Pamela from her earliest years by her family, for example through the nature poetry and Swedenborgian mysticism of her grandparents Samuel and Pamelia Chandler Colman.

Chislehurst

ONE OF THE EARLIEST INFLUENCES ON PAMELA WAS LIKELY THE WORK OF ILLUSTRATOR MARCUS Ward, Illuminator to the Queen. The Ward family, with a large collection of his artwork, lived next door to the Smiths when they were in Chislehurst, on the outskirts of London, from 1879 to 1881. His children's books, *Marcus Ward's Golden Picture Books* and others, comprise "Lays and Legends" and fairytales, with illustrations in color and metallic gold in a medieval style. He also published nursery rhymes and songs for children. An advertisement by the publisher Nimmo in the back of Ward's books offers an apt description.

> "Gorgeously Illuminated after the Medieval manner in Colours and Gold by Marcus Ward Illuminator to the Queen. Each Story or Legend is illustrated with a set of brilliant Pictures designed in the quaint spirit of Medieval times and printed in Colours and Gold by Marcus Ward Illuminator to the Queen. The charm of novelty is still further heightened by the Stories being related in Antient Ballad form with appropriate Music arranged in an easy style for Voice and Pianoforte suited to little folks or great folks and minstrels of all degrees" [11]

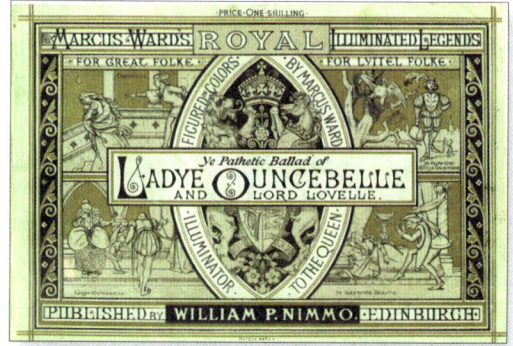

Above: Marcus Ward, *Ye Pathetic Ballad of Ladye Ouncebelle and Lord Lovelle. Marcus Ward's Royal Illuminated Legends for Great Folke for Lyttel Folk. Figured in Colors by Marcus Ward Illuminator to the Queen.* Edinburgh: William P. Nimmo, 1872

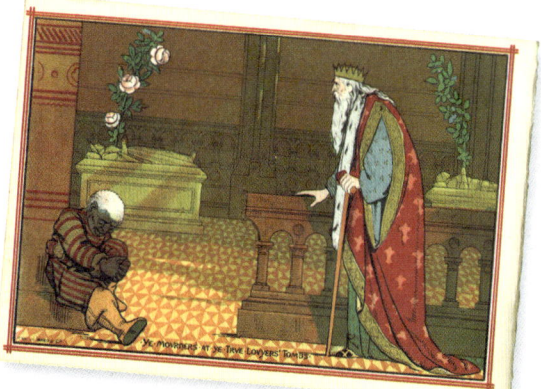

Below: Marcus Ward, "Ye Mourners at Ye True Lovyers' Tombs," *Ye Pathetic Ballad of Ladye Ouncebelle and Lord Lovelle. Marcus Ward's Royal Illuminated Legends for Great Folke for Lyttel Folk. Figured in Colors by Marcus Ward Illuminator to the Queen.* Edinburgh: William P. Nimmo, 1872

The combination of pictures and music must have fascinated young Pamela, who probably had the books read to her by her parents. Her mother Corinne was an extraordinary singer, according to Corinne's brother Samuel Colman, who also was a painter. Corinne likely sang the songs to Pamela, thus reinforcing for her at a very early age the connections among pictures, stories and music, especially "antient music," meaning Renaissance and Baroque music.[12] Ward's work was frequently advertised in *The Publishers' Circular and Booksellers' Record* and has been reprinted more recently.[13] His illustration style uses gold and flat colors with dark outlines and compressed perspective. Depth is generally indicated by overlapping, another medieval stylistic trait. While similar characteristics can be seen in some Japanese art, Ward's work is not Japanese in style—rather, it's an archaic style harking back to the Middle Ages. Although both Pamela and her father Charles collected Japanese Ukiyo-e prints, Pamela worked in many different styles. Much of her work is similar to Ward's archaic style. It's possible that Pamela's later use of yellow backgrounds in the tarot cards was influenced by the flat yellow spaces found so often in Marcus Ward's prints.

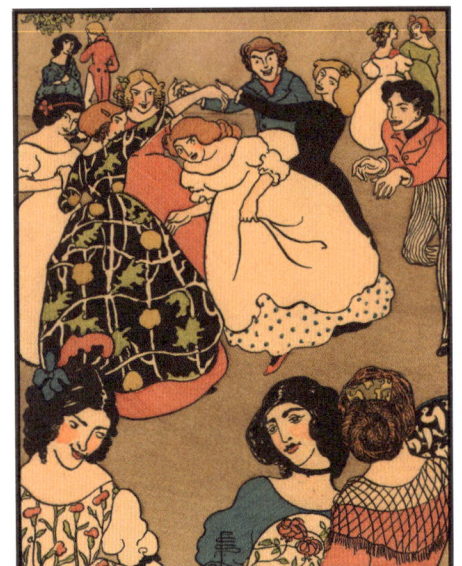

"Twelfth Night Merrymakers" by Pamela Colman Smith, 1898. Courtesy of Melinda Boyd Parsons

Some of Pamela's early books and prints, done shortly after she left Pratt, do show Japanese influence. Examples include the 1898 print, the "Twelfth Night Merrymakers" and a swirling sea image in *The Golden Vanity*, 1899. The Japanese stylistic traits in these works include, first, an "elevated" or "tilted perspective" that creates a sense of looking down on things that are close to the "front" of the image while seeing more distant objects straight on. This is particularly noticeable in "Twelfth Night Merrymakers." Second, the Japanese prints that influenced Pamela tended to cut off figures or other objects at the margins of the picture, which creates the sense of a larger space existing beyond the edges of the picture. This artistic device draws viewers into the work to try to imagine what lies outside their field of vision. Third, Japanese prints use flat, unmodulated color with a lack of the shading that creates a sense of three-dimensional modeling within a picture. The fourth characteristic is the use of black outlines varying between thin and thick, with thin, delicate lines predominating.

During her years in Chislehurst, Pamela's love for the beauty of nature was first manifested. She later told Albert Bigelow Paine in 1901, "[Chislehurst] has lovely woods and clouds of bluebells!" It must have seemed quite a change from London, and later from Manchester, Manhattan and Brooklyn. Chislehurst obviously stayed in her mind as an ideal locale and landscape. Perhaps it contributed to her avid interest in the bucolic Kent countryside, where Ellen Terry's beautiful Tudor house Smallhythe was located.

Spiritualism and Arts and Crafts Movement

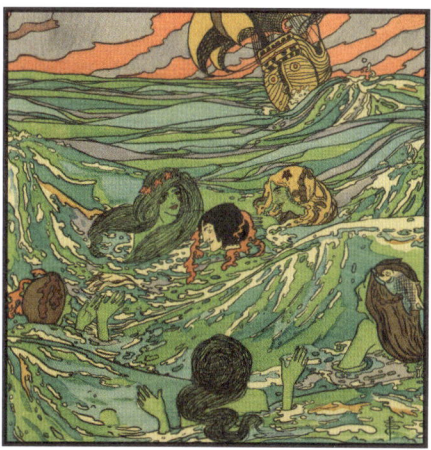

Illustration from "The Golden Vanity" by Pamela Colman Smith, 1899

Upon leaving Chislehurst, the Smiths moved to Didsbury, in Fielden Park, a verdant, quiet suburb of Manchester, England, just north of the River Mersey. The Smiths were a well-to-do middle class family, employing several live-in servants.[14] The new 1880 rail line in Didsbury made for easy commuting into Manchester, where Charles Smith plied his trade in textiles and upholstery. Few other facts are known of their time there, but two elements of life in the Manchester area are likely to have influenced Pamela Colman Smith: Spiritualism and the Arts and Crafts movement.

Manchester's working class—for instance, those who worked in the textile mills—generally led grueling lives, dying young from overwork, poverty, and pollution in the mills and city. Given high mortality rates among these workers, the new 19th-century religion of Spiritualism took strong hold in Manchester and the English Midlands generally, as well as in northern England and London.

> "In mid-nineteenth-century England all manner of persons enjoyed the latest rage of summoning the spirit bands. Throughout the land solemn Victorian furniture creaked, tipped, and danced at the behest of small assembled companies sitting in the darkness in states varying from uncontrolled mirth to ghastly apprehension. But despite the fact that Queen Victoria and Gladstone were known to have dabbled, it was in the Midlands and the North, among the industrialised working class, that spiritualism initially took a firm hold."[15]

The politically progressive middle class in Manchester's suburbs—the Smith family among them—was immersed in the Arts and Crafts movement, which tried to replace cheap, mass produced factory goods and assembly-line construction with a craftsmanly production mode. The aim was to make factory labor more satisfying and enriching, as well as to bring joy and beauty to the lives of the working class through availability of Arts and Crafts furniture, carpets, books and so forth. While this was a wonderful idea, it was incredibly unrealistic. Few factories had an interest in moving away from mindless,

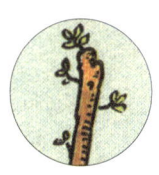

dangerous, underpaid and overworked assembly-line practice since it was good for their bottom line. Further, most Arts and Crafts products, because they were thoughtfully designed and handmade, were too expensive for the lower classes to buy. Nonetheless, Pamela was interested in and knowledgeable about the ideals of Arts and Crafts production, as indicated in her correspondence from 1896 onward. Such ideas also had been central to the curriculum at the Pratt Institute when Pamela was in attendance. Later, it influenced her own methods of hand-producing, hand-printing and hand-coloring her books and print portfolios.

There were links among Arts and Crafts ideals, political radicalism, the pursuit of social justice and Spiritualism. As a religion that attracted suffragists, Spiritualism involved mostly female trance-speakers or mediums claiming to communicate directly with the dead, a comforting thought in a period when early death was so common. One of the most important sources for Spiritualism was 19th-century interest in Emmanuel Swedenborg, the famous Swedish scientist turned mystic and visionary, with whose ideas Pamela's family was involved.[16]

In practice, Spiritualism was not only a way to speak with the dead but it also nourished the seeds of reform politics. In particular, women mediums or trance-speakers often were highly critical of conditions for the working poor and the inequality of women and men, and they worked toward the implementation of socialist, feminist and suffragist agendas. These were subjects that women were not allowed to discuss openly at the time. However, if women Spiritualists were criticized or threatened for their comments, they could say it wasn't their idea. They could claim that it was the spirits speaking through them, using them as an empty vessel, a conduit for their ideas. This was an excellent way to be an activist and avoid culpability for it. But on the other hand, the deflection of blame to the spirits reinforced the widespread idea that women were weak-minded empty vessels incapable of independent thought. So Spiritualism was a mixed blessing.

While Pamela was too young in Manchester to practice trance-speaking, her family's involvement with Swedenborgianism strongly suggests that she was aware of it. She said later that she never was a practicing spiritualist, but after she moved to England she displayed similar orientation in her visionary watercolors and her tarot cards.[17] She claimed that the strong women and assertive goddesses in her paintings "just came to her" as fully formed visions, and that she set them down without alteration. This detached process allowed her to escape censure for the feminist implications of the paintings. Arthur Waite's belief that she was psychic created a similar dynamic around her creation of the tarot card drawings.

The Pratt Institute

In 1893 Pamela matriculated at The Pratt Institute in Brooklyn, New York where she studied art until 1897. Her transcript reveals that her attendance was sporadic due to illness, but there could not have been a better school to nurture her talents and reinforce the ideas to which she had been exposed. Notions of aesthetic and social reform were entwined in the school's commitment to the democratization of art, the integration of fine art and industrial design, and the belief that art and beauty could cure the problems of an intensely materialistic society. As one faculty member stated in the journal *Pratt Institute Monthly*, "[A]waken the power of beauty, by education, in all minds, and the world will quickly become a brotherhood…[and] each student an individual reformer."[18]

Pamela was far from the naïve "primitive" she sometimes pretended to be. She avidly read literature of all sorts—especially Shakespeare—and studied a range of traditional and modern art at Pratt. She attended extracurricular activities, guest lectures, and museums that all stressed the notion of art as a "civilizing" factor useful in social reform. Students were encouraged to study museum objects as varied as Asian porcelain and photographic reproductions of Old Master art. This work was supplemented by mandatory lectures on art history. With so many intellectual resources at her fingertips, Pamela was exposed to a broad knowledge of both historical and then-contemporary art and artists, including the Arts and Crafts movement. Beyond Pratt's feminism and reforming zeal the strongest influence on Pamela was the teaching of Arthur Wesley Dow.[19] His composition and design class was the last she took before leaving Pratt in the spring of 1897. In particular, Dow introduced her to the crucial belief that visual expression paralleled musical expression. To achieve this, he said artists should not imitate the three-dimensional reality of the visual world, but instead should reduce their work to flat areas of color, tone and shape that could be "composed" on a flat surface the way a musician composes tones of music. In both visual art and music, the goal, Dow said, was to create a mood or feeling. That idea stayed with Pamela throughout her life.

Theatrical Influences

Pamela was involved in theatre from almost her earliest years. Her mother Corinne had been known as one of the finest amateur actors from her days in Brooklyn Heights, a love and talent that surely stayed with her after she married Charles Smith.[20] Corinne was known for her passion for London's theatres and may occasionally have performed as a stage *diseuse*, that is, a woman monologist.[21]

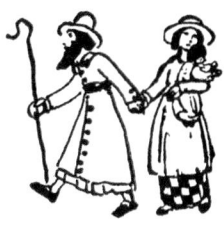

Whenever possible in New York and England, Pamela attended as many plays as she could. While she enjoyed her years in Jamaica, she complained that it had no theatres. As she said in a letter to Mary Reed, "Jamaica is just elegant for some things—air, scenery—rides, etc.—and piggish for others—<u>NO THEATRES</u>!!!"[22] This is probably why she was so enthralled with her miniature theatre, writing plays, drawing extraordinarily expressive figures, designing costumes and elaborate scenery, and then actually staging the plays with music and other sound effects. Her emphasis on the expressiveness of her figures and faces was the subject of her important 1908 article, "Should the Art Student Think?" published in *The Craftsman* magazine.[23] One of the most radical American art journals, *The Craftsman* strongly emphasized the interconnections between the arts and progressive social/political issues. Pamela's article comprises advice to upcoming art students, in particular how they should learn to look through the exterior appearance of people and things to the character and spirit beneath the surface. This, she felt, could best be accomplished by going to the theatre, for as she said, "…the stage is a great school…to the illustrator…. First watch the simple forms of joy, of fear, of sorrow; look at the position taken by the whole body, then the face…. After you have learned to tell a simple story, put in more details, the face, and indicate the dress…. The stage has taught me almost all I know of clothes, of action, and of pictorial gestures."[24] And further, "Keep an open mind to all things…. Think good thoughts of beautiful things, colors, sound, places, not mean thoughts. When you see lot of dirty people in a crowd, do not remember only the dirt, but the great spirit that is in them all, and the power they represent."[25]

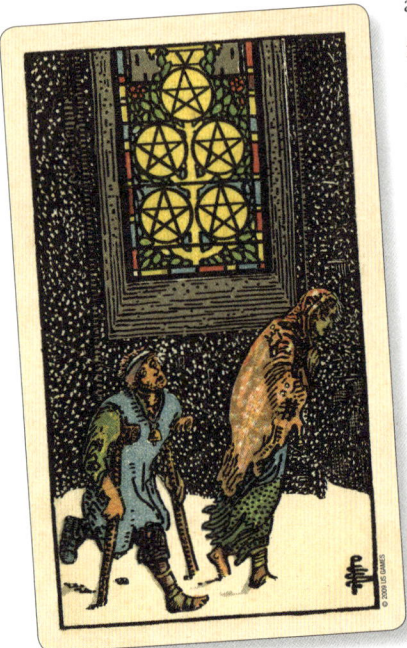

The Five of Pentacles card comes to mind here, depicting a crippled man and an impoverished woman dressed in rags. In a blustery snowstorm, they struggle past a church with five pentacles worked into a stained-glass window design. Their almost-bare feet must be numb. For Waite, the card depicted "mendicants…and [foretold] material trouble above all, whether in the form illustrated—destitution—or otherwise." Such other possible meanings included "disorder, chaos, ruin, discord, profligacy."[26] But for Pamela, surely the card's figures represented the "dirty people seen in a crowd" of which one was "not to remember only the dirt, but the great spirit that is in them all, and the power they represent…. Ugliness is beauty, but with a difference, a nobleness that speaks through all the hard crust of convention."[27] That's a spirit of compassion that might inform the life of a woman like Pamela, who had been struggling on her own since her father died in 1899 and was gradually moving toward the spirit, comfort and community of the Catholic church. Perhaps this outlook is intimated by the design of the Five of Pentacles.[28] She concluded her article with the advice to "Use your wits, use your eyes. Perhaps you use your physical eyes too much and only see the mask. Find eyes within, look for the door into the unknown country."[29]

Tarot Drawings

THE FIVE OF PENTACLES IS A GOOD EXAMPLE OF HOW PAMELA DREW UPON HER OWN PERSONAL experiences in creating the Rider-Waite Tarot. Other influences such as her background in storytelling, theatre and her burgeoning interest in Catholicism become apparent in the card details.

In her tarot drawings, Pamela incorporated several intriguing types of symbolic changes that have their roots in her earlier life and work: the use of androgynous figures and gender-role reversals in some cards, including several Trump cards; the insertion of portraits of her feminist and suffragist friends into the cards; and the development of symbolism in cards that suggests Christian—particularly Catholic—ideas. None of these devices were new, but they were not common at the time. One need only glance, for instance, at the androgynous figure in her Ten of Swords to see just how dramatic and original her designs are and how close they are in their dream-like spirit to her visionary musical paintings.

Ideas both from the theatre and her art background were used as devices to pull the viewer into the world of the card and its illustrations. This device is called "engagement" or "engaging the viewer," and there are various ways it works in Pamela's cards.[30] The most obvious way is to present viewers with an extremely dramatic story of which neither the beginning nor ending are known. Again, the Ten of Swords is an excellent example. How did this poor person end up skewered to the ground by not one, but ten swords? It is a harsh image of an apparently dead figure. In Pamela's time, this person would have been seen as a man, but closer consideration actually reveals no evidence of that—at the very least the figure is androgynous and could be female. Short hair and masculine clothing were worn by many of Pamela's feminist and suffragist friends, including well-known actors like Edy Craig and Cicely Hamilton. In the Ten of Swords, the figure is covered from the waist down, so the clothing makes little difference. Further, the viewer doesn't see the figure's face, which makes it easier for both men and women to imagine themselves in the card, a major factor in engaging the viewer.

Is the figure as dead as it appears? Waite says, in *The Pictorial Key to the Tarot*, that while it suggests "pain, affliction, tears, sadness, desolation… It is not especially a card of violent death." Only a very close examination reveals why Waite makes this statement. Look at the figure's right hand. It makes a gesture in which the third finger and the pinky finger both curve down to meet the thumb, while the index and second finger are also curved but don't touch other fingers or thumb. While similar to the gesture of the Hierophant, it is not identical. The Hierophant's third and pinky fingers are bent straight down and do not touch the thumb, while the index and second fingers are straight up. The hand gesture in the Ten of Swords figure is doubly significant. It indicates that the body is not dead since all muscles relax within minutes of death, (called primary flaccidity) and gestures requiring muscle control similarly relax. The horror of what the figure has gone through is painful even to observe, yet the hand gesture suggests the body will come to life again. Given that the deck was intended by Waite and Pamela to be oriented toward Christianity, not magic, this set of visual clues makes it analogous to the Passion of Jesus and his subsequent resurrection. In fact, the same gesture is seen in representations of *Christ Pantocrator*, the risen Christ as almighty or all-powerful or Ruler over All. The image and gesture are found in both Eastern Orthodox (Pantocrator) and Western Roman Catholicism (Christ in Majesty). In both cases, the gesture is one of blessing, as it is in the Hierophant.

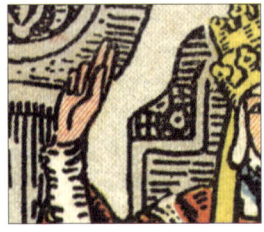
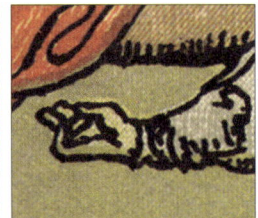

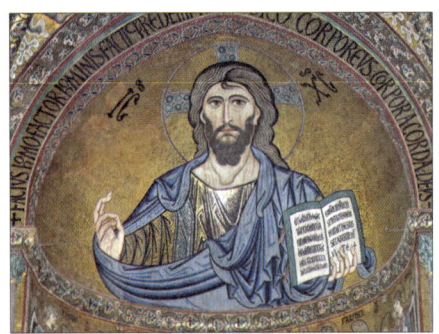
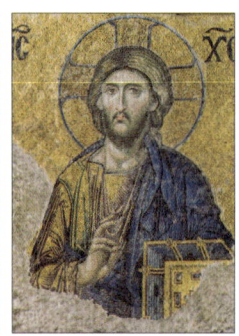

Above left: Christ Pantocrator, Cathedral of Cefalù, Sicily, 12th-13th century

Above right: Christ in Majesty, Hagia Sophia, mosaic, 1261 CE

As with Pamela's paintings to music, what gives her tarot cards their power to engage and inspire the viewer is her almost hypnotic ability as a storyteller, both in pictures and words. One thinks, in this regard, of Arthur Ransome's assertion that much of his subsequent writing was influenced by his early exposure to Pamela's lilted tale-telling: "I think I learned more of the art of narrative from [Pamela's] simple folk-tales than ever from any book."[31]

For Pamela, her facility with storytelling also created a feminist symbol system that was integrated with the spiritual meanings of the cards. Beginning with gender role reversal, the Knight of Wands and the Knight of Swords are clear examples of such reversals. Both knights have delicate features in contrast with other Rider-Waite male characters who generally have broader faces and more chiseled or cruder features, for example the Emperor card. The Knight of Wands also has curling red hair and rosy lips, a conventional way of indicating female gender. While Pamela never discussed her intentions for the cards, she seems to have been influenced by the Joan of Arc imagery pervasive in the suffrage movement. In 1909 there were two stage productions featuring Joan of Arc that Pamela likely saw, given her passion for the theatre, and that probably functioned as the immediate models for her female knights. One American production featured the actress Maude Adams' lavish portrayal of St. Joan in an adaptation of Schiller's *The Maid of Orléans*, which opened at the Harvard Stadium in June 1909, when Pamela was stateside. The other was Cicely Hamilton's *A Pageant of Great Women*, first produced by Edith Craig in London at the Scala Theatre in early November 1909, when Pamela was back in England. As one writer noted of *A Pageant of Great Women*:

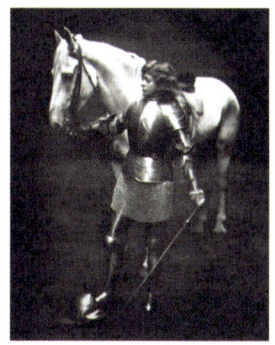

Left: Maude Adams as Joan of Arc in an adaptation of Friedrich Schiller's "The Maid of Orléans." Publicity photograph, 1909, for "The Maid of Orléans" production at Harvard Stadium. Private Collection

> Joan of Arc, patron saint of the [suffrage] movement's most radical wing and equestrian leader of their processions, makes her appearance at the vanguard of the warriors. Her virginity and gender render her the ideal symbol of unsexualized womanliness, [while] her militancy and transvestism preclude containment by conventional domesticity.[32]

Arthur Waite, referring to the Grail story, even described the Knight of Swords as Galahad in *The Pictorial Key*: "In the design he is really a prototypical hero of romantic chivalry. He might almost be Galahad, whose sword is swift and sure because he is clean of heart."[33] What Waite did not mention in *The Pictorial Key* is that earlier decks had occasionally depicted knights as female. One such pack, the Cary-Yale Visconti Tarocchi, is one of several *tarocchi* packs painted in the 15th century for the Visconti and Sforza families.[34] This lushly elaborate deck had sixteen cards in each suit, the extra two being a female knight and female page. While it's unlikely that Pamela saw the actual Visconti deck, which was still in Lombardy, she surely read about the cards in a 1903 article in London's premier art journal *The Burlington Magazine*, where the deck's "four amazons" (female warriors) were discussed.[35]

Female Knight of Coins and female Page of Cups from the Cary-Yale Visconti Tarocchi

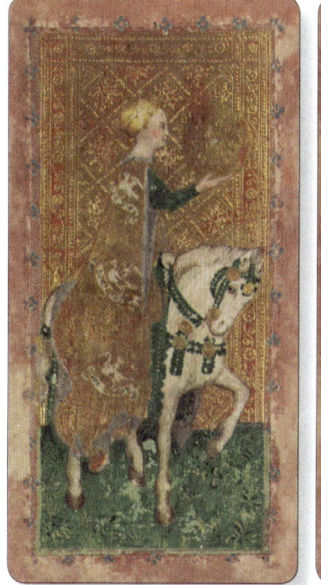
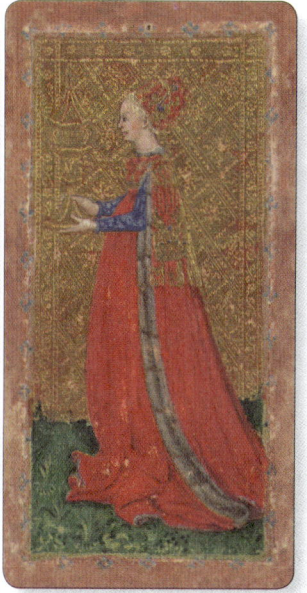

Another possible gender reversal—or at the very least, an androgynous figure—is seen in the Fool card. This figure was discussed in the 1970s by art historian Frances Osborn Robb, who compared the Fool to the actor Maude Adams' portrayal of *Peter Pan*.[36]

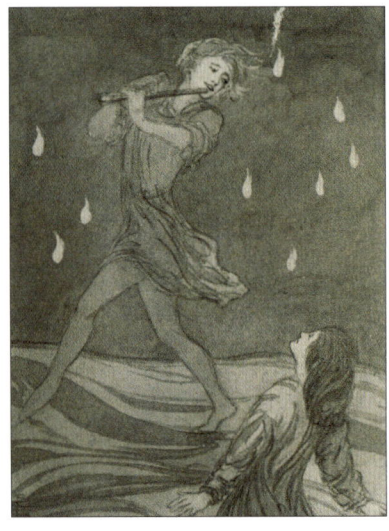

Untitled drawing by Pamela Colman Smith. From the collection of Dorothy Norman, 1997. Courtesy of Philadelphia Museum of Art

Adams' costume is similar to the Fool's, with a short, graceful tunic with wide sleeves, decorated with a botanical motif, worn over a white shirt. Her cap, like the Fool's, sports a feather. The god Pan—of whom Peter Pan is the mythological descendent—complements the spiritual significance of the Fool card. As the lines of the J.M. Barrie's play, *Peter Pan*, reveal, Pan represents the mystical fullness and absolute novelty of life itself: "'Who are you, Pan?' 'I'm the sun rising. I'm poets singing. I'm the new world. I'm a little bird that has broken out of its egg. I'm joy, joy, joy!'"[37]

Another possible clue to the Peter Pan identity of the Fool is Pamela's 1907 painting of Peter Pan, now lost but recorded in this photograph by Alfred Stieglitz. His posture and *joie de vivre* are close to Waite's description of the Fool in *The Pictorial Key*: "…it is as if angels were waiting to uphold him…. He is a prince of the other world on his travels through this one…. [H]e is the spirit in search of experience…. Many of the Instituted Mysteries are summarized in this card."[38] Pamela's addition of drops of light around Pan also suggests this sense of mystery, resembling *Yod*, the tenth letter of the Hebrew alphabet, out of which—in mystical terms—the world is created. Waite wrote about *Yod* in his book, *The Secret Doctrine in Israel*, recently reprinted.[39]

As another source explains it: "Suspended in mid-air [as are Pamela's drops of light], *Yod* is the smallest of the Hebrew letters, the 'atom' of the consonants,…[from] which all the other letters begin and end…. In the Jewish mystical tradition, *Yod* represents a mere dot, a divine point of energy. Since *Yod* is used to form all the other letters, and since God uses the letters as the building blocks of creation, *Yod* indicates God's omnipresence."[40]

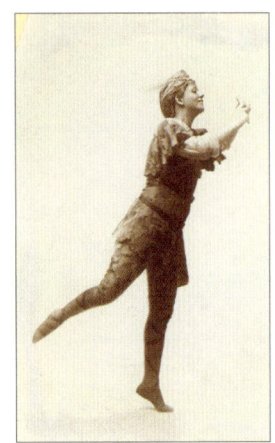

Right: Maude Adams as Peter Pan, cabinet card, circa 1906. Courtesy of Private Collection

An alternative and more feminist interpretation is that the drops of fire may symbolize *Pistis Sophia*, the feminine principle of God, often represented as drops of light falling from heaven—an idea that complements the feminine aspects of Pamela's "Peter Pan." All these spiritual meanings dovetail with the Fool's symbolism, and we believe that both Smith and Waite were interested in *Pistis Sophia*; Waite through his 1908 Hermetic Text Society, and Smith through her knowledge of art history and her preparation for her conversion to Catholicism.[41]

Friendships

Pamela drew inspiration for the tarot deck from the world of the stage and from her personal friendships, and often these realms overlapped. There are several instances of Pamela inserting portraits of her friends into the deck. Ellen Terry shows up in the cards, generally in the sort of womanly role she played in the theatre. We see a young Ellen Terry in the face of the Queen of Wands, whose openness of expression and prominent chin resemble Terry's appearance, for instance in the photo of the actor as Ophelia. An older, wealthy Ellen Terry appears in the Nine of Pentacles, with her estate behind her, as described by Waite in *The Pictorial Key*: "A woman…stands…in the garden of a manorial house. It is a wide domain, suggesting plenty in all things. Possibly it is her own possession…" This domain recalls the background in Pamela's print of Terry as "Mistress Page," where she's shown at her medieval manor house in Kent.

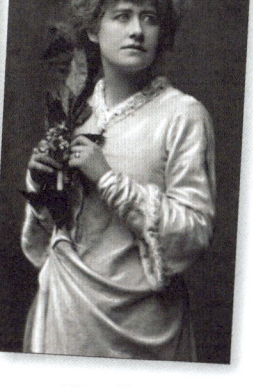

Ellen Terry as Ophelia, cabinet card, undated. Courtesy of Private Collection

In the Nine of Pentacles, Waite specifically mentions the grape motif, which has a long and multifaceted history as a Christian symbol of sacrifice and redemption. One of the themes of Ellen Terry's personal mythology was her self-sacrifice, both for her children, Gordon and Edith Craig and for the greater good of the theatre community—she always called herself merely a "useful" actor. There is a hint of deferred power in the image of the bird she holds in the Nine of Pentacles card. Waite mentions simply "a bird," but Pamela represented a hooded falcon, a symbol of explosive power barely restrained. While Ellen supported the suffrage movement, she never managed to transcend Victorian gender limitations in her career. One might interpret the falcon on her wrist as her audacious daughter, Edy Craig, a powerful personality who transgressed prescriptive gender roles in many ways. This interpretation is reinforced by the similarity in pose between the Nine of Pentacles and Pamela's suffrage poster, "A Bird in the Hand," where the bird symbolizes the still unrealized goals of the suffrage struggle. The Nine of Pentacles holds yet another possible feminist motif suggested by the pattern

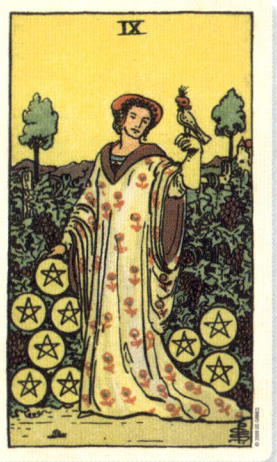
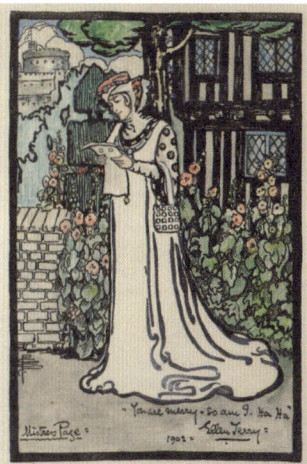

on the woman's gown, which is ostensibly a flower pattern, though it may have been originally designed as a symbol for Venus—a circle with a cross descending from it—long a part of the lexicon of signs denoting women.

Edith Craig as a young girl. Courtesy © National Trust, UK

Edith Craig appears in the cards in several guises. In the androgynous Magician, we see a young Edith Craig looking much as she does in this youthful photograph, this one as a willful child. What makes the comparison of Craig to the Magician more apt is this 1900 caricature by Pamela of herself bowing to Craig's authority. Craig's resolution and strong will were so well known among her family and friends that Pamela stressed those very qualities by depicting Craig as looming like a powerful spirit above a humble Pamela. The robe Craig wears closely resembles the Magician's robes (except in color), with a white undergarment like the Magician's and an open-fronted, loose-sleeved overgarment. That Pamela would see the Magician as an appropriate role for Craig is suggested in Waite's description of the Magician as "A youthful figure in the robe of a magician, having the countenance of divine Apollo…" The figure's association with divinity—especially with the androgynous god Apollo and his twin Aphrodite—recalls the links between feminism and spiritualism, as well as Craig's—and Apollo's—gender fluidity.[42]

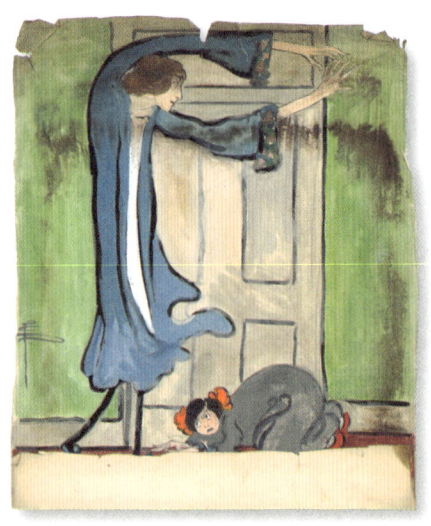

Caricature of Edith Craig, 1900 by Pamela Colman Smith. From "Ellen Peg's Book of Merry Joys," Courtesy © National Trust, UK

The Magician card also refers to the Grail quest, symbolized by the suit signs on the table. Waite said in his 1909 book *The Hidden Church of the Holy Graal*:

> The canonical Hallows of the Grail Legend are of course the Cup, the Lance, the Dish and the Sword. I am wondering now how many critical works have been written on the Holy Grail and yet it has occurred to no one that its hallows may be somewhere else in the world than in old books of Romance. They are in the Tarot. The reason for these Hallows also being in the Tarot reposes in certain secret records now existing in Europe….

While Pamela as a keen Arthurian likely would have agreed with this view, she may also have equated the grail quest with women's quest for political, social and spiritual equality, as many feminists did. Historian Christine Poulson, for instance, "links the popularity of

Grail angels as images of 'female perfection and spiritual authority' to the importance of women in the Spiritualist [and suffrage] movements."[43] In any case, for Waite and Pamela the card was meaningful on many levels, none of which excluded the others. In various parts of his text Waite connects it with Neo-Platonic theory ("as above, so below"), with Christian Gnosticism, and a range of other mystical systems. For Pamela and her feminist friends, these meanings included the image of Edith Craig as the Magician. To recapitulate Waite's phrasing, "On the table are…the symbols… signifying the elements of natural life…which the Magician adapts as he will." Surely Craig's adaptation to her own strong will of what generally was regarded as a "natural" inequality of women and men could qualify her—symbolically at least—to be the Magician. The fact that the equality for which women struggled was believed by some in Pamela's circle to reflect the existing divine order— as, for example, among Spiritualists, or in the Golden Dawn's pantheon of divinities—brought the connection between political and spiritual realities full circle.

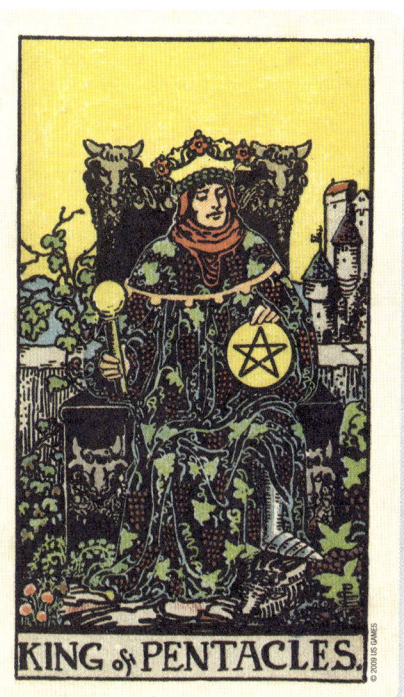

An older Edith Craig recurs in the King of Pentacles, where her achievements have given her a serene appearance. The King wears a crown of lilies and roses and a robe covered in grape designs, designating sacrifice and revival. She sits on a black throne decorated with fierce bulls, symbols of transformation and sacrifice in Egyptian and Christian iconography. Behind the throne, apparently perched on a high parapet, is a broad landscape with a towered castle, the King's domain. The King's face resembles Edith Craig's straight-lipped visage in this well-known portrait photograph used on suffrage postcards. Another hint to the King's identity is the armored foot protruding from beneath her robes. This is the only tarot king who wears armor; Pamela may have been referring to Craig's status as a suffrage warrior. The divinatory meanings of the card recounted by Waite are a virtual inventory of Craig's qualities: valor, intelligence, organizational aptitude and so forth. Hence, in this card and many others, the myriad influences in Pamela's life from her family, friendships, education, religion and social movements all came together in the Rider-Waite Tarot deck.

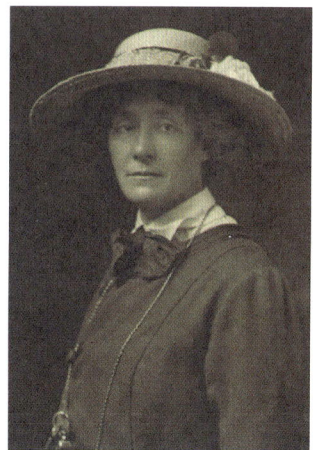

Photograph of Edith Craig used in suffrage literature. Courtesy © National Trust, UK

Stuart Kaplan and I have known each other for over 40 years, from around the time Volume I of his monumental Encyclopedia of Tarot was published and I finished my 1975 exhibitions at Delaware and Princeton on Pamela Colman Smith. Stuart consistently supported me in my research, even in my overseas trips, where I tried to track down Pamela leads (many of which he provided me). He encouraged me to keep going when my efforts flagged, and he shared his vast knowledge of tarot cards and their history. Our friendship has flourished, and I celebrate it on U.S. Games Systems' 50th anniversary and Pamela Colman Smith's 140th birthday!

MELINDA BOYD PARSONS

---

1   There is no parallel to the Page in our modern playing cards.
2   Arthur Edward Waite, *Shadows of Life and Thought: A Retrospective Review in the Form of Memoirs* (London: Selwyn and Blount, 1938), pp. 172-80.
3   Arthur Waite, "The Tarot: A Wheel of Fortune," *The Occult Review* X (July-December 1909): 307-17. I was grateful to Sir Michael Dummett for sending me a copy of this article. The identity of the third person is not known for certain. For discussion, see Mary K. Greer's "Pamela Colman Smith and the Tarot", "Appendix F", in her pioneering book, *Women of the Golden Dawn; Rebels and Priestesses* (Rochester, VT: Park Street Press, 1995), pp. 405-06.
4   Waite was interested in Pythagoras and his mystical theories of mathematics and music, as shown in his early, rather obscure work, *Lives of Alchemystical Philosophers: Based On Materials Collected in 1815 and Supplemented by Recent Researches With a Philosophical Demonstration of the True Principles of the Magnum Opus, or Great Work of Alchemical Re-Construction, and Some Account of the Spiritual Chemistry* (London: George Redway, 1888). A 4th edition dated 1909 is available for free here: https://ia800209.us.archive.org/35/items/manualofcartoman00gran/manualofcartoman00gran.pdf (accessed September 27 2017).
5   Moakley, "Introduction," in Waite, *The Pictorial Key to the Tarot* (New Hyde Park, New York: University Books, 1959), pp. ix-x. Unfortunately for later readers, Moakley's illuminating "Introduction" was deleted from all subsequent editions of *The Pictorial Key to the Tarot*. ("How often this happens!") Upon her 1998 death, Moakley's will left all her research materials and publications to Stuart R. Kaplan, both because she admired his prodigious scholarship and because she knew her own work would be safe in perpetuity in Kaplan's collection.
6   Arthur Edward Waite, *The Hidden Church of the Holy Graal: Its Legends and Symbolism Considered in Their Affinity with Certain Mysteries of Initiation and Other Traces of a Secret Tradition in Christian Times* (London: Rebman, 1909). There is a free download of this in various formats on https://archive.org/stream/hiddenchurchofho00waituoft/hiddenchurchofho00waituoft_djvu.txt (accessed August 30, 2017).
7   Pamela, writing to Paine from "King Arthur's Castle Hotel," excitedly told him that Henry Irving also was there at Tintagel, and that she had shown Irving not only photographs of her toy theatre that Paine had sent but also a portfolio of her prints and drawings. August 23, 1899. Pamela Colman Smith to Albert Bigelow Paine. Letters, The Huntington Library, San Marino, California.
8   Waite used the phrase "meaning behind meaning" in his discussion of the trump card "Temperance" in *The Pictorial Key to the Tarot*. It does not appear in the University Books 1959 text but can be found on the website "Sacred Texts": http://www.sacred-texts.com/tarot/pkt/pkt0102.htm (accessed September 6, 2017).
9   Waite, *The Pictorial Key to the Tarot* (New Hyde Park, New York: University Books, 1959), pp. 46, 62.
10 Ernest Fenollosa, "The Nature of Fine Art," *The Lotos* IX (1896): 759-60.
11 See Google Books: https://books.google.combooks?id=okUDAAAAQAAJ&dq=Marcus+Ward+%22antient+music%22&source=gbs_navlinks_s (accessed October 3 2017)
12 There was an "antient music" revival in London in the opening years of the 20th century, which Pamela was involved with, along with W.B. Yeats, Gordon Craig, Arnold Dolmetsch and others. You can tell by the description of one of Marcus Ward's books that Pamela was primed for that: *Ye Pathetic Ballad*

of Ladye Ouncebelle and Lord Lovelle. Marcus Ward's Royal Illuminated Legends for Great Folke for Lyttel Folk. Figured in Colors by Marcus Ward Illuminator to the Queen. The description also prefigures Pamela's archaic phrasing in her plays for the miniature theatre.

13 Occasionally originals show up on booksellers' sites, such as Abe Books; as well, some originals are held by libraries: for example, *"The Royal illuminated book of nursery rhymes. First series; the old familiar words set to appropriate music, arranged in an easy style suited to little minstrels; each story is illustrated by pictures, designed in the quaint spirit of medieval times, and printed in colours and gold /* by Marcus Ward, Illuminator to the Queen." http://trove.nla.gov.au/work/30303190?selectedversion=NBD10992574

14 The servants' names on the census record are Mary A. E. Sheed and Isabella G. Lang according to Ancestry.com and The Church of Jesus Christ of Latter-day Saints, 1881 England Census, Class: RG11; Piece: 3890; Folio: 99; Page: 23; GSU roll: 1341929 (Provo Utah: The Generations Network, Inc., 2004)

15 See Alex Owen, "Victorian Spiritualism and the Spiritualist Woman", in Owen, *The Darkened Room; Women, Power and Spiritualism in Late Victorian England* (London: Virago Press, 1989), pp.18-40.

16 According to Henry Tuckerman, Samuel Colman II, the publisher, "associated with the Swedenborgians, a sect remarkable for aesthetic proclivities...." Tuckerman, *Book of the Artists* (New York, 1867), p. 559.

17 At least that is what she told George Pollexfen, 17 February 1902. She may have said this because W. B. Yeats was against spiritualism at that time. William Butler Yeats Manuscript Collection 294, Box 120, Stony Brook University Special Collections and University Archives. Later in life, though, W.B. Yeats married Georgie Hyde-Lees. A few weeks after their marriage in 1917, Georgie started to practice "automatic writing" (a written version of spiritualism in which she claimed to channel messages from various spirit controls). Often the messages that came through concerned ways that W. B. could better their marriage, suggesting that Georgie too used spiritualism more actively than passively. For extended discussion, see Ann Saddlemyer, *Becoming George: the Life of Mrs. W. B. Yeats* (Oxford and New York: Oxford University Press, 2002).

18 Katherine Shattuck, "Art in the School Rooms," *Pratt Institute Monthly,* hereafter *PIM* (May 1898), p. 246, cited in Marsha Morton, "Missionaries of Culture," in *Pratt and Its Gallery: The Arts and Crafts Years* (Brooklyn: The Pratt Institute, 1999), p. 8.

19 Regarding feminism, not only were there many female faculty members at Pratt, but the majority of students were women. Both the lecture program and articles in *PIM* reflect this. As one writer in *PIM* noted in 1892, linking feminism and labor reform, "This is the women's era, and the Nineteenth Century ought not to close without the organization of women workers" *PIM*, October 1892, p. 2.

20 According to the U.S. Federal Census of 1870, Charles and Corinne Smith resided together in New York Ward 18, District 20 (2nd enumeration), New York, New York.

21 Phil Norfleet: "Corinne Smith, is said to have been an avid fan of the London theater and occasionally performed as a stage diseuse." (http://pcs2051.tripod.com/index.htm). *Diseuse* is a French term defined by Merriam Webster as "a woman who is a skilled and usually professional reciter" It is a unique type of short performance, not in a play or with a troupe of actors, but an individual monologist reciting or giving readings from stories, soliloquies, poems or dramatic works. This type of performance is very similar to Pamela's later public presentations of her Annancy tales. Interestingly, the extended term of *diseuse* in French is *"diseuse de bonne aventure,"* that is, a fortune-teller.

22 Pamela Colman Smith to Mary Bidlack Reed, November 15 1896. Pamela Colman Smith Collection, Special Collections Department, Bryn Mawr College Library.

23 Pamela Colman Smith, "Should the Art Student Think?" *The Craftsman* XIV: 4 (July 1908): pp. 417-19.

24 Pamela Colman Smith, "Should the Art Student Think?" *The Craftsman* XIV: 4 (July 1908): pp. 417-18.

25 Pamela Colman Smith, "Should the Art Student Think?" *The Craftsman* XIV: 4 (July 1908): p. 418.

26 Arthur Waite, *The Pictorial Key to the Tarot* (New Hyde Park, NY: University Books, 1959). p. 272.

27 Pamela Colman Smith, "Should the Art Student Think?" *The Craftsman* XIV: 4 (July 1908): p. 419.

28 Thanks to Mary Greer for suggesting this connection between Pamela's life between 1899 and 1909 and her depiction of what appears to be a church window. Greer, email to Parsons, October 21 2017.

29 Pamela Colman Smith, "Should the Art Student Think?" *The Craftsman* XIV: 4 (July 1908): p. 419.

30 For detailed discussion of "engagement" of the viewer, see Michael Cohen, *Engaging English Art: Entering the Work in Two Centuries of English Painting and Poetry* (Tuscaloosa: University of Alabama Press, 1987).

31 Arthur Ransome, *The Autobiography of Arthur Ransome,* ed. R. Hart-Davis (London: Jonathan Cape,

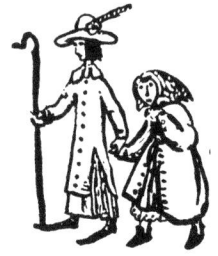

1976), p. 88. Likewise telling is the fact that Pamela's friend, the painter Alphaeus Cole, at age ninety-eight, still was able to recite and sing the folktales and songs he had heard from Pamela seventy years earlier. Alphaeus Cole, audiotape interview in the collection of Melinda Boyd Parsons and transcript in the Stuart Kaplan Collection.

32 Sheila Stowell, 1909 description of Joan of Arc, quoted in Laura E. Nym Mayhall, *The Militant Suffrage Movement: Citizenship and Resistance in Britain* 1860-1930 (New York and Oxford: Oxford University Press, 2003), p. 85 and note 12.

33 Arthur Edward Waite, *The Pictorial Key to the Tarot*, 1959, p. 230.

34 For discussion and illustrations of these cards, see Stuart R. Kaplan, *The Encyclopedia of Tarot I*, pp. 93, 95; II, pp. 28-29, 31, 35.

35 Emiliano Parravicino, "Three Packs of Italian Tarocco Cards", *Burlington Magazine* III, 9 (December 1903): 237-47.

36 Frances Osborn Robb, "Pamela Colman Smith and the Waite Rider Tarot," undated typescript [circa 1973?], pp. 8-9. Typescript formerly in the collection of William Innes Homer; current location unknown.

37 Quotation from J.M. Barrie's *Peter Pan, Or, the Boy Who Wouldn't Grow Up*, printed in Empire Theatre Program, Charles Frohman presentation of Maude Adams' "Farewell Performances" of *Peter Pan*. Undated clipping, The University of Memphis Rare Book Room, McWherter Library.

38 Arthur Edward Waite, *The Pictorial Key to the Tarot*, 1959, pp. 152, 155.

39 Arthur Edward Waite, *The Secret Doctrine in Israel; A Study of the Zohar and its Connections* (Facsimile edition, Whitefish Montana: Kessinger Publishing LLC), 2010.

40 "The Letter *Yod*," in "Hebrew for Christians." http://www.hebrew4christians.com/Grammar/Unit_One/Aleph-Bet/Yod/yod.html, accessed September 12, 2017. What is fascinating is how closely *Yod* and its function parallel the cosmological theory of the creation of the universe from a singularity.

41 In Michelangelo's "Creation of Adam" on the Sistine ceiling, for instance, the figure of Sophia accompanies God as he reaches forward to touch Adam's finger.

42 For more, see G. G. Bolich, *Crossdressing in Context, Vol. 4: Transgender and Religion* (Psyche's Press, 2010).

43 Christine Poulson, *The Quest for the Grail; Arthurian Legend in British Art, 1840-1920* (New York: St. Martin's Press, 1999).

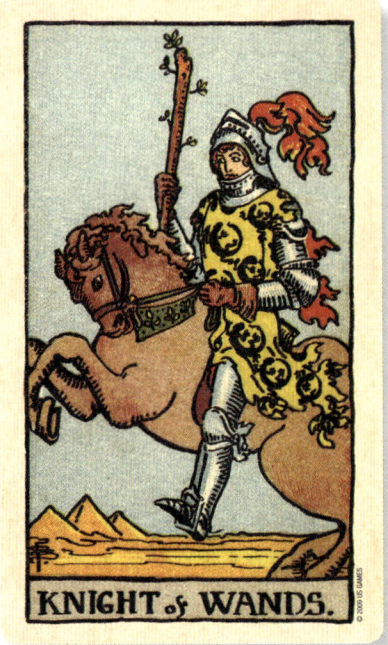
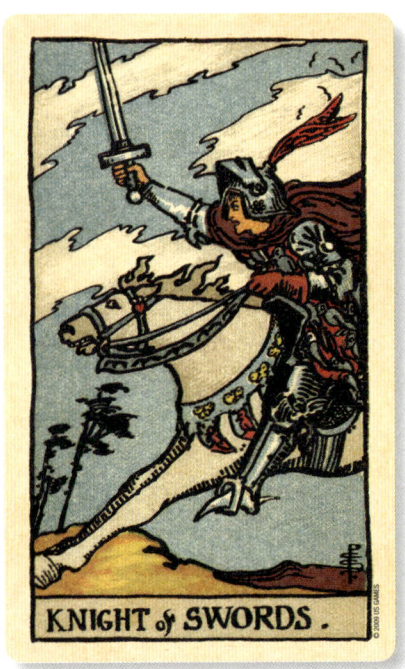

PAMELA'S LEGACY

THE YEAR 2018 MARKS THE 50TH ANNIVERSARY OF THE FOUNDING OF U.S. GAMES SYSTEMS, Inc. and the 140th anniversary of the birth of Pamela Colman Smith. In honor of this, it seems fitting to explore Pamela's legacy as it has been ushered into the world through her publisher and through Stuart Kaplan, who has amassed the most complete collection of Pamela's artworks, references and books, which are now shared in this book. A legacy is something from the past—a gift or inheritance—that is left to those who come after. The Latin root *legate* means "an envoy or messenger sent with a commission," so this chapter explores what Pamela's message to future generations might be.

"Pixie," as Pamela came to be known, found early success at the turn of the 20th century as an illustrator, costume and theatre set designer, poet, and folklorist, as well as editor and publisher of two literary magazines and a feminist press. Despite early success during her career, the artist struggled throughout most of her life to have her achievements recognized. She would be all but forgotten today except for a series of 78 tarot illustrations she prepared in 1909 that are now sold in multiple editions and in over 50 countries around the world. Writing about her legacy, therefore, necessitates a focus first on her tarot designs.

Innovative Tarot Deck

THE NUMBER ONE LEGACY OF PAMELA COLMAN SMITH RESIDES IN THE MILLIONS OF PEOPLE around the world who over the past hundred plus years have been drawn to and continue to draw inspiration from her tarot deck. In addition to those who use the cards as a tool to impart direction and meaning to their own lives and the lives of others, there exists a population of artists, writers and other creatives who use her storytelling style of tarot images as both inspiration and model when creating their own decks, art, films, poetry, as well as fiction and nonfiction books. In fact, most tarot authors take this deck as the standard when writing about tarot. All of these people studying tarot can be viewed as Pamela's legacy students, even those who may not be aware of Pamela Colman Smith as the artist. The deck has variously been known as simply *Tarot Cards*, *The Rider Tarot Cards* and then the *Rider-Waite Tarot Deck* after the publisher, Rider & Company, and the conceptualizer, A.E. Waite. With the 2009 publication of *The Pamela Colman Smith Commemorative Set* from U.S. Games Systems, Inc. (hereafter USGS) on the centennial of its creation, her grateful fans welcomed the inclusion of Smith's name in the deck's title. They were also gifted with a set of postcards of her non-tarot works from the collection of Stuart Kaplan, founder of

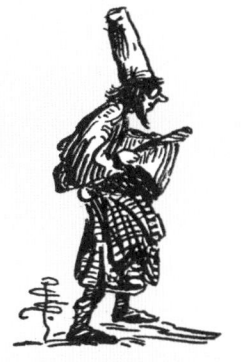

U.S. Games Systems, Inc. and with a book, *The Artwork and Times of Pamela Colman Smith*, acknowledging the full range of her creative endeavors. At long last, Pamela was credited not only with making the deck, but the set also commemorated her other artistic output.

In his first booklet enclosed with the 1971 edition of the Rider-Waite tarot deck, Stuart Kaplan explained that its outstanding feature is its "emblematic designs readily suitable for divination in contrast to the rigid forms of swords, batons, cups and coins previously used in tarot decks." The Rider-Waite deck was, in fact, the first modern tarot to include a Minor Arcana with pictorial scenes illustrating the cards' meanings.

Perhaps because of the limited time Pamela had to create these images—only a few months in 1909—the Major Arcana, rife with details specified by Waite, are highly symbolic and elegant but static in the mode of the Gothic woodcut decks that preceded them. By contrast, the Minor Arcana number (or pip) cards are like animated storyboard sketches and character studies. They convey, for the most part, mobility and action, caught in mid-movement. The Court Cards, based closely on designs by Golden Dawn founder William Wynn Westcott, resemble Victorian photo postcards of actors in costume—stiffly posed (except for the Knights). These postcards may well have served as models for some of the details in Pamela's designs, thus the Minor Arcana pip cards have a certain liveliness to them and a dynamic sense that's missing from most of the other cards in the deck. In readings, they represent the more mundane and pragmatic aspects of life rather than the spiritual and allegorical doctrines and principles of the Majors.

In his few brief mentions regarding their collaboration, Waite says he chose Pamela, who had followed him into his Rectified Order of the Golden Dawn, as she was "a most imaginative and abnormally psychic artist . . . [who] loved the ceremonies without understanding their symbolic import." In an article in the *The Occult Review* (Vol X, No. 12, December 1909), he explained that his purpose in producing the deck was to "rectify the symbolism" of the Major Arcana "by reference to channels of knowledge which are not in the open day." Pamela had only been through the first two initiations in the Golden Dawn (Neophyte and Zelator) and so would have seen only two Golden Dawn tarot cards as they were revealed during the initiation ceremonies. It seems that Pamela's inspiration for creating illustrations for the number cards resulted from viewing a photographic display of the 15th century *Sola-Busca Tarot* recently arrived at the British Museum, for she directly copied a couple of its images.

The appearance, meanings and methods of the cards were not taught to initiates like Pamela Colman Smith until after their entrance into the Inner Order at the sixth initiation. Furthermore, Waite always kept his vows of secrecy, revealing in his book only what he knew from his other, extensive esoteric studies. Waite explained, "She had to be spoon-fed carefully over the Priestess Card, over that which is called the Fool and over the Hanged Man." For instance, Waite described, in *The Secret Tradition in Freemasonry*, the Master Mason entering the temple between Boaz and Jachin (B and J) and through the veil of palms and pomegranates—just as we see on the High Priestess card.

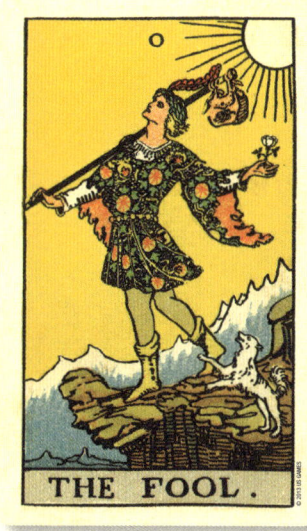 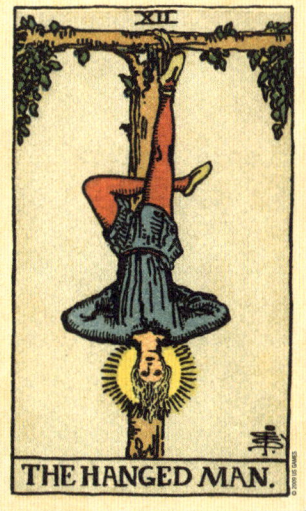 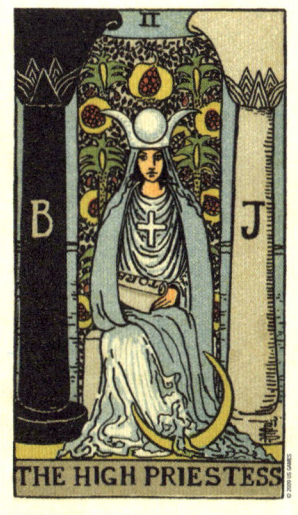

On the Fool's tunic are found twelve wheels with eight radii, with one wheel also containing the Hebrew letter Shin. In the Adeptus Minor ritual of his Fellowship of the Rosy Cross, found in Israel Regardie's *The Complete Golden Dawn System of Magic*, Waite explained,

> "At the meeting point of the arms—in the middle of the Cosmic Cross—is placed the Wheel or Circle of the Spirit, having eight radii, proceeding from the sacred letter SHIN. The doctrine of the Rosy Cross in the Grade of Adeptus Minor is here formulated and symbolised, with intimations of mysteries which lie beyond the Grade."

Few deck creators have been so esoterically well informed concerning the multidimensional import of symbols as was Waite.

The Rider-Waite-Smith tarot deck owes its classic look to a combination of 15th century High Gothic woodcut playing cards favoring strong black lines, the Symbolist/Arts and Crafts amalgam of medieval, romantic and folk styles of decoration, as well as the *Japoniste* use of strong line with flat color and perspective and favoring a diagonal emphasis, which is seen mostly in the Minor Arcana. The Japanese influence found in Ukiyo-e woodcuts (collected by Pamela's father and her Pratt Institute instructor, Arthur

Wesley Dow) is epitomized in the West by the printmaking techniques of fin de siècle French posters. While this effect continued through the 20th century, the newest tarot decks frequently eschew Pamela's design techniques in favor of a great variety of artistic styles including computer-generated art and collage. Still, the storyboard or comic strip character is found in many modern decks, including those from the East with the Japanese and Korean *manga* and *anime* tarots.

The single most significant event in making Pamela Colman Smith well known and her deck the "standard" in the modern world was Stuart Kaplan's acquisition of the rights to publish the tarot deck around the world via USGS. By the close of 1971 the *Rider-Waite Tarot* deck was being sold in chain bookstores and department stores across the United States and soon around the world. In the decades that followed, Stuart Kaplan has written and published books, essays, articles and deck booklets that tell Pamela's story, expanding on it as more and more biographical data has come to light. Following the deck's success, Kaplan commissioned artists to create new, culturally themed and artistic decks modeled on Pamela's designs as well as decks featuring variations on the original designs and coloring. This output resulted in a Rider-Waite-Smith style deck to fit almost every taste and new decks to entice collectors.

Six of Swords, left to right:

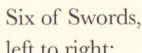
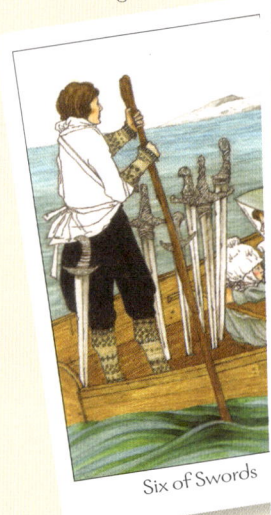
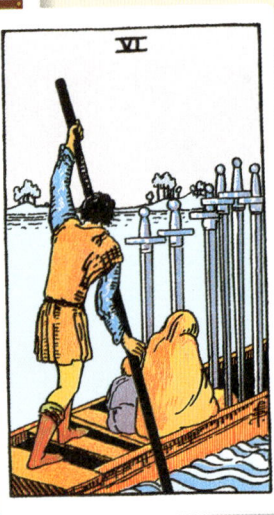
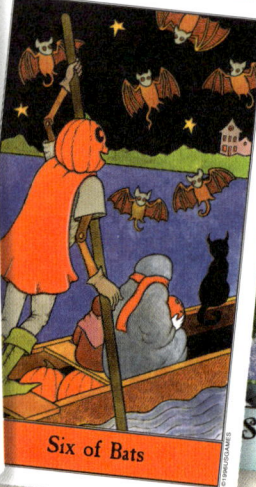
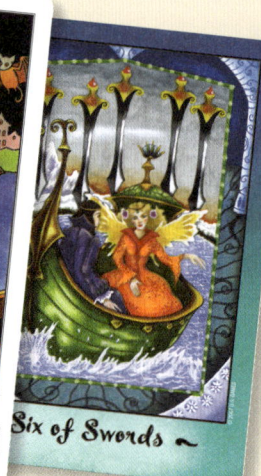

Dreaming Way Tarot by Rome Choi & Kwon Shina (2012, USGS)

Deviant Moon Tarot by Patrick Valenza (2008, USGS)

Rider-Waite Tarot by A.E. Waite & Pamela Colman Smith (1909, 1971, USGS)

The Halloween Tarot by Kipling West (1996, USGS)

Faerie Tarot by Nathalie Hertz (2008, USGS)

USGS decks featuring exact reproductions and close variations on Pamela's original designs:

* The best selling Rider-Waite-Smith deck is the one first published by U.S. Games Systems, Inc. in 1971 and available almost everywhere. *The Rider Tarot Deck* in its brightly colored yellow box is among the Top Ten Tarot Decks of All Time in every survey, and is sold in the standard, giant, pocket and miniature sizes. The back has a blue and white plaid design.
* *The Universal Waite Tarot,* redrawn and recolored by Mary Hanson-Roberts, appeared in 1992. It is known for its softer, warm colors, enhanced depth through shading and additional details, especially in the faces. The back is navy blue with symmetric gold stars.
* In 1993, USGS printed *The Original Rider Waite Tarot Pack*, a replica of the very first edition of the cards, with their "roses and lilies" back design, made especially for the Christmas Arts and Crafts Fair of 1909. The poor quality of the 1909 cardstock necessitated a new edition in 1910 with minor changes to the images and coloring.
* *The Quick & Easy Tarot* of 1999 has small versions of the Mary Hanson-Roberts' recoloring with a few sentences of upright meanings printed above and reversed meanings below the image. The back is gold with a stylized pomegranate design and navy border.
* The *Albano-Waite Tarot* first appeared in 1968 as a recolored edition. The tones are not quite as intense as the original electrically charged ones but still impart a 1960s feel. The backs are white with a gold sun.
* 1999 saw a *Glow in the Dark Tarot,* Major Arcana only, in black and white; the white shows up as a luminescent green in the dark. The back has a double Moon motif.
* The *Radiant Rider-Waite Tarot,* recolored by Virginijus Poshkus, was issued in 2003. It was redrawn as well as recolored in more vibrant tones and aura like effects. Many faces are redrawn to express stronger emotions. The backs are blue violet with gold stars.
* *The Pamela Colman Smith Commemorative Tarot Set* came out in 2009 containing prints and postcards of Pamela's work, plus a 101-page illustrated book, *The Artwork and Times of Pamela Colman Smith* by Stuart R. Kaplan and Lynn Araujo. This exact reproduction of Pamela's original deck has muted colors with ivory borders suggesting the aged appearance of the original cards. The backs feature the Rosicrucian white rose from the banner on the Death card and Pamela's signature against a blue-gray background.
* In 2015-2017, three stand-alone choices of earlier decks were added, all having four additional cards with selections from Pamela's non-tarot art. *The Smith-Waite Centennial Tarot Deck* is identical to the one in the aforementioned set and was also presented as a pocket-sized deck in a tin. The S*mith-Waite Tarot Deck Borderless Edition* (2017) is a full-sized deck but without borders, providing a more immersive reading experience.

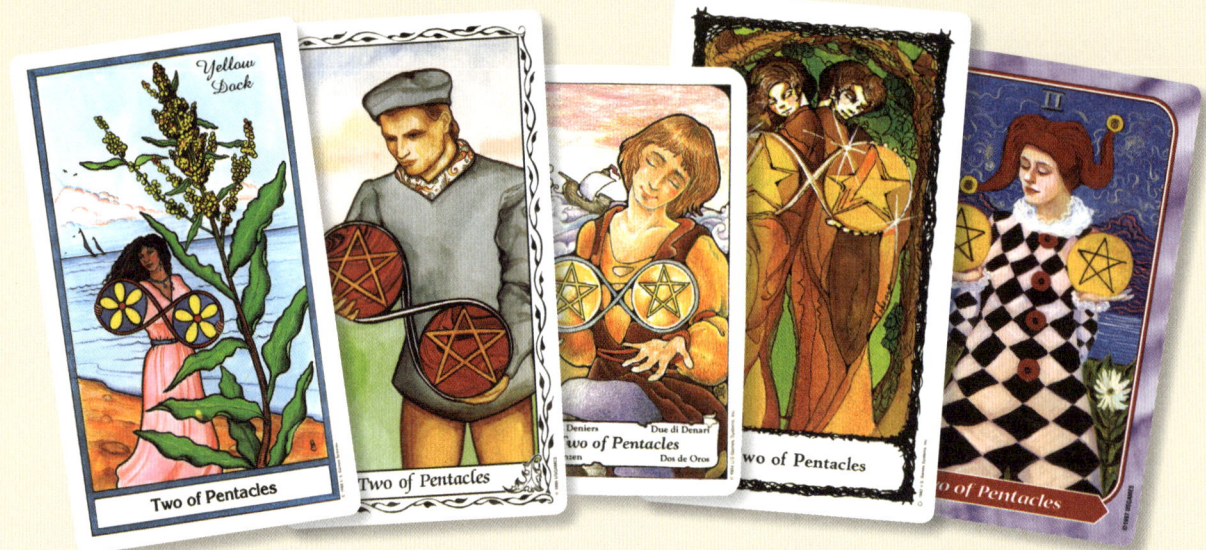

Two of Pentacles, left to right:

The Herbal Tarot by Michael Tierra and Candis Cantin (1988, USGS)

The Hudes Tarot by Susan Hudes (1995, USGS)

The Hanson-Roberts Tarot by Mary Hanson-Roberts (1985, USGS)

The Sacred Rose Tarot by Johanna Gargiulo-Sherman (1982, USGS)

Spiral Tarot by Kay Stevenson (1997, USGS)

Cards in Film, Media and Poetry

PAMELA'S TAROT DECK HAS BECOME ICONIC IN POPULAR 20TH AND 21ST CENTURY CULTURE with instantly recognizable visual symbols that speak more strongly than a thousand words. As a result of this influence, *Rider-Waite-Smith* Tarot cards regularly appear in movies and on television with the following as only a small sampling. The 1947 film noir classic, *Nightmare Alley* with Tyrone Power and Joan Blondell as the carny tarot reader is a must see movie for its allusions to the tarot that go well beyond the depicted readings. It is closely based on William Lindsay Gresham's masterpiece novel of the same name that features a Major Arcana card for each of its 22 chapters. Harking back to the '60s, *A Walk on the Moon* (1999) with Diane Lane and Viggo Mortensen includes one of the great film tarot lines. Lane's tarot consultant mother holds up the card with a line of swords plunged in a person's back (Ten of Swords) and asks, "Does this look like a vacation?" *Things You Can Tell Just by Looking at Her* (2000) has Calista Flockhart reading the Rider Tarot for Glenn Close's character.

The 2008 "Mountain King" episode of *Mad Men* on AMC (2:12) contains one of the best examples of an actual tarot reading to appear on television. HBO's *Carnival* 2003-2005 features a tarot reader using the cards to further the plot and not just to presage disaster via the Death or Hanged Man cards. Even PBS's Masterpiece Theatre *Endeavor* (2017) builds suspense through a series of closing shots of the signature *Rider-Waite* tarot cards, culminating in a reading for the young Inspector Morse.

Pamela's images also have been incorporated into musical albums and performances. For a few of the most notable see Led Zeppelin's untitled fourth album and their Hermit statue made to immortalize it; Madonna's Reinvention Tour "Hollywood Screen"; Roseanne Cash's music video "The Wheel"; and the *Xena: the Warrior Princess* 1998 TV musical episode, "*Bitter Suite*" (3:12).

Among poets, tarot has long been favored for inspiration and for the direct appropriation of its images. This trend goes back at least as far as 1527 with Teofilio Folengo's *Caos del Triperiuno*, which includes a series of poems representing the fortunes of people revealed by the cards dealt them. T.S. Eliot's "The Waste Land" is perhaps the most famous single poem, in which the reader, Madame Sosostris, describes Pamela's Three of Wands as "the man with three staves." From the mid-20th century on, tarot has appeared more and more frequently in poems. Some of the most well-known poets include Sylvia Plath, Anne Sexton, Diane di Prima, Alice Notley, Ted Berrigan, Philip Whalen, John Wieners, Philip Lamantia, Robert Creeley, Charles Olson, and more recently Patti Smith and the 2008-2010 United States Poet Laureate, Kay Ryan, who told the Washington Post (July 17, 2008) that she started her career by writing poems about tarot cards, "She would get out a pack of tarot cards, turn one card over every day and write a poem from it."

The Rider-Waite Deck as Experienced by Tarot Readers

IN THE MODERN COMPUTER AGE THE WORD *LEGACY*, ACCORDING TO THE OXFORD DICTIONARIES, denotes "software or hardware that has been superseded but is difficult to replace because of its continued functionality and wide use." And, in fact, some tarot readers complain that Pamela's scenes sentimentally dramatize what had originally been the unillustrated pips of the earlier and still current Italian, French, Swiss and Spanish decks. Her pictorial scenes in the Minor Arcana are seen as paradoxically both limiting *and* broadening card meaning, resulting in a too particular storyline or a too broad—"whatever you see in the picture"—approach to determining significance in the cards. As an example, while the Two of Pentacles is described by Waite as gaiety, news and agitation; it is often seen, via Pamela's design, as juggling two or more situations in one's life. However, the nearly universal adoption of Pamela's motifs for the Minors show exactly how well understood they are and how valuable for accurate readings they have proven to be.

As a professionally trained artist and book illustrator, Pamela made tarot accessible and even playful. Pamela's images are seemingly simple and uncluttered, relaxing to the eye, and leave empty space suggesting infinite vistas. Through the bright colors and strong lines that characterize classic children's books, the viewer is drawn into a realm of knights and maidens, castles and gardens, fantasy creatures, and objects of risk, enterprise and magic. All is revealed as if by a curtain being pulled back on a stage to disclose a scene in mid action. Memorization of card meanings is no longer essential as the images tell their own tale that often evokes in the viewer the core card meanings described by A.E. Waite and later by Eden Gray. Even more important was Pamela's ability to transcend the personal with her images. Perhaps it had something to do with her reported experiences "seeing" music and fairies. She called it an "inner sight" that would close down if she tried to change anything, teaching her to remain open to what came *through*, but was not *of*, her.

A Therapeutic Tarot

FOR THE CONTEMPORARY TAROT READER AND QUITE A FEW PSYCHOTHERAPISTS, THIS PARTICULAR tarot deck brings up personal memories and reflections that serve as doorways to the active imagination and archetypes of the unconscious that are at the root of the psychology of Carl Jung. The card's personally evocative nature has been found useful in Jungian as well as other transpersonal psychology methodologies such as Transactional Analysis, Gestalt Therapy and Psychosynthesis. Although the figures lack diversity of race, size and, to a lesser extent, age, all of which have become of concern more recently, there are an equal number of male and female figures in the deck and several that appear androgynous—a strength when one is projecting their inner psyche onto the cards. Furthermore, the ambiguity of expression on many faces leads one to perceive different attitudes and emotions at different times. Robert Wang's *Jungian Tarot* deck and books from USGS take this notion as their basis. As a projective device, Pamela's cards can work as well or better than the classic *Thematic Apperception Test* (TAT) according to Art Rosengarten, Ph.D. in *Tarot and Psychology: Spectrums of Possibility* (2000).

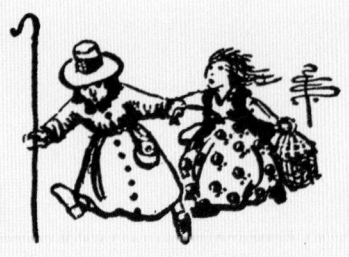

The Mid 20th Century Tarot Renaissance

Pamela's accessibility is in stark contrast to A.E. Waite's abstruse, though brilliant book, *The Pictorial Key to the Tarot*, which is often more confusing than helpful to new tarot readers. It required Eden Gray's *Tarot Revealed: A Modern Guide to Reading the Tarot Cards*, first published in 1960, to encourage everyone to "take the plunge and begin to use the cards in divination and contemplation." It was Eden Gray who coined the term "the Fool's Journey" to describe the Major Arcana, linking it forever to Joseph Campbell's archetypal "Hero's Journey," which it so resembles. Although Waite had referred to the Majors as "the soul's quest," that phrase never caught on. Gray's books and Pamela's cards made for the perfect combination at the perfect historical time.

More than one commentator on the 1960's counterculture claimed that every hippie pad had its requisite tarot reader; the deck was a staple of the lifestyle. Tarot appeared frequently on the hugely popular afternoon TV soap opera *Dark Shadows* (1966-71), featuring vampires and witches. This show may have been the first introduction for many to tarot in the U.S. Pamela's Fool card, with the Fool poised at the edge of a cliff, was adopted as the USGS logo, both because the founding of the company required a leap of faith and because April 1st is the birthday of its founder, Stuart Kaplan. The Fool card also became the signature image of the Summer of Love with his flower, psychedelic tunic and the feather in his hair. Even Waite's description in *The Pictorial Key to the Tarot* of the Fool as "the spirit in search of experience" reflected the outlook of the time. 1970 began with the biggest break yet from the occult tarots of the 19th and early 20th centuries when the young commercial artist, David Palladini, created a totally new rendition of Pamela's illustrations

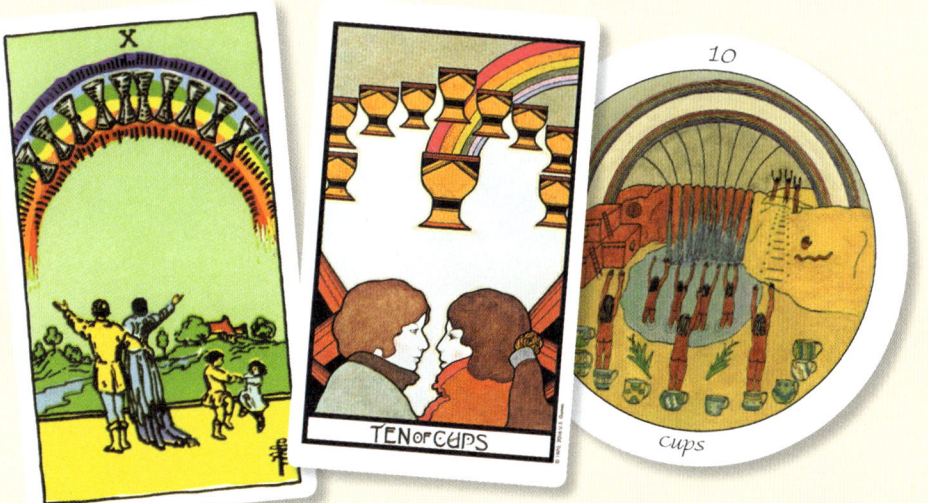

Ten of Cups, left to right: *Tarot Cards* by Frankie Albano (1968, Tarot Productions, Inc.) *Aquarian Tarot* by David Palladini (1970, Morgan Press), USGS. *Motherpeace Tarot* by Vicki Nobel and Karen Vogel (1981, 1983 USGS)

with his *Aquarian Tarot* (1988, USGS). Yet another example of a deck that arose from a contemporary social movement is Vicki Noble and Karen Vogel's round *Motherpeace Tarot* (1981, 1983) proclaiming the intersection of political feminism and women's spirituality, and going much further than prior tarot decks in conveying a social vision that resulted in a radical reconceptualization of Pamela's template.

Waite and the Secret Tradition

WE CAN SEE PAMELA'S PICTORIAL MINOR ARCANA AS AN AMBASSADOR OR ENVOY INTO THE future, a tool for "future telling"—while yet illustrating timeless echoes of long ago: of myth and legend rather than of actual historical events. The style chosen may be a deliberate reference to the "Secret Tradition" of A.E. Waite and "Ageless Wisdom" of Paul Foster Case. Waite's many books and articles on the "Secret Tradition" in alchemy, Freemasonry, Kabbalah and the Grail, as well as in tarot, expounded on a single idea that there exists hidden teachings of a "return to Unity with the Divine." Furthermore, this philosophical belief, expressed also in Blavatsky's "Secret Doctrine," Aldous Huxley's "Perennial Philosophy" and Joseph Campbell's "monomyth," suggests that mystical doctrines and teachings can be traced through the ancient religions of Egypt and Greece to the mystical branches of today's religions as well as into secret and magical orders. The symbols that Waite directed Pamela to use in the Major Arcana and a few of the Minor Arcana cards point to his belief in the power of those symbols to return the soul to its Source. He wrote in *The Secret Tradition in Freemasonry* that "certain high grade Orders do carry a second sense in their symbolism . . . of that Great Experiment which is at the heart of all true religion, being the way of the soul's reintegration in God." There's no doubt that the tarot was meant to carry such import for "the true Tarot is symbolism; it speaks no other language and offers no other signs" as Waite proclaimed in *The Pictorial Key to the Tarot*. Carl Jung suggested something similar when he wrote in *Structure and Dynamics of the Psyche* (1969), "The psychological mechanism that transforms energy is the symbol."

In addition to the images themselves, Pamela left us her legacy of how to read the cards in a 1908 article in the preeminent Arts and Crafts magazine *The Craftsman*. Here, her instructions for viewing a painting also apply to interpreting her cards:

> "Note the dress, the type of face; see if you can trace the character in the face; note the pose. . . . First watch the simple forms of joy, of fear, of sorrow; look at the position taken by the whole body. . . . After you

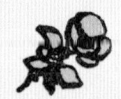

have found how to tell a simple story, put in more details. . . . Learn from everything, see everything, and above all feel everything! . . . Find eyes within, look for the door into the unknown country."

This approach is perfectly suited to reading tarot for oneself or in an interactive relationship with a client.

Susan Wands' mystery novel *Magician and the Fool* (2018, i2i Publishing) features Pamela Colman Smith. The author writes that "Pixie was a free spirit who is remembered because she created and left a pack of cards that have ignited our collective imaginations."

Pamela's Non-tarot Legacy

WHILE THE TAROT IS PAMELA COLMAN SMITH'S MOST WIDELY KNOWN GIFT TO POSTERITY, HER contributions in other fields deserve far more recognition than they've yet received. Pamela's art has been featured in a couple of exhibitions since her death, most notably the Delaware Art Museum exhibitions of 1975 curated by Melinda Boyd Parsons and the 2007-2008 "Georgia O'Keeffe and the Women of the Stieglitz Circle" exhibitions that toured several museums. The Pratt Institute has celebrated Pamela Colman Smith on their website and in their exhibits, writing that they "helped develop such versatile artistic sensibilities that included her tarot deck." Both Melinda Boyd Parsons and Elizabeth O'Connor have written articles in academic journals that made scholars more aware of Pamela's contributions to art and theatre.

But it is this book itself that will be of utmost significance in opening the door of public awareness to Pamela's artistic gifts and previously unknown facts concerning her life. Nowhere else will one be able to hold in their hands the vast evidence of her creative abilities and productions during the relatively short 15- to 20-year period of her known artistic activity—ranging primarily from 1898 to the advent of WWI in 1914. The bibliography in this book details the extent to which she was known and lauded, ranging from her painting exhibitions to her book illustrations, her involvement in the theatre and many performances of Jamaican folktales as well as the chanting of the poems of W.B. Yeats.

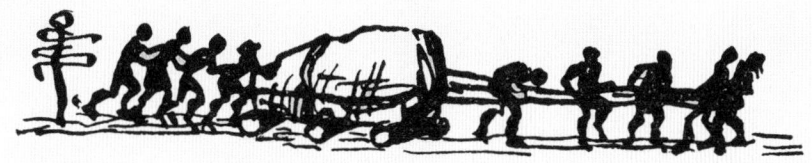

Jamaican Folktales: The Annancy Stories

PAMELA LEFT A NOTABLE LEGACY THAT AROSE FROM HER TELLING AND ILLUSTRATING JAMAICAN folktales. This includes the first use of the Jamaican regional dialect in print through her 1896 contribution of two stories to the *Journal of American Folklore*. In 1899 she published *Annancy Stories*, the first illustrated storybook of the tales of the spider/trickster figure, Anansi, followed by a later self-published book of folktales called *Chim-Chim Folk Stories from Jamaica*. She performed these stories in dialect dressed as a Jamaican nurse, using cut out figures of the characters to enact the scenes as she narrated them. The quasi-human spider Anansi or Annancy demonstrated the ability of the weak and the downtrodden to use brains, wit and cunning to triumph, mirroring the struggles Pamela faced in her own life. Her Annancy Stories are available today in a full color reprint edition, preserving the original hand coloring. Today on YouTube you can watch animated Anansi stories or hear the late Miss Lou (Dr. Louise Bennett Coverley), dressed much as Pamela would have done, sharing stories, songs and poems, keeping alive the dialect and West Indian culture.

A Legacy of Crossed Boundaries

PAMELA REGULARLY CROSSED BOUNDARIES: BETWEEN JAMAICA AND THE U.S., BETWEEN NEW York and London, between our material world and a mystical, magical "unknown country" others called her Dreamland. (She devoted the June 1902 issue of *A Broad Sheet* to the A.E. poem "Gates of Dreamland," for which she created a dreamy painting of a young sleeping figure surrounded by fairies.) She even had a crossing of the physical senses, given that she had a form of *synesthesia*. She also appeared to exist between cultures as she was frequently described as Chinese, Japanese, mixed race or primitive American as well as "a savant with a child's heart." Like much of her art, she herself lived at the borders and edges of accepted social convention as do the majority of tarot readers, many of their clients, post-suffrage feminists, and those in the LGBT community who acknowledge her as a kindred spirit.

Because so little is known about her private life, Pamela Colman Smith has been the focus of tremendous speculation and fantasy. Some admirers claim her as a hero of mixed race and/or with lesbian leanings, although there is nothing but speculation, both during her lifetime and after, to substantiate either. There's no indication that her parents visited Jamaica until ten years after her birth, and while quite a few of her closest friends were publicly notable lesbians, there are no traces of a romantic relationship of any gender in her life. Adding to her air of mystery, her place of burial is unmarked and unrecorded, the former as she died a pauper and the latter as a result of a fire that destroyed church records from the period. Thus, as "goddaughter of a witch and sister to a fairy" (Ransome, 1907) she left a legacy of mystery and intrigue that is enticing because of its hints and potentials, especially to the mystically and magically inclined.

It is ironic that her financial and personal possession legacy went not to her companion, Nora Lake, as per her will, but instead everything was sold to pay the debt she owed primarily to Britain's Inland Revenue service. Whether her failure to pay taxes was some kind of protest, lack of awareness or due to simple poverty will never be known.

The Artist

PAMELA'S NON-TAROT LIFE AND ACTIVITIES HAVE HAD LITTLE EFFECT ON THE MODERN WORLD until recently when she began appearing more frequently in books about Alfred Stieglitz, Ellen Terry, Edy Craig and the Yeats family, mostly regarding her art exhibitions, theatrical designs and *A Broad Sheet* (with artist Jack B. Yeats). Pamela was one of those who helped, through her drawings, to immortalize the great British actress Ellen Terry, as can be seen by searching on Pamela's name at the British National Trust website or by viewing the works at Ellen Terry's home, Smallhythe Place, near Tenterden, Kent where Pamela most likely completed her drawings for the tarot deck. Terry's home and the surrounding countryside can be seen clearly in many of the cards. In the Ten of Cups we see a home nestled in the hills much like a typical country view in that part of Kent. In the Six of Cups we see Smallhythe Place itself but drawn as if next to a tower (found nearby). The windswept trees and distant hills in the Swords Court Cards echo the distant view in the fall from the upper floor of the vicarage across the road.

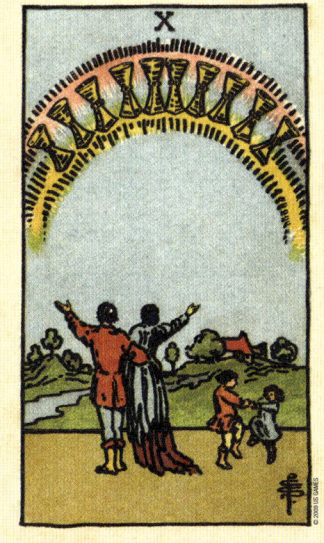
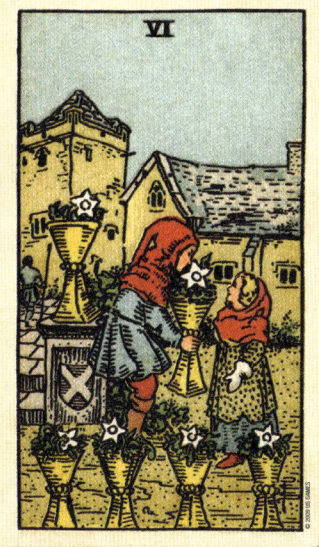

One more area in which Pamela is noteworthy is found in this quote from a Merriam-Webster example of the word *legacy*: "The rights and opportunities that women enjoy today are partly the legacy of early suffragists and feminists." How perfectly appropriate, for Pamela was active as an artist in the British suffrage movement, creating posters that were usually unsigned, in solidarity with her sisters. As in her posters for suffrage, the war effort, relief funds and so on, Pamela left a legacy of fighting against systems that tried to exploit and limit her and others who have been disenfranchised. Indeed, much of her art features women in more independent and active roles than was normally seen in late Victorian and Edwardian England—roles with which the modern woman can easily identify.

Most of Pamela's art was ephemeral, appearing in books and other publications that sold in editions of under 500, which she would color by hand. Drawings and paintings are on inexpensive paper that is, in some cases, disintegrating. Furthermore, her theatre designs are long gone, her performances and toy theatres exist only in commentaries and in a few old photographs. The location of many works described in exhibition catalogs is unknown, if they still remain. All these works including her "music pictures," are discussed in the biography section of this book. Her art and book illustrations are collected avidly by those who have come to love her unique imagination and otherworldly vision..

Our Lady of The Lizard

SOME OF PAMELA'S LEGACY IS LONG FORGOTTEN. HAVING CONVERTED TO ROMAN CATHOLICISM IN 1911 she devoted a significant portion of her later life to caretaking a tiny Catholic chapel that no longer exists in an isolated location in Cornwall at The Lizard, the southernmost tip of the British isles. It is the location where the Spanish Armada was first sighted and from where Marconi sent his early radio transmissions. Pamela and her housekeeper companion, Nora Lake, were lauded, unnamed, in *The Tablet: The International Catholic News Weekly* (1922-1923), which poetically described the chapel at The Lizard as being in an "out-of-the-world spot" where "a devoted benefactress has for some time kept an open chapel" that is "all that is left of Lyonesse on the mainland." Lyonesse was a mythical Arthurian kingdom, site of the story of Tristan and Iseult and of the final battle between King Arthur and his son Mordred. The island supposedly sank off the rocky coast, much like in Pamela's painting of "The Sunken Cathedral." It is easy to imagine Pamela in "Our Lady of The Lizard Chapel" saying prayers for the thirty-six torpedoed WWI vessels and hundreds of ships wrecked there over the ages, as well as for the coast guard and "all those who pass safely by," as mentioned in Catholic news reports. This suggests a spiritual legacy that is well beyond our worldly ability to judge.

Pamela's "Other Worldly" Senses

PAMELA HERSELF HAD PSYCHIC ABILITY AND A FORM OF SYNESTHESIA—SHE SAW MUSIC—AS was mentioned often during her lifetime and detailed in this biography. There is also a tantalizing description in *The Occult Review* (Nov. 1907) of her and Lady Alix Egerton visiting the Peacock's Well in Ireland where they heard faery music and were suddenly surrounded by a throng of men on horses and on foot and a queenly woman who vanished as a salmon appeared in the river in her place, wearing a silver crown.

Pamela has not, except for the articles interviewing her during her lifetime, been discussed in the literature of synesthesia. The public's fascination with her unusual gift is showcased by the heading of the article pictured here. Synesthesia (a crossing of the senses in which numbers and letters have distinct colors, names smells, or music with colors and images), although earlier recognized, was not named until the end of the 19th century; the ancient Greeks called one form "color-hearing." Perhaps, as Pamela's music pictures become better known, her unusual gift will become more recognized and she will be included in future discussions of synesthesia in art.

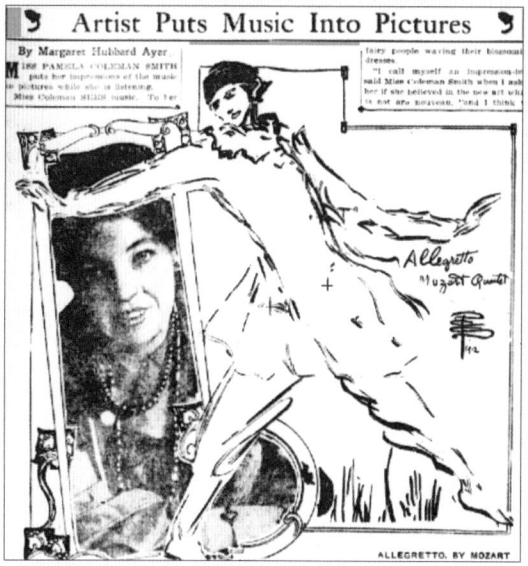

The Los Angeles Herald, March 26, 1912

The *San Jose Mercury News* (March 25, 1924) said that in her music pictures "she can get to the soul within the sounds" and quoted Debussy as saying, "You have not only captured the idea which was in my mind, but you carried it further." The writer also states that Miss Colman Smith's music pictures are in great vogue such that "in many of the big houses in England one may find the music room decorated with friezes and panels illustrative of the movement of various compositions." We have yet to find any of these friezes and panels but are ever hopeful of one coming to light. More and more artists, musicians and poets are coming forward about their own forms of synesthesia saying that it adds so much to their creative endeavors.

Critical Commentaries on the Works of Pamela Colman Smith

It is true that some viewers of Pamela's artworks, both in her heyday and into the 21st century, find her work less stimulating. They declare it relatively sparse, naïve, too primitive and old fashioned with its emphasis on faux medieval and bygone eras. Her color palette is limited, and tones (at least in the tarot deck) are too bright and too flat. Critics say she displays a flawed perspective and faulty figure drawing skills. Her tarot images are not ethnically diverse, being too Western and Christian, leaving out both Eastern and African culture and history. They find her erratic, immature and, dare it be said, "disturbing." Finally, it is felt that her work may not capture the evolving changes in culture and human experience.

This book, however, amply displays a greater range of her styles and themes than has been recognized in the past. The welcoming and tremendous sales of her tarot deck around the world show that it speaks equally to other cultures, even when those people are not fully aware of the myths and symbols to which an image alludes.

A great many people around the world agree that Pamela Colman Smith leaves a legacy of originality, sincerity, unaffected childlike naturalness and harmony of expression. They appreciate her clarity and richness of symbolic detail, the theatrical *'tableau vivant'* quality of the tarot, and her mysterious faux medieval atmosphere. Her scenes are like stories that can be read by a child and ring true as a fairy tale. Emotional energy can be clearly discerned from the expressions and body language of the figures. The flatness, the vibrant colors, the simple faces and stylized movements of her tarot cards form easily recognized patterns and comparisons, linking thematically significant features throughout the work. Pamela's images are quirky and non threatening, with happy scenes that include frailties and unhappy scenes that show strengths.

Conclusion

We now see Pamela Colman Smith as an independent, self-determined, artist, publisher and performer who traveled freely and expressed herself whimsically and colorfully. She kept a sense of humor while upholding the truth and integrity of her own vision, spoke out against discrimination in her profession and insisted on her financial due. Pamela excelled at visual storytelling in the mode of Shakespeare's plays or the Arthurian and Grail legends so prevalent in her beloved Cornwall. People still make pilgrimages to honor her in the Cornish towns where she lived. She died just a short distance from Tintagel, site of Merlin's cave and the reputed castle where Merlin used magic to bring about King Arthur's conception through Igraine and Uther Pendragon. Who can say but the mysteries surrounding her birth and life are just as magical? Her stories are forever young as Pamela will be in our hearts.

If Pamela's legacy is her being an "envoy or messenger sent with a commission" then her charge has certainly been one of keeping the joy and magic of a natural, free creative spirit alive in the world. The richness and bounty of tarot decks that make use of her ingenious template will continue to inspire and delight for generations to come.

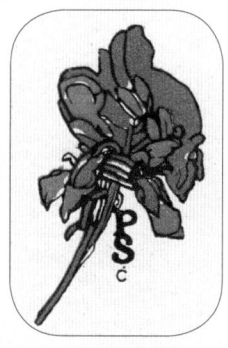

ADDENDUM

1878-1951 Birth & Death Certificate

SHOULD THE ART STUDENT THINK? BY PAMELA COLMAN SMITH

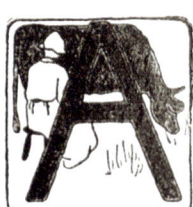LL you students who are just beginning your work in an Art School. Stop—think! First make sure in your own mind what end you wish to work for. Do you know? Perhaps you have not decided. You will leave all that to the time when you have learned to draw and leave the school—a crippled tool—ready to begin your serious work and have a studio—and all the rest of it. Do not wait till then! Put in a corner of your mind an idea—such as, "I wish to paint portraits." Just keep that idea in the corner, and do not forget that it is there. Call it up sometimes and review your work in front of it. Thus—"Am I working at the right beginning for this branch of art? Am I studying the faces of all the people I see—trying to find out their character—imagining how I should paint them if I were to do so? Am I trying to show more of their character than appears on the surface? Can I see it? No. But how shall I find it?" Look for it.

When you see a portrait of an historical person, note the dress, the type of face; see if you can trace the character in the face; note the pose, for often pose will date a picture as correctly as the hair or clothes. Remember the date, if the picture is dated; if not, place it in your mind as second half of the fourteenth century, or first half of the eighteenth, and so on. If you are not sure of the period, make a pencil sketch and take it with you to some reference library. Once a week make a point of looking up all the clothes you have seen (or wish to draw in some composition, perhaps). Some day when you may have a novel to illustrate and a character to portray, you will remember, "Oh, yes, a dress of the kind worn by so and so in the portrait by so and so—that type—or—no! Somewhat more lively."

Go and see all the plays you can. For the stage is a great school—or should be—to the illustrator—as well as to others. First watch the simple forms of joy, of fear, of sorrow; look at the position taken by the whole body, then the face—but that can come afterward.

As an exercise draw a composition of fear or sadness, or great sorrow, quite simply, do not bother about details now, but in a few lines tell your story. Then show it to any one of your friends, or family, or fellow students, and ask them if they can tell you what it is meant to portray. You will soon get to know how to make it tell its tale. After you have found how to tell a simple story, put in more details, the face, and indicate the dress. Next time you go to the play look at the clothes, hat, cloak, armor, belt, sword, dagger, rings, boots,

SHOULD THE ART STUDENT THINK?

jewels. Watch how the cloak swings when the person walks, how the hands are used. See if you can judge if the clothes are correct, or if they are worn correctly; for they are often ruined by the way they are put on. An actor should be able to show the period and manner of the time in the way he puts on his clothes, as well as the way he uses his hands, head, legs.

THIS may be beside the mark, think you! "Of what use is the stage to me? I am to be an illustrator of books! The stage is false, exaggerated, unreal," you say. So are a great many pictures in books, and the books, too, for that matter. The stage has taught me almost all I know of clothes, of action and of pictorial gestures.

Learn from everything, see everything, and above all *feel* everything! And make other people when they look at your drawing feel it too!

Make your training at your art school your a b c. You must learn to hold a brush, to mix paint, to draw in perspective, and study anatomy.

Keep an open mind to all things. Hear all the music you can, good music, for sound and form are more closely connected than we know.

Think good thoughts of beautiful things, colors, sounds, places, not mean thoughts. When you see a lot of dirty people in a crowd, do not remember only the dirt, but the great spirit that is in them all, and the power that they represent.

For through ugliness is beauty sometimes found. Lately I have seen a play, ugly, passionate, realistic, brutal. All through that play I felt that ugly things may be true to nature, but surely it is through evil that we realize good. The far-off scent of morning air, the blue mountains, the sunshine, the flowers, of a country I once lived in, seemed to rise before me—and there on the stage was a woman sitting on a chair, her body stiff, her eyes rolling, a wonderfully realistic picture of a fit.

I believe that in the so-called "composition class" the future of many a student lies. (Professor Arthur Dow, of Columbia University, has proved this, and through his influence I believe a good many schools have begun to teach composition first.)

But let the student begin young, and with all the necessary aids for the broadening of his mind. Composition first, and all the other rules and rudiments, in order as they come. As much literature,

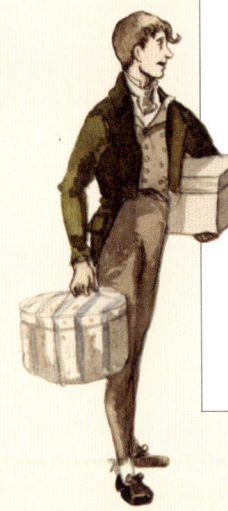

SHOULD THE ART STUDENT THINK?

1908

music, drama as possible (all to be thought of in relation to that idea so safely tucked away in the corner of the student's mind), to be worked at from the vantage point of knowing what they are to aid.

I wish here to say how grateful I am to the writer of an article in an American magazine (*Putman's Monthly* for July, 1907). "An Appreciation and a Protest." An appreciation of Albert Sterner, and a protest against the "ultra-sweetness and oppressive propriety admired alike by the publisher and the public," and "individuality discreetly suppressed."

O! the prudishness and pompous falseness of a great mass of intelligent people!

I do not hold that "the incessant roar of high-power presses" is alone to blame for the stifling of life, but for a lack of inspiration. For it is a land of power, a land of unkempt uproar—full of life, force, energy.

Lift up your ideals, you weaklings, and force a way out of that thunderous clamor of the steam press, the hurrying herd of blind humanity, noise, dust, strife, seething toil—there is power! The imprisoned Titans underneath the soil, grinding, writhing—take your strength from them, throw aside your petty drawing room point of view.

I do not want to see riotous, clumsy ugliness suddenly spring up, but a fine noble power shining through your work. The illustrations that I see in the magazines by the younger people are all dignified and well, carefully and conscientiously drawn, but their appalling clumsiness is quite beyond me,—their lack of charm and grace.

I do not mean by charm, *prettiness*, but an appreciation of beauty. Ugliness is beauty, but with a difference, a nobleness that speaks through all the hard crust of convention.

I have heard it said that half the world has nothing to say. Perhaps the other half has, but it is afraid to speak: Banish fear, brace your courage, place your ideal high up with the sun, away from the dirt and squalor and ugliness around you and let that power that makes "the roar of the high-power presses" enter into your work—energy—courage—life—love. Use your wits, use your eyes. Perhaps you use your physical eyes too much and only see the mask. Find eyes within, look for the door into the unknown country.

"High over cap" on a fairy horse—ride on your Quest—for what we are all seeking—*Beauty*. Beauty of thought first, beauty of feeling, beauty of form, beauty of color, beauty of sound, appreciation, joy, and the power of showing it to others.

1911

Pages from William Rider & Son's four-page brochure advertising a pack of 78 tarot cards, circa 1910

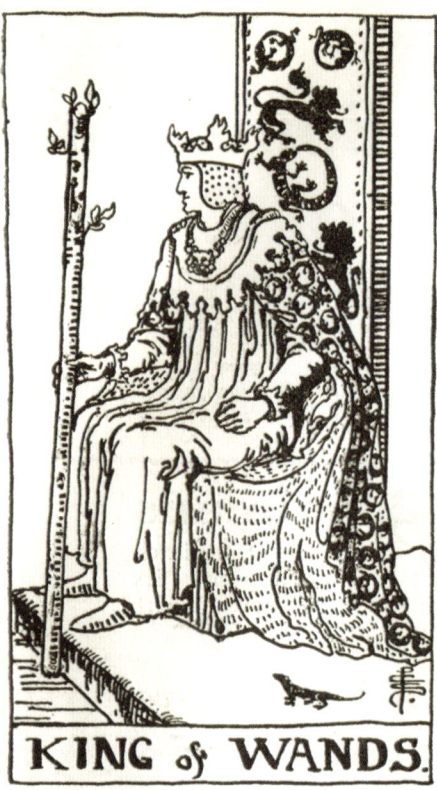
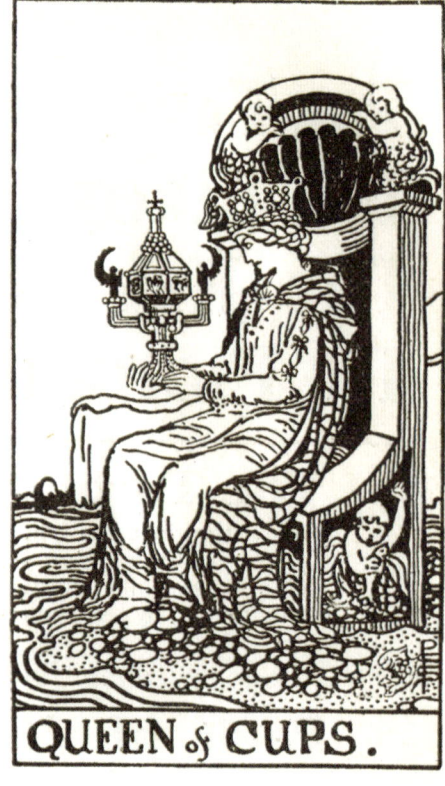
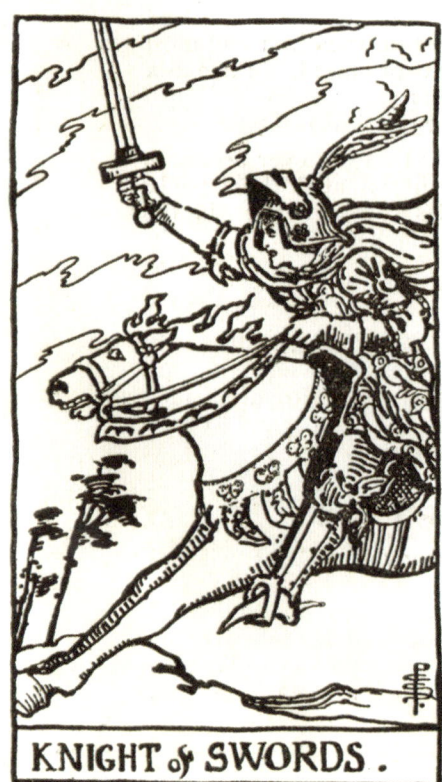
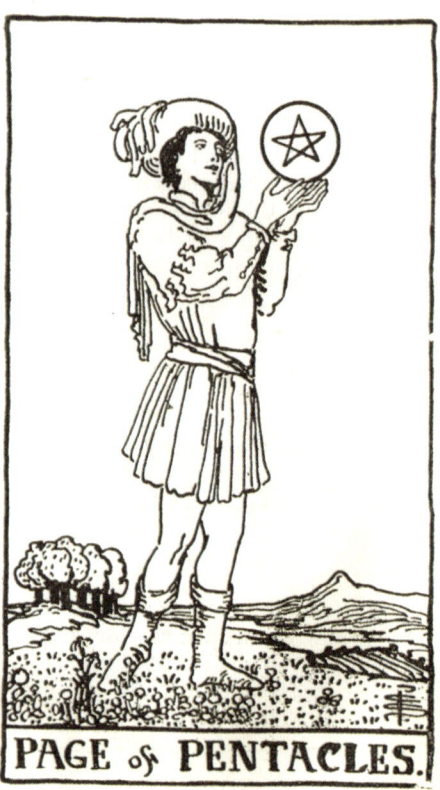

Specimens of Cards (reduced from actual size).

1911

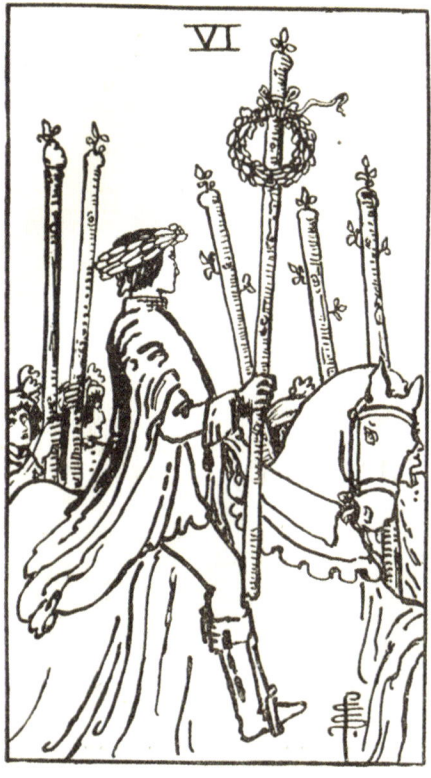
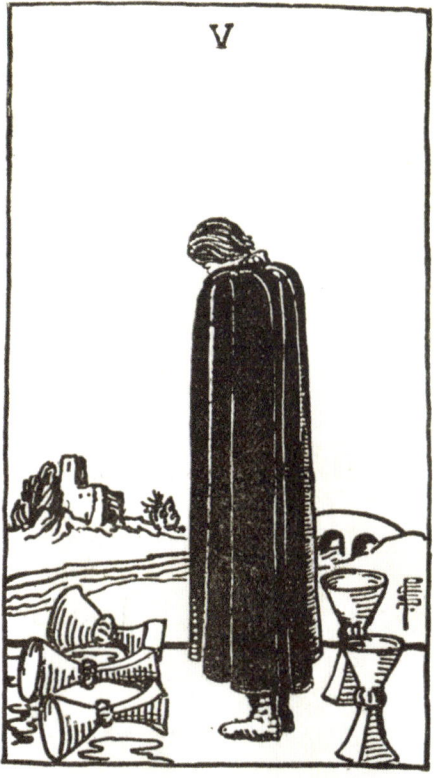

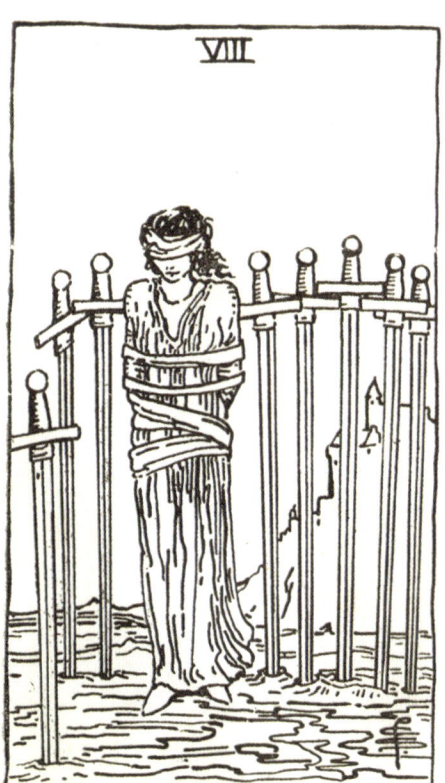
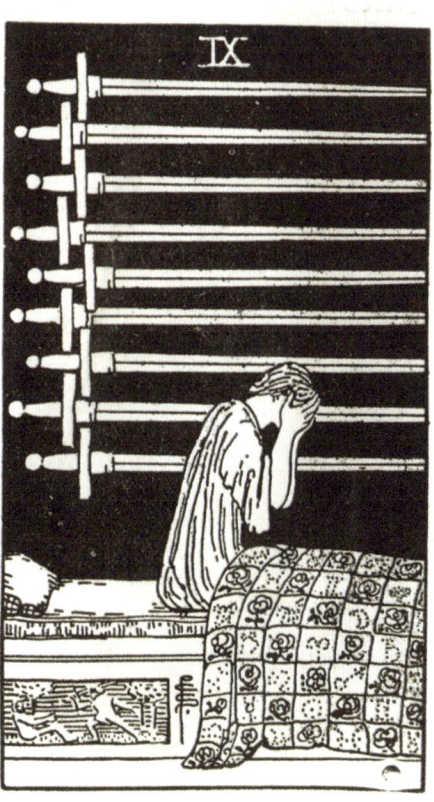

Specimens of Cards (reduced from actual size).

Diplomas

1913

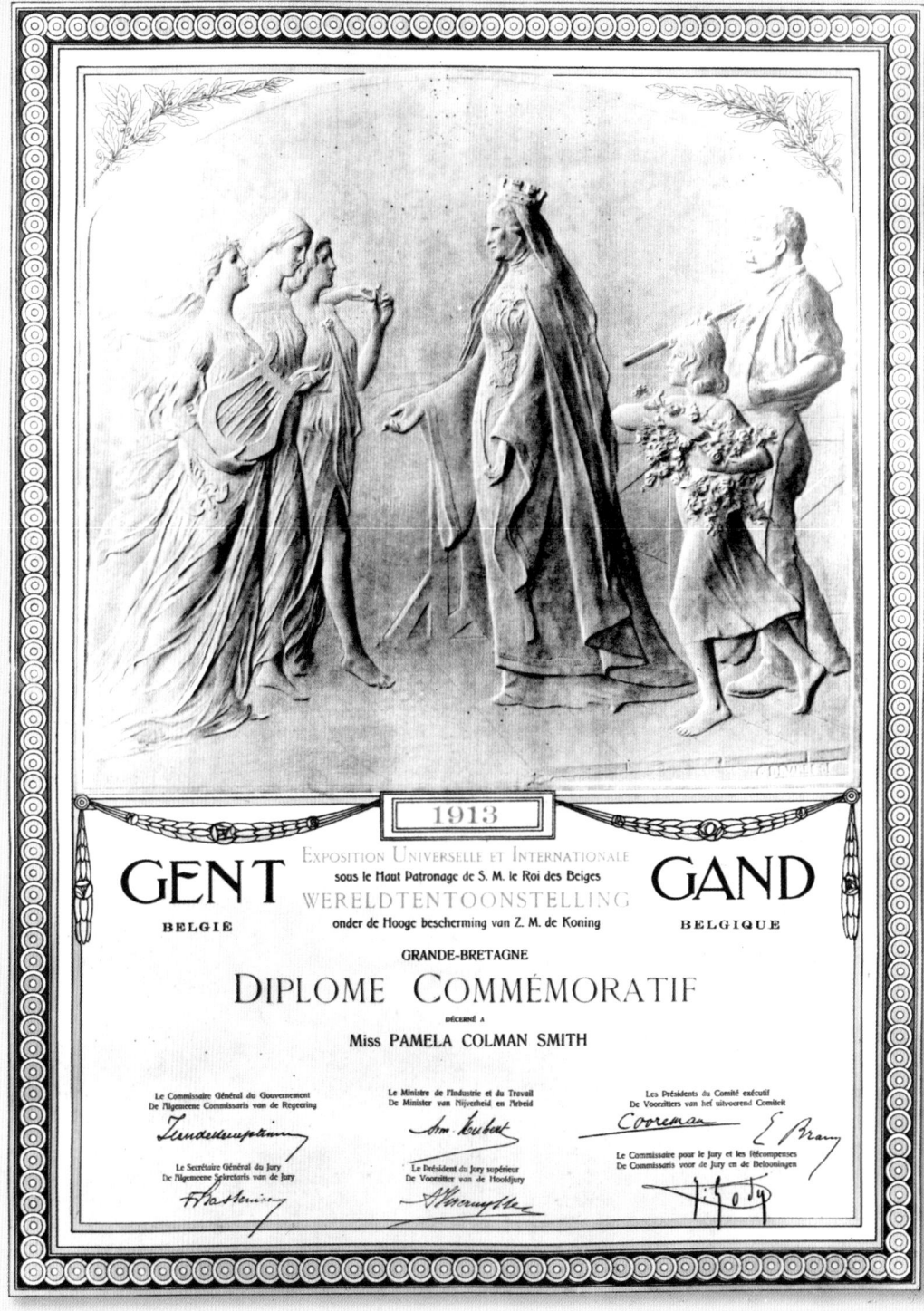

1914

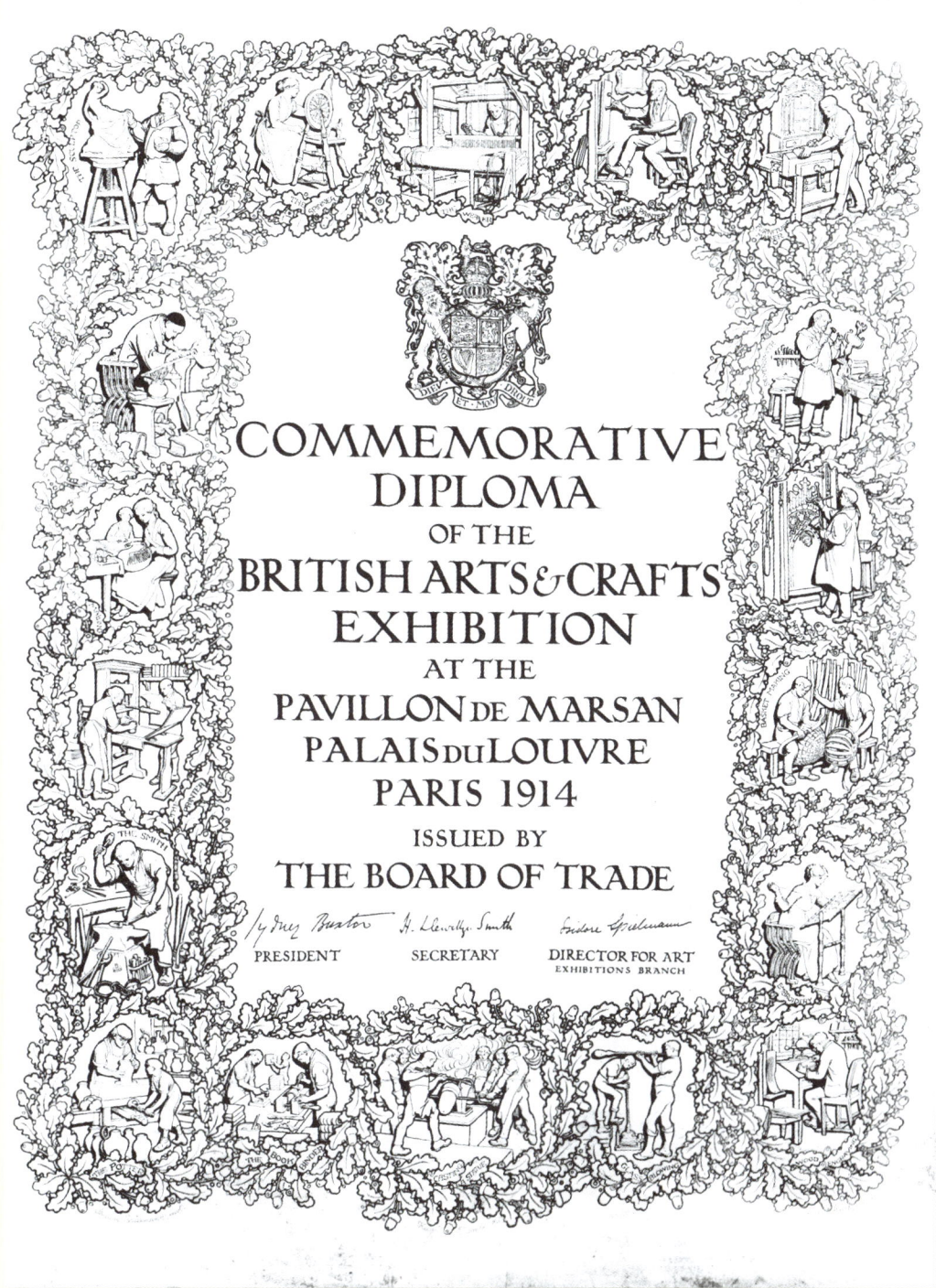

Passport Application

1916

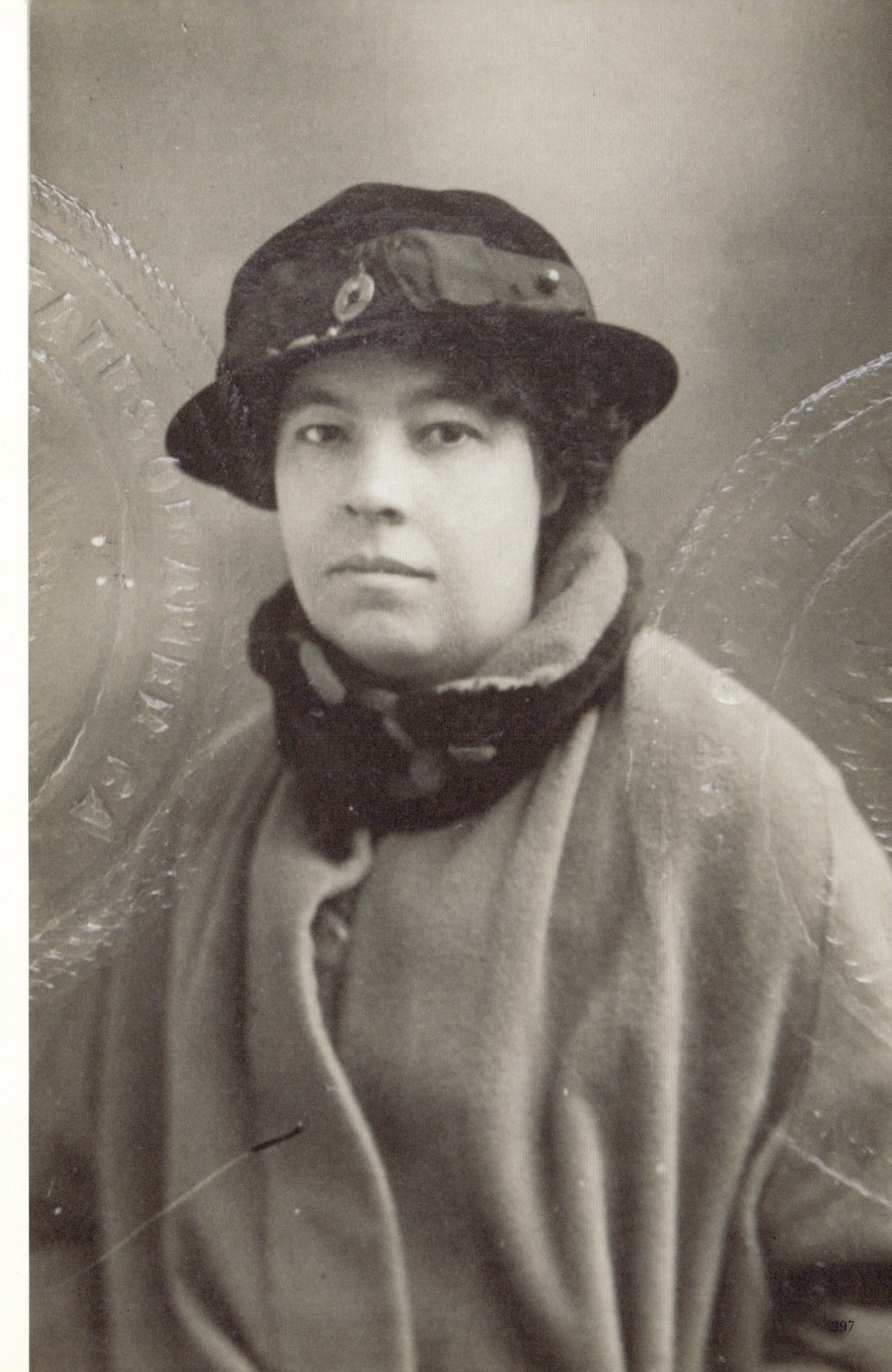

Burial Record, Parish of Bude Haven

1951

Name.	Abode.	When buried.	Age.	By whom the Ceremony was performed.
Beatrice Elma Carey-Dick (No. 1833)	12 Knowenian Terrace, Bude	13th June 1951	63 years	Kingston Kitterhell Minister
Edith Helena MARSHALL (No. 1834)	Elmscott Bungalow, Poundstock	15th June 1951	81 years	Walter Prest Vicar
John James DEACON (No. 1835)	32 Bell Vue, Bude	5th July 1951	85 years	Knowles Minister
Lucy Treweekes HAMBLEY (No. 1836)	Lansdowne Road, Bude	21st July 1951	88 years	Walter Prest Vicar
MARY JANE MAY ROBERTS (No. 1837)	SARATOGA DOWNS VIEW, BUDE	21st AUGUST 1951	56 YEARS	E. Lowell Congl Minister
Clara Louise ASKHAM (No. 1838)	11 Valley Road, Bude	28 Aug 1951	75 years	Samuel Lowndes
The Cremated remains of EDITH ANNIE MILLS (No. 1839)	Rosendale, Lansdowne Road, Bude	17th September 1951	74 years	Walter Prest Vicar
Corinne Prisula Mary Coleman-Smith (No. 1840)	2 Benredon House, Bude	September 20 1951	73 years	J. H. du Mereles Browne R.C. Priest

Last Will and Testament

1951

PROBATE ENGROSSMENT.

I CORINNE PAMELA MARY COLMAN SMITH of No. 2 Bencoolen House Bude in the County of Cornwall Spinster hereby revoke all testamentary dispositions heretofore made by me and declare this to be my last Will which I make this twenty third day of February One thousand nine hundred and fifty one ———

I APPOINT George Lyons Andrew and Richard Hugh Studley Jones both of Bude aforesaid Solicitors to be the Executors of my Will ———

I GIVE devise and bequeath all my estate both real and personal to my friend Nora Lake ———

ANY Executor or Trustee being a Solicitor or other person engaged in any profession or business shall be entitled to be paid all professional or proper charges for business transacted time expended and acts done by him or any partner of his in connection with the trusts hereof including acts which an Executor or Trustee not being in any profession or business could have done personally ———

IN WITNESS whereof I have hereunto set my hand the day and year first above written ———

SIGNED by the above named CORINNE PAMELA MARY COLMAN SMITH as her last Will in the presence of us both present at the same time who in her presence and in the presence of each other have hereunto set our names as witnesses:—

Corinne Pamela Mary Colman Smith

E. Chegwin, The Green Tub, Bude.   Solicitors Clerk.

Jean Walkey, Broadclose Hill, Bude
Clerk to Messrs. Andrew & Jones,
Solicitors, Bude.

LONDON: PUBLISHED BY HIS MAJESTY'S STATIONERY OFFICE. To be purchased directly from H.M. STATIONERY OFFICE at the following addresses: York House, Kingsway, London, W.C.2; 13A Castle Street, Edinburgh 2; 39 King Street, Manchester 2; 2 Edmund Street, Birmingham 3; 1 St. Andrew's Crescent, Cardiff; Tower Lane, Bristol 1; 80 Chichester Street, Belfast; or through any bookseller.

Probate of Will

1951

In His Majesty's High Court of Justice.

The District Probate Registry at Bodmin

BE IT KNOWN that Corinne Pamela Mary Colman Smith of 2 Bencoolen House Bude Cornwall spinster

died there on the 18th day of September 1951

AND BE IT FURTHER KNOWN that at the date hereunder written the last Will and Testament

(a copy whereof is hereunto annexed) of the said deceased was proved and registered in the District Probate Registry of His Majesty's High Court of Justice at Bodmin

and that Administration of all the Estate which by law devolves to and vests in the personal representative of the said deceased was granted by the aforesaid Court to

George Lyons Andrew and Richard Hugh Studley Jones both of Bude aforesaid solicitors the Executors

named in the said Will

And it is hereby certified that an Affidavit for Inland Revenue has been delivered wherein it is shewn that the gross value of the said estate in Great Britain (exclusive of what the said deceased may have been possessed of or entitled to as a Trustee and not beneficially) amounts to £1048 — 11 — 5 and that the net value of the estate amounts to £ Nil

Dated the 13th day of November 1951.

District Registrar.

Extracted by Andrew & Jones Solicitors Bude

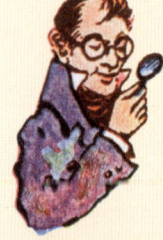

Accounting of Debts, Receipts and Payments

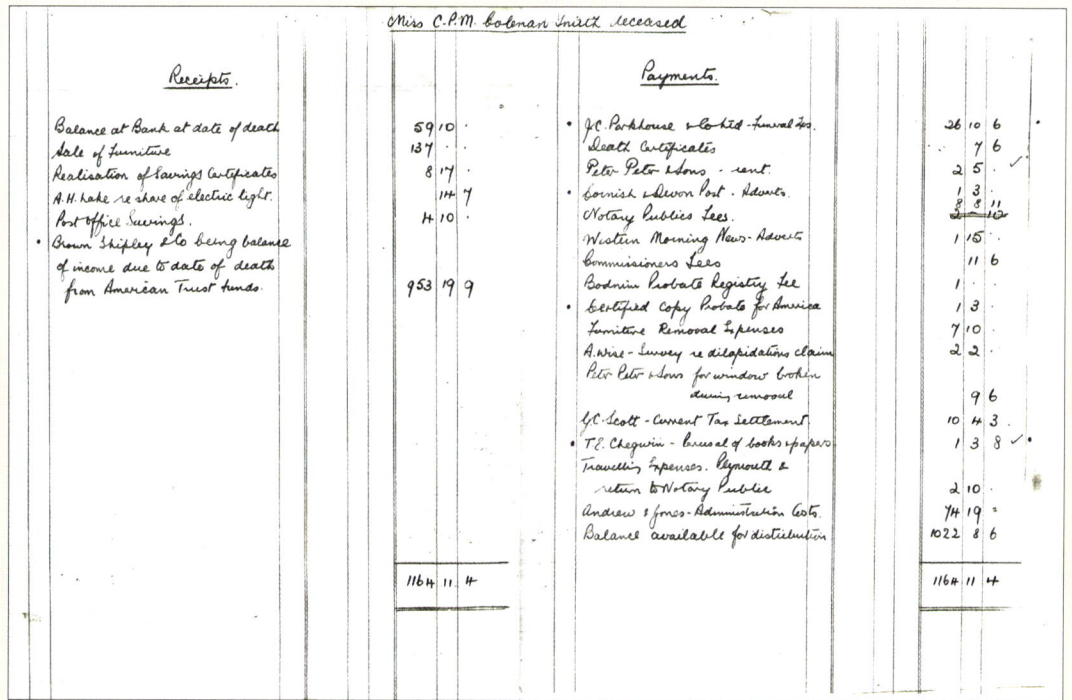

1954

Accounting of Debts, Receipts and Payments

1951

Pamela Colman Smith's personal possessions auctioned by Kivell & Sons, November 15, 1951

PHONE—HOLSWORTHY 4.
" BUDE 95.
Agents to the County Fire Office.

N.° 18

KIVELL & SONS,

Auctioneers, Surveyors, House and Estate Agents,
Licensed Valuers, Certificated Bailiffs.

Offices: BUDE, HOLSWORTHY and STRATTON.

Sale at VILLA HALL, BUDE.

15th Nov., 1951.

Mr.essrs Andrew & Jones. 17, Strand. Bude.

Lot		£	s	d
	F.E.S.L. 15.			
	re: Sale. Villa Hall. 15.11.51			
	re: Miss Coleman-Smith (decd).			
	By sale of Furniture and Effects	133	15	6
	Less sale expenses	6	15	6
	Cheque enclosed	127	—	—
	Detailed list enclosed.			

Detailed list of articles sold re Miss Coleman-Smith (decd).
Sale at the Villa Hall, Bude, on Thursday November 15th 1951.

Lot.		£	s	d
26.	Cooking bowls		11	—
27.	—do—		7	6
28.	Enamel Roaster		6	—
29.	Tray and china		2	6
30.	—do—		3	6
31.	Mincer and squeezer		2	—
32.	Box china		2	—
33.	—do—		1	2
34.	Dishes etc		2	6
35.	Dishes etc			
36.	Bowl china		2	—
37.	Ware and pail		5	—
38.	Antique Chest Drawers	12	—	—
39.	Casseroles		5	—
40.	Kitchen table		5	—
41.	Box Pictures etc		1	—
42.	Box odds		2	—
43.	Box Brass ware		4	—
44.	Box odds		1	—
45.	Box paints etc		4	—
46.	Box materials		6	—
47.	Mirror		7	—
51.	Electric bowl and china		9	—
52.	—do— —do—			
53.	Chest Drawers	1	7	—
54.	Plated Hot water jug.		13	—
55.	Serpentine Bowl and Ornaments		6	—
56.	Angle poise Electric lamp	1	—	—
58.	3'6" Oak Bed, Box spring, & Spring interior	1	9	10
59.	Ware)			
60.	—do—		4	—
61.	Plant bowls		5	—
62.	Round table		15	—
63.	2 Glass water jugs		2	—
64.	Box Lamp glasses		3	—
65.	Tray & Tumblers		1	—
66.	Glass ware		1	—
67.	—do—		1	—
68.	Box—do—		1	—
69.	Decanter & Vase		2	—
70.	Glass Cheese dish & Jar		1	6
71.	Glass ware			
72.	Standard Electric lamp	2	5	—
73.	Oak Gate leg table	5	12	6
74.	Box books		2	—
75.	—do—			
76.	Box odds		1	—
	C/F	39	1	6

		£	s	d
	B/F	39	1	6
77.	Basket books		7	—
78.	Japanese Lacquer Box		6	—
79.	Antique Cabinet	16	—	—
80.	Chest drawers		7	—
81.	Antique Dress chest with Heart shape Mirror on wheels	5	10	—
82.	Antique shaving stand	3	10	—
99.	Chair		8	—
100.	Wheel back chair		10	—
101.	Ornaments		4	—
102.	Filing chest	4	—	—
103.	Pouffe and Hassock		3	—
104.	3 pillows and cushion			
105.	½ row top books		17	—
106.	2nd —do—		17	6
107.	½ row 2nd Shelf books		5	—
108.	2nd —do—1		10	—
109.	Mahogany Book case	6	—	—
110.	Jug etc		3	—
111.	2 jugs and teapot		2	—
112.	—do—		5	—
113.	2 jugs		5	—
114.	Kitchen Cabinet	6	10	—
129.	3' Divan and Mattress	2		
132.	Top row books		2	6
133.	2nd —do—		2	6
134.	Top row books)		1	—
135.	2nd —do—)			
136.	3rd —do—)		2	—
142.	2 mirrors and picture		13	—
143.	Prints		5	—
144.	Stand		4	—
145.	—do—		3	6
146.	Alim Steamer		9	—
147.	Screen & Rack		4	—
148.	2 ring electric grill		8	—
175.	Oak Tall boy	7	—	—
179.	Round table		6	—
180.	Chest drawers		9	—
181.	Small dresser		11	—
193.	Carpet	9	—	—
197.	Wooden arm chair		5	—
198.	Arm chair		15	—
199.	3 rush seated chairs			
200.	Swivel chair	2		
218.	Runner carpet 20'x 3'	3	10	—
219.	—do— 23'x 3'	4		
	C/F	119	14	6

		£	s	d
	B/F	119	14	6
220.	Table		1	—
221.	—do—		1	—
222.	Box books		2	—
223.	—do—		1	—
224.	Cupboard		16	—
225.	—do—		15	—
241.	Piano case		1	—
245.	5 chairs		1	—
261.	2'6" Iron bed		1	—
262.	3' —do—		16	—
263.	Two 2 fold screens			
264.	Easle	1	—	—
265.	Books)			
266.	—do—)		17	—
267.	2 boxes blocks)			
268.	Lawn mower		7	6
269.	Pair shears		7	—
270.	Tresles and easles		11	—
271.	Chest and odds		4	—
272.	Table and canvases		4	—
273.	Trays and Brassware		8	—
274.	Table and pictures		8	—
275.	Small trunk and odds			
276.	Box china		4	—
277.	—do—	1	—	—
278.	Lamps and shades)			
279.	Baskets & Shelves)		2	—
280.	Box odds		3	—
281.	—do—			
282.	Oil heater and can)			
283.	Stand, boxes etc.)		4	—
284.	Coak bucket & Bucket)			
285.	Screen and bedrest		3	—
286.	Tools		11	—
287.	Brushes and mop		3	6
288.	—do—		2	—
289.	Desk chair	1	—	—
290.	Trunk & Vases etc		5	—
292.	Oil heater		5	—
293.	Basket and saucepans		1	—
294.	Tables and stand		2	6
295.	Tea trolley			
296.	Bamboo table)			
297.	Bedside cabinet)		6	—
298.	Commode		3	—
299.	—do—		6	—
300.	—do—			
301.	—do—		1	—
	C/F	131	18	6

		£	s	d
	B/F	131	18	6
302.	Wringer and stand		15	—
303.	Bamboo table and electric ring		2	—
304.	3 clothes horses		6	—
305.	Filing cabinet etc		3	—
306.	Canvases		7	—
307.	Trunk & Pictures		7	—
308.	Pictures	1	—	—
309.	—do—)			
310.	—do—)		2	—
		133	15	6
	Less sale expenses	6	15	6
		£127	—	—

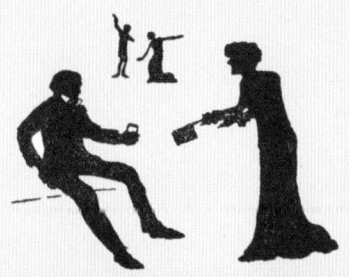

Letter from Parnall, Godwin & Chegwin

1982

PARNALL GODWIN & CHEGWIN

SOLICITORS AND COMMISSIONERS FOR OATHS

HARRY P. GODWIN
JOHN H. B. PARNALL
PAUL H. FINN, A.C.I. Arb.
IAN J. LANGSFORD, LL.B
JOHN BUSBY, B.A

CONSULTANT
R.H.S. JONES, B.A., B.C.L. (OXON)

ALL OUR POST IS INSURED

ALSO AT 16, WESTGATE STREET
LAUNCESTON
(LAUNCESTON 2375)
AND 20, THE SQUARE
HOLSWORTHY
(HOLSWORTHY 253333)

TELEPHONE:
BUDE 2141/2 & 2323

17, The Strand,
Bude,
Cornwall, EX23 8QZ

OUR REF: PRD/RJ/Misc   YOUR REF:

25th November 1982

Dear Sir,

<u>Re: Miss P. Colman Smith - deceased.</u>

Further to previous correspondence, on making a further search we found the file of papers relating to the estate of the late Miss Colman Smith. Mr. Jones the surviving Executor took the file home and read through it and he reports as follows:-

Miss Colman Smith had since 1946 lived in Bude as tenant of a flat which she shared with a Mrs. Nora Lake.

Miss Colman Smith died on 18th September 1951. She left a Will which appointed Mr. G.L. Andrew and Mr. R.H.S. Jones as Executors and bequeathed her whole estate to Mrs. Nora Lake above referred to.

When the Executors came to examine the estate they found that Miss Colman Smith had been in receipt of remittances of income from Manufacturers Trust Company of New York but, that there had not been sufficient to meet her expenditure and that she had died in considerable current debt, including sums owing to the Inland Revenue for income tax. There were no current funds to pay the rent of the flat and this had accordingly to be vacated and the contents disposed of at the local Auction Rooms.

Eventually the Executors arrived at a composition with the creditors under which, after the satisfaction of debts having priority under English Law, the creditors accepted a payment of Five Shillings and five pence (just over 25%) in full satisfaction of their respective debts.

The Executors duly proved the Will in the Bodmin District Probate Registry on 13th November 1951. A plain copy of the Will is enclosed. Official copies can be obtained from Somerset House in London, for a small fee. The obtaining of such official copies is commonly done by Law Stationers in London and, if you so desired, no doubt your business agents in London would arrange this for you.

Thus, the circumstances of the administration were that there was no estate to go to Mrs. Lake under the bequest to her and the flat had to be entirely physically cleared out and the contents disposed of. The file mostly relates to the business and financial side of these proceedings but we think it may be of help to you if we send you a copy of the general account of the estate, which we do herewith.

Continued.......

- 2 -

Stuart R. Kaplan   25th November 1982

With regard to your desire to identify the gravesite, Mr. Jones has made some enquiries without success. It rather appears from the copy letter from Mr. Widdows that Miss Colman Smith may have been cremated. The placing of Memorials in Churches or Churchyards of the Church of England is a complex subject. If eventually the funds justify it you might save time and expense by writing to the Vicar of Bude and enquiring whether you could provide some article of Church use which could bear an inscription of it having been given in Memory of Miss Colman Smith.

Yours faithfully,

Parnall Godwin & Chegwin

Advertisements

2006

I am searching for the grave site of
PAMELA COLMAN SMITH
(1878 - 1951)

I also seek to purchase any items relating to Ms Smith including paintings, books, manuscripts, notebooks, correspondence, personal papers, etc.

Ms Smith died September 18, 1951 at 2 Bencoolen House, Bude

Pamela Colman Smith was an illustrator, writer, artist, costume and set designer and storyteller. I am writing a book about Ms Smith which will be published in 2008. I would also like to locate the grave site in order to erect an appropriate headstone, should one not already exist.

Some of Smith's publications include a series of 24 hand-coloured oversized sheets known as *A Broad Sheet* published in 1902 and 1903, and 13 issues of a small, hand-coloured periodical named *The Green Sheaf*. Other works that she either illustrated, authored and/or published include *In Chimney Corners (1898), Christmas Carol (1898), The Land of Heart's Desire (1898), Twelfth Night Merry-makers (1898), The Golden Vanity (1898), Annancy Stories (1899), The Green Bed (1899), Sir Henry Irving and Miss Ellen Terry in Robespiere, Merchant of Venice (1899), Trelawny of Wells (1899), Fair Vanity (1899)* and *Widdicombe Fair (1899)*. Ms Smith also contributed numerous works to a magazine called *The Kensington*.

The Green Sheaf also published numerous books including *Tales from My Garden* (illustrated by Smith) and FOUR PLAYS by Laurence Alma Tadema (1905), *The Book of Hours* by Lady Alix Egerton (1905), *A Sheaf of Songs* by Alfred G Calmour (1905), *Tales for Philip and Peter* by E Harcourt Williams (1905), *Saints among the Animals* by Margaret Ward and Alphaeus P Cole (1906), *In The Valley of Starts There Is A Tower of Silence* by Smara Khamara (1906), *The Book of Good Advice* by Reginald Rigby (1906) and Chim-Chim (1905), another of Smith's own books of Jamaican folklore. During 1909 Smith prepared 78 illustrations for the Rider-Waite Tarot deck.

In 1913 Smith illustrated *The Russian Ballet* by Ellen Terry followed by *Bluebeard*, Smith's own book. *The Book of Friendly Giants* by Eunice Fuller (1914) contains over 100 illustrations by Smith. A set of 30 cards illustrated by Smith, called *The Way of the Cross* with verses by Paul Claudel and translated into English by Rowland Thurnam, appeared in 1917.

Unpublished manuscripts and illustrations by Smith include *Little Charles, The Railings of Drift, the Cuckoo Bird, Greenfinger* and *Fisher of Men*.

Smith often painted while listening to classical music. Her paintings reflect the musical mood she felt while listening to Bach, Beethoven, Chopin, Debussy, etc., and these musical-inspired paintings bear musical titles. Smith's works usually carried her monogram, a composite of her 3 initials, PCS, each letter on top of another with the initials reading from top to bottom.

Around 1918 Ms Smith leased a house known as Park Garland in The Lizard. She became active in the local Catholic Church and served as sacristan for Our Lady of The Lizard Church. On the wall of her home were *14 Stations of the Cross* in wash, sepia and Indian ink presumably drawn by Ms Smith.

By 1942 Smith had moved to Bude and shared a flat with her friend Nora Lake at Gorseland, Upton Cliff. Present at the time of Smith's death in 1951 was Mrs Elsie T Bate, a friend who occasionally cleaned her flat. Smith is believed to have been a member of St Michael's Church, Bude. Funeral arrangements for Smith were arranged by J C Parkhouse and Co. The executor of Smith's estate was Richard Jones Esq. of Parnall, Wilson & Chegwen, Bude. On November 15, 1951 Kivell & Sons auctioned at Villa Hall all her belongings including paintings, prints, drawings, sketches, boxes of books, personal records, filing cabinets, etc.

Anyone having information about Pamela Colman Smith, or knowing the whereabouts of her grave site, or owning any of her possessions or works, or having for sale any of her possessions or works, kindly contact the undersigned by email at skaplan@usgamesinc.com. I will be at The Falcon Hotel, Bude, at telephone number 01288 352005 on Thursday, May 25 from noon to 2.00 pm and on Friday, May 26 from 10.00 am to noon or kindly leave a message and I will contact you upon arrival.

Stuart R Kaplan, Chairman, U.S. Games Systems, Inc.
179 Ludlow Street, Stamford, Connecticut 06902 USA
Tel 001-203-353-8400, ext. 301, fax: 001-203-353-8431,
email: skaplan@usgamesinc.com

The Post & Weekly News, Thursday, May 25, 2006

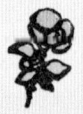

IN MEMORIAM

She was born February 16, 1878, in Middlesex, England, of American parents. Her childhood years were spent between London, New York, and Kingston, Jamaica.

During her teens, she traveled throughout England with the theatre company of Ellen Terry and Henry Irving. Thereafter, she took up formal art training at the Pratt Institute of Brooklyn, New York, graduating in 1897.

Although American by birth, she returned to England, where she became a theatrical designer for miniature theatre and an illustrator, mainly of books, pamphlets and posters.

She excelled in reciting folktales and stories drawn from her experiences in Jamaica. Her circle of friends included William Butler Yeats and his brother, Jack Yeats, plus notable theatrical and literary personalities of the day.

Around 1903, she joined the Order of the Golden Dawn and began to paint visions that came to her while listening to music, including Beethoven, Bach, Chopin and Debussy.

She turned to writing and illustrating books which realized only minor success. She became disillusioned with commercial publishers who rejected much of her work, forcing her to self-publish or to publish in collaboration with her literary friends.

She opened a small shop specializing in hand-colored prints and illustrations, but it proved financially unsuccessful. Her small press of limited edition books and posters never realized the sales necessary to succeed.

Events turned in her favor in 1907 when Alfred Stieglitz selected her art as the first non-photographic work to be shown at the Little Galleries of the Photo-Secession, later called 291, on Madison Avenue. She realized some praise from critics, and thirty-three of her drawings sold, but by the end of the year her financial situation worsened.

In 1909, under the guidance of Arthur Edward Waite, she undertook for token payment a series of seventy-eight allegorical paintings described by Waite as a rectified tarot pack. The designs, published in the same year by William Rider and Son, exemplify the mysticism, ritual, imagination, fantasy and deep emotions of the artist.

Despite occasional art shows and favorable reviews by critics, the continued slow sales of her works and rejections by commercial publishers left her deeply disappointed. Her disillusionment reached a climax in 1914 when she confided to a friend that she didn't care for people anymore.

Years earlier she had written and published a poem, *Alone*, which provides insight to her isolation and despair.

ALONE

Alone and in the midst of men,
Alone 'mid hills and valleys fair;
Alone upon a ship at sea;
Alone—alone, and everywhere.

O many folk I see and know,
So kind they are I scarce can tell,
But now alone on land and sea,
In spite of all I'm left to dwell.

In cities large—in country lane,
Around the world—'tis all the same;
Across the sea from shore to shore.
Alone—alone, for evermore.

After World War I she received a small inheritance and leased a house on the English coast in the artist's colony called The Lizard.

Despite further attempts to write and illustrate books, most of her works failed to reach publication.

Suffering from physical and financial decline, she moved during World War II to Bude, Cornwall. Despite continued output of stories and illustrations, she failed to realize any commercial success.

She never married. She had no known heirs except for an elderly female companion who shared her flat.

She died on September 18, 1951, penniless and obscure.

There was no funeral procession to honor her life.

There was no memorial service to touch upon the impact one day her work would have upon her admirers.

No obituary about her appeared in any local newspapers.

Her grave site, if one exists, remains unknown.

She died disappointed that her paintings and writings failed to achieve success, yet she never stopped believing in herself.

All of her personal possessions were sold at auction—books, manuscripts, prayer books, paintings, drawings, furniture, even her personal letters—to satisfy her debts. Thus, despite her last wishes, her companion and heir was deprived of any inheritance, and everything went to strangers.

Except for a few exhibitions during her early career that had moderate success, much of her work has disappeared.

Pamela Colman Smith would be all but forgotten except for the seventy-eight tarot paintings known as the Rider-Waite Tarot pack. She would no doubt be astonished and gladdened to know that today the deck touches the hearts and emotions of millions of people.

Reprinted from *The Encyclopedia of Tarot*, Vol. III, by Stuart R. Kaplan

Songs of Praise Hymnal

Pamela Colman Smith's personal hymnal published by Oxford University Press, London, 1931 filled with pencil illustrations, notations, clippings and prayer cards

(Handwritten on facing flyleaf:)

Away in a manger —
no crib for a bed
The little Lord Jesus
laid down his
sweet head

The stars in the bright
sky looked down
Where He lay
The Little Lord Jesus
asleep on the hay.

SONGS OF PRAISE

Enlarged Edition

OXFORD UNIVERSITY PRESS
LONDON: HUMPHREY MILFORD
1931

---

28 MORNING

Praise for the sweetness
Of the wet garden,
Sprung in completeness
Where his feet pass.

3. Mine is the sunlight!
Mine is the morning
Born of the one light
Eden saw play!
Praise with elation,
Praise every morning,
God's re-creation
Of the new day!

31 *J. Keble, 1792–1866.*

NEW every morning is the love
Our wakening and uprising prove;
Through sleep and darkness safely brought,
Restored to life, and power, and thought.

2 New mercies, each returning day,
Hover around us while we pray;
New perils past, new sins forgiven,
New thoughts of God, new hopes of heaven.

3* If on our daily course our mind
Be set to hallow all we find,
New treasures still, of countless price,
God will provide for sacrifice.

4 Old friends, old scenes, will lovelier be,
As more of heaven in each we see;
Some softening gleam of love and prayer
Shall dawn on every cross and care.

7 ⛤ Pentacles

MORNING 29

5 We need not bid, for cloistered cell,
Our neighbour and our work farewell,
Nor strive to wind ourselves too high
For sinful man beneath the sky:

6 The trivial round, the common task,
Would furnish all we ought to ask,—
Room to deny ourselves, a road
To bring us daily nearer God.

7.*Only, O Lord, in thy dear love
Fit us for perfect rest above;
And help us this and every day
To live more nearly as we pray.

32 *H. Albert, 1604–51. Tr. H. J. Buckoll‡ (1842).*
Gott des Himmels und der Erden.

NOW the morn new light is pouring:
Lord, may we our spirits raise,
Through thy grace our souls restoring;
So, on thy great day of days,
We with joy its dawn may meet
Fearless at the mercy-seat.

2 Jesus, who our steps art guiding
By thy word's celestial light,
Now and evermore abiding,
Our defence, our rock of might:
Nowhere, save alone in thee,
Can we rest from danger free.

3. Lo! we yield to thy direction
Soul and body, heart and mind;
Keep thou all by thy protection,
To thy mighty hand resigned.
Thee our glorious God we own;
Let us, Lord, be thine alone.

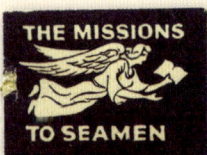

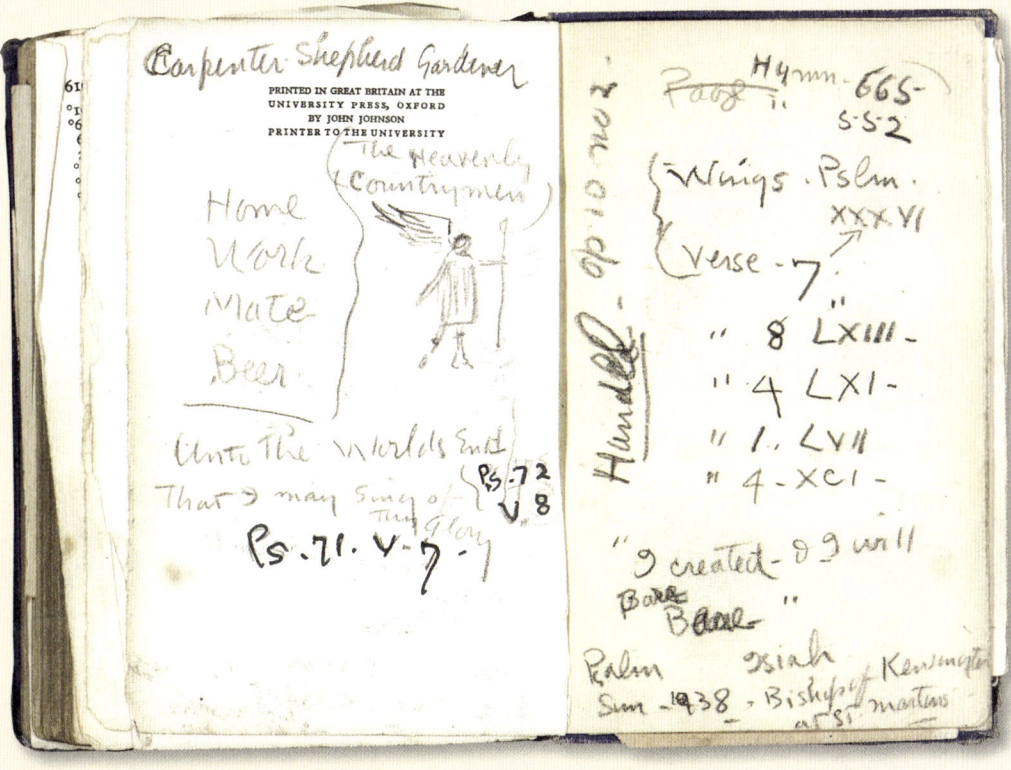
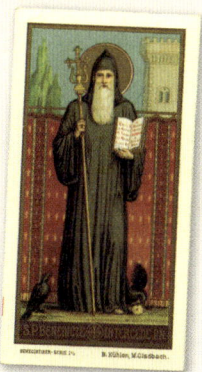

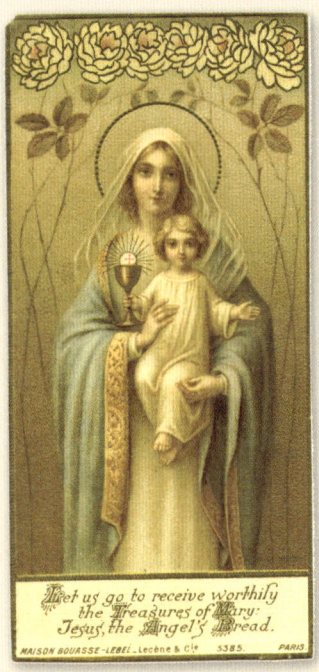

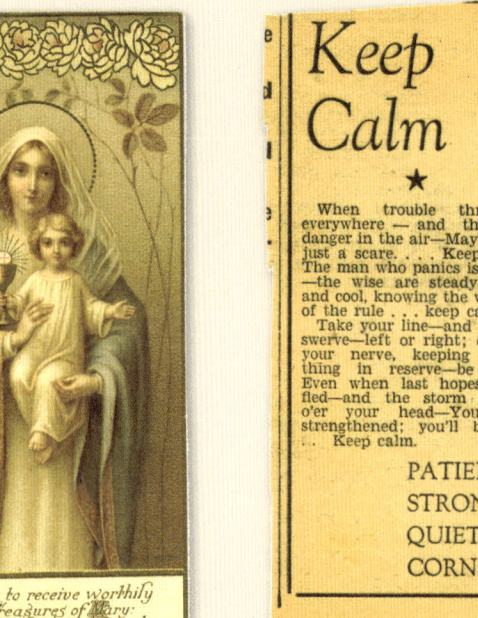

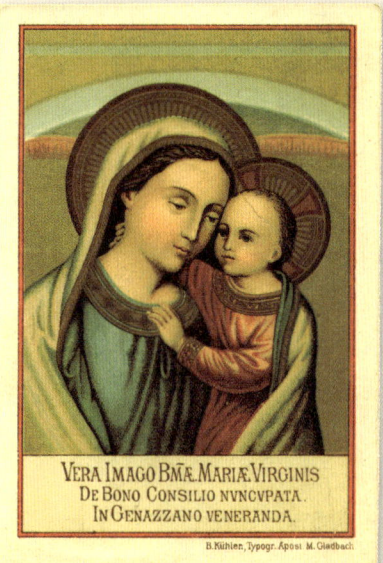

Keep Calm

★

When trouble threatens everywhere — and there is danger in the air—Maybe it is just a scare. . . . Keep calm. The man who panics is a fool—the wise are steady, quiet and cool, knowing the wisdom of the rule . . . keep calm.

Take your line—and do not swerve—left or right; control your nerve, keeping something in reserve—be calm. Even when last hopes have fled—and the storm breaks o'er your head—You'll be strengthened; you'll be led. . . . Keep calm.

PATIENCE STRONG'S QUIET CORNER

Let us go to receive worthily the Treasures of Mary: Jesus, the Angel's Bread.
MAISON BOUASSE-LEBEL, Lecène & Cie 5385. PARIS

VERA IMAGO B. MAE. MARIAE VIRGINIS
DE BONO CONSILIO NVNCVPATA.
IN GENAZZANO VENERANDA.

B. Kühlen, Typogr. Apost. M. Gladbach.

Our Prayer

Give us peace with honour,
Peace that's true and real
Peace that rests securely
On a great Ideal,
Peace without betrayal
Of a weaker power,
Give us strength and guidance
In this bitter hour.

We are sick and weary
With the world's unrest
Yet Hope flames, undying
In the human breast.
Faith still lifts her banner
Love still points the way,
Here now at the cross-roads
Let us pause—and pray

PATIENCE STRONG'S QUIET CORNER

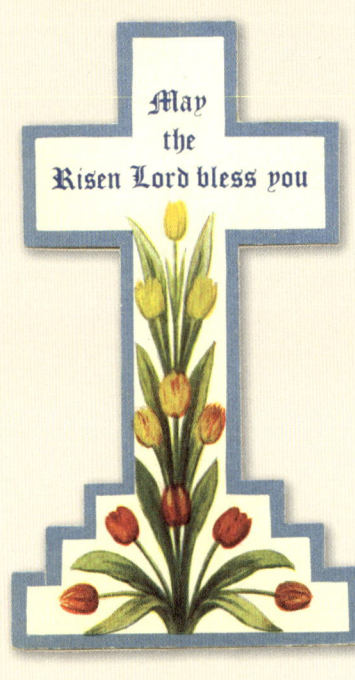

May the Risen Lord bless you

CLOUDS IN THE NIGHT

The clouds that fly through the sky at night,
And loom so large in that great black space,
Are swift and grey and lit by the light
Of a silver moon in their fleeting race.

Silver and grey they fly by the moon
And the twinkling stars so blue and bright,
Silver and grey they disappear soon,
Into the vast unlit abyss of night.

In their ever-changing shapes they race
Across the depths in the heavens above,
And each cloud touches the shining face,
And secretly whispers a word of love.

Each one of them woos the moon a space,
She scorns them all, she is far too fair,
The clouds fly happily to her face,
But sadly away, through the clear cold air.
FRANCIS J. LUCE.

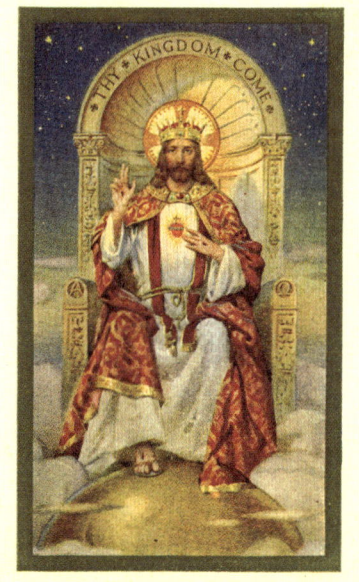

CHRIST THE KING

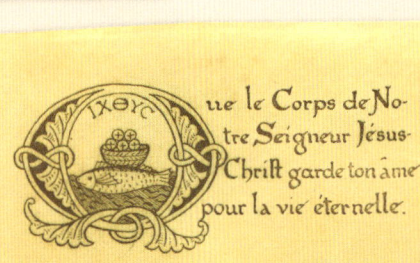

ue le Corps de Notre Seigneur Jésus-Christ garde ton âme pour la vie éternelle.

IPPLEPEN

O there are apples at Ipplepen,
Apples for the master, apples for the men,
And the sweep of the scythe in the August sun,
And the scent of hay when scything's done.

And peace there is upon Ipplepen,
Peace on its maids, peace on its men,
The peace of the humble who till and toil
From dawn to eve at the rich red soil.

Peace of the open 'neath tranquil skies,
Of the thymy common, the loud bees' prize,
Of grassy bank and hedgerow tall,
Of narrow lane and grey stone wall.

Peace of the matins the glad birds sing,
Of the drifting dragonfly's gauzy wing,
Of wealth of dainty wayside flowers,
And the blessing of unharried hours.

But most when from its church tower swells
The benison of Sabbath bells
Across the yellow harvest lands
To where, enshrined in leafy dells,
The twin church of Torbryan stands.
                                    E. B. W. CHAPPELOW.

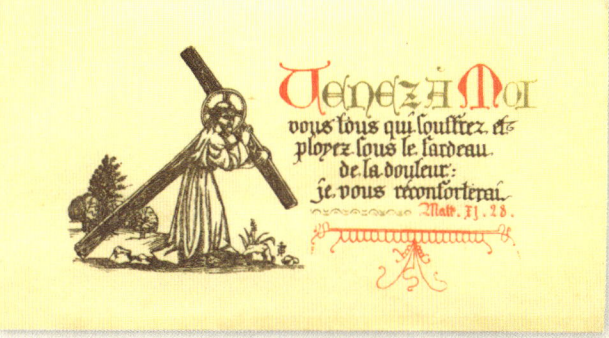

Lines of Comfort

WITH the passing of each day, some thread of Life gets worn away; some hope will fade, some wish will fall, some heart will break, but that's not all: for lovelier things will also start, the hope renewed, the mended heart, the coming true of longed-for things all these and more Tomorrow brings.

AND so it is that we will find that clouds are always silver-lined, and though Today slips out of sight, Tomorrow's coast is always bright. Time takes away but also gives, events must go but memory lives. Then pass brief day your toll to take, you rob my heart for my soul's sake.
                                    Jean Morton.

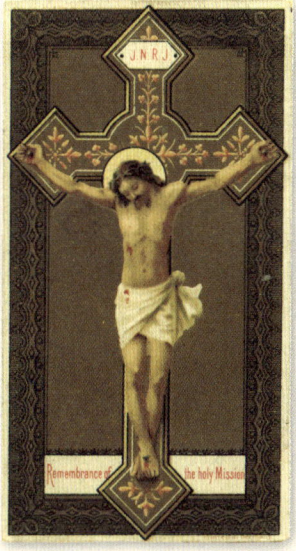

'All the World doth worship Thee'

When the birds sing, O Lord, let my heart sing
    Some melody
When earth pours forth her fragrance, I would bring
    My praise to Thee,
When flowers lift up fair faces, I, my heart,
    Would fain uplift,
And so, in humble gratitude take part
    In Nature's Easter Gift.
                        A. R. G.

He hung a lantern in the sky
    The way to show;
        Then slipped below
    Into a stable shed,
        That so
The simple and the wise
    Might see, and know
That God hath not His dwelling
    In the skies!

                    R. E. CLEEVE.

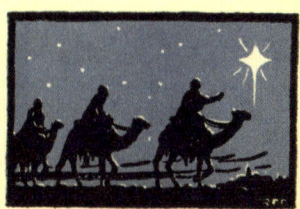

Portrait of Pamela Colman Smith

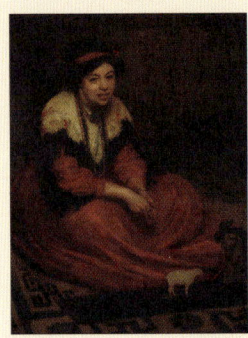

"I first met Pamela at a reception given by W.B. Yeats the poet in his garret. That was one evening in 1901 or 1902. I was intrigued by her and asked to one of her weekly evenings. I was charmed by the people I met there, Yeats was the dominant figure and the guests his admirers. Pamela sat on the floor and told Jamaican folk lore stories or served her guests with "Opal Hash," christened by Yeats; it was merely cheap red wine mixed with warm water and sugar. Thus enlivened Yeats would lilt his poems while Pamela's guests joined in. Needless to say I became one of her regular friends at her parties."
From a letter dated August 5, 1974 from Alphaeus P. Cole to Dr. William I. Homer, Department of Art History, University of Delaware.

"On Friday, January 19, 1906, got Pixie to pose for proposed portrait. On 21st started to draw portrait of Pamela Colman with admirable success/Wednesday, 24th. Pixie couldn't sit/Friday, 26th. Pixie posed. January 28. Sunday. Pixie sat all day for the portrait. February 10 - worked in AM on portrait of Pixie. David Murray, R.A. came to visit. Murray was interested in Pamela Colman Smith. She told him stories and he remained to listen. …. sent the portrait of Pamela Colman Smith…. finished with difficulty because Pixie seldom had no time to sit. Monday, April 30th. Varnishing day at Academy. My painting of Pamela Colman Smith hung in room…. holds its own well."
From Alphaeus P. Cole's diary.
[Note: David Murray (1849-1933) was a noted Scottish landscape painter. He was knighted in 1918.]

* * *

I FIRST BECAME AWARE OF THE EXISTENCE OF ALPHAEUS P. COLE'S OIL PAINTING OF PAMELA Colman Smith from a 1975 exhibition catalog entitled "To All Believers – The Art of Pamela Colman Smith" by Melinda Boyd Parsons.

The exhibition was co-sponsored by The University of Delaware and Delaware Art Museum in association with the Delaware Chapter, The Victorian Society in America.

Although the painting was not on exhibit, a black and white picture of the painting appeared in the catalog with the caption: "Alphaeus Cole (1876-), Pamela Colman Smith, oil on canvas, collection of Irving Seidman, Esq., New York. [Not in exhibition.]"

I located the address of Attorney Seidman in New York City and contacted the family. The painting hung in the Seidman's bedroom. It was one of Mrs. Seidman's favorites and she had no interest in selling it. I learned that the Seidmans were friends of Alphaeus and his wife, and that Irving, although a patent lawyer, had drawn up Cole's will and had done other legal work for the artist, and Cole paid him with several paintings including Pamela's portrait.

During the next several decades, I stayed in contact with Mrs. Seidman. I called her several times. I sent her a copy of Volume III of *The Encyclopedia of Tarot*, which featured a chapter about Pamela and her art. I told her of my plans to eventually publish a full-color book on the non-tarot art of Pamela.

When I acquired Pamela's 1901-1905 Visitors book, I was intrigued to see several rough sketches by Alphaeus Cole of a seated Pamela in the same pose as the eventual oil portrait.

On March 23, 2013 I received a message on my office phone from a Steven Seidman. Professor Seidman is an author and teaches on the faculty of Ithaca College. I returned the call and learned that Sylvia Bernice Seidman was his mother and that she had passed away in September 2012 at the age of 100. While going through her belongings, Dr. Seidman found a note next to *The Encyclopedia of Tarot* that she kept on a table. The note requested Steven to please contact Stuart Kaplan and let him know that the painting of Pamela Colman Smith would be going up for auction.

I was overwhelmed by Mrs. Seidman's thoughtfulness. For almost four decades, I had hoped to acquire the painting of Pamela Colman Smith so that it could be displayed in our company offices. U.S. Games Systems publishes Pamela's Rider-Waite tarot deck, which it distributes throughout the world. I have collected Pamela's non-tarot art for decades, traveling several times to southern England in search of her paintings and personal possessions, and for her grave site. Although the deck was called Rider-Waite by Rider & Company when it was first published in 1909, I have always felt that insufficient recognition was given to the artist. For that reason, I have sought to make people more aware of Pamela's talent not only as the tarot artist, but also her extensive non-tarot art, and her wide-ranging other interests largely unknown up to now. To help rectify this oversight, several years ago USGames issued a facsimile edition of her original tarot deck, aptly entitled, "Smith-Waite Tarot."

The painting of Pamela was scheduled for auction on Monday morning, April 22, 2013 at Doyle Auctions New York City. I stayed the night before the auction at a hotel across the street from Doyle. The next morning, accompanied by Bobbie Bensaid, Vice President of USGames, we arrived at the auction house at 8:00 AM, an hour before the doors opened. Having waited so long for the opportunity to acquire the painting, I was taking no chances of missing the auction.

When bidding started for the painting. I raised my bid paddle. For me, it was a once-in-a lifetime opportunity. But one or more people were bidding against me. I kept the paddle up, never taking it down. I remember Bobbie tugging at my arm and whispering in my ear, "how high will you go?" I was determined in my reply, "It's now or never."

When the bidding ended, and auctioneer's hammer came down, I had won the painting. It was only later that day did I learn that it was Melinda Boyd Parsons who was bidding against me.

The oil portrait of Pamela "Pixie" Smith by Alphaeus P. Cole that is the frontispiece of this book is proudly on display at the offices of USGames for all employees and visitors to enjoy.

Stuart R. Kaplan

BIBLIOGRAPHY

The bibliography is organized in seven parts, each in chronological order

---

Part 1 - WORKS BY PCS BY DATE

1896
Smith, Pamela Colman. *Henry Morgan: A Play for the Miniature Theatre.* Typescript prepared by Melinda Boyd Parsons from Pamela Colman Smith letters.

Smith, Pamela Coleman [sic]. "Two Negro Stories From Jamaica." *The Journal of American Folklore.* Volume 9, Number 35, October-December 1896. p. 278.

1897
"A School-Girl Song of Spring" with illustration by Pamela Coleman [sic] Smith. *Pratt Institute Monthly.* Volume V, Number 6, March 1897. p. 199.

1898
Waugh, Edwin. *Christmas Carol.* Designed by Pamela Colman Smith. New York: R.H. Russell, Publisher, [1898]. fo, unpaginated.

1899
Smith, Pamela Colman. *Annancy Stories.* New York: R.H. Russell, 1899. 4to, 79 pp.

MacManus, Seumas. *In Chimney Corners:* Merry Tales of Irish Folk Lore. Illustrated by Pamela Colman Smith. New York: Doubleday & McClure Co., 1899. 8vo, 281 pp.

The Golden Vanity and the Green Bed: Words and Music of Two Old English Ballads. With pictures by Pamela Colman Smith. New York: Doubleday & McClure Co., 1899. fo, unpaginated.

Stoker, Bram. *Sir Henry Irving and Miss Ellen Terry in Robespierre, Merchant of Venice, the Bells, Nance Oldfield, the Amber Heart, Waterloo, etc.* Drawn by Pamela Colman Smith. New York: Doubleday & McClure Co., Publishers, [1899]. fo, unpaginated.

Baring-Gould, Rev. S. and Rev. H. Fleetwood Sheppard. *Widdicombe Fair.* Illustrated by Pamela Colman Smith. New York; London: Doubleday & McClure Co., 1899. 4to, unpaginated. Edition limited to 500 copies.

Smith, Pamela Coleman [sic]. "Story of Six Poached Eggs." *Salt Lake Herald* (Salt Lake City, UT). January 1, 1899. Fourth Section. p. 25.

1900
William Gillette in Sherlock Holmes: As Produced at the Garrick Theatre, New York. William Gillette. Published with the authorization of Mr. Charles Frohman. New York: R.H. Russell, Publisher, 1900. 4to, unpaginated.

1901
The Kensington: A Magazine of Art, Literature and the Drama. London: Simpkin Marshall Hamilton Kent & Co., 1901.

The Page. Volume IV. Nos. 1 & 2. Edited and published by Edward Gordon Craig, at the Sign of the Rose, Hackbridge, Carshalton, Surrey, England. 1901. 8vo, unpaginated.

"The Wind," a hand coloured illustration by PCS.

Smith, Pamela Colman. *The Basket Maker: And Other Tales That Will Suit the Young or the Old with Pictures.* London: [s.n.], 1901.

1903
A Celtic Christmas 1903: The Irish Homestead Christmas Number. Dublin: Published by J.J. Jennings at the Office of the Irish Homestead, Dublin; Printed for the Irish Agricultural Organisation Society at the Sackville Press, 1903. 4to, xii, 24 pp.

The Green Sheaf. Edited and published by Pamela Colman Smith. London: Sold by Elkin Matthews, 1903-1904. 4to.

"Miss Ellen Terry." *The Lady's Realm.* Volume XIV, 1903. p. 141.

1904
Calmour, Alfred C. *A Sheaf of Songs.* London: "The Green Sheaf", 1904. 12mo, 57 pp.

A Celtic Christmas 1904: The Irish Homestead Christmas Number. Dublin: Published by J.J. Jennings at the Office of the Irish Homestead, Dublin; Printed for the Irish Agricultural Organisation Society at the Sackville Press, 1904. 4to, x, 26 pp.

MacManus, Seumas. *In Chimney Corners: Merry Tales of Irish Folk Lore.* Illustrated by Pamela Colman Smith. New York: McClure, Phillips & Co., 1904. 8vo, 281 pp.

1905
Alma-Tadema, Laurence. *Four Plays.* London: "The Green Sheaf", 1905. 8vo, 143 pp.

A Celtic Christmas 1905: The Irish Homestead Christmas Number. Dublin: Published by J.J. Jennings at the Office of the Irish Homestead, Dublin; Printed for the Irish Agricultural Organisation Society at the Sackville Press, 1905. 4to, x, 26 pp.

Cole, Margaret Ward. *Saints Among the Animals.* Pictures by Alphaeus P. Cole. London: "The Green Sheaf", 1905. 8vo, 71 pp.

Egerton, Alix. *The Book of Hours.* London: "The Green Sheaf", 1905. 12mo, 70 pp.

Smith, Pamela Colman. *Chim-Chim: Folk Stories from Jamaica.* London: "The Green Sheaf", 1905. 12mo, 62 pp.

Theobald, Edith M. "Letters from the Beasts to Dina." *The Dream Garden: A Children's Annual.* 1905. pp. 42-53.

Venture: An Annual of Art and Literature. London: John Baillie, 1905. 8vo, 187 pp.

Autumn Leaves appears opposite p. 26.

Williams, E. Harcourt. *Tales for Philip and Peter.* London: "The Green Sheaf", 1905. 8vo, 103 pp.

Yeats, Jack B. *Catalogue of .. Sketches of Life in the …. West of Ireland.* [London]: [Elkin Mathews], [1905?]. 8vo, unpaginated.

Advertisement on inside back cover "A broadsheet with pictures. Coloured by hand. By Pamela Colman Smith and Jack B. Yeats."

1906
Alma-Tadema, Laurence. *Tales from My Garden: Three Fairy Tales.* Illustrations by Pamela Colman Smith. London: "The Green Sheaf", 1906. 8vo, 94 pp.

A Celtic Christmas 1906: The Irish Homestead Christmas Number. Dublin: Published by J.J. Jennings at the Office of the Irish Homestead, Dublin; Printed for the Irish Homestead, Ltd. at the Sackville Press, 1906. 4to, x, 26 pp.

Khamara, Smara. *In the Valley of Stars There is a Tower of Silence: A Persian Tragedy.* London: "The Green Sheaf," 1906. 12mo, 61 pp.

1907

"A Reincarnation of Ellen Terry." *The Literary Digest.* Volume XXXIV, Number 6, February 9, 1907. pp. 213-214.

"The Indomitable Youthfulness of Ellen Terry." *Current Literature.* Volume XLII, Number 3. March 1907. pp. 302-304.

Smith, Pamela Colman. "A Protest Against Fear." *The Craftsman.* Volume XI, Number 6, March 1907. p. 728.

Williams, E. Harcourt. "Ellen Terry." *The Metropolitan Magazine.* Volume XXV, Number VI. p. 737.

"Ellen Terry in Two Plays." *Harper's Weekly.* Volume 51, March 2, 1907. pp. 316-317.

1908

Terry, Ellen. *Story of My life.* London: Hutchinson & Co., 1908. 8vo, 381 pp.

Wilson, Robert Burns. "Let No Man's Soul Despair!" Drawing by Pamela Coleman [sic] Smith. *Metropolitan Magazine.* Volume XXVII, Number IV, January 1908. p. 514.

Young, Ella. "How the Son of the Gobhan Saor Shortened the Road: An Irish Folk Tale." Illustrated by Pamela Colman Smith. *The Idaho Daily Statesman.* April 12, 1908. p. 5.

1909

Original Prospectus for "The Tarot of the Bohemians", "The Tarot Pack of Cards", "The Key to the Tarot" and "The Pictorial Key to the Tarot." London: William Rider & Son, Ltd., (ca 1909). 4 pp.

1910

Smith, Pamela Coleman [sic]. "Appropriate Stage Decoration." *The New Age.* Volume 7, Number 5, Supplement, June 2, 1910. pp 7-9.

1911

Waite, Arthur Edward. *The Pictorial Key to the Tarot.* London: William Rider & Son Limited, 1911. 12mo, 340 pp.

Stoker, Bram. *The Lair of the White Worm.* London: William Rider and Son, Limited, 1911. 12mo, 328, 16 pp.

1912

Smith, Pamela Colman. *Catalogue of an Exhibition of Drawings Suggested by Music, Paintings on Silk and Other Original Works by Pamela Colman Smith.* New York: Berlin Photographic Company, [c.1912].

Smith, Pamela Colman. "Susan and the Mermaid. Told and Pictured by Pamela Colman Smith." *The Delineator.* Volume LXXX, Number 6, December 1912. pp. 421-424.

1913

Blue Beard. Pictures by Pamela Colman Smith. New York: Duffield & Company, 1913. 12mo, 25 pp.

Terry, Ellen. *The Russian Ballet.* With drawings by Pamela Colman Smith. London: Sidgwick & Jackson, Ltd., 1913. 8vo, 52 pp.

1914

Fuller, Eunice. *The Book of Friendly Giants ... With Introductory Verses by Seymour Barnard and Drawings by Pamela Colman Smith.* New York: The Century Company, 1914. 8vo, 325 pp.

1915

Shanks, Edward. *Songs.* London: The Poetry Bookshop, 1915. 8vo, 32 pp.

1917

Thurnam, Rowland. *The Way of the Cross: From the French of Paul Claudel.* Passion drawn by Pamela Colman Smith. Text written by Beatrice A. Waldram. London: Art and Book Co. Ltd., 1917. 12mo, unpaginated.

1919

Smith, Pamela Colman. "Producing a Village Play." *Drama: The Organ of the British Drama League.* October 1919. pp. 47-50.

1926

Lyttelton, Edith. *The Sinclair Family.* With 12 drawings by Pamela Colman Smith. London: Heath Cranton Limited, 1926. 12mo, 253 pp.

Part 2 – WORKS ABOUT PCS BY DATE – ARTWORK

1896

"The Poster Art Craze." *The Brooklyn Daily Eagle.* May 24, 1896. p. 18.

"School Entertainment at Half-Way Tree." *The Daily Gleaner* (Kingston, Jamaica). December 14, 1896. p. 3.

"Teachers – Students – and – Things." *Pratt Institute Monthly.* Volume IV, Number 10, June 1896. p. 311-312.

1897

Haskell, I. C. "The Decorative Work of Miss Pamela Colman Smith." *Pratt Institute Monthly.* Volume VI, Number 3, December 1897. pp. 65-67.

"Pratt Institute." *The Brooklyn Daily Eagle.* December 5, 1897. p. 30.

"Pratt Institute." *The Brooklyn Daily Eagle.* December 19, 1897. p. 32.

1898

"In Local Studios." *The Brooklyn Daily Eagle.* February 13, 1898. p. 12.

"Books and Authors." *The New York Times.* December 10, 1898. Saturday Review of Books and Art. p. BR834.

"Colored Illustrations of Pamela Colman Smith." *Boston Evening Transcript.* December 21, 1898. p. 16.

"Literature." *The Times* (Washington, DC). December 25, 1898. p. 15.

"Teachers – Students – and – Things." *Pratt Institute Monthly.* Volume VI, Number 5. February 1898. pp. 147-148.

1899

"American Studio Talk." *International Studio.* Volume VI, Number 1, January 1899. p. xx.

"Appreciation." *Pratt Institute Monthly.* Volume VII, Number 3, January 1899. p. 62.

"Art Notes." E. von Windeck. *Book-Notes.* Volume 2, Number 1. January 1899. pp. 64-66.

"The Lounger." *The Critic.* Volume XXXIV, Number 859, January 1899. p. 15-16.

"The Progress of One Student of the Regular Art Class." *Pratt Institute Monthly.* Volume VII, Number 3, January 1899. p. 71.

"The Rambler." *The Book Buyer.* Volume XVII, Number 6, January 1899. pp. 577-578.

"In Local Studios." *The Brooklyn Daily Eagle.* January 15, 1899. p. 16.

"An American de Monvel." *The Atlanta Journal Constitution* (Atlanta, Georgia). January 22, 1899. p. 23.

"An American de Monvel." *Omaha Daily Bee* (Omaha, Nebraska). January 29, 1899. p.9.

"Among the New Books." *San Francisco Chronicle* (San Francisco, California). January 29, 1899. p. 4.

"In the Book Room." *The Brooklyn Daily Eagle.* February 25, 1899. p. 7.

"Here and There." *Brooklyn Life.* February 25, 1899. p. 17.

"Notes and News." *The New York Times.* February 25, 1899. Saturday Review of Books and Art. p. BR124.

"Pretty Souvenirs." *The Literary News.* Volume XX, Number 3, March 1899. p. 78.

"Literary Notes." *The Times* (Washington, DC). October 22, 1899. Second Part. p. 8.

"Literature." *The Philadelphia Inquirer.* October 22, 1899. p. 46

"About Books & Authors." *The Tennessean* (Nashville, Tennessee). November 5, 1899. p. 20.

"Modern Irish Art." *Dublin Daily Express* (Dublin, Ireland). November 11, 1899. p. 3.

"In Local Studios." *The Brooklyn Daily Eagle.* November 12, 1899. p. 21.

"In the Country Beyond." *The Brooklyn Daily Eagle.* November 18, 1899. p. 8.

"Literary Chat." *The Courier-Journal* (Louisville, Kentucky). November 18, 1899. p. 7.

"More Irish Folk-Tales." *Brooklyn Life*. November 18, 1899. p. 6.

"New Books." *Hartford Courant* (Hartford, Connecticut). November 18, 1899. p. 8.

"Literary World." *The Farmer and Mechanic* (Raleigh, North Carolina). November 21, 1899. p. 8.

"Literary Notes." *Virginian-Pilot* (Norfolk, Virginia). November 26, 1899. p. 11.

"The Theatrical World." *The Record-Union* (Sacramento, California). November 26, 1899. p. 7.

"Children's Gift Books." *Pall Mall Gazette* (London). November 28, 1899. p. 9.

"Books and Periodicals." *The Inland Printer.* Volume XXIV, Number 3, December 1899. p. 438.

"Guide for the Christmas Book Buyer: Art" *The Critic.* Volume XXXV, Number 870, December 1899. p. 1145.

"Literary Clippings." *The Tennessean* (Nashville, Tennessee). December 3, 1899. p. 20.

"The Golden Vanity." *The New York Times.* December 16, 1899. Saturday Review of Books and Art. p. BR883.

"Notes and News." *The New York Times.* December 16, 1899. Saturday Review of Books and Art. p. BR886.

"Literary Notes." *Kilburn Times* (London). December 22, 1899. p. 3.

"Literary Notes." *Willesden Chronicle* (London). December 22, 1899. p. 3.

"Glimpses of the New Books." *San Francisco Chronicle* (San Francisco, California). December 24, 1899. p. 21.

1900

"Department Notes." *Pratt Institute Monthly.* Volume VIII, Number 3, January 1900. p. 70.

"About Books and Authors." *The Tennessean* (Nashville, Tennessee). January 14, 1900. p. 13.

"Society." *Brooklyn Life.* January 20, 1900. p. 20.

"In Local Studios." *The Brooklyn Daily Eagle.* April 8, 1900. p. 21.

"Two Interesting Books." *Omaha Daily Bee* (Omaha, Nebraska). April 20, 1900. p. 7.

"About Books and Authors." *The Tennessean* (Nashville, Tennessee). April 22, 1900. p. 20.

"About Books and Authors." *The Tennessean* (Nashville, Tennessee). April 29, 1900. p. 20.

"In Local Studios." *The Brooklyn Daily Eagle.* April 29, 1900. p. 32.

Teall, Gardner. "Cleverness, Art, and an Artist." *Brush and Pencil.* Volume 6, Number 3, June 1900. pp. 135-141. Six examples of PCS artwork.

1901

"Illustrious Women Illustrators." *San Francisco Chronicle* (San Francisco, California). August 4, 1901. Sunday Supplement. p. 25, 36.

"Talk of the Town." *Weekly Irish Times* (Dublin, Ireland). November 2, 1901. p. 10.

1902

Stone, Wilbur Macey. *Women Designers of Book-Plates.* New York: Published for the Tryptych by Randolph R. Beam, 1902. 16mo, unpaginated.

"Grantham Industrial Exhibition." *Grantham Journal* (Lincolnshire, England). January 25, 1902. p. 2.

"A Literary Letter." *The Sphere* (London). November 29, 1902. p. 192.

1903

"Ladies' Pages." *Illustrated London News* (London). April 11, 1903. p. 556.

De Cordova, Rudolph. "The Women Editors of London." *Cassell's Magazine.* Volume 26, May 1903. pp. 680-686.

"The Rambler." *The Lamp.* Volume XXVI, Number 6, June 1903. pp. 417-428.

"Woman Editors." *Lake's Falmouth Packet and Cornwall Advertiser* (Cornwall, England). June 27, 1903. p. 7.

"Writers and Readers." *The Reader.* Volume II, Number 4, September 1903. pp. 331-333.

"Miss Pamela Smith's Drawings." *Morning Post* (London). November 19, 1903. p. 9.

1904

"Society." *The Richmond Item* (Richmond, Indiana). February 2, 1904. p. 8.

"Art and Artists." *The Daily Palladium* (Richmond, Indiana). February 5, 1904. p. 4.

"Literary Notes." *The Academy and Literature.* Volume LXVI, Number 1657, February 6, 1904. p. 139.

"News of the Book World." *Minneapolis Journal* (Minneapolis, Minnesota). February 6, 1904. p. 4.

"Art Notes." *The Academy and Literature.* Volume LXVI, Number 1663, March 19, 1904. p. 307.

1905

"London Art." *New-York Tribune.* January 20, 1905. p. 10.

"The Varied Work in Pratt Institute's Show." *The Brooklyn Daily Eagle.* November 17, 1905. p. 15.

"A Celtic Christmas." *Northern Whig* (Antrim, Northern Ireland). December 9, 1905. p. 10.

"Art Notes." *Pall Mall Gazette* (London). December 28, 1905. p.3.

1907

"In the World of Art and Artists." *The New York Times.* January 6, 1907. p. X4.

"The Looker-On." *Brooklyn Life.* January 12, 1907. p. 9.

"Some Special Exhibitions." *The Sun* (New York). January 15, 1907. p. 6.

"Notes." *The Craftsman.* Volume XI, Number 6, March 1907. pp. 769-771.

"The Week in Society." *Brooklyn Life.* March 2, 1907. p. 16.

"The Editors' Page." *Camera Work: A Photographic Quarterly.* No. 18,

April 1907. pp. 37-38.

"Photo-Secession Notes." *Camera Work: A Photographic Quarterly*. No. 18, April 1907. p. 49.

"Exhibitions at the Little Galleries." *Camera Work: A Photographic Quarterly*. No. 20, October 1907. p. 26.

"Gallery Notes." *The Morning Post* (London). November 8, 1907. p. 2.

"Art Notes." *Pall Mall Gazette* (London). November 26, 1907. p. 9.

"The Baillie Gallery." *The Morning Post* (London). November 26, 1907. p. 2.

"Our London Correspondence." *Manchester Courier* (Manchester, England). November 29, 1907. p. 6.

"Exhibitions Open During December." *Burlington Magazine for Connoisseurs*. Volume 12, Number 57, December 1907.

"Music Pictures." *The Observer* (London). December 1, 1907.

1908

"Around the Galleries." *The Sun* (New York). January 14, 1908. p. 6.

"London Letter." *American Art News*. Volume 6, Number 8, February 15, 1908. p. 5.

"Around the Galleries." *The Sun* (New York). February 25, 1908. p. 6.

"Art Exhibitions." *New-York Tribune*. February 26, 1908. p. 7.

"Variety of Art Exhibits." *The New York Times*. March 1, 1908. p. 8.

"Around the Galleries." *The Sun* (New York). March 4, 1908. p. 6.

"Art Exhibitions." *New-York Tribune*. March 10, 1908. p. 7.

"The Photo-Secession Galleries." *Camera Work: A Photographic Quarterly*. No. 22, April 1908. p. 44.

"Pictures in Music." *The Strand Magazine*. Volume XXXV, Number 210, June 1908. pp. 634-638.

"Publications." *Kent & Sussex Courier* (Kent, England). June 3, 1908. p. 2.

"Publications." *Taunton Courier, and Western Advertiser* (Somerset, England). June 3, 1908. p. 2.

"Reviews." *Bath Chronicle* (Bath, England). June 4, 1908. p. 6.

"Literary Notes." *Royal Cornwall Gazette* (Cornwall, England). June 11, 1908. p. 6.

"Messrs. Newnes' Publications." *Northern Times and Weekly Journal for Sutherland and the North* (Sutherland, Scotland). June 11, 1908. p. 8.

"Notices & Magazine Cuttings." *Banbury Advertiser* (Oxfordshire, England). June 11, 1908. p. 6.

"June Magazines." *Northern Whig* (Antrim, Northern Ireland). June 12, 1908. p. 10.

"June Magazines." *Cheltenham Looker-On* (Gloucestershire, England). June 13, 1908. p. 14.

"Literary Notices." *Alloa Advertiser* (Clackmannanshire, Scotland). June 20, 1908. p. 4.

"Art Topics of the Day." *The Brooklyn Daily Eagle*. June 21, 1908. p. 23.

"Pictured Music." *Current Literature*. Volume XLV, Number 2, August 1908. pp. 174-177.

"Recent Publications." *Desert Evening News* (Salt Lake City, Utah). August 13, 1908. p. 4.

"Notes on Fine Arts." *The Brooklyn Daily Eagle*. October 2, 1908. p. 7.

1909

"Lecture at Pratt Institute." *The Brooklyn Daily Eagle* March 14, 1909. p. 12.

"Art Notes." *The Sun* (New York). March 17, 1909. p. 8.

"Art Notes Here and There." *The New York Times*. March 21, 1909. Part Six. Fashions and Dramatic Section. p. 6.

"A Lecture on Art." *The Brooklyn Daily Eagle*. March 25, 1909. p. 11.

"Pamela Colman Smith Talks to Pratt Art Club." *The Brooklyn Daily Eagle*. March 25, 1909. p. 11.

"The Week in Society." *Brooklyn Life*. March 27, 1909. p. 15.

De Casseres, Benjamin. "Pamela Colman Smith." *Camera Work: A Photographic Quarterly*. No. 27, July 1909. pp. 18-20.

"New Members." *Camera Work: A Photographic Quarterly*. No. 27, July 1909. p. 28.

"Photo-Secession Notes." *Camera Work: A Photographic Quarterly*. No. 27, July 1909. p. 27.

"General Notices." *The Scotsman* (Midlothian, Scotland). October 12, 1909. p. 1.

"Notes of the Month." *The Occult Review*. Volume X, Number 6, December 1909. pp. 300-301.

Waite, Arthur Edward. "The Tarot: A Wheel of Fortune." *The Occult Review*. Volume X, Number 6, December 1909. pp. 307-317.

1910

"The Photo Session: Exhibitions." *American Art Annual*. Volume 8, 1910-1911. p. 202.

"Ladies Letter." *Northern Whig* (Antrim, Northern Ireland). January 11, 1910. p. 10.

1911

Jean-Aubry, Georges. ""Visualized Music" de Miss Pamela Colman Smith." *Le Mercure Musical* (La Revue Musicale S.I.M.). Volume VII, Number 2, 15 February 1911. pp. 44-46.

"Music Pictures." *The Guardian* (London). June 1, 1911. p. 6.

"Studio Talk." *International Studio*. Volume XLIV, Number 174, August 1911. pp. 144, 146.

"Literary Gossip." *Belfast News-Letter* (Antrim, Northern Ireland). November 14, 1911. p. 10.

1912

White, Sara Peirce. "Group Industries as Related to the Arts and Crafts Movement." *Handicraft*. Volume IV, Number 11, February 1912. pp. 388-391.

"Calendar of Special New York Exhibitions." *American Art News*. Volume 10, Number 23, March 16, 1912. p. 2.

"Interesting Things Seen in the World of Art." *The Sun* (New York). March 17, 1912. Fourth Section. p. 55.

"News and Notes of the Art World." *The New York Times*. March 17, 1912. p. SM15.

"Unusual Exhibit by Local Artist." *The Brooklyn Daily Eagle*. March 18, 1912. Picture and Sermon Section. p. 4.

"Art." *Star Tribune* (Minneapolis, Minnesota). March 24, 1912. p. 47.

"Homespuns, Baskets, Pottery and Tapestry Turned Out by Craft Workers." *The Sun* (New York). March 24, 1912. Third Section. p. 33.

"Tête-à-Tête with the Musicians." *The Houston Post* (Houston, Texas). March 24, 1912. p. 59.

Ayer, Margaret Hubbard. "Artist Puts Music into Pictures." *Los Angeles Evening Herald*. March 26, 1912. p. 10.

"Truly the Sister Arts." *The Charlotte News* (Charlotte, North Carolina). March 28, 1912. p. 5.

"Exhibitions at the Galleries." *Arts & Decoration*. Volume 2, Number 6, April 1912. pp. 227-228.

"Reviving Home Industries." *The Hutchinson News* (Hutchinson, Kansas). April 6, 1912. p. 11.

"Revival of Old Industries." *Journal Gazette* (Mattoon, Illinois).

April 26, 1912. p. 9.

"Revival of Old Industries." *Dakota County Herald* (Dakota City, Nebraska). May 3, 1912. p. 3.

"Revival of Old Industries." *The Atchison Daily Champion* (Atchison, Kansas). May 8, 1912. p. 2.

"Revival of Old Industries." *The Cape County Herald* (Cape Girardeau, Missouri). May 10, 1912. p. 3.

"Revival of Old Industries." *Courtland Journal* (Courtland, Kansas). May 10, 1912. p. 3.

"Revival of Old Industries." *Belvidere Daily Republican* (Belvidere, Illinois). May 11, 1912. p. 6.

"Revival of Old Industries." *The Red Cloud Chief* (Red Cloud, Nebraska). May 30, 1912. p. 3.

"Revival of Old Industries." *The Greensboro Patriot* (Greensboro, North Carolina). July 18, 1912. p. 10.

MacDonald, M. Irwin. "The Fairy Faith and Pictured Music of Pamela Colman Smith." *The Craftsman*. Volume XXIII, Number 1, October 1912. pp. 20-34.

"Current Art Magazines." *The Brooklyn Daily Eagle*. October 2, 1912. Picture and Sporting Section. p. 6.

"The Latest Books and Literary News." *The Inter Ocean* (Chicago, Illinois). October 5, 1912. p. 5.

"Timely Talks on the Library." *The Star Press* (Muncie, Indiana). October 13, 1912. p. 24.

"Pamela Colman Smith: She Believes in Fairies." *The Delineator*. Volume LXXX, Number 5, November 1912. p. 320.

"Along Literary Pathways." *The Times-Democrat* (New Orleans, Louisiana). November 3, 1912. p. 50.

"Believe in Fairies." *The Pantagraph* (Bloomington, Illinois). November 13, 1912. p 15.

1913

"Revival of Old Industries." *The Evening Index* (Greenwood, South Carolina). January 16, 1913. p. 17.

"Miss Ellen Terry…" *Pall Mall Gazette* (London). January 30, 1913. p. 5.

"Coming Theatrical Productions." *Derby Daily Telegraph* (Derbyshire, England). February 7, 1913. p. 4.

"The Russian Ballet." *Globe* (London). February 13, 1913. p. 5.

"New Books." *The Guardian* (London). February 21, 1913. p. 5.

"The Russian Ballet." *Pall Mall Gazette* (London). March 3, 1913. p. 7.

"Books to Read and Books to Use." *Yorkshire Post* (West Yorkshire, England). March 5, 1913. p. 4.

"The Russian Ballet." *Illustrated Sporting and Dramatic News* (London). March 8, 1913. p. 26.

"In the Realm of Literature and Art." Evening Star (Washington, DC). November 1, 1913. p. 11.

"Ellen Terry Discusses the Russian Ballet." *The Baltimore Sun* (Baltimore, Maryland). November 2, 1913. p. 20.

"Ellen Terry Discusses Russian Ballet." *The Courier-Journal* (Louisville, Kentucky). November 3, 1913. p. 6.

"Literary Notes." *The Morning News* (Wilmington, Delaware). November 5, 1913. p. 5.

"Book News and Comment." *Pittsburgh Daily Post* (Pittsburgh, Pennsylvania). November 8, 1913. p. 8.

"British Empire Shakespeare Society – Edinburgh Branch." *The Scotsman* (Midlothian, Scotland). December 8, 1913. p. 8.

"Modern Art on View at the Modernist Studios." *Brooklyn Life*. December 20, 1913. p. 22.

1914

"Les Livres." *Le Mercure Musical* (La Revue Musicale S.I.M.). Volume X, 1 January 1914. p. 39.

Pierce, Lucy France. "The Littlest Theatre." *The Drama: A Quarterly Review*. Volume IV, Number 13, February 1914. pp. 84-92.

"Notes." *The Academy*. Volume 86, Number 2187, April 4, 1914. p. 428.

"For Every Woman." *Pall Mall Gazette* (London). March 28, 1914. p. 4.

"For Young Readers." *The Courier-Journal* (Louisville, Kentucky). November 9, 1914. p. 8.

"Books for Young Readers." *The Brooklyn Daily Eagle*. November 21, 1914. Holiday Book Number. p. 5.

1915

"The New Lady Traveller in Toys." *Sheffield Weekly Telegraph* (South Yorkshire, England). October 16, 1915. p. 11.

"'291' the Mecca and the Mystery of Art in a Fifth Avenue Attic."

The Sun (New York). October 24, 1915. Fifth Section, Special Feature Magazine. p. 6.

"Real Russian Ballet to be Here Three Days in March." *The Indianapolis News* (Indianapolis, Indiana). November 20, 1915. p. 14.

1916

"Diaghileff Ballet Russe Makes Debut in New York." *Indianapolis News* (Indianapolis, Indiana). January 18, 1916. p. 18.

"The Books They're Talking About." *The Cincinnati Enquirer* (Cincinnati, Ohio). March 13, 1916. p. 5.

Gerrard, Thomas J. "Art After the War." *The Living Age*. Volume CCLXXXVIII, Eighth Series, Volume 1, Number 3741, March 18, 1916. pp. 715-724.

"The Chelsea Fair." *Chelsea News and General Advertiser* (London). June 16, 1916. p. 2.

"Temple of Mystery." *Pall Mall Gazette* (London). June 29, 1916. p. 9.

1919

Waite, Arthur Edward. "The Tarot and Secret Tradition." *The Occult Review*. Volume XXIX, Number 3, March 1919. p. 157.

Blaikie-Murdoch, W. G. "The Cuala Press and Its Bookplates." *The Bookplate Booklet*. Volume 1, Number 1, May 1919. pp. 9-20.

1920

Yeats, Jack B. *The Treasure of the Garden*. A play by Jack B. Yeats. Coloured by the author. London: Elkin Mathews, [192-?]. 8vo, unpaginated. PCS advertising on last page and inside back cover.

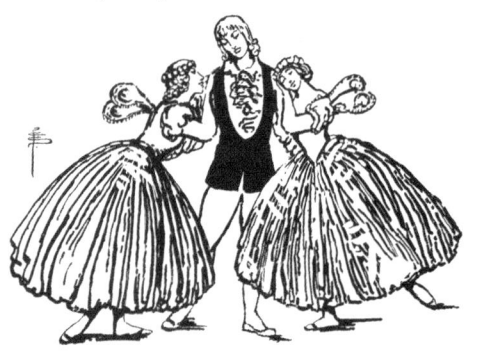

1924

Calkins, Earnest Elmo. *"Louder Please!": The Autobiography of a Deaf Man*. Boston: The Atlantic Monthly Press, 1924. 8vo, 260 pp.

Craig, Edward Gordon. *Nothing or the Bookplate...with a Handlist* by E. Carrick. London: Chatto & Windus, 1924. 8vo, 26 pp. 50 plates.

"Music Pictures." *The Mercury* (Hobart, Tasmania). March 25, 1924. p. 10.

"Books of the Hour." *Brooklyn Life*. October 18, 1924. p. 14.

1927

Forbes-Sempill, Honourable Mrs. "Music Made Visible: An Unmusical Artist's Lightning Impressions Recorded While Listening to Music: The Remarkable Drawings of Miss Pamela Colman Smith." *The Illustrated London News*. February 12, 1927. pp. 258-260.

"Can Music Be Interpreted in Terms of Pictorial Art?" *Sikeston Standard* (Sikeston, Missouri). May 3, 1927. p. 3.

1938

"Footlight Footnotes of the Little Theatre." *Wilkes-Barre Times Leader, the Evening News* (Wilkes-Barre, Pennsylvania). April 2, 1938. p. 11.

1954

Moakley, Gertrude. "The Waite-Smith Tarot." *Bulletin of the New York Public Library* (New York, NY). Volume 58, Number 10, October 1954. pp. 471-475.

1966

Moakley, Gertrude. *The Tarot Cards Painted by Bonifacio Bembo for the Visconti-Sforza Family: an Iconographic and Historical Study*. New York: New York Public Library, 1966. 8vo, 124 pp. Author's personal copy with corrections.

1974

Harper, George Mills. *Yeats's Golden Dawn*. New York: Barnes & Noble, 1974. 8vo, 322 pp.

Homer, William Innes. "Pamela Colman Smith." *Music & Letters*. Volume 55, Number 4, October 1974. pp. 508-509.

1975

Parsons, Melinda Boyd. *The Rediscovery of Pamela Colman Smith*. Thesis. M.A. University of Delaware, 1975.

Parsons, Melinda Boyd. *To All Believers: The Art of Pamela Colman Smith*. Delaware Art Museum, September 11 - October 19, 1975; The Art Museum, Princeton University, November 4 - December 7, 1975. Wilmington, DE: Delaware Art Museum, 1975. 4 to, unpaginated.

1977

Pamela Colman Smith: An Exhibition of Her Work, arranged by Joan Coldwell and Ann Saddlemyer. McMaster University Art Gallery, 15-24 February, 1977. Hamilton, Ontario: Canadian Association for Irish Studies, 1977.

1978

Whitney Museum of American Art, Downtown Branch. *The Symbolist Mood Around 1900: Whitney Museum, 55 Water Street, November 2-December 6, 1978*. (New York, N.Y.): Whitney Museum of American Art, Downtown Branch, 1978.

1987

Parsons, Melinda Boyd. "Mysticism in London: The Golden Dawn, Synaesthesia, and Psychic Automatism in the Art of Pamela Colman Smith." *The Spiritual Image in Modern Art*. Edited by Kathleen Regier. Wheaton: Quest Books, 1987. pp. 73-101.

Parsons, Melinda Boyd. "Theatrical Productions, Symphonic Music, and the Rise of 'Musical Painting' in the Late Nineteenth Century." *Nineteenth-Century Studies*. Volume 1, Spring 1987. pp. 49-72.

Gover, Jane. "Women of the Photo-Secession and Alfred Stieglitz." *AB Bookman's Weekly*. Volume 80, Number 16, 1987. pp. 1690-1698.

1990

Kaplan, Stuart R. *The Encyclopedia of Tarot*. Volume III, Stamford, CT: U.S. Games Systems, 1990. pp. xvii, 1-45.

1996

Parsons, Melinda Boyd. "Pamela Colman Smith and Alfred Stieglitz: Modernism at 291." *History of Photography*. Volume 20, Issue 4, 1996. pp. 285-292.

2008

"The Art of Pamela Colman Smith." Mary K. Greer. n.p., 17 April 2008. Web. https://marygreer.wordpress.com/tag/pamela-colman-smith/.

2009

Kaplan, Stuart R. and Araujo, Lynn. *The Artwork & Times of Pamela Colman Smith*. Designed by Jody Boginski. Stamford, CT: U.S. Games Systems, 2009. 12mo, 101 pp.

2010

Smith, Pamela Colman. *Susan and the Mermaid*. Adapted from a story in the December 1912 issue of *The Delineator* magazine, with notes by Corrine Kenner. [United States]: [CreateSpace], [2010]. 8vo, 27 pp.

2013

Greer, Mary K. *Secrets and Sources of the Rider Waite Smith Minor Arcana*. n.p. 2013. Recorded Webinar. Global Spiritual Studies. http://globalspiritualstudies.com/product/secrets-and-sources-of-the-rider-waite-smith-minor-arcana/.

2014

Brown, Ruth. *The Compleat Psychic*. n.p.: Creative Commons 3.0 License, 2014. 445 pp.

http://www.themista.com/freeebooks/compleatpsychic.pdf

Caples, Garrett T. *Retrievals*. Seattle, WA: Wave Books, [2014]. 8vo. 280 pp.

2016

Meier, Allison, et al. "Pamela Colman Smith, the Forgotten Artist Behind Your Tarot Cards." *Hyperallergic*, 27 Oct. 2016, hyperallergic.com/330790/the-unnamed-woman-artist-revealed-in-the-monogram-of-your-tarot-cards/.

O'Connor, Elizabeth Foley. "'We Disgruntled Devils Don't Please Anybody": Pamela Colman Smith, The Green Sheaf, and Female Literary Networks." *The South Carolina Review*. Volume 48, Number 2, Spring 2016. pp. 72-89.

Part 3 – WORKS ABOUT PCS BY DATE – FOLKTALES

1898

"Annancy Stories - A Literary Event: The Amusing Tales that Old Negro Nurses Tell to the Children of Jamaica, Collected and Illustrated by Pamela Colman Smith." *New York Herald*. December 11,

1898. Fifth Section. p. 3.

"Mother Calbee and Her Cruel Present" and "A Lesson for the Ungrateful Ones."

Pittsburgh Daily Post. December 25, 1898. p. 16.

"Ticky-Picky-Boom-Boom" and "Mother Calbee." *New York Herald*. December 25, 1898. Colored Section. p. 7.

1899

"Six Poached Eggs – And How the Judge Administered Justice." *The Atlanta Constitution* (Atlanta, Georgia). January 1, 1899. p. 19.

"Jamaica Spider." *The Times* (Washington, DC). January 15, 1899. p. 17.

"A Young Girl Becomes a Brilliant Artist." *The Courier-Journal* (Louisville, Kentucky). January 15, 1899. p. 25.

"Our Anancy Stories." *The Daily Gleaner* (Kingston, Jamaica). February 4, 1899. p. 16.

"Bits for Bookworms." *The Daily Herald* (Delphos, Ohio). May 11, 1899. p. 3.

"New Books and Magazines." *Omaha Daily Bee* (Omaha, Nebraska). December 14, 1899. p. 7.

"Books for Children." *Saint Paul Globe* (St. Paul, Minnesota). December 17, 1899. p. 18.

"Annancy Stories." *The Indianapolis News* (Indianapolis, Indiana). December 20, 1899. p. 6.

1900

"Book Talk." *San Francisco Chronicle* (San Francisco, California). February 11, 1900. p. 24.

"In the World of Books." *Seattle Post-Intelligencer* (Seattle, Washington). February 25, 1900. p. 32.

1903

"The Week." *The Speaker: The Liberal Review*. Volume VIII, May 16, 1903. p. 152.

"London Correspondence." *Sheffield Daily Telegraph* (South Yorkshire, England). December 9, 1903. p. 6.

1904

"Some Women Who Have Achieved Fame." *The Lady's Realm*. Volume XVI, 1904. pp. 544-545.

"The Café Chantant for Princess Christian's Infant Nursery." *The Observer* (London). January 24, 1904. p. 3.

"Theatre Notes." *Morning Post* (London). February 5, 1904. p. 5.

"Literary Gossip." *Wigan Observer and District Advertiser* (Lancashire, England). February 10, 1904. p. 8.

"Furnivall Sculling Club." *West London Observer*. February 12, 1904. p. 2.

"Mr. Thomas Hardy…" *Wigan Observer and District Advertiser* (Lancashire, England). February 12, 1904. p. 8.

"Novel Methods of a Lady Storyteller." *Riverine Grazier* (NSW). April 1, 1904. p. 4.

"Jamaican Folk Lore." *Evening Star* (Washington, DC). April 4, 1904. p. 14.

"Delightfully Employed." *The Spokane Press* (Spokane, Washington). May 3, 1904. p. 1.

"Delightfully Employed." *The Tacoma Times* (Tacoma, Washington). May 5, 1904. p. 2.

"Delightfully Employed." *The Pittsburgh Press* (Pittsburgh, Pennsylvania). May 6, 1904. p. 20.

"Weird Entertainment in English Society." *St. Louis Post-Dispatch* (St. Louis, Missouri). May 15, 1904. Sunday Magazine. p. 8.

"A Pleasant Employment." *The Decatur Herald* (Decatur, Illinois). June 5, 1904. p. 16.

"Literature of the Week." *Hampshire Advertiser* (Hampshire, England). September 3, 1904. p. 5.

"Reviews." *Grantham Journal* (Lincolnshire, England). September 24, 1904. p. 6.

"Minutes of Meetings." *Folklore*. Volume XV, Number 3, September 29, 1904. p. 243.

The Lamp. October 1904. p. 294.

"West Indian Folklore Stories." *Sterling Standard* (Sterling, Illinois). October 21, 1904. p. 2.

"West Indian Folklore Stories." *The Winfield Daily Free Press* (Winfield, Kansas). October 21, 1904. p. 3.

"West Indian Folklore Stories." *The Columbus Journal* (Columbus, Nebraska). October 26, 1904. p. 6.

"West Indian Folklore Stories." *The Marquette Tribune* (Marquette, Kansas). October 27, 1904. p. 3.

"Wins by Witchery in London Drawing Rooms." *The Brooklyn Daily Eagle*. November 1, 1904. p. 9.

"West Indian Folklore Stories." The Marshfield News and Wisconsin Hub (Marshfield, Wisconsin). December 1, 1904. p. 6.

1905

"The Twenty Seventh Annual Report of the Council." *Folklore*. Volume XVI, Number 1, March 25, 1905. pp. 7-8.

1906

"Theatre Notes." *Morning Post* (London). July 7, 1906. p. 5.

"Arrangements." *Morning Post* (London). July 9, 1906. p. 7.

"Arrangements." *Morning Post* (London). July 10, 1906. p. 7.

The Guardian (London). July 11, 1906. p. 6.

"An Afternoon of Folk-Lore." *The Sunday Times* (London). July 15, 1906. p. 6.

1907

"What is Doing in Society." *The New York Times*. January 25, 1907. p. 9.

"The Week in Society." *Brooklyn Life*. January 26, 1907. p. 28.

"Italian Officials Guests." *The Brooklyn Daily Eagle*. January 30, 1907. p. 10.

"The Entertainment Club Dines." *The New York Times*. January 30, 1907. p. 9.

"Italian Ambassador Entertained by Entertainment Club at Waldorf." *New-York Tribune*. January 30, 1907. p. 14.

"Women's Clubs." *Brooklyn Life*. February 2, 1907. p. 22.

"The Week in Society." *Brooklyn Life*. February 9, 1907. p. 16, 18.

"Pamela Colman Smith to Entertain the Packer Alumnae." *The Brooklyn Daily Eagle*. February 10, 1907. p. 13.

"In the Women's Clubs." *The Brooklyn Daily Eagle*. February 16, 1907. Picture Section. p. 3.

"Announcements." *Brooklyn Life*. February 16, 1907. p. 3.

"Women's Clubs." *Brooklyn Life*. February 16, 1907. p. 38.

"The Packer Associate Alumnae and Pamela Coleman [sic] Smith." *The Brooklyn Daily Eagle*. February 17, 1907. News. Editorial. p. 3.

"Announcements." *Brooklyn Life*. February 23, 1907. p. 3.

"Packer Alumnae at Home." *The Brooklyn Daily Eagle*. February 24, 1907. p. 36.

"Made Veteran Humorist Laugh." *The Evening Statesman* (Walla Walla, Washington). February 27, 1907. p. 3.

"Reading Club Anniversary." *The Brooklyn Daily Eagle*. March 17, 1907. p. 39.

"The Week in Society." *Brooklyn Life*. March 23, 1907. p. 17.

"The Story that Amused Mark Twain." *The World's News* (Sydney).

April 6, 1907. p. 13.

Campbell, Lady Archibald. "Faerie Ireland." *The Occult Review*. Volume VI, Number 5, November 1907. pp. 259-274.

1908

"Miss Colman-Smith's Story-Telling." *The Times* (London). February 4, 1908. p. 9.

"A Pretty Story-Teller." *The Sketch: A Journal of Art and Actuality*. Volume LXI, Number 790, March 18, 1908. p. 306. With photograph of Pamela Colman Smith.

"League of Mercy." *Morning Post* (London). April 14, 1908. p. 6.

"The Fair, Told and Pictured by Pamela Colman Smith." *The Junior Call* (San Francisco) (San Francisco Call). September 12, 1908. p. 4.

"Stone." *Bucks Herald* (Buckinghamshire, England). December 26, 1908. p. 5.

1910

"Matinee for Children." *The New York Times*. April 3, 1910. Part Six. Society – Fashions – Drama. p. 8.

"Plays for the Children." *The Brooklyn Daily Eagle*. April 3, 1910. News. Editorial. p. 9.

1912

"At the Bechstein Hall." *The Tatler* (London). January 24, 1912. p. 40.

"In the Audience." *Brooklyn Life*. March 16, 1912. p. 14.

"Miss Jean Sterling MacKinlay." *Kent & Sussex Courier* (Kent, England). May 17, 1912. p. 7.

"Miss Jean Sterling MacKinlay." *Kent & Sussex Courier* (Kent, England). May 31, 1912. p. 7.

"Chit Chat." *The Stage* (London). July 11, 1912. p. 17.

1913

"Old Songs and Ballads." *Eastbourne Gazette* (East Sussex, England). January 15, 1913. p. 3.

"Old Songs and Ballads." *Eastbourne Gazette* (East Sussex, England). January 22, 1913. p. 8.

1917

"Tableaux at the Savoy Hotel." *The Times* (London). February 9, 1917. p. 3.

"Pamela's Tales." *The Sketch* (London). February 14, 1917. p. 138.

"Boudoir Gossip." *Pall Mall Gazette* (London). February 20, 1917. p. 8.

2015

O'Connor, Elizabeth. "Pamela Colman Smith's Performative Primitivism." *Caribbean Irish Connections: Interdisciplinary Perspectives*. Edited by Alison Donnell, Maria McGarrity, Evelyn O'Callaghan. Kingston, Jamaica: The University of the West Indies Press, 2015. pp. 157, 173.

Greer, Mary K. "Category Archive." *Storyteller—Pamela Colman Smith*. n.p., 15 Apr. 2015. Web. 22 July 2017. <https://marykgreer.com/category/pamela-colman-smith/>.

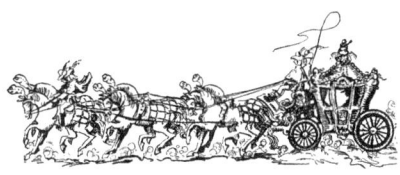

Part 4 – WORKS ABOUT PCS BY DATE – ADVERTISEMENTS

1899

"From Day to Day." *Dublin Daily Express* (Dublin, Ireland). August 12, 1899. p. 4. [*In Chimney Corners*]

"Notes and News." *The New York Times*. August 19, 1899. Saturday Review of Books and Art. p. BR558. [*Golden Vanity*]

"Autumn and Holiday Books." *The New York Times*. October 7, 1899. Saturday Review of Books and Art. p. BR662. [*Golden Vanity and Widdicombe Fair*]

"The Newest Books." *St. Louis Post-Dispatch* (St. Louis, Missouri). October 14, 1899. p. 4. [*In Chimney Corners*]

"Books and Authors." *Albany Ledger* (Albany, Missouri). November 3, 1899. p. 2. [*Golden Vanity and Widdicombe Fair*]

"The Book World." *The Buffalo Commercial* (Buffalo, New York). November 7, 1899. p. 5. [*Golden Vanity*]

"New Publications." *The Globe* (London). November 8, 1899. p. 4. [*In Chimney Corners*]

"Publications Received." *Morning Post* (London). November 10, 1899. p. 9. [*In Chimney Corners*]

"Beautiful Gift Book." *Dublin Daily Nation* (Dublin, Ireland). November 11, 1899. p. 4. [*In Chimney Corners*]

"Books and Authors." *The Plain Speaker* (Hazleton, Pennsylvania). November 11, 1899. p. 2. [*Golden Vanity and Widdicombe Fair*]

"Now Ready." *Dublin Daily Nation* (Dublin, Ireland). November 13, 16, 17, 18, 20, 21, 22, 24, 25, 30, 1899. p. 8. [*In Chimney Corners*]

"Literary Notes." *The Times* (Philadelphia, Pennsylvania). November 18, 1899. p. 12. [*Irving/Terry souvenir*]

"Ready at all Bookstores." *The Sun* (New York). November 18, 1899. p. 7. [*Annancy Stories*]

"Books and Authors." *The Westville News* (Westville, Mississippi). November 23, 1899. p. 2. [*Golden Vanity and Widdicombe Fair*]

"Christmas Books." *Scribner's Magazine Advertiser*. Volume XXVI, Number 6, December 1899. p. 33. [*Annancy Stories*]

"Now Ready." *Dublin Daily Nation* (Dublin, Ireland). December 2, 4, 6, 8, 14, 16, 19, 20, 21, 22, 28, 1899. p. 8. [*In Chimney Corners*]

"In the Literary World." *The Atlanta Constitution* (Atlanta, Georgia). December 3, 1899. p. 11. [*Annancy Stories*]

"Books and Authors." *The Bossier Banner* (Bellevue, Bossier Parish, LA). December 7, 1899. p. 4. [*Golden Vanity and Widdicombe Fair*]

"Christmas Books." *The Philadelphia Inquirer* (Philadelphia, Pennsylvania). December 8, 1899. p. 10. [*Golden Vanity and Widdicombe Fair*]

"New Publications." *Democrat and Chronicle* (Rochester, New York). December 9, 1899. p. 7. [*Annancy Stories*]

Suitable Holiday Books." *New-York Daily Tribune*. December 11, 1899. p. 8. [*In Chimney Corners*]

1900

"Now Ready." *Dublin Daily Nation* (Dublin, Ireland). January 3, 6, 9, 11, 16, 19, 22, 24, 25, 30, 31, 1900. p. 8. [*In Chimney Corners*]

"Now Ready." *Dublin Daily Nation* (Dublin, Ireland). February 1, 5, 7, 9, 12, 14, 15, 16, 17, 19, 20, 22, 23, 24, 26, 1900. p. 8. [*In Chimney Corners*]

"Now Ready." *Dublin Daily Nation* (Dublin, Ireland). March 1, 2, 3, 5, 6, 7, 8, 12, 15, 16, 19, 21, 1900. p. 8. [*In Chimney Corners*]

1901

"Books for Little." *The Times* (Philadelphia, Pennsylvania). February 23, 1901. p. 12. [*Annancy Stories*]

1905
"To-Day's Books." *Morning Post* (London). December 12, 1905. p. 5. [*Chim-Chim*]

1906
"To-Day's Books." *Morning Post* (London). October 18, 1906. p. 3. [*Tales from My Garden*]

1910
"Rider's Occult Publications." *The Occult Review*. Volume XII, Number 6, December 1910. Rear cover. [*Rider Tarot*]

1911
"Bookland." *Berwickshire News* (Scotland). November 28, 1911. p. 5. [*The Lair of the White Worm*]

1912
"Rider's New Books." *Globe* (London). May 8, 1912. p. 4. [*The Lair of the White Worm*]

"Rider's Latest Publications." *The Tatler* (London). May 15, 1912. p. 50. [*The Lair of the White Worm*]

"The Delineator." *The Times-Democrat* (New Orleans, Louisiana). November 13, 1912. p. 16. [*Susan and the Mermaid*]

"Along Literary Pathways." *The Times-Democrat* (New Orleans, Louisiana). December 1, 1912. p. 50. [*Susan and the Mermaid*]

1913
"Book Received." *The Era* (London). February 15, 1913. p. 15. [*Russian Ballet*]

"Books for Children." *The Sun* (New York). November 8, 1913. p. 8. [*Bluebeard*]

"Pictures for Children." *The Brooklyn Daily Eagle.* November 29, 1913. Holiday Book Number. p. 6. [*Bluebeard*]

"The Bobbs-Merrill Company." *The Sun* (New York). December 3, 1913. p.8. [*Russian Ballet*]

"The Bobbs-Merrill Company." *The Indianapolis Star* (Indianapolis, Indiana). December 14, 1913. p. 7. [*Russian Ballet*]

1914
"New Books Received." *The Los Angeles Times* (Los Angeles, California). November 22, 1914. Part IIIa. p. 11. [*Book of Friendly Giants*]

1917
"Books Received." *Evening Star* (Washington, DC). January 21, 1917. p. 2. [*Russian Ballet*]

1920
"Drama." *Coterie: A Quarterly: Art, Prose, and Poetry.* Number 4, Easter 1920. p. 96. [*Drama* magazine]

Part 5 – WORKS ABOUT PCS BY DATE – BIOGRAPHICAL, OTHER

1867
Tuckerman, Henry T. *American Artist Life, Comprising Biographical and Critical Sketches of American Artists.* New York: G.P. Putnam & Son, 1867. 8vo, 639 pp. [Samuel Colman]

1896
"Died." *The Daily Gleaner* (Kingston, Jamaica). July 14, 1896. p. 2. [Corinne Colman obituary]

1899
"No More? No More?" *The Brooklyn Daily Eagle.* November 16, 1899. p. 8. [Brooklyn history]

"Charles Edward Smith." *The Brooklyn Daily Eagle.* December 2, 1899. p. 18. [Obituary]

"Charles Edward Smith." *New-York Tribune.* December 2, 1899. p. 9. [Obituary]

"Died." *New York Times.* December 3, 1899. p.7. [Charles Edward Smith obituary]

"Pastoral: Diocesan Works." *The Tablet.* December 9, 1899. p. 954. [Chapel at Lizard]

"In Local Studios." *The Brooklyn Daily Eagle.* December 17, 1899. p. 30. [Charles Edward Smith death announcement]

1900
"Announcements." *Brooklyn Life.* May 26, 1900. p. 16. [Travel to London]

"Society." *Brooklyn Life.* May 26, 1900. p. 12. [Travel to London]

1901
Smith, Pamela Colman. *Visitors.* 1901-1905. 8vo, 151 pp. Manuscript. Pamela Colman Smith's personal Visitors book. Signatures, sketches, witticisms, poems, etc. throughout.

1904
"Pamela Coleman [sic] Smith, Closely Related to Many Prominent Brooklyn Families, and Her Strange Career." *The Brooklyn Daily Eagle.* November 1, 1904. p. 9.

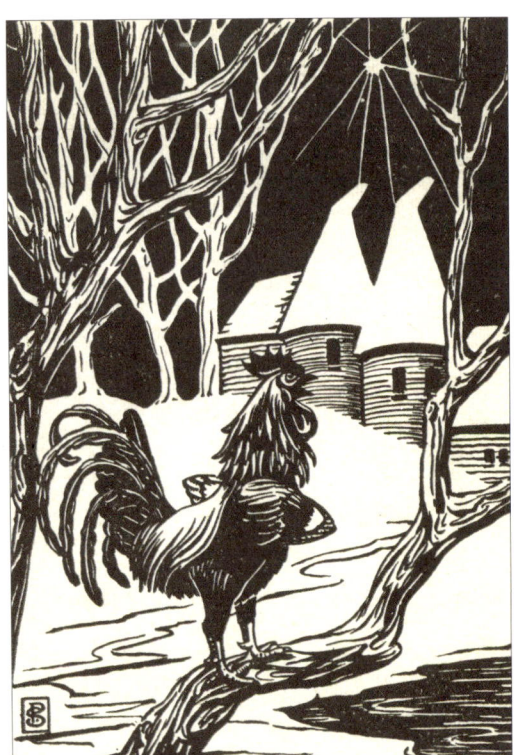

1906

Elton, Oliver. *Frederick York Powell: A Life and a Selection from His Letters and Occasional Writings. Vol. II: occasional writings.* Oxford: Clarendon Press, 1906. 8vo, 464 pp. Reprint.

1907

Jekyll, Walter. *Jamaican Song and Story: Annancy Stories, Digging Sings, Ring Tunes and Dancing Tunes.* Collected and edited by Walter Jekyll. London: David Nutt, 1907. 8vo, 288 pp.

Ransome, Arthur. *Bohemia in London.* With illustrations by Fred Taylor. New York: Dodd, Mead & Company, 1907. 8vo, 293 pp.

"The Week in Society." *Brooklyn Life.* March 30, 1907. p. 26. [Irving and Terry]

1914

"The Travelers." *Brooklyn Life.* March 28, 1914. p. 24. [Travel to London]

1920

"Samuel Colman." *American Art News.* Volume XVIII, Number 25, April 10, 1920. p. 4.[Obituary]

1922

"Advent Pastorals." *The Tablet.* December 16, 1922. p. 15. [Chapel at Lizard]

1923

Nevinson, Henry Wood. *Changes and Chances.* London: Nisbet & Company, 1923

"The Chapel at the Lizard." *The Tablet.* February 10, 1923. p. 32. [Chapel at Lizard]

1929

Shaw, Martin. *Up to Now.* London: Oxford University Press, H. Milford, 1929. 8vo, 218 pp.

1934

America & Alfred Stieglitz: A Collective Portrait. Edited by Waldo Frank, Lewis Mumford, Dorothy Norman, Paul Rosenfeld & Harold Rugg. With 120 illustrations. New York: The Literary Guild, [1934]. 8vo, 339 pp.

"Old Families Ruled in Own Communities." *The Brooklyn Daily Eagle.* April 8, 1934. p. 101.[Brooklyn/Family history]

1938

Waite, Arthur Edward. *Shadows of Life and Thought: A Retrospective Review in the Form of Memoirs.* London: Selwyn and Blount, 1938. 8vo, 288 pp.

1939

The Catholic Who's Who: 1939. London: Burns, Oates & Washbourne LTD, 1939. p.468.

1944

Yeats, John Butler. *J.B. Yeats: Letters to His Son W.B. Yeats and Others 1869-1922.* Edited with a memoir by Joseph Hone. London: Faber and Faber Limited, 1944. 8vo, 296 pp.

1946

Yeats, John Butler. *J.B. Yeats: Letters to His Son W.B. Yeats and Others 1869-1922.* Edited with a memoir by Joseph Hone. New York: E.P. Dutton & Co., 1946. 8vo, 304 pp.

1949

Adlard, Eleanor, editor. *Edy: Recollections of Edith Craig.* London: Frederick Muller Ltd., 1949. 8vo, 156 pp.

1951

Robinson, Lennox. *Ireland's Abbey Theatre.* Port Washington, NY: Kennikat Press, 1951. 8vo, 224 pp.

1954

The Letters of W.B. Yeats. Edited by Allan Wade. London: Rupert Hart-Davis, 1954. 8vo, 938 pp.

1960

Doty, Robert. Forward by Beaumont Newhall. *Photo Secession: Photography as a Fine Art.* George Eastman House monograph number 1. Rochester, NY: George Eastman House, 1960. 8vo, 103 pp.

1961

Greene, David Herbert and Edward M. Stephens. *J.M. Synge.* New York: Collier Books, 1961. 8vo, 319 pp.

1965

Hone, Joseph M. *W. B. Yeats, 1865-1939.* London: MacMillan & Co., 1965. 8vo, 503 pp.

1970

Pyle, Hilary. *Jack B. Yeats: A Biography.* London: Routledge & Kegan Paul, 1970. 8vo, 228 pp.

1973

Norman, Dorothy. *Alfred Stieglitz: An American Seer.* New York: Random House, 1973. 4to, 253 pp.

Homer, William Innes. "Stieglitz and 291." *Art in America.* Volume LXI, Number 4, July-August, 1973. pp. 50-57.

1974

Harper, George Mills. *Yeats's Golden Dawn.* New York: Barnes & Noble, 1974. 8vo, 322 pp.

1977

Homer, William Innes. *Alfred Stieglitz and the American Avant-Garde.* Boston: New York Graphic Society, 1977. 8vo, 335 pp.

Coldwell, Joan. "Pamela Colman Smith and the Yeats Family." *The Canadian Journal of Irish Studies.* Volume 3, Number 2, November 1977. pp. 27-34.

1983

Homer, William Innes. *Alfred Stieglitz and the Photo-Secession.* Boston: Little, Brown and Company, 1983. 4to, 180 pp.

1988

Tickner, Lisa. *The Spectacle of Women: Imagery of the Suffrage Campaign, 1907-14.* Chicago: University of Chicago Press, 1988. 8vo, 334 pp.

1989

Pyle, Hilary. *Jack B. Yeats: A Biography.* Savage, MD: Barnes & Noble Books, 1989. 8vo, 228 pp.

1991

Ransome, Arthur and Rupert Hart-Davis. *The Autobiography of Arthur Ransome.* London: Jonathan Cape, 1991. 8vo, 368 pp.

1992

"'Holy Pagan Innocence': Spirituality and Primitive Purity in the Stieglitz Circle." Melinda Boyd Parsons. *No: An Independent Quarterly of the Visual Arts.* Number 17 (1992), 14-17; and Number 18 (1992), 10-13.

Pyle, Hilary. *Jack B. Yeats: A Catalogue Raisonné of the Oil Paintings.* London: Andre Deutsch Ltd., 1992. Volume I. p. xliv, 1115.

1995

Greer, Mary K. *Women of the Golden Dawn: Rebels and Priestesses.* Rochester, VT: Park Street Press, 1995. 8vo, 490 pp.

Murphy, William Michael. *Family Secrets: William Butler Yeats and His Relatives.* Syracuse, NY: Syracuse University Press, 1995. 8vo, 534 pp.

Whelan, Richard. *Alfred Stieglitz: A Biography.* Boston: Little, Brown and Company, 1995. 8vo, 662 pp.

1997

Parsons, Melinda Boyd. "Pamela Colman Smith." *Dictionary of Women Artists.* Edited by Delia Gaze. London: Fitzroy Dearborn, 1997, pp. 1289-1292.

1998

Cockin, Katharine. *Edith Craig (1869-1947): Dramatic Lives.* London; Washington: Cassell, 1998.

2001

Cockin, Katharine. *Women and Theatre in the Age of Suffrage: The Pioneer Players 1911-1925.* Houndmills, Basingstoke, Hampshire; New York: Palgrave, 2001. 8vo, 239 pp.

2004

Hoffman, Katherine. *Stieglitz: A Beginning Light.* New Haven, CT: Yale University Press, 2004. 8vo, 381 pp.

2006

Jensen, K. Frank. *The story of the Waite-Smith Tarot.* Melbourne: Association for Tarot Studies, 2006. 8vo, 221 pp.

2007

Pyne, Kathleen. *Modernism and the Feminine Voice: O'Keeffe and the Women of the Stieglitz Circle.* Berkeley, CA: University of California Press, 2007. 8vo, 339 pp.

2008

Schuchard, Ronald. *The Last Minstrels: Yeats and the Revival of the Bardic Arts.* New York: Oxford University Press, 2008. 8vo, 447 pp.

2009

Holroyd, Michael. *A Strange Eventful History: The Dramatic Lives of Ellen Terry, Henry Irving, and Their Remarkable Families.* New York: Farrar, Straus and Giroux, 2009. 8vo, 620 pp.

2011

"Biography of Pamela Colman Smith (1878-1951)." Phil Norfleet. n.p., 30 March 2011. Web. http://pcs2051.tripod.com/index.htm.

Rachlin, Ann. *Edy Was a Lady.* Leicester: Troubador Publishing, 2011.

2012

Morton, Tara. "Changing Spaces: Art, Politics, and Identity in the Home Studios of the Suffrage Atelier." *Women's History Review.* Volume 21, Issue 4, September 2012. pp. 623-637.

Stoker, Bram. *The Forgotten Writings of Bram Stoker.* Edited by John Edgar Browning; foreword by Elizabeth Miller; afterword by Dacre Stoker. New York: Palgrave Macmillan, 2012. 8vo, 266 pp.

2013

Cockin, Katharine. *The Collected Letters of Ellen Terry.* Volume 4 (1899-1904). New York: Routledge, 2013.

2014

Caples, Garrett T. *Retrievals.* Seattle: Wave Books, 2014. 8vo, 280 pp.

Cockin, Katharine. *The Collected Letters of Ellen Terry.* Volume 5 (1905-1913). New York: Routledge, 2014.

"Fool's Journey: The Fascinating Life of Pamela Colman Smith." Beth Maiden. n.p., 12 December 2014. Web. https://www.autostraddle.com/fools-journey-the-fascinating-life-of-pamela-colman-smith-267673/

2015

Cockin, Katharine. *The Collected Letters of Ellen Terry.* Volume 6 (1914-1928). New York: Routledge, 2015.

Katz, Marcus and Tali Goodwin. *Secrets of the Waite-Smith Tarot: The True Story of the World's Most Popular Tarot: with Previously Unseen Photography & Text from Waite & Smith.* Woodbury, MN: Llewellyn Publications, 2015. 8vo, 458 pp.

Thomas, Zoë. "At Home with the Women's Guild of Arts: Gender and Professional Identity in London Studios, c.1880–1925." *Women's History Review.* Volume 24, Issue 6, 2015. pp. 938-964.

Robinson, Dawn G. *Secret Bude.* Gloucestershire: Amberley Publishing, 2016. 8vo, 95 pp.

2016

Skal, David J. *Something in the Blood: The Untold Story of Bram Stoker, the Man Who Wrote Dracula.* New York: Liveright Publishing, 2016.

2017

Cockin, Katherine. *Edith Craig and the Theatres of Art.* London; New York: Bloomsbury Methuen Drama, 2017. 8vo, 312 pp.

Wands, Susan. *Magician and Fool.* n.p.: i2i Publishing, 2017. 8vo, 382 pp.

Part 6 - PCS CORRESPONDENCE

Letters to Albert Bigelow Paine from Pamela Colman Smith, 1898-1907, from The Huntington Library, Art Collections, and Botanical Gardens. Manuscripts Department. San Marino, California.

Letters to Mary B. Reed from Pamela Colman Smith, 1896-1900, from the Special Collections Department, Bryn Mawr College Library, Bryn Mawr, Pennsylvania.

Letters to Alfred Stieglitz from Pamela Colman Smith, 1907-1909, from the Alfred Stieglitz/Georgia O'Keeffe Archive. Yale Collection of American Literature, Beinecke Rare Book and Manuscript Library, Yale University, New Haven, Connecticut.

Part 7 - BOOKS FROM PCS'S PERSONAL LIBRARY
Listed by author

Alma-Tadema, Laurence. *Four Plays.* London: "The Green Sheaf, " 1905. 8vo, 143 pp.

Buchan, John. *John Burnet of Barns*: A Romance. London: Thomas Nelson and Sons, Ltd., 1922. 16mo, 445 pp.

PCS handwriting on flyleaf, "My dear Badger a book to bring you joy at Easter. From your P. Mole. Easter 1942," with small illustration (a mole?).

Buchan, John. *The Three Hostages*. London: Thomas Nelson and Sons, Ltd., 1926. 16mo, 447 pp. PCS handwriting on flyleaf, "Pamela – Birthday. 1942."

English Association. *Poems of To-Day*: An Anthology. London: Published for the English Association by Sidgwick & Jackson, 1918. 12mo, 174 pp. PCS initials and "June, 1919" on half title page.

Grisewood, Frederick. *Our Bill: Guide- Counsellor- Friend*. With illustrations by Joan Hassall. London: George G. Harrap & Co. Ltd., 1939. 12mo, 167 pp. PCS handwriting on flyleaf, "Dear Badger. Every good wish from Moley. Christmas 1939," with small illustration.

Hymns Ancient and Modern for use in the services of the church. With first and second supplements. London: William Clowes and Sons, Limited, 1916. 16mo, 799 pp. PCS initials and handwriting on front cover and flyleaf.

Irving, Laurence. *Godefroi and Yolande: A Medieval Play in One Act*. London and New York: John Lane at the Sign of the Bodley Head, 1908. 8vo, 89pp. PCS bookplates, handwriting.

Laboulaye, Edouard. *Fairy Tales*. With two hundred and fifty-one illustrations. London: George Routledge and Sons, [1887]. 8vo, 357 pp. PCS handwriting at top of title page, "Pixie Pamela," with a small drawing.

Masefield, John. *The Nine Days Wonder (the Operation Dynamo)*. London: William Heinemann Ltd., 1941. 12mo, 57 pp. PCS handwriting on flyleaf, "A.H.L. Dear Bear. Happy Easter. From P. Mole. Bude 1941."

Paine, Albert Bigelow. *The Hollow Tree*. Illustrated by J.M. Condé. New York: R. H. Russell, MDCCCXCIII. 8vo, 128 pp. Inscribed to PCS by the author, December 1898.

Pyle, Katharine. *The Counterpane Fairy*. Written and illustrated by Katharine Pyle. New York: E. P. Dutton & Co., 1898. 12mo, 191 pp. PCS handwriting on flyleaf, including an explanation of her relationship to Pyle.

Ransome, Arthur. *Bohemia in London*. With illustrations by Fred Taylor. New York: Dodd, Mead & Company, 1907. 8vo, 293 pp.

Sabatini, Rafael. *Anthony Wilding: A Romance*. London: Hutchinson & Co., [192-?]. 12mo, 288 pp. PCS bookplate? map glued to flyleaf.

Sabatini, Rafael. *Bardelys the Magnificent: Being an Account of the Strange Wooing Pursued by the Sieur Marcel de Saint-Pol, Marquis of Bardelys, and of the Things That in the Course of it Befell Him in Languedoc, in the Year of the Rebellion*. London: Stanley Paul, n.d. 12mo, 254 pp. PCS bookplate, with handwritten note.

Sabatini, Rafael. *Chivalry*. London: Hutchinson & Co, [1935]. 12mo, 287 pp. PCS handwriting on half title page, "To Growly Bear. With all good wishes for Christmas. 1935. From the Mole"

Sabatini, Rafael. *The Shame of Motley: Being the Memoir of Certain Transactions in the Life of Lazzaro Biancomonte, of Biancomonte, Sometime Fool of the Court of Pesaro*. London: Hutchinson & Co, [192-?]. 12mo, 252 pp. PCS initials and handwriting on inside front cover. "Xmas 1924." Some artwork and two newspaper clippings regarding Sabatini affixed to flyleaves.

Sabatini, Rafael. *St. Martin's Summer: A Tragi-Comedy*. London: Hutchinson, [1924?]. 12mo, 284 pp. PCS initials and handwriting on inside front cover. Artwork affixed to flyleaf.

Shakespeare, William. *A Midsummer Night's Dream*. Illustrated by Robert Anning Bell. Edited with an introduction by Israel Gollancz. London: J.M. Dent & Co. 1895. 8vo, 128 pp. PCS handwritten name on bookplate.

Songs of Praise. Enlarged edition. London: Oxford University Press, 1931. 32mo, 615 pp.

Von Arnim, Elizabeth. *The Solitary Summer*. New York: The Macmillan Company, 1899. 8vo, 190 pp. PCS initials and small drawing on inside cover.

The Westminster Hymnal: the only collection authorized by the hierarchy of England and Wales. Complete edition of words. London: Burns Oates & Washbourne Ltd., 1912. 32mo, 320 pp. PCS handwriting on flyleaf, "Church of Our Lady of the Lizard. December 1920. Not to be taken away.," with small drawing.

Yeats, W. B. *Fairy and Folk Tales of the Irish Peasantry: Edited and Selected by W.B. Yeats*. London: Walter Scott, Ltd., [1888]. 12mo, 326 pp. PCS bookplate, handwriting ("Please return to PCS 1899") and illustration on flyleaf.

Yeats, William Butler. *The Wind Among the Reeds*. London: Elkin Matthews, 1903. 12mo, 108 pp. PCS handwriting on inside cover, "Pixie Pamela. 1903."

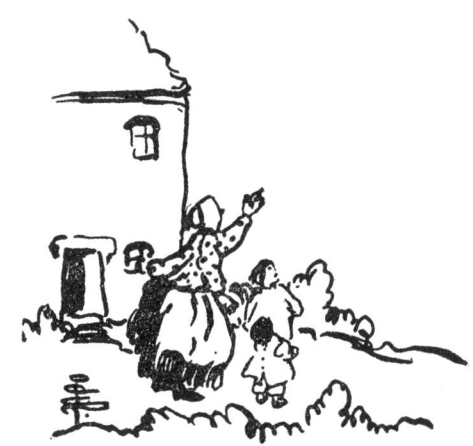

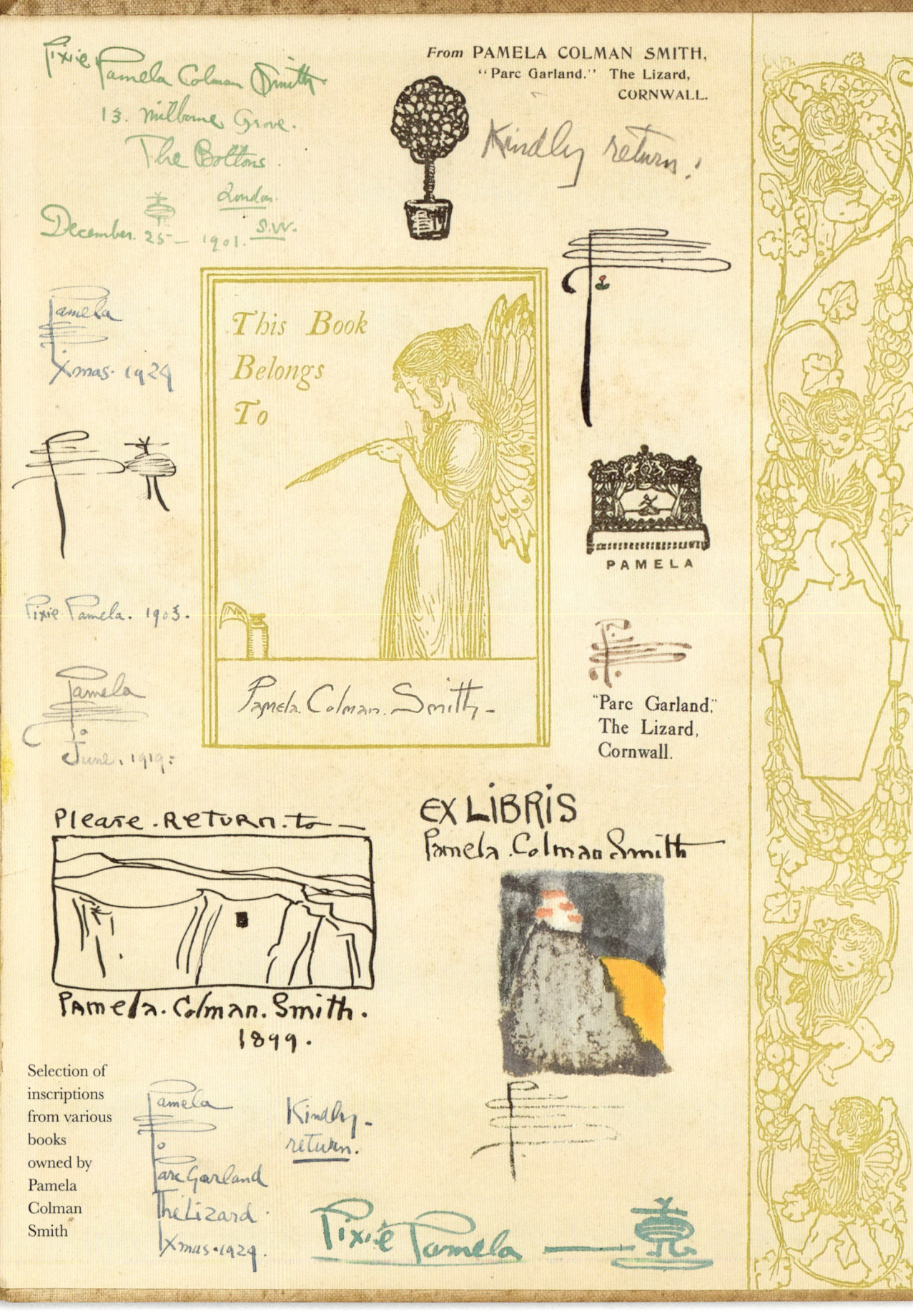

Selection of inscriptions from various books owned by Pamela Colman Smith

INDEX

PCS stands for Pamela Colman Smith. Artworks and writings are by PCS, unless otherwise noted. Italic page numbers refer to illustrations and captions.

A

The Academy and Literature (magazine), 54
Acebos, Helena Euthalia, 149
Ace of Cups, *351*
"Ace of Swords" (drawing, design for a Set of Tarot Cards), 69
actors, cabinet cards depicting, 350
Actresses' Franchise League, 76
Adams, Maude, 25, 66, 363, *363*, 364, *364*
Adams, R., 149
A.E. (George Russell), 43, 49, 181, 182
 "The Gates of Dreamland," illustration for, 46, *47*, 382
Aeolian Hall, London, 71
Aesop's Fables, 29
Ageless Wisdom (of P.F. Case), 380
air element, 350
Albano, Frankie, *379*
Albano-Waite Tarot, 375, *379*
Alexander, L.H., 149
Alice (character), 246
Alice sit by the fire (play by J.M. Barrie), 246
"All arts are branches of one tree" (quote), 288, 350
"All Round My Hat" (ballad), 284
All the World doth worship Thee (prayer), 409
Alma-Tadema, Laurence, 84
 Four Plays, 58
  book cover, *57*
 Tales from My Garden, 58
"Alone" (hand-colored print), 69
"Alone" (poem and illustration), 50, *52*
The Amber Heart (play), 104
Anansi stories, 70
 PCS's book of. *See Annancy Stories*
 PCS's recitals of, 42, 48, 211
Anansi the spiderman, character, 11, 28, 29, 71, 382
Andersen, Hans Christian, 29
angels, 367
"Angels at a Well" (drawing), 251
"Annancy and Chim-Chim" (story), 132
"Annancy and Death" (story), 66, *207–208*
"Annancy An' De Nyam Hills" (story), 27, 29, 100
"Annancy and Guinea Fowl" (drawing), 251
"Annancy An' Tiger Ridin'" (story), 30
"Annancy an' Tiger Ridin' Horse" (illustration from Annancy Stories), 134
"Annancy is you comin' down?" (illustration from 'Death in the House'), 66, 208
Annancy Stories, 11, 27–30, *28*, *29*, *30*, *32*, 56, 70, *129–137*, *130*, 211
"Anne, Sister Anne, do you see any one coming?" (illustration), *304*
Anti-Suffrage Alphabet (of Laurence Housman, PCS's contributions to), 78

Aphrodite, 366
Apollo, 366
"Appropriate Stage Decoration" (essay), *288–289*
Aquarian Tarot, *379*, 380
Arabian Nights, 29
"Ariel" (Shakespeare Series, 1898) (drawing), 251
"Arlequin" (Schumann's Carnival, drawing), 251
art
 vs. materialistic society, 359
 relation of visual and musical arts, 359
 and social reform, 359
Arthur legends, 353–354, 385, 387. *See also* Grail Legend
Artist Suffrage League, 76
Arts and Crafts Movement, 357–359, 373
Asquith, Herbert Henry, 76
assembly lines, 357–358
Associate Alumnae of Packer, 249
"At De Party" (illustration from The Green Sheaf, 1903, No. 2), 184
Aubry, G. Jean, 60
Ayton-Lee, Claudia A., 149

B

Baby Rabbits (costume design), 328
Bach, J.S., 60, 62
 Aria in G (illustration), *61, 324*
 Chromatic Fantasy, 65, *276*
 Concerto Brandenberg No. 2 in F (drawing), 283
Baillie, John, 56, 149
 The Dream Garden: A Children's Annual, 58, *212*
Baillie, R., 149
Ballet Russe, 82
"The Balloon" (illustration), 89
Barbauld, Anna Laetitia, 49
 illustrations of book by, *192*
 Lessons for Children project, 44
 "Little Charles" (illustration), *59*, 185
Baring-Gould, Rev. Sabine, 34–36, 123
Barnard, Seymour, 335
Barrie, J.M., 71, 149, 246
 Peter Pan (play), 364, *364*
 painting from, 67, 364
"The Basket Maker" (poem and illustration), *160–161*
Bates, Elsie T., 90
Bath, England, PCS recitals in, 71
Battersea Park Studio, 71
Beardsley, Aubrey, 23, 66, 284
Beethoven, Ludwig van
 Egmont/Opus 84, *217*
 Overture 'King Stephen' (drawing), 282
 Piano Sonata, Opus 57 (drawing), 69
 Piano Sonata, Pathétique (drawing), 65, 69, *278*
 Sonata No. 11, Opus 22 (drawing), *223*, 282
 symphonies, 62

Symphony No. 5 in C, 65, *278*
Symphony No. 5 in C (drawing), 282
Symphony No. 5 in C (illustration in The Strand Magazine), 278
Symphony No. 7 (drawing), 283
Beggerstaff Brothers, 76
"Behold Him Getting Fatty..." (drawing), *247*
Beinecke Rare Book and Manuscript Library, 223–235
Belfast, exhibition in, 69
The Bells (play), 40, 104
Bencoolen House, Bude, 90
"Benedictus" (drawing), 251
Berlin Photographic Company, exhibition at, *68–69*, 69
Bernhardt, Sarah, portrait of, 41
Berrigan, Ted, 377
"The Better Horse is the Old Grey Mare, or Married to a Pirate's Widow" (illustration from A Broad Sheet, March 1902), 168
"Billy Beg and the Bull" (story), 30
Binyon, Laurence, 56
Bird, Miss, 234
"A Bird in the Hand is worth Two Mocking-Birds in the Bush" (poster), 76, *77*, 365
Birnbaum, Martin, 88
"Birth of the Sun" (drawing), 69
Bishop, A.M., 149
"The Black Bull of the Castle of Blood" (story), 30
Blackburn, Kate, 149
Blake, Sir Henry, 17
Blake, William, 49, 66, 284
Songs of Innocence and *Songs of Experience*, proposed edition, 43, 56, 58
Blanchard, Margaret, 149
Blavatsky, Madame, 380
Blessed Virgin Mary, 84
Blondell, Joan, 376
Blue Beard illustrated book, 81, *303–307*
"The Blue Cat" (watercolor), 9, *224–225*
"Blue Smoke" (painting on silk), 68
Boas, Franz, 27
Bobbs-Merrill Company, 82
The Boltons, South Kensington, London, 41
Book Buyer, 25
book covers by PCS, 57, *57, 58*
bookplates by PCS, 41, *289*
book publishing by PCS, 11, 44, 56–58
hand production of, 358
books written by PCS, 33–36, 44
limited editions of, 33
Bottomly, Gordon, 149
Boughton, Alice, 89
Bowner, Albert, 149
Boys' High School, Brooklyn, 72
Braisse, Sheila E., 149
"Bramy Joker" (illustration), *40*, 41
Brentano's, 8
Brer Fox (costume design), 329
Brer Rabbit (costume design), 327
"Brer Rabbit and Mr. Fox" (musical frolic), costumes for, 83

Brer Terepin (costume design), 329
Brer Rabbit and Mr. Fox. See Dearmer, Mabel
Bridges, Robert, 49
Bridges, Victor, 49
Brighton, England, 41
A Broad Sheet (magazine), 11, 46, *47*, 48, 166, *166–177*, 181–182, 382, 383
broadsheets, 46
Brodda Gingy Fly character, 71
Brompton, England, 71
Brooklyn
Brooklyn Heights, 14, 15, 72
development of, 16
Brooklyn Barnard Club, 249
Brooklyn Daily Eagle, 12, 40, 81
Brooklyn Life, 32, *70*, 284
Broughton, Alice, *70*
Brush and Pencil, 19, 23
Bryn Mawr College Library, 18
"Buckingham" (Shakespeare Series, 1898) (drawing), 251
Buckinghamshire, 71
Bulldog Soldiers & Sailors Club, 84
"Bull-Garshananee" (story), 29
bull motif, 367
The Burlington Magazine, 363
Busch, Mrs, 235
Bush, Mrs, 234
Byrd, William, 62
Byron, Marjorie, 149

C

cabinet cards, 350
"Caliban" (Shakespeare Series, 1898) (drawing), 251
Calkins, Earnest Elmo, 21
"Louder Please!" 14
Calkins, Maud L., 284
"Call to Earth, Prelude" (painting on silk, based on Franck), 68
Calmour, Alfred C.
A Sheaf of Songs, 58, 196
book cover, 58
"Good Bye" (poem), *196*
Calvert, Edward, proposed book of, 56, 58
Cambridge, England, exhibition in, 69
Camera Work, 68
Campbell, Audrey Cecil, 149
Campbell, Joseph
Hero's Journey, 379
monomyth, 380
Campion, Thomas, "A Hymn in Praise of Neptune," *190*
"Candoo" (illustration from Annancy Stories), 133
Cantin, Candis, *376*
Carbery, Ethna, 32
card games
early woodcut playing cards, 373
tarot decks used in, 350
Cargill, Sidney, 149
Carnarious, Rusty, 9
Carnival, HBO, 376–377
Carr, J. Comyns, illustration for play, *239*

Cary-Yale Visconti Tarocchi tarot deck, 363
Case, Paul Foster, Ageless Wisdom of, 380
Cash, Roseanne, 377
"The Castle of Pain" (drawing), 251
"Catch Me" (watercolor based on Schumann's Opus 10, No. 4, 1904), 63, *63*, 197, *197*
Catholic Who's Who, 89, *344*
A Celtic Christmas, 43, *200–201*, 213
The Century Company (publisher), 335
Century magazine, 17
"Charles and Auntie" (hand-colored print), 69
Charpentier, Marc-Antoine, 84
Chelsea Fair, 84
"Chiarina" (Schumann's Carnival, drawing), 251
Chim-Chim bird character, 28, 29, 71
Chim-Chim: Folk Stories from Jamaica, 11, 58, 66, *204–211*, 382
    book cover, *57*
Chislehurst, London, England, 16
    childhood years in, 355–357
Choi, Rome, *374*
Chopin, Frédéric, 66, 284
    Ballade No. 1 in G Minor, 65, *277*
Christ, Passion of, 353
Christianity
    mystical tradition of, 353
    symbols of, in PCS's tarot deck, 361
Christ in Majesty, Hagia Sophia, *362*
"Christmas Card" (hand-colored print), 69
Christmas cards by PCS, 25
Christmas Carol (song and booklet), *24*, *102–103*
Christ Pantocrator, 362
    in Cathedral of Cefalù, Sicily, *362*
Christ the King (prayer), 408
"The City of Coral" (illustration from Susan and the Mermaid), 80
Claudel, Paul, 84
    Way of the Cross, illustration for, *344*
"The Clay Chickens" (illustration from The Green Sheaf, 1903, No. 8), 191, *191*
Close, Glenn, 376
"Close to the casement, always at his work" (illustration from The Book of Hours), 199
"Cloud" (drawing), 251
"Cloud Choir" (drawing), 251
"Cloud Faces" (fan, painting on silk), 68
Clouds in the Night (prayer), 408
Clubs suit, 350
Coburn, Alvin Langdon, 218–222
"A Cobweb Cloak of Time" (poem and drawing), 46, 172
"The cobweb cloak of Time has dropped between the world and me" (illustration from A Broad Sheet, July 1902), 172
"The Cold Women" (illustration from A Celtic Christmas, 1905), 201
Cole, Alphaeus P., 149
    oil portrait of PCS, *4*, *410–411*
    sketch for oil portrait, *12*, 410
Cole, Madge (aka Peggotty), 150
Cole, Margaret Ward and Alphaeus P., *Saints Among the Animals*, 58
Coleman (sic) Pamela, Smith, 100
Collier's Weekly, 25
Collinson, Walter, *144*, *145*, *146*

Colman, Corinne Chandler (mother), 15
    death of, 17
    singing talent of, 356
    theatre talent of, 360
Colman, Pamelia Chandler (maternal grandmother), 15, 355
    LuLu Tales of, 15
Colman, Samuel (maternal grandfather), 15, 355
Colman, Samuel (uncle), 15, 356
color prints by PCS, 25
"Columbine and Pantaloon" (Schumann's Carnival, drawing), 251
Conciliation Bill, 76–77
Connecticut Colony, 16
Conrad, Joseph, 60
Cooke, Fannie J., 284
"Coquette" (Schumann's Carnival, drawing), 251
Cornwall, England, 11, 354, 385
    PCS moves to, 86–90
    pilgrimages to, 387
"The Corse" (drawing), 251
court cards, 350–351, 372, 384
Coverley, Louise Bennett (Miss Lou), 382
Coyle, Heather Campbell, 36
The Craftsman, 65, 67, *298*, 360, 380
Craig, Edith (Edy), *40*, 43, 49, 56, 76, 78, *78*, 79, 88, *144*, *145*, *148*, *238*, 361, 363, 365, *366*, *367*, 383
    also signed Visitors book as Pealope, Geraldine, or Ailsa, 150
    PCS's first acquaintance with, 40–41
    portrayed in Rider-Waite Tarot Deck, 366–367
    Theatre of the Soul, 78
Craig, Edward Gordon (Gordon), 40–41, 49, 60, 181, 182, 365
    "The Harvest Home Masque," 49
Crane, Walter, 23, 43
Creeley, Robert, 377
Critic, 33
"Crow and Pitcher" (poster, PCS's first sale), 21, *21*
"The Cuckoo Bird" (story), 88, 89
Cups tarot suit, 350, 354

D

"Dancing Cloud" (painting on silk), 68
"Dancing in General" (essay), *312*
"Dancing Trees" (painting on silk, based on Suite by Dvorak), 68
Dark Shadows (soap opera), 8, 379
Dearmer, Mabel, *Brer Rabbit and Mr. Fox* children's play by, costume designs, *325–331*
Death card, 377
"Death in the House" (drawing), 251, 284
"Death in the House" (painting), 66, 208
Debussy, Claude, 65
    comment on PCS's painting, 386
    'En Sourdine' (drawing), 69
    friend of PCS, 62
    'Il pleure dans mon coeur' (drawing), 69
    Submerged (Sunken) Cathedral, *342–343*, 385
De Casseres, Benjamin, 68–69
"De Golden Water, De Singin' Tree An' De Talkin' Bird" (story), 30, *135–137*
de Groux, Henry, 66, 284
Delaware Art Museum, 381, 410

Delineator, 14, 79
de Pratz, Claire, 150
"De Story of De Man An' De Six Poach Eggs" (story), 27, 73, 100, 134
Deviant Moon Tarot, *374*
Diaghilev, Sergei Pavlovich, 82
Diamonds suit, 350
Dibby Dibby Tree character, 71
Didsbury, England, 357
di Prima, Diane, 377
"A Dirge" (drawing), *231*
Dolmetsch, Arnold, 60, 150
Donegal County, Ireland, 32
Doubleday & McClure, 36, 44, 104
　　royalties from, 34
"Doubt" (Schumann, drawing), 251
Dow, Arthur Wesley, 17, 21, 34, 354, 359
　　art collection of, 374
"Down the turret stair she flew quickly" (illustration), *291*
Doyle, Arthur Conan, *Sherlock Holmes* (play made from), stage illustrations for, 36, 39
Doyle Auctions, 411
"Do you not see them?" (illustration from Deirdre, Act II, from The Green Sheaf, 1903, Supplement to No. 7), 189
Drama Magazine, 86
Dreaming Way Tarot, *374*
Dreamland, PCS's so-called, 382
"Dreams Returning Home, Nachtstuck No. 4" (painting on silk, based on Schumann), 68
Drew, Nicole, 150
Dublin Daily Express, 32
Dublin Daily Mail, 32
"Duet" (watercolor), 89, *349*
Duffield & Company, 305
　　letter from, *89*
Duncombe-Jewell, L.C. (Louis Charles), 150
Dvorak, Antonin, New World Symphony, 62

E

"Earth (Lot's Wife)" (drawing), 251
earth element, 350
Eastbourne, PCS recitals in, 71
Eckford, Quincy Oliver, 17
Edinburgh, Scotland, 41, 233
　　exhibitions in, 67, 69
Educational Theater, 73
Egerton, Lady Alix, 49, 150, 181, 182, 385
　　The Book of Hours, 58, 198–199
　　"The Lament of the Dead Knight," 49
Eight of Cups, *351*
Eight of Swords, *393*
"Elegy" (painting), *244*
Eliot, T.S., "The Waste Land," 9, 377
"Ellen Peg's Book of Merry Joys" unpublished folio, *40, 41, 143–148*, 366
Ellen Terry's Story of My Life, 286–287
Elliot, Bianca, 150
Elliot, Hugh (S.R.), 150
Emery, Florence (Beatrice), 150

Emperor card, 363
"The Enchantment of Cathvah" (illustration from A Broad Sheet, November 1902), 176
Endeavor, PBS Masterpiece Theatre, 377
England, PCS return to live in, 40
English ballads, 34
Ensor, James, 66, 284
Entertainment Club, 72, 249
Erskine, Beatrice, 41
"ET," 236
Exeter, move to, 89
exhibitions of PCS work, 65–69
　　British, 67–69
　　first, 21–23
　　international, 69, *394–395*
　　number of, 11
　　of 1900, 38
　　of 1907, 65, 66–67, *251*
　　of 1912, 68
　　recent, 381

F

factory goods, 357–358
Faerie Tarot, *374*
Fair Vanity, 27
"Fairy Balloon" (illustration), 89
"Faith (also called The Triumph of Faith)" (illustration), 232
"Faith" (Shakespeare Series, 1898) (drawing), 251
Fantin-Latour, Henri, 66, 284
"The Farm" (illustration dedicated to Mrs Robertson), 237
"The Farmhouse" (poem and illustration), *162–163*
Farm Street Church, London, 74
Farncombe & Son, 48, 49
Farr (Emery), Florence, 33, 43
Farrow, W.E., 150
fear, PCS essay/manifesto on, 67, *216*
Feilring, Alice, 150
Fellowship of the Rosy Cross, 373
feminism, 358, 366
Fenollosa, Ernest, 354
"Figures Parading Before Dame Ellen Terry" (illustration), *237*
films, appearance of tarot in, 376–377
Fine Arts Club, 249
"Finn and Diarmid" (illustration from A Broad Sheet, January 1902), 166
fire element, 350
"Fisherman and Genii" (drawing), 251
"Fisher of Men" (story), 88
Fisher of Men (story), 89
Fitzgerald, Lord George, 17
Five of Cups, *351, 393*
"Five of Cups" (drawing, design for a Set of Tarot Cards), 69
Five of Pentacles, 360–361, *360*
Flecker, James Elroy, *Brumana*, 89
"Florestan" (Schumann's Carnival, drawing), 251
"Fluellen and Henry V" (Shakespeare Series, 1898) (drawing), 251
Folengo, Teofilio, Caos del Triperiuno, 377
Folk-Lore Society, 284
folk songs, sung by PCS, 71

Folk Stories from Jamaica, West Indies (brochure), 72
folktales
　　PCS's illustrations for, 83
　　PCS's interest in, 11
"Folly" (drawing), 251
The Fool card, 75, 350, *350,* 364, 373, *373,* 379
Forbes-Robertson, Beatrice, 150
Forbes-Robertson, Sir Johnston, *The Sacraments of Judas,* 41
Forbes-Sempill, Hon. Mrs., "Music Made Visible," 60, *61,* 62, 87, 346–348
Ford, Emily, 150
"Forest and Hill" (drawing), 251
Fortescue, Mrs., 56
"A fountain that shot up in a silver torrent" (illustration), 337
Four of Cups, *351*
"Four of Wands" (drawing, design for a Set of Tarot Cards), 69
"Four Place Cards" (hand-colored print), 69
Franck, César
　　Prelude (drawing), 69
　　Prelude Corale and Fugue (drawing), 69
　　Quintette (drawing), 69
　　Sonata for Violin, Last Movement (drawing), 69
Franco bon Bonadice, Nora, 150
French, Cecil P., 49, 50, 150, 181, 182
Frogs (costume design), 330
Frohman, Charles, 36
Frothingham, William H., 150
Fryer-Fortescue, Ethel P.F., 150
"The Fugitive" (painting, from Chopin's Ballade No. 1 in G Minor), 65, 251
Fuller, Eunice, *The Book of Friendly Giants,* 83, *332–341*

G
Gaelic mythology, illustrated edition of, proposed, 43
The Gallery, London, 54
"Gardens in the Rain" (painting on silk, based on Debussy), 68
Gargiulo-Sherman, Johanna, *376*
"The Gates of Dreamland" (illustration from A Broad Sheet, June 1902), 171
Geiger, Willis, 68
"Gelukiezanger" pseudonym of PCS, 56–58
George Eastman Museum, 218–222
George G. Harrap & Co., rejection letter from, *88,* 89
"Georgia O'Keeffe and the Women of the Stieglitz Circle" exhibitions (2007-2008), 381
Gestalt Therapy, 378
Ghent, exhibition in, 69
"The Giant of the Band Beggar's Hall" (story), 30
"Giants should always be brotherly with giants, but only with good giants" (maxim of Pantagruel), 335
Gillette, William, 36, *39,* 138, *142*
Gingy Fly character, 29, *209–210*
Girls' Realm Guild of Service, 70
Glasgow, Scotland, 41
Glazounow, Alexander, Quartet, Opus 15 (drawing), 69
Glinka, Mikhail, Russian Airs (drawing), 69
Globe, 83
Glow in the Dark Tarot, 375
God, 364

Goddard, Ethel, *The First Sorrow of Fergus,* 202–203
Godefroi and Yolande, a Medieval Play in One Act (script), *41*
"God save you merry gentlemen may nothing you dismay" (drawing), *298*
Golden Dawn, 43, 350, 372–373
　　PCS in, 74–75, 372
　　vow of secrecy, 353, 372–373
The Golden Vanity and The Green Bed, 27, 33–34, *33,* 113–118, 356, *357*
　　illustrations, 50
"Good-bye," he roared. "And don't forget the giant Riverrath" (illustration), 334
"Good Bye" (illustration from A Sheaf of Songs, 1904), 196
"The Good Hope" (play), *240–241*
"Good-Night" (drawing), 251
Gorseland, at Upton Cliff, outside Bude, PCS move to, 89–90
Graham, Helen, 150
Graham (name in inscription on illustration), 237
Grail Legend, 353, 366–367
　　four Hallows of (Cup, Lance, Dish, Sword), 353–354, 366
Grantham Industrial Exhibition, 41
grapes, symbol of self-sacrifice, 365
Gray, Eden, 379
　　Tarot Revealed: A Modern Guide to Reading the Tarot Cards, 8, 378, 379
"Gray Fisherman" (illustration), 89
Greeks, ancient, 386
The Green Bed, 119–121
green color, 48
"Greenfinger" (story), 88, 89
The Green Sheaf (magazine), 46–55, *182–195*
　　advertisements in, 56, 70
　　announcement of founding, 181–182
　　editing of, 11
　　price, 33, 48
　　reviews of, 50–54
　　title, 47–48, 182
Green Sheaf press, 11, 33, 44, 56–58
Greer, Mary K., 8, 350
Gregory, Lady Isabella Augusta, 43, 49, 150, 181, 182
Gresham, William Lindsay, *Nightmare Alley,* 376
Grieg, Edvard
　　Sonata (drawing), 282
　　Spring Song (drawing), 282
Grimm Brothers, 29
Grog (horse), 17
The Guardian, 83
Guinea Fowl character, 29

H
Half-way Tree Infant Kindergarten, 19
Hall, Millicent, 150
Halloween Tarot, *374*
Hamer, Leslie Price, 150
Hamilton, Cicely, 78, 361
　　A Pageant of Great Women, 363
"Hamlet" (painting on silk), 68
"Hamlet" (Shakespeare Series, 1906) (drawing), 251
handbills by PCS, 78
hand coloring, PCS's school for, 54
handcraft by PCS

429

painted wooden box, *236*
  sale of, 40
hand production, of the Arts and Crafts Movement, 358, 384
Hanged Man card, 75, 373, *373*, 377
Hans Andersen Bazaar, London, 70
Hanson-Roberts, Mary, 375, *376*
Hanson-Roberts Tarot Deck, *376*
Harris, Joel Chandler, 83
Hartwell and Stone school, 71
Harvey, H, 150
Haskell, I.C., 21
"Hath a dog money? Is it possible a cur can lend three thousand ducats?" (Merchant of Venice, Act I, Scene 3), 106
"Haylefayly An' Pretty Peallope" (illustration from Annancy Stories), 28, 30, 133
"Headpiece: Les Sylphides" (illustration for the Russian Ballet), 309
Hearn, Ethel A. Cade, 150
Hearn, Isabel, 150
Hearn, James, 150
Hearts suit, 350
Hebrew alphabet, 364, 373
"He had a wife and ten children" (illustration), 341
He hung a lantern in the sky (prayer), 409
Heineman (publisher), 44
"He kept his eyes fixed on Lilla" (illustration), *292*
Henry Altemus Publishing Company, 44
Henry Morgan (miniature theatre play), 19–20, *20*
Herbal Tarot, *376*
Herman, Pollie, 150
Hermetic Text Society, 364
Hertz, Nathalie, *374*
Hicks, Alice, 143
Hierophant card, 362
High Priestess card, 75, 373, *373*
"The Hill of Heart's Desire" (illustration from The Green Sheaf, 1903, No. 1), 184
Hobby Horse, 48
Holy Grail. *See* Grail Legend
homosexuality, 48, 383
Hooker, Lydia Lewis (paternal grandmother), 16
Hooker, Thomas (ancestor), 16
Hope, Christopher G., 150
Horton, W.T., 49, 150, 182
"Hotspur" (Shakespeare Series, 1898) (drawing), 251
Housman, A.E., 76
Housman, Clemence, 76
Housman, Laurence, 76, 78
"How Annancy Went To Fish Country" (illustration from Annancy Stories), 133
"How Annancy Win De Five Dubbloon" (illustration from Annancy Stories), 29, 133
Howard, Pamela Atkins Colman (aunt), 15
"How many legs have fishes?" (illustration from A Broad Sheet, December 1902), 177
How the Vote Was Won (play), 78
Hudes, Susan, *376*
Hudes Tarot, *376*
Hudson River School, 15
"Humoresque" (Dvorak, drawing), 251

Huneker, James, 66
"Hushwood" (possibly a drawing), 232
Huston, W. Shafman, 150
Huxley, Aldous, Perennial Philosophy of, 380
"A Hymn in Praise of Neptune" (illustration from The Green Sheaf, 1903, No. 6), 190

I

"Iachiamo" (Shakespeare Series, 1898) (drawing), 251
The Illustrated London News, 60, *61*, 65, 87
illustrations by PCS, 11
  for books, 25, 27, 29–32, *31*, 41, 50, 79–83, *111–112*, *192*, *290–296*
  for magazines, 41, 46
  for own work, 50
  for theatre, 82, *239*
"Impressions of New York" (series of drawings in 1907 exhibition), 248
"In a long-before time—before Queen Victoria came to reign over we." (introduction to PCS's stories), 71
"In a Garden" (drawing), 251
"Incantation" (drawing), 251
Independent and Rectified Order of the Golden Dawn, 74, 372
International Studio, 34
"In the Fields" (Mrs. Bardauld, drawing), 69
Iphetonga (tribe and place), 12–13
Ipplepen (prayer), 409
Irish folktales, 11
Irish Homestead, 43
Irish Literary Revival, 46, 49
Irish Literary Society, 43
Irish myth and fairies, 26–27
Irish poets, in PCS's circle, 42
Irvine, Beatrice, 150
Irvine, J. Harry, 150
Irving, Sir Henry, 27, 36, *38*, 40, 41, 105–108, 143, *145*, *148*, *286*, 354
Irving, Laurence, 49, 143, *144*, *145*, *148*
  portrait of, *41*
Isis-Urania Temple of the Hermetic Order of the Golden Dawn, 43, 74–75, 352
"It Is September" (illustration from A Broad Sheet, September 1902), 174
"It is well for the little child" (illustration from The First Sorrow of Fergus in A Celtic Christmas, 190), 202
"I've just finished a big job for very little cash!" (quote), 235

J

Jack character, 30
Jackson, Amy L., 150
Jackson, Theresa, 150
Jamaica, 11
  PCS in, 17–18, 25, 360
  Smith family move to, 16
Jamaican folktales, 11, 27–30, 46, 48, 100, 382
  performances by PCS, 70–73, *70*, *72*, 284
  See also Annancy Stories
Jamiesen, Alexander, 150
"Jan A Dreams" (illustration from The Green Sheaf, No. 2, 1903), 184
Japanese influence on PCS's work, 12, 66, 356, 373–374
Jardin, Lindsay, 150
Joan of Arc, 363, *363*
Jockey Coat (costume design), 331

John (costume design), 327
John Baillie Gallery, 71, 284
"John of Gaunt" (Shakespeare Series, 1898) (drawing), 251
Johnson, Fanny, 150
Jonny, Myrna C., 150
Journal of American Folklore, 27, *100,* 382
Joyce, James, 49
"June" (drawing), 251
Jung, Carl, 378
    Structure and Dynamics of the Psyche, 380
Jungian Tarot deck, 378
"Juveniles" (illustration from The Green Sheaf, 1903, No. 5), 188

K

Kaplan, Stuart R.
    advertisement, seeking whereabouts of PCS's grave and personal effects, *404*
    collection of PCS's artworks, 371, 410–411
    Encyclopedia of Tarot, 410–411
    first encounter with tarot, 8
    founding of U.S. Games, 379
    letter from attorneys in England, relative to PCS, deceased, *403–404*
    promotion of PCS's work, 371–372
    publishing of Rider-Waite Tarot Deck, 374
    research on the tarot, 368
    Tarot Cards for Fun and Fortune-Telling, 8
Kaplan, Stuart R., and Lynn Araujo, *The Artwork and Times of Pamela Colman Smith,* 372, 375
Kaplan, Stuart R., and others, *Pamela Colman Smith: The Untold Story of the Rider-Waite Tarot Artist* (this book), 381
Keats, John, 49
Keep Calm (prayer), 408
Kelso, Tessa L., 150
Kensington Magazine, illustrations, 41
Kent countryside, 357, 383
Kerby, Marion Gordon, 71, 78
Khamara, Smara, *In the Valley of Stars There Is a Tower of Silence,* 57, 58, *214–215*
King, Frederick Allen, 42, 89, 150
King cards, 350
"King Deer's daughter (costume design), 325
King of Pentacles, 367, *367*
King of Swords, *351*
King of Wands, *392*
Kingston, Jamaica, 19, 25
Kingston *Daily Gleaner,* 17, 19
"The kite was shaped like a great hawk" (illustration), *294*
Kivell & Sons, auctioneers, *402*
Knight cards, 350
Knight of Coins, *363*
Knight of Pentacles, *351*
Knight of Swords, 362, *370, 392*
Knight of Wands, 362–363, *370*

L

"Lady Arabella was dancing in a fantastic sort of way" (illustration from Lair of the White Worm), 79, *293*
"The Lady of the Scarlet Shoes" (illustration from A Broad Sheet, October 1902), 174

Lady's Home Magazine, 70–71
L'Aiglon (illustration), 41, *238*
Laird, Helen, 150
Lake, Nora, 86, 89, 90, 385
Lamantia, Philip, 377
"The Lament of a Lyceum Rat" (illustration from The Green Sheaf, 1903, No. 5), 187, 188
"The Lamp," 180
Landewednack Primary School, Cornwall, 86
Lane, Diane, 376
Lane, John, 48
Lane and Duckworth (publisher), 44
Lasner, Mark, 324
"Launcelot and Gobbo" (Shakespeare Series, 1898) (drawing), 251
League of Mercy, 71
"Lear" (Shakespeare Series, 1898) (drawing), 251
"Le Carnaval" (illustration for the Russian Ballet), 309, *314–316, 318*
Le Carnaval ballet, 83
Led Zeppelin, 377
lesbianism, 383
"Les Bouffons (Pavillon d'Aramide)" (illustration for the Russian Ballet), 309
Les Sylphides ballet, 83
"Les Sylphides" from *The Russian Ballet,* 309, *312, 317*
Let us go to receive worthily (prayer), 408
Levy, Henry, 8
"Lighting the starfish" (illustration from Susan and the Mermaid), 301
Lines of Comfort (prayer), 409
"L'Isle Joyeuse" (painting on silk, based on Debussy), 68
Liszt, Franz
    Polonaise in E Major (drawing), 283
    Symphonic Poem 'Les Préludes' (drawing), 283
Litany of Loreto, 84
The Literary Digest, 42
"Little Charles" (Mrs. Bardauld, drawing), 69
Little Galleries of the Photo-Secession, 11, 68, 72, 284
    checklist of PCS exhibition, *251*
Little Jack of all Trades (published 1804), *160–161*
little magazines, 46, 48
"The Little Shepherd" (painting on silk, based on Debussy), 68
"Little Sir William" (ballad), 284
Little Truthes (published 1807), *162–163*
Liverpool, England, 41
Lizard, Cornwall, England, 385
Lloyd George, David, 76
London
    exhibitions in, 67, 69
    PCS born in, 11
    PCS recitals in, 71
    Smith family in, 15–16
"London Bridge" (watercolor), 38
London *Morning Post,* 32, 54–55
Los Angeles Herald, 383
Lowndes, Mary, 150
Lyceum Theatre Company, 11, 36, 38, 41, 143
"Lyke Wake Dirge" (drawing), 251
"A Lyke-Wake Dirge" (poem and illustration from The Green Sheaf, 1903, No. 11), 193, *193*
Lyonesse (mythical), 385

Lyons, Frank, 150
Lyttelton, Edith, 87
    The Sinclair Family, illustrations for, 87, *345*

M

Macbeth, William, 54. *See also* William Macbeth's Gallery, New York
"Macbeth" (Shakespeare Series, 1898) (drawing), 251
MacCathmhaoil, Seosamh, "In Tenebris" (poem), *213*
Macdonald, Biddy, 150
Macdonald, M. Irwin, 65
Mackenzie, Evelyn, 150
Mackinlay, Jean Sterling, 71
Maclagan, Eric R.D., 150
MacManus, Seumas, 30–32
    In Chimney Corners: Irish Folktales, 30–32, 110
        illustrations, 27, 29–32, *31, 111–112*
"Madame Knowledge" (watercolor), *281*
"Madame-sans-Gene" (illustration), 239
Mad Men, AMC, "Mountain King" episode, 376
Madonna, 377
Maeterlinck, Maurice, 66, 284
magic, practice of, 352
The Magician card, 350, *350*, 366, *366*, 367
"Magic Spectacles" (talk), 73
Major, Gladys, 150
Major Arcana, 76, 350, 372, 379
Malory, Thomas, *Le Morte d'Arthur*, 354
"Mamma's Birthday" (drawing), 251
Manchester, England, 16, 41, 357
Markino, Yoshio, 150
"Marnin'!" (illustration from Gingy Fly in Chim-Chim), 209
Marshall, Anne, 150
Marshall, Christabel, 150. *See* St. John, Christopher
Marshall, Jenny Owlett, 150
Mary (costume design), 327
Mary Evans Picture Library, 346–348
Masefield, John, 49, 150, 182
the Masquers, 43, 60
Mathews, C. Elkin, 150
Mathews, Editte Elkin, 46, 48, 54, 56, 150
"May" (drawing), 251
Mayor, Susannah, 143
May the Risen Lord bless you (prayer), 408
McLaughlin, D.S., 68
media, appearance of tarot in, 376–377, 379
mediums, spiritual, 358
Menomenee, S.S., 40–41, 143, *145*
"The Mer-children returning from the coral fields" (illustration from Susan and the Mermaid), 300
"The Mer-lady taking the little girl to a party" (illustration from Susan and the Mermaid), 301
Merlin, 387
"The merry wind" (illustration and poem from A Broad Sheet, April 1902), 169
Methuen (publisher), 56
Metropolitan (magazine), *285*
miniature theatre performances
    PCS's, 11, 19–20, 43
    popularity of, 46

    stage settings, *22*, 360
Minnehaha, S.S., 232
Minor Arcana, 76, 350, 372, 377
Miss Meddows (costume design), 326
"Mistress Page" (print), *178*, 365, *365*
Moakley, Gertrude, 353
modernist poetry, 50
Monsell, E., 181, 182
Monsell, J., 181, 182
Monsell, Lily M., 151
"The Moon," 235
Moore, George, "Blood Bond" illustration, 46
Mortensen, Viggo, 376
"Mother Calbee" (illustration from Annancy Stories), 133
Motherpeace Tarot, *379*, 380
Moulin-Browne, Rev. John de, 90
"The Mountain Lovers" (illustration from A Broad Sheet, August 1902), 173
"Mountains" (drawing), 251
Mountcharles village, Ireland, 32
Mozart, W.A., 65, 84
    Concerto in A Major (drawing), 69
    Concerto No. 4 in D Major (drawing), 69
    Sonata in F Major, *228*
    String Quartet in D Major (drawing), 69
    Symphony in D 'Prague' (drawing), 283
Mr Kildee (costume design), 327
"Mrs. Barbauld" (illustration from 'How Master Constans Went to the North' from The Green Sheaf, 1903, No. 2), 186
"Mrs. Barbauld" (illustration from The Green Sheaf, 1903, No. 4), 185
"Mrs. Barbauld" (illustration from The Green Sheaf, 1903, No. 9), 192
Mrs. Hitchcock's Entertainment Club, 249
"Mr. Titman" (illustration from Annancy Stories), 134
Munch, Edvard, 66, 284
music, visualization of, 60
"Music" (drawing), 251
"Music Pictures" (handwritten manuscript), *62–63*
music pictures of PCS, 60–69, 87, 89, *276–284*, *346–348*, 354, *383*, 386
mysticism, 352–353

N

Nance Oldfield (play), 104
    illustrations for, 109, 239
"Narcisse" (illustration for the Russian Ballet), 309
"The Narrow Way" (drawing), 251
National Trust, 236–246, 366, 367
Nativity play for children, 86–87
nature
    divine spirit in, 355
    PCS's love of, 356
Nelessarse, Lena, 151
Neo-Platonic theory, 367
Nevinson, Henry Wood, *Changes and Chances*, 14
Newcomb, Mr and Mrs H, 151
Newman, Pollie, 151
New York
    PCS as artist in, 11, 21, 25, 70
    PCS early life in, 11–25
    PCS return to (1907, 1909), 72, 73

New York Herald, 29
    letter from, 89
"New York—Steam" (drawing), 251
The New York Sun, 66, 284
New York Sunday Herald, 44
The New York Times, 68
New York World, 72–73
Nichols, Colshaw & Co., 16
Nicholson, William, 76
Nietzsche, Friedrich, 49
Nightmare Alley (film), 376
Nijinsky, Vaslav, 83
Nine of Cups, *351*
Nine of Pentacles, 365–366, *365*
Nine of Swords, *393*
"Nine of Swords" (drawing, design for a Set of Tarot Cards), 69
1960s counterculture, 379
"No," said Granua, "I'm down in the valley, picking bilberries" (illustration), 338
Nobel, Vicki, *379*, 380
Noguchi, Yone, 49
Norman, Dorothy, collection of, 252–268, 270–275, 364
Notley, Alice, 377
Notman, Mr, 234
"Now who should be goin' by, but de king an' chief counselor" (illustration from Annancy Stories), 136
number cards. *See* pip cards

O

obeah, 28–29
Obeah woman character, 29
occultism, 352
The Occult Review, 385
O'Connor, Elizabeth Foley, 9, 381
Ogden, Alice Lydia, 151
Ogden, Willis L., 151
O'Keeffe, Georgia, 21, 68
Olsen, Rachel, 324
Olson, Charles, 377
"On board the Fjord ship" (illustration), 345
"Oolanga's black face . . . peering out from a clump of evergreens" (illustration), *295*
opal lush (a drink), 42
"O' Pines of Sister Pines" (watercolor), 89, *90, 91*
Original Rider Waite Tarot Pack, 375
"Our Adventures" cartoon, 41, *286–287*
Our Lady of the Lizard chapel, 86, *86*, 385
Our Lady of the Lizard Fund, 86
Our Prayer (prayer), 408
"Out of the World" (drawing), 68
Owen, Mary Price, 151
Oxford University Press, 406–407

P

"Paarat, Tiger, An' Annancy" (story), 56
Paarat character, 29
Packer Institute, 72
"A Pagan Rhyme" (illustration from The Green Sheaf, 1903, No. 3), 188
Page, Thomas Nelson, 28, 130

The Page (little magazine), 41
A Pageant of Great Women (play), 78
Page cards, 350
Page of Cups, *351, 363*
"Page of Cups" (drawing, design for a Set of Tarot Cards), 69
Page of Pentacles, *392*
"Page of Pentacles" (drawing, design for a Set of Tarot Cards), 69
Paine, Alfred Bigelow (Tutter), 32, 44, *45*, 46, 356
    "The Boat of Dreams," 44
Palestrina, Giovanni Pierluigi da, 84
Palladini, David, 379–380, *379*
Pall Mall Gazette, 32
Pamela, Pixie, 151
Pamela Colman Smith Commemorative Tarot Set, 371, 375
Pan (god), 364
Pappsajannopoulo, Euphrosyne Stefan, 151
Papus (Gerárd Encausse), *Tarot of the Bohemians*, 76
Parc Garland, home in Cornwall, 86, *86, 87*, 89
Paris, exhibition in, 69
Parnall, Godwin & Chegwin, letter from, *403–404*
Parsons, Melinda Boyd, 9, 381, 410, 411
Passion of Christ, 353
Paterson, James, 233
Patterson, James, 67
"Pavillon d'Armide" from *The Russian Ballet*, 309, *313*
Pavlova, Anna, 83
Peacock's Well, Ireland, 385
Peg Woffington character, 41
Pen & Brush, 249
Pennsylvania Academy, 67
Pentacles tarot suit, 350, 354
Pentz, Arthur J., 151
"People of the Rain" (painting on silk), 68
performances by PCS, 70–73, *70, 72*, 284
    as extra, 40–41
    testimonials to, 71–72
Perrault, Charles, 29
Person, Evekyn, 151
"Peter and Ann in Stockholm" (illustration), 345
"Peter Pan" (drawing), 251
Peter Pan character, 66, 364
"Phantom Inn" (painting on silk), 68
Philadelphia Inquirer, 36
Philadelphia Museum of Art, PCS artwork in, *252–275*, 364
Photoerone Reading Club, 72
photo postcards, Victorian, 372
Photo-Secession Galleries. *See* Little Galleries of the Photo-Secession
"Pictures in Music" review in *Strand Magazine*, *276–280*
"Pierrot" (Schumann's Carnival, drawing), 251
Pigeon character, 205–206
"pigs" (PCS's term for publishers), 11, 44
Pinero, Arthur Wing, *Trelawney of the 'Wells'*, illustrations for, 27, 36, *37*
Pioneer Plays, 78
pip cards, 351
    pictorial scenes on, 351, 352, 372
Pistis Sophia, 364
Pittsburgh Daily Post, 29
Pixie's Poetry Book project, 44
"Plague" (drawing), 251

Planches, Baron Mayor des, 72
Plath, Sylvia, 377
Plymouth, Bishop of, 86
poetry
    appearance of tarot in, 377
    modernist, 50
poetry of PCS, 49, 50
Polish Victim's Relief Fund, 84
    poster, *85*
political radicalism, 358
"Portia Hurrying to the Railway Station" (illustration), *237*
Poshkus, Virginijus, 375
posters by PCS, 78, 85
    for businesses, 18
    wartime, 84
The Pot and the Kettle (play), 78
Poulson, Christine, 366
Pound, Ezra, 49
Powell, F. York, 49
Power, Tyrone, 376
Pragnell, Kate, 71, 72
Pratt Art Club, 73, 284
Pratt Institute, Brooklyn
    Arts and Crafts Movement at, 358
    exhibition of PCS work (1900), 38
    PCS celebrated by, 381
    PCS performances at, 19, 249
    PCS's art studies at, 11, 17, 21, 248, 354, 359
    PCS's friends from, 18
Pratt Institute Monthly, 17, 20, 21, 359
"Pray, Fisherman, what is this great water?" (poem and illustration from The Green Sheaf, 1903, No. 13), 195, *195*
Pre-Raphaelites, 18
"Prince Igor" (illustration for the Russian Ballet), 309
"Prince Siddartha" (illustration from The Green Sheaf, 1903, No. 3), 188
Princess Christian's infant nursery, Windsor, 71
prints by PCS, 34, 54
"A Protest Against Fear" (essay/manifesto), 67, *216*
Pryde, James, 76
Psychosynthesis, 378
psychotherapy, tarot used in, 378
publishers
    correspondence with, *88–89*
    PCS's view of, 11, 44
    royalties from, 34
Pulowech character, 341
Purcell, Henry, 62
Puritans, 16
Pythagoras, 353

Q

Queen cards, 350
"Queen Katharine" (illustration), 239
"Queen Margaret" (Shakespeare Series, 1898) (drawing), 251
Queen of Cups, *392*
"Queen of the Tides" (drawing), 251
"The Queen of the Tides" (illustration from Susan and the Mermaid), 300
Queen of Wands, *351*, 365, *365*
Queen's Hall, London, 60
"The Queen of the Golden Mine" (story), 30
Que le Corps de Notre Seigneur Jesus Christ (prayer), 408
Quick & Easy Tarot, 375
Quod Tibi Id Allis ("To Yourself as to Others"), 43

R

Radford, Dolly, and G.M. Bradley, *Shadow Rabbit: A Story of Adventure*, 58
Radford, Ernest, 49
    "Eventide," 50, *51*
Radiant Rider-Waite Tarot, 375
"The Railings of Drift" (story), 88, 89
"Rain" (drawing), 251
"Rain Passing through a Valley, Suite by Dvorak" (watercolor painting on silk), 68
Ramsden, Omar, 151
Ransome, Arthur M., 151
    Bohemia in London, 14, 42, 383
Ravel, Maurice, Valley of Clocks, 62
Reade, Charles
    Peg Woffington (novel), illustration for, 41
    play by, illustration for, *239*
The Reader, 21
"Realism is not art" (quote), 288
Recess (print), *22*, 25
"The Recitation" (hand-colored print), 69
"The Recitation" (illustration from A Broad Sheet, February 1902), 167
"Red Cloak" (watercolor), *230*
Red Cross, PCS contributions to, 84
Reed, Mary Bidlack, 17, *18*, 19, 40, 354, 360
The Reeds" (Loaned by Miss Mildred Howells) (drawing), 251
Reeke, Dorothy, 151
reform politics, 358, 359
"Regan" (Shakespeare Series, 1898) (drawing), 251
Regardie, Israel, *The Complete Golden Dawn System of Magic*, 373
Remembrance of the holy Mission (prayer), 409
Renaissance cards, 350, 352
reviews of PCS work, 19–20, 23, 32, 54, 65, 68–69, 83, 180
    quoted, *248–249, 284*
R.H. Russell (publisher), 25, 27, 36
    royalties from, 34
"Richard II" (Shakespeare Series, 1898) (drawing), 251
Richards, Miss A., 151
Richards, Grant, 44
Richards, Mrs W., 151
Richardson, R.J., 41
Rider & Company, 371, 411
Rider-Waite-Smith Tarot Deck, name of, 373
Rider-Waite Tarot Deck, *74*, 350–368, 371–374, *374*
    accessibility of, owing to PCS's images, 378, 386–387
    androgynous figures in, 361
    appearance in films, media and poetry, 376–377
    collecting of, 411
    composition of, 350–352
    diversity of figures, lacking in, 378
    first edition (1909, reissued 1910), 375
    gender-role reversals in, 361, 362–364
    male figures in, 362

names given to, 371, 373
other tarot deck designs based on, 375
PCS chosen to illustrate, 74–76
PCS's greatest claim to fame, 90, 371–374
PCS's process of drawing the cards, 361–364, 372
portraits of PCS's friends in, 361, 365–367
publication rights, 8–9
worldwide popularity of, 74, 386
Ridley, Ada P., 78
Rigby, Kessie, 151
Rigby, Reginald, 49, 151
  The Book of Good Advice, 58
"The Rim of the Sea" (illustration and poem from The Green Sheaf, 1903, No. 6), 194, *194*
Robb, Frances Osborn, 364
Roberts, Grace E., 151
Robertson, Mrs (name in inscription on illustration), 237
Robertson, Nora Murray, 151
Roman Catholicism, PCS conversion to, 75, 84
"Romantic Landscape" (hand-colored print), 69
"Rosa mystica" (drawing, design for The Litany of Loretto), 69
Rosengarten, Art, *Tarot and Psychology: Spectrums of Possibility*, 378
Rossetti, Dante Gabriel, 49
Rostand, Edmond, *L'Aiglon*, illustration, 41, *238*
"The rude fish who stared" (illustration from Susan and the Mermaid), 300
"Ruined Temples and Spilt Wine" (painting on silk), 68
Russell, Archibald G.B., 151
Russell, George. *See* A.E.
Russell, Robert H., 44. *See also* R.H. Russell (publisher)
The Russian Ballet (book). *See* Terry, Ellen
Ryan, Kay, 377

S

Sacred Rose Tarot Deck, *376*
"The Sailor and the Shark" (illustration from A Broad Sheet, May 1902), 170
St. Andrew Sketching Club, 18
St. Andrew's Parish, Jamaica, 17
St. John, Christopher (Chris) (Christabel Marshall), 41, 49, 78, *78*, 151, 181, 182
  The Decision: A Dramatic Incident, 78
  Henry Irving, 58
  The Russian Ballet, 82, 308–323
St. Louis Post-Dispatch, 32
St. Nicholas Magazine, 44
Salberg, Lily, 151
San Jose Mercury News, 386
Sant, Pauline, 151
Sardou, Victorien, *Robespierre*, 40, 104, 108–109, 236
Savin, Poppie, 151
Scarlatti, Domenico, 62
"Scene from an Unwritten Play" (drawing), 251
"Scheherazade" (illustration for the Russian Ballet), 309, *310*, *311*, *321*, *322*
Scheherazade ballet, 83
Schiller, Friedrich, *The Maid of Orléans*, 363, *363*
Schumann, Robert
  Carnaval, 62, 69, 284
  Concerto in A Minor, "Castle of Pain," 279
  Intermezzo No. 5 (drawing), 69
  Opus 10, No. 4, 63, *63*
  Overture 'Manfred' (drawing), 282
  Papillon (drawing), 69
  Symphony No. 1 (drawing), 69
  Symphony No. 2, Opus 61 (drawing), 69
  "Träumerei" (drawing), 251
  'Warum' (drawing), 69
  watercolor based on music of, 227
"Schumann Carnival" (Nijinsky and Nijinska, drawing), 68
"A Scotch Farm" (drawing), 251
"Sea Creatures" (painting), 63, *64*
Secret Tradition, 353–355, 364, 373, 380–381
Seidman, Irving, 410
Seidman, Steven, 411
Seidman, Sylvia Bernice, 410–411
Semple, Helen C., 151
Seven of Cups, *351*
"Seven Princesses" (Maeterlinck, drawing), 251
"Seven Towers of Fairie" (painting on silk), 68
Severac, Déodat de, Song of the Land, 62, 69
Sexton, Anne, 377
Shakespeare, William
  Henry VIII, 239, 242
  Macbeth, Lady Macbeth in (print), 25–26, *26*
  Merchant of Venice, 40, 104, *106*, 243
  PCS's early reading of, 359
Shakespearean alphabet for children project, 25
Shakespeare's Heroines (calendar for 1899), 25, *128*
Shaw, Martin Edward Fallas, 49, 50, 151, 325
  "The Harvest Home Masque," 49
Shedlock, Marie L., 151
"She got a shore tailor" (illustration from A Broad Sheet, April 1902), 169
Sheppard, Rev. H. Fleetwood, 123
Sherlock Holmes, 138, *142*
Shina, Kwon, *374*
Shin Hebrew letter, 373
"Ship O Dreams" (drawing), *302*
"Ship of Dreams" (painting on silk), 68
"The Shrew" (Shakespeare Series, 1898) (drawing), 251
Sidgwick & Jackson, Ltd., 82, 308
Simmons, Kate, 284
Sinding, Christian, Impromptu (drawing), 283
Sir Henry Irving and Miss Ellen Terry (brochure), *104*
"Sir Henry Irving as Cardinal Wolsey" (illustration), *242*
"Sir Henry Irving as Robespierre" (illustration in *Brooklyn Eagle*), 13, *105*
"Sir Henry Irving as Shylock" (illustration), *243*
"Sisters" (drawing), 251
Six of Cups, *351*, 383, *384*
Six of Swords, *374*
Six of Wands, *393*
The Sketch, 71
"Sleep" (drawing), 251
Smallhythe Place, Kent, 143, 236–246, 357, 383–384
  PCS artwork collection at, 236–247
Smith, Bryan (uncle), 16
Smith, Charles Edward (father)

art collecting by, 356, 374
in business, 16, 357
death of, 40, 361
family background, 15
Smith, Cyrus Porter (paternal grandfather), 16
Smith, Hilda Robinson, 151
Smith, Pamela Colman, 11–97
appearance, 12, 14
art. *See also* exhibitions of PCS work; reviews of PCS work; *individual arts, e.g. books; handcraft; illustrations; paintings; poetry; posters; prints; writings; etc.*
contributions to art and theatre, poorly recognized, 381
femininity of, perceived, 23
feminist implications of, 358
imaginative and psychic qualities of, 75–76, 352, 358
influences on (medieval, Japanese), 356
lasting artistic value of, 90
location of many pieces unknown, 384
musical character of, 354
negative criticism of, 386
originality of, noted, 21, 23
present location of, *236–247, 252–275,* 384
recent recognition of, 383–384
sketchbooks, 143
visionary character of, 350
art career
art studies, 11, 17, 21, 354, 359
diplomas awarded, *394, 395*
early school years, 17–18
early years as professional artist, 25–39
first sales, 21
FRSA professional honor, 89
artworks by year
1896, 100
1898, 102–103
1899, 104–137
1900, 138–148
1901, 160–165
1901-1905, 149–159
1902, 166–178
1903, 179–182
1903-1904, 182–195
1904, 196–197
1905, 198–212
1906, 213–215
1907, 216–233, 236–283
1908, 285–287
1909, 234–235
1910, 288–289
1911, 290–297
1912, 298–302
1913, 303–323
1914, 325–341
1916, 342–343
1917, 344
1926, 345
1927, 348
1946, 349
birth certificate, *388*

books about, 372, 375, 381
business ventures
bookstore of, announcement, *55,* 56
little magazines, 46–55, 181–182
school for hand coloring, 54
small press, 56–59
crossing boundaries in art and personal life, 382–383
family background, 11–16
featured in a novel, 381
fellow of the Royal Society of the Arts (F.R.S.A.), 89
final years, 89–90
burial record, *398*
burial spot unknown, 90, 383
death (1951), 90
death certificate, *388*
last will and testament, 90, 383, *399*
probate of will, *400*
search for grave site and personal effects, advertisement, *404*
finances
accounting of debts, receipts and payments, *401*
auction of personal possessions, *402*
debts at death, 90
failure to pay taxes, 383
money-making ventures, 54
old age poverty and debts, 88–90, 383
PCS's care with, 48
In Memoriam, printed in *The Encyclopedia of Tarot, 405*
legacy of, 371–387
letters
to A.B. Paine, 32, 44, *45,* 46
to Mary Reed, *18,* 40, 354, 360
to Alfred Stieglitz, 67–68, *232–235, 282–283*
to Ellen Terry, *246*
to W.B. Yeats, 56
life events
birth (1878), 15
childhood, 15–16
death (1951), 90
move to Cornwall, 86–90
move to England, 40
lifetime struggles of, 371
misunderstandings about, 11–14, 54
motto, *Quod Tibi Id Allis* ("To Yourself as to Others"), 43
newspaper stories about, 12, 14, 60, 62
nicknames
"Constance," 18
"Gypsy," 42
"Melia," 15
"Pixie," 11, 40
passport application, *396*
personal characteristics
career, not marriage, life choice, 11–12
compassionate spirit of, 360
nonconformity of, 67–68
private life, little known about, 382–383
sexuality of, 48, 383
as storyteller, 362
strong character of, 387
unconventionality of, 11–12, 54

portraits of
    by Alice Broughton, photograph, *70*
    by A.P. Cole, oil, *4, 410–411*
    by A.P. Cole, sketches, *12*, 410
    by Kate Pragnell, photograph, 72
    passport photo, *397*
    photograph by Russell & Sons, *16*
    photograph with theatre friends, *78*
    self-portraits (caricatures), 12, *12, 145, 148, 366*
    by unknown photographers, *10, 73*
    by J.B. Yeats, *6*
quotes, 288, 350
racial origins of, unclear to many, 12–14, 382–383
residences
    Chislehurst, 16, 355–357
    Cornwall, 86–90
    London, 41–42
social status, 14
spirituality of
    initiations into Golden Dawn, 75, 372
    other worldly senses, 385–386
    psychic ability, 385–386
    Roman Catholic faith, 75, 84, 86, 90, 352, 354, 361, 364, 385
studies of art and literature by, 359
studio/salon run by (1901-1914), 42
    Visitors book, *42, 83, 149–159*, 410
Smith, Patti, 377
Smith, Theodore Eanes (Teddy) (uncle), 16, 86, 151
Smith-Waite Centennial Tarot Deck, 375
Smith-Waite Tarot Deck Borderless Edition, 375
Smith-Waite tarot deck facsimile, 411
"Snow is Dancing" (painting on silk, based on Debussy), 68
socialism, 358
social reform, 359
Sola-Busca deck, 76, 352, 372
Songs of Praise Hymnal (doodles and scribblings), 406–407
"The Son of the Goban Soar" (illustration), 89
Spades suit, 350
"Spanish Ladies" (folk song), 50
"Spanish Ladies" (illustration from The Green Sheaf, No. 3, 1903), 184
"Spectre de la Rose" (illustration for the Russian Ballet), 309, *312, 319, 320, 324*
Spectre de la Rose ballet, 83
"Sphinxes" (drawing), 284
"Sphynxes" (Schumann's Carnival, drawing), 251
Spiral Tarot Deck, *376*
"Spirit of the Rose" (Nijinsky, drawing), 68
"Spirits of Pain" (drawing), 251
spiritualism, 357–358
"Spring Carried by Showers, Aria by Foote" (watercolor painting on silk), 68
Sqeeter (costume design), 329
Stations of the Cross cards, 84
Staves (Wands) tarot suit, 350, 354
"Stella matutina" (drawing, design for The Litany of Loretto), 69
Stevenson, Kay, *376*
Stewart, Nona, 151
Stieglitz, Alfred, 11, 66–68, 72, *232–235, 282–283*, 364, 383
Stoker, Bram, 36, 40, 143, *146*

Dracula, 79
Lair of the White Worm, 79
    illustrations, *79, 81, 290–296*
Lyceum Souvenir
    illustrations, *38*
    theatre review by, 109
Stone, Wilbur Macey, *Women designers of book-plates*, 41
story-telling, public, 71
    by females, 71
    by PCS, 362
"Straggling wooden houses" (illustration), 345
The Strand Magazine, *62–63, 276–280*
"A Strange Sanctuary" (watercolor), *297*
Stratford-Upon-Avon, exhibition in, 69
Strauss, Richard, 65
    Don Quixot (sic) (drawing), 69
    Song 'Nachtgang' (drawing), 283
    Till Eulenspiegel's Merry Pranks, Opus 28 (drawing), 69
Stravinsky, Igor, Duet, *349*
"Strolling Players" (play), 41
The Studio (magazine), 21
Stuyvesant Apartments, New York, 25
"Submerged Cathedral" (painting), *342–343*, 385
Suffrage Atelier, 76, 77
suffrage movement, 76–78, 363, 365
    contribution of spiritualism to, 358
    dramatic performances in support of, 78
    PCS's contributions to, 384
Suk, Josef, Fantasia in G Minor, Opus 24 (drawing), 69
Summer of Love (1968), 379
"A Sun God" (drawing), 251
"Sunken Cathedral" (painting), *342–343*, 385
"Sunset" (Corelli, drawing), 251
Supplement to the New Age, PCS essay in, *288–289*
"Susan and the Mermaid" (story), 79–81, *299–301*
    "City of Coral" (illustration), *80*
    "Ship of Dreams" (illustration), *299*
Swedenborg, Emmanuel, 358
Swedenborgianism, 15, 355, 358
Swords tarot suit, 350, 354
    court cards of, 384
Symbolism, 21, 373
synesthesia, 21, 60, 382, 385–386
Synge, J.M., 49

T

"T" (illustration from 'A Dream of Angus Oge' from The Green Sheaf, 1903, No. 4), 186
The Tablet: The International Catholic News Weekly, 86, 385
"Tailpiece: Le Carnaval" (illustration for the Russian Ballet), 309
"Tailpiece: Scheherazade" (illustration for the Russian Ballet), 309
"Tailpiece: Spectre de la Rose" (illustration for the Russian Ballet), 309
"Tamar" (illustration for the Russian Ballet), 309, *323*
Tamar ballet, 83
Tarock (card game), 8
tarot
    mid 20th century renaissance, 379–380
    reading the, 377–378
tarot decks

composition of cards in, 350–352
designs based on the Rider-Waite-Smith Tarot Deck, 375
early, 76, 350, 352, 363, 372
hidden meanings of, 353, 354
Italian, French, Swiss and Spanish, 377
Japanese and Korean, 374
modern designs, 374–375, *374*
Renaissance predecessors of, 350, 352
sales of, 8–9
See also Rider-Waite Tarot Deck
Tatum, Mrs, 234
Taylor, Horace, 83
Tchaikovsky, Pyotr Ilych
1812 Overture, *280*
Variations, Opus 33 (drawing), 69
Violin Concerto in D, Opus 35 (drawing), 69
Teall, Gardner, 19, 23
Temple of Mystery bazaar, 84
Ten of Cups, *351, 379,* 383, *384*
Ten of Swords, 361–362, *361,* 376
hand gesture of, promising resurrection, 362
Terry, Ellen, *38,* 144, *145, 147,* 286, 365
brochure about, 27
country house of, 357, 383–384
death of, 88
friendship with PCS, 36, 40–41, 60, 365
legacy of, promoted by PCS, 383
letter from PCS, *246*
nicknamed T Peg, 246
PCS sketchbooks in the possession of, 143
photograph of, *78*
portraits of, 41, *178, 179, 237, 238, 239, 240–241, 250*
portrayed in Rider-Waite Tarot Deck, 365
The Russian Ballet (written with Chris St. John), *308–323*
cover, *82,* 308
illustrations, 82
testimonial from, 72
"That's worth eighteen pence to me" (from *Nance Oldfield*), 109
theatre works of PCS, 11
theatre world
New York, 19
PCS's interest in, 36, 359–360
"The Faithful Wife Dancing Before the Robbers" (illustration), 41
Thematic Apperception Test (TAT), 378
"Then three girls and the puss-fish" (illustration from Susan and the Mermaid), 301
Theobald, Edith, "Letters from the Beasts to Dina," 58, *212*
"There, stuck on the rocks, was a tremendous wooden box" (illustration), 340
"They could follow the tall white shaft" (illustration), *296*
Things You Can Tell Just by Looking at Her (film), 376
Thornby, Charles, 151
Three Easy Pieces, 89
Three of Cups, *351*
Three of Wands, 377
"The Three Sisters" (story), 29, 30
Thurnam, Rowland, 84
Tierra, Michael, *376*
Tiger character, 29, 56

"Time" (watercolor), *229*
The Times (London), 284
Tintagel castle, 354, 387
Toad character, 29
"To All Believers" (dedication page), 336
Todhunter, John, 49
"A Dream," 49
"Touchstone" (Shakespeare Series, 1898) (drawing), 251
The Town (poem and illustration), 50, *53*
Transactional Analysis, 378
"Träumerei" (Schumann, drawing), 251
"Tree of Dawn, Aria" (painting on silk, based on Mozart), 68
"A tremendous palace, all of ice" (illustration), 339
"Triumph of Laughter" (drawing), 251
"Tropical Fruits" illustration in *Pratt Institute Monthly*, 22
Turkle character, 205–206
"Turris Davidica" (drawing, design for The Litany of Loretto), 69
"Turris eburnea" (drawing, design for The Litany of Loretto), 69
Twain, Mark, 44, 72–73
"Twelfth Night Merry Makers" (print), 25, 356, *356*
"Two Children" (painting), *245*
291 Gallery, 66–67, 68, 226
Two of Cups, *351*
Two of Pentacles, *376,* 377–378
Tyars, Frank, 41
typing services, invoice to PCS for, *88*

U

"U" (illustration from 'A Deep Sea Yarn' from The Green Sheaf, 1903, No. 6), 186
Ukiyo-e prints, 21, 356, 374
Uncle Remus (costume design), 329
Unger, Gladys, 288
Unicorn Press, 56
The Universal Order, 218–222
Universal Waite Tarot, 375
University of Delaware Library, 324–331
Untitled artwork by PCS
costume figure of a woman in green cloak, *101*
photographic reproductions of, *218–222*
possible poster for 291 Fifth Avenue, 226
possible sketch for advertising on glass, *226*
Stieglitz Platinum Prints, *252–275,* 364, *364*
three fish on a plate, 122
twenty-four untitled drawings from the collection of Dorothy Norman, *252–268, 270–275*
U.S. Games Systems, Inc.
anniversary of, 8, 368, 371–372
logo, 379
offices, 411
rights to publish Rider-Waite Tarot Deck, 374
tarot decks and sets published by, 8–9, 371, 374–375

V

Valenza, Patrick, *374*
"Vas Spirituale" (drawing, design for The Litany of Loretto), 69
Vaughan, Scorpana Mary, 151
Vaun, Russell, 151
Nicandra, 79

Venus, symbol for, 366
Victorian era
    cabinet cards, 350
    illustration practice, 23, 34
    photo postcards, 372
"Viola" (Shakespeare Series, 1898) (drawing), 251
Visconti Tarocchi tarot deck, *363*
Visitors Book of PCS, *42, 83, 149–159*, 410
    given by her to F.A. King, 150
Vogel, Karen, *379*, 380
Vulliamy, Blanche Georgiana, 151

W

Wagner, Richard, 65
Waite, Arthur Edward, *353*
    autobiography, *Shadows of Life and Thought*, 75
    Catholic background, 352
    commissioning of tarot deck, 74–76, 352–353, 358, 371, 372
    The Hidden Church of the Holy Graal, 353, 366
    meets PCS, 43, 352
    The Pictorial Key to the Tarot: Being Fragments of a Secret Tradition Under the Veil of Divination, 74, *74*, 352, 353, 363, 364, 365, 377, 379, 380
    The Secret Doctrine in Israel, 364
    The Secret Tradition in Freemasonry, 373, 380
    Secret Tradition of, 380
    writings, 353, 380
Waldorf-Astoria, 249
Walker, Dorothy, 151
Walker, Emery, 151
A Walk on the Moon (film), 376
Wallace, Margaret, 151
Wands, Susan, *Magician and the Fool*, 381
Wands tarot suit, 350, 354
Wang, Robert, 378
Ward, Alfred Marcus, 151
Ward, Dorothy P., 151, 181, 182
Ward, Marcus
    children's book illustration, influence on Pamela, 355–356
    Ye Pathetic Ballad of Ladye Ouncebelle and Lord Lovelle, 355
Ward, William A. Hardcastle, 151
War Refugee Relief Fund, 84, 87
Washington Times, 19, 36
"The Watchers" (drawing), 251
"Water" (drawing), 251
water element, 350
Waterloo (play), 104
Waugh, Edwin, 25
Waugh, Frederick J., 151
"The Wave" (drawing), 235, 251
"The Wave" (watercolor), *268-269*
"Weeping Trees and Falling Stars" (drawing), 69
"Weeping Wave" (drawing), 251
Weiser, Donald, 8
Wentz, Arthur, 151
West, Kipling, *374*
Westcott, William Wynn, 372
West India Improvement Company, 16
West Indian folklore, 11

Whalen, Philip, 377
"What a fine thing I have seen to-day" (illustration from A Broad Sheet, April 1902), 169
"What the West Wind Saw" (painting on silk, based on Debussy), 68
Wheeler, Ethel (Rolt), 151
Wheelock, Warren F., 284
Whistler, James McNeill, 23
"Why Toad Walk 'Pon Four Leg" (illustration from Annancy Stories), 28, 134
Widdicombe Fair (book), 27, 33–34, *34, 35*, 123–127, *123, 125–127*
    "Widdicombe Fair" (drawing in), 251
Wieners, John, 377
"The Wigwam Giants" (story in Fuller's *Friendly Giants*, 341
Wilcox, Beatrice C., 151
Wilde, Oscar, 48
William Gillette (book), 138–141
William H. Russell publishing firm, 44. See also Russell, Robert H.
William Macbeth's Gallery, New York, 21–23, 25, 38
William Rider and Son, London, 74, *392–393*
Williams, Duncan, 151
Williams, E. Harcourt, 49, 71, 151, 181, 182
    "Ellen Terry" poem, illustrated, *250*
Williams, Peggy, 151
Wilson, Robert Burns, "Let No Man's Soul Despair!" illustration for, *285*
"The Wind" (drawing), *22*, 41
"The Wind" (poem and illustration), *164–165, 238*
Windsor, England, 71
Winkley, Hilda, 151
women
    depicted by PCS, 65
    PCS's deviation from expected role of, 11–12
    portraits by PCS, 26, 34
    short hair and masculine clothing of feminists, 361
    story-telling by, 71
women painters
    exhibitions of, 68
    PCS as inspiration for, 14
women's rights, 78
Women's Social and Political Union (WSPU), 76
Women Wartime Workers, 84
women writers, in PCS's magazine, 49, 58
Woodward, Alice B., 78
Woodward, Lillian, 71
working class, 357–358
    mortality rate of, and attraction of spiritualism, 357
World War I, 84–85
writings of PCS, 11
    "A Protest Against Fear," 67, *216*
    "Should the Art Student Think?" 360, 380–381, *389–391*

X

Xena: the Warrior Princess, "Bitter Suite" episode, 377

Y

Yale University, Beinecke Rare Book and Manuscript Library, 223–235
Yeats, Jack Butler (brother of W.B. Yeats)
    PCS collaboration with, 11, 46, 48, 166, 383
    in PCS's visitors book, 151

Yeats, John Butler (father of W.B. Yeats), 12
    portrait of PCS, *6*
Yeats, Mary "Cottie," 46
Yeats, W.B.
    Cathleen ni Houlihan, stage makeup, 43
    collaborations with, 12, 33, 182
    consulted about *The Green Sheaf*, 47
    The Countess Cathleen, 33
        stage design, 43
    Diarmuid and Grania illustrations, 46
    and the Golden Dawn, 75, 352
    Hour-Glass, 47, 182
    The Land of Heart's Desire (triptych print), 25, 26–27, *27*, 29
    PCS friendship with, 42–43, 74
    in PCS's visitors book, 151
    poetry, 60, 72, 284
    publishing work of, 48, 49
    Where There is Nothing stage designs and costumes, 43
    writing in A Broad Sheet, 181, 182
Yeats family, books about, 383
Yellow Book, 48
Yod Hebrew letter, 364
"Yorick" (Shakespeare Series, 1898) (drawing), 251
"The youngest daughter began to think the master of the house a very civil gentleman" (illustration), *306*

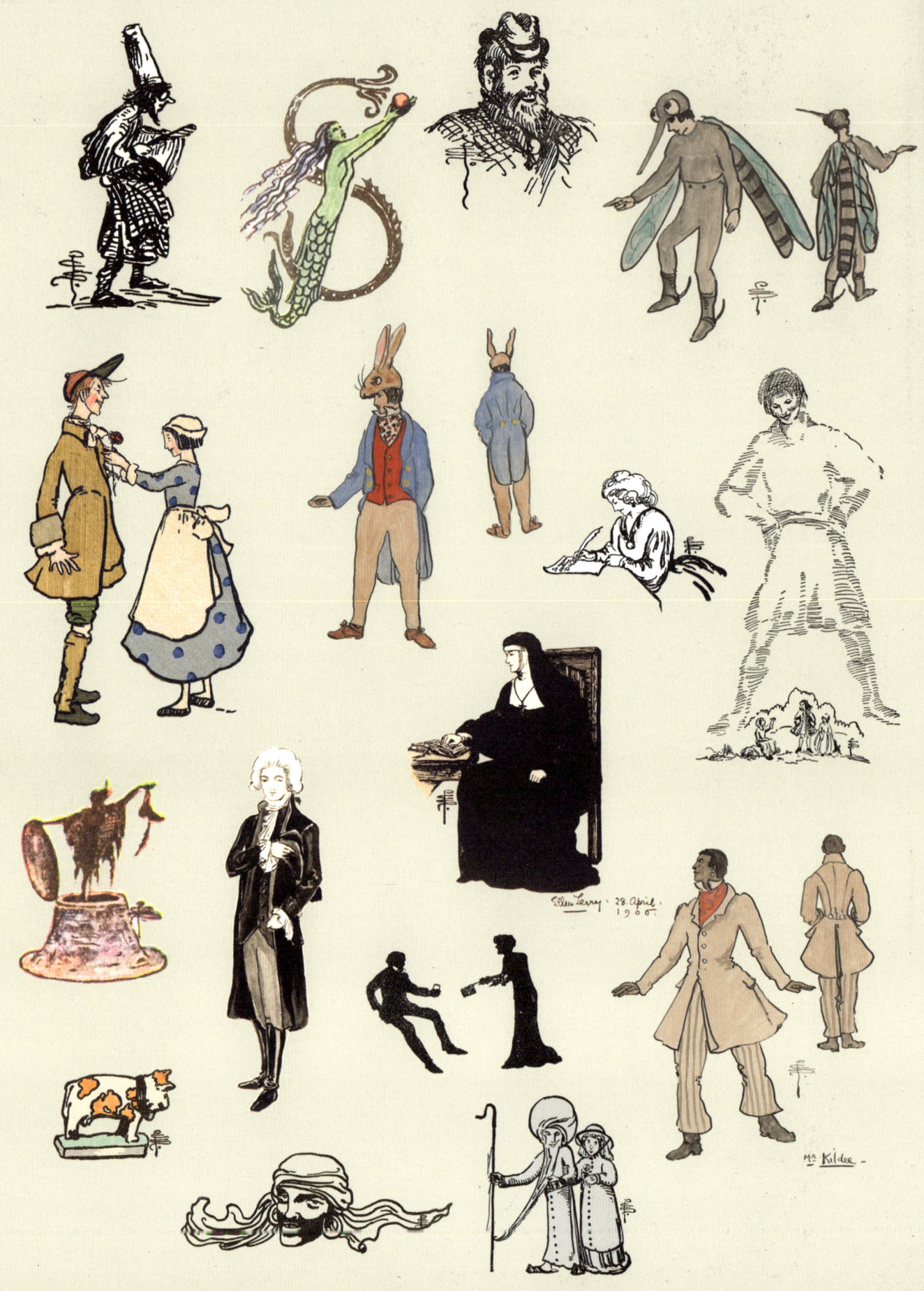